Praise for Henry Kamen's

Philip
OF SPAIN

'formidably learned, impartial and just: a worthy achievement'
– *Economist*

'a valuable contribution . . . The arguments he puts forward will
provoke reflection and debate'
– J.H. Elliott, *New York Review of Books*

'his book supersedes all [previous biographies] in respect of his
presentation of Philip the man . . . This excellent book . . .
is a fine achievement. Since it is well written, it can also be read for
pleasure by the general reader'
– Hugh Thomas, *New York Times Book Review*

'Henry Kamen is perhaps the most challenging of historians of early
modern Spain . . . [This book] has set a standard of scholarship
that [will be] hard to match'
– I.A.A. Thompson, *Times Literary Supplement*

'a remarkable achievement . . . what a good read!'
– Peter Gwyn, *Daily Telegraph*

'although scores of authors will write about Philip II, few will
marshall such an impressive range of new material'
– Geoffrey Parker, *The Times*

'masterly . . . a work of marvellous scholarship' – *Library Journal*

'a highly impressive work, sympathetic but not uncritical . . .
a subtle and highly intelligent portrait'
– John Adamson, *Sunday Telegraph*

'Despite an abundance of specialised studies of his reign, there has
been no full-length biography of Philip II. Henry Kamen's
impeccable scholarship provides it.' – Raymond Carr, *Spectator*

Philip of Spain

Philip of Spain

Henry Kamen

Yale University Press
New Haven and London

I don't know if they think I'm made of iron or stone. The truth is, they need to see that I am mortal, like everyone else.

Philip II, 29 Nov. 1578, Biblioteca Zabálburu, Madrid (142 f.9)

Copyright © 1997 by Henry Kamen

First published in paperback 1998

Set in Palatino by Best-set Typesetter Ltd, Hong Kong
Printed in Great Britain by the Bath Press

Library of Congress Cataloging-in-Publication Data

Kamen, Henry Arthur Francis.
   Philip of Spain/Henry Kamen.
   Includes bibliographical references and index.
   ISBN 0–300–07081–0 (cl.: alk. paper)
   ISBN 0–300–07800–5 (pb.)
   1. Philip II, King of Spain. 1527–1598.   2. Spain—History—Philip
II. 1556–1598.   3. Spain—Kings and rulers—Biography.   I. Title.
DP178. K36   1997
946'.043'092—dc 21
[B]   96–52421
                                                                              CIP

A catalogue record for this book is available from the British Library.

10 9 8 7 6 5 4 3

Contents

Illustrations and Maps

MAPS

Preface

Philip II refused to let his life be written during his lifetime. He thereby saved himself from adulators, whom he hated. But he left the field wide open to detractors. Since then he has consistently been given a bad press. Denigrated in his own day by political foes abroad, by Protestants everywhere, and even within Spain by enemies such as his former secretary Antonio Pérez, he acquired a sinister reputation that the passing of time only succeeded in blackening yet further.

The image presented by both his defenders and detractors has barely changed over four centuries. On the whole, biographies by his defenders have been appallingly bad. The scholarship of his enemies has by contrast usually been excellent. The splendid research done by modern Belgian, Dutch and English-speaking historians has completely altered our knowledge of aspects of his policies, but barely touched Philip's personal image. 'To historians he is an enigma', the most eminent historian of our time, Fernand Braudel, was obliged to conclude.

The American J. L. Motley penned in 1855 the classic portrait of Philip as the incarnation of evil: 'mediocrity, pedant, reserved, suspicious, his mind was incredibly small . . . bigot, grossly licentious, cruel . . . a consummate tyrant'. Some Spanish contemporaries of Motley shared the same view. One of them affirmed (in 1889) that 'the figure of Philip has always been a sombre page in our history . . . Suspicious, cruel, vengeful . . . He committed authentic crimes with terrifying cold-bloodedness.' In an influential Spanish study of 1948, notable for its attempt to be fair to Philip, Gregorio Marañón could still portray him as suspicious, weak, indecisive and an accomplice in murder.

Through the centuries no historian dared to look closely into Philip the man. The only attempt at a purely biographical study was that by the

Dane, Carl Bratli in 1912. Nearly all the multi-volume accounts (by Prescott, Merriman, and Forneron) are in reality political histories of the reign. The recent short life by Geoffrey Parker (1978) includes several personal details, but is also mainly a political survey and has significant differences of presentation from my own. Until now, in short, we have known very little about the thoughts, motives and preferences of the man who for half a century, during one of the most crucial epochs in history, governed the most extensive empire in the world.

This is the first full-length and fully researched biography of the king ever written. It has been made possible by the use at every point of entirely new manuscript sources, many of them hitherto unknown. Previous 'biographies' have dedicated themselves largely to foreign politics; this study by contrast places special emphasis on the king and on his principal environment, Spain. At the same time due attention has been paid to the part played by America in forming his outlook. As in all biographies, a strictly chronological plan has been followed; and for the first time a reliable itinerary of the king's movements, both in Spain and abroad, has been given. I have attempted both to present a new vision of Philip on the basis of original documentation, and to understand his policies through his own perspective and words. Those who know the riches of the published material on, for example, art, religion and politics, will understand my disappointment that more on these and related themes could not have been integrated into the picture. A fuller treatment of such aspects would, quite apart from producing a very much larger book, have run the risk of losing sight of Philip himself. My primary purpose was to bring to life for non-specialist readers a king who till now has languished in the realm of uninformed mythology.

On many key points the presentation here differs very radically from the traditional one. I have therefore felt it necessary to give a reasonable number of supporting references. Very occasionally, the notes point out where my conclusions differ from those of other scholars. Fuller discussion of these points would, again, have inflated the notes unduly.

All the major studies of the king were written by non-Spaniards. This has inevitably contributed to his unfavourable image. The superb Belgian scholar Gachard, for example, was uniformly unsympathetic to Philip II. In Spanish, curiously enough, not a single researched biography has been produced since the seventeenth century. The voluminous compilation by Cabrera, who knew the king and also had access to original papers, is confused, derivative and otiose. A recent generation of Spanish scholars, notably Alfredo Alvar, Fernando Bouza, J. I. Fortea Pérez and Fernando Checa, has fortunately made very important contributions to our understanding of aspects of the king.

Research for the book was financed principally by the Higher Council for Scientific Research (CSIC), Madrid. My special thanks are due to help from the research programmes of Dr Maria Teresa Ferrer and Dr Manuel Sánchez, of the Institució Milà i Fontanals (CSIC), Barcelona. I am grateful also for grants conceded by the Generalitat of Catalonia, and by the Austrian Academy of Sciences. It is a pleasure to acknowledge the kindness of very many archivists, in particular at the archive of Simancas, and at the Zabálburu Library in Madrid. I am specially indebted to Professor David Lagomarsino of Dartmouth College; Professor Friedrich Edelmayer of the University of Vienna; and Professor Francis Higman of the Institut d'Histoire de la Réformation, Geneva. Professor William Maltby of St Louis University and Professor Geoffrey Parker of Ohio State University generously looked over the text and saved me from several errors. No small part in the whole enterprise of creating *Philip* was played by my wife Eulàlia.

CSIC,
Barcelona

Note to the 2nd edition

For this edition identified slips have been corrected. The fine research that continues to be done on the reign of Philip II, notably on aspects (such as finance and the economy) not dealt with here, will certainly modify some of the conclusions in my book, which is a biographical essay rather than a survey of the entire reign. New studies are about to be published by Geoffrey Parker on imperial policy, and by Manuel Fernández Alvarez on the whole reign, while my own *Spanish Inquisition* (1998) looks in more detail at cultural aspects.

Some reviewers have questioned a line on the final page asserting that Philip 'cannot be held responsible for more than a small part' of what happened during his reign. The comment, which I combined with a similar phrase from Fernand Braudel, was a gesture to the problems raised by the role of the ruler in history. At what stage does a policy mistake become a moral crime? Historians, guided hopefully by the available documentary evidence, will continue to disagree on the verdict.

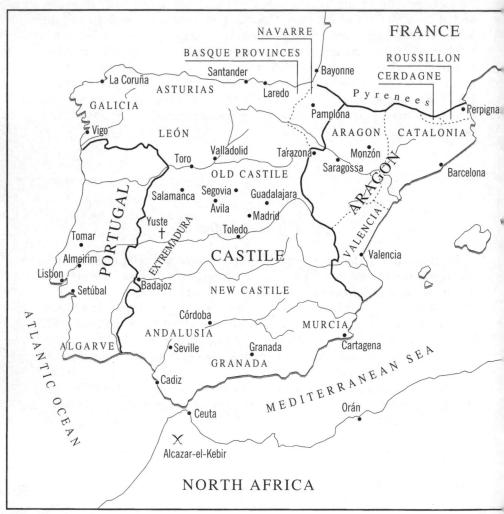

Spain under Philip II

SCOTLAND

NORTH
SEA

DENMARK

BALTIC SEA

ATLANTIC OCEAN

IRELAND

ENGLAND

London

Plymouth
Dover
Calais
Antwerp
Cologne
Brussels
St Quentin
Rhine
Mainz
BOHEMIA
Prague
Paris
Heidelberg
Regensberg
Seine
Augsburg
Vienna
Blois
Munich
Franche-Comté
Innsbruck
AUSTRIA
FRANCE
Milan
Trent
Danube
Turin
Genoa
OTTOMAN EMPIRE
La Coruña
Santander
Perpignan
Marseille
Siena
Madrid
Barcelona
Rome
Naples
Lisbon
Valencia
Seville
Cadiz
Lepanto
Algiers
Palermo
MEDITERRANEAN SEA
Bougie
La Goletta
Tunis
MALTA
DJERBA

Europe in the Age of Philip II

The House of Habsburg in the Sixteenth Century

The Family of Charles V

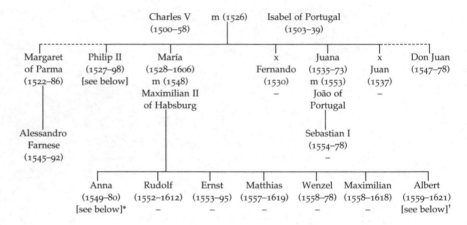

Charles V (1500–58) — m (1526) — Isabel of Portugal (1503–39)

| Margaret of Parma (1522–86) | Philip II (1527–98) [see below] | María (1528–1606) m (1548) Maximilian II of Habsburg | x Fernando (1530) – | Juana (1535–73) m (1553) João of Portugal | x Juan (1537) – | Don Juan (1547–78) |

Alessandro Farnese (1545–92)

Sebastian I (1554–78) –

| Anna (1549–80) [see below]* | Rudolf (1552–1612) – | Ernst (1553–95) – | Matthias (1557–1619) – | Wenzel (1558–78) – | Maximilian (1558–1618) – | Albert (1559–1621) [see below]† |

The Family of Philip II

Philip II
(1527–98)

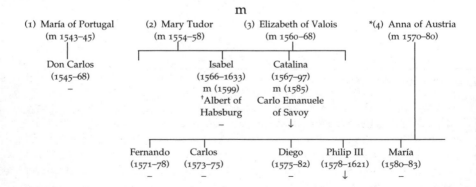

m

| (1) María of Portugal (m 1543–45) | (2) Mary Tudor (m 1554–58) | (3) Elizabeth of Valois (m 1560–68) | *(4) Anna of Austria (m 1570–80) |

Don Carlos (1545–68) –

| | Isabel (1566–1633) m (1599) †Albert of Habsburg – | Catalina (1567–97) m (1585) Carlo Emanuele of Savoy ↓ | |

| Fernando (1571–78) – | Carlos (1573–75) – | Diego (1575–82) – | Philip III (1578–1621) ↓ | María (1580–83) – |

xvi

1

The Formative Years
1527–1544

I cannot find words to express the need and straits in which these realms find themselves[1]

In July 1522 the Emperor Charles V returned to his Spanish dominions. Over two years previously he had sailed from them, just as revolution was breaking out in the major cities of Castile. His journey abroad took him to the lands over which he ruled in northern Europe. In Germany he was formally elected Holy Roman Emperor of the German nation. During the sessions of the Imperial Diet in Germany he paid due attention to the scandal caused by the preachings of the monk Martin Luther. His absence did not prevent him following closely the course of events in Spain. He was gratified to learn of the defeat of the rebels, the Comuneros, at the battle of Villalar in April 1521. On his return, the royal council under his direction decreed a further number of exemplary executions, but Charles soon declared that 'enough blood has been shed'[2] and on 1 November 1522 in a solemn ceremony in the town square of Valladolid, he issued a general pardon to the rebels. It opened the way to a reconciliation between the king and his alienated subjects.

Over the next few months the king did his best to correct the errors that had thrown the beginning of his reign into turbulence. Born in Ghent, in the Netherlands, in 1500, endowed with the square face and low-hung jaw typical of his Habsburg family, he was an accomplished soldier and a proficient scholar. But it took him time to acquire political experience. He succeeded to the crowns of Spain in 1516, and arrived in the peninsula in 1517. In Castile he at first ruled jointly with his mother, the crazed queen Juana, daughter of Ferdinand and Isabella. It was a purely nominal col-

1

laboration, for she was already in retirement. During his first weeks as ruler, Charles was criticised for being insensitive to the interests of his new subjects. He soon made up for his mistakes. From 1522 he prudently made concessions to all the major demands that had inspired the revolt of the Comuneros. They had complained about his absence. He now stayed for seven years, the longest of his sojourns in the peninsula. High up on the list was their demand that the king marry, by implication within the realm. He was young, the most eligible bachelor in western Europe (and already father, by a Flemish girl, of a daughter, Margaret). The Castilian deputies to the Cortes (or parliament) of 1525 hoped that he might marry his cousin Isabel, sister of the king of Portugal. Charles was virtually pledged to marry the daughter of Henry VIII of England, Mary. But by 1525 he had drifted from the idea of an alliance with England and accepted the link with Portugal. The marriage took place at Seville on 10 March 1526. It was a political union, but Charles fell in love with his beautiful wife, three years younger than he. When the heat invaded Seville they escaped to spend the honeymoon in the Moorish splendour of the Alhambra at Granada. In December the couple, and the whole court with them, moved back to Castile. It was there, in one of the palaces of Valladolid, that a son was born to Isabel in the afternoon of 21 May 1527.

She was thirteen hours in labour, but Charles stayed by her side throughout. The proud father was 'so overjoyed and delighted by his son',[3] that he spent his time doing nothing but arranging celebrations and festivities. The infant was not baptised until six weeks later, by the archbishop of Toledo in the monastery of St Pablo in Valladolid. His godparents were the Constable of Castile (who bore him in his arms), the duke of Béjar, and Charles's elder sister Eleanor, queen of France. The emperor laid on 'tourneys and ventures like those described in *Amadis*, but far more daring and accomplished than those in the book, so that neither before nor since had such celebrations been held'.

The happiness of the occasion was clouded by serious political problems. Just over a year before, Charles had released from captivity in Madrid the king of France, Francis I, captured at the battle of Pavia in northern Italy in 1525. Although Francis was to keep his promise, made in captivity, to marry Eleanor, he almost immediately on his release refused to honour the main political concessions he had made. Francis's ally, pope Clement, took heart at these events and challenged the emperor's forces based in Milan. In reply the emperor's army, strengthened by German mercenaries, moved south and on 6 May 1527 attacked and sacked the city of Rome. The outrage to the capital of western Christendom shocked all Europe. The news reached Charles in Valladolid in midJune, and dampened the festive atmosphere. The emperor's attention had of necessity to be diverted to these serious events, and his departure soon became unavoidable. Pressure of affairs of state meant that in the coming years he was fated to play little part in the rearing of his infant son.

Twelve months later, on 10 May 1528, representatives of the Cortes met in the monastery of St Jerónimo in Madrid and recognised the infant as heir to the throne of Castile. They also recognised the empress Isabel as regent of the realm during Charles's impending absence. On 27 July 1529 the emperor set sail from Barcelona. He was not to return until 1533.

Every aspect of the prince's upbringing was catered for with great care. Isabel's circle was largely Portuguese. It gave to her son a propensity for things Portuguese which he never lost. Of the many nurses assigned to him the most influential was the Portuguese Leonor Mascarenhas, in her twenties when she began to care for him.[4] Philip's affection for and confidence in her made him appoint her, years afterwards, as nurse to his son Don Carlos. He was also assigned 'governors', the first of whom was Pedro González de Mendoza, son of the duke of Infantado. From abroad Charles kept in close touch with all those in charge of the heir to his Spanish throne. Infant mortality in those times was a permanent threat. It carried off the majority of the royal children in Spain, and in the population as a whole eliminated one out of every two infants. As a consequence, questions of health featured prominently in letters sent to the emperor. Isabel's own private correspondence expressed her fears. 'The prince my son is ill with fever,' she wrote to a friend in mid-June 1532, 'and though the illness is not dangerous it has me very worried and anxious.' Three weeks later Philip was ill again: 'I'm very anxious,' she wrote.[5]

Shortly before Charles's departure, a daughter, María, was born to the empress on 21 June 1528 in the royal palace of the Alcázar in Madrid. Mendoza in 1531 informed the emperor that 'the Infanta grows bigger and fatter by the day, and the prince entertains her like a genteel gallant'. But the prince was not always a model of gentility: 'he is so mischievous that sometimes Her Majesty gets really angry; she spanks him, and the women weep to see such severity'.[6] Mother and son seem to have had a good relationship. Isabel gave him the only semblance of a family circle he was to have in his childhood. Deprived of a father, he looked only to her as the example for his character and conduct. On his side, unfortunately, a child's respect never had the opportunity to mature into abiding affection: her early death cut that link.

When Charles returned to Spain in April 1533 it was time to begin the next stage in the training of the prince. In July 1534 he appointed a tutor for Philip, 'to teach him to read and write'. Juan Martínez de Siliceo, aged forty-eight at the time of his appointment, was a priest and graduate of Paris and Salamanca. The next year the prince was given a new governor, Juan de Zúñiga, a noble companion of the emperor who from 1532 enjoyed the title of grand commander of Castile. Charles left Spain again in April 1535 and was periodically absent for the next few years (he was abroad when Isabel gave birth on 24 June 1535 to their third child, Juana). Before leaving, he arranged for the prince to have his own separate household. This meant that he had lodgings, attendants and chapel independent of the queen. Siliceo and Zúñiga were entrusted with his education.

Booklets on reading and grammar were specially written for Philip's instruction by a humanist member of the royal household, who also translated Erasmus's *Institution of a Christian Prince* into Spanish for the same purpose.[7] Illness occasionally interrupted his schooling, but he made fair progress. Siliceo commented in November 1535 that 'he shows promise of learning a lot in a short time'.[8] By February 1536, 'he has made a lot of progress in reading and learning prayers in Latin and Spanish'. By September that year, 'he knows the conjugations and some other principles; soon he will start to study authors, the first of whom is Cato'. By March 1540, 'he has improved a lot in speaking Latin, and speaks no other language during classes . . . He has started to write in Latin.'

An important place in the prince's education was assigned to music. The aristocratic households of this time – the great Mendoza family is an example – had their own musicians and put on musical entertainments. Spain could draw on its own popular songs, on Moorish music, and on imported influences from Italy, France and the Netherlands. Inevitably, music was central to the activities of the royal court. Each of the royal households had its own chapel, with accompanying musicians and choristers. Both in chapel and out, the tastes of the court were especially influenced by foreign styles. Philip's sisters learned to dance in the French way. The prince was always interested in music. Around 1540 the Granada composer Luis Narváez was his music tutor and taught him to play the guitar (*vihuela*). Significantly, Philip appears in these years in the dedication of several books on guitar music.[9]

Non-academic interests soon asserted themselves, as Siliceo's letter of June 1540 pointed out. 'Though hunting is at present what he is most inclined to, he doesn't neglect his studies a bit. And we have to be grateful that at this age of fourteen when the weakness of the flesh begins to assert itself, God has given the prince such a passion for hunting that he spends most of his time in this and in his studies.' In September, 'his favourite pursuits after study are going hunting and jousting'.[10] It is fair to doubt whether Siliceo was right to think that the sexual urges of adolescence were wholly consumed by hunting and study.

Shortly after, in February 1541, Siliceo was appointed bishop of Cartagena. The fact is that Charles was not satisfied with Philip's educational progress. He told him flatly that Siliceo 'has not been nor is the most suitable teacher for you; he has given in to you too much'.[11] The tutor's appointment to Cartagena paved the way for his removal, though he did not leave for his see till 1544. In 1541 Cristóbal Calvet de Estrella[12] was appointed to teach Philip Latin and Greek, Honorat Juan to teach mathematics and architecture, and Juan Ginés de Sepúlveda to teach geography and history. These illustrious humanists and scholars were, however, unable to bring the prince to the level of excellence desired by his father.

Philip, like any normal schoolboy, did not like school. 'He studies well enough when he is in school,' Zúñiga wrote to the emperor in 1535, 'although when he has to go there he resembles his father at the same age.'[13] By the same post he sent Charles the first of several letters written by the prince 'in his own hand'. None of these appears to have survived. Zúñiga received reports from Siliceo and sent them on to Charles, together with comments on the progress made by the prince in other matters. From the grand commander Philip picked up a passion for hunting. 'He continues with his studies as when Your Majesty was here, and in the hunting season goes to the country twice a week,' wrote Zúñiga in January 1540. Two weeks later Philip 'went to Alcalá for four days . . . He enjoyed himself greatly, specially in the woods, where he killed nine rabbits with the bow, and nicked others.' A week later, 'yesterday he went hunting and killed four fowl and brought down another two'. In the following week, 'he went to the Pardo and shot two arrows . . . He came and went by litter, but in the country was a good six hours on horseback, which seemed to him like two and to me more like twelve.'

Zúñiga was aware of the importance of studying Latin. 'I consider it essential that a prince be a good Latinist, to be able to discipline both himself and others, especially one who is going to rule over so many different tongues'. Sepúlveda too was concerned that through Latin the prince should learn to speak to ambassadors directly and so avoid interpreters.[14] It was a goal which the emperor enjoined on the prince repeatedly. But in classes when his humanist tutors addressed him in Latin, Philip insisted on replying in Spanish. The prince was neither a model pupil nor in any way outstanding. His command of Latin remained always average, his literary style at best mediocre, and his handwriting generally ill-formed. Educated as a humanist, he never became one. His Greek always remained very rudimentary. When his then secretary Gonzalo Pérez in 1547 dedicated to him his Castilian translation of the *Iliad*, he hoped that Philip 'may see in his own tongue what many famous princes have read in Greek'.[15]

But his refusal to become a scholar did not mean that he could not appreciate the value of scholarship. His tutors, notably Calvet de Estrella, were given funds to build up a library for the prince. Philip grew up surrounded by books written by the geniuses of western civilisation. Among volumes acquired for him by Calvet in 1545, bought in Salamanca and Medina del Campo but for the most part printed abroad, were items by Sophocles, Virgil, Aquinas, Boccaccio, Savonarola, Petrarch, Vitruvio,

Copernicus, and the collected works of Erasmus.[16] His library in 1553 contained 'books in different subjects and languages', including works by Dürer, Dante and Machiavelli.[17] The collection grew over the years, as he continued to purchase items on his special interests: architecture and art, music and warfare, magic and theology. The prince undoubtedly dipped into the volumes. The rich selection also stimulated his urge to collect further.

From 1535, when Philip was put under Zúñiga's care, his classes included a number of noble pages. Among them was Zúñiga's son Luis de Requesens, who was mercilessly teased by the others for his strong Catalan accent. The group in 1537 totalled six. 'Of those who study with the prince,' reported Zúñiga's wife Estefania in 1537, 'little Luis is the youngest . . . Two days ago the prince and six other children took part in a prank.'[18] From a very young age, the prince organised infant tourneys and dances among his group. In 1537, for example, 'a little joust and in the evening a dance . . . the prince and the Infanta danced'.[19] Philip was to remain for the rest of his life a devotee of dancing, court festivities, and rites of chivalry. When he was sixteen Zúñiga claimed that he was 'the most accomplished man of arms in this court, and this can be said without flattery; this week he and the duke of Alba put on a contest in the country'. He was 'very good at fighting both on foot and on horseback', he added.[20]

Through his childhood years the prince seems to have suffered periodic illnesses, which Zúñiga took care to report in detail to the emperor, since they concerned his only male heir. It is doubtful if we should conclude that he was sickly by nature. He led an active, vigorous life, and took part in all activities. His constitution and diet laid him open to digestive ailments and fevers, but he resisted severe illnesses successfully.

His major privation was the absence of his father, which Isabel endured with difficulty. 'The empress and her children are very well,' reported Estefania in 1538, 'but Her Majesty is pained by the emperor's departure, for fear that he will be absent longer than he says; and she is right, for her life is very dreary when he is not here.'[21] Charles returned that summer, and at the end of October was in Toledo to take part in the Cortes called for those weeks. It was one of the decisive political moments in Castile's history. The nobles stubbornly refused to grant any money towards the emperor's campaigns in Germany. Charles angrily dissolved their session and they were never again summoned to a meeting of the Cortes. 'You are not required any longer,' the cardinal of Toledo, Tavera, informed the grandees, 'you may go home or wherever you wish.'

Shortly after, during spring 1539, Isabel fell ill in Toledo. At the end of April she suffered a miscarriage, from which she died on 1 May. Philip at the time was almost twelve, possibly too young to appreciate the blow. Charles, who despite his long absences (and occasional dalliances) abroad, loved his wife deeply, was grief-stricken.[22] He immured himself in a convent for seven weeks. On 2 May the empress's body was accompanied to the outskirts of the city by ministers and grandees. Philip was unwell and went only part of the way with the procession. He withdrew and took to his bed. From the city border Isabel's body was accompanied to the royal resting-place at Granada (where the tombs of Charles's grandparents Ferdinand and Isabella also were) by members of her household and other officials, led by the marquis of Llombay, Francisco de Borja, equerry of the empress. Two weeks later the prince presided over the solemn obsequies held for the empress in the church of San Juan de los Reyes.[23]

No sooner did Charles emerge from his convent at the end of June than he received news of a revolt in his home city of Ghent, in the Netherlands. In November, as a consequence, he had to leave once again, this time at the head of a small force which passed through France on its way to Ghent. Before he did so he left a short written *Instruction* to guide his son. Government was left in the hands of cardinal Tavera as regent, with the duke of Alba and Francisco de los Cobos as his colleagues. Philip, for the first time without either parent to turn to, remained under the capable guidance of Zúñiga, from whom he seems to have picked up the traits of seriousness and piety that marked his character in later years.[24] Zúñiga was the prince's decisive support throughout his early development, helping him both in personal matters and in decisions of state. It was not the best of times for a child to be handed responsibility. The year 1540 was one of famine and misery throughout most of Castile.[25]

Charles's main preoccupations in the north of Europe were the German princes and the king of France. The princes questioned his authority in German politics, and many gave their support to Luther's Reformation. France, concerned to restrict the apparently immense power of the emperor, encouraged them in both their political and religious aspirations. The French also had claims on Italian territory, principally the strategic duchy of Milan, which Charles controlled.

From about 1540 the Turkish question, a constant threat, became more menacing. The armies of the Ottoman empire, under their ruler Suleiman the Magnificent, had so far failed to break through the line of Christian defences on the Danube. But in the Mediterranean they were considerably more successful. Spain was in the front line of the conflict. Muslim corsairs, led by Khair al-Din Barbarossa and Dragut, used the north African coast as the base for their attacks on Christian shipping in the western Mediterranean. In 1535 Charles had won a famous victory by capturing Tunis and the fort of La Goletta from the corsairs. Now in 1541 he planned a similar descent on Algiers. In October he arrived in Mallorca from Italy, in the fleet of the Genoese admiral Andrea Doria. A general rendezvous was set for the coast south of Algiers. It was a vast international force of

65 galleys and 450 other ships, with 24,000 troops from Italy and Spain. Among the Spaniards were the duke of Alba and Hernán Cortés the conqueror of Mexico. Unfortunately, a violent storm wrecked the vessels before the attack could start. With difficulty Charles made his way to the safety of Bougie,[26] and from there to Cartagena in early December. Travelling overland, he was met at Ocaña, south of Aranjuez, by Philip, who accompanied him back to Valladolid.

*

By May 1541 Philip had spent two years in official mourning for his mother. He was given permission by Charles to exchange his black garments for more colourful ones, and to wear gold. He was also now, at fourteen, deemed to be of age, and so made his first communion that year. Looking over this period of his mother's death and his coming of age, it is difficult to believe that Philip had any real experience of childhood or domestic affection. His distant father, for whom he always retained an unshakeable respect, was an object of reverence rather than of tangible love. His need for love from his mother was, because of her early death, never allowed to mature. His affections settled, as a consequence, exclusively on his sisters María and Juana. The three shared a deep dedication to each other that lasted all their lives. The only other persons for whom he felt a bond of familial affection were the Catalan household of Zúñiga, his wife Estefania and their three sons, who were all destined to become Philip's friends and collaborators. Whenever he went to Barcelona he made a point of visiting Estefania and her family.

The lack of a loving childhood was not unusual in the sons of kings. They were brought up to be men rather than children. Love was not one of the emotions normally permitted to men of state. There is no doubt that for years after his mother's death Philip faithfully controlled and repressed his instinct for affection. This by no means made him overly serious or old beyond his years: he was capable of all the pleasures and distractions to which young men devote themselves. But childhood was a phase lost somewhere in the process of growing up.

Emergence into manhood was signalled by plans to find him a wife. The candidate chosen by his father was the princess of Portugal, Maria, to whom he became formally betrothed in December 1542, an agreement ratified on 13 January 1543.

*

From this point forward he was rapidly propelled into the role prepared for him. From 1541 he was given his own personal secretary, the humanist Gonzalo Pérez, a gruff and bossy career priest who served him faithfully for the next twenty-four years. In 1543 his small private household, presided over by Zúñiga as chamberlain, was made up of personnel assigned to cater for his daily needs: porters, a clerk, a physician, stable hands. He had his own kitchen staff. The two largest groups in his household were those in the chapel (Siliceo and ten other chaplains, with several attendants), and his bedchamber. He also had the occasional services of seventy-three pages, sons of the aristocracy and of bureaucrats. The personnel came in all to some 110 persons.[27] The running cost in 1543 appears to have been 32,000 ducats a year, one-eighth the cost of the king's own much larger household.[28]

The prince's eating habits followed normal practice for noble households. His kitchen accounts for January 1544 reveal a daily diet based on a lot of meat ('for stewing, roasting and soup'), backed up by bread, chicken, and eggs. Fish, consumed in the coastal areas of Spain rather than inland, never featured. Twice a week lettuce and endives were bought. Once a week the royal table had fruit (melon, oranges). In summer the diet varied little (pears replaced oranges).[29] In 1549 in the Netherlands he continued to have fruit, cheese and salads.[30] During those months in northern Europe, beer appeared on the table, but it is likely that Philip never took to it. The item disappeared from the accounts after 1551, when he returned to Spain.[31] From 1550 wine, which he had drunk occasionally before, was a regular item with meals.

In these early years the prince became perfectly acquainted with the royal residences, particularly the hunting estates, of central Castile. He knew most of the principal towns in the centre of the peninsula. But he was ignorant of the rest of Spain. On 22 May 1542 his father, who had returned the preceding December from his disastrous expedition to Algiers, set out with him from Valladolid. It was a formal trip that involved taking with them a huge number of officials and attendants. The emperor, who spent most of his life on the move, was familiar with the routine. He was always accompanied, for example, by officials from the different realms he ruled; among them were several secretaries, to whom he dictated in the different languages of his territories.

For Philip, it was his first experience of a royal journey. Their route took them to the eastern provinces of Aragon, Catalonia and Valencia, known collectively as the crown of Aragon. Each of the realms of Spain had its own constitution, and it was a long-standing obligation for the heir to the throne to visit each realm and be formally sworn in. The royal party went first to Burgos. From here they left on 2 June for Navarre, and eventually on 22 June reached Monzón, in Aragon, where the meeting of the Cortes of Aragon, Catalonia and Valencia had already commenced. Philip fell ill with fever, which kept him indisposed the whole of July and August.

That summer the emperor also had to cope with a threatened invasion by France. Defences had to be strengthened all along the Pyrenees. The threat became real when French forces laid siege to Perpignan, on the

Catalan frontier. Charles sent the duke of Alba off in July to deal with the problem.[32] It was not until September and early October that the Estates extended their recognition to prince Philip.[33] The prince's next obligation was to go to each realm to swear to their privileges. On 12 October he set off for Saragossa.

Charles in the meantime went on to Barcelona, where he arrived on the sixteenth. Philip returned to join him early in November. He was scheduled to make a solemn entrance into the city on 8 November, but arrived the day before and had to spend the night in a convent outside. Not to be outdone, he slipped secretly into the city on the evening of the seventh, visited his father, and then went 'by night to see the distractions in the town' before going back to sleep outside the walls.[34] This experience of enjoying night-life and celebrations when in disguise, appealed to him hugely. He repeated it frequently in later years. The following afternoon he made his formal entry, and swore to the constitutions of Catalonia. On the ninth he received the homage of the authorities. Francisco de Borja was now viceroy of Catalonia, and the festivities put on for the royal party went on for two weeks. There were 'illuminations, dances and masked balls', in which the prince played a leading part. On the fourteenth he was taken on a special tour of the business area of Barcelona. On 21 November, in pouring rain, the emperor and Philip set out for Valencia. Having made sure of Philip's constitutional position as heir in Valencia, the emperor made his final preparations for departing abroad. The court left Valencia on 16 December and returned to Castile.

On 1 March 1543 Charles and Philip once more left Madrid. The latter accompanied his father as far as Alcalá de Henares. Charles then went on to Saragossa and Barcelona. In the first week of May he set sail from Palamós, on the Catalan coast, after naming his son as regent of Spain. It was a momentous step, for Charles now entered on his longest absence from the peninsula, an incredible fourteen years during which he tried in vain to bring his imperial commitments to a successful conclusion, ruining his health in the process. Philip, by contrast, now became effective and permanent ruler of Spain. These early years of his regency were certainly only an apprenticeship, but they helped to shape the king, and their relevance to his later development should not be underestimated.

*

Before he sailed from Palamós the emperor left with Zúñiga two hand-written letters of *Instruction* for his son, one dated 4 May, the other 6 May.[35] The first, headed 'Confidential', and consisting of advice on his personal and public behaviour, was to be handed to Philip by Zúñiga and read in his presence, since Zúñiga was still responsible for his conduct. In it, Charles said he was leaving him 'in my place during my absence, to govern these realms'. Philip was adjured to keep two principles always before him: to 'keep God always in mind'; and to 'accept good advice at all times.' He must serve God above everything: 'never allow heresies to enter your realms; support the Holy Inquisition . . . and on no account do anything to harm it'. He must be 'an upholder of justice' and uproot all corruption among his officials. He must be 'temperate and moderate in all you do. Keep yourself from anger, and do nothing in anger'. He must avoid flatterers, but accept the good advice given him by his counsellors and 'preserve their freedom so that their opinions are given freely'. Great care must be taken not to say, or sign, anything that might create problems for the future. He must exercise caution in the crown of Aragon, 'because you are more liable to make mistakes in this government than in that of Castile'. In giving audiences he must be patient, 'and you must also find time to go among and talk with the people'.

The *Instruction* then turned to his personal life. First of all, to his disinclination for study. 'As I told you in Madrid, don't think that it is childish to study.' Study helped to make the man. Being a man was not a question of body but of mind, and only study could achieve this. Moreover, he was to rule over many different peoples and languages, and to communicate with them all it was essential to know Latin. 'Nor would it be amiss to know a bit of French.'

He must now also enter the adult world. 'Till now your company has been that of children . . . From now on, you must not associate with them.' The change would be brutal. 'Your company will be above all that of grown men.' But he must enter the world of public affairs slowly and with caution, consulting always, and especially with Zúñiga. 'You will soon marry'; but once married he must be moderate in his pleasure, 'because besides being harmful both to bodily growth and strength, often it impairs the capacity to have children and can kill', as was the case with prince Juan, son of Ferdinand and Isabella. He must therefore limit access to his wife and 'keep away from her as much as possible', and when with her 'let it be briefly'. In this he should be ruled by Zúñiga's advice. However, he must remain faithful to her and once married must not go with other women. And in all matters, if in any doubt, he should have recourse to Zúñiga.

The *Instruction* of 6 May was headed 'Private' (*secreta*), for him to keep 'under lock and key, so that nobody not even your wife sees it'. In it Charles regretted his departure, and the penury of his treasury, but trusted that God would favour him in his struggle against the king of France. The advice concerned delicate matters of state.

Criticising the factions among his ministers, he recommended that Philip consult with the president of the royal council, cardinal Tavera, and with the secretary of state Francisco de los Cobos. 'Although they are the heads of differing factions, I wanted to have both of them available so that you should not fall into the hands of either.' Philip must never put himself in the hands of any one minister. 'Rather, deal with many and do not bind yourself to one alone.' For example, the duke of Alba had ambitions in government: 'he has set his sights on great things and on rising as high as he can', but 'you must be careful not to let him or other grandees get a firm footing in government, or you will regret it afterwards'. However, Alba should be employed in matters of war, 'since he is the best that we have at present in these realms'. As to Cobos, he had been a good servant and no one knew affairs of state better than he, but he was also grasping and had many enemies. In conclusion, Charles hoped to be able during his journey to sort out the current problems and so clarify the issues facing them both.

From abroad, the emperor continued to take a close interest in the training of his son. Outside of politics and war, the main business of 1543 was Philip's marriage. The princess of Portugal was aged just sixteen, six months younger than Philip. The prince wrote to his father how with a small escort he had gone out at the beginning of November to witness secretly the princess Maria's progress from the frontier. At Aldeanueva 'I saw her without her being able to see me'. On Monday, 12 November Philip made a ceremonial entry into Salamanca. The princess entered a few hours later, and the couple were married by cardinal Tavera on the same day.[36] The celebrations continued till the early hours.

A few days later the royal pair, with their retinue, set out for Valladolid. They made a courtesy stop at Tordesillas to visit queen Juana, mother of the emperor and Philip's grandmother. The unhappy, crazed queen had ruled Castile briefly in the early years of the century. Her parents, Ferdinand and Isabella, had been well aware of her mental affliction but hoped it would not affect her political capacity. When her husband, the Flemish Philip the Handsome, died unexpectedly, she went out of her mind. Out of respect for her, as long as she lived she was accepted as queen jointly with her son. During his period as regent, Philip got used to signing decrees in the name of 'the Catholic Queen and the emperor and king, my lords'. In practice, she did not stir from her strange retreat in her palace at Tordesillas, where Philip made regular courtesy visits to see her. She died, a prey to her imaginings, in April 1555.

*

Immediately his father left the country in 1543, Philip applied himself with enthusiasm to his new role. 'His Highness received the *Instructions*,' Zúñiga reported to the emperor, 'together with the powers which Your Majesty sent for governing these realms and those of Aragon. After he had read it all, he sent the special instructions to the tribunals and councils. He has begun, conscientiously and with resolution, to study what he has been ordered to do. He is in touch always with the duke of Alba and the grand commander of León [Cobos].'[37] The prince continued at the same time with his habitual interests and diversions, notably jousting and hunting. Zúñiga kept him company. 'His Highness arrived here in good health this afternoon,' the grand commander wrote in May 1543; 'his grandmother was pleased to see him, and he also enjoyed being in Alcalá eight days with his sisters. The day after he left Alcalá he killed a large, fat stag which he sent to his sisters. One day when he was in the Segovia woods he killed two or three, as well as a roe; I myself killed a very large stag.'[38]

Philip was still obliged to follow his daily classes with his tutors in Latin and other subjects, but more and more he was introduced into the routine of business undertaken by the councils. His mentor was Francisco de los Cobos. As secretary to Charles for Spanish affairs, and administrator of the treasury, the grand commander of León was effective director of government machinery in the emperor's absence. He used his position to build up a reliable team of state officials. He also, on the side, made himself extremely rich. Philip was encouraged by him to assist at meetings of the lesser councils and also to make decisions. Cobos informed Charles shortly after his departure that 'two meetings on matters of administration have been held with His Highness, and I must say that he really is very good in these affairs'.[39] The prince's first recorded decision was in this meeting in July 1543 of the royal council, when 'His Highness has through his councillors ordered all necessary steps to be taken' in a matter involving an argument with the papacy.

Government in those days was a simpler affair than today. The areas in which the state had competence were limited, no proper bureaucracy existed, and the main business of the king was to raise a few taxes in order to keep the peace or wage war. As responsibilities increased, the crown relied on selected counsellors to help it arrive at decisions. Most advisers were traditionally from the high nobility and formed councils for specific areas of government. In 1543 there were about nine councils advising the king of Spain, of which the most important was the royal council (often also called the council of Castile). Staffed since 1493 by legal experts, it was the highest court in Castile and had competence over most aspects of government. Questions of foreign policy were dealt with by a number of grandees sitting in the council of State, which when it convened for military business was known as the council of War. Other specialist councils existed for America (the council of the Indies), the Inquisition, and affairs of finance. The eastern realms of the peninsula, and the kingdom of Naples, sent representatives who sat on the council of Aragon. The councils met on allotted days, during specific hours, in the royal palace. They gave their opinions in the form of a written report known as a *consulta*. The secretaries of the councils directed all the paperwork, and liaised directly with the king. They became, inevitably, powerful men who effectively controlled business.

From the summer of 1543 Philip began to append his signature, with the words 'Yo el Principe [I, the prince]', to all official letters. His annotations, written in the scrawl of one who had refused to subject himself to writing lessons, began to appear in the margins of state papers. It seems that Philip's education may have been adversely interrupted by these political duties, for Siliceo reported in August that 'about his studies I can say that he understands what he reads in Latin, although he practises little, partly because he is busy with government and partly because he spends his time in pursuits of arms and chivalry'.[40]

At this early stage, most real decisions in Spain were being made by Cobos, who ruled his colleagues with an iron fist. But by the end of 1543 the prince – with Cobos's guidance – was participating in most aspects of business, and also took a close interest in American affairs. Financial matters were from the very beginning put his way, the emperor's instruction to the council of Finance stating specifically that 'matters arising should be discussed with the prince my son, so that he can see the accounts of what is needed'.[41] Most major decisions were still reserved for the emperor, but in practice day-to-day matters were resolved in Spain. This left Philip free to follow policies that the emperor might not always agree with. The council of the Indies, for example, complained to Charles in August 1543 that the prince was diverting silver which came to them from America to other projects.[42]

Philip also began to give audiences, one of the most important duties of the crown. Among his earliest was that given to the marquis of Mondéjar, who travelled to Valladolid from Andalusia in order to lay before him a plan to bring peace and security to the lands peopled by the Moriscos of Granada.[43] With effective power in nearly all areas of decision-making, Philip was now the real master of Spain. Thirty years later he had no doubts in dating the fact: 'I began to govern in the year 1543'.[44]

The favourable noises made about the prince's role at this date, when he was still only sixteen, smack of polite flattery. Fernándo de Valdés, president of the royal council, felt that 'His Highness is very able in his duties, to the great contentment of these realms'. Cobos felt that 'since Your Majesty left him he has grown in body and even more, in my opinion, in judgment; he takes part enthusiastically in all business'.[45] There is, all the same, clear evidence that Philip was indeed working at his new job. He now took on, for example, the role of principal correspondent with the emperor. Guided by secretaries who put together the several pieces of information which had to be reported to Charles, Philip helped to compose official letters into which he was expected to slot his contribution. From the autumn of 1543 all the ministers deferred to the prince's letters. Alba and Cobos, though they still conducted their own correspondence with Charles, told him also that 'there is no need to repeat what the prince is writing, since he will write all that is necessary'. Tavera,

rounding off one of his missives, added that 'on all the other matters that
have been discussed in the council of State on the prince's orders, you will
be informed through the letters of His Highness'.[46] These were not polite
gestures, but a real division of tasks, in which the prince was allotted
considerable responsibility.

A report drawn up by Cobos in 1544 gives an intimate (and suspi-
ciously favourable) sketch of the prince at work.[47] Philip is described as

> always immersed in matters of government and justice ... His daily
> business and activity is always on these matters and with men of
> judgment ... Sometimes he asks questions even though he knows the
> answer, and this is no doubt his greatest virtue, since he does it in order
> not to err. In weighty matters for which special committees are set up,
> he listens to each opinion with great care and attention, and when
> everything is aired and explained he criticises with courtesy and pru-
> dence that which he disagrees with. Afterwards he alone decides. He
> often shuts himself up with me for hours to deal with business of the
> council of State. He does the same with the president [of the royal
> council] on questions of justice, with the duke of Alba on those of war,
> and with others on other different areas.

The report, obviously designed to please the emperor, gives an exaggerated picture of the prince's competence, claiming for example that
'instead of giving him advice, we all accept and respect his'. For all that,
it seems to coincide with other evidence of Philip's impressive immersion
in the world of government. Most official correspondence within the
peninsula was addressed to him, though in practice he dealt with only
some of it. By contrast, virtually all official correspondence emanating
from the central government carried his signature, proof that he dedicated considerable time to the formality of putting his name to letters.[48]

When the emperor left Spain in 1543, war had already broken out with
France. He went to Germany, from which he launched an invasion of
Francis I's kingdom. It appeared the most direct way of stopping aggression in Italy by the French, and their schemes with German Protestants
and the Turks. The major difficulty was the lack of adequate finance for
the war.

Philip tried to find funds in Spain. Serious debates took place in
Valladolid in August 1543 over the desperate situation of the treasury.
Charles was committed to heavy military expenditure in northern
Europe, and looked to the Castilian exchequer to help him. 'Aware of the
pressing need,' wrote Cobos, 'His Highness summoned the councils of
State and of Finance to see what could be done.' In their deliberations, the
councils agreed that some silver be seized from the ships recently arrived
laden with silver from America, but that the Cortes should not be asked to

pay more taxes. Cobos reported the matter in constitutional terms to his king. 'In the end it was decided that these are not matters to be treated of in Your Majesty's absence', since only the king should summon the Cortes.[49] In a parallel letter written on the same day to Charles, and summarising the same debate, Philip expressed a quite different perspective, that of a people oppressed by taxes:

> It was debated whether to ask the cities for money. On looking at the matter, many points emerged from which it appeared that to ask for money would be very long and arduous, since the countryside is poor and exhausted and every day the towns present petitions about the expenses they had during the last campaign. Because of all this, it was suggested that it would be better if this army were raised at Your Majesty's own expense.[50]

The sentiments were so direct as to be naive. Charles needed money, and did not have to be reminded that his people were over-taxed. He was to find to his surprise that over the next few months Philip lined up very readily with those ministers who thought that Castile could not be bled further. But only the prince was courageous enough in his letters to express these sentiments boldly. He took part conscientiously in meetings. In February 1544 he informed his father that 'I ordered a meeting of the council of State, to be attended also by the president and two members of the royal council, as well as the members of the council of Finance. In several meetings which they had in my presence they debated' how one could meet the request for money.[51] The conclusion to which he and they came was, he wrote in September, that peace was necessary, 'for the well-being and succour of Christendom and of these realms, which are so needy and exhausted that I cannot find words to express their state, except to assure you that only your return to these realms can be the real remedy for everything'.[52]

Evidently those who were unhappy about the wars abroad were influencing the prince. On the same day that Philip sent his September letter, Cobos wrote that 'the prince's letter deals so exactly with all details of business, that it leaves me with nothing to say except to refer to it'.[53] It was a convenient subterfuge. Cobos had always opposed Charles's imperial commitments,[54] and he could now rely on Philip to support him. The prince however was no passive tool. He continued to devote himself to hunting, and participated in occasional jousts (unimpressively, according to one witness, who commented that 'the prince has taken part in two superb tourneys, though I feel the tourneys were better in Piedmont').[55] But he was capable of using his own initiative, and when his sister María fell ill in the autumn he personally decided when and where the court should move in order to protect her health.[56] That November, his wife's pregnancy was confirmed, which increased his domestic commitments but did not deter him from some of the most important political steps he was to take in these years.

News of the peace of Crépy (September 1544) between the emperor and France reached Valladolid in October. Spaniards, who had little to gain from the war, were overjoyed, but for Charles there were complications. The peace made him think of offering one of two alternative marriage alliances to Francis I's second son, the duke of Orléans. He could offer either his daughter María, with possession of the Netherlands at his own death; or his niece Anne of Hungary, with possession of Milan a year after the marriage. The emperor consulted his advisers in Spain and the Netherlands on the matter. In Spain Philip took charge of the discussions. In late November he went to Madrid to consult personally with his sister María, since 'she will open her mind to no one more than to me'.[57] 'I hope to be back soon,' he wrote to his friend Francisco Borja, duke of Gandía, 'at the latest before Christmas.'[58] He came back to Valladolid rather earlier, on 29 November, and took part in the debate in the council of State, which had convened during his absence.

Philip took a close interest in the question (which we shall touch on later), and introduced a procedure by which formal opinions would be expressed individually, so as to guide his own decision-making. He first ordered the council to have four or five meetings in which the members could elaborate their thinking.

> Afterwards when I came the council met immediately in my presence, and I wished to hear all that they had discussed and debated. They debated again and discussed the matter at length, and although they were settled in their views I ordered them to think more about it. On the third day, I said, they should meet again in council and come to it with their minds made up so we could arrive at a decision. It was so done. Since we learned from our contacts that their opinions were divided, I ordered each member to express his view.[59]

This remarkable initiative, laying down a procedure which Philip was to follow throughout his tenure of power, shows his determination to elicit considered advice and to consult all opinions, as his father had advised, before making decisions.

In subsequent weeks Charles was to find that his son was no compliant servant of his policies. At the end of December 1544 the prince wrote that he and a majority of the council were opposed to the emperor's wish to seize the silver that had come from America for private merchants. 'Above all since it would undo what has cost me many meetings, consultations and agreements to achieve, there being so little silver.'[60]

The resistance of Spanish officials to the wars in the north was expressed most clearly in the prince's important letter to the emperor of March 1545.[61] In it he stressed that 'I do not need to repeat the situation of the treasury of these realms, how everything up to the year 1548 is assigned and spent, leaving nothing for expenses, and the same is the case with the taxes on the poor people of these realms'. There was no point in the emperor citing the ability of the king of France to raise a grant of taxes, for France was bigger and richer than Castile. Each nation must be treated according to its own laws and customs, 'and these realms will not tolerate being treated in that way, for each nation must be approached with respect and dealt with differently according to the nature of its people'. Philip stressed that he had consulted with his advisers and they had agreed (the failure of 1538 was in their minds) that it would be futile to convene the Cortes of Castile. The emperor's suggestion to convene the Cortes of Aragon was also not viable, because of 'the universal poverty in those realms, especially in the principality of Catalonia as a result of several barren years and the wars in Perpignan'.

This firm refusal of money was accompanied by a spirited presentation of the plight of the people of Castile:

> With what they owe for other things, the common people who have to pay the taxes are reduced to such extremes of misfortune and poverty that many of them go naked without clothing. And the misery is so universal that it afflicts not only Your Majesty's subjects but even more those of the nobility, for they cannot pay their taxes nor have the means to do so. The prisons are full, and all are heading for ruin. Believe me, Your Majesty, if this were not true I would not dare write it to you.

In fact, the financial situation was so acute, and the demands of the emperor so insistent, that eventually meetings of the Cortes in Castile and Aragon were held. In Aragon proper a small grant was obtained, but in Valencia and Catalonia the Cortes refused to vote anything without the royal presence.

In Castile the prince personally supervised the negotiations for the Cortes that opened in Valladolid in March 1544. The Cortes of Castile consisted in theory of three estates, with representatives from the higher clergy, the great nobles and the leading (at this period, eighteen) towns. In practice, for some time now only the deputies of the towns normally met, since the main business tended to be taxation, from which the other estates were in principle exempt. The nobles, we have already seen, ceased to be summoned after 1538. The standard procedure was for the towns to send two deputies each. If all the deputies attended, the assembly with its secretaries and officials would not have numbered more than about fifty people. The king or his representative would open the session with a speech setting out the purpose of the summons. This would be replied to formally by a member of the Cortes, and the debate or negotiations would then begin.

'I ordered the deputies to meet,' Philip wrote to his father, 'and after I said a few words the proposal was read to them and they replied in the usual way.' The speech consisted of a plea for money to help the emperor against France and the Turks. 'And after debating and arguing with them on the matter, and about the great distress and poverty in which these realms are, or at least the people who have to pay the taxes, it appeared superfluous to talk about other matters, and it was agreed to consult with all the cities' represented in the Cortes.[62] Negotiation usually went on for weeks. The Cortes invariably presented a number of petitions (in 1544 they totalled nearly sixty), with which Philip had to deal if he hoped to get a grant of money. He was asked to make sure that the assembly would be called at least every three years. Cautious but firm, he promised to do what seemed best.

By 1544, on all the evidence, Philip was a fully committed head of government,[63] influenced certainly by the views of those in power but with initiatives and ideas of his own which he expressed freely in his letters to the emperor.

*

From Germany Charles kept a watchful, but liberal, eye on his son's progress. He was aware of Philip's fondness for women, and instructed Zúñiga shortly after Philip's marriage to control contact between the young couple. The governor faithfully made sure that Philip followed Charles's wish 'that the prince absent himself sometimes from his wife, and in particular that they should not be together during the day'. The question was in part resolved by an attack of scabies which Philip suffered shortly after the wedding and which obliged him to sleep apart from Maria for over a month.[64] At the same time there was growing evidence that the prince seemed not to be as enamoured of his bride as was expected.

In these weeks Charles warned the grand commander to 'moderate the great lust you always had for hunting', since it was leading the prince to hunt excessively and indiscriminately. Philip must also continue to study, despite his marriage and affairs of state. Zúñiga, the emperor complained, was not giving him enough information. He had heard from other sources 'of the coldness the prince adopts to his wife in public, which distresses me very much'. He put it down, nonetheless, to 'the timidity of someone of his years'. There were other matters about the prince's style of living which worried both Zúñiga and the emperor: the excessive time Philip spent in going to bed and getting up, expensive parties, going out at night.[65] Philip also enjoyed tournaments, which he mounted on a big scale. 'The prince is in good health,' Gonzalo Pérez wrote in May 1544; 'in March he organised a tournament and put on another yesterday in the countryside; it was a great success, with close on a hundred taking part.'[66] Seen in perspective, despite his father's worrying, all this looks like the relatively harmless life-style of a young aristocrat.

Philip's coldness to his wife was to be expected in an arranged marriage between two very young people. In January 1544 the emperor was informed that 'the prince is somewhat distant with the princess, and in Portugal they feel strongly about it'. Later, in the autumn, the best that Cobos could report was that the couple 'get on together very well', and that the prince was not making inordinate sexual demands on his wife.[67] Whatever the young prince's sentiments for his wife may have been, they were not allowed to mature. In giving birth to a son, Carlos, on 8 July 1545 she suffered a serious haemorrhage that led to her death four days later. She was just over seventeen. Cobos informed Charles that 'the prince felt the loss deeply, which shows that he loved her; although,' he felt obliged to add, 'some took a different view of his outward reactions.'[68] Aged eighteen, Philip had left his childhood world behind. He was now a father and a widower, and apprentice head – since 1543 – of the Spanish state.

2

The Renaissance Prince
1545–1551

Believe me, Your Majesty, if this were not true I would not dare write it to you.[1]

'I cannot think where this will stop,' the Castilian religious reformer Teresa of Avila commented around mid-century. 'I have seen so many changes in my lifetime that I do not know how to go on. What will it be like for those who are born today and have long lives before them?'[2]

The Spain over which prince Philip presided in his father's absence was indeed changing in several ways. Like many countries in Europe, 'Spain' was not a unified state but an association of provinces sharing a common king. The majority of provinces were grouped under the crown of Castile, which included Castile but also the kingdom of Navarre and the autonomous Basque provinces. The eastern provinces, forming the crown of Aragon, comprised the autonomous territories of Aragon, Catalonia and Valencia. Most provinces enjoyed their own laws, institutions and monetary system, and were subject to the political control of their local nobility.

The king – above all an absentee king like Charles – was in no position to rule by absolute authority. He exercised control instead through agreements and the judicious use of influence. Royal power was strongest in Castile, where tradition allowed the king to raise taxation and an army. Fortuitously Castile, which also ruled directly over America, was the largest realm of Spain and contained three-quarters of its population. It became the base upon which Charles, and later Philip, constructed their policies.

Charles's grandfather, Ferdinand the Catholic, had begun the nation's emergence as a European power by his active foreign policy. In 1504, after years of war in southern Italy, he won sovereignty over the kingdom of Naples. Ferdinand's wife Isabella had given particular attention to the conquest in 1492 of the Muslim kingdom of Granada, and had backed Columbus in his voyages to the New World. Charles, on his accession to the Spanish throne, was drawn into this immense range of imperial interests. As sovereign of the Netherlands he enjoyed the title of duke of Burgundy; to his many other titles he subsequently added that of Holy Roman Emperor in Germany. Ruler of the biggest accumulation of states ever known in European history, he drew Spain into an imperial role it had never before experienced.

Spain in mid-century was well poised to make its mark on the world. Charles's empire was not created by the Spanish, but they were beginning to play an important part in it. Spain's military fame rested chiefly on its long, valiant battle against the advancing forces of the Turkish empire. In 1535 the emperor, with forces drawn mainly from Italy and Spain, had scored a brilliant victory over the Muslims by capturing the north African city of Tunis. Since then the small Spanish fortresses scattered around the western Mediterranean, such as La Goletta, were the only protection of the Christian west against Islamic power. On constant guard against the great external threat, fearful of the enormous potential Muslim threat at home (in Granada), Spain was uniquely fitted to lead a crusade in defence of the west. Spanish military detachments could be found in Italy, Germany and Flanders. The presence of these troops in other states was inevitably resented. 'They are loved by nobody,' a courtier of prince Philip observed.[3] Hostility was the price to be paid for Spain's growing imperial role.

In good measure, the outside world was suspicious because it did not know Spain. Some non-Spaniards had served in the wars against the Muslims of Granada, some had gone on pilgrimage to the shrines at Santiago in Galicia or Montserrat in Catalonia. Cultured foreigners visited the peninsula, however, only if the royal court was there. It is significant that the Italian humanist Castiglione, who made Spain his home early in the century, dedicated himself to producing a book on the theme of *The Courtier*. Charles's continuous absence deprived the country of a regular court. Castile without its king tended to become a cultural backwater.

Spain's isolation from the outside world was commented upon by travellers and ambassadors. Envoys of the republic of Venice, who made frequent visits, seldom failed to present the country in an unfavourable light. In very many ways, the peninsula was indeed off the beaten track. Yet Spaniards who had done a bit of travelling thought their own country quite satisfactory. 'Of everything that I have seen,' commented one, 'the best is Spain . . . The people there are liberal but not so bookish as in Italy, courageous but not so barbarous as the Germans, humane and amiable but without the placidity of the inhabitants of Flanders.' In Spain there was more tranquillity, more freedom for everyone. 'How little the Spanish peasant would complain about the taxes he pays if he knew what happened elsewhere and to what taxes others are subjected!'[4]

*

In Europe it was a time of growth, expansion and exploration. Spaniards were in the forefront of the movement, building their new frontiers beyond Europe. In America in 1521 the adventurer Hernán Cortés had overthrown the capital of the Aztec empire and founded the city of Mexico. Ten years later, the Pizarro brothers launched the expeditions which overthrew Inca power in Peru. America since that time had become a prey to wealth-hungry settlers. In 1542, shortly before he sailed for Italy, Charles signed the text of the 'New Laws', which attempted to protect the native population of America against Spanish exploitation. In 1543 the merchants of Seville banded together to form a 'Consulate' to organise trade to the New World. It was the first stage of an adventure that also caught the imagination of the young prince Philip. 'Our Spaniards,' his historiographer-royal later wrote, 'traversed the Equator, discovered the other pole, and in many things disproved through direct experience the astrology and geography of the ancients, gaining for the world another world besides.'[5]

Few Spaniards were unaware that overseas discoveries were playing a part in the economic changes at home. The ports of Andalusia, which traded directly to America, were booming; Seville tripled its population; and silver and exotic goods from the New World began to enter Spain's economy. Many Spaniards got richer, among them a brother of Teresa of Avila, who went to America, made himself wealthy, and returned to live in comfort in Avila.

Others, similarly, tried to better their lot by going to the new lands in America. Some of them were trying to escape the restraints of the social system. By about 1540 at least 20,000 Spaniards, mostly of humble origin, had crossed the Atlantic. The repercussions of this emigration were soon felt at government level in Spain, where important issues of colonial policy were raised.

Amid all this, as Teresa of Avila well knew, disquieting changes were beginning to affect the tranquillity of the people of Spain. The cost of living was rising: in the half-century to 1550, the cost of food in Valladolid rose by half, around Seville it more than doubled. Money no longer bought what it used to; 'gentlemen, commoners and clergy cannot live on their incomes,' an Italian visitor commented some years later. There was arguably a bright side to the picture. The birth rate was rising; and more people meant more demand for food and supplies. In Castile, population rose by half during the early part of the century; in some towns it doubled or tripled. But demographic growth also meant more problems in the towns, and more poverty.

Spain's expansion could not disguise its backwardness. The crown of Castile had a population of some five million; the crown of Aragon about a million and a half. Spain regularly had to import grain to feed these people, but the aridity of much of the countryside meant that in times of drought it faced severe difficulties. When Philip was entrusted with the realm in 1543, a new poor law to deal with begging had just been issued, cardinal Tavera had just founded in Toledo a hospital for the poor, and at Salamanca university the theologian Domingo de Soto was giving lectures on the problem of poor relief.[6] Two prominent studies of poverty which appeared in 1545 were presented by their authors to the prince, who despite his privileged environment was made aware of the problems facing his people.[7] Philip's concern for the poor was to remain one of the recurring themes in his correspondence.

For all the problems, mid-century Spaniards could feel some confidence in the prevailing stability of their country. A generation earlier, things had been very different. The political violence of the Comunero rebellion of the 1520s had left wounds. Now that was little more than a memory. Religious violence had also been intense. Prior to the 1520s there had been a bloody persecution of Christians of Jewish origin, the *conversos*. Thousands of those who refused to leave Spain when the expulsion of the Jews was decreed in 1492 converted and attempted to continue practising their religion in secret. They were ruthlessly punished by the Inquisition. During Philip's childhood, this too was almost a thing of the past. Though anti-Semitism continued, as elsewhere in Europe, *conversos* by mid-century were loyal Christians and often accepted into public life.

Spaniards may on the other hand have been worried about the new Lutheran heresy which was gaining a foothold in Germany and the north. Though there were frequent alarms, normally set off by the Inquisition, in the 1540s there were no significant signs of heresy in the peninsula. Ideological hostility, where it existed, was directed mainly against the very large population of Christianised Muslims, known as Moriscos. Converted by force in the early century, they lived principally in the south of the peninsula and numbered well over a quarter of a million people. Virtually all continued to practise their Islamic religion. One of the first matters Philip had to deal with as regent was the situation of the Moriscos of Granada, who in 1543 presented a memorial with their grievances. The prince and the Inquisition were consulted on the problem.[8]

Despite its relative isolation the country was not closed to ideas and influences. Cultural currents emanating from Italy and the Netherlands were making their mark on poets, scholars and artists. In 1543, the year that Philip became regent, one of the most important works in Spanish literature came out in Barcelona: an edition of the poems, composed in the Italian style, of Juan Boscán and Garcilaso de la Vega. Intellectuals did not look only to Italy. Since the 1520s the works of the Dutch humanist Erasmus had enjoyed considerable popularity in the peninsula. The Inquisition later prosecuted a number of people who shared his views, but Erasmus continued to be an influence on intellectuals well into the later part of the century.[9] Philip grew up in an atmosphere influenced by his ideas, and read and studied Erasmus when young. Many in his entourage were sympathetic to Erasmus: his secretary Gonzalo Pérez, a humanist of *converso* origin, was a symbol of the outward-looking intellectual changes of the period.

The common people of Spain were, of course, untouched by these intellectual currents. Apart from a small minority in the upper classes, few could read or write, and books were to be found only in the major cities. The culture of most people was dictated by their religious practice, which had changed little through the centuries. Spaniards were to all appearances Catholic, but their everyday religion was a free-wheeling mixture of official doctrine, popular folklore and ancient superstition. By mid-century, a few hesitant changes were being introduced into this old-time religion. The source of reform was Italy, where the council of Trent had been holding sessions dedicated to the reform of the Church. From Italy, too, came a stream of new religious orders, prominent among them the Jesuits.

In 1543 Bernal Díaz de Luco, one of Philip's advisers in the council of the Indies and later bishop of Lugo, published his *Advice to Curates*. For him the key problem in Spain was the need to overcome ignorance among both clergy and people. He was also alarmed by the vogue for reading books of chivalry, which emphasised adventure, travel and gallantry. Seen by critics as a peril to good literature and morals (which did not stop Teresa of Avila reading them when she was young), the books provided staple reading for the conquistadors in America as well as for ordinary citizens at home. Prince Philip was second to none in his dedication to this literature.

While excited by the possibilities offered by the New World, Spaniards were also beginning to open their minds to Europe. Trade links with the Netherlands and Italy had ensured that regular cultural contacts took place: the bulk of Castile's wool was sold to buyers in the international market at Bruges. The Netherlands sent to the peninsula its artists and some of its spiritual influences. From the north too came printers, who soon monopolised the trade in the major Spanish cities. Links with Italy were closer than with northern Europe, thanks to proximity and to similarity of culture. Spaniards went to Bologna and Rome to be educated; to Venice to buy books. But they also went to Italy to serve as soldiers. In the long run, it was the Spanish military presence that had the most unfavourable consequences for the way in which other Europeans viewed the peninsula and its rulers.

*

When the emperor left his son in charge of Spain (and, with it, America) in 1543, he retained for himself the ultimate right to make decisions. This required the maintenance of a reliable system of communications, with postal couriers using at least three routes to northern Europe: via Barcelona, Genoa and northern Italy; or through France; or by sea to Flanders. When matters were referred to Charles by post, several weeks might elapse before a decision was made.[10] In practice, virtually all matters of daily government had to be handled on the spot in Spain by the small team of administrators led by Tavera and Cobos. In at least two areas consultation with Charles was indispensable, since serious conflicts of interest might be involved. These were finance, and the granting of jobs and pensions.

Philip was eased almost painlessly into the practice of government. Major decisions were referred to his father, and Cobos with his staff took care of administration. The circle of ministers with whom he worked did not change significantly over the next dozen years. Its members were divided into two groupings, one headed by Cobos, the other by Tavera. Political clans at the time were formed through the use of influence, but there were also strong elements of family connection.

The existence of sharply antagonistic groupings, which managed all the same to cooperate in the king's business, was a fact of life that Philip came to recognise and accept. He benefited from the advice of all. Cardinal Juan de Tavera, president of the council of State, archbishop of Toledo and Inquisitor-General, was aged seventy-one in 1543. Among those associated with his circle was the grand commander of Castile, Juan de Zúñiga. At the other pole was the Cobos grouping, including the ambitious Fernándo de Valdés, aged sixty-one in 1543, president of the royal council and a fierce rival of Tavera. The grouping also contained Francisco García de Loaysa, an influential sixty-four-year-old Dominican friar who had occupied nearly every post of importance in government.

The duke of Alba, Fernando Alvarez de Toledo, aged thirty-six in 1543, did not yet side with either group, though he later came to ally with Cobos. Tall, small-headed, with sharp piercing eyes, he had already displayed evidence of the ability that was to make him the leading soldier of his time. Subsequently he distinguished himself in the wars in France, Germany and Italy. He was general of the militia, councillor of state, and high steward of the household, which gave him charge over the palace. A knight of the elite Burgundian order of the Golden Fleece, he came from one of the oldest and most powerful families in the realm. Totally loyal to the crown, Alba expected in return to receive the highest consideration.

This prompted Charles in his *Instructions* to warn Philip of his 'ambition'. 'You are younger than he: take care that he does not dominate you. Be careful not to let him or other grandees get a firm footing in government.' For the next thirty years, his stern, commanding figure was to play a crucial part in Spanish politics.

The most significant of those who aided Philip in routine work was Gonzalo Pérez. He was born in the first decade of the century to a *converso* family from Aragon, and studied humanities at Salamanca university, which gave him a lifelong interest in the arts. Immediately after his studies he entered the royal Latin secretariat, and was groomed in administrative matters by Cobos. In 1541 he became Philip's personal secretary. In 1543, on Charles's departure, he was appointed secretary of the council of State.

To these different influences on Philip's early years in government we may add that of the Portuguese connection. Outside Castile, Portugal was the only part of the peninsula with which the prince had any cultural contact, and whose language he could understand. His mother Isabel's household was strongly Portuguese. Her Portuguese ladies-in-waiting married into the highest aristocracy of Spain (one married Francisco de Borja). The subsequent marriage of Philip to a Portuguese princess simply underlined what was by now a firm development. Out of this Portuguese background, which continued to influence Philip throughout his reign, the most remarkable figure to emerge was Ruy Gómez de Silva, whose mother had come to Spain as a lady of the empress Isabel. Subsequently he was selected to form part of the small group of noble pages who studied with the prince. A self-effacing but strong personality, Ruy Gómez owed his success to the way in which he became the prince's shadow. Philip, for his part, found in him a companionship and fidelity which he always appreciated.

Philip's visit to Monzón in 1542 had brought him into touch for the first time with the threat of war against France. Otherwise, these years were for the prince, as for Castile, years of peace. The emperor's military disputes in Germany were conducted without implicating Spain. Castilians sent occasional troop detachments, and responded to appeals for money, but otherwise kept clear of the wars. The realms of Aragon, which claimed the privilege of not having to send soldiers, contributed with periodic grants. Spaniards were reluctant to be dragged into a north European role, for them in some measure still a new experience. Most preferred the familiar environment of the south, where they knew the Mediterranean and continued their old conflicts with the Moorish enemy.

*

The first full debate over which Philip presided as regent took place in the council of State in December 1544. Its theme, as we have seen, was the relative value to Spain of Milan and the Netherlands. Which of the two could the emperor afford to give away as a dowry to the duke of Orléans? The majority of councillors, among them Tavera and Zúñiga, argued that the Netherlands contributed to vital Spanish economic interests and must never be relinquished. Alba, Cobos and their friends argued by contrast that Milan was essential for the strategic protection of Naples, Sicily and Spain, and offered the only secure land routes to northern Europe.[11] It was a key debate, airing all the policy interests that had influenced the crown in past decades, and was highly instructive to the young prince. There was, at least, common agreement that the principal danger came from France. Philip had a personal interest in the debate, for in October 1540 his father passed on to him the right of succession to the duchy of Milan.[12] Charles's final decision, communicated to France in March 1545, was for the cession of Milan,[13] but the untimely death of Orléans in September the same year terminated the negotiations with France and put an end to the debate.

Over these months, Philip continued his triple role as pupil ('Honorat Juan is in continual attendance on the prince,' Cobos informed the emperor), husband and political apprentice. But he was soon forced to rely on his own resources. The loss of his wife in July 1545, followed almost immediately by that of the venerable Tavera on 1 August were only the first of a series of blows. Three more senior members of the council died over the next eight months.[14] Then on 27 June 1546 it was the turn of Juan de Zúñiga, on whom Philip had relied for every type of advice. The prince remained in touch with Zúñiga's widow Estefania, then in Barcelona, and wrote to her occasionally from Madrid. But the loss of the grand commander, who had been as a father to him, was irreparable. Finally, on 10 May 1547, Cobos himself died. Of the senior figures who had taken part in the debate over Milan, Alba alone remained, but he was not available, either. In January 1546 he had joined the emperor in Germany, to help Charles prepare his forthcoming offensive against the Protestant princes.

The emperor evidently did not intend to leave Philip without firm guidance. Among the figures who rose to importance now was Fernando de Valdés, the third of the advisers appointed by Charles in 1543. He was made archbishop of Seville in 1546 and Inquisitor-General the following year. Over the subsequent decade he began to exercise a considerable influence in internal affairs. Also appointed in these months was Luis Hurtado de Mendoza, second marquis of Mondéjar, who brought the illustrious house of Mendoza into the councils of state.[15] Though important, these personages were not, like their predecessors, men who could influence the prince. Philip had grown up under the shadow of weighty men whose counsels he had followed to the letter. Freed of their tutelage, he continued to rely on the advice of others, but asserted the right to choose his advice and make his own decisions. His father still controlled all appointments (Mondéjar's nomination was made from Regensburg) and determined all policy, but Philip in Spain began palpably to exercise the reins of power.

There was nobody else to do it. In the months after Zúñiga's death, Cobos became seriously unwell. 'Loaysa is ill and the cardinal [Tavera] has gone to Toledo. In short, the whole load falls on me,' Cobos confided to his secretary early in 1545. 'I'm so weary that I don't know what to do with myself.'[16] Though tired, he was still in fair health. In the summer of 1546, however, he fell seriously ill so the prince took over effective direction of affairs. He wrote to Cobos expressing his worry that business was being affected by his illness. 'Since you are now able to walk about,' he wrote in his own hand, 'it would be sensible for you to come and convalesce here, since the business there can be left, and important matters can also be dealt with here.' In September: 'I am distressed that your illness is continuing, but hope that it will improve and that you will soon be able to take part in affairs.'[17] At this juncture Charles took steps to reinforce Philip's authority by having him invested as duke of Milan in a private ceremony conducted at Guadalajara by the marquis of Mondéjar and notarised by Gonzalo Pérez. The act took place on 16 September 1546.[18]

Philip assumed responsibility over decisions in Castile. He took over full direction of the loan which was to be requested that year from the cities of Castile and responded to official correspondence from the emperor, without waiting for Cobos. Philip wrote to Cobos in September: 'This mail has come from the emperor; I have opened the package and taken the letter for me in his hand, and have read that [to Cobos] written in the secretary's hand.' Philip reported directly to the emperor on the steps he had taken to raise money.

All state revenue up to 1550, he stated frankly, was spent:

So that to my way of thinking, and according to what the grand commander indicated to me before his indisposition, the plain truth must be put to Your Majesty: we have reached the end of the line. We do not know from where nor how to seek ways and means of finding money. The problem has immersed us all in a far greater anxiety than you can imagine, and is certainly the main reason to have put the grand commander in the state he is, and worsened his condition.[19]

Preparations were meanwhile under way for holding a meeting of the Cortes of the crown of Aragon in Monzón. Charles issued the official summons from Bohemia in April 1546. Responsibility for the session fell entirely on the prince, who since 1544 had also busied himself in the 'affairs of Aragon'[20] and knew something of the issues there. There were, besides, other matters concerning the world-wide monarchy which awaited attention.

Philip was aware of the problems of the Spanish presence in America. He was in Barcelona in November 1542 when his father signed the New Laws which had been drawn up by a committee inspired by the veteran priest Bartolomé de las Casas. Las Casas himself was in Barcelona early in 1543, and Philip talked to him there as well as in Valladolid, where the laws were officially confirmed in June. Las Casas in those months had tried to persuade Philip to 'order it decreed throughout this realm [he was referring to Andalusia] that all the Indians in it be set free'.[21] The government was serious about its intention to enforce the New Laws, as we see by the contract issued to Orellana, discoverer of the river Amazon, in 1543. In its very first clause the contract ordered that 'no harm be done to the Indians', and that 'in no way must war be waged against the Indians', who were stated to be 'human beings and subjects'.[22] In July 1544 Las Casas sailed for America, endowed with new authority as bishop of Chiapas. His famous New Laws were about to provoke a tide of rebellion among the Spanish settlers in America, who refused to accept an end to their control over the native Indians.

The rebellion was most serious in Peru, where the new viceroy, Blasco Núñez de Vela, used high-handed methods to introduce the laws, and failed to stifle a rebellion by the conquistador Gonzalo Pizarro. In January 1546 Pizarro defeated and killed the viceroy in battle. On receiving news of the troubles in Peru, the prince in 1545 called a meeting of the council. Eight members were present including Tavera, Cobos, Zúñiga and Alba. Alba was alone in suggesting that the rising should be crushed 'with great strength and force' and 'a large and powerful armada'. All the others considered this wholly impracticable.[23] They were anxious to make concessions (some of the New Laws were revoked at the end of 1545), but at the same time refused to condone rebellion. Since it was logistically impossible to despatch an army, they decided to send a lone emissary as 'pacifier'. The man chosen was the priest Pedro de la Gasca, a member of the council of the Inquisition who also had considerable military experience. The emperor followed events closely from Germany, and sent Gasca his instructions from there,[24] but all the practical steps were directed by the council and the prince.

Gasca's success story began with his landfall at Nombre de Dios in July 1546. He was armed with absolute powers, but little else. With amazing skill, he won sufficient support to raise an army and bring about the defeat and execution of Pizarro in April 1548. For Philip it was his first contact with armed rebellion. Early in May 1547 he wrote to Gasca hoping 'that the land be pacified through the path of clemency, without any need for severity or punishment'. Two weeks later he recognised that if the rebels did not submit, 'it seems that an exemplary punishment may be exercised on the leaders and on the most guilty'.[25] Gasca's total success in Peru made a lasting impression on Philip. Seven years later, when there were further troubles in the same region, he wrote from London commenting that it might be necessary to call again on Gasca's services.[26] The example of Peru decisively affected his approach to the problem of rebellion.

*

Throughout 1547 Philip was actively in control of affairs in Spain, consulting when necessary with the ailing Cobos. He was also developing what came to be one of his great hobbies, an interest in building. The emperor had for some years been planning to restore and rebuild parts of the half-neglected royal palaces, notably the Alcázars (medieval fortresses) in Madrid and Toledo. In 1543 he charged his architect Luis de Vega to construct a palace on the site of the hunting-lodge at El Pardo. His absences shifted the work on to Philip's shoulders. In May 1545 the prince set up a special department, the Committee for Works (*Junta de Obras y Bosques*), to oversee the royal residences and administer justice on the royal estates. It developed with time into a major government body. In August 1548 Philip commissioned a report on the Alcázar in Madrid and the house at El Pardo. 'Look into this and remind me about it,' runs one of his marginal comments that year on papers related to the palaces.[27] El Pardo was the first building which bore witness to his evident interest in design and architecture. His commitment dated from the occasion when he and his father had to spend an uncomfortable night in the cramped space available there. When he complained to Charles, the latter replied that 'kings do not need to have residences'.[28] This did not satisfy Philip. A few days later he set about making his own arrangements for the building. When in 1552 a treatise by the Italian architect Serlio was published in Toledo, the translator (himself a distinguished practitioner) recognised that the prince had 'a taste for architecture'.[29]

*

In January 1547 Philip gave his approval to a plan by Valdés and Cobos to pay salaries to the officials of the Inquisition (who had so far lived only off confiscations from the property of those whom they sentenced). He recommended the plan to Charles, 'since you know better than anyone how important it is to support the Inquisition in these realms'.[30] At the end of May he set out for Monzón. 'Accompanying me are the archbishop of Seville, the marquis of Mondéjar, and a few grandees and other persons who I thought should come with me.'

Before leaving Valladolid, he gave his approval to a highly controversial measure, demanded insistently by his father, for the seizure of gold and silver from the churches of Castile in order to pay for the wars in

Germany. Philip's personal opposition to such seizures confirmed the attitude he had maintained since he took over the regency: unswerving respect for his father's wishes, but a no less firm resolution to follow the more realistic views of his advisers. He wrote: 'I cannot omit to mention to Your Majesty that what was written and commented to you on this matter, was not from a wish to cause difficulties or create impediments, but because it appeared most necessary to act in this way'.[31]

The emperor had learned by now that his son was no mere puppet. Over the next decade they continued to have major disagreements on many matters, both political and personal,[32] but Charles never demonstrated impatience with Philip and never publicly overrode him. He may even have been proud of his son's independent spirit. At any rate, precisely in these weeks the emperor decided that the prince was ripe to enter into his European inheritance. In April 1547 he achieved a resounding victory over the Protestants at the battle of Mühlberg, and felt it was time to put his house in order. Plans were made to bring Philip to visit Germany.

The prince was at Monzón, where on 5 July he opened the joint session of the general Cortes of Aragon, Catalonia and Valencia. His experience of the Castilian assembly of 1544–5 had given him adequate background. But his performance on this occasion was by any standard remarkable, since he had none of his well-tried advisers, neither Zúñiga nor Cobos, to back him up. The term 'general Cortes' was used for what in reality were completely separate sessions of the representatives of the eastern realms, which tended to meet in Monzón because of its proximity to all three realms. The king or his proxy, who alone could summon the Cortes, would pass from one building to another to deal with each Cortes individually.

Business from all over Spain was directed to Monzón. Philip corresponded directly with the ambassador in Lisbon over the precarious health of the king of Portugal, and received letters from Ruy Gómez in Germany.[33] He had to deal with a mass of petitions. Among them was one, which he eagerly supported, asking for the building of more and better houses in Monzón. Neither the court nor the deputies had any enthusiasm for holding sessions in the town. Monzón was a sleepy, inhospitable place, insufferably hot in the summer, with none of the amenities its distinguished visitors might expect. Philip had to resign himself to several further visits. On this occasion he took part conscientiously in the sessions. 'I have seen His Highness in the Cortes,' reported a member of his household, 'pass whole nights without sleep in order to bring his business to a close.'[34]

Shortly after the prince's arrival in June, the indefatigable Bartolomé de Las Casas also turned up. Now aged seventy-seven but as active as ever, he had just returned from America and made haste to visit Philip, who greeted him cordially[35] and listened sympathetically to his account. The two had several meetings during the weeks the royal group was in Monzón. Philip wrote letters on his behalf to the authorities and clergy of the diocese of Chiapas. Las Casas succeeded in obtaining the prince's permission to change the name of the territory where he was currently conducting one of his colonising experiments, from Tuzulutlán to True Peace (*Vera Paz*).[36]

Philip's patronage was a decisive help to the Dominican friar in this critical period. In 1547 the humanist Juan Ginés de Sepúlveda (Philip's former tutor) was beginning the anti-Las Casas campaign which reached its climax in 1550 in a famous debate before the royal council in Valladolid. In the summer of 1547 another well-known Dominican, Melchor Cano, obtained his chair at Salamanca university and entered the lists against Sepúlveda. The controversy over the Indians of America was a debate that embroiled all Spanish intellectuals, and Philip did not remain neutral. He (like his father) gave his continuous support to Las Casas, corresponded with him, and advanced him money. A few years later, he was obliged to make decisions against the advice and opinion of Las Casas, but by then other factors had intervened. It did not affect the considerable esteem in which the old campaigner was always held by Philip.

Among the business that crossed the prince's desk was a matter involving his old tutor, Siliceo. In 1546 Siliceo was promoted by Charles to the archbishopric of Toledo, the principal see in Spain. The new archbishop soon fell out with his cathedral chapter, the body of canons responsible for running the see. He particularly objected to the fact that a number of the canons were of *converso* origin. On the excuse that *converso* origin made one suspect in matters of religion, Siliceo and a majority of the canons in July 1547 voted through a new statute, disqualifying from membership of the chapter anyone who could not prove his purity (*limpieza*) from Jewish blood.

Purity regulations of this type had long existed in a few religious bodies in Castile, but they had always been strongly criticised as racialist and were falling out of use. Philip was in these years no supporter of anti-Semitism: indeed in 1546 he had proposed appointing a *converso* to the see of Granada.[37] Revival of the issue by Siliceo caused a storm of protest, which soon reached the prince in Monzón.[38] The city authorities of Toledo complained energetically to the prince and to the council against a measure which, they said, was certain to stir up enmities and resurrect all the bitterness of the Comunero movement 'twenty-six years ago'. Those canons who opposed the statute also protested, and one of them obtained a resolution from the university of Alcalá condemning the decision. In response to the petitions sent to him (which included a personal letter from Siliceo to his former pupil), Philip sent out for appropriate opinion.

The bishop of Sigüenza consulted with his clergy and informed the prince that the statute would cause 'great problems', and should be withdrawn. The royal council, the highest court in the land, agreed that 'this statute is unjust and scandalous and if put into effect could cause many problems'. The matter could clearly not be allowed to proceed, particularly since in September a special magistrate sent out by Philip informed him that 'in the city there are many persons who would be affected by it'. To let the measure take effect would undoubtedly cause serious disorder in Toledo, so the prince at the end of September 1547 signed an order suspending the statute, and in November informed Siliceo that he was consulting the emperor.

In December, immediately after closing the Cortes, he left Monzón: 'I left Monzón on Friday the ninth, and am going to Alcalá de Henares to spend Christmas with the Infantas my sisters'.[39] The family reunions with María and Juana were always a special pleasure.

Philip's stance in favour of Las Casas, and against the anti-Semitism of Siliceo's statute, was neither original nor daring. Controversy over the Indians of America, and the place of *conversos* in Spanish society, had been around for many years. Among the elite, very many supported Las Casas and saw little problem in living side by side with *conversos*. Philip's position accorded with the attitude taken by people in educated circles. The 1547 Toledo statute, his biographer was later to write, was 'detested by those who lay down the guidelines for good government'.[40]

*

From Germany, Charles V expressed his anxiety and impatience to see Philip. He was concerned by the instability in many of his territories, and the state of his own health. The gout, which afflicted nearly every personage of the time, was laying waste his body. He wished to make arrangements to pass on a secure succession to his son. Moreover, a whole epoch in European history ended in the year 1547. On 28 February, Henry VIII of England died. Just over a month later, on 31 March, Charles's great antagonist Francis I of France also passed away. The previous year, 1546, when Martin Luther died, also marked the end of the career of the scourge of the Mediterranean, Khair al-Din Barbarossa. It became urgent to prepare Philip for the new scenario in European politics. Fortunately, the west was now at peace.[41] Charles's victory over the German Lutheran princes at the battle of Mühlberg in April 1547 restored some tranquillity to central Europe. It was safe for the prince to travel abroad. Early in 1548 Charles sent the duke of Alba to Spain with instructions to reform the ceremonial of the Spanish court, and bring Philip back with him. In January in Augsburg he drew up a long set of *Instructions* which he sent to Spain with Alba, for the prince to consider before he left the country.[42]

When Alba arrived he brought the emperor's orders to introduce into Spain the ceremonial of the court of Burgundy.[43] Charles was conscious of the poverty of royal ritual in Spain and wished to prepare the prince for the more elaborate forms used in the north. The new ceremonial was officially inaugurated (despite the hostility of many Castilian nobles and of Alba himself) in the Spanish court on 15 August 1548, to coincide with the festivities of the feast of the Assumption. The personnel of Philip's household before this had formed two distinct groups: his gentlemen, pages and servants, including those in the kitchen and stables; and the chaplains and choir of the chapel. Before 1548, as we have seen, they totalled at least 110 persons. The Burgundian ritual brought about changes at the top. There had been only one chamberlain before; after 1548 the prince had a high steward and five assistant chamberlains. He also gained over fifty 'gentlemen' with various ceremonial duties. Little change occurred at the lower levels of the household. Altogether, the immediate personnel after 1548 added up to about 200 persons, without counting the members of the guard.[44]

In February 1548 Philip summoned the Cortes of Castile to Valladolid to settle outstanding matters, mainly of finance. When the deputies assembled on 4 April the prince informed them of his impending departure, but his message was not well received. Castilians had already lived nearly six years without their king; now they were losing their prince as well. They petitioned Philip not to leave the realm, and sent a letter of protest to Charles.[45] 'If the absences of their rulers continue,' they said, 'these realms will be left even poorer and more ruined than they are.' 'Castile does not accept the absences of its princes,' a historian of the time observed.[46]

On 13 September the archduke Maximilian, who was due to exercise the regency during Philip's absence, arrived from Vienna with his retinue of Austrian and Czech courtiers. A marriage had been arranged between him and Philip's sister María. Son of the emperor's Spanish-born brother Ferdinand, Maximilian spoke perfect Spanish, as well as five other languages. Since April this year he had borne the honorary title of king of Bohemia. Two days after his arrival he was formally married to the Infanta María. The extensive celebrations included the staging of a comedy by Ludovico Ariosto.[47]

At daybreak on 2 October Philip's party set out from Valladolid for Barcelona. The prince left the bulk of Cortes business in the hands of his administrators. A summary of the petitions of the Cortes, well over 200, was brought to him in Catalonia shortly before his departure. He gave his formal assent to half of them; the most pressing ones, expressing opposition to his departure, were studiously ignored.

It was a bad time to leave. The Castilian countryside was afflicted by drought. Grain was scarce, with prices 'never before seen in Castile'.[48] In

Valencia there had for months been rumours of an insurrection among the Moriscos, who constituted a third of the population of the province. One of Philip's last acts before leaving was to set up a special committee under Inquisitor Valdés, made up of eighteen persons including 'theologians and lawyers from all the councils', to discuss the problem. After each had given his view in writing, 'I have now ordered them to meet again and reduce their opinions to only one,' the prince informed his father.[49]

The royal party was a large and distinguished group that included Alba, Ruy Gómez, and a number of leading nobles. There were noted humanists, among them Gonzalo Pérez as secretary, Honorat Juan as tutor, Constantino Ponce de la Fuente as preacher, and Cristóbal Calvet de Estrella as chronicler. Foreigners in the entourage included the German cardinal of Trent, who was with Philip during the entire journey. The prince was also accompanied by his musicians, among them his guitar-teacher Luis Narváez and the blind composer Antonio de Cabezón. The prince's steward, Vicente Alvarez, went along to supervise food arrangements, and in his spare time wrote a journal of the whole trip.

Although the travellers encountered violent rainstorms in Catalonia, Philip managed to make a three-night stay at Montserrat. In Barcelona, which he entered on 14 October, he resided at the palace of Estefania de Requesens, who over the years had been as a second mother to him. A sumptuous banquet was laid on by the cardinal of Trent for the prince and other guests, during which over 150 different dishes were served. At the three-hour feast, the prince became exceptionally merry and 'began to drink a bit more than he was used to'.[50] The group left Barcelona on 18 October and headed north for the port of Rosas, where bad weather delayed their departure. They eventually sailed in the fleet of fifty-eight galleys commanded by the great Genoese admiral, the eighty-two-year-old prince Andrea Doria, on 2 November.[51]

*

Philip's excitement at his first sea voyage shines through in the letters he wrote on arriving in Italy.[52] The bad weather of the past few days continued, so for security the ships kept close to the coastline and Philip slept ashore. On 3 November he passed the night in Cadaqués. The next few days were spent mainly on land, visiting Cotlliure and Perpignan. Not until the ninth did the fleet manage to sail from Cotlliure, but off Aigues Mortes they were held up for six days by the wind, and could neither land nor continue. Provisions had to be ferried out. After they resumed the journey, visits ashore were made at the isles of Hyères and Lérins. Thereafter the weather improved. Doria decided to press on straight to Italy, so they sailed past Nice and Monaco without stopping. The first landfall was made just before dusk on 23 November at Savona, where the feast of welcome, put on by the Spinola family, was remarkable for the presence not only of the highest nobility of northern Italy but also of agents from all the chief Italian banking-houses, the Lomellini, Pallavicino, and Grillo. The prince was not used to such cosmopolitan company, and had difficulty with the language. He spoke very little. His formality seemed rather 'austerità e severità',[53] noted an observer.

When not faced with formal courtesies, Philip was very much more at ease. He participated wholeheartedly in festivities, dancing and tournaments; his energy on social occasions was formidable. The voyage ended on 25 November, when the entire fleet sailed into the harbour of Genoa. Philip was the guest for sixteen days of prince Andrea Doria at his palace outside the city. Head of Genoa's leading noble family, the great seafaring admiral had allied himself to Charles V twenty years before. Since that time, his private fleet had been the mainstay of Spain's naval power in the Mediterranean. The high point of the stay was Philip's formal attendance at mass in the cathedral on 8 December. The city was packed with nobles, soldiery and populace. The Spanish guard wore the prince's livery: yellow, white and red. The only event marring the visit was a small public disturbance to protest against the conduct of the Spanish soldiers.

The party left Genoa on 11 December. It was cold, and snowing. They took the route through Alessandria and Pavia, and in each town did a bit of touring and admired the fortifications. On the nineteenth, as they approached Milan, they were met by the duke of Savoy, Carlo III, who accompanied them into the city. Philip himself was duke of Milan, by gift of his father, and entered to a suitably triumphant welcome. The stay, which lasted nineteen days, was taken up with tours, feasts, banquets, tourneys, theatre visits and balls. On New Year's Day the governor, Ferrante Gonzaga, put on a great feast followed by dancing. Philip stayed up until it ended at four in the morning. His gallantry to women was evident. At the feast he gave up his seat of honour to the governor's daughter and let the fair ladies drink from his glass, 'something no one had ever seen before'.[54] At the tourney held a few days later, he was 'looked at admiringly by the ladies because he fought with such spirit and agility'. But the stay was not all gallantry. Philip took time off to meet the great artist Titian, and commissioned some portraits from him.[55]

The journey resumed on 7 January. The route took them through Cremona and Mantua (a four-day stop, as guests of the duke of Ferrara). From here they began the ascent up the mountainous valley of the river Adige. They crossed out of Italy now, into German territory, and on the twenty-fourth arrived at Trent.

Philip was welcomed into the city by the cardinals of Trent and Augsburg, and by Charles V's ally the young twenty-seven-year-old Elector of Saxony, Maurice. Triumphal arches covered the streets. Trent was a centre of world attention because of the Church council which should have been in session there. In 1547, however, the prelates at the council were instructed by the pope to move temporarily to Bologna, because of an outbreak of plague. Only the prelates dependent on Charles V – the Germans and Spaniards – disobeyed the pope and stayed on at Trent. It was this small group which now took part in welcoming the prince of Spain. Philip managed to speak to the prelates, but the greater part of his time in Trent was occupied in festivities. Every night there was a banquet. On the first night, 'the dinner was joyous and very German because everyone drank a lot; it ended at ten and then the celebrations began'.[56] There was dancing: 'the first to dance was the prince, who was picked out by the most beautiful of the Italian ladies.'[57] The next two nights, Friday and Saturday, the prince dined alone. It was a self-discipline which he had practised for many years, and which he apparently continued for the rest of his life. Twenty years later an ambassador reported that he was still following the practice.[58] The last of the five nights the party spent here took the form of a masked ball that lasted almost until dawn. The prince, Elector Maurice and the other nobles wore masks. The gaiety was so general that the cardinals of Trent and Augsburg also danced with the ladies.[59]

The journey to the Netherlands lasted a full six months, an extended pleasure tour which was also intended to be educational. As they went north they were preparing for the cold and snows of the Alps. At Bolzano, where they spent the night of 30 January, Philip was presented with a large block of silver ore, mined in the region. His companions noted the well-being of the people in the Tyrol, the wayside crucifixes, the beauty of the women, the gradual disappearance of vineyards. On 3 February they made their way up to the Brenner pass, and then descended towards Innsbruck, which they entered on the fourth.

From this point the cardinal of Trent acted as Philip's translator into German. After a rest at Innsbruck, where Philip spent a day hunting in the woods, the entire group embarked in boats and sailed down the river Inn as far as Rosenheim. It was a relaxing journey which they broke every night in order to sleep ashore. From Rosenheim they pressed overland, spending the night at the abbey of Ebersberg. On 13 February the party arrived at Munich where they were greeted by duke Albert of Bavaria and his family. The Spaniards were immediately impressed by the beauty of the town, its little houses and clean streets. There were banquets nearly every night. On the second day they went hunting in the woods round Munich, and had a splendid picnic in the country. That night there was a sumptuous dinner with 'sweet music and ladies'.[60] 'During all these entertainments, His Highness was as happy, relaxed and sociable as if he understood the language; as a result everyone was enchanted, above all the duke's daughter.'[61]

Two days after leaving Munich the party, which since Trent also included Maurice of Saxony, entered Augsburg. It was 21 February.

Philip for the first time learned what it was like to live among heretics, since the area was largely Lutheran. It did not affect his conduct. His father's firm policy was one of unavoidable coexistence with Lutherans and Philip accepted it without protest. Maurice of Saxony, his close companion during the journey, was an active Lutheran and leading ally of the emperor. The prince greeted the city councillors cheerfully, and spent four days in the partly Protestant city. He took the opportunity to visit the magnificent palace of the Fugger family, financiers who had enriched themselves by lending money to his father. The day after departing from Augsburg, Elector Maurice took his leave in order to return to Saxony.

The next important stop was Ulm, where they spent the last two days of February. The entertainment here was a joust between boats on the Danube. The losers were tipped into the river. Philip was now travelling through the solidly Lutheran territory of Württemberg. His party made their way north, towards the Rhine. At Vaihingen they were met by the Grand Master of the Teutonic Knights, the Lutheran duke Albert of Hohenzollern, with a military escort which accompanied them as far as Speyer. In this way they reached Heidelberg, capital of the Palatinate, on 7 March.

The remarkable city, set on a hill overlooking the woods of the river Neckar, was at this time a Catholic area surrounded by Lutheran states. Philip spent four days here. On the second, he went out hunting at the mountains and picnicked in the woods. On the third, there was jousting in the castle courtyard, followed that night by a ball and a banquet. As in the other feasts along the route, the prince took pains to follow German drinking habits. There was a series of toasts, and each time he dutifully raised his glass and drank the wine. But 'that was hazardous, for His Highness was not used to these practices'.[62] The wine was, all the same, delicious,[63] of a quality unknown in Spain. The Germans expressed their satisfaction at seeing the prince doing 'many things against his inclination and habits' simply to please them.[64] Philip could not have been happier. He wrote from Heidelberg to Ferrante Gonzaga that 'I have been very well received by all these princes and cities of Germany, with great demonstrations of affection'.[65]

The group left on the eleventh and arrived in the evening at Speyer, on the river Rhine. They were met by a Netherlands military escort under the command of the duke of Aerschot, and by the archbishop of Mainz who came downriver to greet the prince. They then struck out westward instead of going down the valley of the Rhine. Passing through Kaiserslautern, Zweibrücken and Saarbrücken, they arrived in Luxembourg late on 21 March. Philip stayed only one day in the town, in which he spent the time examining the walls and defences. He had a passionate interest in military fortifications, and had inspected the defences of every city through which they passed on the journey. He was now on home

ground, in the states of his father. The party spent the last three days of
March in Namur.

A few miles outside Brussels, a reception was put on for the approaching travellers by queen Mary of Hungary, sister of the emperor and regent
of the Netherlands. Towards nightfall on 1 April, Philip made a formal
entrance into the capital. The streets were brilliantly decked and illuminated, there were triumphal arches everywhere and torches in the windows. Over 50,000 people, a witness estimated, were gathered in the city
centre to greet the prince.[66] Philip made his way to the royal palace, where
he was received formally by Mary and by her sister the queen of France,
Eleanor. The two queens accompanied him to a room where the emperor
was waiting to receive him. The two embraced. Philip had not seen his
father in six years.

*

The political team with which Philip came into contact in these years was
his father's. It was made up of men whose professional horizon was the
whole of Europe. They usually had a university background, were trained
in the humanities, and spoke several languages. They focused their loyalty not on any single nation but on the emperor, a personage transcend-
ing nations. When prince Philip was in the north, the most important of
these officials was the emperor's chancellor, Antoine Perrenot. A native of
Besançon in the Franche-Comté, Antoine (born in 1517) was the eldest of
the five sons of Nicolas Perrenot, chancellor for over twenty years. During
that period, father and sons worked together in the emperor's service.
Antoine pursued his career through the Church, and was appointed
bishop of Arras in the 1530s. When Nicolas died in 1550, Antoine succeeded him as the emperor's closest counsellor. During Charles's last,
difficult years in the Netherlands, Perrenot directed policy. In the process,
his approach clashed with that of the nobility of the Netherlands.

The Netherlands were (as the name implied) a small group of
unspectacular, low-lying provinces whose economic sustenance came
mainly from the sea. The major port, Antwerp, was a hive of trading
activity. Despite its unassuming aspect, the country was always a potential source of problems. Its seventeen provinces had no political unity
beyond their allegiance to a common ruler, Charles. They technically
formed part of the Holy Roman Empire ruled by Charles, but the emperor
had some years before secured their effective autonomy. The Netherlands
had a common constitutional assembly, the States General, but real political power rested with the great nobles and above all with those who were
governors (*stadhouders*) of the leading provinces. Charles had attempted
to strengthen control in the capital, Brussels, by setting up a system of
three central councils. Differences between the provinces were aggravated by cultural divisions: the greater part, roughly the northern areas

down as far as Brussels, spoke Dutch; in the south, economically richer and more densely populated, the principal language was French.

The dual culture affected politics. The Netherlanders felt themselves kin to both the Germans and the French. Most greater nobles had French origins, but they frequently married into German families. The most prominent grandee was William of Nassau, prince of Orange, six years younger than prince Philip. Holder of extensive estates in both France and Germany, he became in 1559 *stadhouder* of the provinces of Holland, Zealand and Utrecht. In 1561 he married, as his third wife, the daughter of Elector Maurice of Saxony. Another of the magnates of the country was Lamoral, count of Egmont, four years older than Philip and *stadhouder* of the French-speaking provinces of Flanders and Artois. The cosmopolitan links of Netherlands nobles tended to make them the focus of international interest.

The complex situation in the Netherlands was at its most delicate in religion. The Dutch had a well-deserved reputation as religious liberals. It was the country of Erasmus, guiding light of European humanism. But it was also the country where the radical Anabaptists most flourished, and where they were (during the 1530s) the most bitterly persecuted. In the months that he was in the Netherlands, Philip became familiar with an environment where the existence of heresy was accepted as almost natural.

For the first three and a half months of his stay he remained in Brussels. In part this was because of the emperor's health. The French ambassador had reported from Brussels in February 1549 that Charles had 'tired eyes, a pale mouth, face more dead than alive, his speech weak, his breath short, his back bowed'.[67] He managed all the same to make his son's visit agreeable. 'During all this period there were fine celebrations, banquets, dances, elegant masked balls, hunting parties and tournaments.'[68] Philip got to know all the young men who in later years would play a key part in his policies. He jousted shoulder to shoulder with William of Orange (with whom he shared a passion for the literature of chivalry) and Lamoral of Egmont. He went with them on hunts and to balls. There was no problem of communication. Many, like Egmont, spoke perfect Spanish. Several were companions in chivalry, as knights of the elite Burgundian order of the Golden Fleece. Philip also had his fair share of the ladies. The French ambassador commented on his interest in the beautiful young duchess of Lorraine, and 'the frequent kisses and extremely great courtesies that the prince offers her'.[69] But Philip could not avoid work. The emperor made him come 'every day for two or three hours to his study to instruct him person to person'.[70] On 12 July Charles set out with his son on a tour of the provinces.

Even before he entered Germany a controversial item was put on Philip's plate. Consequent on his victory at Mühlberg Charles took as prisoners the Lutheran leaders the duke of Saxony and the Landgrave Philip of Hesse. They were kept under honourable custody in Brussels. Among the first letters the prince received while in the Empire was one from the duke, asking him to mediate with the emperor for his release.[71] The requests did not stop. Elector Maurice, who was married to the daughter of the Landgrave, asked Philip when he met him at Trent to intercede with Charles.[72] Philip said he would try. Shortly after leaving Heidelberg he was pursued by a similar request from the princess Palatine. This time the prince explained that he could not, because the emperor was very angry over the whole matter.[73] The issue remained with him to the end of his stay in Germany.

Philip's tour had as its purpose the swearing-in of the prince of Spain as heir to each province. Charles intended that Philip should get to know his future northern subjects. For the next few months the cities vied with each other in the complexity of their triumphal arches and celebrations. The royal party included the households of the emperor, the prince, Mary of Hungary, and the leading nobility. The journey was done in two phases. In July and August 1549 they toured the southern provinces and returned afterwards to Brussels. Then in September and October they went round the northern provinces. As in the trip through Germany, there was much to wonder at and admire.

The highlight of the first part of the tour was the entertainment put on by Mary of Hungary for her guests in the last week of August 1549 at her palace in Binche. Mary had converted the old château into one of the most sumptuous Renaissance palaces of northern Europe. The stay there left an unforgettable impression on Philip. His suite of rooms was richly furnished and decorated in a way that he was later to imitate. The little chapel contained a painting of *The Descent from the Cross* by Roger van der Weyden which the prince so admired that he later (in 1574) acquired it for the Escorial and also, before that (in 1569), had a copy painted for him by the Flemish artist Michel Coxcie. On 24 August a great tourney was mounted in the palace courtyard, with the prince participating. Over the next two days the queen staged a splendid chivalric feast, based on the popular book of chivalry, the *Amadis of Gaul*. Knights (one of them was Philip) had to traverse several obstacles in order to gain entrance to the Dark Tower, liberate the prisoners there, and afterwards make it to the Happy Isles. On the twenty-ninth the guests went out to Mary's nearby château at Mariemont, where there was a feast served by pretty girls dressed as nymphs and huntresses. This was followed by the storming of a mock castle by knights who had to liberate imprisoned maidens. The next day there was another tourney, with sixty knights participating. After nine days at Binche, Philip continued the tour, this time northwards.[74]

On 11 September the prince made a formal entry into Antwerp, the commercial metropolis of northern Europe, where he was accorded the privilege of a magnificent 'Joyous Entry', as the ceremonial was called. Unfortunately, a heavy downpour dampened the occasion.[75] The visitors were particularly impressed by the opulence of the city, 'which could with good reason be called the market-place of the world'. The Spaniards next paid special attention to Rotterdam, which they visited on 27 September. It was the birthplace of Erasmus who was still highly regarded in Spain, and Philip went specially to mass at the church near Erasmus's family house, and 'the leading lords and gentlemen of the court' went inside the house to pay homage.[76]

The long and tiring tour ended with the return to Brussels on 26 October. Philip had seen every corner of the seventeen provinces, and been sworn in at every principal city. He now took a rest from travel, and turned to other matters. He consulted with the emperor over planning a reunion of members of the Habsburg family. He wrote to Spain to congratulate his sister María over the birth of her first child, and in passing urged Maximilian to come to Germany for the reunion.[77] The feasts, the hunts, the tourneys, the balls, started up again. In December the prince received a splendid gift of eight falcons from the Lutheran king of Denmark. He wrote back, thanking the king profusely: 'they are so fine that we hope to make use of them many times; and if we could please Your Serenity in some matter we shall do so with as much appreciation as our good friendship demands'.[78]

Carnival in Brussels in February 1550 was particularly notable. A joust over the god of love was held at the court. The god was displayed with a noose round his neck and an armed guardian (the Spaniard Alonso Pimentel, aided by count Lamoral of Egmont) at his side. Every time a challenger bested the guardian, the noose was raised. If the guardian scored, the noose was lowered. Unfortunately the challengers triumphed, and love was hanged. That evening a banquet was given by the prince. The god of love was brought in in his coffin, set before the queens of France and Hungary, and a requiem was sung over him. But the musicians played, and the god came suddenly to life again. Everyone danced to celebrate the event, 'even the monks, who joined in without a jot of shame'.[79]

Lent brought a more sober prospect. In February, news arrived which deeply affected both the prince and his friend Luis de Requesens. Estefania had died in Barcelona. Requesens left immediately for Catalonia. During the weeks of Lent, the Spaniards, almost without exception ignorant of French and Dutch, were fortunate to have the services of three good Spanish preachers, Constantino, Bernardo de Fresneda, and Agustín de Cazalla.[80] The names of the first and third of these were, in time, to evoke rather different memories in the minds of the courtiers.

On 31 May Philip was due to leave with the emperor to go to join the Imperial Diet at Augsburg. The last night in Brussels was a time for leave-taking. There were farewells and partings of lovers and friends. The feasts lasted all night.

> That night His Highness did not go to bed. He stayed in the main square, conversing with the ladies as they sat at their windows. A few gentlemen, young and even some old, accompanied him. The talk was of love, stories were told, there were tears, sighs, laughter, jests. There was dancing in the moonlight to the sound of orchestras that played all night.[81]

The imperial party set out for nearby Louvain on the thirty-first. No sooner had they arrived there than Philip decided that he had to gallop back to Brussels. He did so, and spent the night there. 'I do not know,' commented his steward tactfully, 'if he slept under the stars or under a roof.'[82] At any rate, he returned to Louvain the next day 'very worn out'.

After this the journey continued without incident, to Maastricht. The next major stop was Aachen, on 8 June, where the prince admired the quantity of relics in the cathedral and visited the tomb of the emperor Charlemagne. On the tenth they arrived at Cologne, where they stayed four days. The Spaniards were dazzled by the large, beautiful and pros-perous city, 'the splendid countryside along the Rhine', and the green cornfields stretching into the distance.[83] Many of the vast quantity of religious relics in the city were for sale, and were dutifully bought by the visitors. 'Tomorrow,' Philip wrote to Maximilian on 12 June, 'I shall be at the German hunts which are the best anywhere. I would very much like Your Highness's company in them.'[84] They left Cologne and arrived at Bonn the same day, the fourteenth. At this point the travellers changed their mode of transport, for here a small fleet of river boats awaited them. The emperor and Philip were allotted a large, spacious vessel. The con-voy, which left Bonn on the fifteenth, spent the next four days sailing in summer sunshine up through the spectacular gorges of the river Rhine. The emperor relaxed on deck, enjoying the breeze and dictating his memoirs (in French) to his secretaries.[85] Each night they slept on land, in Andernach, Koblenz, Boppard and Bacharach. In this way they reached Mainz, where the emperor and Philip stayed as guests of the archbishop.

The rest of the journey was overland. Leaving Mainz on 21 June, they headed south towards Worms and Speyer. After three days in Speyer, they retraced the route that Philip knew well from his previous trip. Early in July they finally reached their objective, the Imperial city of Augsburg.

*

On 8 July 1550 they entered Augsburg, to which the Imperial Diet (the parliament of German princes and cities) had been summoned by the emperor. Delegates to the Diet were already assembling, though sessions did not commence until the last week of the month. The emperor was concerned to obtain their help against a threatened invasion by the Turks up the Danube. For their part, most delegates were more interested in clarifying the religious situation in Germany. The Protestants were particularly concerned to obtain the release of the duke of Saxony and the Landgrave of Hesse. Philip was able to observe at first hand the comings and goings among Protestant and Catholic princes. It was an atmosphere that benefited from the freedom of religion laid down by Charles's toleration decree (known as the Interim) of 1548.

Philip spent an entire year in southern Germany. It must have been one of the most formative periods in his life, but curiously he never referred to it in later years. He made an attempt to get on with the young German nobles, whose manners he found brutish. 'Our prince is doing his best,' it was reported of him. 'He often goes out to join in their sports, and is to take part in a tourney next Thursday.'[86] But he seems to have found living among them for an extended period rather different from the casual festive pleasures he had got used to during his travels. If Philip's views coincided in any way with those of his steward, Vicente Alvarez, he probably found the Germans excessively restless, given to violence, drink and newfangled ideas. By contrast with conflicts in Germany, Spain seemed an isle of tranquillity.[87]

Apart from social pleasures, the prince busied himself with art. In September he was writing to the Spanish ambassador in Venice to make sure that Titian was coming to Augsburg, 'as soon as possible'.[88] When Titian arrived, Philip gave him one of his most important commissions, for a series of mythological paintings known as the 'Poésies'. In Augsburg the artist completed what became Philip's favourite portrait of himself, in armour with his hand resting on a helmet. The prince also had time for architecture. In the same weeks he went over plans, drawn up by an Italian engineer sent by Ferrante Gonzaga, to rebuild the fortress in the Italian city of Siena.[89]

For Charles the most pressing item on the agenda was, after the Diet, a reunion of the Habsburg family. He hoped eventually to leave his inheritance entire to Philip; but to do it he needed the support of the other members of his family. This, he found, was extremely difficult to obtain. The chief members of the Habsburg clan gathered in the city and for six months the debate continued. Charles had over the years consolidated control of the hereditary Habsburg lands – mainly Austria and Bohemia – in the hands of his brother Ferdinand. Since 1531 the latter had been 'king of the Romans', a title that gave him the right to succeed to the Imperial crown. Strongly supported by most German opinion, Ferdinand wished the succession, and the Imperial crown, to pass to his eldest son Maximilian, king of Bohemia and currently standing in for Philip in Spain. Germany, the cardinal of Augsburg declared in November, could only be ruled by a German. The princes would prefer the Turk to Philip, reported an ambassador.[90] Ferdinand insisted to his brother that Maximilian be brought from Spain to express his views. Mary of Hungary came expressly from Brussels in September to lend support to Charles. The discussions (conducted in French, with only Philip using Spanish) seemed for a while to calm down, and Mary returned to the Netherlands after a fortnight. But Maximilian arrived from Spain in early December, and insisted firmly on his rights. Ferdinand and Charles quarrelled violently both in private and in public. They had bitter disagreements over how money then being voted in the Diet was to be spent. The Diet closed in mid-February 1551, but the family dispute went on. Mary returned on New Year's Day from Brussels in response to an appeal from Charles for support.

It became clear that full agreement was impossible, so Charles decided to impose a settlement. A statement was drafted for him on 9 March 1551 by Antoine Perrenot, bishop of Arras.[91] It was signed by all parties. The documents[92] declared that the Imperial crown would pass to Philip after going first to Ferdinand. After Philip it would pass to Maximilian. The family accepted this, but as time would show, Ferdinand had little intention of observing the decision. Maximilian, who had long disagreed with Charles over many matters, was even less inclined to cooperate.

Philip during these months mingled work with leisure. He accompanied the emperor to sessions of the Diet. He gave his support to Charles's policies on religion. At the conclusion of the Diet, Charles guaranteed respect for the Lutheran faith in Germany, and referred outstanding religious disputes to the judgment of the council of Trent. Neither then nor later did Philip express disagreement with this policy. It is probable that he accepted the need for religious coexistence within the context of the political loyalty which the Diet offered. During more than two years in the Empire, he had spent much time in the intimate company of Lutherans. He had attended dinners and balls with them, jousted shoulder to shoulder with them and gone on excursions in their company. It had never bothered him, nor should it have: in this early period of the Reformation the nobles in Germany, the Netherlands, France and England continued to treat each other with respect even if they differed in belief. All the Lutherans he knew were, at the time, allies of the emperor. If their political loyalty could be preserved, the religious question could in time be resolved. Religious war and rebellion were not yet, in European politics, the order of the day.

There were, meanwhile, lighter moments. At the end of July 1550 he accompanied Charles on a five-day trip to Munich.[93] They then went out to Starnberg and spent a whole day hunting in the woods. Because of his gout, Charles did not often have the opportunity to indulge in a sport which was always the prince's favourite. On 8 August the party returned to Augsburg. Philip evidently liked Munich, and made another trip there, for four days, in April 1551, just before leaving for Spain. Augsburg had its own diversions as well. In mid-October 1550 a big tourney was staged in the courtyard of the palace in Charles's presence with Philip among the leading participants. For Carnival in February 1551 another big joust was staged. Among the principal knights were Philip, Maximilian, and William of Orange. At the end of the day a ball completed the festivities.

*

In May 1551 the prince prepared to leave for Spain. On the afternoon of the twenty-fifth, Charles left Augsburg for a brief visit elsewhere. Three weeks before, Philip had received a letter from Maurice of Saxony, wishing him well for his journey and asking him one last time to intercede with the emperor for the release of Philip of Hesse. His reply confirmed the good relations he had always had with the Lutheran Elector. He had tried again over the release, he said, 'but I have not managed to achieve anything for the moment'. For the rest, he said he was 'deeply grateful for the care and affection you have shown to me in so many ways since I came to Germany'.[94] He had spent many months in the company of Maurice of Saxony and the other German and Netherlands nobles. He knew that he was leaving behind him a Germany full of problems for Charles. He did not know that, in those weeks, Elector Maurice was preparing to betray the emperor.

Philip left the city in the evening of 25 May with a small escort that included the duke of Savoy. A separate group, which included Maximilian, went by a different route. Philip's party made leisurely progress through the beautiful mountain valleys of the Tyrol, spending three days in Innsbruck, from where he wrote to tell his father that he was well. In the evening of 6 June the travellers arrived at Trent. The famous council had now, with the pope's approval, overcome its previous internal differences. A new, second session had just – on 1 May – begun, with a full complement of delegates. Later there were even Protestant delegates, some of them sponsored by Maurice of Saxony. Their rights at the council were defended by the emperor's Spanish officials Francisco de Vargas and Francisco de Toledo.[95] The meetings received Philip's close attention. He had a talk with archbishop Guerrero of Granada, leader of the Spanish delegation, and during the sessions he got to know fray

Alfonso de Castro, whom he appointed a few years later as his confessor. He also met the Dominican Bartolomé Carranza, whom he appointed as a court chaplain when the latter returned to Valladolid in 1553. Festivities were not forgotten. There were entertainments, and delightful ladies.[96] At dawn on 9 June Philip left Trent. In subsequent months he continued to maintain an active interest in the Spanish contribution to the council, though overall policy towards the council was decided directly by his father. His party made its way across Lombardy. They spent a couple of days in Mantua, where they were fêted by the duke. On Sunday, 14 June, the prince's mass in Mantua was celebrated by Pedro Gasca, who was passing through on his way to report to the emperor on his activities in Peru. Gasca spent the entire afternoon giving the spellbound Philip an account of events in America.[97] The next day the prince left for Milan.

In Milan the governor, Ferrante Gonzaga, welcomed them and took Philip on yet another guided tour of the fortifications. From here the royal group passed through Padua and arrived on 1 July at Genoa, where a political crisis within the governing elite was brewing. The group were joined in the city by Maximilian and his party, and, on 6 July, they set sail in a huge fleet under the command of Andrea Doria. The thirty-eight galleys included Doria's vessels as well as the galleys of Naples under García de Toledo and those of Spain under Bernardino de Mendoza.[98] They put ashore briefly at Nice, where they enjoyed the inevitable feasts and comely ladies.[99] The fleet entered the port of Barcelona on 12 July. Philip wrote off to the duke of Savoy to say that he had had 'the most perfect voyage that one could wish for'.[100]

An ambassador of Venice some time later dismissed Philip's entire tour as a disaster. The prince's demeanour, he suggested, was 'little liked by the Italians, disliked by the Flemings and hated by the Germans'.[101] Like so much else written by the Venetian ambassadors, the conclusion was barely a half-truth. Philip was perfectly aware that he was, at every step of his tour, vulnerable to pressure from all sides. Wherever he went there were bitterly conflicting interests that attempted to corner his support. His response was to follow scrupulously the advice given him by those who directed his movements, whether the cardinal of Trent in Germany or the bishop of Arras in the Netherlands. This apparently sensible policy had the result that, for example, those who disagreed with Arras would complain to the emperor. In Germany Philip had the most difficult time of all. He was condemned for nearly a year to play a purely passive role in his father's policies. The constant efforts to have him intervene on behalf of the Lutheran prisoner princes show that he was not regarded even by Protestants as a diehard. Within the limits of what the prince might have expected from the long trip, there is no reason to take a pessimistic view. He and his Spanish courtiers undoubtedly looked on it as a success. Philip certainly made many errors, and his inability in languages was a constant stumbling-block. But he learned an enormous amount and expanded his horizons in every direction. From a personal viewpoint, he genuinely enjoyed himself.

Maximilian had disembarked on 11 July at the port of Rosas. He set off immediately for Saragossa, where he was due to be reunited with his wife. Philip preferred to remain in Barcelona, where his host was young Luis de Requesens. The stay perplexed the city authorities. It did not fit within the usual norms, and they were unsure what entertainment could be offered. Philip was keen to keep the festive mood going. He met the city council, the Consell de Cent, and demanded that they hire musicians to play music in the streets. This was done: the music went on for three days and nights. He then wanted to know why they had suspended a festivity they normally held in that month. They explained that it was because in the past it had led to excesses and deaths.[102] Disappointed, the prince accepted their decision. On 19 July he informed Maximilian that 'I have decided to leave at the end of this week and take the road through Montserrat'.[103] But he stayed on a few more days in the city. The city records discreetly say nothing of his revelries. Years later, remembering the beauty of the Catalan girls, he warned the young Don Juan against them.

Philip left Barcelona on 31 July and went on to Saragossa. Here he took leave formally of María and Maximilian, who left on 15 August for Barcelona, where they took ship for Italy. Philip left the same day, but in the opposite direction. He went north to Tudela, where on 19 August a special session of the Cortes swore fealty to him as lord of Navarre. From Navarre his party went south to Soria and then headed for Valladolid. On the twenty-ninth he was met at Roa by princess Juana and Don Carlos. Together, they entered Valladolid on the first day of September.

3
Soldier and King
1551–1559

If there is no way to avoid an engagement before I arrive, I cannot enjoin you too strongly to inform me post haste.[1]

(eve of the battle of St Quentin)

By the time Philip returned to Valladolid in the autumn of 1551 the world was again moving towards war.

After three years of feasts, gallantry and women, the prince found it difficult to adjust to the sober reality of politics. The week after arriving in Valladolid he went to Tordesillas for the customary visit to his grandmother. The visits were a painful duty. Juana did not always recognise those who came to see her. For years she had refused to attend mass, or go to confession or communion. She identified all her attendants as devils. Her conversation seemed normal until, suddenly, she would say something which showed that she was not in her right mind.[2] After the visit he went on to stay with his sister Juana at her palace in Toro, 'where I think I shall relax for a week or ten days before going to work in Madrid'.[3]

In fact he remained most of the month at Toro. During his stay he put on a grand tourney at Torrelobatón, in which two groups, each with sixty knights, jousted against each other. Those who took part were 'men at arms I found here'.[4] The entertainment went on for two whole weeks in late September.[5] He was to repeat the exercise from time to time in later years. The Renaissance cult of chivalry, one of his most passionate interests, was reflected too in his collections of weapons and armour, and above all in his reading. Yet despite the excitement of the jousting, Philip felt morose. He had returned home only to be immediately separated from his sister María, to whom he had always felt particularly close. After the tourney, he wrote to Maximilian from Medina del Campo, 'I felt so depressed that I left at once . . . Today I left Toro, feeling absolutely alone.'[6]

The rest of the year was spent alternating between Madrid and Aranjuez. He spent the Christmas of 1551 at Toro. The day after New Year he wrote to Maximilian: 'I came here for the holidays and after them I shall return to Madrid. Before that, my sister will be married.'[7] His youngest sister, sixteen years old and strikingly attractive, was due to marry prince João of Portugal. About to lose her as well, Philip made sure he could spend the maximum amount of time in her company. 'At Easter I'm going to Toro,' he wrote in April.[8] At this juncture international events broke into his domestic preoccupations. The situation abroad was rapidly deteriorating.

Distracted by his ill-health, too confident over his victory in Germany and the secure succession agreed at Augsburg, the emperor was caught unawares by his enemies. In August 1551 the Turks captured Tripoli and prepared to move in the Mediterranean. In October the French forged an alliance with the German Protestants. In 1552 the whole scenario exploded.[9] Maurice of Saxony, on whose friendship Charles had depended heavily, joined the other Protestant princes and came to an agreement with Charles's principal enemy, France. Henry II of France immediately laid claim to the Habsburg lands in Italy. He also sent an army into Lorraine while the German princes massed another army in Franconia. The emperor was at Innsbruck, without sufficient forces. His brother Ferdinand would not or could not help him. Virtually alone, in late May 1552 Charles was forced to flee for safety over the Brenner pass, in the midst of a raging snowstorm.

Philip tried to prepare the treasury for the crisis. A Cortes had been summoned to meet in October 1551. It did not give substantial help, so another session was called for the end of the year. When news from Germany reached Spain there was indignation; the news of his father's humiliation angered Philip. Those who remembered Maurice as a friend were the most indignant. 'What Maurice did was an act of great villainy,' Ruy Gómez protested.[10] Several Castilian nobles, among them Alba, set off at once to help the emperor and Philip intended to follow their example. In June he wrote to Andrea Doria (who was ferrying Alba to Italy): 'I have decided to go to serve His Majesty, and to this effect I am writing the present letter to implore you. When you arrive in Genoa you will do me a very great favour by coming back at once with the galleys, without losing a moment, so that I can cross over.'[11] In the event, no doubt dissuaded by his father, he stayed behind and dedicated himself to raising men and money. Letters were sent throughout Spain to raise volunteer soldiers and cash; the Church was tapped for money.

No sooner was all this set on foot than the prince convoked the joint

Cortes of Aragon for July 1552 at Monzón. Madrid was his base in the first half of 1552. During these months he and Ruy Gómez put into effect in Castile an overhaul of the government and a purge of institutions. The measures (as we shall see, in Chapter Four) brought about the first clashes between Gómez and the duke of Alba. Philip took a break at Easter, which he spent with his sister at Toro, with courtesy stops at Tordesillas to see his grandmother. In mid-June he took leave of Juana, who set out towards Portugal for her marriage to prince João. Philip went in the opposite direction, arriving at Monzón on 30 June.

He braved heat and discomfort to assist at the Cortes. With good reason, he never had favourable memories of his stays at Monzón. This time he remained there a full six months, giving him an opportunity to play a closer role in the affairs of the crown of Aragon. Catalans, Valencians and Aragonese used the occasion to direct their petitions to him. The opening speech was made on 5 July. Subsequent discussions, as often happened, dragged on. To escape from the boredom of the setting, the prince spent his leisure hours hunting and work was left to the end of the day. Secretary Zayas wrote to Gonzalo Pérez from Monzón in November: 'His Highness returned from hunting at about ten, supped at once, and afterwards he and the duke of Máqueda read your letter and were a great while discussing the matter . . . It is now past midnight.'[12] Sometimes the prince returned too late for work. A secretary apologised to Pérez for not replying to a letter sooner: 'because His Highness the day before yesterday spent all day hunting, until late at night'.[13] The Cortes did not close formally until 27 December. Philip stayed to spend Christmas at Monzón, then took his leave and headed for Saragossa. He spent an enjoyable New Year's Day in the Aragonese capital, then returned with the court to Madrid in mid-January 1553.

From October 1552 the emperor had been besieging the city of Metz, then in French hands with a large Imperial army commanded by Alba. But Charles was forced to raise the siege at the beginning of January 1553. It was a humiliating withdrawal, and the emperor's last military action. He felt old, ill and depressed. For some time, he had considered the possibility of abdication. In the autumn of 1552, before the siege of Metz began, he had been opposed to the idea of Philip coming to Germany with reinforcements. Now things looked different. In Brussels, to which he withdrew after Metz, the emperor consulted with Mary of Hungary. She had wanted Philip to come the previous year; now she persuaded Charles to agree that only the prince's presence would give some dignity to the emperor's straits. A letter was accordingly sent in late March from Brussels. The main business, Charles told Philip, was the latter's impending marriage with princess Maria of Portugal. But Philip must also come again to the Netherlands. 'I have represented to you many times how you need to win the confidence and affection of these states, giving them through your presence and contact more satisfaction than they had in your last stay here, since they were not able to get to know you as well enough as was required to keep them happy and gain their goodwill.' Besides, something must be done about the insupportable cost of the wars. He had tried not to touch the wealth of America, which he wished to reserve for Philip, 'so that after my death you may have a source of supply, should some necessity arise when I am not here.' They must discuss this, and also the threat from France. The prince must come north. 'I very much doubt whether these states, of whose importance you are aware, can be sustained without your presence and aid.' Then, after settling these issues and the abdication, 'together we can return to Spain and conclude those matters which I had left aside for until then'.[14]

The letter crossed with one from Valladolid in which Philip expressed his deep regrets at his father's situation. He was doing his best, he wrote, to raise money from every quarter. But Castile's resources were also desperate. Available ships were old and rotting; only a quarter of treasury expenses could be covered; income from America was pledged for several years. Steps were being taken to sell patents of nobility, sell township status to villages, and alienate fiscal rights. 'God knows how much pain and worry it gives me to see affairs in this state at such a time.'[15]

*

The matter of Philip's second marriage was virtually decided. Charles had suggested that the princess Maria of Portugal (Philip's cousin, as daughter of queen Eleanor's first marriage to the king of Portugal)[16] was the most suitable choice, and negotiations were opened. But by 1553 the desperately poor health of the emperor took priority over other business. Charles wished his abdication to take place in his home country of the Netherlands, which he now saw as the centre of his strategy.

The journey to Brussels could not be postponed long. In the autumn of 1553 Philip received a confidential report from the court:

In the opinion of his doctors His Majesty cannot expect to live long, because of the great number of illnesses that afflict him, especially in winter and in times of great cold. He puts on a show of being in better health when he is in fact most lacking in health, since the gout attacks him and frequently racks all his limbs and joints and nerves . . . and the common cold affects him so much that he sometimes appears to be in his last straits, for when he has it he cannot speak nor when he speaks can he be heard . . . and his piles put him in such agony that he cannot move without great pain and tears. All these things, together with his very great mental sufferings, have completely altered the good humour

and affability he used to have, and turned him into a melancholic . . . And on many occasions he weeps and sheds tears as
copiously as if he were a child.

Charles refused to see ambassadors, or even his own gentlemen. 'His
Majesty will not allow anyone, lord or prelate, into his presence, nor does
he want to deal with papers or sign the few prepared for him. He spends
night and day in adjusting and setting his countless clocks, and does little
else . . . And he has spent many days in reading and having read to him
the psalms of David.'[17]
The proposal to marry Maria of Portugal meanwhile took second place
to a far more important possibility. In July 1553 the young Edward VI of
England died. The succession to the still largely Catholic country fell to
his elder sister Mary. It was a heaven-sent opportunity to create an Anglo-
Imperial alliance against France. Charles had himself been briefly
betrothed many years before to Mary. He now proposed that she marry
Philip. In August 1553, when his ambassador Simon Renard first
broached the issue indirectly to Mary, 'she began to laugh, not once but
several times, and looked at me as if to say she found the theme very
much to her liking'.[18] Once the marriage seemed a possibility, Charles contacted Philip, who immediately put himself at his father's disposal. When
Charles made a formal proposal on his son's behalf, Mary's nervous response quickly turned to active interest. She bombarded Renard with
searching questions about the prince, and asked for a portrait. On no account would she marry without seeing what her prospective husband
looked like, so a copy of Titian's splendid portrait of a handsome Philip in
armour (now in the Prado) was sent to her. From the beginning Mary
made clear to Charles what she did and did not expect from the marriage.
'If Philip were disposed to be amorous,' she told Renard, 'such was not
her desire, for she was the age your Majesty knew of and had never harboured thoughts of love.' She would love and obey him, 'but if he wished
to encroach in the government of the country, she would be unable to permit it'.[19] On 29 October, in her private chapel and attended only by a lady-
in-waiting and by Renard, Mary swore to accept Philip as her husband.
Philip accepted the marriage with Mary as a purely political move. He
was not enthusiastic about it, but deferred to his father's wish absolutely.
His agreement was given even before he received a portrait of her (now
also in the Prado), executed by Antonis Mor. In 1553 he was twenty-six
years old, eleven years her junior, and had been unmarried for eight
years. In contrast to his reserved attitude to his first wife, during these
eight years he had built up a reputation for his adventures with ladies. On
his grand tour, in Italy, Germany and the Netherlands, he had been a
great success with the young women. Mary Tudor pointedly asked

Renard about this aspect of the prince. At the very time that the negotiations with her were in progress, Philip in Valladolid was enjoying a
relationship with a court lady-in-waiting, Isabel Osorio.[20] It was a serious
affair that lasted a few years. Philip apparently gave her a secret document declaring that she was his wife. He took care of her (she remained
unmarried) and she died, wealthy, in 1590.[21] Subsequent to the English
wedding, when Philip went to the Netherlands in 1555 he immediately
had love affairs with at least two ladies, one of whom apparently bore him
a daughter.[22] After her marriage to Philip, Mary commented to the
Venetian ambassador in England that 'if she did not have a chaste king, at
least he was free from the love of any other woman'.[23] She may sincerely
have believed this.

In England there was strong opposition at every level to the marriage,
fomented assiduously by the French ambassador Noailles. Though the
English and Spaniards had been allies for a long time, the former were
reluctant to be dragged into Charles V's wars, and wary of the problems
posed by the presence of Protestantism in their country. Most of the royal
council disapproved, and on 31 October the House of Commons suppli-
cated the queen not to marry a foreigner. With typical Tudor determination, Mary persisted. On 16 November she called a hurried meeting of
the Commons (only about twenty members managed to attend) and
announced her decision. The marriage contract, signed on 12 January
1554, attempted to allay English fears. Philip would share responsibilities
and titles with Mary, conform to all English laws and customs, admit no
foreigners to office in England, and not involve England in the wars of his
other realms. If Mary pre-deceased him, he would relinquish his powers.
The conditions were very similar to those which rulers of Spain were used
to (and which king Ferdinand of Aragon accepted when he married
queen Isabella of Castile). There was therefore no problem about
accepting them.

Frustrated by Charles's success in arranging the marriage, Henry II of
France plotted with discontented English nobles and sent money through
Noailles. In January 1554 the leader of the council, bishop Stephen
Gardiner, issued orders for the arrest of the chief plotters. The only part of
the scheme to proceed to the stage of a rising was the movement led from
Kent by Sir Thomas Wyatt. The rebels marched on London, but Mary
stood her ground, and appealed directly to the people in a speech at the
Guildhall on 1 February. The rising collapsed and Wyatt surrendered; the
whole affair lasted just a week.

Because leniency towards plotters at the beginning of the reign was
seen as a cause of the rebellion in 1554, clemency was put aside. About
fifty people, most of humble origin but with some prominent casualties
such as the guiltless Lady Jane Grey, suffered the death sentence. Early in

March, with England tranquil again, the count of Egmont came over from Brussels to ratify the marriage in the name of the emperor and Philip. Before Egmont and the lords of the council, Mary pledged her vows and placed on her finger the ring sent by Charles. On 2 April parliament approved the marriage.

English ambassadors had meanwhile gone to Spain to escort Philip to England. Philip in return sent to England the traditional gift of a wedding jewel, taken by the marquis of Las Navas. At Valladolid the preparations for the journey and wedding were on a grand scale. Philip estimated that he would be arriving with a personal retinue of between 3,000 and 5,000 persons, not to mention the 6,000 soldiers and mariners who would escort the ships.[24] He apparently thought the proposed retinue was modest, but was later persuaded that it looked more like an invasion force. Arrangements were made to leave as regent in Spain his younger sister Juana, whose husband the prince of Portugal had died on 2 January, three weeks after she had given birth to a son, Sebastian. Aged only nineteen when widowed, Juana was attractive but austere; 'discreet' and 'religious' were terms applied to her.[25] She chose to spend the rest of her life in the service of the crown and of religion and, once she had settled her affairs in Portugal, returned to Valladolid. Philip went to the frontier in May 1554 to meet her.

The Cortes of Castile assembled in the city under the presidency of princess Juana, who now took over the government. Philip and his entourage left Valladolid on 16 May and travelled north to Santiago, where the English ambassadors were waiting. He signed the marriage contract brought from England by the duke of Bedford. On Sunday, 24 June the prince and the English nobles attended high mass together in Compostela cathedral.

Philip sailed from Coruña in the afternoon of 13 July. The fleet consisted of seventy large vessels and several lesser ships, bearing the leading lords and ladies of Castile as well as a now reduced force of 4,000 troops. An escort of thirty armed ships brought up the rear. It was an uncomfortable voyage and Philip became violently seasick. 'I nearly died of seasickness,' Ruy Gómez reported.[26] The ships were met off the Isle of Wight by armed vessels from England, under Lord Howard of Effingham, and from the Netherlands. They entered Southampton in the afternoon of 20 July.

The Spaniards were greeted by typical English weather – wind and pouring rain that did not stop for several days. Philip thought better about disembarking his whole retinue at once, and went ashore accompanied by only nine nobles, among them Alba and the counts of Egmont and Hornes. With the reception party was the Earl of Arundel, who presented Philip on the queen's behalf with membership of the medieval chivalric Order of the Garter. The following day the rest of the fleet disembarked, while the soldiers continued on to Plymouth. The prince rested a couple of days in Southampton, then proceeded to Winchester. He entered the town on the twenty-third with a numerous escort. He was 'riding on a faire white horse in a rich coate embroidered with gold, with a white fether in his hat',[27] and was received at the cathedral by the chancellor, Stephen Gardiner, who escorted him to meet Mary. He spoke in Spanish to her, she spoke French. The daughter of a Spaniard, Mary understood Spanish but did not speak it well.[28] 'After they had talked together half an hour they kissed and departed.'

On the night of Tuesday the twenty-fourth he and Mary were paid a special visit by Charles's personal envoy Juan de Figueroa, regent of Naples.[29] Figueroa brought a very special wedding gift: formal investiture as king of Naples and duke of Milan. Charles, in effect, abdicated from these realms and passed them on to his son. The royal pair agreed that the title of king of Naples should be publicly and formally bestowed immediately before the wedding rite in the cathedral the following day. Philip was now in his own right a king, and could marry Mary on equal terms. From this week, he signed his letters as 'king-prince', *el rey príncipe*. In a typical display of independence, he refused to allow any mention of Milan. That, he said, 'was an old matter', and his father had granted him the succession in 1540.[30]

The wedding took place, with appropriate splendour, in Winchester cathedral on 25 July, feast-day of St James, patron saint of Spain.[31] From the beginning, and mindful of his father's urgent advice, Philip tried his best to make a good impression on the English. He instructed his retinue to 'adapt and adjust to their customs, which we all have to accept as our own'.[32] Though all too aware of the recent uprising and the general lack of security in England, he cut down on the size of his Spanish escort and took some English nobles into his retinue. He attempted some words in English. When taking leave of Mary at their first meeting, the hour was late so she taught him how to say 'Good-night' to her ladies, but he forgot it in a second and came back to ask her again.[33] He went walking among the people, despite the rain, and played gallant to the ladies. He drank the tepid beer of the English, so as not to offend. The item appears regularly in the accounts of his kitchen.[34] 'He has shown,' an ambassador commented, 'such great sweetness of temper and such affability as not to be surpassed.'[35]

Work was not forgotten. The day after the wedding, he was up at 7 a.m. and despatched business (for Flanders and Italy) until 11 a.m. Writing to Juana, Philip reported that after the marriage at Winchester 'we came to London where I was received with demonstrations of affection and general contentment'. The entrance to the capital in fact took place many days after the wedding. The royal pair took ship down the Thames and made their entrance by water on 18 August, sailing under Westminster bridge and disembarking in the heart of the city. 'After staying in London six or seven days,' Philip's account continues, 'we came to pass what remains of summer in this house' of Hampton Court. By September, 'I have begun to deal with the business of this kingdom and a good start has been made.'[36] With his arrival, a large number of notables and diplomats from all Europe gathered in London. Gonzalo Pérez judged that eighteen different languages were being spoken at court. But Philip, in his view, handled the situation superbly.[37]

The Spanish nobles were excited by England. For them it was the legendary island of chivalry, the home of king Arthur and of Amadis.[38]

> He who thought up and composed the books of Amadis and other similar books of chivalry, with imaginary countrysides and dwellings and enchantments, must without doubt have first seen the customs and strange ways in use in this realm, before he wrote about them. There is more to be seen in England than is written of in those books, because the dwellings that there are in the country, the rivers, the fields, the beautiful flowered meadows, the cool fountains, are in truth a pleasure to see and above all in summer.

In Winchester, 'we went to see in the castle the Round Table of king Arthur'.[39]

Apart from the wonders of legend and landscape, however, there was little to delight them. They found the English 'white, pink, and quarrelsome'. 'All their celebrations consist of eating and drinking, they think of nothing else.' 'They have a lot of beer, and drink more of it than there is water in the river at Valladolid.'[40] Above all, however, there was tension and hostility. 'We are in an excellent land, but among the worst people in the world. These English are very unfriendly to the Spanish nation. This has been seen very well from the many incidents, some of them important, that have taken place between them and us.' In London there were several incidents in the street, and Spaniards were frequently set upon and robbed. 'There are great thieves among them, and they rob in broad daylight,' Ruy Gómez wrote. Nobody walked at night through the streets for fear of thieves. When the nobles complained, they were told 'that it is in the interests of His Majesty's service to cover up all this'. Not surprisingly, 'some say they would prefer to be in the slums of Toledo rather than in the meadows of Amadis'.[41]

They found the ladies of court 'quite ugly'. One disappointed noble commented that 'I do not know why this should be so, because outside the palace I have seen some very beautiful women.' The Spanish opinion of Mary was unequivocal: 'the queen is in no way beautiful; she is short, frail rather than fat, and very white and fair-haired; she has no eyebrows; she is a saint; she dresses very badly'.[42] The description, which accords perfectly with her portraits, is more generous than that of the Venetian ambassador. He described her as unattractive, wrinkled, 'very short-sighted' (so that books had to be brought up to her eyes) and with a voice 'rough and loud, like a man's'.[43] The queen was sincere and devoted in her relations with Philip, while he was generous and courteous towards her. On both sides, it was accepted that love was not part of the contract. Ruy Gómez observed tactfully in the week after the wedding that 'the queen is a fine lady, though older than we were told. But His Highness comports himself so well and gives her so many presents that I am certain that both will be very satisfied with each other.' 'The king,' he added a few days later, 'is trying to be as gracious as possible to her so as not to fall short in any way of his duty.'[44] In one pithy phrase, he summed up Philip's attitude: 'the king understands that this marriage was effected not for the flesh but for the restoration of this realm and the conservation of those states [that is, Flanders]'. Sandoval, the official chronicler of the emperor, put it even more cogently: 'he acted in this like Isaac, letting himself be sacrificed to the will of his father'.[45]

In the months after the wedding Philip abstained scrupulously from interfering in English domestic affairs,[46] and devoted himself closely to the politics of Spain, Italy and America. In none of these areas did his views coincide with those of his father. Philip had obediently accepted Charles's proposal of the English marriage. But on matters of government, which had effectively been in his hands now for ten years, his perspective was consistently different and independent. Charles, anxious that his son come to Brussels and enable him to proceed with the abdication, sent his secretary Francisco de Eraso to London with a message. Writing in September, Philip explained why some delay was necessary.[47]

The settlement of religion (in which he helped substantially)[48] was going smoothly, he said. At the end of September 1554, his letter continued, he and Mary left Hampton Court for London. On 30 November they presided over a moving joint session of parliament in which the reconciliation of England with Rome, after twenty years of schism, was made law. Although 'I greatly desire to kiss your hands and see you and talk to you, I beg you again to accept that when this is over I shall be able to come.' Besides, 'since the queen is pregnant it will be easier later, and I think it will be around January'. He was not, as some have supposed, anxious to escape from England and from Mary.

On specific matters of policy, he felt bound to disagree with his father. One issue was whether the use of the labour of Indians in America, known as *repartimiento,* should be conceded to the settlers there as a right. He had before him the views of theologians in Spain. He had also now set up in London a special committee of twelve, which debated the issue for three days. The discussion was so violent that a couple of the participants almost came to blows. The two – both of them chaplains of the prince – were the stocky, bushy-browed Bartolomé Carranza, a friend of Las

Casas, and the portly Franciscan Bernardo de Fresneda. Philip did not mention the conflict, only the resolution of the meeting. 'It appears that a majority from both sides agree that one should and can concede the said *repartimiento* in perpetuity, and that there is no other solution for the security and peace of those lands.' He then listed further reasons for this conclusion. 'For all these and other reasons, I have decided that the matter be put into effect.' In a marginal note for secretary Eraso, he scribbled: 'Tell His Majesty firmly that this matter cannot be resolved any other way.' It was a thorny problem, which Philip did not press, and which he allowed everybody to discuss for two more years. Not until September 1556 did he inform the council of the Indies (which solidly opposed the idea) that 'I have resolved to concede it and to order it put into effect without delay'.[49] There was a powerful motive inducing the concession: the settlers had offered the crown five million ducats in gold. Philip explained to the council that 'I cannot find supplies anywhere else to pay the great amount that is owed'.

As for finding funds for a future war with France, Philip wrote to his father, he was opposed to raising any money from the Netherlands. This was, he felt, 'the first campaign in which I am pledged to gain or lose honour [*reputación*], for now and for the future, and on which all have their eyes fixed. Besides, the campaign has to be launched from the direction of those states, and it would be better if I did not under any circumstances need to ask them for new contributions.'

Finally, he insisted that Charles's officials in the Italian states, which were now definitively in his hands, answer only to him. 'It is unreasonable that after Your Majesty has granted me those states, the officials should feel that the grant is only in name and that the situation is the same as before Your Majesty made the grant to me.' The matter was important, for Philip was very shortly to attempt the use of force in Italy to resolve differences with the papacy. Committed as he was to bringing his father's wars to an end, he regretted the turn of events in Siena, where Spanish troops had to be used to put down a revolt. 'I would very much like to explain my actions before the world, to demonstrate that I have no claims to the territory of others,' he informed Charles shortly after. 'But I would also like it to be understood that I must defend that which Your Majesty has granted to me.'[50]

Charles had long since accepted the independent line taken by his son. He swallowed Philip's Italian policy without demur. But he registered his dissent concerning the decision on the Indians. Charles, like Las Casas, felt that a deep moral principle was involved. Philip agreed with them on the principle, but saw the force of his advisers' arguments that if no concessions were made to the settlers then permanent rebellion would be the outcome. Charles wrote: 'I have never been easy on this question, as you know, and have always wished to keep clear of it.' While he remained king, he would never put his signature to the decision. It would be better if Philip waited until Castile and the Indies were passed to him; he would then be free to go ahead. 'You will be able to do it according to your wishes and as something that is your own, and sign the orders; and you will unburden me of this scruple.'[51]

The problems of America were, however, too pressing to be set aside. Las Casas continued to be in close touch with Philip during the latter's absence abroad. The island of Hispaniola, principal centre of Spanish settlement in the New World, was going through a serious crisis. To plead its case it sent a special representative, who took care, before visiting Philip in England and in Flanders, to come armed with letters of recommendation from Las Casas.[52] The supply of gold from America was drying up, and the economy was suffering from a lack of labour. Philip gave his approval therefore to further imports of African blacks as slaves, and to the seizure of Caribbean Indians (thought by the Spanish to be cannibals) as slaves.[53] It was a significant step. Only just over a year before, Philip had accepted the views of theologians that the trade in blacks to America was immoral, and had ordered a trading licence to be suspended.[54] Curiously, in this matter the views of Philip and of Las Casas seem to have coincided absolutely. Both were concerned to strengthen the Spanish presence in Hispaniola (an island which many, including Las Casas, thought was larger than Spain itself) in order to make it rich and powerful. It would become 'a realm greater even than Spain, the very thought of which would make the king of France tremble', as Las Casas put it in 1559.[55]

Very soon after,[56] Las Casas became a firm opponent of black slavery and an outright defender of the Caribs. Philip continued to respect the veteran's views and maintained his favour.[57] 'In consideration of the services of fray Bartolomé de las Casas to the emperor, and his services past and present to me,' runs a royal order of 1560, 'it is our wish that for as long as he resides in this my capital, he be lodged in it in the manner that befits his standing.'[58] For these last years of his life, the aged campaigner followed the court. In 1561 Philip joined Las Casas in a public debate on the American question held in the Dominican monastery of Atocha in Madrid.[59] It was here that Las Casas died five years later. In some respects at least, his ideas continued to influence the king. In May 1565 he presented to Philip the text of his *Twelve Doubts*, a brief summary of his views.

In England, meanwhile, the religious settlement was taking a new and tragic turn. At the end of 1554 a number of bishops' courts began proceedings for heresy against selected persons. On 1 February 1555 the first victim of the persecution was sent to the stake. Many European observers in London, who felt from their experience that burning was no solution, were appalled. On 5 February Simon Renard wrote urgently to Philip: 'I do not think it well that Your Majesty should allow further executions to take place.'[60] The king, however, had no power to intervene in the Church courts. He approached the problem another way. On the following Sunday, 10 February, his confessor fray Alfonso de Castro preached before the court a sermon in which he 'did earnestly inveigh against the bishops for burning of men, saying plainly that they learned it not in scripture to burn any for conscience sake; but the contrary, that they should live and be converted'.[61] There were no further burnings for the rest of the month, possibly as a result of the sermon.

Philip's first direct response to the problem of religious persecution was evidently one of moderation. He seems not to have disagreed with Castro's sermon, and shortly after appointed him to Spain's second see, that of Santiago.[62] The king and his advisers wished to assuage rather than agitate the issue of religion, but several Spanish clergy, including Bartolomé Carranza, supported the English bishops in their campaign of persecution. Mary's own view, that 'the punishment of heretics ought to be done without rashness',[63] was not translated into a policy of moderation. The persecution, and the inevitable rumours about bringing in Spain's Inquisition, helped sow a further seed of distrust between the two nations.

Philip's detachment from English affairs was exemplary. If asked for an opinion he always referred matters to the queen. The Venetian ambassador commented that he was not only popular but also well loved, and would be more so if the Spaniards round him could be got rid of.[64] There was no doubt over English attitudes to the Spanish presence. Protestant voices and French insinuations encouraged English xenophobia. Little incidents served to fan distrust. However, there were also entertainments which soothed tempers. There were masked balls at court, and several tournaments, one of them in the great yard at Westminster at Easter 1555, where the king and his men, dressed in blue, challenged the English knights.[65]

Philip's stay in England lasted little more than a year. He intended to cross over to Brussels in the spring to confer with the emperor, but was held back by Mary's suspected pregnancy. The queen was large. Philip treated her respectfully, but doubts over the pregnancy were all too soon confirmed. By the summer it was accepted at court that the child was 'mere wind'. Philip wrote ruefully to Maximilian: 'the queen's pregnancy turns out not to have been as certain as we thought. Your Highness and my sister manage it better than the queen and I do.'[66]

As soon as everyone became reconciled to the reality, Philip hastened his departure. The bulk of his court stayed behind in London when he took his leave of the queen at Greenwich on 29 August. Mary was disconsolate. She fought back her tears at the leave-taking. Philip, for his part, took delight in kissing all the ladies farewell. His group departed on barges downriver and the queen returned to her apartments. 'Placing herself at a window which overlooks the river she gave free rein to her grief by a flood of tears, nor did she once quit the window as long as he was in sight.' The king stood on the top of his barge to be better seen, and waved his hat in farewell.[67] His large party, which included a good part of the English Privy Council, made slow progress. The river breeze was a welcome relief from the stifling heat of that year's summer, which had provoked forest fires in southern England.[68] Overnight stays were made at Sittingbourne and Canterbury. At Dover high winds delayed embarkation until 4 September, but then they made it in three hours to Calais. On the eighth he met the emperor in Brussels.

*

Philip's presence was necessary in order to carry out Charles's firm decision to abdicate from all his realms. The chief officials of the Netherlands, and the delegates to the States General, were instructed to assemble in mid-October though continuous bad weather forced the date to be put back to 25 October. Invitations were sent out to members of the Habsburg family, knights of the Golden Fleece and neighbouring princes. In the afternoon of the appointed day the emperor, accompanied by Philip and a tiny group of attendants, rode through Brussels to the great hall of the royal palace.

The hall was packed.[69] The emperor made his entrance, walking slowly. He supported himself with his left hand on a stick, his right hand leaning on the shoulder of the prince of Orange. Behind them came Philip, Mary of Hungary, the duke of Savoy, the knights of the Fleece and the high officials of Burgundy. The emperor went up to the dais and sat down. Philip sat down on his right, Mary on his left. A courtier began by explaining briefly to the assembled dignitaries the purpose of the session. Then the emperor, seated because of his infirmities,[70] put on his spectacles and glanced rapidly at some notes in his hand. He raised his head and began to speak.

Before announcing his decision he gave a short and moving summary of his life and his struggles.

> I have been nine times to Germany, six times to Spain, and seven to Italy; I have come here to Flanders ten times, and have been four times to France in war and peace, twice to England, and twice to Africa . . . without mentioning other lesser journeys. I have made eight voyages in the Mediterranean and three in the seas of Spain, and soon I shall make the fourth voyage when I return there to be buried.[71]

While he spoke, the English envoy observed, there was 'not one man in the whole assemblie that poured not oute abundantly teares'. The wave of emotion overtook Charles, who also began to weep. The emperor bade his son kneel before him, asked for his hand and embraced him. He placed his hands on Philip's head and blessed him. The prince then rose to accept the duties entrusted to him. However, he limited his own intervention to apologising, in a few halting words of French, for the fact that he could not speak the language, the official one of the States General.[72] The bishop of Arras, he said, would speak for him. Antoine Perrenot then delivered his address. After him, Mary said a few words. At the end of the ceremony Charles formally invested his son as new sovereign of the Netherlands.

Mary had intimated that she also wished to resign. Charles accordingly appointed as governor of the Netherlands the young duke of Savoy, Emanuele Filiberto. The remaining acts of abdication were made much later. On 16 January 1556 Eraso notarised the act transferring Spain and its dominions. Subsequently, in a confidential document, Charles passed to his son authority over the territories of the Holy Roman Empire in Italy. This (as Perrenot explained carefully many years later) was in contravention of the agreement made at Augsburg, by which only Ferdinand could concede the 'vicariate'. Aware of this, Philip never made use of the privilege.[73] In Spain the absent Philip was proclaimed king on 28 March, in the town square of Valladolid. On 5 February Charles transferred to him the province of Franche-Comté, the other integral part of the duchy of Burgundy. Formal abdication of the imperial crown to Charles's brother Ferdinand did not take place until May 1558. From the spring of 1556, Philip was ruler of the most extensive empire in the world, comprising Spain, England, America, the Netherlands with Franche-Comté, and half of Italy.

Philip's prolonged stay in the Netherlands was dominated by two items of business: the contribution of the States General to Imperial finances, and the settling of differences with the pope. Behind both problems, however, loomed the shadow of France. Surrounded on all sides by the Habsburgs, Henry II of France looked for support to the papacy, headed since May 1555 by the eighty-year-old and violently anti-Spanish Paul IV. In December 1555 both signed a treaty directed against Imperial power. But France was also deeply involved in the Netherlands, a French sphere of influence where the leading nobles were blood relatives of the French aristocracy. In taking over the western inheritance of his father, Philip was also plunging himself into a potential war with France.

War was the last thing he wanted. After his constant strictures to Charles, he knew only too well that the treasury could not finance a conflict. In February 1556 he brought off a surprising peace agreement with France (the treaty of Vaucelles). The core problem remained Italy. At the end of 1555 the duke of Alba had been appointed viceroy of Naples. In September 1556, after months of provocations and sparring between

Paul IV and the Habsburg authorities, Philip ordered Alba in to harass the papal states. The pope managed to win French support, in January 1557 the duke of Guise invaded Italy in the pope's interest, while the Admiral of France, Coligny, attacked the Netherlands. The war became general.

The complex diplomatic moves involving France and the papacy exercised an enduring influence on the soldiers, courtiers and diplomats assembled in Brussels.[74] It was unlikely that Germans, Flemings, Franche-Comtois, English, French, Italians and Spaniards would see eye to eye over matters of policy. Many Flemish nobles, among them Egmont, found common ground with Ruy Gómez and other Spaniards in Philip's retinue. Ruy Gómez and the Flemings, for their part, disagreed profoundly with Antoine Perrenot's political approach. The seeds were sown for serious contention in the future.

Philip could, at least, count on the unwavering support of his cousin Maximilian. On 17 July the king and queen of Bohemia came to Brussels. Philip demonstrated his sincere affection for them, and fêted them with dinners and tourneys during the three weeks they spent there. Apart from wishing to take his leave of Charles, Maximilian came with a special request from his father: that the emperor not abdicate yet in Germany, since the political situation there was still uncertain.[75]

On 17 September 1556, two weeks after Alba marched into the papal states, the emperor Charles V sailed from Vlissingen for Spain. He was accompanied by his two sisters, Mary of Hungary and Eleanor of France. On the twenty-eighth the little fleet of Flemish, English and Spanish ships arrived at Laredo. From here the Imperial party made their way slowly south. After the obligatory stops to meet Juana and other officials, they arrived at the monastery of Yuste (Extremadura) late in November. Charles travelled sometimes in a chair, sometimes in a litter. The construction of the little palace he had planned was not complete, and he did not move into his apartments there until February 1557.

When he came to Yuste Charles had no intention whatever of continuing his political role. Bit by bit, however, he drifted back into touch, conducting an active correspondence on a broad range of matters. In May 1558, for example, he alerted Juana to the need for a hard line against the Lutheran cells discovered in Castile. Meanwhile he relaxed, took the sunshine, and ate like a horse, to the dismay of his medical advisers. At the end of August 1558 he was taken seriously ill, and in the early hours of 21 September he died, holding in his hand the crucifix which his wife Isabel had held when she died.

*

England was not left out of the developing struggle in western Europe. In the king's absence Mary had been managing the government, and cardinal Pole the restoration of the old Church. Constant messages were sent by the lovelorn queen urging her husband to return and attend to affairs. She had need of his support, particularly after the death in November 1555 of her chief councillor the bishop of Winchester. Philip wrote back explaining that the conflicts with France and the pope tied him down in the Netherlands. His commitments were not all war and politics. He had, according to unverifiable reports by ambassadors, at least two love affairs. He also performed good works. The month of December 1556 was bitterly cold and the rivers froze; the poor died in the streets. Philip organised emergency relief in Brussels. 'He had some wooden shelters built for 800 of them and ordered distribution of bread, beer, straw and firewood.'[76] The unaccustomed climate encouraged the Spanish lords in Philip's retinue to try skating on the frozen lake in the park in Brussels. The king looked on and laughed.[77]

In February 1557 he sent Ruy Gómez back to Spain to see what money was available for the war. It was also now important to get some military help from the English. On 18 March 1557 he sailed for England from Calais. On St George's Day he held a splendid ceremony of the Order of the Garter. But while he assisted at ceremonies, in an attempt to win English support for the war, the situation in the country was slowly slipping from his grasp. Mary was ill. There were plots brewing. One of these, fomented by Henry II, finally persuaded the Privy Council on 7 June to declare war on France. It was still an age in which the rituals of chivalry were practised. The declaration of war was taken overland by a herald, who recited it to the face of Henry II at Rheims. Philip hoped with the help of the English to bring about a final drive that would end in peace. He had virtually no claims on France, and even less on the papacy. But only a show of force could impose peace. 'He knows very well,' his ambassador in England declared, 'that war in Italy is contrary to his interest, for if he loses his states are lost, and if victorious he conquers nothing', since the papacy could not be touched.[78] Agreement was reached on the military help to be given by the English and Philip took his leave again in the first week of July. Mary accompanied him this time as far as Sittingbourne, where they spent the night. He took his leave of her there, and went on to Canterbury. On 6 July he sailed from Dover just before dawn. It was to be his last sight of England and of the queen.

In Brussels he was plunged directly into the war. Charles V had made sure that his son would be brought up as a soldier. Philip's entire training, his long familiarity with tourneys and games of war, his skill at hunting, meant that he could adapt easily to a military role. He had, for all that, never been in action. The emperor gloried in war as a dimension of personal prowess, participating personally in campaigns, sieges and voyages. In this (as in many other respects) Philip differed from his father. He preferred the model of his great-grandfather Ferdinand the Catholic, who commanded armies but did not commit his own person.[79] That at least was his opinion in 1555. It may be that he forgot it during the enthusiasm of the summer of 1557. The young nobles who gathered in Brussels were eager for action and Philip, exactly thirty years old, was in his prime. The regent of the Netherlands and commander of its forces, Emanuele Filiberto, duke of Savoy and first cousin to Philip, was twenty-eight and had just (in 1553) succeeded his father in the title. Slim, austere and excitable, with a commanding presence,[80] Savoy was an exile from his homeland, which was occupied by the French. He was eager to strike at the enemy, and the opportunity soon arose when the French chose to launch a surprise assault upon the border towns of the Netherlands.

Among the invading army figured the most illustrious of France's aristocracy. The forces were commanded by the Constable of France, Anne de Montmorency, with the support of the Admiral of France, Gaspard de Coligny, and the Marshal Saint-André. In the ranks served dukes and princes such as Montpensier and Nevers, Enghien and Condé. Philip had, by mid-July, assembled a counter-force of 35,000 under the orders of Savoy, seconded by the prince of Orange and all the nobles of the Netherlands. The cavalry were entrusted to Lamoral, count of Egmont.

In Brussels Philip combined the roles of commander-in-chief and paymaster-general. He coordinated the movement of all the troops and their supplies, planned strategy with a council of war, and scrupulously doled out the little money available for the campaign. After a few days of indecisive campaigning in the borderlands of France and the Netherlands, it was decided to make a stand. Philip and his advisers had at first thought of doing this at the nearby town of Rocroi, but Savoy dissuaded them. 'Taking into account all opinions,' the king wrote to Savoy, 'and the difficulties that you say exist over Rocroi, and the debates that we have had here, it was decided that the most convenient and suitable move is to invest St Quentin.'[81] The latter town was defended by troops under Coligny. By a strange twist of fate, Rocroi nearly a century later was to be the scene of a historic French victory over the army of Spain.

St Quentin was seen to be crucial, both for blocking the French advance and for clearing the way for a march on Paris and the king threw himself into the campaign with energy.[82] In the last week of July he was busily organising for the scattered Italian and German troops under his command to rendezvous at St Quentin. He also made scrupulous arrangements for supplies of munitions and food to be available. He cancelled all other plans and decided that 'I shall go straight to Cambrai. And I shall prepare myself immediately in order to arrive in good time at the camp, which I think will be on Tuesday.'[83] The timetable he set himself could not be kept to. After one week in Cambrai, as he informed Savoy on 6 August, he was still waiting for the English troops under the earl of Pembroke to join him. After his efforts to obtain English help, courtesy required that he not engage in action without them. He made use of the delay to arrange for further cavalry and cannons to be sent on, and for field-kitchens to be prepared for making bread for the troops. 'It greatly distresses me,' he wrote in his own hand at the end of the despatch, 'not to be able to come today as I intended. But in order not to hold up these men I am sending them without me, and shall await the others and bring with me the rest of the artillery.'[84]

The next day, Saturday the seventh, he was deeply worried. In moments of personal anxiety, he always wrote his letters in his own hand. He did so now to Savoy. 'I am extremely displeased at not being able to come nor is it possible to come soon, for the English have written that they will not arrive here until Tuesday, although I have urged them to hurry up.' And there were other troops, Germans, who could not arrive before the tenth. 'I am quite desperate.'[85] On Monday he received news at last that the English were arriving, but would need one day to rest. 'I shall leave on Wednesday', with the English, a German regiment, and a troop of Walloon archers. He knew however that a French relief force might provoke Savoy into a military action. He adjured the duke: 'Touching your point about engaging in battle in the event that they provoke it, what I can say is that the first concern must be to take care that they do not relieve the town. Unless absolutely necessary to prevent them relieving it, *you must avoid engaging in battle until I arrive.'*[86] If, however, there was no option, Savoy must decide as seemed best. The haunting fear that there might be a battle without him, made him add in his own hand:

> If there is no way to avoid an engagement before I arrive, I cannot enjoin you too strongly to inform me post haste, so as to give me the means and opportunity to arrive in time. Since I know that you desire my company in such an eventuality, I do not wish to press you further, but I beg you to have spare horses waiting day and night to be able to inform me.

'Seeing that the late arrival of Münchhausen with his regiment,' Savoy wrote back on the eighth, 'has forced Your Majesty to delay coming until the English arrive, I can only say that it is infinitely important that Your Majesty cut the delay as short as possible.'[87] 'Make all possible haste,' he also wrote to secretary Eraso, 'so that His Majesty comes immediately.'[88]

Events turned out as the king feared. In the afternoon of the ninth he learned that Montmorency had set out with a large force to relieve St Quentin. Without knowing the precise location of the French troops, Philip dared not move. On Tuesday, 10 August, the feast of St Lawrence, the Constable with some 22,000 infantry and cavalry advanced upon Savoy's positions before St Quentin. In a short but bloody action the troops under Savoy and Egmont routed and destroyed the Constable's army. A contemporary estimate put the number of dead in the French army at 5,200, with thousands taken prisoner. Possibly no more than 500 of Savoy's army lost their lives.

It took some time to appreciate the scale of the victory. Philip first heard of it at 11 p.m. He remained awake until around three in the morning, receiving further despatches. Early on the eleventh, encamped at the village of Beaurevoir, he finally wrote to the emperor to confirm the news. 'I arrived here today and will be in the camp tomorrow,' he wrote. 'I found here a message from my cousin [Savoy] telling me that he has seen the Constable and that the rest are prisoners.'[89] The victors were unsure who had been taken prisoner. When they received details, they could hardly believe it. The prisoners included Montmorency and three of his sons, together with the Marshal Saint-André, the duke of Montpensier, the prince of Condé, and the duke of Longueville. The French dead included the duke d'Enghien and viscount Turenne. The king arrived at the camp on the thirteenth, but with no signs of disappointment. He had been handed one of the most brilliant military victories of the age. On the battlefield before St Quentin, 'accompanied by the princes and commanders of his army in full military regalia' and flanked by the captured French standards, he proceeded slowly down the long lines of distinguished prisoners and paid his respects to each of them.

Official mythology later claimed the victory as Spanish. It was far from being that.[90] Of Philip's total army of some 48,000 – not all of whom took part in the battle – only 12 per cent were Spaniards. Fifty-three per cent were Germans, 23 per cent were Netherlanders, and 12 per cent were English. All the chief commanders were non-Spaniards. They included Savoy, Egmont, duke Eric of Brunswick and baron von Münchhausen.

The week after, Ruy Gómez, freshly returned from Spain, remarked that the victory had evidently been of God, since it had been won 'without experience, without troops, and without money'.[91] The comment reflected a real problem about what could practically be done next. Philip, advised by his close friend Ferrante Gonzaga,[92] favoured an immediate exploitation of the victory by an advance on Paris. All the other members of the Netherlands council of State were opposed. There was no money to pay for a further campaign, the Netherlanders were reluctant to go on the offensive, and France had more forces in reserve. Philip was assured that there was nothing more honourable than retreat when victorious. The arguments seemed irrefutable. He duly accepted the advice, returning to Brussels 'sound, cheerful and full of glory, and to universal satisfaction'.[93] When his council some weeks later told him that nothing more could be done, Philip replied angrily: 'Yes, at present nothing else can be done, but at the time much might have been achieved.'[94] There was, all the same, every reason for satisfaction.

Just under two weeks later the town of St Quentin, defended by a very small force under Admiral Coligny, fell to the renewed siege. Philip led the assault. 'In the afternoon of the twenty-seventh,' according to his own account, 'we entered in strength . . . from every side, killing all the defenders.'[95] It was his first direct experience of the brutal carnage of war. Despite the king's efforts, the town was sacked by the German mercenaries who, reported the earl of Bedford, accompanying the victors, 'showed such cruelty as the like hath not been seen'.[96] Admiral Coligny was made prisoner. With both the Constable and the Admiral in his power, Philip had a strong negotiating hand. He had also, as he informed his sister Juana, won his spurs. 'Our Lord in his goodness has desired to grant me these victories within a few days of the beginning of my reign, with all the honour and *reputación* that follow from them.'[97]

In October the English troops went home, and the king prepared to wind down the campaign. The autumn was one of torrential rain, completely unsuited to any military action.[98] The king returned to Brussels where he met the States General. The immediate problem was money for the troops. Already in 1556 – omen of much graver events to come – a Spanish regiment had mutinied when not paid. 'I am extremely sorry,' Philip wrote to the duke of Savoy, 'not to be able to send you the money for paying off this army, but I simply do not have it. You can see that the only possibility is to negotiate with the Fuggers.'[99]

The costs of war, not only in the Netherlands but also in Italy, were already insupportable. In letter after letter, he had pleaded to Juana from England and the Low Countries for more money. In May 1558 he insisted that if urgent needs were not met, peace could not be made and he could not go home to Spain. And he wanted to return, 'and leave matters here settled so that I am not obliged to come back'. 'The lack of money is so great that I don't know what to say,' he wrote apologetically. 'I am in worse straits that you could possibly imagine.'[100]

The war also went favourably in Italy where Alba forced the papacy into a peace settlement in September. It was an accord that, for the rest of the century, bound the papacy closely to Spain.[101] But it was too early to prepare for peace. In France the duke of Guise, who had just returned from an unsuccessful campaign in Italy, recruited a new army and took the field. He appeared before Calais on New Year's Day 1558. The town, England's last possession on mainland Europe, fell on 10 January. Its loss infuriated the English, and grieved their queen mortally.

Philip was forced to review his strategy. Writing to the duke of Savoy in January, in despatches which show his perfect familiarity with the geography of the Netherlands and northern France,[102] the king attempted to control the situation. French forces continued to make attacks across the border. They suffered a further crushing defeat in mid-July 1558, at Gravelines, at the hands of an army commanded by Egmont. Peace talks became inevitable and in October the plenipotentiaries met near Cambrai.

On Philip's side they were the prince of Orange, Alba, the bishop of Arras, Ruy Gómez and Viglius, president of the council of State in Brussels. For Henry II they were the Constable, Saint-André, and three others.

*

Philip was at Arras when he received on 1 November, All Saints' Day, firm news of his father's death at Yuste.[103] The news was expected, but he immediately changed his plans and set off for Brussels. On the way there he was given news that Mary Tudor had died on 17 November. This created a problem of protocol, since he did not wish the ceremonies for the two deaths to be confused. He sent instructions ahead for funeral rites to be held for his queen, to be presided over by Savoy, in his absence. He himself refused to enter Brussels until the city had prepared the funeral ceremonies for the emperor. A formal, glittering service of mourning was held for his father in Brussels on 28 November. The regalia and colour of the knights of the Golden Fleece were dominant. Three days later, he held further ceremonies, for his wife the queen, and for his aunt Mary of Hungary, who had also died in Spain in November.

On New Year's Day 1559, for the first time since the death of his father, the king dined in public in Brussels. Acute differences over policy had never affected the profound and lifelong veneration in which he held the emperor. As seen through the engravings done for Philip by the Dutch painter Heemskerck in 1566, Charles was the prototypical military hero, whose victories over the Lutherans in Germany were on a par with his triumphs over the papacy, over France and over the Turks at Vienna in 1529. Philip came to see in time that military solutions were not always the most effective. But his admiration for his father's prowess in war was absolute and it affected his own character. He accepted the need to be a soldier. His favourite portrait of himself was the full-size one done of him in armour, by Titian which held the place of honour in his chamber in 1553,[104] together with one of his father. As a young man, his tastes centred on war and hunting. Well before his English marriage, he had an impressive collection of arquebuses, swords and bows. The campaign at St Quentin fulfilled in some measure his dreams of glory in battle, but it was obvious to observers that he had no real military inclinations. He never attempted to equal the achievements of the emperor. He could continue to venerate his father while in practice adopting a quite different approach to problems. 'The emperor,' commented the Venetian ambassador, 'was inclined to things of war, the king dislikes them. The former threw himself with ardour into great enterprises, the latter avoids them.'[105]

Philip was also profoundly influenced by the aesthetic tastes of his father. The programme to rebuild (and rethink) the royal palaces in Castile was one that he took over directly. He inherited his father's architects, just as he inherited his artists. The difference was that Charles was never long enough in Spain to give a personal impulse to artistic projects. Philip, by contrast, started where Charles left off. The prince's boundless admiration for Titian arose from the meeting arranged by Charles in Augsburg in 1550. The painter (then aged sixty, but with many years of work ahead of him) immediately captured Philip's imagination. In 1553 his bedroom was dominated by Titian canvases. While adhering to much of what was passed to him by his father, Philip nonetheless branched out into a positive expression of his own preferences.

He always followed scrupulously the advice given by his father in matters of religion and politics; there is no respect in which he ever diverged from the instructions received through Zúñiga. On specific policies, it is true, the two were often poles apart although Philip in later years played down these differences. He always regretted, for example, Charles's need for military alliances with the Lutheran princes. But years later, when referring to these things, he refused to find fault with anything his father had done then.

*

In England, meanwhile, changes of enormous importance were taking place.

With Mary's death, Philip's powers and authority in England automatically lapsed. But he was by no means disposed to pull out. Even before Mary was dead Philip's ambassador the duke of Feria was sounding out the possibility of a marriage to Elizabeth (whom Philip had, two years earlier, thought of as a wife for his son Don Carlos). Philip was not put off by her Protestant tendencies. Elizabeth toyed with the idea. In April 1559, when she learned that Philip's peace negotiators were also proposing a marriage alliance with Elizabeth Valois, the queen commented with a smile to Feria that Philip 'could not have been much in love with her, since he did not have the patience to wait four months'.[106] Philip subsequently tried to find her an alternative husband, and broached the idea of the archduke Charles, son of the emperor Ferdinand. The idea was still around as late as 1567. For her part, Elizabeth wanted no link with Spain. But she could surmise that Philip had no intention of turning his back on England. France at that moment had a direct claim to the English throne, through the marriage of the dauphin in April 1558 to Mary Stuart, the next direct heir. It was in Philip's interest to keep England, where Elizabeth's position was still weak and the religious situation unstable, out of the hands of the French.[107] He extended his stay in Flanders until he could be certain of a firm peace settlement that would guarantee the security of England. For some time to come, Philip of Spain was to be the protector of the Elizabethan regime, even when the evidence for its Protestantism was plain for everyone to see.

Early in 1559 the peace talks with France were moved to Cateau-

Cambrésis. A settlement was urgently needed. 'I tell you that it is totally impossible for me to sustain the war,' Philip affirmed in January.[108] In moments of leisure, he went hunting in the woods at Binche, 'excellent country for it, and for the benefit to my health from the exercise and the open air'.[109]

There was disquieting news from Castile, where the Cortes during that spring petitioned him 'to return and reside in these realms without delay'.[110] Against his advice, his sister and her advisers had sanctioned an ill-fated military expedition into north Africa under the veteran soldier the count of Alcaudete. Philip also had before him reports, dated May 1558, from his sister and from Inquisitor-General Valdés, on the recent discovery of a Protestant group in Valladolid. Valdés was particularly forceful. He was aware that reports unfavourable to him had managed to reach Philip, sent (he said) by 'some people whose intentions will one day be exposed'. Concerned to ensure his own political survival, he painted an alarming picture of Lutherans active in Seville, Valladolid and Salamanca, Jews active in Murcia, and Moriscos in the throes of discontent. The only remedy, he said, was to put the Inquisition in charge.[111] Philip had no other machinery available to handle the situation, and agreed with him about the need for quick action. He wrote off at once, authorising whatever measures might be required. His sister was instructed to set up a committee of lawyers and theologians to advise him on the matter. Writing from St Quentin, he also told Valdés that 'in nothing could you give me greater satisfaction than in proceeding with all severity against those who have been arrested, in order to check and punish so great an evil'.[112] In subsequent months, he followed closely the religious situation in the peninsula, urging his sister in February 1559, for example, to exercise 'all care and diligence'.[113]

The emperor, at his retreat in Yuste, was horrified to learn of the appearance within Spain of the very plague which had torn Germany apart. He wrote in May 1558 to Juana, urging her to take the harshest possible measures against the accused, 'as creators of sedition, upheaval, riots and disturbance in the state . . . punishing the guilty thoroughly to prevent this thing spreading'. Juana's profoundly religious temperament rose to the challenge. Over the next few months, aided by Valdés, she brought in a number of measures of control, including a stringent new censorship law.

*

The final peace between the Habsburgs and France was signed on 3 April 1559, in the little village of Cateau-Cambrésis. It was one of the decisive treaties of western history. It satisfied France, which kept Calais and three key fortresses in the Rhineland and immeasurably strengthened Spain, which was confirmed in its domination of Italy. The duke of Savoy was restored to his duchy, and given the hand in marriage of the king of France's sister Marguerite. Peace returned to Europe. The enmity between the Valois of France and the Habsburgs was laid to rest. Friendship between France and Spain was sealed by Philip agreeing to marry Elizabeth Valois, eldest daughter of Henry II and Catherine de' Medici. His ambassadors to the peace negotiations, Alba, William of Orange, and Lamoral of Egmont, arrived in Paris on 15 June 1559, bringing with them a gift of a jewel to formalise the marriage proposal. Precisely seven days later a magnificent proxy wedding was celebrated in Notre Dame cathedral, with Alba standing in for the king.

The marriage celebrations in Paris were, suddenly, interrupted by an unprecedented disaster.

As part of the festivities, a tournament was held at the French court on 30 June. The forty-year-old king, Henry II, armoured and on horseback, took on his challengers. During a joust the lance of a young captain of the Scots Guard, the count of Montgomery, accidentally plunged through the king's visor into his right eye. He was immediately attended to by his surgeons, but lapsed into unconsciousness and died on 10 July. His fifteen-year-old son François, married to the Scottish Mary Stuart, was proclaimed king. Mary, daughter of a sister of the duke of Guise, was in her own right also queen of Scotland.

Philip, then in Ghent, was informed of the accident and on 24 July he ordered special services to be held for the late king. He was shocked by the death, but he hoped that the peace treaty would not be called in question by France's new rulers. He then made his final arrangements to leave for Spain. 'It is unbelievable,' reported a French diplomat, 'how this prince bestirs himself and urges on his affairs so as not to be left with any obstacle to delay him' returning home. He set himself a departure date of 8 August, 'expressing, whenever he spoke of it, a singular warmth and desire to be in the land of his birth'.[114]

The homesickness was genuine, and aggravated by fears for his own health ('I have not been very well recently').[115] But there were other serious matters. Apart from the news about heresy in Spain, his principal worry was the military debt, which he preferred not to resolve by taxing the Netherlands. As he explained to Perrenot in June,

> I am hard pressed to go and seek a remedy for these problems, and the further away the remedy appears the greater my haste to go and seek it, since I am disappointed at not being able to find it here. Were I to stay, nothing would be gained. The best thing is for all of us to seek a solution, as I shall to the best of my ability, and if it cannot be found here I shall go to seek it in Spain.[116]

From 29 July into the opening days of August he presided over the chapter of the Order of the Golden Fleece. 'I feel shattered,'[117] he commented after a tense session with the knights, who included Egmont and Orange. On 7 August he opened the session of the States General of the Netherlands in Ghent, and explained to delegates the motives for his departure.

Though a satisfactory peace had been concluded, Philip was aware that he was leaving many matters in the Netherlands unresolved. The States General wanted him to withdraw the Spanish troops, which were an expense for them. The debts of the government remained to be covered. Above all, there was the increase in heresy, which nobody seemed capable of dealing with. Philip, in line perhaps with the caution he had displayed in England over the same question, refrained from any firm attitude on the last matter. He was aware that a bloodbath of heretics, of proportions unsurpassed in the Spain he knew, had recently taken place in the Netherlands. Viglius, president of the council of State in Brussels, estimated in 1556 (with considerable accuracy) that some 1,300 heretics had been 'burned, hanged or drowned' in the provinces. Precisely because of this, Viglius felt that some sort of toleration was inevitable.[118] Philip had the facts before him. As yet there was no indication of how he might deal with the problem.

He left the government in the hands of his half-sister Margaret of Parma. Aged thirty-seven in 1559, she was the illegitimate daughter of Charles by a Flemish girl. In the 1530s the emperor had sent her off to Italy to marry first a Medici prince and then a Farnese, the duke of Parma. She came back to her home country thoroughly Italianised. In appearance she was almost masculine. She walked like a man and her enemies made unkind remarks about the thick growth of hair on her upper lip.[119] But they respected, for the moment, her firm handling of the political situation in Brussels.

Though there were Spaniards in the Netherlands council of State on whom Philip could count directly, he preferred to put his confidence for the moment in the bishop of Arras. Thanks to Philip's support, Antoine Perrenot in 1561 received a cardinalate from the pope. He retained the see of Arras, but was from then on known as cardinal Granvelle. When he got back to Spain, it was through Granvelle that Philip introduced his most important measures. This increased tensions between the great nobles and the cardinal.

*

The Venetian ambassadors observed Philip closely during these years, spoke frequently to him, and have left us a vivid – though not always reliable – impression of his appearance and character.[120] His medium height, fair complexion and hair, large blue eyes, the thick lower lip and short pointed beard, appear in their reports exactly as in the superb portrait by Antonis Mor, painted at this time.[121] 'He suffers from stomach and digestive disorders and for that reason has begun recently on the advice of his doctors to make frequent outings.' The problem was that he 'eats excessively of certain foods, above all sweets and pastries'. 'His habit is to partake only of highly nutritious food, and he abstains from fish, fruit and similar aliments, which have a tendency to produce ill humours.' (It is true that he avoided fish, but fruit and salad appeared regularly in his menus.) His general demeanour was quiet. 'His habits of life are of a tranquil character', and he was almost 'melancholic'. On the other hand, he was much given to night life. 'He is dissipated with women, likes to go in disguise at night, and enjoys all types of gaming.'

His conduct to others, by contrast, could not be faulted. His rigid manner in Italy on the first journey was a thing of the past. 'He tends more to gentleness than anger, and displays a special courtesy to ambassadors and other persons . . . He frequently tells amusing witticisms and enjoys listening to jokes. But at meal-time though the buffoons are admitted to his presence he does not give himself to laughter so much as in his own rooms, where the merriment is unconfined.'

Those who had political dealings with him found him formidable. He perused all the memorials and petitions he received. In audiences, 'he pays great attention to what is said to him, but normally does not look at the person who is speaking to him, and keeps his eyes down, raising them only to look from side to side'. (It was a manner he had acquired with experience.) 'He replies succinctly and promptly to all questions.' When discussing serious business he abhorred vagueness and generalities. In Brussels he gave audiences after breakfast and lunch. Before supper every evening he went through correspondence with Gonzalo Pérez and in the course of the day he consulted regularly with other secretaries and councillors.

> Although his time of life is apt to engender an insatiable desire to govern, his efforts are directed not to increase his possessions by war but to preserve them by peace . . . Although he resembles his father in his features, he is dissimilar in many respects . . . The emperor governed entirely according to his own views, but the king governs according to the views of others, and he has no esteem for any nation except the Spanish. He consorts only with Spaniards, and with these only he takes counsel and governs.[122]

On the whole, the Venetian reports then and later give a fair picture of Philip's subdued character. But they are tainted throughout by a barely concealed hostility to things Spanish, and often lapse into wilful distortion. They have been used sometimes as evidence for the image of a timid, diffident king, crippled by a feeling of inferiority before the imposing personality of his father.[123] But it is an image for which no basis can be found in the letters of other ambassadors or in contemporary reports.

For Philip it had been a successful absence, perhaps much more than the visit ten years before. 'He looketh for long time to live in rest for any wars with France,' the English envoy wrote home. 'As for Italy, he counteth them all at his beck. The pope he now feareth not . . . So as (it is said) upon his getting into Spain he mindeth not to return unto these parts.'[124]

Philip's anxiety to leave did not arise from any disdain for the Netherlands. In the north he was ill at ease in many respects, but he also came to know and cherish the culture. He valued the humanist environment, and specifically selected as tutor for his son the philosopher Sebastián Fox Morcillo, then a professor at Louvain. (Fox's appointment remained valid even though the king probably knew that his brother Francisco was one of those arrested for heresy in Spain in those weeks.)[125] Above all, he was captivated by the artistic creativity of the north. His first journey had been decisive in determining his tastes; the second confirmed his preference for things Flemish.[126]

Flemish art had long exercised a crucial influence in the peninsula. It had been favoured under Ferdinand and Isabella and during the reign of Charles V.[127] Philip now brought his personal enthusiasm to bear, arranging for paintings and artisans to be brought to Spain. He was the first to introduce into Spain the landscaped gardens of Flanders. His experience of buildings in the north had given him further ideas on what could be done in Spain. Continually, during the years of his absence, he sent instructions and suggestions for the reconstruction of the Spanish palaces. In August 1559 he signed in Ghent a letter to Juan Bautista de Toledo, then in Naples, inviting him to Madrid to become his principal architect. In childhood he had come to know the Netherlands music that his father had made standard at the Spanish court. Philip went further by taking back with him to Castile his Flemish choristers. From then on, he always had two sections to his chapel, the Flemish and the Spanish. His contact with the north was for him a positive experience which he fully appreciated and about which he never uttered a single criticism.

His anxiety to leave, however, is easy to understand. He had been away for over five long years. He was happy to return to a land whose climate, language, and people he knew; 'desiring, above all, to obtain some rest and ease in his native land'.[128] Of the sixteen years since 1543 that Philip had been governing Spanish affairs, he had spent eight out of the country. He had visited northern Italy, the Alps, southern Germany, the Rhineland, the Netherlands, parts of France, and southern England. For him, Augsburg, Milan, London, Cologne, Antwerp and Trent were not faraway places but towns whose streets he had trodden. His father excepted, no other European ruler of the time had travelled and seen so much, or accumulated so much practical experience of international relations. He had lived with the Protestant problem in Germany at close quarters, seen heresy punished in England, and been present in person on the battlefield against France. He had met in person, both in peace and in war, most of the prominent personalities of his time. In later years all this accumulated experience filtered through into his letters and influenced his decision-making. During the years abroad, his inability to speak any language other than Castilian (and Latin) may have limited his contact with others and reinforced the impression of a tight-lipped king. But his keen and sensitive eye took everything in, eagerly devoured what evidently pleased him and rejected what did not suit his temperament. Though brought up in Castile, he was never limited to the horizon of Spaniards. The new king of Spain who came home in 1559 was very much a European.

But he was also, by the vicissitudes of power, now primarily a southern European. The reluctance of the emperor Ferdinand to let the Imperial crown out of the hands of his family, in time made permanent the division between the two halves of Charles V's empire. But there was not, under Philip, any rupture. The new king of Spain continued to maintain close and active links with the empire and the German princes.[129] In the west, the inopportune death of Mary Tudor dissolved the Anglo-Spanish alliance and a friendship which went back to the Middle Ages suddenly ground to a halt. Spain emerged on the world stage as a great power. With a firm base in northern Europe (the Netherlands), and a key position in Italy (through Milan and Naples), it stood poised to dominate western Europe. France, clearly, could never tolerate this.

The royal party arrived in Vlissingen on 11 August, but had to wait for a favourable wind. Philip occupied himself on excursions to the islands in the area. After supper on Wednesday the twenty-third, he moved into his cabin. Early on the twenty-fifth the formal leave-taking commenced. First the great lords, among them Egmont and Orange, said farewell.[130] Then at midday it was the turn of Margaret of Parma, accompanied by her son Alessandro Farnese, who took ship with the king. In mid-afternoon 'the king embarked with his whole fleet towards Spain, with an easterly wind, very small, next to a calm . . . The number of his ships was twenty Spanish, thirty Hollanders, and forty of others of less sort', the English envoy in the Netherlands reported.[131] The journey home was uneventful. They put into Laredo on the evening of Friday, 8 September, and the king disembarked. At midday on Saturday, before everything from the ships could be unloaded, a storm hit the coast. Some of the ships capsized, with the loss of men, property and papers. Undeterred, after only a short rest, Philip set off directly for Valladolid. He entered the city, which was decked out with triumphal arches, on Thursday, 14 September.

4

The Cross and the Crescent
1559–1565

Had there been no Inquisition, there would be many more heretics.[1]

Philip returned only to plunge into severe problems at home. There were food shortages. In 1559 torrential spring rains fell, the river Duero flooded, and southern Castile was suffering from grain scarcity. In Aragon, there was political uproar provoked by an attempt of the Inquisition to extend its control over the Moriscos of the nobility.[2]

The first priority was financial. One week after arriving in Valladolid, he summoned a Cortes to meet in a month's time in Toledo. In his opening proposal, which he read in person, Philip expressed his satisfaction at being home again. He reported on the peace, on the threat from foreign heresies, and concluded by hoping the Cortes would grant the money necessary to his policies. He expressed his willingness to satisfy the petitions they presented, promising for example (a promise he did not keep) not to sell off any more property from the crown's patrimony.[3]

The next priority was the question of the discovery of Protestants. It was an issue that gripped the imagination of Spaniards for the next three years.

Astonishingly, Reformation heresy had made little impact on Spain. Nearly forty years had passed since the dawn of the German Reformation, and of all western countries Spain alone seemed immune to its appeal. There was in Spain, unlike other western countries, a refreshing absence of repression. 'We interpreted everything freely', a priest commented. 'There was no need at that time to be suspicious of anyone.'[4] Persecution of *conversos*, at its most intense over a generation before, was now only sporadic. Suddenly, the discovery in 1557–8 of groups of alleged

Lutherans in Seville and in Valladolid itself, with well-known clergy, nobility, and royal officials among them, shook the government out of its complacency. With Charles V urging her on from his retreat in Yuste, the regent Juana took a number of urgent measures. All those under suspicion were arrested by the Inquisition, a stringent censorship law was decreed for Castile, and a new Index of forbidden books was rushed through. In May 1559 the first of a series of *autos de fe* was held in Valladolid, at which some of those arrested were executed.

The star of Inquisitor-General Valdés had been waning in government circles; now the discovery of 'heretics' enabled him to recover the initiative. In long and confident letters to the king in Brussels he described the efficiency with which the Holy Office had acted and the impressive number of people it had arrested and punished.[5] Meanwhile, he also brought off another coup: the arrest on charges of heresy of Spain's leading prelate, the archbishop of Toledo. The Dominican Bartolomé Carranza, chaplain and court preacher to Philip, had accompanied Philip during the visit abroad. Impressed by the swarthy Navarrese priest, Philip in 1558 appointed him to the archbishopric. Carranza was consecrated by Granvelle in Brussels in February 1558, and returned to the peninsula that August. Exactly a year later, as a result (many said) of the personal enmity of Inquisitor Valdés, he was arrested by the Inquisition. He was accused, among other charges, of making heretical statements in a *Catechism* he had just published in Antwerp. The case became one of the most famous of the century.

The figures Valdés cited to the king for Protestants could not fail to alarm. Philip returned in time to be able to preside over an *auto de fe* in Valladolid on 8 October 1559. The ceremony attracted much attention, for it was a novelty in Spain. Up to the 1520s, when the great persecution of *conversos* began to die down, many *autos* had been held, but they were simple religious ceremonies with no pomp or ritual. In the following generation there had been very few. The king had previously attended only one, a humble affair in Toledo on 25 February 1550.[6] The Valladolid display, like the *auto* held there in May and another held in Seville in September, was intentionally impressive.

The ceremony was staged by the Inquisition in the main city square of Valladolid, with the assisting public crowding around the sides. The proceedings began at 6 a.m. A formal sermon was preached, then the king, baring his sword before the inquisitors, took an oath to uphold the authority of the Holy Office. The central spectacle was a procession of penitents, whose sentences were read out by the officiating inquisitors. This occupied the most time. Those who repented were publicly accepted back into the bosom of the Church; the unrepentant were condemned to the relevant punishments. Solemn mass brought the proceedings to a close. The whole ceremony, witnessed by several thousand spectators, lasted some twelve hours. By its combination of faith, punishment and spectacle, the *auto* was deliberately devised as a piece of theatre which would both impress and deter.

Philip was particularly impressed by the fact that among those condemned were some well known to him. The previous *auto*, in May, had included Dr Agustín Cazalla, at whose sermons he had often assisted. The present one, in October, included the civil governor of Toro, Carlos de Seso. There was a total of thirty accused, most of them members of the newly discovered groups. Though accused of 'Lutheranism', no more than a handful of them had identifiably Protestant beliefs. During the procession Seso is said to have called out to the king, 'How could you permit this to happen?' Philip is said to have replied sharply, 'I would bring the wood to burn my own son, if he were as wicked as you.' It is possible that he said it, for three years later he used a similar phrase in front of the French ambassador.[7] But it was more likely a later invention. Almost exactly the same words had been used by the pope in an interview with the Venetian ambassador in Rome twelve months before![8]

The *auto* ended after the mass, and most of the public drifted back to their homes. The king did not go to the sequel, carried out on the confines of the city. One of his aides, the Netherlander Jean de Vandenesse, went to see out of curiosity and was shocked. Twelve accused, among them four nuns, were burnt at the stake; two were burnt alive. 'It was a very sad spectacle,' Vandenesse limited himself to commenting.[9] The king never assisted at executions. Like all heads of state, he had to deal with problems of crime and punishment, but managed to do it without disturbing his own equanimity. An *auto de fe* was for him, as for all those who saw it, a deeply moving experience which uplifted faith. He never witnessed the burnings.

Immediately after the *auto* Philip went off to visit his palace at Valsaín. Over the next three months he alternated between Valsaín, Aranjuez and the Alcázar. In November 1559, he issued a decree ordering Castilians who were studying at foreign universities to return home. The decree may have been inspired by a suggestion he had received many years before from a friar; at that time he had simply set the paper aside, with a note: 'file this'.[10] Issuing the decree now, he was aware that it was little more than a gesture. There were few Castilians studying abroad. The decree in any case did not apply to students from the non-Castilian realms of Spain, who remained free to go to foreign universities of their choice. But there was no doubt in his mind about the need for action against a Lutheran threat. Shortly after his return, in September, placards were found posted up on public buildings in Toledo, attacking the Catholic Church as 'not the Church of Jesus Christ but of the devil and his son, the Antichrist pope'. Early in November heretical leaflets were found during mass in Toledo cathedral; the doors were shut at once, and all foreigners were searched.[11]

Just over a year later, in Seville pamphlets circulated attacking 'these thieving inquisitors, who publicly robbed and burnt the bones of Constantino out of jealousy'. The leaflets also asked the public to 'pray to God for his true Church, so that it may firmly and steadfastly endure the persecution by the synagogue of Satan' (that is, the Inquisition).[12]

The events of 1559 were probably decisive in shaping Philip's attitude to the religious question in Spain. Nipping heresy in the bud would save Spain from going the way of other nations. He had seen at first hand the consequences of diversity of religion in northern Europe: the disorder and blood-letting there must not be repeated here. The English authorities under Queen Mary had executed nearly three times as many heretics as died in Spain in the years just after 1559, the French under Henry II at least twice as many. In the Netherlands ten times as many had died. 'The healthiest case is Spain,' he observed with some justice to the Inquisitor-General.[13] After hearing of the good work done at Valladolid, the bishop of Pamplona commented with satisfaction: 'We have great peace and tranquillity, and the best of it is that we are free of Luther.'[14]

The efficiency of the Holy Office in identifying and dealing with the problem marked it out as being the ideal weapon to counter subversive doctrine. Time and again in later years the king would revert to these two basic ideas – timely repression, and the efficacy of the Inquisition – as proven truths. He gave, as a result, unswerving support to the Inquisition. When he was at Monzón three years later he was sent an account of an *auto de fe* that the inquisitors of Barcelona had just held and in which they had punished some 'Lutherans', all French. 'We have seen the account,' he wrote back to the inquisitors, 'and urge you to keep up the good work. I shall always order special favour and attention to be paid to the interests of the Holy Office.'[15] From that date his sentiments never changed. 'We cannot and must not agree [the statement is of 1571] to anything that is in any way unfavourable to the Holy Office, seeing from our experience every day the necessity that there is for it.'[16] It was a lesson he did not cease to press untiringly on other European rulers.

His conviction of the need for a firm hand in religious matters was born of his first-hand experience of political disorder in northern Europe. It did not arise from any unusual intensity of faith among Spaniards. Ironically, at the very time that Protestants were discovered, clergy in Spain were becoming aware of the ignorance and unbelief among their own people. In 1554 a well-known friar, Felipe de Meneses, confessed that 'I find a greater inclination to liberty in Spain than in Germany or any other nation.'[17] With good reason might the king fear contagion spreading to his lands. This explains his failure to lift a finger to help the imprisoned Carranza. The archbishop had many personal enemies and rivals who envied his promotion to the wealthy see of Toledo. Their number included inquisitor Valdés, and the royal confessor Fresneda. In the atmosphere of crisis and danger from heresy which reigned in Castile, the alarmists prevailed. Carranza's trial was allowed to drag on. He was fated to spend nearly seventeen years in confinement in Spain and later in Rome.

The controls of 1559 are sometimes presented as imposing a regime of repression and fear. The controls were, it is true, unprecedented. Yet they were similar to steps being taken in other countries. Despite them, after the crisis of 1559 Spain provided an extraordinary spectacle of normality. Repression did not increase, nor were there signs of Protestantism. Some of Erasmus's works were prohibited, but he continued to be bought, read and cited without fear.[18] The trade in books from abroad was not interrupted. Spaniards travelled freely and several came into direct contact with the new ideas in Europe.

Taking advantage of the discovery of Protestants, Inquisitor-General Valdés in 1558 tried to persuade the king that he should (almost literally) hand the country over to the Inquisition. More tribunals should be set up in the provinces, licences for printing books should be issued only by the Inquisition, all book sales should be subject to the Inquisition, the Inquisition should have vigilantes everywhere.[19] 'I desire only that the interests of the Holy Office be respected,' the king replied tactfully from St Quentin.[20] But he ignored the proposals.

Brought up in an environment where anti-Semitic attitudes were common, Philip was also sensitive to the warnings he received from Valdés about the implication of 'Jews' (a term used by anti-Semites when referring to *converso* Christians) in the new heretical movements. In 1547 he had rejected Siliceo's statute of blood purity in Toledo. Nearly ten years later, the situation appeared different. He now apparently felt that 'all the heresies in Germany, France and Spain have been sown by descendants of Jews, as we have seen and still see every day in Spain'.[21]

But there is good reason to doubt whether Philip ever expressed such extraordinary sentiments. There is no evidence, either in his statements or his policies up to this time, that he could either believe or harbour such strange anti-Semitic ideas. The phrase was, in fact, derived from the memorial that Siliceo had sent him some time before in defence of the statute.[22]

In Brussels he also rejected a tempting offer from the leader of the exiled Spanish Jews, Jacob Abravanel. The Jewish presence was still strong in the western Mediterranean,[23] and many Spanish Jews expelled from Spain in 1492 were active in the Italian states. Some had taken refuge in Naples, from which they were forced out in 1541. Abravanel was among those who then went to live in the republic of Venice. In 1558 he wrote to Philip, offering a handsome sum in gold if the king would permit his people to return to Naples for a guaranteed twenty-five years.[24] Philip had serious financial problems but rejected the offer.

On his return to Spain, the king was to find evidence that seemed to link *conversos* with heresy. Some of the 'Protestants' in both Valladolid and Seville were of *converso* origin. Inquisitor Valdés, anxious to maintain his influence, did not hesitate to feed Philip with information about *converso* conspiracies. Another bishop, earlier that year, had warned the king that '*conversos* are the source from which this accursed doctrine first arose'.[25] Alarmed by the appearance of the Protestants, suspicious of 'Jewish' activity, Philip assumed from this time a more anti-Semitic stance in his policies, and became more than ever convinced of the need to support the Inquisition. He was kept informed of the discovery and arrest by the Inquisition of Murcia, in that decade, of a group of judaising *conversos*.[26]

The king also became a more convinced supporter of blood purity. In 1554 he approved purity statutes in the four cathedrals of the realm of Granada.[27] In 1566 he introduced a purity statute into the city council of Toledo, against the bitter opposition of most of its members. He looked carefully at the racial origins of nominees to bishoprics and other public posts, although, he confessed, 'I don't know if one has slipped through my fingers.'[28] In reality, his prejudice – dismissed bitingly by the Spanish founder of the Jesuits, Ignatius Loyola, as 'a whim of the Spanish king and his court' – was out of step with the thinking of many educated Spaniards of the day. Nor did he himself enforce it consistently. On several occasions he refused to accept or approve purity statutes. In 1566, the very year he had given permission for a statute in Toledo, he instructed the university of Salamanca to refrain from adopting one.[29] *Conversos* continued to occupy key posts at all levels in his administration (even in Toledo, despite the city statute), and the king never interfered. Sympathy for blood purity was already on the decline.

*

On Philip's return the control of government was in some disarray. Different influences had been at work during his absence, and up to 1556 many key appointments had been made by his father. The rising star was Ruy Gómez (prince of Eboli from 1559),[30] who both in England and in the Netherlands had been working closely with the king. Three factors gave him influence. Ten years older than the king, he had been brought up at court with him, and Philip found his character congenial. Second, he had regular and direct access to the king. Since the household reform he had been a chamberlain (*sumiller*), which gave him the duties of waking the king in the morning and seeing him to bed at night. Third, from 1557 he held the post of chief accountant (*contador mayor*) of the treasury, which enabled him to control payments and thereby influence policy. Despite his key position Gómez was neither aggressive nor thrusting, and was content to play a subdued role. He was solely and absolutely dedicated to the person of the king[31] and owed his survival in politics to his gentleness and prudence, 'clean hands and an open character'.[32] He became the focus for a grouping of interests to which courtiers attached themselves. Through his wife he had a direct link with the most powerful of Castilian grandee families, the Mendozas. Ana de Mendoza, daughter of the libertine Diego Hurtado de Mendoza, duke of Francavilla, was later to play a crucial part in the Antonio Pérez affair. She was aged only thirteen when the marriage contract, arranged in part by Philip,[33] was signed in 1553. When the court was in the Netherlands, Gómez also struck up links with key figures there, such as Egmont. By the mid-1550s, well before Philip returned in 1559, the network of influence associated with Gómez was securely in place.[34] The Venetian ambassador claimed that 'everybody calls him *rey* [king] Gómez rather than Ruy Gómez'.[35]

In the days of the emperor, influence and control had been exercised largely by Cobos and his associates, among them Alba. In the early 1550s, when Philip gradually took over, there was a scramble among officials to place themselves in the orbit of Gómez. From as early as 1552, for example, the emperor's secretary Francisco de Eraso gravitated to Gómez as political patron,[36] and was subsequently rewarded with key posts in the treasury, the council of the Indies and the council of State. Several other notables were associated at this period with the Eboli interest. Among them were Don Juan Manrique de Lara, and the king's confessor fray Bernardo de Fresneda.

The birth of a Gómez group, and its clear split from that of the duke of Alba, can be dated back to the year 1552. The group had, it seems, formed round Philip in the three years of sojourn in the Netherlands, Italy and Germany. Logically, its supporters could be found among courtiers in these three countries. When Gómez and his friends came back to Spain, they prepared for a cleansing of the Augean stables. 'It was utterly necessary,' confided Ruy Gómez to his friend Francisco de Eraso, 'for His Highness to return to these realms. Every day one discovers things which, had they been allowed to go on, would have occasioned great concern. Now there is profound fear among those involved, and they make great efforts to appear snowy white.'[37] Progress was slow. 'Affairs proceed in the Spanish way,' Gómez complained; 'slow and disordered. His Highness does all that he can.'[38] Major scandals were uncovered, notably in the country's principal court of justice, the chancery of Valladolid.[39] Inevitably, the duke of Alba felt he was being edged out. He went off to his estates. Ruy Gómez observed to Eraso: 'The duke of Alba has gone off in a huff but he has no reason to do so, because the prince extends a great deal of favour to him and gives him a part in everything without exception. In spite of this, he is not satisfied, because he doesn't have every-thing. As you and I have discussed on occasion, I don't know if this conduct helps him.'[40]

On Philip's second return to Spain, the same thing happened. Perhaps the man most disappointed in 1559 was Alba. As high steward he con-trolled the king's household as well as the public functions of the court. Exactly twenty years Philip's senior, he had aided and advised him at every step of his political career. Head of the powerful noble house of Toledo and Europe's foremost soldier, Alba had every reason to hope that his pre-eminence and his services would on the king's return guarantee him the leading place in the government.[41] This did not happen. Philip had a profound respect for the duke, but little in common with him in personality or in outlook. It is likely that he did not like being overawed by Alba, though he continued to consult him extensively. On Flanders the duke's advice was essential.[42]

The elite groupings of the period were bound together first by family ties and then by ties of loyalty to great houses. But, above all, they were proud of their service to the crown. Loyalty to the king overrode rivalries. Alba's kinsman and brother-in-law Don Antonio de Toledo, prior of León, was the duke's closest ally, yet continued also to be a leading official of the government in the years when the duke's star had waned. This fluidity blurred many of the differences between factions. They might in practice fight over every conceivable matter,[43] but it was more difficult to identify radical disagreement over principles.[44]

Whenever he felt slighted, as he did after returning in 1559 and finding that the court was not in his control, the duke would retire to his country estates to sulk. This did not offend Philip, who employed members of Alba's grouping equally with those attached to Ruy Gómez. Gonzalo Pérez, a close ally of Alba, continued to be secretary. Up to 1579 the rivalry of interest between the Alba and the Eboli groupings dominated all aspects of court politics. But the king, in accord with practice under his father, allowed differences of opinion and policy to flourish; he was willing to learn from all sides.[45] Unpleasant incidents might occur, but he pretended not to notice. Gonzalo Pérez admired his ability to govern with a council where everyone was at each other's throat. 'I don't know,' he commented soon after the return to Toledo, 'how he was able to bring together sixteen councillors so different in character and in other respects, but I believe that His Majesty will surmount this and will know what to do.'[46] It was one of his more remarkable achievements that, until the 1580s, members of his councils complained frequently about each other but never about the king. Nor was he bound to the two groupings. Other persons with regular access to him – such as his new wife – were freely consulted and could sometimes play a decisive role, but in the end the king relied on himself to be able to keep the balance between conflicting groups. Since it was the rule in government at that time for only the king to make decisions, differing opinions and advice could help rather than hinder efficiency.

*

Philip also returned to find the treasury in desperate straits. In Zealand his hope in coming to Spain had been 'to seek what is required for there and for here'. But from Toledo he informed Granvelle that 'I promise you that I have found things here worse than over there . . . I confess that I never thought it could be like this . . . When I find the remedy I will act on it, because I esteem and very much love the Netherlands, and now more than ever.'[47] He unexpectedly yearned for the north, but there were serious problems here at home. The debts of Castile were in large measure inherited from his father. 'Apart from nearly all my revenues being sold or mortgaged,' he reported, 'I owe very large sums of money and have need of very much more for the maintenance of my realms . . . I am greatly distressed to see the state in which things are.'[48]

Finance had been the issue over which he had most often disagreed with his father and it was what caused him most problems with his sister Juana. Their correspondence on the matter in early 1559 was strained. 'You need to find the money from there,' she wrote in June, 'because here all is consumed and spent.'[49] In July: 'not only can Your Majesty not be supplied [from Spain] with as big a sum as you say you need, but with any sum at all, however small it be'. This was the response to a memorandum from him on his needs in the Netherlands. Philip was furious. 'I know,' he commented, 'that they laughed a great deal over there at some things in the memorandum. Others they have at least looked at. One thing I can say: they should not get the wrong idea, thinking that I intend to take advantage of them.'[50]

Juana in all conscience could promise no comfort. Her officials were considering desperate measures. They were, for instance, taking seriously the offer by an army paymaster from Valladolid, Luis Ortiz, to double the king's revenues and liquidate the debt.[51] The debt, consisting of money owed by the crown to financiers and other creditors, was consuming over two-thirds of ordinary income. Extraordinary sources of money, such as silver from America, were infrequent and unreliable. In 1559, for example, no silver came for the crown. There was no option but to renege on paying creditors. In June 1557, when in London, Philip had already arranged a suspension of payments. When he came back to Spain, he attempted another suspension in November 1560. The burden of debts inherited from his father remained round his neck for the rest of the reign, worsening with each further military enterprise.

The biggest problem of all, and his overriding preoccupation for the next ten years, was the Ottoman threat.

*

The six years following Philip's return to the peninsula were dominated by fear of the Turks. They were also the last great years of Turkish supremacy in the Mediterranean.[52] The powerful Ottoman empire, with its capital in Istanbul, had now overrun the entire eastern Mediterranean, the whole coast of north Africa, was pushing into Russia, and after occupying all the Balkans had been checked only at the frontiers of the Habsburg lands in Germany. Much of this successful expansion was the achievement of the sultan Suleiman the Magnificent. The Turks were able to draw on seemingly endless resources of military manpower and their huge navies swept all before them in the Mediterranean.

At approximately the same time that Philip's envoys were negotiating the peace of Cateau-Cambrésis, the emperor Ferdinand was concluding a truce with the Turks before Vienna. Philip did not see the need for a formal truce on Spain's behalf. In any case he was more concerned about security in the western Mediterranean, where the threat to Spain came not directly from the Turks but from their allies the Muslim states in north Africa. Based principally on Tripoli and Algiers, these states controlled a significant naval force which, led now by the corsair Dragut, preyed on Christian shipping.

In June 1559, from Brussels, Philip gave his approval to a Spanish–Italian expeditionary force designed to capture Tripoli.[53] The expedition was the idea of the duke of Medinaceli, viceroy of Sicily, and Jean de La Valette, grand master of the knights of Malta. Long delays transpired before the huge force, some ninety ships with 12,000 men, finally set out from Syracuse in early December. Bad weather compelled them to shelter in Malta till late February 1560. They set out again in March and occupied the island of Djerba. The delay allowed the Turks in Istanbul to put together a relief fleet. The Christian ships, commanded by admiral Gian Andrea Doria, who had just succeeded his uncle as head of Spain's Mediterranean fleet, were caught by the Turks in May on Djerba. Half of the fleet was sunk and the soldiers, led by their officers, fled in panic. Doria and Medinaceli managed to escape. What was left of the force was besieged by the Turkish fleet. Over 10,000 men eventually surrendered in July, and were led in triumph a few days later through the streets of Istanbul.

The disaster stunned the court and all Europe. Spain had never suffered a military reverse of these dimensions in all its history. 'You would not believe,' reported the French ambassador from Toledo, 'how much this court, and Spain, and all that depend on them, have felt the loss of the fort and how ashamed they are of it, blaming the delays in the council of War which has so disgracefully abandoned so many good men without making any relief effort.' The king accepted the disgrace: 'it appears that His Majesty is willing to swallow this pill meekly'.[54] Djerba brought home to him the need to reform the entire position of Spain in the Mediterranean. In 1561 Dragut destroyed seven more of Spain's galleys. Then in 1562 a freak storm wrecked another twenty-five off the Málaga coast.

The vulnerability of Spain to heresy, bankruptcy, rebellion and military defeat had never been more patent. Starvation also loomed. The poor harvests of 1559 led to problems in 1560. In 1561 once again the harvests failed. Philip felt deeply that his absence from the country had exposed it to dangers which were unthought of in the earlier years of his rule. He now took steps to restore order to Spain, and strengthen its defences.

The only bright spot on the horizon was his marriage, negotiated at Cateau-Cambrésis.

In mid-December 1559 Elizabeth Valois arrived at the Spanish frontier and spent a few days in Pamplona. She then entered Castile and on 28 January reached Guadalajara, where a festive reception for her was laid on by princess Juana. Philip, as he had done before in the case of Maria, 'went roaming about all day in disguise among the crowd to witness the reception'.[55] The marriage to the king of Spain was formalised on the morning of 31 January 1560 in the palace of the dukes of Infantado. The bride was almost fourteen years old, with a dark Italian complexion, bright eyes and long flowing black hair. She was attractive but 'not greatly beautiful',[56] in the opinion of the Venetian ambassador. The judgment is confirmed by the fine portrait of her done that year by Sánchez Coello. For the wedding she wore a silver dress bordered with pearls and precious stones, and a magnificent diamond necklace. Philip was nearly twenty years older and twice a widower. He presented himself in a white doublet and a crimson cloak. 'Both parties,' an observer noted, 'are very pleased with each other.'[57] Philip was captivated by the vivacious Elizabeth, and shared with her the entertainments of the season. The wedding was followed by a banquet and a ball. The next day there were bullfights, jousting, and the inevitable hunt. It is likely that the marriage was physically consummated soon after. In October Gonzalo Pérez reported that the queen was 'somewhat indisposed, they say it is because of pregnancy', though he had doubts about this.[58] To one so close to the king, the idea would not have occurred if he did not know for certain of the consummation.

For Carnival, in February, the royal couple moved to Toledo, which they entered on the twelfth. The new queen was greeted at the Alcázar by the three young gallants of the court: Don Carlos, Don Juan of Austria and Alessandro Farnese. The celebrations in the palace fulfilled Philip's love of dance and festivity. A courtier reported that Elizabeth was 'every day more lovely, and very well considered by these realms'.[59] In Holy Week Philip retired to a monastery, a pious practice that he had followed all his adult life. Apart from short absences, or the visit both made for a few days to Aranjuez in May 1560, the king and queen made Toledo their home. Together they attended an *auto de fe* which the Inquisition staged in the

Zocodover Square on 9 March 1561. It was a small ceremony, with only twenty-four accused. It was also the only *auto* that Elizabeth ever had occasion to witness.[60]

Despite the marriage, Philip continued to divert his sexual energies elsewhere. From 1559 his lover was Eufrasia de Guzmán, a lady-in-waiting of his sister Juana. In 1564 she became pregnant, so he married her off to a court noble, the prince of Ascoli.[61] He may have had other lovers, but they are not documented. In 1563 an ambassador reported that his favourite recreations were hunting, tourneys and, above all, 'ladies'.[62]

In time, the principal lady in his life came to be Elizabeth. A lady-in-waiting reported to Catherine de' Medici, who was anxiously waiting for the news, that the queen began to have her periods in August 1561. The king normally slept with her. The lady-in-waiting reported in January 1562 that Elizabeth 'had a good supper and slept all night with the king her husband, who never fails to be there except when there is good reason'.[63] Gradually, Philip seems to have got used to the idea of fidelity. Ruy Gómez informed the French ambassador in October 1564 that the king's 'past love affairs have ceased, and everything is going so well that one could not wish for more'.[64]

*

The king began to be faced with the problem of accommodating his now considerable court. Previous rulers of Spain, including his father, had had no central capital. They had moved around, taking their officials with them. Valladolid was the effective government centre, but Philip looked round for other options. It was some time before he decided, in 1561, to fix the court in Madrid.

The decision (which we shall consider in Chapter Seven) followed logically from the steps he took, on returning home, to improve the royal palaces. His head full of the splendours of Netherlands architecture and art, he gave instructions to his builders to adapt structures, roofs and gardens to the style he had seen in the north. When Philip visited the Alcázar in Madrid, he turned his nose up at the Mudéjar decorations. Everything would have to be changed. But it would take time. A report was asked for from the architect Gaspar de Vega, who had been with Philip in the Netherlands and England and had made a special visit to the French palaces in the area of Paris. Flemish experts and artisans were contracted to come to Spain. Above all, he awaited the arrival from Naples of Juan Bautista de Toledo, a distinguished architect and humanist of Spanish origin who had lived all his life in Italy.[65]

The king's activity in building marks a turning point in Spanish architecture. He had seen the sumptuous palaces of Germany, England and Flanders. A convinced European, he saw no reason why Italian and Flemish tastes should not be implanted in the peninsula. Already in 1556 he was sending back sketches of gardens and buildings, in his own hand, to the directors of works at Aranjuez and at Aceca.[66]

The network of residences in the vicinity of the capital was slowly put in order. In these months another plan, bold and wholly innovative, took shape in the king's mind. Since the victory at St Quentin he had been considering the possibility of founding a religious house in honour of the event. Sending for Juan Bautista from Ghent in 1559 was the first definite step. The architect arrived in Spain early in 1560 and was given his instructions: to think about the new foundation, and to apply himself meanwhile to the works at Aranjuez, Madrid and Aceca. Philip subsequently contacted the Jeronimite order, who were to staff the new monastery. The friars had several meetings with the architect and with Philip's secretary for works, Pedro de Hoyo. In January 1561 a rough sketch of the building, done by Juan Bautista, formed the basis for discussion.

As yet no site had been chosen. By the end of that year, however, Philip had decided on a place in the sierra de Guadarrama, next to the little village of El Escorial. By March 1562 Juan Bautista had his sketches ready. Philip was excited: 'Bring it when you have finished, and all the better if it's tomorrow.'[67] After this the next stage was the construction of a model, which was completed by December, after several disagreements.

The king's idea at this stage was summarised by the future librarian and historian of the Escorial, fray José de Sigüenza. Philip planned (said Sigüenza) a monastery for about fifty friars, adjoining a residence for himself, the royal family, and part of the court. Between the two residences there would be a church. Very soon the idea changed and plans were modified. But the work was commenced. On 23 April 1563 the first stone was laid of the building dedicated to San Lorenzo (St Lawrence), the saint on whose feast-day the battle of St Quentin had been won.

*

Among Philip's most pressing worries was the question of his son. Don Carlos was fourteen years old in 1559 and the prince's strange character was already a subject of gossip in every European court. The Venetian ambassadors reported as fact hair-raising stories of his cruelty to animals, and his curious temperament. Striking portraits of him done in 1557 and 1564 by Sánchez Coello[68] give some hint of Don Carlos's physical defects, his twisted face and misshapen legs.

Early in 1562 the prince had a serious accident. On 19 April, while trying to enter a part of his lodgings at Alcalá to see a serving girl, he fell down some steps and hit his head. He was found bleeding and unconscious. Later he developed a fever. The doctors, following their traditional method, bled him. Ten days later, the wound on his head looked even uglier and he was extremely feverish. The king, then in Madrid, was interrupted in the middle of an audience with the French ambassador. He set out at once for Alcalá, accompanied by his own doctor Vesalius, and by Alba and Ruy Gómez. Other members of the council followed. On 5 May Don Carlos fell into a coma. His death appeared imminent and public prayers for him were ordered throughout the realm. The king was desperate. An Italian noble who was present reported his extreme distress, as he waited hours by the bedside of his son and heir, his eyes full of tears.[69]

On 9 May, following a suggestion made by the duke of Alba,[70] the embalmed body of a local saint, the Franciscan Diego de Alcalá, was brought in from a local convent. The prince was made to touch the body. The six doctors, meanwhile, had recourse to an alternative. They agreed to try the balms recommended by a Morisco doctor from Valencia.[71] The balms, one white and one black, were applied on 8 and 9 May. The doctor was also sent for and arrived on 9 May. The balm was used for a few more days. One way or another, through the intervention of the saint or the Morisco, by 20 May the fever had disappeared. By mid-June Don Carlos was walking about without problems. In gratitude for the recovery, Philip subsequently obtained from the pope the official canonisation of Diego of Alcalá.

*

In 1562 the outbreak of religious conflict in France opened up a new source of concern. Throughout the winter of 1561–2 there were small, bloody, conflicts between Catholic and Protestant groups all over France. In March 1562 the killing of a group of Protestants at Vassy by the duke of Guise's men was denounced as a 'massacre' and religious fury spilled over into civil war. Instability in France would certainly affect the neighbouring Netherlands, and might touch Spain itself. Philip had grown up in the shadow of the Comunero revolt and was deeply convinced of the evils of rebellion and civil war. To the end of his life he retained a dislike of the Comuneros.[72] In 1560 he lectured the French ambassador l'Aubespine (and through him the French king) on 'the time of the Comuneros and civil wars in Spain, when the emperor his father came to the throne, and the steps he then took'.[73] He was preoccupied less with heresy, which from his experience of Germany and England he knew could be handled according to circumstances, than with rebellion and public order. Diversity of religion was bad, but from the state's point of view it was bad primarily because it encouraged rebellion. Philip's careful approach to the problem in France had to take into account the fact that there was a bewildering diversity of political interests to deal with. His mother-in-law Catherine de' Medici, the king, the chancellor l'Hôpital, the princes of Bourbon, the dukes of Guise, the duke of Montmorency in Languedoc, all had differing approaches to both religion and politics. He consequently relied heavily for information on his diplomats at the French court. From

1559 until 1564 his ambassador there was Thomas Perrenot de Chantonnay, a brother of Granvelle.

When the French government in January 1562 granted toleration to its Protestants, Philip's scepticism was borne out by events: the concession did not avert rebellion. He accordingly sent some military support from Flanders to help queen Catherine. In October Alba informed the French ambassador in Madrid, Saint-Sulpice, that military help would continue provided no further toleration were permitted, since this might destabilise the Netherlands. 'It would almost be better,' Alba said, 'for the kingdom of France to destroy itself than to allow such a breach in questions of religion.'[74] Other advisers of the king gave Saint-Sulpice the clear impression that they were quite happy to see a France weakened by dissension.[75] The very difficult Franco-Spanish diplomacy of the next few years was made more difficult by Spanish inability to understand the complexity of affairs in France. Philip was kept informed by his subsequent ambassador, the Basque Francés de Álava, who served in France from 1564 to 1571, and sent home brilliant but sternly conservative despatches.

French affairs were closely related to two other questions: the Netherlands, and Mary queen of Scots. The Netherlands were Spain's economic lifeline, as Philip and his ministers were well aware. Three-quarters of Spain's chief export, wool, went there to be marketed. Over four-fifths of the ships plying the trade route between the north and the peninsula were from the Netherlands.[76] The loans which had helped to finance the late emperor's wars were largely negotiated there. But this fortunate inheritance could be destabilised by dissension, civil and religious, or by the greed of neighbouring states. Cardinal Granvelle, whose advice weighed most with Margaret of Parma, favoured a firm hand against religious and political opposition. He also warned Philip against the commercial ambitions of England and the expansionist ambitions of the French.

The issues that Philip had left unresolved in Brussels continued to provoke discontent. The nobles resented in particular Granvelle's control over government and his influence with Margaret. When in 1559 Philip launched a scheme to reform the structure of bishoprics in the provinces, Granvelle was accused of being its author. In July 1561 Egmont and Orange wrote to Philip in the name of the nobles, protesting that they were not being consulted. A bitter campaign was launched against the cardinal by his enemies. In 1562 the nobles sent the baron Montigny to Spain to present their point of view. Philip asked Montigny what the main grievances were. Montigny replied that they were three: the bishoprics, the Inquisition, and Granvelle. Rumours were evidently being spread that the king wished to introduce the Holy Office. Philip was indignant. 'Never in my imagination,' he assured Montigny, 'have I thought of introducing into Flanders the Inquisition of Spain.'[77]

Finally, in March 1563, three leading nobles – Orange, Egmont and Philippe de Montmorency, count of Hornes – sent an ultimatum to Philip. Granvelle, they said, must resign. They were leaving the council of State until he did so. The crisis continued into the summer months, with Margaret refusing to budge from her support for the cardinal, and Philip trying vainly from Spain to placate the angry nobles.

The anti-Granvelle campaign was backed in Madrid by the royal secretary Francisco de Eraso, who had close links with Ruy Gómez. Granvelle was an old friend of Alba. This, and other considerations, served to align the groupings in Madrid with those in the north. Egmont and Orange looked to Ruy Gómez and Eraso for support; Granvelle looked to Alba. Other dimensions also developed. In 1561 a zealous Augustinian friar, Lorenzo de Villavicencio, became alarmed at the extent to which heresy was spreading in the Netherlands[78] and teamed up with an army paymaster there, Alonso del Canto.[79] The two, sponsored by Eraso, began sending the king confidential, detailed reports on personalities in Brussels. Their spying was not limited to cases of heresy. Eraso encouraged his men to send him information about Granvelle and about the situation in the Netherlands. The king in this way had access to a direct and unofficial source of information about affairs in the north.

Philip was quite aware of the rivalries and interests involved. An incident at court in 1560 occurred in his very presence. He was immersed in a consultation with Eraso. The secretary, to ensure privacy, locked the door and left the key in it. Later, Alba turned up to see the king. Finding the door shut, he tried to use the key which gave him, as high steward, right of access throughout the palace. When it would not enter, he banged on the door. The king and Eraso went on with their business. Alba was left to wait outside for an hour, fuming among the other courtiers, until Eraso came out. Alba then stormed off, complaining loudly, 'Even the doors!'[80] Shortly after, he retired to his estates, in another of his periodic sulks. The incident seemed to demonstrate that Philip was relying more on the advice of the Ruy Gómez group.

This was not quite true. Alba's sulks were a reflection of his own hurt pride, not of Philip's policy inclinations. The king in the 1560s felt himself buffeted between conflicting waves of interest, and was at no moment so sure of his position that he could afford to do without good advice. He was particularly vulnerable in matters concerning the Netherlands. Like all the other territories ruled by the Spanish crown, the Netherlands had an autonomous government. The king issued general directives, but the details and implementation were left to the government there. In the mid-1560s the heresy laws, and other measures which excited the anger of the nobles, were never referred to the king for his approval.[81] Hence the opposition to Granvelle and to Margaret arose from a local situation for which Philip was not entirely responsible. The king, as a consequence, could not fully control events. This was a dangerous position from which to make the important decisions to which he must subsequently commit himself. He was more anxious than ever to consult with everyone, and especially with Alba.

*

At the end of February 1563 Philip and Don Carlos attended the opening of the Cortes in Madrid. Formal sessions began on 1 March and the deliberations continued for several more months, concluding in October. Finance was inevitably the central topic, but the deputies were also concerned that Don Carlos should marry, and that the king should visit the cities of the realm.[82] Since his return from Brussels, Philip had not found time to go round the provinces of the peninsula. It was an error on his part, which he tried to remedy immediately. The deputies also, in a period of spiralling inflation, pressed for controls on luxury in dress. The king replied to this with a law which he issued at the end of October.

In response no doubt to the complaints that he had not visited his people, Philip was once more on the move during 1563. 'I have to leave here early in June,' he reflected, 'and go to visit the coasts and frontiers on the Atlantic, as well as the mountains of Biscay, Guipúzcoa and Navarre, and have my son the prince sworn to; this will keep me busy until I go to Monzón, where I have to hold the Cortes of the realms of Aragon.'[83] It was a formidable programme, but he could not carry it out as planned. The idea had been to swear in Don Carlos in the different realms, but the prince fell ill, and after some delay Philip had to set out without him. He left Madrid later than planned, on 18 August, the height of the summer, stopping briefly at the Escorial to lay the foundation stone of the future monastery. Flanked by clergy and nobles, with Juan Bautista by his side, on the afternoon of Friday 20 the king presided over the ceremony.[84] After a few days at Valsaín, he made his way to Valladolid, Saragossa and eventually to Monzón.

The meeting of the Cortes of Aragon was an event he dreaded because of the sheer discomfort. 'You no doubt know,' he complained, 'of the availability of lodging in Monzón. It is so wretched and cramped that I daren't take the queen there.'[85] On seeing the town, a Flemish courtier referred to it as a 'hole'.[86] Its central location in the realms of Aragon had made it, through long usage, the place where the Cortes met, but Monzón was not equipped with adequate buildings or services to cater for the influx of well-heeled lords and ladies. Deputies who came could not leave fast enough. Unfortunately, political business could prolong Cortes meetings inordinately.

The sessions were opened by the king on 13 September 1563, the day after his arrival. The three realms of Aragon, Catalonia and Valencia met in separate session, and in each the king made an opening speech.

Catalonia alone continued its sessions the year afterwards in Barcelona, in the presence of the king. One of the major points at issue at Monzón was the Inquisition. Since 1558 the realm of Aragon had been in uproar because of attempts by the Inquisition to control the Moriscos of the nobles. At Monzón the nobles pressed the attack further. Philip refused to tolerate this. 'He summoned some of those in the Estates and told them indignantly that they must not raise this matter in the Cortes.'[87] Attacks on the Inquisition were so fierce that Philip, despite his reluctance, was obliged to take note. The result was an agreement or Concordia issued five years later (1568) by the Inquisitor-General, cardinal Espinosa, which in some measure limited the actions of the Holy Office. There were similar grave conflicts in Catalonia. The king was, as always, stubborn when it came to the Inquisition. The Venetian ambassador, who was at Monzón, said he had heard from Alba that the king felt the Inquisition to be 'the only way to maintain the people in the faith'.[88]

During the days of heat and discomfort at Monzón the king had to come to grips with the crisis in the Netherlands. In October 1563 Thomas de Armenteros, Margaret of Parma's secretary, arrived with a special message. The regent had finally given in to the pressure in Brussels, and now requested Philip's permission to sack Granvelle. There was no lack of voices to support the move. Eboli and Eraso were accompanying Philip, and they were in favour. But Granvelle's friends were not absent.[89] The king continued to consult Alba (then in another of his sulks, at his estates in Huéscar)[90] about what to do. The duke's reply was typically aggressive. 'Every time I see letters from those gentlemen in Flanders,' he fumed, referring to the dissident nobles, 'I get so enraged that if I did not try to control myself Your Majesty would take me for a madman.'[91] On no account, he advised, should Granvelle be removed.

But Philip decided to accept Margaret's decision and beat a retreat. He wrote personally to Granvelle in January 1564, advising him to leave the country temporarily under the pretence of visiting his ailing mother in Besançon. A month later, which gave time for the cardinal to act out his part, he wrote to the nobles ordering them to return to the council. Granvelle left Brussels early in March and the nobles shortly afterwards resumed their duties. The crisis was over. Granvelle went into a short enforced retirement, which he seemed to enjoy. Nothing, he wrote to correspondents, was better than the green hillsides and fresh air of Besançon. He grew his beard long. Some said he had sworn not to cut it until he returned to the Netherlands.

The anti-Granvelle interest in Madrid, represented by Eraso, felt strong and confident. But it is unlikely that Philip accepted the turn of events with good grace. He had, in general terms, supported Granvelle's policies, especially in matters of religion where the cardinal favoured a firm application of the heresy laws (known as *placards*). Now, in his absence, the religious situation in 1564 seemed to be getting worse. The nobles and Margaret appeared to be unable (or unwilling) to act. A stream of alarmist reports from Villavicencio alerted Philip to the gravity of the situation.[92]

The Cortes of the Aragonese at Monzón dragged on despite Philip's haste to get away. In the last days of December 1563 the king went daily after supper to the sessions and stayed there till one or two in the morning. On Christmas Eve he actually had his supper in the church where the Cortes was being held. He then had his bed brought in.[93] The hint, however, was lost on the Aragonese (the session went on till three in the morning). Finally the king declared that he was going to leave on 20 January. The deputies prevailed on him to stay a bit longer. Eventually, the last session was wound up formally on 23 January, typically at three in the morning. The very same morning, Philip set out for Barcelona.

After first visiting Montserrat, he was met at Molins de Rei on 6 February by the city authorities. 'He came on horseback, dressed in a velvet doublet, cloth cloak and hat of black taffeta with a white feather.' He made a formal entry into a city bedecked with Renaissance arches and flowers. There were festivities and balls and Philip participated fully in the celebrations. He wanted to 'cast off the melancholy of four and a half months in Monzón', an ambassador commented. 'There are frequent masked entertainments, when he goes mingling with everybody.'[94] The visit coincided with Carnival, one of the king's favourite events. There were 'dances, sounds, masks and costumes as never seen before'. The count of Aitona put on a great two-day feast in his house, 'and the king went one day masked to visit the celebration and the ladies'.[95]

The main reason for the royal visit was the postponed meeting of the Catalan Corts, which took place in Barcelona. Philip swore to the constitutions of the province on 2 March. Three days later, on 5 March, he attended an *auto de fe* held by the Inquisition in his honour. The ceremony, which lasted from dawn to lunchtime, two o'clock, was held in the Born, a square just outside the city. Philip and his attendants watched from a window overlooking the site. The sessions of the Corts dragged on, but final agreement was reached on 23 March.

A secondary reason for the visit to Barcelona was the king's wish to receive personally his nephews the archdukes Rudolf and Ernst, who arrived in the port on 17 March.[96] The two eldest children of the emperor Maximilian[97] by Philip's sister María, the archdukes were aged eleven and twelve respectively in 1564. Philip may have been thinking of one of the nephews as a possible heir to his throne, though this had not been on his mind when he first suggested the visit three years before.[98] The possibility of a Bohemian succession in Spain had been considered seriously in 1561, during Don Carlos's illness. The idea helped to keep Maximilian continually hopeful, and brought him more into line with Spain on religious

matters. The archdukes disembarked to a full-scale government reception. Bewildered, they refused to give their hands to any of the dignitaries
present.[99] Philip became very attached to both boys, who were to remain
in the peninsula for over seven years.

After the closing of the Corts in Barcelona, the court set out immediately for Valencia. Here, once again, there were non-stop tourneys, balls
and banquets. The night before the king departed, there was a big ball at
which the ladies were 'dressed as queens', according to the French ambassador. Philip left Valencia on 25 April. On the way back to Madrid he
stopped at Cuenca, as a gesture to honour the new bishop there, his
confessor Fresneda.

*

Though Elizabeth of Valois certainly resented the king's infidelities, their
domestic life appears to have been harmonious. In October 1562 Philip
commented with pride to the French ambassador on his new residence
of Valsaín in the woods of Segovia, praising 'the hunting round about,
and the enjoyable stay that he and the queen his wife and the princess
[Juana] had had these past two months'. Elizabeth was fond of the place
'because of the tranquillity of the galleries, garden and fountains,
but above all because she saw the king more frequently there than here
in Madrid, where he is occupied in business virtually the whole day
long'.[100]

From these months, domestic pleasures took second place to the
momentous issues which pressed on the king's attention from every side.
In Spain itself, a courtier reported that people were 'all very dissatisfied
with His Majesty'.[101] Abroad, four problems stood out: the Netherlands,
France, the council of Trent and the Turks.

The Netherlands were approaching another crisis point. Removing
Granvelle had not solved problems. The religious question, which
affected the rights of the nobles within the areas they controlled, posed
special difficulties. Many magistrates refused to implement the anti-
heresy laws (the *placards)* and in December 1564 William of Orange made
an impassioned speech in the council in Brussels in favour of liberty of
conscience. The nobles decided that their complaints should be presented
personally to the king by the count of Egmont. Philip did not want him to
come, but consented once the council of State in Brussels had made the
decision. Margaret wrote to him urging him to receive Egmont 'with a
happy face and Your Majesty's accustomed good will'. In these same
weeks the king agreed to a top-level meeting with Catherine de' Medici to
discuss issues outstanding between France and Spain.

Egmont travelled southwards through France, stopping in Paris for a
few days. He arrived in Madrid on 23 February 1565.[102] The Netherlands'
most distinguished soldier, victor of St Quentin, charming and cultured,

fluent in several languages including Spanish, Lamoral of Egmont was then aged forty-three. He brought with him a fifteen-page memoir in French listing the programme of the nobles, who wanted an increased role in the Brussels government, and moderation on the heresy laws. Though he resented being pressurised, the king was disposed to listen. When Egmont arrived at the palace Philip went to embrace him effusively and would not let him kneel to make the customary obeisance. Later Gonzalo Pérez sent the king the Spanish translation of the memoir and copies were supplied to Ruy Gómez and Alba. Philip carefully read and commented on every point of substance. Meanwhile, Egmont was entertained at Valsaín. He was in regular touch with his friends Eboli and Eraso, and also met Don Carlos and exchanged views.

On 24 March the king convened a meeting of the council of State to discuss the matters raised, as well as a further brief memoir by Egmont. He then set about drafting an *Instruction* which Egmont was to take back with him and give to Margaret. Philip was irritated by the nobles' demands, and displeased with those at court who supported them. 'I feel,' he commented to Pérez on the day of the council meeting, 'that there is reason to investigate the aims of those people, both there and here, who have encouraged Egmont to suggest these things.'[103] His displeasure probably influenced his attitude to Ruy Gómez.

Gonzalo Pérez unfortunately became bedridden with gout, forcing Philip to carry out most of the drafting of the *Instruction* himself. The king had before him the report of his advisers in council, but the approach he adopted was his own. He set out to reassure and mollify, rather than make outright concessions.[104] He agreed, for example, on changes in the administration without specifying the changes in detail. To Egmont's proposal of a conference in the Netherlands to reconsider the heresy laws, he agreed but specified who should attend and that the meeting must not be public. Passing between Pérez and Philip, the text took two days and nights to prepare. In the early hours of 26 March Philip looked over the final version. He asked Pérez to correct any errors, because 'it is one o'clock, and I am falling asleep'. He kept on writing until well past two in the morning.[105]

The final *Instruction*, dated 2 April, was to be handed by Egmont to Margaret. Philip's notes to help Pérez with the drafting were clear enough. 'In the question of religion, what most concerns me and what I can least permit is any change, and I should count it as nothing to lose a hundred thousand lives if I had them, rather than allow it.' As for the proposed committee, it should 'discuss whether there is any other way to effect the punishment of heretics, not to leave them unpunished for that is not my intention, but only that they should discuss to see if there is any other method of punishment'. Egmont saw and approved the text. He spent a few more days with the king, who transferred to Aranjuez on 3

April. Philip gratified several personal requests of the count. On 6 April Egmont left the court to begin his journey back. The king had made a major effort to accommodate him, and was exhausted by the meetings and by lack of sleep.[106] Egmont, by contrast, wrote to Philip from Valladolid to say that he was the most contented man in the world. A courtier got the same impression. Egmont, he reported, 'is very pleased over his own business and that of his friends, and was very well treated by His Majesty'.[107]

The count was returning under the impression that the king was making concessions. He said as much to his colleagues when he arrived in Brussels. But on 13 May Philip signed letters for Margaret, drafted in Valladolid by his French-language secretaries Tisnacq and Courteville, which touched on the religious question and expressly ordered the execution of six Anabaptists whose plea for clemency had been referred to him. Any hopes of toleration vanished. There was a general outcry, and Egmont and the Flemish nobles protested that they had been tricked. Margaret wrote back to explain precisely why the nobles felt aggrieved. She also explained that the committee sanctioned by Philip had met and had recommended a policy of toleration, so that she was suspending executions for the time being.

In Spain the king, his advisers, and the council, were startled by Egmont's claims. Philip had never intended to deceive.[108] 'My intention,' he had told Pérez at the time, 'is neither to resolve the count's demands at present, nor disabuse him about them . . . If we refused outright we would never see the end of him.'[109] But the misunderstanding hardened attitudes on both sides. The council in Madrid affirmed that on the implementation of the heresy laws 'there is little hope that Madame will do it, judging by her letters, since she is dominated by the gentlemen in those states'.[110]

In a more detached tone, Gonzalo Pérez explained later that the misunderstanding arose out of Philip's policy of consulting on different matters with different secretaries and officials:

In many things His Majesty makes and will make mistakes, because he discusses matters with several people, now with one then with another, hiding something from one but revealing it to others, and so it is no surprise that differing and even contradictory letters emerge, and this happens not just in Flanders but in other provinces as well. This cannot fail to cause great harm and many problems. Neither Tisnacq nor Courteville knew of my Egmont letter, nor did I and Ruy Gómez know about the letter they wrote from Valladolid.[111]

For his part the king was never in any doubt about policy. During Egmont's visit he had, apparently,[112] consulted a committee of theologians in Madrid over whether he must grant toleration in the Netherlands. They assured him that although in the circumstances it would be licit to grant it, he was under no obligation to do so. The king's marginal comments on the subsequent report from the Netherlands' theologians recommending toleration, leave no doubt about his views. 'In these times one has seen from experience that whenever heretics have been treated with moderation they have taken greater liberties. And so it is my wish that the *placards* of the emperor be observed.' The stance was far from being an ostrich-like defence of the old order. He was also preparing, in these weeks, to implement the decrees of the council of Trent in his realms. Reform, for him as for many other Catholic leaders, did not imply concessions to Protestants. Quite the reverse: reforms would make concessions unnecessary. 'In carrying out the *placards* it is to be hoped that the evil will be best remedied, but at the same time one must attend to reforming the clergy and teaching the people.'[113] He had before him the ideal of the new, reformed Church which was emerging from Trent. He urged on Margaret the need to implement its decrees. The old, corrupt Church would be reshaped and given new life; heresy would disappear.

*

Throughout Egmont's visit Philip was very busy with preparations for the meeting with Catherine de' Medici which explains in part his impatience with his guest. The death of Catherine's husband Henry II had produced extreme instability in Spain's most powerful neighbour and traditional enemy. The Calvinists (known in France as 'Huguenots') were daily increasing in number. Their strength came in great measure from the support given by members of the aristocracy, notably the Bourbon family. After Henry's death the noble factions began to jostle each other for control of the monarchy. The young king, François II, reigned for barely a year, dying in 1560. His successor and brother Charles IX was only ten when he came to the throne. As queen mother, Catherine effectively controlled the government. But dynastic rivalry added to religious tension was an explosive mixture. The 'massacre' of Huguenots at Vassy in 1562 has traditionally been regarded as the beginning of the so-called 'Wars of Religion'. It was a conflict that affected Spain's interests directly.

The king wanted to persuade France to adopt a firm policy against the Huguenot leaders. He was drawing on his direct experience of what had happened in Germany with the Lutheran princes. Philip was also extremely concerned about France's barely disguised support for Turkish corsairs in the Mediterranean. For her part, Catherine wanted Spain's public support for her dynasty, menaced by conflicting noble interests. Both sides were aware of the very great gap that separated them. The French were actively in alliance with the Turks, and had ambitions in

America; Spain was committed to obstruct both. The queen mother in 1564–5 was making a tour of the nation with the intention of securing the loyalty of the provinces to Charles IX. The venue eventually selected for a meeting with the Spaniards was Bayonne, close to Spain's frontier, which the royal party was due to reach early in 1565.

Philip was sceptical of the advantages to be gained from a meeting, and from the first made it clear that he personally would not go. The event was instead given the official status of a reunion between Catherine and her daughter the queen of Spain. In March Philip decided that Eboli, who was due to accompany Elizabeth, might be too soft in his dealings with the French, and assigned Alba to take his place. Eboli protested and persuaded Saint-Sulpice to intercede for him with Philip,[114] but to no avail. It was a clear sign of the hard line that the king was beginning to adopt. He informed Catherine that he would cancel the meeting if either Jeanne d'Albret queen of Navarre or the prince of Condé, both well-known Protestants, were present.

Elizabeth's enthusiasm for the visit to her homeland and reunion with her mother was boundless. Philip gave her complete freedom to plan the journey as she wished. She took him at his word, and spent a fortune on clothes and jewels. Her chamberlain Juan Manrique in despair informed the king that 'the queen has spent most of the money on clothes which she has ordered at great cost'.[115]

The king and queen spent Holy Week in different monasteries, the king at Guisando, the queen at Mejorada. From 3 May they were in Valladolid together. The queen made excursions on most afternoons into the countryside, in the company of Don Carlos and Don Juan. Philip then accompanied her to Cigales, where he took his leave on 15 May. She made her way north with her numerous escort,[116] which included one of her favourite painters, the Italian Sofonisba Anguisciola. Philip, meanwhile, had to deal with the Barcelona escapade (which we shall refer to later) of the impetuous Don Juan.

At Bayonne Philip's emissaries, Alba and Juan Manrique, found themselves in the position of supplicants. The French nobles to whom they talked had differing views about the situation in France and the remedies required. Only the veteran soldier Blaise de Montluc saw eye to eye with Alba. The king, Charles IX, told the Spaniards that 'taking up arms is not the solution, I would destroy my kingdom'. Catherine refused to meet Alba, complained about Philip's apparent distrust, and threatened that 'this is the short-cut to war'.[117] The two emissaries had no option but to turn to Elizabeth, who was asked to bring her mother into the talks. Although Philip felt that allowing his wife into the meeting 'is not right', Elizabeth proved her worth as a parry to her mother's outbursts. The talks were conducted in French, which Alba spoke. At the first full meeting Catherine accused Spain of mistrust. When Elizabeth denied it, her mother rounded on her: 'You've turned into a right Spaniard (*Vous estes devenue bien espagnole*)!'

Rather than coming to Bayonne with a clear set of demands which they might force on Catherine, the Spaniards were trying to formulate their own options in respect of France. Agreement with France would clarify what could be done about the Netherlands and the Turks. Alba was outspoken on the religious question. He had no doubt, after talking to Montluc and the rigid Catholics, that an immediate solution would be to 'cut off some heads', namely those of the Huguenot leaders. But, as he wrote to Philip, he told Catherine he was opposed to any general move against the Protestants: 'I told her that I saw no reason at the moment for taking up arms, nor would Your Majesty advise it'. Elizabeth wanted to know why her mother would not accept the council of Trent in France. Catherine replied that 'the situation in France is different', and that collo-quies (or discussions between spokesmen for the two religions) were preferable and 'were very necessary for the tranquillity of conscience of many in the realm'.[118]

The talks were not all business. A huge amount of money was spent by Catherine and the king on celebrations. At a special dinner given by the king some 2,000 lords and ladies sat down to feast.[119] The talks ended on 29 June, when a lavish tournament in costume was put on by the French.[120] Charles IX dressed as a Trojan; the duke of Guise and his men dressed as 'Scottish savages'. On 1 July the whole royal party set off towards the Spanish frontier at Irún. Though Philip expressed his 'satis-faction' with the meeting, no agreement nor even any coincidence of views emerged from it. The impression gained at the court in Madrid was that 'nothing has been achieved'.[121] Catherine came away with the convic-tion that any firm action she took would be supported by Spain. 'But,' she told Francés de Álava, 'as you said to me the other day great caution is necessary, for many are already very agitated and afraid of what the future might bring.'[122] Since the talks were held completely in private, the Huguenots quickly came to the conclusion that some sinister plot had been hatched between the crown and Spain. Philip, however, had gained nothing from the meeting except vague words and considerable expense. Unable to rely firmly on the French crown, he was obliged to make his own political agreements with those French nobles whose interests coin-cided with his.

*

Philip's pressure on France to accept the council of Trent touched on a vital issue of European politics. The pope, as leader of the Catholic Church, accepted the need for reform but tried to use its agents, princi-pally the general council of the Church which had been meeting sporadi-cally at Trent since the mid-1540s, to reaffirm papal authority. Some

Catholic countries, such as France, were suspicious of papal interference and preferred to introduce reforms in their own way. Spaniards were no less suspicious of the pope. But Philip felt that acceptance of the decisions of Trent, where his own bishops had made a powerful contribution, was absolutely essential to any reform programme. The council, he and his bishops felt strongly, had a spiritual authority that was completely independent of the pope. Already in 1553 he was instructing his government to adopt each of its decrees as they emerged.[123] In 1560 he subjected the French ambassador to 'a long discourse on the value of general councils and how it would be difficult for a national council to deal with matters concerning belief'.[124] He made efforts to send the best possible men from Spain to the new sessions that began in 1561. They were by no means yes-men, and the king made little attempt to control them. Some of his nominees were accused by other Spaniards of supporting 'excessive freedom in religion'.[125] But this was typical of the broad range of opinions to be found both among Spaniards and in the council as a whole.

During the last stages of the council Philip was at Monzón, from where he handled a voluminous correspondence relating to its sessions, through his special envoy the count of Luna. Philip reiterated his view that the council was 'the one true remedy that remains'.[126] He sent proposals for reforms, in his own handwriting. He instructed Luna to block moves by English clergy to outlaw the queen of England, a move that 'would be futile'.[127] The council of Trent closed at the end of 1563 and its decrees were issued formally by the pope in June 1564. Two weeks later, on 12 July, Philip in Madrid accepted the decrees as the law of Spain. He was the first European ruler to do so.

Almost simultaneously, following conflicts over precedence between the French and Spanish ambassadors in Rome, he broke off relations with the papacy. 'Touching the Council,' he explained, 'His Holiness sent me the text of its decrees printed in Rome, and I accepted them and ordered them observed in all my realms and lordships, as an obedient son of Holy Mother Church . . . Touching the question of precedence, I ordered the recall of my ambassador and his return to these realms, and have decided to have no ambassador or any other agent there.'[128]

The king's remarkable dual policy, of accepting Trent while questioning papal politics, won extensive support among Catholics in Europe. When Catherine de' Medici, who was struggling to keep the allegiance of her own Catholics, heard that Philip had accepted the council, 'she was taken aback, and said, "Surely not all of it?"'[129] But the acceptance was indeed complete. The following January Philip convened his royal council in order to prepare plans for implementing Trent in Spain.

The provincial councils called by Philip in 1565 were a landmark in the history of the peninsular Church.[130] Philip's religious policy was forward-looking, and by no means a mere imposition of traditional Catholicism.

He gave full and enthusiastic support to the novelties introduced by Trent. Root and branch reform of all religious orders, the disciplining of all clergy, education of parish priests, reform of religious practice among both laity and clergy, abolition of the old mass and old rites, adoption of a new mass, a new prayer book, a new calendar, the training of missionaries and the establishment of schools: all of this was a formidable modernising programme which the king attempted to implement.[131] His attempts to reshape the religious orders were no less ruthless than the measures undertaken by reformers in the England of Henry VIII. Monasteries and convents all over Spain were occupied by soldiers and closed, monks and nuns expelled, property confiscated. Never a religious conservative, Philip accepted changes with enthusiasm and contributed personally to textual changes in the Spanish mass.[132] By contrast, many of his clergy refused to accept in any way the changes resulting from Trent.

At the same time, the progress of heresy in the Netherlands and France made the king aware how vulnerable Spain was. The apparently firm measures taken in 1558–9 appeared, in retrospect, inadequate. Spaniards continued to go abroad to study and to trade, books continued to enter the peninsula without hindrance. The 1558 measures had applied not to all Spain but only to Castile. This left the entire northern frontier of the Pyrenees, and the entire Mediterranean coast, unaffected. In 1565 there were Aragonese, Navarrese and Catalan students at the university of Toulouse. When Philip heard of it, he made a note to recall them.[133] But it was three years before he eventually, in 1568, extended to the crown of Aragon the order not to study in France. In an age when no adequate border controls existed, and few were aware of or paid attention to the laws, little could be done to enforce the wishes of the government. Friars and nuns crossed the frontier and went to Geneva, the centre of international Calvinism. Books printed in Spanish and Basque were smuggled across the frontier.[134] In Catalonia the inquisitors claimed they were unable to stop the quantity of books crossing into Spain.

As part of his policy, the king tried to keep a watch on Spaniards living outside the country. Around 1560 his ambassador in London, Quadra, reported that Spanish Protestants were flocking to that city. 'Every day they arrive, with their wives and children, and many more are expected.'[135] Philip's father had in the 1540s condoned the occasional seizure outside Spain of Castilians who became active Protestants. They were packed off home and made to face the music there. The intention was not, as a subsequent ambassador of Philip in England explained, to eliminate them but to keep an eye on them and hope that others would take the hint and mend their ways.[136] The selective kidnapping was carried out most actively by Villavicencio and Alonso del Canto, who were sponsored by secretary Eraso. With the help of special funds, they set up a little network to spy on Spanish *émigrés* living in England, the Netherlands and

Germany. Their most notable success was in persuading the famous
humanist Furió Ceriol to return to Spain in 1563. In the process, they
collected valuable information on Spanish Protestants abroad,[137] and also
became experts on the religious situation in the north. Philip came to
value highly Villavicencio's information-packed but often venomous
reports on personalities in the Netherlands.

*

Throughout the spring of 1565, while Philip was busy with the immediate
issues of Egmont, the provincial councils, and Catherine de' Medici, a
major preoccupation haunted his thoughts and his correspondence: the
Turkish threat. From his foreign ambassadors he kept trying to obtain the
latest information about the movements and intentions of the Ottoman
naval forces. Meanwhile a major shipbuilding programme was put in
hand.[138] Subsidies which Philip was receiving from the pope could now be
seen to be well spent. 'The pope has his eyes on us,' the king commented.[139] In August 1564 the newly appointed commander of Spain's
Mediterranean ships, García de Toledo, managed to put together an
impressive fleet which captured the rocky fortress of Vélez de la Gomera
on the north African coast.

Next year it was the turn of the Turks. When news arrived of a Turkish
fleet in April 1565 the first impression was that it was headed for the
fortress of La Goletta. In May 1565, however, the fleet attacked the island
of Malta, which was defended principally by the knights of St John, under
their commander Jean de La Valette. The island was overrun, and the
knights were left defending a few forts. The position of the Christian
forces became desperate. While they continued to resist, García de Toledo
was able to put together a large relief fleet which effected troop landings
and, in early September, forced the Turks to raise the siege. The news
reached Spain in early October. The success made up for previous disasters and Philip's reputation was immeasurably enhanced.

After Malta, there could be no doubt of Spain as a serious Mediterranean power. But Philip did not set his sights on dominating the inland
sea. He was neither an imperialist nor a crusader.[140] Even less was he, like
Don Juan later, an adventurer. He limited his horizons strictly to a defensive role, and was always watchful of the cost.

Tension continued within Spain, where the events of the year excited
the Morisco population and gave rise all autumn to rumours of uprisings
and of an invasion to be sponsored by Algiers.[141] The relief of Malta was,
for all that, a significant advance. It enabled Philip immediately to re-
adjust his priorities in western Europe. Above all, it brought the Netherlands to the forefront of the agenda.

*

In the course of 1565 a significant shift in policies and personnel began to take place in government. Ruy Gómez felt that the changes had begun in 1564, when the king appointed him as chamberlain to the household of Don Carlos. Philip explained at the time that he would not entrust his heir to anyone except Eboli. But Eboli felt, with reason, that his new duties would remove him to some extent from the politics of the court. His fears were justified. Replacing him for the talks at Bayonne was a clear pointer. Other changes in state personnel, notably the rise to influence of the obscure priest Diego de Espinosa, also affected Eboli's position. There were, however, clear policy reasons for Philip's change of tack. Ruy Gómez was a personal friend of Egmont, Hornes and other leading Flemish nobles. He had worked with them at Philip's side in the Netherlands and in England, appreciated their views and interceded for them with Philip. The king now began to distance himself from Eboli's approach to these problems. At this juncture the disgrace of secretary Francisco de Eraso took place.

Since Philip's return Eraso had, through his links with Ruy Gómez, exercised a firm control over several aspects of administration. He was also actively in touch with the parties in the Netherlands. Egmont and Orange found him sympathetic. Granvelle, by contrast, quickly discovered that Eraso was his enemy. The turbulent politics of the Netherlands was in this way directly linked to personal ambitions at the Spanish court. Early in 1565 an investigation (*visita*), of the sort which the king sprang from time to time on his officials, was ordered into aspects of financial administration.[142] Eraso and Francisco de Garnica were the chief officials affected. Eboli was obliged to distance himself from Eraso, and was in fact given the job of announcing the verdicts, early in April 1566. Eraso was fined a large sum and deprived of several of his offices. 'He resented it and complained bitterly' because his friends (by implication, Ruy Gomez) had failed to support him.[143] He continued to play a role in the administration, until his death in 1570, but his changed functions signified a shift of the king's sympathies away from Eboli's group to the tougher line being pushed by Alba and Granvelle.

5
Towards Total War
1566–1572

The flames are spreading everywhere.[1]

Philip's incessant search for peace was fuelled by his knowledge that Spain did not have the means to wage war. He had always said so. Other nations, seeing the vast range of his territories, preferred to believe that he had expansionist aims. From 1566, the outbreak of seemingly minor conflicts in different parts of the globe forced Spain to upgrade its war capability, a move that had profound implications for the Castilian treasury.

Philip ruled over a collection of states that both then and later was dubbed an 'empire' but in reality was more like a confederation. The major partners in the confederation (or 'monarchy', as Spaniards of the time called it) were in principle independent of each other. They shared a common sovereign, the king of Spain, to whom they periodically contributed sums of money as a gesture of loyalty. Apart from this, the various states had no obligations to each other and few to Spain. Over the years, the presence of Castilian officials, and the demands of the emperor for money, had made inroads into this theoretical autonomy. Like his father before him, Philip found that the great advantage in ruling so many states was the ability to raise war revenues from them.

The disaster of Djerba and the urgent demands of the relief of Malta brought the problem of war to the fore. Philip's entire lifetime had been one of peace within the country. The Spain that he knew, though occasionally menaced by alarms, had not been at war with any other state. In 1568 the Sevillan writer Juan de Mal Lara celebrated the 'calm enjoyed in general happiness by the entire kingdom'.[2] War was a distant reality, fought in Italy or Flanders or on the Danube. Only the marauding of north African corsairs disturbed this tranquillity. 'The peace that has reigned here for so many years'[3] was blamed by a minister in the 1560s for the poor state of defence. Another commented that 'our Spain . . . is badly in need of the practice of arms and warfare'; and claimed that 'since our time has been one of universal peace, military discipline is much decayed'.[4] A visiting ambassador shared the same opinion. 'The lengthy peace, quiet and tranquillity', in his view, contributed to the lack of military vitality among Spaniards.[5]

Surprisingly for a world power, Spain had no standing army or navy. If Spaniards became soldiers, they did so in order to serve abroad, as minority contingents in other armies. When the duke of Alba commanded the forces that unsuccessfully besieged Metz in 1552, about a sixth of his men were Spaniards. Most serving soldiers came inevitably from Castile, but there were never enough of them to meet needs. The government relied heavily on being able to recruit foreign troops, mainly Germans, Netherlanders and Italians.[6] They were used even in the peninsula, where foreign troops defended Perpignan against the French in 1542. Spain also had no regular navy. Fleets were pieced together when occasion demanded, by contributions from different states. For normal security needs in the Mediterranean, the government used the contracted services of the fleet owned by the Genoese admiral, prince Andrea Doria. The Castilian treasury, which oversaw military expenditure, was still trying to work off the debts of Charles V, and was in no position to take on new commitments. The only priority adopted was defence against the Turk.

Spain had little money to spare for war. The different states of the monarchy, including the provinces of the crown of Aragon, raised money largely for internal needs. The cost of war abroad consequently fell mainly on Castile. Government income here was totally pledged, thanks largely to the expenditure of Charles V, and the accumulated debt was immense. This made it difficult to obtain loans from international bankers like the Fuggers. The king was helped to some extent by the silver that arrived from America, but he also had to fall back continually on the Castilian taxpayer.

From the 1560s the king tried to build up Spain into the military power it needed to be. His first concern was the Mediterranean. Within a decade he managed to secure a fleet of galleys possibly four times as large as that which had been available to his father,[7] an achievement that would not have been possible without the contribution of the Italian states of the monarchy. Despite the build-up, Spain never became self-sufficient in defence matters. It continued to rely heavily on help from its partners in the monarchy. When the Morisco rebellion broke out in Granada in 1569, the government had to import virtually all the weapons it required for its campaigns. Field-guns, which Spain did not have, were imported in quantity from Milan and Flanders.[8] Thanks to this military expenditure, from 1566 Philip's relations with the Castilian taxpayer, as represented in the Cortes, deteriorated rapidly. In December 1566 Cortes deputies were beginning to complain about the cost of fitting out an army for Flanders.[9] The king, however, had no option but to press for more revenue, both from the Cortes and from the clergy.

Spain was the only European country with direct access to American silver. In some sense, the resources of the New World made Spanish foreign policy possible. The monopoly was therefore vigorously protected and, where possible, firm action was taken against intruders. At the beginning of 1566 the French ambassador in Madrid, Fourquevaux, received firm news about a massacre of his fellow-countrymen in Florida. A group of Huguenots, patronised by the Admiral of France, Gaspard de Coligny, had begun since 1562 to colonise the Florida coast. The Spanish authorities considered them heretics, pirates, and intruders in territory that was patently Spanish. Consequently the French settlers were surprised in September 1565 by a special expedition under the command of Pero Menéndez de Avilés. Over 250 Frenchmen were killed and their women and children taken prisoner. The news did not become public in Madrid until mid-February 1566 whereupon Fourquevaux immediately asked the king for an audience. Not until 1 April did Philip concede him one.

In an angry protest the ambassador denounced the carnage and brutality of the attack. 'I have borne arms for forty years,' he said, 'and in that time the forces of the two crowns have often combated each other, but never once has such an execrable deed occurred.'[10] With his accustomed courtesy, the king heard him through. At the end he spoke. 'I told him [Philip reported] that I was distressed that the matter should have come, as it had, to the shedding of blood'.[11] They were, however, invaders and heretics, who had obviously gone to Florida without the approval of the French government. The action (which the king described as 'an exemplary punishment') would serve to discourage others. He made use of a telling phrase in his explanation to Fourquevaux: 'to preserve kingdoms and states it is sometimes necessary to depart from the norm in order to repel aggression (*une violence*)'.[12]

America was the back door through which unexpected threats might materialise. Since it was quite impossible to resort to normal methods of defence there, the king knew he had to strike hard if at all possible. Other states of the monarchy helped with their resources. In 1566, the Spanish government was shipping large quantities of armaments from the Netherlands to Florida.[13] But problems continued to emerge in the New World. In Peru the long-standing rebellion of the Incas, secure in their mountain fortress of Vilcabamba, called for a strong Spanish response. Rebellions by white Spanish settlers also continued to pose difficulties.

Because America had the status of a mere colony, it did not possess constitutional privileges that the king had to respect. Rebels there could be punished out of hand. This tough line, pursued by Philip's officials in America, was not so easy to adopt in Europe. The Netherlands, now the king's number one problem in the Old World, was an autonomous state. His advisers, both in Brussels and in Spain, urged him to go there in person to settle affairs.

*

From around October 1565 there were strong rumours at court that Philip was going to Flanders. For months the advice to go there had been proffered to him. But, as del Canto complained in September to Granvelle, 'His Majesty does not have even one person with him who will tell him how important it is to come to these lands.'[14] The impression grew among those in the north that Philip or his advisers were indifferent. Ironically, both opposing tendencies shared this view. The aggrieved Flemish nobles wanted him to deal with the situation personally. Granvelle, no friend of theirs, felt that Philip needed to go himself to see how the nobles were mismanaging affairs.

The king was undecided. In the summer of 1565, he eagerly welcomed fresh and direct reports made to him personally at Valsaín by Villavicencio, who had just returned from the Netherlands. In several audiences lasting up to three hours, Philip spoke alone and directly to the friar, quizzing him about both persons and events in Brussels. Villavicencio, a tireless writer, also heaped a number of memorials upon the king, who looked at them with care and passed them for attention to secretary Gonzalo Pérez. Though he did not share all the friar's views, the king was most impressed by his information. His reports appeared to be in accord with what was really happening. Late that summer, Philip received correspondence from Margaret in which the regent firmly supported concessions to the nobles and a measure of toleration. It was the drift against which the friar had warned him. The king consulted closely with Gonzalo Pérez, and through Pérez with Alba. 'There is so much to consider here and it is so important that we get it right,' he told the secretary.[15]

At the end of August the king and Pérez, with the active help of Villavicencio, drew up a policy document on the measures to be adopted in the Netherlands.[16] At crucial points, and notably in religious matters, the advice of the friar was explicitly accepted. Philip had at last made up his mind. The policy was to be hard-line: no easing of the *placards*, no increase in the political role of Egmont, Orange and the nobles. Philip arrived at this policy not because he was a resolute diehard, but because the arguments of Villavicencio, Granvelle and – at one remove – Alba, made more sense to him.

He was still not sure how to implement it. Other major preoccupations, principally the provincial councils in Spain and the battle for Malta, kept him up to his eyes in work. He also, early in September, became ill with the severe headaches that periodically afflicted him. His instinct was for writing to Margaret of Parma, telling her to take a firm line. Villavicencio, however, insisted to him that only his presence there would resolve matters. In the event, Philip decided to do both things. From September onwards, the air was alive with rumours of the king's impending visit to the Netherlands. His work in Spain done, Villavicencio returned to the north in October. In the same month, Philip wrote to Granvelle in his retirement at Besançon and invited him to go to Rome to represent Spanish interests there.

The way in which decisions had been reached during 1565, particularly over Bayonne and the Netherlands, confirmed the diminishing role of Ruy Gómez at court. At crucial points, the king consulted only with Gonzalo Pérez and a couple of members (Don Antonio de Toledo and Alba) of the council of State. It was, for him, a significant change of direction. Normally, he consulted as much opinion as possible. Now, however, the convincing testimony of Villavicencio helped him to take a more rigorous stance. The policy change had profound implications: it confirmed the shift of influence in favour of the Alba grouping, and it determined, for better or worse, the way in which the problem of Flanders would evolve. In mid-October, amid the beauty of the autumn woods at Valsaín, Philip signed and sent off to Margaret the letters which set out the policy he offered the Netherlands leaders.

The instructions arrived in Brussels in November. When the content of the king's letters was made known, there was uproar. Orange, Egmont and Hornes withdrew from the council of State. There were protests in the provinces. Rumours swept the country, once again, that Philip intended introducing the Spanish Inquisition. Nothing could have been further from his mind. He was convinced, he told Granvelle, that the Spanish model of Inquisition was unsuitable for export to the Netherlands or Italy.[17]

At the end of the year a number of the Calvinist-inclined lesser nobility of the Netherlands, led by Henry de Brederode and Louis of Nassau (younger brother of the prince of Orange), made a secret agreement to oppose the enforcement of the *placards*. Philip, meanwhile, reiterated his intention to go to Brussels. 'From the day I grasped that my presence was necessary in order to remedy the affairs of Flanders, I resolved to go there in person.' So far he had not been able to, 'because of waiting for the queen's childbirth; because both of us were taken ill for several days; and because of the need to settle the affairs of these realms so that they are adequately governed during my absence'. Now, however, the situation seemed better. He would go as soon as possible, but preceded by an army.

'My going is the true road' towards peace in Flanders and with France, he said.[18]

In April 1566, Brederode and Nassau at the head of some 300 armed confederates presented to Margaret of Parma a 'Request' demanding toleration. The nobles were sneeringly dismissed as 'Beggars' (*Gueux*) by a minister at Margaret's side, but she was powerless to refuse their demands. On 9 April she issued an order modifying the application of the heresy laws. It was greeted with satisfaction by the leading Catholic clergy and officials, who felt a policy of total suppression to be unworkable. That same week the leading grandees, Orange, Egmont and Hornes, presented an ultimatum to the regent that they would resign from the council of State if the king did not give it a greater voice in government (which they saw as being dominated by the court in Madrid) and if the policy of toleration were not continued. Once again, Margaret had to give in. It was agreed that two spokesmen, the baron Montigny and the marquis of Berghes, go to Madrid to explain matters. Floris de Montmorency, baron Montigny, was the brother of Hornes. He had been to Madrid in 1562 and knew his way around the politics of the court.

The support of moderate Catholics in Flanders for a policy of toleration was not wholly outrageous to Spanish opinion.[19] Philip himself had favoured moderation in England. The situation in Germany also supplied a precedent. There, as the king well knew from personal experience, princes could decide the religion of their subjects. But in the case of the Netherlands, Philip was inflexible. When Elizabeth of Valois was asked early in April 1566 why her husband did not adopt an Interim for the Netherlands, as Charles V had done in Germany, she replied that 'she knew the king, and he had told her often that he would never permit it to his subjects, and would sooner renounce ruling over them'.[20] There was no possibility of compromise on this point. The issue was never simply one of religion. Philip could see the need for moderation instanced by his father's Interim, just as in England he had advised caution over the persecution of heretics. In the Netherlands, by contrast, he was now convinced that any concession to the nobles would lead to a rapid collapse into the situation that France was currently facing. The threat came primarily from the recalcitrant nobles, only secondarily from their religious demands. The issue was rebellion, much more than heresy. He could see the same danger materialising in France. 'The flames are spreading everywhere and if those realms [he was referring to France] do not make haste to quench them they could be consumed in them beyond remedy.'[21]

At the end of April 1566, long before any disorders had taken place, he was preparing for the possibility of military intervention in the Netherlands. 'Every day,' Fourquevaux noted, 'the council of War meets over the Netherlands.'[22] Military commanders were coming and going all day in the palace. There were rumours that the preparations might be against the

Turks, but Flanders seemed the most probable objective. 'It must be something very important,' a correspondent informed the emperor, 'and so secret that they say the king himself always takes the papers to and from the council personally, and does not leave them in the hands of secretaries.'[23]

The pope, for his part, saw the situation less as rebellion than as a threat from heresy. From the beginning of 1566, in every meeting he had with Spain's ambassador Luis de Requesens or with cardinal Granvelle, he insisted that the king must go urgently to settle matters in person.[24]

Philip still kept all his options open. What remained undecided was whether the king himself would go. In May 1566 several conservative advisers, who favoured the harsh *placards*, were also firmly against armed intervention. Both cardinal Granvelle in Rome and fray Villavicencio in Brussels argued that the presence of the king would be sufficient to remedy matters. Philip accordingly confirmed his intention to go in person. His letters to his brother-in-law the emperor, and to the pope, emphasised that the decision was firm.

In reality, events delayed him. Significant changes had taken place at court. In April 1566 Gonzalo Pérez died depriving the king of one who for eighteen years had been his closest and most reliable aide. Pérez was literally irreplaceable. His responsibilities were, from the summer of 1566, divided between his son Antonio Pérez, and Gabriel de Zayas, a nominee of Alba. Another new development was the rise of Diego de Espinosa. A Navarrese priest and university-trained lawyer with a long career on judicial tribunals, Espinosa was appointed president of the royal council in 1565. He was admitted to the council of State, and in 1566 appointed Inquisitor-General in succession to Fernándo de Valdés. He accumulated further posts, and in 1568 Philip obtained for him the rank of cardinal. It was a meteoric rise, and destined to be short; but for a short while he was the most powerful man in the monarchy after the king. He brought with him his personal secretary, Mateo Vázquez de Leca.

In the midst of this flurry of changes, Montigny and Berghes arrived in June from Flanders. It was an unpropitious time to show up. Philip was about to retire with the whole court to Valsaín. He was immensely tied up with his wife's imminent childbirth in August. But in spite of this he and his advisers concentrated their minds on the issue of the Netherlands.

In the tranquillity of the woods of Segovia the king attempted to reach some firm decisions.[25] He left the whole apparatus of government behind in Madrid, but summoned particular officials. Over several days, he had talks with the council of State and other selected ministers. At a crucial meeting of the council on 22 July the nobles were supplemented by three Netherlanders, the secretaries Tisnacq and Courteville and the newly arrived Joachim Hopperus, official representative of the States General in Spain. The king was already in possession of a memorial from Montigny whereby he had access to a representative range of opinion. In the event, the meeting did little more than summarise the options available and Philip was left to make his own decision. Four days later he announced his course of action: he would go to the Netherlands in the spring. This was not new, for it simply reaffirmed an old decision, but at least it met a basic demand of many Netherlanders. His next decision was not so palatable: he rejected categorically the demands made by Egmont, Orange and the nobles.

When Montigny was told by Hopperus and Tisnacq about the decisions, he could not conceal his anger and demanded to speak to the king. That evening he was given an audience. He 'spoke very freely', according to a witness, 'to the point of bringing the colour to His Majesty's cheeks'.[26] The information he was receiving from the Netherlands, however, could hardly have led Philip to make any other decision. In July, he heard from del Canto that Brederode and the *Gueux* were raising men for an insurrection, and that Calvinist preachers from France and Geneva were entering the country and preaching sedition.[27] The great nobles were doing nothing to stop this. Letters that arrived from Margaret on 21 July told the same story. The king must either act firmly, the regent urged, or concede the demands. This was more than enough to concentrate the king's mind. For over a year, ever since Egmont's visit, he had allowed events to take their course. Now, it appeared, was the time to call a halt.

The council of State convened every day in the last week of July. On the thirty-first the king wrote to Margaret. His instructions were, on the face of it, an attempt at moderation. The *placards* must be enforced, but with various modifications. A general pardon would be issued, but religious offences were excluded. No sooner had the letters gone than Philip regretted even his few concessions. In a small legal ceremony, witnessed only by the officiating notary together with Alba and two other councillors, on 9 August he retracted the offer of a pardon, on the grounds that he had issued it under duress. Shortly after, he instructed Margaret to raise troops in Germany.

During that summer he was kept informed of the recruitment of soldiers by the Calvinist nobles. By August 1566 he had clarified the issues to himself. In a letter to Requesens he explained that if he went north it must be with an army, because 'it would be pointless and of little use if I went without strength'. He went on, in one of his most quoted declarations: 'you can assure His Holiness that rather than suffer the least injury to religion and the service of God, I would lose all my states and a hundred lives if I had them, for I do not intend to rule over heretics'.[28] The apparently uncompromising statement, framed in terms of religion, was meant above all to reassure the pope, who had repeatedly, through his nuncio in Madrid, demanded to know why Philip tolerated heresy in the Netherlands. 'He has told me several times,' the nuncio reassured His Holiness, 'that he has no wish to rule over heretics.'[29] A fuller guide to the king's intentions were the words that followed his quoted declaration. Philip stated: 'if possible, I shall attempt to settle affairs of religion in those states without the use of arms, because I know that it would be their total destruction to resort to them. But if matters cannot be settled as I wish without using arms, then I am determined to resort to them.'

Philip also made a further move to reassure the pope in August, by agreeing, against his own instincts and certainly against the wishes of the Inquisition, to allow the imprisoned archbishop Carranza to be transferred to Rome to have his case examined there. The archbishop sailed from Cartagena for Rome in December.

On 3 September a sheaf of letters from Margaret arrived at Valsaín. They reported widespread anti-religious riots and destruction of images in the cities of the Netherlands. 'Defilements, abominations, sacrileges', were the words Margaret used. In a subsequent letter she said that 'matters are worse than you could possibly imagine'.[30] In Ypres cathedral the Calvinists had blasphemed in the pulpit and had then spent all day sacking the building. In west Flanders alone some 400 churches were sacked.[31] After this, a shocked Philip was in no doubt that a state of rebellion existed. His views were shared by the Spanish public. In Madrid anger against Netherlanders was so great that, said one of them, 'we daren't go out in the street'.[32] But the king was still hesitant. He was literally sickened by the news, and let it be known, in the despatch sent to Brussels, that he had 'received the information with immense grief, but have been unable to reply because of my indisposition'.[33] He came down with fever almost immediately after hearing what had happened,[34] and had to be bled. The news and the illness were not necessarily connected, for other members of the court, including the queen, were also laid low with fever.[35] But the illness conveniently helped him to put off a decision. Not until 22 September was a special meeting of the council convened. There was now no doubt at all that an army must be sent in. The day after the council meeting Philip looked relaxed and confident.[36]

In a special council meeting at the end of October, the argument for armed intervention was reconfirmed. The king, exceptionally, presided over the session.[37] In December, when all military preparations had been made, Alba stated that 'in this question of Flanders the issue is not one of taking steps against their religion but simply against rebels'.[38]

Meanwhile, at the end of 1566 the king had to deal with a proposal, put forward by Montigny and Berghes, that Ruy Gómez be sent to the Netherlands if he himself could not go. When spring 1567 came the only certainty was that an army would be going, and that Alba would be leading it. Knowledge that the duke, appointed in November 1566, would be coming north with an army, helped powerfully to concentrate the minds of the Catholic leadership in the Netherlands. Some remained openly scornful. 'What can an army do?' Egmont asked Margaret. 'Kill 200,000 Netherlanders?'[39] During the winter and early spring Margaret and her officials, with the help of Orange, Egmont and other aristocrats, used troops to eliminate the centres of Calvinist sedition. In April 1567 Brederode fled. Margaret sent an emissary to report to Philip that armed intervention was not now necessary. It was too late. The very day that the emissary arrived at court, 27 April, Alba set sail from Cartagena, on the Mediterranean coast. His destination: Italy, the Alpine passes, and then Flanders.[40]

The sixty-year-old general, in poor health and riddled with gout, was not the king's first choice for command of the army.[41] He would have preferred the duke of Parma – Margaret's husband Ottavio Farnese – or the duke of Savoy. Both were in good standing with the Netherlanders, and (possibly more important) were not Spaniards. When he failed to enlist their support, Philip turned instinctively to Alba. His choice was made easier by the fact that Alba's rivals in the council considered this a good opportunity to get him out of the way. The duke had firmly supported the decision that the king go to Flanders. He also understood that a small army must accompany the king in order to restore order. But at no time had he lent support to the idea of a punitive force, *without the king*, being sent north.[42]

On 22 August Alba entered Brussels at the head of his army of 10,000 Castilian troops. He came armed with few precise instructions, and in the belief that he would soon be followed by the king. Philip gave him full military powers, with instructions to arrest and punish the rebel leaders before the king's arrival. The idea, as the king had explained to the pope some months before, was to 'avoid bloodshed' by taking firm action.[43] On 5 September a special court, called the 'Council of Troubles', was set up to instil order into the affairs of the Netherlands.

In the four months of 1567 that it took Alba to reach Brussels, the king must have been beset with doubts about the correctness of his decision. His advisers in the council of State were evenly divided about the wisdom of intervention, and most outside the council were against it.[44] Fourquevaux reported the feeling, 'general in this court', that what he called 'this Turkish-type army' would merely unite Catholics and heretics in Flanders against it.[45] The news from Margaret in April that the situation was under control, served only to deepen the king's worry.

But two separate events helped to confirm his resolve. The decisive factor, strangely enough, may have had nothing directly to do with the Netherlands. In the spring of 1567 Philip received information about a plot by a group of young nobles in Mexico to seize power there. They were allegedly led by the marquis del Valle, Martín Cortés, son of the famous conqueror and a personal friend of the king. Some of the 'conspirators' were summarily executed in Mexico in July 1566. A new viceroy arrived two months later, and ordered the transportation to Spain of the marquis, together with the relevant papers. Cortés and the documents reached Spain early in 1567.[46] With memories of the Pizarro revolt in his mind, and evidence now of yet another possible insurrection, the king had no doubts. Revolt could not be tolerated, either in the Netherlands or in Mexico. He sent a team of judges to Mexico to deal with the case.[47]

The second item to strengthen Philip's resolve came that summer. In the first week of August a letter arrived from his brother-in-law, the emperor Maximilian II, informing Philip of the military leagues between German Protestant princes, Orange (who had fled to Germany in April 1567) and other Flemings. The news brought tears to the king's eyes.[48] He had been fully justified in sending the army.

It was a more confident Philip (cheered, moreover, by the birth to Elizabeth in October of another daughter, Catalina) who now faced the Netherlands problem. On 9 September Alba began the great repression by arresting Egmont, Hornes and a number of other Flemish notables. Philip could almost see the end in sight. 'I am thoroughly pleased and satisfied with everything you are doing,' he wrote in reply to Alba's letter of 9 September. 'I cannot but stress that you have greatly satisfied me'.[49] 'With the energy and vigour you are applying to affairs, I feel that their resolution is in sight . . . Here too the arrest was made at the opportune time of M. de Montigny, whom I ordered taken to the castle of Segovia . . . After the imprisonment of Montigny, I also ordered the arrest of Vandenesse and his transfer to the same castle.'[50] At court Fourquevaux observed that 'they say here that the need now is not for soft words with the Flemings but severity and the bloody sword. Never was the king more happy and content.'[51] In November the king wrote to Alba: 'you have a free hand'.[52]

The duke's campaign was ruthless and struck terror into all. Both Calvinists and Catholics were swept into the net. The policy shocked since it appeared to be indiscriminate. The first executions and confiscations were limited to those who had participated in the troubles of 1566–7. Any government trying to impose order would have done the same. By the end of 1567 the Netherlands lay passive under the hard heel of Alba. All the Calvinist leaders and dissident Catholic nobles were either in confinement or had fled abroad. As though conscious of the outrage done to two of the leading knights of the Golden Fleece, Egmont and Hornes, Philip on 30 November did not celebrate the order's feast-day publicly in Madrid, as he usually did, but crept away to the convent of Esperanza, near Aranjuez, where he celebrated it alone.[53]

Up to this point Philip seems to have approved wholly of Alba's policy. Rebels could expect no quarter. 'The worst corner into which princes can be driven,' he observed at this time, 'is having to make agreements with rebel subjects.'[54] He was less clear about what came next. 'The king has no intention,' Alba reassured a correspondent, 'of shedding blood. If he can find another way of resolving this business, he will take it.' The same day he told the king that 'the peace of these states cannot be achieved by cutting off heads'.[55] In November Philip forwarded to Alba for his consideration some papers from Villavicencio. Philip seems to have considered the friar's views reasonable; they were, indeed, both interesting and prophetic. Villavicencio claimed that Alba's task was now done. The situation, he insisted to the king, could not be resolved with an army. Nor must force be used against the Netherlanders, for that would unite them all against Spain. They would fight to defend what was theirs. Spaniards could not be allowed to govern in the country, 'for they neither know the language nor understand the laws and customs'. The only solution was for the king to go there at once.[56] It was one of the tragedies of this complex situation that Philip ignored the policy advice and simply sent the documents on to Alba. He did the same thing three months later when Hopperus sent him papers with similar advice and,[57] and the duke was allowed to make the decisions.

The king's decision to go in person to Flanders had been put off several times. Philip was not enthusiastic about going, but faced the commitment squarely. In December a special meeting of the Cortes was called. At the opening ceremony on the eleventh in the Alcázar of Madrid Francisco de Eraso read the king's speech in which he confirmed his intention of going north. The dismayed deputies protested against yet another absence, but in June 1567, when he finally dissolved the Cortes, Philip insisted on the need to go. By July the final details were arranged. Ships, provisions and soldiers, all put together at great expense, were standing by in the northern port of Laredo. The costs were frightening: Eboli estimated they came to 200,000 ducats. It was proposed that Juana act again as regent, since Don Carlos was to accompany the king and Elizabeth was advanced in pregnancy.

Still the king delayed. He was waiting, he explained later, for news from Alba. At last, on the night of 21 August, he heard for the first time of Alba's safe arrival in Brussels. By then it was obviously too late to sail. The weather conditions would not allow it. In September 1567 orders were given for the supplies in Laredo to be removed from the ships, and for the soldiers to be dismissed. Foreign observers suspected that the king had never intended to go. The preparations, some felt, had been part of an elaborate deception. The French ambassador was more realistic: the formal assurances and costly preparations were, he considered, too real to be a mere smokescreen. Above all, Philip's explanation to the pope, who more than anyone had urged the visit, had the ring of truth about it. There were two preconditions for his trip, the king wrote.[58] First, he had to hear of Alba's arrival; but the duke had been delayed. Second, Alba had to carry out 'certain acts which must precede my departure'. These acts included, apparently, the arrest of Egmont and Hornes, which Philip learned of only on 19 September. The strategy, explained the king, was 'first to use the severity of justice, then afterwards use clemency and kindness'. The former had to be done in his absence, the latter in his presence.

There was also another reason for the cancellation, impossible to divulge. Philip in 1567 feared for the stability of his throne in Spain. There was no way he could leave the country now, risking his life in the hazards of the journey to Flanders. The problem was his son and heir, Don Carlos.

*

Don Carlos's health remained poor after his accident in 1561. He was unwell in the spring of 1564 and could not accompany Philip on the visit to the crown of Aragon. That June, when the new Imperial ambassador Adam von Dietrichstein arrived, he appeared to be much better. Dietrichstein sent the emperor a description of the prince: 'brown curly hair, long in the jaw, pale of face . . . One of his shoulders is slightly higher than the other. He has a sunken chest, and a little lump on his back, at waist height. His left leg is much longer than his right . . . he has weak legs. His voice is harsh and sharp, he has problems in speaking and the words come with difficulty from his mouth'. Unlike the Venetian ambassador, who thought the prince downright ugly, Dietrichstein thought he had a normal aspect. He noted, however, Don Carlos's violent nature, his intemperate speech, and his gluttony.[59]

Despite his obvious deficiencies, the prince was intelligent and usually gentle. Philip had no doubts about letting him take part in meetings of the council of State from June 1564 onwards. A year later, in June 1565, he also let Don Juan of Austria participate. The idea of marriage for the prince was mooted. There was no lack of possibles for the hand of the heir to Spain. Mary queen of Scots seemed in 1563 a strong candidate. Then in 1564 it was virtually agreed that he would marry Anna, the daughter of the emperor Maximilian.

Don Carlos's life pursued two parallel courses, one normal and one bizarre. The bizarre aspects became the subject of court gossip and of grave concern to the king. The prince developed an attachment to the queen which took the form of buying her expensive jewels. He periodically vented his temper on servants and was particularly cruel to animals. On one occasion he took a liking to a horse that the king specially prized. He persuaded Philip's master of the horse, Antonio de Toledo, to let him ride it. The horse was ridden cruelly, and died of its wounds.

The political aspects of Don Carlos's behaviour were the most serious. In his farewell speech to the States of the Netherlands in 1559, the king had promised to send Don Carlos to govern the provinces. But the prince's conduct made it plain he was not suited to the task. That he did not go to the Netherlands became Don Carlos's most profound grievance against his father. When Alba in April 1567 was taking his leave of the king at Aranjuez, Don Carlos protested that it was he, not Alba, who should be going to Brussels. He openly threatened (in one version, he actually attempted) to kill the duke. His only comfort was that his father was also planning to go, taking himself and Don Juan. When Philip later cancelled the sailing, Don Carlos was furious. He threatened to kill his father. The tension at court was profound. 'If God does not send a remedy,' the French ambassador reported, 'some great mischance may happen.'[60]

From threats Don Carlos proceeded to action.[61] He wrote letters to the grandees, asking for their support. He plotted to escape from court and take ship for Italy. He asked Don Juan to help in his schemes. After trying in vain to reason with him, Don Juan galloped off to inform the king at San Lorenzo. It was Christmas Day, 1567. Philip consulted with his councillors. He returned to Madrid on 17 January, his mind made up. Just before midnight on 18 January, he called together the four active members of the council of State, and went with them and four aides to the bedroom of the prince. The king wore armour and a helmet. They entered silently, and seized all the weapons and papers in the room. The prince stirred, and asked sleepily, 'Who is it?' The answer came, 'The council of State.' Don Carlos rose, and saw his father, in armour. 'Has Your Majesty come to kill me?' he asked. Philip reassured him. The aides removed all heavy objects and nailed up the windows. In a brief exchange of words with the prince, Philip said he would now treat him not as a father ought to but as a king should. The councillors and king withdrew. The prince remained shut up in a tower of the Alcázar, watched over by a permanent guard of two, doing shifts of six hours at a time.

It was the beginning of the most profoundly depressing period in the whole of the king's life. On the following day he began sending out brief letters of information, first to the Imperial ambassador and then to other governments, realms and authorities in Spain. The queen, who was informed that morning, burst into tears. Don Carlos had never been anything but kind to her. 'She has not stopped crying for two days,' the French ambassador reported.[62]

The king was very likely in a state of shock. Outside his small circle, few understood the real situation. Weeks later, Philip sent an intimate explanation of the whole matter to the pope, written in his own hand. The prince, he said, was guilty neither of heresy nor of rebellion, as rumours had alleged. He was, quite simply, 'completely lacking in the capacity needed for ruling over states'. The pope sympathised, hoping that this chastisement would set the prince to rights. It was the common impression in Vienna, Rome and London, that the king was simply meting out a punishment. The truth is that something more terrible than mere punishment was involved. The king had by his own decision deprived himself of a successor. 'What has been done,' he wrote in his own hand to the emperor in May, 'is not temporary nor susceptible to any change in the future.'[63] Don Carlos's confinement was to be permanent. The gravity of the decision clearly left Philip shaken. He did not stir from the Alcázar in months, not even to go to Aranjuez or San Lorenzo.[64] When in subsequent weeks foreign ambassadors screwed up the courage to express their sympathy, the king scowled at them. 'His Majesty always speaks to me and to the others with a smile,' said the Genoese ambassador, 'but on this point he was sharp, curt, and diffident.'[65] The French ambassador said the king looked 'gloomy and depressed'.[66] Astonishingly, he still entertained hopes of going to Flanders. He wrote in mid-March to Francés de Álava in France: 'the matter of the prince will not be an obstacle to my visit to Flanders, which I desire and must carry out now more than ever'.[67]

The reaction outside the palace was one of total stupefaction. In France and the Netherlands the wildest stories circulated. Madrid itself was full of rumours. The most shrewd found it wisest not to talk about the matter; others expressed the opinion that the king had been too severe.[68] Flemish officials writing home from the capital spoke of incredible rumours, and of murmuring among the nobility. The palace, said the French ambassador Fourquevaux, was in a state of fear.[69] He conveyed to the French king the explanation he had received from Ruy Gómez on behalf of Philip. For at least three years Philip had been convinced that the prince 'was even more unwell in mind than in body'. The king had waited in the hope that matters would improve, but in vain.[70]

In confinement the conduct of Don Carlos grew worse. He tried to kill himself by not eating for weeks. Then he swallowed one of his rings in the belief that diamonds are poisonous. The king meanwhile tried to justify his severity by holding a public inquiry into the prince's conduct.[71] He personally attended some of the sessions in an attempt to provide some background information. As summer approached, Don Carlos subjected himself to extreme changes of temperature by covering his bed with ice. All this had its effect. He fell ill, and died in the early hours of 24 July, aged twenty-three. His body was buried with honours in the church of St Domingo in Madrid. From there it was transferred in 1573 to San Lorenzo. The court went into mourning for a year.

Antonio Pérez claimed later that the king 'wept three days for his son'.[72] If he wept, it was probably not from mere sorrow, for Philip had never felt close to his son. The whole story, rather, had been a tragedy. The loss was soon overtaken by another. Elizabeth never fully recovered from the birth of Catalina the preceding October. She became pregnant again, but also fell ill. In mid-September she began to have fevers and faints. The king was at her bedside when she died, aged only twenty-two, on 3 October 1568. Philip reported that she died 'after a still-birth an hour and a half before of a girl of four or five months, who was baptised and went to heaven with her mother'. His grief was profound, 'to suffer so great a loss after that of the prince my son. But I accept to the best of my ability the divine will which ordains as it pleases.'[73]

The sequence of deaths in Philip's family could not fail to arouse rumour and speculation. The most extravagant stories circulated in Madrid. Foreign opinion, in large measure unsympathetic to the king, lapped up the gossip and further elaborated the narrative. Respectable historians of the time, such as the French annalist de Thou, published accounts which hinted at foul play. Philip's private grief was therefore only one aspect of the cross he had to bear. The other was the irredeemably sinister reputation that the tragedies in his family, joined to the tragedies being perpetrated in his name in Flanders, bestowed on him in the eyes of many contemporaries.

*

The repression in the Netherlands, instead of solving a crucial problem, elicited bitter criticism from every major European state. Alba was unrepentant about his tough policy convinced that the population must remain in a state of fear, 'so that every individual has the feeling that one fine night or morning the house will fall in on him'.[74]

Of the leading dissidents who escaped from Alba's hands, only William of Orange remained. Tall, dark-haired, with a small moustache and a short peaked beard, the prince of Orange-Nassau was aged thirty-five at the moment that fortune left him in the unenviable role of defender of his country.[75] A comrade-in-arms of Philip during the latter's years abroad in mid-century, he never made a secret of his concern for the privileges of his class or of his dislike for religious dogmatism. Widowed in 1558, in 1561 he married Anne, the Lutheran daughter of the late Maurice of Saxony. The marriage, celebrated in Leipzig,[76] gave him a useful link with the princes of the Holy Roman Empire. When news came of Alba's departure from Spain, Orange opportunely took refuge in Germany. It became clear that the only way to regain the Netherlands was by the use of an army. In the course of 1568 Orange sponsored invasions by several small forces, which entered from France and from Germany. All were defeated. Captured prisoners gave details of Orange's links with Protestants in several countries. The invasions could not fail to affect the fate of the distinguished prisoners in Alba's hands. On 5 June 1568, in the public square of Brussels, the counts of Egmont and Hornes were beheaded for high treason.

The executions shocked opinion throughout Europe. The two nobles, as knights of the Golden Fleece, could be tried only by their peers. But Philip, grand master of the order, had cleared the way for the trial by a special patent which he had drawn up in April 1567 and sent to Alba in December.[77] There is no doubt that Philip considered Egmont responsible for much of the trouble in Flanders, but the pressure for an exemplary punishment came rather from the members of his council, particularly (it seems)[78] from cardinal Espinosa. Alba had always regretted the need to arrest the two counts, whom 'I have always loved and esteemed as my own brothers'.[79] According to some, he was reluctant to proceed to execution.[80] Philip wrote formally to Alba: 'I very deeply regret that the offences of the counts were so serious that they called for the punishment that has been carried out'.[81] The remorse, which came too late, was probably sincere. The counts were victims of a political crisis. Their names, interestingly enough, continued to be held in honour at the Spanish court. A book on the events of Flanders published in Castile a few years later, when all books had to be licensed by the royal council, referred to them as 'outstanding princes, well loved and of the highest and finest character'.[82]

The policy of repression continued. In popular parlance the council of Troubles became known as the council of Blood. In the months since Alba's arrival over a thousand people, including people from all social echelons, were executed after being tried by the council. The scale of the repression was well known to many in Spain. A study published there in 1577 estimated, with considerable accuracy, the number of executed at 1,700 persons.[83] By the end of 1568 the liberties of the Netherlands were finished.

Though there was outrage throughout Europe at Spain's policy, the king had no misgivings. He wrote to his ambassador in France that he was 'surprised at the sinister interpretation' put on events in Flanders by the French court, where the Huguenots had considerable influence. His policy was exclusively 'concerned with punishing rebels and not with religion'. 'I have never written or said otherwise'.[84] He was not about to launch an anti-heresy crusade. Moreover, after the successful repression it was time to arrive at a settlement. In February 1569 he wrote to Alba: 'let us talk about the general pardon, since I feel that it is now time to concede it'.[85]

In Germany the criticism, on the part of both Catholics and Protestants, was particularly strong,[86] since the Netherlands had always had close links with the Holy Roman Empire. Philip tended to pay special attention to German views. His long stay there had given him good insight into the complexity of German politics. Above all, he needed the emperor's support if he was to continue to be able to recruit German soldiers – valued above those of any other nation – for his armies in Flanders and Milan. He periodically sent money[87] to help Maximilian's war effort against the Turks and through his ambassador Chantonnay, the brother of Granvelle, he kept Maximilian in close touch with his policy in the Netherlands. In May 1568 he explained that he was going to perform his duty there even if 'the whole world should fall in on me'.[88] The execution of Egmont and Hornes, however, stretched relations between the two branches of the Habsburg family to breaking point. The emperor's ambassador in Madrid, Dietrichstein, in August delivered to the king a firmly worded letter from his master.[89] So strong was the feeling among the German princes that the emperor on their behalf sent his younger brother, the twenty-eight-year-old archduke Charles of Styria, to try and mediate with the king. He was also to discuss the case of Don Carlos.

The archduke left Vienna at the end of October 1568 and reached Madrid on 10 December.[90] During his journey news arrived in Vienna of Elizabeth's death. Charles was thereupon instructed to offer Philip the hand of the emperor's daughter Anna, who had originally been proposed for Don Carlos. The suggestion was opportune. At the end of January 1569 the cardinal of Guise, Louis de Lorraine, came to Madrid on behalf of Catherine de' Medici.[91] Among the matters he discussed was the possible marriage of Philip to Elizabeth's sister, Marguerite of Valois. After considering the alternatives, Philip and his advisers opted for Anna, apparently because it was felt the Valois girls did not produce sons. Moreover, the king said, 'I have such scruples about marrying two sisters, that I could never agree to it'.[92]

The theme opened up several possibilities. A suitable marriage alliance, Philip wrote to Granvelle, might be the path to peace in Europe. As a widower of advancing years, although 'I would be very happy to remain in the state in which I find myself', this 'would not satisfy my duty to God and to my subjects, which must always be put before my own happiness'. He was therefore thinking of a triple marriage arrangement involving himself and the emperor's daughter Anna, the Infanta Isabel and the king of France, and the French king's sister Marguerite and the king of Portugal. The alliances would, he thought, 'bring peace and universal quiet to all Christendom, hurt the Turk our common enemy, and extirpate heresies everywhere'.[93]

Charles's visit was the first occasion since the Augsburg family reunion that the Habsburgs had put their heads together. The frank and open interchange of views between the two members of the family offers an unusual glimpse into the justifications offered by the king. Charles brought from Maximilian a plea for less rigour in the Netherlands, and for reconciliation with the prince of Orange. He presented the proposals in a memorandum which the king's ministers discussed and debated.

In a reply of January 1569, meant for the eyes of the German princes,[94] Philip put forward four main points. His concern, he claimed, was defence of the faith. Experience showed that any compromise on religion led to

the ruinous and sad state in which matters of religion stand. The example of events in the Netherlands, caused by laxity, licence, and consentment, is sufficient to make one see clearly that a different road has to be pursued. If there is division and disagreement over religion,

neither government nor state nor the authority of princes nor peace and
concord and tranquillity among subjects can be maintained.

Second, the punishments in Flanders had caused him 'great distress
and sadness', but were necessary. Those arrested were tried by legal
process: 'they were heard and defended before competent judges, and
were found guilty of their offences fully and entirely'. The only people
punished were 'the leaders and heads of the plot and conspiracy'. Third,
no part of the laws or constitution of the Netherlands had been altered. 'I
have not till now made any change in the form of government or in its
laws and tribunals.' Finally, the Spanish troops were no threat to any
other state, and had not crossed the frontiers of the Netherlands. Any
aggression would be contrary to his 'line of conduct, which has always
been far from causing harm or hurt to anyone'.[95]
The defence can obviously be faulted. The council of Blood was not a
normal court; and changes had certainly been made, if not in the government then at least in the way it operated. The remarkable thing is that
Philip was willing to defend his policy in public. The archduke disagreed
strongly with the king's arguments, and came back immediately with a
strongly worded reply. He accepted Philip's sincerity, but denounced the
policy of blood. 'Many will not cease to criticise Your Majesty for this until
you have ordered a complete stop to killing so many poor people . . . One
cannot fail to affirm at every step, now as before, that there has been an
excessive and abominable use of rigour.' Those in the empire advised
'kindness and compassion rather than naked rigour'. 'Apart from this,' he
concluded, 'His Imperial Majesty is of the opinion that anyone who thinks
he can control and govern Flanders like Italy or Spain, is very much
deceived.'[96]

*

By 1569 Spain was being driven into a position of isolation. Philip felt
keenly that the Catholic side was 'very divided, while the heretics stand
united and together'.[97] The execution of Egmont and his colleagues
shocked and alienated opinion everywhere. Only Granvelle commented
sardonically that until the Spaniards caught Orange the hunt was still
on. Even in Rome, from which Granvelle was writing, opinion was
not in favour of Spain, and the papal Curia was still trying to reach a
conclusion on the highly sensitive Carranza case. Philip put a brave
face on the presence at court of the archduke Charles (who left Spain
only in April 1569), but it was hardly the right moment to have a foreign
observer on his doorstep. Montigny and Vandenesse had recently been
imprisoned in the castle of Segovia, and the court was alive with rumours
about their fate.
Jacques Vandenesse, a Flemish gentleman of the king's chamber, aged

thirty-five when arrested in September 1567, was accused of passing information from the king's office directly to the prince of Orange. As early as the spring of 1566 a leak was suspected and it did not help when Egmont publicly claimed to know everything that went on in the king's bedchamber.[98] Vandenesse was also too free and open about his hostility to Alba's expedition. Once, when told to keep quiet in case the king overheard, he answered angrily that he would be even more outspoken in the king's presence. He was arrested on Alba's request and confined. His case was dealt with confidentially in 1569.[99] In December 1570 he was moved to the fortress at Santorcaz,[100] where he died of an illness.

Montigny's position had been untenable from the first. His arrival in 1566 coincided with news of the image-breaking. Thereafter he became involved in various efforts, both open and covert, to change policy decisions affecting the military intervention in Flanders. At one stage he and Berghes may even have spoken to Don Carlos. They received information from Vandenesse and others, which they sent on to Orange. Montigny was arrested shortly before Vandenesse in September 1567, and confined likewise in Segovia. Sentence of death against him was decreed by the council of Troubles in Brussels on 4 March 1570,[101] and was received by the king at the end of June. In August Montigny was moved to the castle of Simancas, outside Valladolid. He was the last of the group of important nobles implicated in the troubles in Flanders. After the protests against the 1568 executions and the visit of the archduke, Philip would have been unwise to send Montigny, scion of the great Montmorency family of France, back to face punishment in Flanders. It also made little sense to carry out a public execution in Spain. Public executions were meant to edify, and the point would have been lost.

Montigny had every reason to hope that his offences would be overlooked and he would be restored to favour. In default of this, he attempted to escape early in 1570. The harsh punishment meted out to those who took part in the plan – of the seven private servants and jailers involved three were sentenced to death, the rest to the galleys – was a clear sign that no mercy was forthcoming. By late September 1570 Philip, who never in his life erred on the side of mercy, decided that the execution must be carried out, but in Spain and in private. On 1 October a special instruction was sent to the bailiff (*alcalde*) of the high court at Valladolid. At the same time one of Philip's chaplains, fray Hernando de Castillo, was instructed to go to Simancas and prepare the prisoner. Montigny was informed twenty-four hours in advance of his impending execution. He prepared a short written testament and was garotted in the early hours of 16 October 1570.[102] The body was buried soon after. Inexplicably, the government decided to give out that the baron had died from natural causes. This was the message that secretary Zayas told Alba to communicate to the grieving widow.[103]

The execution has often been presented as a secret and private crime of the king.[104] The manner of death, certainly, was shrouded in secrecy. But the execution itself was openly decreed, by a tribunal in whose decisions the king (as was his custom) did not intervene, and the details of its implementation were known to the king's council and several other persons. It was a political act for which the king bore final responsibility, but which he himself did not decree.

The true fate of Montigny remained secret and was unlikely to provoke reactions. What most embarrassed the king was the outbreak, soon after the archduke's arrival, of a full-scale rebellion among the Moriscos of the kingdom of Granada.

*

Since the fall of the Muslim kingdom of Granada in 1492, the rulers of Spain had pursued an equivocal policy of repression and toleration towards their Islamic subjects. The Inquisition, established in Granada in 1526, began to prosecute Moriscos for not observing their new religion. However, in many parts of the peninsula, above all where Moriscos were subjects of the nobility, there was by contrast an effective tolerance of the practice of Islam.

Philip had little direct experience of the situation of his Morisco subjects, and seems not to have had fixed views about them. It is likely that he found the current mixture of persecution and toleration, not so different from medieval practice in the peninsula, to be acceptable. There were occasions when he personally had contact with individual Moriscos. A Morisco doctor was among those called upon to attend to Don Carlos during his illness in 1561, and another Morisco managed to cure prince Philip in 1586.[105] When prince Fernando, then nearly two years old, fell seriously ill in September 1572, the king did not rule out consulting a Morisco doctor.[106] In 1573 the king asked Alonso del Castillo, Morisco scholar and physician, to come to the Escorial to help catalogue the priceless collection of Arab manuscripts.[107] For security reasons, perhaps because of the permanent threat from Muslim states, Philip kept his distance from Moriscos as a people. They were, for instance, not permitted to work on the construction of the Escorial (a prohibition also extended to French immigrants). Most educated Spaniards looked down on the Moriscos, who were generally poorer, tended in some parts of the country to dress differently and spoke Castilian with a thick accent. Some respected their culture; very many others despised them as a race.

Numbering about 300,000 in the 1560s (some 4 per cent of Spain's population), the Moriscos lived mainly in the southern half of the country. Most cherished Spain as their home but resented their inferior status. The majority remained practising Muslims and looked for help to their co-religionists in Africa and the Ottoman empire. It was an explosive situation that bred constant violence. Disaffected Moriscos in Valencia and Granada were active as bandits.

Traditional aristocrats like the third marquis of Mondéjar, captain-general of Andalusia, whose family had helped to govern the province for half a century, favoured a policy of benevolent subjugation, keeping the Moriscos in their place but treating them and their culture with tolerance. The view was common among feudal nobles, who appreciated the Moriscos as a workforce and as taxpayers. In some measure the king shared this attitude. When a Valencian noble had to deal with a Morisco rebellion on his lands in 1568 the king urged him to use 'moderation and mildness, and let them off with light punishments'.[108] Others, like cardinal Espinosa, took the opposite view and felt that only a vigorous policy of cultural assimilation would convert the Moriscos into Spaniards. Church leaders had just been holding their provincial councils. In December 1565 the council held in Granada petitioned the crown to put into effect the existing laws (above all, those of 1526) prohibiting Moorish customs, language and dress.[109] Early in 1567 the government began to do so. Mondéjar protested vigorously but was overruled. He forecast a rebellion, which in fact broke out at Christmas 1568.

At the time Philip must have seen 1568–9 as possibly the worst year of his reign. Though the situation in the Netherlands seemed to be stabi-lising, it was at the cost of men, money and the understanding of other countries. Meanwhile, there were potential threats from France and Eng-land, and in America the news from both Mexico and Peru, racked by problems and rebellions, was depressing. In the Mediterranean it was obvious that the Turks were on the offensive, which made the Granada rebellion doubly dangerous. Ambassador Juan de Zúñiga wrote from Rome to Philip in October 1569: 'It seems that there is a wave of rebellions in the world.'[110]

The Morisco rebellion drew its support primarily from the villages of the Alpujarra region, rather than from the population of the city of Granada. Numbering only 4,000 at the beginning, by 1569 the rebels amounted to perhaps 30,000. With Spain's crack troops away in Flanders, the threat to internal security was serious. Two independent forces under the marquises of Mondéjar and Los Vélez carried out an energetic repres-sion from January 1569. But support for the rebels among the Moriscos increased. Muslims in north Africa sent arms and volunteers, and quar-rels among the Christian commanders hindered efficiency. In April 1569 it was decided to put the campaign under the overall command of Don Juan of Austria. By now it was no longer a question of mere rebellion. Virtually the entire population of the kingdom of Granada was up in arms, in a ferocious war in which little mercy was shown. There was a real risk that the conflict would also bring in the large Morisco population of Valencia and Aragon. Just across the straits, in north Africa the Turkish governor of Algiers, Uluj Ali, chose this moment (January 1570) to seize the city of Tunis.[111]

In December 1569 Philip had already made the decision to hold the next Cortes in Andalusia, in Córdoba as he wanted to visit the confines of the battle zone. From January 1570 Don Juan succeeded in imposing his strategy on the military campaign. There were massacres on both sides. Particularly notable was the resistance put up in February 1570 by the town of Galera. When it fell, all its 2,500 inhabitants, women and children included, were slaughtered, the town was razed and salt poured over it. Slowly and brutally, the cruel war drew to its close. On 20 May the rebel leader came to the prince's camp and signed a peace treaty. Resistance continued everywhere, above all in the Alpujarra mountains. But the end was in sight.

Philip's visit to the south of the peninsula was historic. It was his only visit as king to the major cities of Andalusia. The entire government accompanied him; he left the two princesses behind in Madrid, but took with him the archdukes Rudolf and Ernst. They set out from Guadalajara on 9 February 1570. It was an opportune moment to visit. The poorest of all the regions of Spain, Andalusia had suffered drought since 1568. In Granada the war had meant that most of the land was not being culti-vated.[112] Philip wanted to be in Andalusia specifically, as he said, 'to give more direct support and help to resolving affairs in Granada'.[113] At the end of February the Cortes of Castile met in special session in his presence in the chapter hall of the spectacular mosque-cathedral of Córdoba. The opening speech made it clear that the crown needed money, and that lack of it would put the nation in peril. After the money was voted, the king postponed further sessions to Madrid, where the Cortes resumed in July.[114] Debates in Córdoba revealed deep differences between the two sides over the problem of taxes. Both crown and cities were, for all that, only too aware of the threat to their existence posed by the Morisco rebellion only a few miles away.

Philip took time off to relax. Seville, which he visited on 1 May, turned out *en masse* to greet him. Triumphal arches were erected along the streets, and in the Guadalquivir the massed ships unfurled their sails. The king was dressed in black, still in mourning for his wife and son, but had a cheerful aspect. He walked through the streets, holding by his left hand the archduke Rudolf. Behind him came Espinosa, leading the archduke Ernst. As the royal group, accompanied by ministers and ambassadors, passed under the arches they were showered with rose petals.[115] After ten days in Seville, Philip returned to Córdoba, where he received news from Don Juan that the Muslim leaders had agreed to capitulate. From Córdoba Philip moved on to Jaén at the end of May, and then to Ubeda. After Ubeda the royal party returned directly to Toledo.

By the summer of 1570 the Morisco revolt was effectively over. Help from Muslims abroad – there were 4,000 Turks and Berbers fighting with the rebels in spring 1570 – was not enough to keep it going. What turned the tide was the mass import of arms from Italy, since the Spanish troops had few of their own. Guns and powder in quantity came from the factories in Milan.[116] In August 1570 three more Morisco representatives met Don Juan's secretary and agreed in principle to surrender. By November, 'it's all over'.[117] Don Juan left Granada at the end of the month.

It had been the most brutal war to be fought on European soil during that century. Luis de Requesens reported having killed thousands during the mopping-up. 'I have become ruthless with these people . . . An infinite number have been put to the sword.'[118] The deaths were not, for all that, the only terrible aspect of the war. In the late summer the decision was made by the king's council, under Espinosa, to expel a part of the Muslim population of Granada to other parts of Spain. The proposal was an old one; eight months before the rebellion the French ambassador reported that ministers were thinking seriously of removing the entire Muslim population from Granada and transferring it 'to Galicia and the mountains'.[119] The operation began on 1 November 1570. Over the subsequent months a total of probably 80,000 Moriscos, men, women and children, were forcibly expelled for ever from their homes. They were distributed through parts of Castile where their presence was till then unknown. Very many died of their hardships during the march. Don Juan, watching the exiles, could not repress his pity. It was, he wrote to Ruy Gómez, 'the saddest sight in the world, for at the time they set out there was so much rain, wind and snow that mothers had to abandon their children by the wayside and wives their husbands . . . It cannot be denied that the saddest sight one can imagine is to see the depopulation of a kingdom.'[120]

The expulsions aggravated rather than solved the religious and security problems raised by the Morisco presence. Years later, in 1579, the king commented that 'it seems to me that the proper solution has not been applied'. He was particularly critical of 'the protection given by certain nobles to these Moriscos. I think that this has been and is most harmful. To tell the truth, just to see what the Moriscos did at the time they rebelled, killing so many priests and other Christians, would be sufficient to justify a tough line with these people.' A committee should look into possible solutions. 'I think that among other ideas it would be good to order that children not be brought up with their parents.'[121]

In Lisbon in mid-June 1582 he convened a special committee. They held sessions for three months, and took advice from all those who in previous years had spoken on the question. In September they were agreed on a course of action. The Moriscos were a threat to religion. They were also, as their bandit activity showed, a threat to public order. But above all they were a threat to the nation, because of their link with the Turks. The solution, decided upon was that all of them should be expelled from Spain.[122]

Critics of such a solution were not wanting, either then or later. But the idea had powerful supporters, among them cardinal Quiroga. The hoary old Inquisitor-General felt that 'at the time that they have to be expelled from Spain, there should be no delay because of the few who might genuinely convert, since far more important and more widespread is the harm they cause with their blasphemies'.[123] There was, however, no way of putting the proposal into effect. An army would be needed to round up the Moriscos, and a navy to take them away: neither was available. After Philip's return to Madrid in 1583 the idea was virtually shelved. Attention reverted to the possibility of instructing Moriscos in the faith. In June 1587 the king set up a special committee to consider the question.[124] Chaired by Quiroga, it included eight others, among them confessor Chaves and secretary Mateo Vázquez. Meetings were held regularly until the end of September. One may suspect that little new emerged. Thereafter the issue was never far below the surface. Morisco agitation in Valencia and Aragon inspired the creation of a new committee, in January 1591.[125]

*

Hostility to Spain's actions was the order of the day in virtually every European court. Ironically, at this period Philip looked for support to a nation with whom he had every cause to quarrel: Protestant England.

Since Tudor times the dynastic link between Spain and England had created a special bond. Philip's marriage to Mary, intended to cement that bond, had the opposite effect of arousing tensions and severing the link. But neither the king nor his advisers ever gave up hope. Faced with an insecure Netherlands and an unstable France, Philip regarded England as an essential ally. He persisted, often against his advisers (notably Granvelle and Alba), in holding out the olive branch to Elizabeth. The French ambassador St Sulpice in the 1560s got the distinct impression that Philip's policy was pro-English and anti-French.[126] Alba subsequently accused the king of being too much under the influence of the duke of Feria (an ally of Ruy Gómez) and his English wife, Jane Dormer.[127] Some of Philip's ministers in the Netherlands were even more pronounced in their pro-English views: the suggestion that Don Carlos marry Elizabeth was made there. Even if Elizabeth turned out not to be amenable, Spain could count on the likely sympathy of her direct heir, Mary queen of Scots, and of the numerically significant Catholic nobles and population of England, Scotland and Ireland.

The arrival in the Netherlands of a Spanish army under Alba wrecked hopes of an understanding. English commercial interests, as well as English security, felt threatened. Against this background several incidents deepened distrust. In 1568 five small Spanish pay-ships were sailing up-Channel to deliver bullion to the duke of Alba. Threatened by a storm, they took refuge on the English coast. Elizabeth impounded the ships and then seized the precious cargo. When the newly arrived Spanish ambassador, Guerau de Spes, protested, he was put under house arrest. Relations were further prejudiced by a parallel incident in September 1568 at the port of San Juan de Ulúa, in Mexico. A small group of seven ships under John Hawkins, trading illegally in American waters, was surprised in the port by the Spanish fleet and destroyed. Only one vessel, commanded by Hawkins and including among its crew the young Francis Drake, limped back home to tell the tale and complain of Spanish perfidy.

A break with England seemed inevitable. The tension was exacerbated by the expulsion in 1568 of the English ambassador in Madrid, Dr Man, for undiplomatic remarks about the pope. Early in 1569 the Spanish authorities, in retaliation for the seizure of the pay-ships, embargoed all English ships and property in the Netherlands and in Spain. The English did the same to Spanish property. Furious at the loss of bullion, Philip still saw a bright side: the queen had gone as far as she dared. Elizabeth, he confided to Alba, 'has gone so far that it makes me think, and in this I think the same as you, that she will not dare declare war or have me as an open enemy'.[128] However, there were Spanish diplomats who felt that the only solution was a direct attack on Elizabeth, an 'enterprise of England'. The phrase occurs for the first time in a report drawn up by Guerau de Spes.[129]

There were various ways of dealing with England. But Philip refused to be dragged into the dangerous schemes implicating Mary queen of Scots, who fled into England from Scotland in 1568 and put herself under Elizabeth's protection. However, Philip still saw her as a key figure in the politics of the Guise family, and had no intention of furthering their ambitions. Even more significant was his refusal to support the abortive rebellion that a group of Catholic earls in the north of England carried out at the end of 1569. Interference in English politics promised little benefit to Spain, which only wanted from Elizabeth her neutrality, and security on the seas. While apparently serious threats to the queen were emerging in England, Philip limited himself to supporting Alba's concern for good trade relations. He even blocked papal moves to excommunicate Elizabeth. None of this earned him thanks in London. In January 1570 he remarked to Alba that 'we are in a virtual state of war',[130] since English corsairs continued to attack Spanish shipping. The following month the pope issued his excommunication of the English queen. Its publication infuriated Philip. Alba advised moderation, so as not to drive Elizabeth into French hands. This, rather than any pro-English sentiment, lay behind his advice of 'war with the whole world, but peace with England'.[131] Philip assented. His constant wish to stay friends with England was motivated by fear of France. In May 1570 he instructed his ambassador in France to tell the English ambassador that 'on my side, I shall not break the ancient friendship and alliance between us'.[132]

De Spes, unfortunately, got caught up in a plot inspired by an Italian adventurer named Ridolfi. The aim was to overthrow Elizabeth, proclaim Mary as queen, and send in a force from the Netherlands to support a rising by the Catholic nobles. Alba distrusted Ridolfi, and Philip made it clear that he was not interested.[133] In Madrid the councillors of state were more enthusiastic,[134] but stressed that nothing could be done until the king gave his support. This he did not do. Years later he complained bitterly to the Imperial ambassador Khevenhüller that rumour had falsely implicated him.[135] It is likely that Ridolfi was a double agent in the pay of England's chief minister, the anti-Spanish Sir William Cecil. At any rate, the plot was revealed by Cecil's spies in September 1571. The nation's leading nobleman, the duke of Norfolk, was arrested for his apparent complicity, and later executed. De Spes was expelled from the country. There was still no open rupture with Spain, but the plot had decisive consequences. It broke once and for all England's traditional pro-Spanish connection. It pushed Elizabeth towards an alliance with France. And it confirmed the emergence of a pro-Protestant foreign policy in the English Privy Council.

*

Back home, the war in the Alpujarras had provoked differences of approach among the Spanish nobility, and it also brought to the fore the problem of Don Juan.

Don Juan of Austria, born in 1547, was the fruit of Charles V's love affair with a burgher's daughter from Regensburg, Barbara Blomberg. He was brought up secretly in Spain on the orders of his father, and allowed to emerge only when Juana was regent in 1554. In 1559 Philip on his return was officially introduced to his half-brother. Don Juan was welcomed into the court circle, given a residence, and brought up in the company of Don Carlos and Alessandro Farnese. Philip was understandably intrigued by the prince, nearly twenty years his junior. But it soon became clear that their characters were not suited to each other. The king, forever seeking a son to whom he could give both his confidence and his affection, sought in others what God had not given him in Don Carlos. Don Juan, some felt, made a perfect heir. After Don Carlos's death in 1568, the question of a male successor to the throne became urgent. Without infant sons, the king could turn only to his nephews, the Austrian archdukes, or to the young heir of Portugal, Sebastian.

Don Juan impressed all contemporaries. Energetic and handsome, with a touch of beard, long moustaches and long flowing blond hair, always elegantly dressed, he quite simply glittered. 'He is agile, incomparable in riding, jousting and tourneys . . . He is learned, judicious, eloquent, gifted . . . His speech is all of enterprises and victories.'[136] A soldier-diplomat described him as 'splendid'.[137] He was a constant success with ladies, who gave him several bastard children. One of his daughters was Anna, who became involved years later in the Madrigal conspiracy. Though busy in love, he never neglected affairs of state. His correspondence was enhanced by his elegant handwriting, almost feminine in its perfection. He spoke French, and understood some Dutch and German. It is logical to suppose, as many have done,[138] that Philip envied his charm and viewed him as a rival. This romantic version must be rejected. Philip merely saw in him an impetuous youth in whom he could not place entire confidence. Dashing in love, spirited in war, Don Juan was adventurous to the point of irresponsibility. In the spring of 1565, while the attention of the court was centred on the impending meetings at Bayonne, he could think of nothing but the hazardous state of Malta. His repeated requests to the king to be allowed to participate in the relief of the garrison there were turned down. Ignoring the king's wishes, he teamed up with a group of other young nobles (one of them the brother of Eufrasia de Guzmán) and galloped off to Barcelona.[139] The gallants were detained there and sent back on the king's orders. The incident was typical of Don Juan's enthusiasm. The king never held back from giving him the role that befitted his rank as a prince, but always took care to place a more seasoned person at hand to advise. Don Juan, for his part, was resentful that despite his qualities and achievements, and his position as the son of his father, he did not yet possess his own titles and kingdom.

In May 1568 the king appointed him, at the age of only twenty-one, captain-general of the Mediterranean fleet in succession to García de Toledo. He gave him handwritten instructions[140] which touched primarily on the prince's weak points. He must set a good example, keep his word, avoid gaming, moderate his language, eat moderately, be courteous to others. The instructions given at the same time to the nobleman placed in charge of the prince are rather more specific about Don Juan's known weakness for women: 'he should not go around at night, because Barcelona is noted for its women, and there's no lack of disease'.

Immediately the Morisco rebellion broke out in Granada, Don Juan offered his services. Not until the spring of 1569 was he given supreme command. Philip warned him explicitly that he must always consult with his colleague and tutor, the grand commander of Castile, Luis de Requesens. The prince chafed at this rein on his actions. Impatient and haughty, he also fell out with the powerful Mendoza nobles who had always regarded Andalusia as their fief. Their spokesman, the marquis of Mondéjar, protested to Madrid and retired in disgust to his estates. Philip carefully distanced himself from these quarrels,[141] which he disliked because they upset the very men whose support made stability in Spain possible.

The resounding success of Don Juan at Granada was, in these circumstances, flawed. His correspondence shows him to be highly volatile and undisciplined.[142] A possible heir to the throne, he never won support among the high nobility because of his manner. Philip, whom the prince regularly disobeyed, kept him at arm's length. When the king came to Córdoba for the Cortes, he did not respond to Don Juan's request to be allowed to come and see him. Six months after the campaign, the restless prince was once again given a job away from court. He was appointed to the highly desirable post of commander of the naval expedition which the Holy League was preparing against the Turks.

*

In the autumn of 1569 Philip made arrangements for the marriage with his niece Anna.[143] Twenty-two years younger, she had been born in Spain in 1549 when Maximilian governed the realm during Philip's absence. It was at first intended to bring her to the peninsula via Genoa, but news of Turkish naval movements caused a change of plan. The final arrangements, drawn up by Philip while he was visiting Andalusia in the first half of 1570, were that Anna accompany her father to Speyer, where an Imperial Diet was to be held, and travel from there to the Netherlands, where Alba would organise her sea route to the Cantabrian coast. She was meant to arrive at Laredo, but the bad weather made her ships beach instead at Santander, on 3 October. She came accompanied by her younger brothers Albert and Wenzel. An immense welcoming party of 2,000 persons awaited her. Among them was a musical group of over a hundred minstrels, who accompanied her for the rest of her journey to relieve the tedium.[144]

After resting for ten days in Santander, Anna's retinue made their way to Burgos, where a sumptuous reception greeted them, and then to Valladolid. Just outside Valladolid they were met by the archdukes Rudolf and Ernst. They all then proceeded to Segovia, where Anna arrived on 12 November and was received with great pomp in the Alcázar, specially decorated for the occasion. The king delayed his own entry until that afternoon. Two days later, on the fourteenth, the formal wedding took place. The weather was bitterly cold, and the city was almost cut off by snowstorms.[145] The royal couple managed to get through to Valsaín and some days later went off to visit San Lorenzo and El Pardo. On the twenty-third they made their formal entry into Madrid, where the fireworks, triumphal arches, fountains and musical displays outdid in magnificence the reception in Segovia.

Philip was enchanted with his new wife and fell deeply in love with her. Petite and elegant,[146] with a strikingly white complexion, deep blue eyes and flowing blonde hair, Anna could not have been more different from Elizabeth Valois. Philip expressed 'my great joy and contentment that God has given me all the happiness I could wish for on this earth', and spoke of 'the great love there is between us'.[147] A diplomat observed that 'the king loves her deeply'.[148] She became pregnant in the spring. On 4 December 1571 their first child, Fernando, was born. The throne had, at last, a male heir. The event was celebrated with great rejoicing. Titian subsequently produced a triumphal canvas which combined the theme of the birth with the other great news, known only a month before, of the naval victory at Lepanto. At the same time news came of the safe arrival of the richly laden treasure fleets from New Spain and Peru. Truly, the king's biographer commented later, the year 1571 was a happy one for the monarchy.[149]

Treasure from the New World was opportune help. While the king was preoccupied with the threat from Muslim expansionism in the Mediterranean, he found time to make a series of far-reaching decisions concerning America. In 1569 he appointed to the viceroyalty of Peru a member of Alba's family, Francisco de Toledo, who had already distinguished himself in the royal service. During his twelve momentous years in Peru, Toledo put into effect a series of reforms that pacified the territory and laid the basis for Spain's colonial rule. In 1572 he managed to seize and then execute the last emperor of the Incas, Tupac Amaru. It was the opening of a new phase of consolidation in America. In 1568 Philip had summoned a special committee in Madrid to revise the laws governing the New World territories. The new legislation, issued five years later, emphasised the government's commitment to the principle of peaceful imperialism. When Miguel López de Legazpi began his settlement of the Philippine Islands in 1569, he was specifically ordered by the king not to use force. Philip's instructions were based on the views of the Salamanca professor Francisco de Vitoria, and those of Las Casas, who aimed to avoid the bloodshed that had marked the conquest of Mexico and Peru a generation before. By the time of Legazpi's death in 1572 he had brought about a relatively bloodless occupation of the islands.[150]

In 1571 the king appointed Juan López de Velasco as 'cosmographer-chronicler' of the Indies, to draw up a survey of America and compose an official history of the conquest. This was the period when other great cultural enterprises, such as the *General History* of the Franciscan Bernardino de Sahagún, received royal backing. It appeared to be the beginning of an era of promise in the New World. But the promise was one-sided. Viceroy Toledo's measures severely disadvantaged the Indians. New harsh measures were taken against their religion. The Inquisition, which had operated in an informal way until now, was set up in Lima in 1570 and in Mexico City in 1571. The Indians were soon exempted from its control, but the very presence of the new tribunal was a sign of the times.

*

The successful relief of Malta by Spanish forces did not lull western Christendom into a false sense of security. On the Hungarian frontier an enormous Turkish army, estimated at 300,000 men,[151] was moving against the emperor Maximilian in the spring of 1566. Fortunately, the attack melted away. The reason was the death on 6 September of the great architect of Ottoman power, Suleiman the Magnificent. The Turks withdrew to settle their domestic conflicts. The war against the west was not, however, abandoned, and by sea it continued without a break. A new factor had entered the scenario. In January 1566 the cardinals at Rome elected as their new pope the elderly and zealous ascetic Pius V. Almost immediately he gave priority to the crusade against the crescent of Islam. Philip had the Netherlands to deal with and was not enthusiastic. Subsequently he had the war of Granada on his hands. Only much later, after the fall of the island of Cyprus to the Turks in 1570, did the continuing Turkish menace oblige Philip in May 1571 to participate in an anti-Ottoman 'Holy League' with Venice and the papacy. The alliance took concrete shape in a joint naval force which was to be sent to the eastern Mediterranean to relieve Cyprus and repulse the Turkish navy.

It was agreed that the supreme commander of the fleet would be Don Juan of Austria. Don Juan was in Barcelona from 16 June, waiting impatiently for the Spanish contingent to be put together. He was also waiting for the arrival of the archdukes Rudolf and Ernst, who were going home and whom he had to escort to Genoa. While in the city he received his instructions from Philip, but they left him deeply dissatisfied. Philip continued to address him with the standard title of 'Excellency' instead of the royal 'Highness' that he claimed. The king also, knowing Don Juan's temperament, placed several restrictions on his powers.

The massive Turkish fleet of over 300 galleys was ravaging the coastline of settlements in the eastern Mediterranean. In the west, Don Juan was determined, against the advice of more experienced sailors, to test to the full the resources put at his disposal. At the end of August he was in Messina, the appointed rendezvous for the ships of the Holy League. The assembled Christian fleet was supplied and paid for by the papacy, Venice and Spain. Although Philip II's treasury was the biggest single contributor to costs, the so-called 'Spanish' contribution was in fact largely Italian: four-fifths of the galleys supplied by Spain were built and paid for in the Italian states of the monarchy.

The fleet left Messina on 16 September and headed towards Corfu. There they were informed that the Turks were in the Gulf of Lepanto. The two massive formations came upon each other on the morning of 7

October in the Gulf. Calculations of the ships and men on each side vary widely. It is likely that the Turks had some 230 ships and well over 50,000 men. The Christians had some 200 vessels, not all of which took part in the battle, and about 40,000 men. By the end of the day Don Juan's ships had won a decisive victory. The Turkish vice-admiral, Uluj Ali, escaped with about thirty galleys; all the others were captured or destroyed. The Turks suffered 30,000 casualties and 3,000 prisoners. Christian losses were by comparison small: ten galleys, and some 8,000 men killed.

In the afternoon of 29 October 1571 a courier from Venice brought to the Venetian ambassador and to Philip, then in Madrid, reliable news of the victory at Lepanto. 'The king's joy at receiving the news was extraordinary,' the ambassador reported. 'In that very moment he ordered a Te Deum sung.'[152] Over the next few days all Madrid exploded in an orgy of celebration. A solemn procession was held, in which the king insisted on having the Venetian ambassador at his side. Don Juan's own special envoy, Lope de Figueroa, did not arrive until much later, on 22 November. The king at the time was at San Lorenzo. One of his gentlemen, fat, excited and breathless, burst in to say that a messenger had come from Don Juan. 'Calm down,' the king said; 'let the messenger in, he will say it better.'[153] Philip quizzed Figueroa eagerly. 'For the first half-hour he did nothing but ask, "Is my brother well?" and all sorts of questions,' the latter reported. The queen came in with her ladies and also questioned him. 'Thus I passed an hour in the most agreeable manner possible,' Figueroa wrote to Don Juan.[154] Philip displayed 'great delight and joy',[155] ordered the prior to have a Te Deum sung, and went to his rooms highly contented.

Don Juan was given his full share of public glory. Philip wrote to him, 'I am pleased to a degree which it is impossible to exaggerate . . . To you, after God, ought to be given, as I now give, the honour and thanks.'[156] Don Juan featured duly in the six large canvases which Philip commissioned some years later from the Genoese painter Luca Cambiaso, to hang in the summer lodge of El Monesterio. The military hero of Spain, victor first of the Alpujarras and now of Lepanto, Don Juan was fêted right across the peninsula. The king continued to distrust his character, but gave him all due honour for his successes.

Lepanto was a victory for Christendom, but it was never simply a Spanish victory. Without the resources of the Italians, Spain would have been powerless to act. Philip was perfectly aware of this. It explains his refusal to participate in the daydreaming to which less realistic men, such as Don Juan and pope Pius V, lent themselves. They imagined a possible liberation of the Holy Land, and even of Istanbul. The legend of Lepanto would continue to live on. One of the many who sweated through the battle, an unknown writer called Miguel de Cervantes, described it as 'the greatest occasion that past or present ages have seen, or that future ones can hope to see'. Philip shared the enthusiasm. But he 'opted for the possible, not for the grandiose'.[157] Searching always for peace, Philip looked for a settlement in the Mediterranean. Spain must, first of all, have security in north Africa. Without this, it was difficult to devote resources to the north.

*

Success in the Mediterranean was important compensation for the uncertain situation in northern Europe. In the Netherlands a group of Calvinist exiles who had been based in England, known as the Sea Beggars (*Gueux de Mer*), seized the port of Brill in April 1572. It gave them for the first time a base from which to attack the Spaniards. Alba was confident he could contain their activities, but his attempts during 1571 to collect a new tax, the Tenth Penny, had aroused fierce opposition in the towns who now collaborated with the exiles. In May the town of Mons opened its gates to a force under Louis of Nassau, Orange's brother. Other small forces, aided by Huguenots, invaded.

Events in France gave even greater cause for concern. Exposure of the Ridolfi plot persuaded Elizabeth to agree on a formal alliance with the French in the same month of April (the treaty of Blois). The accord threatened to be extremely damaging to Spanish interests. The young king Charles IX was at this period strongly influenced by the Admiral of France, the Huguenot Gaspard de Coligny. He also had meetings with Louis of Nassau, who attempted to persuade him to form an alliance against Spain. A marriage had already been arranged between the king's sister Marguerite and the Protestant king of Navarre, Henry of Bourbon. French diplomats tried to extend the marriage arrangements to include one between the king's younger brother François, duke of Alençon (later, duke of Anjou), and Elizabeth. The latter, now thirty-eight years old, refused to think seriously about marrying someone twenty-two years younger than herself.[158] Despite this, the scenario opening up for Philip and Alba was the frightening one of an international Protestant front, backed by France.

'There have been no other speeches but war with Spain,' the English envoy wrote home from Blois.[159] Coligny was pressing Charles IX to intervene in favour of the rebels in the Netherlands. Spain was in no doubt about the reality of this threat. In July Alba's aide Albornoz told the royal secretary Zayas that 'I have in my possession a letter of the king of France which would strike you with astonishment if you could see it'.[160] The letter, from Charles to Louis of Nassau, reassured the count that he intended to use his armies to free the Netherlands from its oppressors. But the force sent by Coligny and the king to help Nassau was destroyed by Spanish troops just south of Mons. Queen Elizabeth, who was kept well informed what was going on, did not intend to get drawn into a war with

Spain, nor did she relish the idea of France dominating the Netherlands. In June 1572 she promptly withdrew from the alliance made at Blois.

Charles IX was faced with the unappetising alternative of going it alone against Spain, or pulling back and betraying his Huguenot allies. There remained a third alternative: to break with the Huguenots. It was the solution pressed on him by his mother Catherine de' Medici. Subsequent events are well known. All the great leaders of France, Protestant and Catholic, were gathered in Paris for the marriage on 18 August 1572 of Henry of Navarre to the princess Marguerite. On 22 August an unsuccessful attempt was made on the life of Admiral Coligny. Two days later, on St Bartholomew's Eve, he was brutally murdered. His death was made the signal for the massacre of some 3,000 Huguenots in Paris and a further 25,000 or more in various parts of the country.

The news shocked Europe. The emperor Maximilian protested to the papal legate that the sword was no answer to religious differences. The first firm news of the event reached Madrid on 6 September, when the king was residing in the monastery of St Jerónimo. He called secretary Gracián over the next day to ask him to translate an account in French of the killing of the Huguenot leaders.[161] Philip had always entertained an unjustifiably narrow image of what had really been agreed at Bayonne, and saw the events as a fulfilment of that meeting. His ambassador Diego de Zúñiga, writing from Paris, made it clear that Catherine and the king were responsible, but that the killing of so many Protestants was not part of the plan.[162] On the day after Coligny's murder, Catherine wrote in her own hand to Philip, who replied at once to congratulate her on 'this glorious event'. He also wrote to Zúñiga with his reactions to 'the good news'. 'I had one of the greatest moments of satisfaction that I have had in all my life, and will have yet another if you continue writing to me of what is happening in the other parts of that realm. If things go as they did today it will set the seal on the whole business.'[163] The French ambassador, St Gouard, was invited to visit him the day after he received the news. 'He began to laugh, with signs of extreme pleasure and satisfaction . . . He said he had to admit that he owed his Low Countries of Flanders to Your Majesty.'[164]

Philip was thoroughly relieved and did not disguise it. The threat from the French Protestant leaders, which since the early 1560s had been the chief obstacle to Spain's policies, was now removed. The way lay open to peace in Flanders and perhaps to security in western Europe. The mass killings, a corollary of the elimination of the leaders, were never at the centre of his mind.[165] They were irrelevant to his 'contentment'. He was thinking of the Netherlands. His confidence in the new situation was so great that, a week after receiving the news of St Bartholomew's, he took the unprecedented step of proposing to transport bullion to Alba *through* France, given the insecurity of the Channel route. 'The money being taken is to serve to mop up those rebels of mine who are your enemies as well,' he informed Charles IX.[166] The resolution of the threat from France would also enable him to disarm in Italy. He wrote immediately to the governor of Milan, Requesens, instructing him to pay off 4,000 German mercenaries who had been brought in to defend the duchy. 'Seeing that affairs in France are now in a different state thanks to the recent events, it appears that one need not entertain the suspicions that until now we have had of the French.'[167]

Even the massacres might be turned to profit. Protestant England's indignation might be used to sour its relations with France. 'It's not a bad idea to set the English against the French,' he informed Diego de Zúñiga; 'keep at it . . . But do not in any way try to ally me with the English. What I want is that all the Christian princes join together against England.'[168] In spite of these sentiments, what transpired was an agreement with England. Elizabeth had already made favourable overtures to Spain. As from 1 May 1573 the two countries renewed mutual trade, to the immense satisfaction of merchants on both sides. Further agreement came in 1576. Following talks in Madrid between Alba and the English envoy, Lord Cobham, English traders were exempted from the attentions of the Inquisition provided they caused no scandal over religion.[169] For at least ten years, an uneasy peace between the two nations was assured. England continued to sympathise with and aid William of Orange, but studiously avoided offending Spain.

There was cause for concern only in the Netherlands, where Philip was already considering a change of tactics and had sent a new governor, the duke of Medinaceli. Even here there was some room for optimism. The failure of an invasion mounted by William of Orange, and the successful recovery of rebel towns by Alba, caused a Spanish observer in October to hope that 'before long they will all be back in the obedience of His Majesty'.[170]

6

Dropping the Pilot
1572–1580

I am trembling with fear at what the next post from Flanders will bring.[1]

Although a victory in military terms, Lepanto won little more than a breathing space. There still remained, at least for Spain, the question of the Muslim threat from north Africa. Philip was keen to use the advantage to obtain greater security on his flank, and he encouraged Don Juan to undertake the seizure of Tunis. This was captured successfully on 10 October 1573, almost exactly two years after Lepanto.

The picture is often given of a Philip who, after these years of conflict in the Mediterranean, accepted a truce and turned his attention to the north. The reality was more complex. Time would show that there were no more battles to be fought in the inland sea, but the Mediterranean could never be abandoned. The entire Levant coast of Spain was still largely defence-less. In 1574, when there was pressure once again on the king to resolve the problems of the Netherlands by going there in person, he was ada-mant that it could not be done. 'There's nothing in this life I more wish,' he commented, 'than to see my subjects there, but it is not possible for now to absent myself from here, because of the war against the Turk.'[2] The threat was all too real. In September 1574 a massive Turkish fleet of over 230 vessels recaptured the city of Tunis. The fortress of La Goletta, which overlooked the city and was manned by a Spanish garrison, had surren-dered a fortnight before. The loss was bitterly criticised in both Spain and Italy. 'I cannot but lament,' observed ambassador Juan de Zúñiga in Rome, 'that all that has been spent this year has been to no avail.'[3] The pope blamed Spanish incompetence. He asked Don Juan, who passed through Rome in November, to express his concern to the king. Zúñiga bluntly blamed 'the way they manage things in the council in Spain'.[4] In 1575 the cardinal of Tarragona asked what might happen if the Turks overwhelmed them and 'if Spain is lost, and we ourselves and all that we have?'[5] His answer, surprisingly, was that the king could still go and rule over America: 'he has powerful kingdoms in the Indies.' The comment reflected the profound insecurity still felt on the coastline. At the end of 1576 Philip was trying to reduce his costs in the Mediterranean by cutting the fleet to one hundred galleys.[6] But at the same time he took care to keep all the forces there on alert. In March 1577 the royal council had before it an alarming report that the Moriscos of Valencia and Aragon were preparing to rise on the arrival of a Turkish fleet.[7] In January 1578 the king was warning the governor of Milan to be vigilant 'in case the Turkish armada comes'.[8] It was a long time before the government could think of relaxing its defences. The battle for north Africa was still on.

In any case, Philip had no intention of committing himself to northern Europe, from which he was patently trying to withdraw. After five years, Alba's policies had brought a solution no nearer. The duke himself was old, ill, worn out and fed up. 'He is so desperate,' his secretary Albornoz reported in 1569, 'that he could leave it all and just march off.'[9] The expense of the Spanish presence was formidable. The attempt early in 1572 to introduce the new tax of the Tenth Penny was a failure, and it aroused bitter protests, not only from Netherlanders but also from Spanish officials. In spring that year Philip, already half convinced that an alternative policy was possible in the Netherlands,[10] sent as his new governor the duke of Medinaceli, Juan de la Cerda.

Medinaceli, a friend of Ruy Gómez, had served as viceroy of Sicily[11] and then of Navarre. From the start he was dogged by bad luck. His fleet sailed from the northern coast on 1 May 1572 but was forced back by bad weather and resumed its voyage two weeks later. In the Channel it was harassed by the Dutch, who destroyed many of the ships. Once in Flanders, he quickly saw that the situation was desperate, and Alba's position completely untenable. The latter in his turn bitterly resented Medinaceli's interference. But he found no support in Madrid, where he was now accused of following his own whims rather than the wishes of the king.[12] The new governor seemed to adopt the viewpoint of the Netherlanders. 'Excessive rigour, the misconduct of some officers and soldiers, and the Tenth Penny, are the cause of all the ills,' he affirmed, 'and not heresy or rebellion.'[13] He held up for emulation the policy of Charles V, who had pacified the Comuneros of Spain through clemency and had limited punishment of the rebellion of Ghent to 'a handful'. It was an argument to which the Netherlanders listened with satisfaction, and to which Philip was being obliged to turn.

Alba's attempts to repress revolt with brutal efficiency promised initial success but were in the end counter-productive. In October 1572 he allowed his troops to sack and massacre in the town of Mechelen, which had supported Orange. The horror of it provoked Spanish officials to protest directly to the king.[14] In the next few weeks it was the turn of Zutphen and Naarden. Haarlem put up a stubborn resistance from December 1572 to the following July, but surrendered after receiving reassurances. Philip was ill in bed at San Lorenzo when he received the news on 24 July. It was hailed as a great success. Secretary Gracián, who read him the despatch, reported that to the king 'the news of Haarlem has been better medicine than a great many doctors'.[15]

Philip was of course informed of the merciless methods used by Alba and his commanders. On entering Haarlem, the Spaniards had methodically executed the entire garrison, over a thousand persons, in cold blood.[16] This would serve as a further lesson. But many Spanish advisers were horrified at the cruelty. Deep fissures opened up among Philip's policy-makers. Medinaceli was determined to stop the war, and to issue a general pardon along lines approved of in principle by the king. But when he and Alba met in November 1572 to discuss it, no agreement was possible. Medinaceli insisted that the pardon would encourage 'the innocent'. Alba replied grimly 'that he did not know who the innocent were. If His Excellency knew, could he tell him?'[17]

Philip's secretary Gabriel Zayas, who handled most of the relevant correspondence and was in principle a supporter of Alba, was faced with the unenviable task of sending on to the king bitter criticisms from Spanish officials. A senior officer with Medinaceli reported 'the abhorrence in which the name of the house of Alba is held'. 'Cursed be the Tenth Penny and whoever invented it, since it is the cause of all this.'[18] Writing to the king, a correspondent urged that 'Your Majesty not let yourself be persuaded' that there was any way forward other than clemency and pardon. Rigour had failed, despite the fact that over 3,000 people had been executed in just over five years.[19] A Spanish captain in the trenches, suffering through the freezing winter of 1572–3, confessed that 'I don't understand this war nor do I believe that anyone understands it', and expressed dismay that the king did not seem to realise how terrible the situation was. 'I do not think that, the way things are going, it will be possible to take this country.'[20]

Granvelle, now viceroy of Naples, also saw no victory in Haarlem. 'We are still losing. The hatred that the country has for those who now rule is greater than you can imagine.' The whole of Alba's regime, he summed up, amounted to 'many millions ill-spent, and the complete ruin of those provinces'.[21] In Milan the viceroy, Luis de Requesens, strongly disapproved of what had happened at Haarlem. He had already had occasion to disagree strongly with the duke's methods. 'Mercy,' he urged, 'is very necessary.'[22]

In these months, the opinions of the humanist Benito Arias Montano, then in Antwerp preparing a new royal edition of the Bible, were crucial.

The king asked him to consult with the Netherlanders to find out 'what is the real solution that one can apply'.[23] Philip treated with great respect the reports he received from the illustrious scholar. Montano had, like the king, been a strong supporter of Alba. Now the king allowed himself to take an alternative view. He would discuss Montano's reports with secretary Gracián as they walked up and down the length of the great library in the Escorial.[24]

Alba's methods were not working. Opposition among the people of the Netherlands was hardening, not weakening. The military toll was appalling. To add to the misery of conditions and climate, the soldiers suffered a high death rate. The taking of Haarlem, for example, may have cost the besiegers some 10,000 men. Finally, the burden on the exchequer was insupportable. Juan de Ovando, president of the council of Finance, drew up an estimate in August 1574 which showed that current annual income of the treasury was around six million ducats, while obligations came to eighty million.[25] The current debt in Flanders was around four million, or two-thirds of all the available income of the government of Spain. To this had to be added the current costs there, over 600,000 ducats a month, the biggest single burden on the treasury. The monthly expense in Flanders was over ten times the cost of defence in the peninsula, and twenty times the cost of the royal household and government.

Alba, from a different point of view, was equally desperate about the war. In February 1573 he wrote to Zayas, appealing for a diversion of resources from the Mediterranean and towards the north:

> I beat my head against the wall when I hear them talk of the cost here! It is not the Turks who are troubling Christendom but the heretics, and these are already within our gates . . . For the love of God, ask for the new supplies that I have detailed to His Majesty, because what is at stake is nothing less than the survival of his states.

Throughout the year, he continued to rage, plead, and rail against those in authority in Madrid. 'Until those who serve in his councils are dead or sacked, His Majesty will achieve nothing here.' That was in April. 'I can't go on,' he wrote in July.[26]

In sending Medinaceli to Brussels Philip had effectively dropped his all-out backing for Alba. But by the end of 1572 he was clear in his mind that the tandem of the two dukes was unworkable, and he decided to withdraw them both. He had already warned Alba explicitly. 'I shall never have enough money to satisfy your needs,' the king wrote, 'but I can easily find you a successor able and faithful enough to bring to an end, through moderation and clemency, a war that you have been unable to end by arms or by severity.'[27] On 30 January 1573 he signed and despatched an order appointing his old friend Luis de Requesens, grand

commander of Castile and currently governor of Milan, to the governorship of the Netherlands.

Requesens, who had been in fragile health for many months, was
aghast at being asked to take on this cross. He confided to his brother Juan
de Zúñiga that Flanders was 'lost', that 'I am no soldier', and that he
understood neither French nor Dutch, the two languages of the country.
In short, 'I find a thousand reasons for not accepting'.[28] When, six months
later, he had made no move to obey, the king insisted that he accept
without question.[29]

In October Philip sat down and wrote, in his own hand (a sure sign that
he was expressing his own intimate thoughts), a confidential letter to
Requesens.[30]

He laid bare his thinking on the problems of the north. The key to
regaining the Netherlands was command of the sea. But a primary
obstacle was money: the cost of the war had exceeded all predictions.
Deciding policy was very difficult, since his advisers were split. 'Some say
that the cause of these rebellions is religion, and that there is no solution
other than punishment and rigour.' This was the view of Alba 'and all his
allies'. 'Others say the contrary', blaming bad treatment, the army and the
Tenth Penny; 'and that the solution is moderation and a general pardon'.
This was the view of 'all those from those states and even some from
Spain'. Among these was Arias Montano, who was perhaps too inclined
to the views of the Netherlanders, but whom Requesens must consult.

> With such difference of opinions I have found myself very confused.
> And since I don't know the truth of what is going on there, I neither
> know the solution that is necessary nor what to think. It seems to me
> that the most reliable is to believe neither one side nor the other, since
> I think that both go to extremes. I think that the best view to take,
> though with great discretion, is in the middle.

Philip noted that Requesens would be receiving two sets of instructions, one in Castilian, and one in French. They would reflect differing
points of view, but he was to feel completely free to follow either. The
king insisted only on one principle: 'that you treat the people there with
love and goodwill, since in this there is nothing to be lost'.

Alba's self-defeating rigour, and the corresponding failure of his son
Don Fadrique to capture Alkmaar in 1573, turned the tide of events in the
Low Countries. But there were also important developments in Spain
which signalled a change of direction. Between 1572 and 1573 familiar
faces disappeared from the political scene. The death in September 1572 of
Espinosa removed a diehard conservative. Philip had raised him to positions of eminence because he admired his efficiency, but he soon came to
disagree with the cardinal's work methods. Espinosa often executed deci-

sions verbally instead of putting them on paper. This made for speed, but Philip felt that it cut out the possibility of reflection. He also disapproved of the cardinal's discourteous attitude to the grandees. In a brief exchange over a matter concerning Flanders, Philip called the cardinal a liar. The incident almost literally killed Espinosa.[31] He died on 5 September 1572, of apoplexy during an illness. The king was at the monastery of St Jerónimo in Madrid when he heard the news, and paid grudging tribute to his minister. 'I am not among those who will not miss the cardinal,' he commented.[32] Shortly after, with the death of Ruy Gómez on 29 July 1573, the Eboli group lost its spokesman. Friends of Alba commented on Philip's genuine and evident grief for the man who had been his friend and adviser for two decades.[33]

Espinosa bequeathed to the king the services of his private secretary, the priest Mateo Vázquez de Leca.[34] Twenty-four hours after the cardinal's death, Vázquez entered the royal service. He treasured thereafter 'the first note that His Majesty wrote to me',[35] a little scribbled note in Philip's hand which the secretary carefully dated to 6 September 1572. Swarthy, plump and balding, Vázquez was of Corsican origin. Educated by the Jesuits in Seville (where one of his schoolmates was the young Cervantes), his pious, fatherly demeanour won the confidence of all. He gained the trust of the king and became his 'arch-secretary'.[36] But he also earned the rivalry of secretary Antonio Pérez and the hostility of the widowed princess of Eboli, who more than once referred to him (because of his complexion) as 'this Moorish dog'.

In the late autumn of 1573 the new governor of the Netherlands travelled up the 'Spanish road' (the military route to the north) with two companies of Italian troops. He entered Brussels on 17 November and formally took over from Alba. The duke, who left for Spain in December, did his best to persuade Requesens that the war must go on. He said that he had advised the king to 'lay waste in Holland all the country that our people could not occupy'.[37] The grand commander of Castile was horrified at this warmongering solution. 'From the very first day,' he was to comment later, 'I have had the water up to my teeth.'[38]

Philip had always been aware that Spain must be a naval power. He had devoted years to building up a strong fleet in the Mediterranean. In the Netherlands, as he reminded Requesens, it was essential to get control of the sea. The governor responded by pleading in December 1573 for the king to 'send a mighty armada and make a final effort'.[39] But a substantial naval force being planned by Pero Menéndez de Avilés in the port of Santander in 1574, never got under way. The death of Menéndez that September, and an outbreak of typhus among the crews, forced cancellation.[40] During 1575 further attempts were made to send naval help. In September and again in November fleets were sent out from Santander. The first was hit by storms and dispersed along the English coast. The second, crippled by mutiny and bad weather, never made it to sea. At the end of December the king decided to postpone the naval effort.[41]

Officials lamely recognised that the Dutch were far superior to them at sea.[42] Outside the Mediterranean, Spain's naval power in Europe was virtually zero. To keep trade going, Philip tolerated the transport of goods to and from Spain by Dutch rebel ships. From Seville it was reported that 'Flemings, English and Dutch control all the trade'.[43] In 1574 the king was offered the use of a Baltic port, on the Swedish coast, from which to strike against the rebels and cut off their wheat supplies.[44] It was the first of several proposals of this type.[45] The offer could not be taken up. In the north, as a consequence, Spain lost out to the maritime superiority of the Protestant powers. It was a fatal weakness that with time assured the Dutch their freedom, and created continuing problems for Spain.

Arias Montano's reports on Flanders were sent to Requesens. In Madrid meanwhile Philip encouraged the search for solutions. The day after Alba's return to Madrid the king received a note from Vázquez: 'it is clear that nothing will be achieved through force, and it could be the right time to reach a solution in those states'. As though to remove any notion of defeatism from such a move, the secretary concluded: 'In moments of greatest need God always sends Your Majesty his greatest marks of favour: St Quentin, Lepanto, Granada, all turned out well.'[46]

Could Flanders also be turned into a small victory? In Castile, which had suffered most from the rise in war taxation, criticism of foreign commitments was intense. There was no imperialist fervour at court, only a reluctance to drag out the agony in the north. Dropping Alba, the pilot of Spain's imperial pretensions, was one step towards a possible peace.

Nor was America immune to dissension.

*

In these years, there was a serious crisis of stability in Spanish Peru.[47] Among the discontented Indians a millennarian movement known as Taqui Ongo took shape. It predicted an end to the reign of the Christians, and a return of the ancient gods. Although the viceroy, Francisco de Toledo, put an end to native resistance the discontent was rooted in the minds of thinking Spaniards in America. A Dominican friar in Peru, Francisco de la Cruz, had dreams in which he foresaw the 'destruction of Spain' because of the king's policies. In a statement of 1575, he claimed that 'it is commonly said among those who come from Spain, that the officials there are more concerned about ways of squeezing silver from the realm than about how to govern it in the interests of public welfare and peace'. He criticised 'what the king has done with the revenue he has received and receives from Spain and its realms, squandering it and falling into debt'.[48] Concern for the over-taxed inspired, in Cruz's visions, dreams of a new order in which God would 'wreak justice and punishment on behalf of the poor and humble', both in America (where the Indians would become his chosen people) and in Spain. Cruz's confused views reflected those of many colonists in the New World, who felt that Spain and its Church had let them down. The friar was arrested in 1575 by the Inquisition, interrogated over a period of three years, and eventually burnt at the stake in 1578.

Philip was attentive to voices from America, though he may not have known of Cruz's case. The problems of the New World crossed his desk routinely. Since his contact with Las Casas thirty years before, and the subsequent debates over the Indians, Philip had limited his intrusion into American affairs largely to the question of law and order, or 'pacification' as it came to be called. Viceroy Toledo's successful term of office seemed to have achieved the pacification of the Andean peoples. The introduction of the Inquisition into America in 1571 offered protection for the faith. But, for many missionaries, there were still fundamental problems to be solved before a secure peace could be achieved. It was precisely the new regime in America – a regime of viceroys, inquisitors and bishops – to which they (like Francisco de la Cruz) objected.

Unhappy about aspects of Toledo's regime in Peru, the Jesuit father José de Acosta wrote to the king to protest against the unjust taxes levied on the Indians. Elsewhere he referred to the colonists as 'the shit of Spain' (*Hispaniae faeces*). Philip was taking some steps to mitigate the injustice of the colonial regime. The most notable was his important Ordinance on Discoveries, of 13 July 1573, which definitively banned further conquests in America, and emphasised the preaching of religion and the protection of the Indian as primary objectives. The aim was to stop further and fruitless expeditions, and to consolidate control over the vast area already subject to Spanish rule. Though naive in its ideals, the ordinance was a substantial advance on the more aggressive guidelines that preceded it. Las Casas's own writings were used in framing its text.[49] From now on, Spain recognised a frontier to its American domains. The only people authorised to move the frontier forward were the missionaries, aided if necessary by small military escorts.[50] The king also tried to undo some aspects of Toledo's harsh policies, and ordered repayment to the Indians of money which the viceroy had extorted. When Toledo returned to Madrid, Philip is said to have rebuked him, and to have condemned the execution of Tupac Amaru.[51] He had been sent to America, Philip told him, to govern kings, not to kill them.

But it was not possible now, any more than it had been a generation before, to control events in the New World. The protest of Francisco de la Cruz was typical of much informed opinion. Fray Luis de León, in a discourse at Salamanca in 1579, denounced the colonists for 'committing murder and exterminating peoples and entire races'. Although the king officially took no sides in the disputes over America, there is no mistaking the forward-looking tone of the laws he passed in Spain.[52] The fact that such legislation had little effect in practice exposes the naivety of the government without calling in question its good intentions. In January 1588 Philip conceded the first of several audiences to José de Acosta, who had just returned from America and undoubtedly came to present him with a copy of his new book, *On the Salvation of the Indians*, the first powerful Jesuit contribution to the debate. He also pressed some other memorials into the king's hands.[53] Philip later commented that they were 'important, and he told me certain things which also are'.[54] It is unclear whether the meeting influenced the passing that year of a decree which relaxed the racialist practices of the American Church and allowed men of mixed Spanish-Indian parentage (*mestizos*) to be ordained priests.[55] There can be no doubt that the king's active favour over the years for both Las Casas and Acosta helped the views of these men and of their mentor Francisco de Vitoria to 'triumph over all others' (the phrase is Acosta's)[56] in Spain. By contrast the opposing view was officially discouraged, and its chief proponent Sepúlveda, Philip's one-time tutor, died virtually forgotten and blind in 1573, at the age of eighty-three.

Writing in 1592, exactly a century after the discovery of the New World, the Franciscan friar Mendieta in his manuscript history of the missions looked back to the 1560s as the end of the golden age of the Church in America. Many other friars at the time had also entertained hopes that Spain would achieve something special in the New World. But by the 1570s those hopes were collapsing. In Mexico the great scholar fray Bernardino de Sahagún considered that the Church had lost out in much of Europe, leaving its torch to pass on to the New World. Now, he felt, the flame even in America was flickering, and the torch must pass on to Asia.[57] There seemed, in short, to be a parting of the ways. The efforts of Philip's government, and the colonial system introduced by Francisco de Toledo, did not appear to Spanish colonists of benefit either to themselves or to the Indian population.

*

At the beginning of 1574 the king carried out a long-planned act of piety. The site of the Escorial was intended to be in part a basilica for members of the royal family. Till then their principal resting-place had been in Granada, where Ferdinand and Isabella lay (and were left undisturbed). Philip meant that the members of the Habsburg dynasty should have a site of their own. In June 1573 the bodies of Elizabeth and Don Carlos were brought from Madrid to the Escorial. Now, in January 1574, Philip gave the order to translate the rest of the family. His parents Charles V and Isabel were brought from Yuste and Granada respectively. His first wife Maria of Portugal was brought from Granada (she had been transferred there from Valladolid in 1559). His aunt Eleanor, Charles's sister and queen of France, was brought from near Mérida. Charles's other sister Mary, queen of Hungary, was brought from Valladolid. Queen Juana the Mad was brought from Tordesillas. Finally, Philip's brothers Fernando and Juan, who had both died in infancy, were brought from Granada and Valladolid. The coffins were kept in an alcove under the high altar. Twelve years later they were moved to the special vault prepared for them.

Philip was also able to bring to an end the long-drawn-out saga of archbishop Carranza of Toledo, imprisoned by the Inquisition since 1559. The king's conduct in the affair was little short of shameful. From the first, he took the view that the reputation of the Inquisition was at issue, and should never be compromised. He therefore accepted without question the views of Carranza's accusers, and kept himself aloof from the proceedings. He and other members of the court made a formal declaration in Carranza's favour at the beginning of the case.[58] After that, at no stage did he lift a finger to intervene or help. When eventually in 1565 Carranza's lawyer was allowed to appeal to the king, Philip is reported to have replied: 'Tell him that I have always protected and will protect his rights and honour. My desire is that no harm befall the archbishop and that justice be done.'[59] But neither in the years before nor in following years did the unfortunate archbishop receive the slightest gesture of sympathy from his king.

Philip's concern to protect the Inquisition, and to stop the pope intervening, were certainly among the reasons why Carranza's cause stood little chance in Spain. But his diatribes against the archbishop went beyond politics. When the pope and cardinals attempted to assume jurisdiction over the case, the king fumed and accused them of prejudging the issue by assuming Carranza to be innocent. In 1569, in a letter penned for him by Jerónimo Zurita, the famous historian and secretary of the Inquisition, he referred to Carranza as 'a person of discredit and ill-fame not only in these realms but throughout Christendom',[60] a verdict so untrue that it betrays an evident blind spot in the king's judgment. In 1571 he tried to influence the pope's verdict on the case by eliciting further denunciations from theologians in Castile.[61] In 1574 he went further. He made Inquisitor-General Quiroga force those bishops who had originally approved the archbishop's *Catechism* to reverse their views.[62]

It can be said in Philip's favour that he allowed pro-Carranza views to circulate. His normal policy was never to interfere with the free expression of opinion. He commissioned his own annalist, Ambrosio de Morales, to write an official narrative of Carranza's arrest; the account turned out to be favourable to Carranza. Other books published in the king's lifetime usually mentioned Carranza in terms of respect and admiration. Despite the king's attitude, the archbishop's name continued to be held in high repute among his contemporaries in Spain.

*

In 1574 Philip, willing as always to follow the logic of events, prepared to turn his back on discredited policies in Flanders. They were policies, moreover, he could no longer afford in financial terms. In his council of State the majority now favoured an end to the violence in the Netherlands. From France Francés de Álava wrote advising against the further use of force: 'In my poor judgment,' he wrote to the king, 'another way must be sought, even though it may seem in part to prejudice our honour (*reputación*).'[63] From his position in Italy as viceroy of Naples, cardinal Granvelle also urged the king to change his approach. In his correspondence with others the cardinal did not mince his words. Spain's policy was a disaster: 'If they do not win the goodwill of the people there, even sending 20,000 Spaniards will achieve nothing.' As for Alba, for whom he had nothing but praise as a person, 'the states of Flanders have been ruined under his government'. In short, he reflected in July 1574, the king's advisers had not the slightest idea of the affairs of the Netherlands: 'they do not understand nor will understand in very many years'.[64] The cardinal was no less frank in his letters to the king. 'For the last ten years,' he told Philip in 1576, 'I have always written that the policy adopted was very mistaken.'[65]

The debate in 1574 among those who governed Spain was one of the most momentous ever to occur in the history of an imperial nation. Philip well remembered the debates over America, when his father had taken the unprecedented step of suspending the conquests. Now, a quarter of a century later, his own measures were being scrutinised. The matter virtually monopolised his time, leaving (commented his secretary) 'little space to attend to other things'.[66]

In the Netherlands, some part in the debate was played by two Spaniards who questioned the policies of their country. In Madrid, a Flemish minister also made a decisive contribution.

Benito Arias Montano and Fadrique Furió Ceriol were major scholars and humanists in their own right and the king specifically sought their advice on the situation in the Netherlands. A product of the Erasmian generation at the university of Alcalá, theologian at Trent, chaplain to Philip II and the most distinguished Hebraist in Spain, Montano was sent by the king to Antwerp in 1568 to prepare a new multilingual edition of the Bible. In 1573 the king also asked him to advise on events in the Netherlands. His letters helped powerfully to change Philip's attitude to Alba. Subsequently, the king asked him to stay on and advise Requesens, who consulted closely with him. In his letters Montano condemned certain Spanish attitudes and defended the views of the Netherlanders. 'When a whole people clamours that there is oppression,' he wrote to Philip, 'it is certain that it is so.'[67] Montano retained Philip's full confidence, and was later appointed by him librarian of the Escorial. But the humanist had many other battles to fight before he left Flanders in April 1575. The Inquisitor-General and bishop of Cuenca, Gaspar de Quiroga, who now and later adhered to a hard line on Flanders,[68] in 1574 tried to have him recalled 'because of the harm he might do there if he shows his true colours'.

Furió had first been recommended to Philip by Charles V in the 1550s, and for the rest of his life enjoyed the king's protection. From 1546 to 1564 he had lived outside his native Valencia, mainly in Flanders but also travelling widely throughout the continent. A distinguished humanist,[69] he published at Antwerp in 1559 a manual of guidance for the young king, *The Counsel and Counsellors of the Prince*. Philip valued his advice, but in 1563 ordered him back to Spain, for fear that heterodox influences were at work on him. In 1573, encouraged by the king's new policy on the Netherlands, Furió wrote his important *Remedies*, a full-scale programme for change in the north. Its main points seem to have been acceptable to Philip. In 1574 the king sent him back to the Netherlands to reconsider options in the light of the policy pursued by Requesens. Furió recommended in the summer of 1575 that the only way to split the southern provinces from Orange was to restore their old privileges in full.[70] The departure of the Spanish troops early in 1577 – a concession favoured by Furió, who accompanied the army to Milan – did not, unfortunately, bring a solution any nearer. From this date the king lost confidence in Furió. He continued to protect him, but no longer consulted him.[71]

Joachim Hopperus, representative of the States of the Netherlands in Spain, had been resident at the Spanish court since 1565. Like Granvelle, he tended to support a tough line, and was in favour of the king's decision in April 1565 to prosecute heresy. But he was also openly opposed to Alba's intervention. From as early as 1566 he tried without success to interest Philip in an alternative policy.[72] Granvelle some years later expressed the view that 'Hopperus preferred to please everybody and push his own interests rather than carry out his obligations with the required application and energy'.[73] In addition to his excessive fawning, Hopperus suffered from the handicap that he never learned Spanish well enough to be able to write it, and his memoranda in Madrid had to be translated before anyone could read them.[74] Despite all this, his role in the making of policy was outstanding.

The debates of 1574 were frank and open. In a remarkable session of the council at Aranjuez on 28 January 1574, the duke of Medinaceli and Diego de Covarrubias attacked the Tenth Penny, and Dr Andrés Ponce de León astonishingly claimed that the Flemish had a right to their liberties just as the Aragonese had a right to theirs.[75] Philip was left little option. In March he sent letters to Requesens authorising him to abolish the council of Troubles and the Tenth Penny, and issue a general pardon. The grand commander was already convinced of the need for an about-face. Alba, he said, had arrived in a pacified Netherlands, but he had left it in ruins. The only viable solution – it was perhaps the first time the idea was suggested, over twenty years before Philip adopted it – was for the Infanta Isabel to be made ruler of an independent Netherlands, with a son of the emperor as her husband.[76]

The concessions failed to achieve their desired effect. The pardon was considered inadequate. The States General met on 7 June and repeated its demands, of which the most fundamental had always been that the Spanish troops be withdrawn. By now the troops had begun a series of mutinies which ended by paralysing the whole Spanish war effort.[77] In May 1574 the soldiers at Antwerp mutinied for their pay. In November those in Holland mutinied, deserted, and left the province to the enemy. For a helpless and despairing Requesens it was 'the most terrible time in the world'.[78] The king, preparing to celebrate Christmas in the monastery of St Jerónimo, was cast into gloom by the mutinies. 'The situation is desperate over there,' he reflected, 'and every day more so for us over here.'[79]

In December 1574, Philip recognised 'that it is not possible to make progress on Flanders through a policy of war'.[80] He set up a special committee of four to meet urgently and reconsider policy.[81] The committee had two main tasks: resolve serious internal differences in order to agree on aims; and offer a new deal to the Netherlanders. It met seven times between 14 and 30 December. Both Hopperus and Alba were consulted at every stage.

The failure to find a speedy solution disposed Requesens in September 1574 to recommend a further resort to military force. But he quickly realised that this too was impracticable. In January 1575 he summarised the situation:

> I shall say only that matters here are in such a terrible state, and so impossible to sustain, that we will have to give in to all they want, so long as religion is excepted. And we will have to act so quickly that there will be no time to consult . . . I agree with Hopperus's opinion: that Your Majesty should send someone of the blood royal, remove all foreigners, and restore the old form of government.[82]

In short, capitulation. At this stage the mediation of the emperor Maximilian II was sought. With his help, talks between the parties began at Breda in March 1575. Requesens set up a parallel committee at Antwerp.

When the negotiations with the States General began in 1575, from being a marginal figure at the Spanish court Hopperus was suddenly propelled into a key role. The negotiators at Breda dealt directly with him.[83] Philip turned to him for advice, carefully read all his memoranda, and adopted his ideas as his own. Even finance was affected. One of the king's main bankers, the house of Fugger, 'will not make a move [Philip reported with chagrin] without the opinion of Hopperus'.[84] All the ministers were bypassed in favour of Hopperus. 'Everything has to go through his hands,' some of them complained.[85] Philip's special committee of four grumbled loudly but recognised that 'it is necessity' that forced acceptance of the new conditions.[86] In a note to Hopperus in April 1576 the king wrote: 'I am very pleased that you agree with the decision I have taken . . . I am so satisfied with all you say that I have decided to keep you at my side for this period.' He accepted fully Hopperus's proposal that a general pardon, with no exceptions whatever, be issued. On points of detail, Philip would claim to have had the same idea before Hopperus: 'This was a good idea, which also occurred to me . . . In this your opinion is the same as mine.'[87] When Hopperus wanted to see him, Philip made himself immediately available. 'Hopperus has pressed me for an audience,' he wrote in September, 'and so I want you to come tomorrow so as not to waste time.'[88] Unfortunately, not much time remained. Hopperus's good services were terminated by his death in December 1576.[89] To the end he retained the king's confidence, though Philip was already beginning to see that Hopperus's policies were not bearing the fruit he hoped for.

The king's remarkable ability to change both policy and advisers when the need arose demonstrates that he did not have a closed mind and was capable of accepting realities. But he was most unhappy about the situation. 'The truth is,' he told Quiroga in August 1576, 'that the affairs of Flanders keep me so busy and preoccupied that they don't leave me time to attend as I should to other matters.'[90]

*

The volte-face over Flanders came at a time when discontent had reached a peak in Castile. To help meet its debts, the government from 1573 raised the rate of indirect taxation. There were sharp conflicts with the members of the Cortes of Castile, which held periodic sessions between April 1573 and September 1575. As was normal, a committee from the Cortes negotiated with the president of the council of Finance, Juan de Ovando, and other officials. At the same time the government put direct pressure on the cities to give their deputies powers to grant extra taxes. The summer and autumn of 1574 were particularly full of intense discussions on how to resolve the problem of income. 'Our money runs out in months, not years,' the king noted in May 1574. Flanders was the main headache: 'that is the biggest risk: so many soldiers, and no money'.[91] 'I believe that the Flanders thing will collapse for lack of money, as I have always felt'.[92] The business of the committee on Finance displaced other business. Philip was snowed under with paperwork, 'a pile of papers' in his own words. In the heat of the last Saturday of June in Madrid, he sighed: 'I shall be happy to escape from here in two or three days, I can't do it before'.[93] He had to suffer a few more days in the capital ('I've been over three hours with Juan de Ovando,' he complained five days later, 'and the matter is still left over for another day')[94] before fleeing to San Lorenzo.

The king frequently downplayed his own ability in financial matters. Reading a proposal by a Genoese banker to resolve the current situation, he noted: 'it seems to me that he is right in some things, but he must understand them better than I do, since I don't understand them at all'.[95] It was not true that he did not understand. He had been dealing with these problems for some thirty years. No other ruler of his time had more experience of and perception in matters of state finance. He took in both the broad perspective and the minute detail, but there were elements which inevitably escaped him. Early in 1576 he refused to spend time looking at some documents handed him by one of his accountants. 'You know that I don't understand this subject.'[96] They were referred to another minister.

Through the summer and autumn of 1574 he devoted much of his time to the urgent issue of resolving the financial situation. The cities in the Cortes had offered in December 1573 to raise more money if they were given the right to administer the taxes permanently. The treasury opposed this, suggesting simply that Castile's principal indirect tax, the *alcabala*, be increased. The Cortes deputies came up with a counter-proposal, to introduce a tax on flour.[97]

A committee with members from the Cortes and the treasury met in regular session. In the afternoon of 9 September 1574 Philip had a meeting with two of the Cortes deputies, and discussed the financial situation with them. That night he sat down and wrote a long memorandum on how to balance the current budget. He had for months been struggling with the cities to reach agreement over taxation, and he now expressed some sympathy with them. But they were mistaken to oppose a rise in the *alcabala*. Either the *alcabala* had to rise or a tax must be put on flour, the basic item of sustenance:

> And it is quite clear that there is more reason for choosing the *alcabalas* rather than the flour. Flour has to be paid for by both rich and poor, since the poor man has to eat just like the rich man. This doesn't happen with the *alcabala*, which is paid according to the quantity of goods that is bought or sold, which means that the rich man pays more and the poor man less.[98]

Persuading the deputies on the committee was only the first stage of the fight. 'The matter has many obstacles to get through, and even if it gets through the committee there are still the Cortes deputies and then the cities, which is worse.'[99]

Eventually agreement was reached in February 1575. The government was allowed to take the step it had not yet dared take: raise the rate at which the *alcabala* was levied. It was now to be collected at its full legal rate of 10 per cent. But many cities objected, and refused to collect the tax. The government had to send in its own officials. There were protests and conflict. 'All Spain was tense, angry and in turmoil,' a friar of the Escorial noted.[100]

The Cortes of Castile met again in January 1576. The king personally prepared the opening speech. The sessions, among the most important of the reign, lasted until December 1577. A compromise was reached: in October 1577 a new *alcabala* was agreed, at a lower rate. The agreement was to last for four years, and renewal had to be negotiated. Philip never again attempted to touch the *alcabala*. Instead, the Cortes agreed to grant him special short-term subsidies as the need arose. By accepting subsidies (called *servicios*), the king in effect conceded control of the tax system in Castile to the cities. One way or another, the tax burden rose. In broad terms, government tax revenue in Castile in 1577 was about 50 per cent higher than in 1567.[101] The increase was extremely unpopular. Discontent was aggravated by the drought conditions prevailing in Castile in 1577.[102]

Opposition to taxes gave rise to periodic incidents. Pasquinades against the king were posted on the doors of the main public buildings of Toledo in July 1577. The civil governor of the city failed to find those responsible.[103] Street opinion in Madrid was influenced by the prophecies of the ex-soldier and seer Miguel de Piedrola Beamonte, whose words did not at first worry the king. In November 1578, however, Philip commented that 'there is so much fuss here about prophecies, that I must look into it', and he requested Quiroga and his confessor Diego Chaves to summon Piedrola and 'question him and try to find out from where he gets these prophecies'.[104] The seer's activities were judged to be innocuous, and he was allowed to continue his career.[105]

The criticisms and discontent of the late 1570s marked a decisive shift in the attitude of Castilians to their king. It was the custom of moralists to exaggerate complaints, but the exaggerations reflected a sombre reality. Philip at the time asked his grand almoner, Luis Manrique, to put down on paper his views on the current situation. Manrique suggested that the king 'had deliberately and bit by bit made himself inaccessible and shut himself in a tower without doors and windows'. Dedicated only to his papers, he had isolated himself from the people. Throughout Spain 'the people are despondent, expecting that everything is going to collapse'. If taxes are not lowered, 'in a very short time Your Majesty will have neither treasury nor subjects, everything will collapse'. The king seemed to be unaware 'that his subjects are discontented and that he is no longer in command of their affections'.[106] Much the same words were used in a private letter which a prominent Jesuit, Pedro de Ribadeneira, addressed some time later to Quiroga. Many in the kingdom, he commented, were 'embittered and discontented with His Majesty', who was no longer 'as loved as he used to be, nor so much in command of the hearts and good wishes of his subjects'.[107]

*

The king's health was moderately good in these months, but the combination of heavy work and gout provoked problems. An occasional heavy cold did not help. In February 1576 he complained that 'there are a great many files that I have been unable to look at, tomorrow if I can I'll see them because today I can't take any more. It's late and this thing in my chest won't go away, it's what most wears me out. Although the gout hurts now and then it doesn't affect my head, the cold affects it more.'[108] Gout in his foot, and a heavy cold, continued to be problems in spring 1577, when he had to be bled.[109] He still managed to put in an astonishing amount of hours on administrative work. Even his leisure was work. In San Lorenzo in July 1576 he spent his moments of rest supervising the hanging of his precious Titians. The pictures must be hung high up, he explained, so that when the floors are washed down the canvases do not get splashed.[110] In May 1577 at Aranjuez, a month and place he normally chose for relaxation with the family, he could show signs of fatigue. 'It's ten o'clock,' he signed off a letter, 'and I'm shattered and dying of hunger since today is a fast day. This will have to wait until tomorrow, it can't be done now.'[111]

As the other pieces of his policy fell into place, the king became more conscious of the fragment he could not control: England. In August 1576 Quiroga informed him that 'today the nuncio told me that the pope was determined to launch the enterprise of England', and was looking for the money and the means. Philip replied: 'The nuncio said the same to me, and I'm considering it.'[112] But at the moment it was not a priority. For some years more he refused to entertain seriously the idea of invading England. His message to the nuncio was concise: 'Nobody desires more than I that the matter be put in hand, but the when and how depend on the way things go in Flanders, and on many other considerations.'[113]

Of these considerations, the most pressing was evidently the financial crisis of 1575. Flanders was eating up both government revenue and American silver. In 1573 Philip's expenditure on Flanders was roughly four times what he spent in 1566. About one and a half million ducats a year was being sent to Brussels. The scale of expenditure and debt became insupportable and in September 1575 Philip declared the third 'bankruptcy' of his reign. The treasury suspended payments to its creditors but undertook to pay them in the long term with annuities. The readjustment of debts to his financiers was unavoidable, but precipitated the very problems he wished to avoid. In the Netherlands the unpaid troops mutinied and deserted. At this juncture the governor of the Netherlands, Requesens, died on 5 March 1576. 'God willed,' he commented when he first arrived in Brussels, 'that I come here to pay for my sins.'[114] He had tried, but failed. 'The Netherlands,' he wrote to Philip's confessor Fresneda shortly before his death, 'were for me the Promised Land. God showed them to me, as he did to Moses, from the heights of the mountain.'[115]

Philip, repeatedly pressed by all his advisers to send a prince of the blood to succeed Requesens, had little hesitation in appointing the victor of Lepanto, Don Juan. In April the prince, who was then in Naples, was instructed to proceed directly to Brussels. But Don Juan had far-reaching plans of his own, which he insisted on presenting to the king. Disobeying instructions, he came personally to Madrid. One of his plans, he felt, was so important that it must be put to Philip. As commander in the Netherlands, he would invade England, marry himself to Mary queen of Scots, and thereby become in time ruler of England and the Netherlands. The result would be what Philip had always wanted: peace in western Europe.

At the Escorial, Philip listened politely but shrugged off the plan.[116] Instead, he turned to the pressing business. He gave Don Juan clear instructions (drawn up by Hopperus) to concede all the points demanded by the Netherlanders. 'Saving above all religion and my obedience', everything else could be given away. There were to be no recriminations: 'everything must be pardoned'.[117] In a somewhat dramatic gesture thought up by the king,[118] Don Juan made the northward journey overland through France in secret. He wore his beard and hair dyed, and was disguised as the servant of his only companion, the Italian noble Ottavio Gonzaga. On the evening of 3 November 1576 the weary pair crossed into the territory of the Netherlands.

One day later the Flanders mutineers, mostly unpaid Spanish troops, burst into the city of Antwerp, sacking, looting and killing at will. The principal buildings of the rich commercial metropolis were destroyed; over 6,000 people were massacred. The 'Spanish Fury' shocked Europe, and destroyed Spain's credibility in the north. The delicate negotiations between Philip and the Netherlanders were suspended. The States General moved rapidly to make its own peace with the rebels and Orange. Their agreement, known as the Pacification of Ghent, was signed in that city on 8 November.

Don Juan, faced with a situation he could not control, was obliged in the following February to agree to the terms of the Pacification, by a document inappropriately titled the Perpetual Edict. Its terms were accepted by Philip, who at this stage felt that all possible concessions should be made to Orange in order to secure peace.[119] The most cogent clause of the Edict provided for the immediate removal of all Spanish troops, who began departing southwards for Italy in April 1577. Philip's new governor was left without authority and without troops. As evidence filtered through of a possible anti-Spanish coup, to protect his vulnerable position Don Juan in July seized the fortress of Namur, and appealed to Philip to send the troops back. In his letters he virtually called for a return to Alba's policy, with executions of leaders if necessary. After much hesitation the king agreed to a partial change of policy. In a confidential note he commented that 'the plot against my brother cannot be blamed on the States as a whole but only on a few individuals. What is bad is what has happened afterwards. The situation must be taken very seriously and approached with determination. I have decided that the soldiers return to Flanders.'[120] He continued to maintain the need for concessions to the States, but (for the moment) with an army to guarantee them.

The Netherlands were in an impasse. The States General, at war with Don Juan, invited Orange back to Brussels and put on a hero's welcome for him in September 1577. But they were not yet prepared to appoint him as their ruler. Instead, the following month they announced that the archduke Matthias of Austria had accepted the post of governor-general. It was a move designed to win international support, and Philip's friendship with Matthias was counted on. Quite the reverse happened. A very angry Philip summoned ambassador Khevenhüller and complained that the emperor was interfering in the Netherlands.[121] The members of the council in Madrid were furious, and demanded that the king remove Matthias.[122] Don Juan was compelled to stand by while William of Orange consolidated his position. In January 1578, when Matthias was sworn in to govern the Netherlands in Philip's name, his appointed deputy was Orange. The stalemate with Don Juan did not last long. Ten days after the swearing-in, his troops once more under his control, Don Juan attacked and routed the rebel forces at Gembloux.

The attack appeared to promise positive results and there were other good signs in 1578. The problem of the succession in Spain seemed resolved. In the early hours of 14 April the queen gave birth to another son, Philip, in the Alcázar of Madrid. By good fortune he was to survive, and eventually succeeded to the throne. Philip was overjoyed but also extremely overworked. While Anna rested, he took a break. To clear his head, he told his secretary,

> I am thinking of going tomorrow for a few days to Aranjuez, to have a look at it before going to Monzón since I shall not be able to afterwards. I haven't been there for some time, nearly a year I think. The idea is I shall go tomorrow to sleep at San Martín de la Vega and the next day in the afternoon see the celebrations they put on at Aranjuez.[123]

A month after the birth, Anna accompanied the king to San Lorenzo. Philip celebrated the occasion by putting on another of his grand chivalric tournaments. In the fields at the village of San Salvador de Muñico, some five miles distant from the monastery at Parraces, he and 800 chosen knights re-enacted the splendour of medieval warfare.[124] It lasted for three days. We may imagine, as with the village innkeeper in *Don Quixote*, the peasants thronging in to see the spectacle and 'the furious and terrible blows the knights deliver'.[125] Philip, a father again, felt in superb condition. A courtier commented sardonically on 'the king who despite his fifty years acts like a young gallant'.[126] Philip returned to San Lorenzo on 21 June to pass the midsummer festival there with the court. In the first week of July he and Anna returned to Madrid. Two weeks before, his nephew, king Sebastian of Portugal, had set sail from Lisbon, in another splendid re-enactment of chivalry. His purpose: the crusade against the Moor.

In Madrid, Philip could take comfort from a number of promising signs on the political front. A one-year truce was formally signed in July 1578 between Spain and the Turks. Only six months before, lack of finance had forced the king to order a drastic reduction in the size of the Mediterranean fleet, 'since it is not possible for my fleet to be numerous enough to be able to face the enemy'.[127] It was the first of a series of truces, and came none too soon. Gembloux, meanwhile, gave the initiative to the Spanish forces in the north. The danger of French intervention was assuaged by agreements which Philip's ambassador in Paris, Juan de Vargas Mexía, made with the powerful Catholic grouping headed by the duke of Guise.[128] There was still no end in sight to the conflict, but the Catholic provinces of the south were now inclined to make some sort of an agreement with Spain. Calvinist extremism alienated the sympathies of many Netherlanders.

Don Juan did not survive to see the fruit of his efforts. In poor health, he died on 1 October 1578 near Namur, aged only thirty-one. Six months later his body was disinterred and transported back to Spain, where he was reburied in the Escorial. Before his death he named as his successor the prince of Parma, Alessandro Farnese, who had been serving as an officer in the Netherlands since 1577. Philip approved the appointment, possibly the most fortunate one of his entire reign.

*

On this clear and promising horizon, a small grey cloud appeared.

During the governorship of Don Juan in Flanders, there had been considerable opposition in Madrid to his policies. The differences coincided with a bitter rivalry which had developed between Antonio Pérez and Don Juan's secretary Juan de Escobedo, one of the court noblemen associated with the Eboli group. Early in 1575 he was appointed by the king as secretary to Don Juan of Austria, then serving in Italy and soon became an enthusiastic proponent of Don Juan's ambitious schemes. Among these was one to solve the problems of the north by marrying himself, Don Juan, to Mary queen of Scots, heir to the English throne.

Since his entry into the administration in the 1560s, Pérez (born in 1540) had become one of the bright stars at court. Dark-haired, slim and always impeccably dressed, sporting a moustache and small goatee beard, Pérez combined intelligence and elegance. The king at first kept somewhat aloof from a young man he considered 'dissolute',[129] but soon grew to admire his efficiency. As secretary to the king, Antonio's special care was the affairs of Italy. As friend and colleague of Eboli, he was also concerned with the issue of Flanders. When Eboli died, he became the most prominent representative of the Eboli view within the administration.

Pérez, who corresponded on his own account with Don Juan and Escobedo, was unhappy about the latter's schemes and denounced them vigorously to Philip. In January 1576 he urged the king to 'consider and think of a remedy' to Don Juan's ideas. Philip, never enthusiastic about Don Juan, seemed to agree, but urged patience. Three months later his reaction was sharper. 'I am surprised by what you say about Escobedo,' he informed Pérez in April.[130]

At this juncture Philip appointed Don Juan, then serving in Italy, to succeed Requesens in Flanders. The prince, wilful as ever, was glad of the appointment but wished to link it to his own plans for the Scottish marriage. In June 1576 he sent Escobedo to Madrid with a letter outlining his ideas. Philip insisted on seeing Escobedo at once. 'If he arrives tonight,' he wrote to Pérez on 30 June, 'you can talk to him tomorrow, and come here on Tuesday to lunch and to stay a couple of days.' Tuesday was not soon enough, and on Sunday, 1 July, Philip wrote to Pérez: 'Both you and he can come here tomorrow to lunch, and I shall look over what he brings.'[131]

The king was unimpressed by his half-brother's pretensions, and took a dislike to Escobedo's bold way of presenting his master's case. In subsequent weeks, he refused to see Escobedo and found excuses for not answering his letters. In a confidential letter the king explained what the problem was: 'Going by some of the things that Escobedo says, I can only fear that there will be some terrible demands [by Don Juan] which will be impossible to meet, such as a lot of money, and a lot of soldiers, and a lot of freedom in carrying out his instructions.' On all three questions, he insisted, 'I cannot and must not agree'.[132] He sent a letter to Don Juan in which he ignored the prince's requests to come and see him and ordered him to proceed directly to Flanders. When Don Juan arrived in Spain (contravening the king's express orders), Philip went off to San Lorenzo so that he would not have to receive the prince formally in Madrid. Don Juan visited him there. At the Escorial, the king communicated his instructions but otherwise put him off with vague talk. He was urgently trying to reach a solution in Madrid along the lines suggested by Hopperus, and none of his advisers would have supported Don Juan's proposals.

After reaching Brussels, Don Juan was forced to play an unheroic and therefore uncongenial role as peacemaker. Pérez, the king and other ministers were aware that the prince entertained thoughts of a grand design to invade England from Flanders. Philip was not completely opposed to the idea. Pérez, however, tried to present to Philip an image of a bellicose prince, abetted by Escobedo, whose warlike designs would wreck the delicate financial state of the monarchy. He referred specifically to 'deception'. Philip was perplexed. 'Although I don't understand this very well, I think that I grasp the substance.'[133] Pérez, taking his campaign against Escobedo further, worked on other members of the council. 'This afternoon', he informed Philip in mid-February 1577, 'I was with Quiroga[134] and read him all the recent despatches from Flanders, and he was very disturbed to see how little Don Juan and Escobedo trust us.' He also spoke with others, and got the same reaction. Philip agreed with Pérez's insistence that 'it is necessary to avoid using arms'. He commented that in Flanders 'it would not be possible to supply all that is required, and if we supplied it that would be at the expense of what is needed against the Turkish fleet and everything else'.[135]

It soon became obvious in the Netherlands that Don Juan was not getting the material support he required. He sent Escobedo back to Spain in July 1577 to find out what was happening. The secretary found that Pérez was intriguing not only against his master but even against the king. Before he could do anything about it, he was murdered in March 1578, while riding through a dark Madrid street. Rumour quickly pointed to Pérez as the author of the crime. The king, for the moment, did nothing about the incident except press for inquiries.

No proof exists for the subsequent charges by Pérez that he had acted at the king's instigation. There is no evidence that the king was implicated, or that he encouraged his secretary.[136] Philip, especially in those crucial years of debate, was surrounded by men who passionately espoused wildly different policies. He never silenced dissent by eliminating people. Unlike Henry II of England, whose anger against Thomas à Becket prompted murder, Philip did not suffer mortal rages. Only in cases of alleged treason did he consider action necessary. And then, as with the arrest of Vandenesse, he always followed due judicial process. Nor were his methods uniformly harsh. In 1583 an official of secretary Zayas was arrested 'on suspicion of being a spy and having been in touch with the prince of Orange'. There was no concrete proof and Philip simply transferred the man to serve in Naples.[137] After a while, he was recalled and given posts in Spain and in Flanders.

Philip's innocence in the affair cannot be proved. But the most convincing argument against his implication in Escobedo's murder is that it was not his style and he stood to gain nothing by it. Involvement would lose him the respect he required for his role as king. He always made plain his refusal to tolerate murder. 'It's a bad business,' he commented to his secretary a few years later, 'that there are so many murders and all difficult to solve.'[138] He was referring specifically to the murder in Madrid of the brother of the marquis of Montemayor. In 1578 he tried to cover up for Pérez. But this was, or so he said, because he had been grievously misled. As he scribbled late one night on a report from the committee investigating the case in 1590: 'all the things he [Pérez] says arise out of what he said to me; they are contrary to the truth, though he tricked me into believing them'.[139]

Much of the evidence is wholly circumstantial. All the documents implicating Philip come from Antonio Pérez alone, and many were heavily doctored by him when he came to publish them. The archives have yielded few other secrets.[140] The king's own reactions may certainly be read in different ways. But he was not a master of duplicity, and his closest colleagues saw nothing to suspect. The murder took place on Easter Monday, 31 March 1578. Early the next morning Philip in San Lorenzo was woken with the news. The first note he sent off said: 'The news is very strange, and I don't understand what the officers say.'[141] A subsequent note to Mateo Vázquez stated that 'it's all very strange; it was very bold for someone to kill so important a person under my very eyes'. Father Chaves, his confessor, commented later that 'His Majesty is very concerned'.[142]

We know from other sources that immediately after the murder the king tried to protect Pérez.[143] In subsequent weeks Vázquez broached to the king his suspicions of Pérez, but Philip usually deflected the comments. It is quite reasonable to believe that he did this from a wish to protect his secretary rather than because he himself was implicated. On 12 April Vázquez sent the king a note explicitly pointing a finger at Pérez. Inexplicably, the king sent the note to Pérez to obtain his reaction. Pérez sent back to the king the draft of a suggested reply, which Philip accordingly sent in his own hand to Vázquez. 'Since they are no more than suspicions,' he wrote, 'we should not give credit to them.'[144] By acting in this way, the king immediately made himself the accomplice of a man under suspicion.

But Philip did not intend to become enmeshed in the Escobedo case. In November he scribbled to the persistent Vázquez another note about Pérez:

> Over what you say in the paper that came here and that I have burnt, I gave you my response once before, and do so again . . . If it's a question

of rumour, I don't believe there's anyone who is not the subject of talk. But it's necessary to get at the truth rather than at suspicions, for these have always existed in the world. But you can tell me by word of mouth, without him or anybody else to hear, so that I can see whether or not they are matters that have some basis. Don't say anything about all this.[145]

By this time it was virtually official news in Madrid that Antonio Pérez had engineered Escobedo's death. As with scandals today,[146] the political elite preferred at first to stick together. Within a few weeks, it was as though nothing had happened to disturb the normal rhythm of life in the capital. But factional interests and rivalries were simmering. Vázquez and Pérez were at each other's throats. The king himself was concerned to discover more about what had happened. And there was, intriguingly, the princess of Eboli.

Ana de Mendoza y de la Cerda, only daughter of Diego de Mendoza, count of Melito, was born in 1540, the same year as Antonio Pérez. In 1553, at the age of thirteen, she was married to Ruy Gómez, later prince of Eboli, twenty-four years her senior. Because of her years as well as her husband's absence abroad with Philip II, the marriage was not consummated until 1559. Young, attractive,[147] energetic and ambitious, the princess of Eboli propelled herself into the social and political life of the court. From 1561 she entered into the first of her non-stop pregnancies (she had a total of ten children), but still found time to cultivate the friendship of the highest in the land, including Elizabeth Valois. When Eboli died in July 1573, the princess went into reclusion for three years. She emerged, to take part once again in the ebullient life of the court. Among her close friends was Antonio Pérez. It was rumoured that she was his lover. When Escobedo found this out, some said, his fate was sealed. But others in Madrid also considered that La Eboli had been the king's lover.

The story of a liaison between Philip and the princess is both unproven and absurd.[148] By contrast, her link with Pérez is certain. But it was probably based on political scheming, not on passion.[149] At the subsequent inquiry into Escobedo's murder a witness stated that Pérez 'was with the princess so many hours and so frequently that they suspected that the secretary was talking of many confidential matters of his state'. Another claimed that 'the princess knew secrets of state' which could only have come from a senior minister. As suspicion of La Eboli's role in the Escobedo affair grew, the president of the royal council, Pazos, commented to the king that 'we suspect that she is the leaven of all this'.[150] Philip had every reason to think that the killing of Escobedo was merely a detail in a turbid matter involving his secretary and Ana de Mendoza.

The king had always kept his distance from La Eboli. His attitude was encouraged by Vázquez, whose serious differences with Pérez had a crucial influence on events. When Vázquez in July 1578 made a critical observation about the princess, the king commented firmly that 'if it can be believed of anybody it is of that lady, of whom as you know I have always been cautious, because I have known of her ways for some time'.[151] A few weeks later he emphasised 'the great care that I have taken all my life not to meddle in the affairs of these persons'. By 'these persons' he meant La Eboli, her father and Antonio Pérez. As though he had said too much, he warned Vázquez: 'all this is directed only to you, you are not to say a word to anybody else'.[152]

The crux of the matter, forming the substance of the subsequent legal accusations against Pérez, was that the secretary had misused his office to leak secrets of state. When it appeared that Escobedo might reveal this, Pérez had him killed. A labyrinth of political schemes and personal interests led simply to this.

Within those schemes, high affairs of state were involved. It explains why the king busied himself with the case, which has not ceased to fascinate historians. There are signs that La Eboli, at the most delicate of moments in the struggle for the Portuguese succession, was hoping to marry one of her daughters to the son of the duke of Braganza.[153] It was a flagrant interference in Portuguese politics which also offers an explanation for the date of the arrest of Pérez and Eboli on the king's orders, in July 1579.

Immediately after the murder of Escobedo, Philip ordered a secret investigation, which he entrusted to his secretary, the judge Rodrigo Vázquez de Arce.[154] In those same weeks, Philip was refusing to accept Pérez's guilt. By the end of the year, information and rumours obliged him to change his attitude. In March 1579 he decided to bring the matter out into the open. 'I cannot manage to clear my conscience,' he mused. 'I shall go to confession and communion and trust God to guide me to make the proper decision. I am encouraged a bit to see that the matter is now public, which is no surprise considering a woman is involved.'[155] It was not only his conscience that weighed on him. The king also received a direct rebuke from one of his chaplains, fray Hernando de Castillo, the man who years before had assisted at the secret execution of Montigny. 'I neither know nor understand,' the aged Dominican reproved him, 'what reason you have in conscience for withholding punishment.'[156] Three weeks later, on 30 March, precisely a year after the murder, Philip wrote to cardinal Granvelle in Rome, summoning him immediately to Madrid to take charge of affairs of state. The letter, ironically, was drawn up by Pérez. But the king had still not made up his mind. In April and May he was still assuring the secretary of his support. 'I shall not let you down,' he wrote.[157]

That June the king went with Anna and the family to Aranjuez for a brief stay, and then to Toledo for the Corpus Christi celebrations. On 20 June they left Toledo and made their way to San Lorenzo, arriving there in three days. The family settled down to their routine of leisure, but the king had other things on his mind. To everybody's surprise, and completely breaking his normal pattern, on 9 July he suddenly left for Madrid, citing important affairs of state.[158] It was thought that some development in Flanders or Portugal had emerged. Over the next few days the king in the Alcázar was largely absorbed in sorting out the problems raised by the activities of Pérez and the princess of Eboli.[159] He also had before him a report of a threat, presumably by these two, to Vázquez's life. Events moved to their climax on the night of 28 July. Antonio Pérez, unsuspecting, had been working on papers with the king until ten that night. 'Your business,' the king commented to the secretary, 'will be dealt with before I leave.'[160] When Pérez returned home, at eleven, he was detained and placed under house arrest. Moments later the captain of the royal guard detained the princess and conducted her to prison in a castle at Pinto. The king stayed up all night.[161] He spent the time writing letters, countersigned by secretary Gaztelu, to explain his decision. They were directed to the duke of Infantado, the duke of Medina Sidonia, and other grandees related by blood to the princess.[162] This done, he returned the next day to San Lorenzo.

Granvelle arrived in Madrid on 28 July. The capital was soon buzzing with news of the arrests, which seem to have caused general satisfaction to the public.[163] Among friends of Pérez (like Quiroga) and powerful relatives of La Eboli (like Medina Sidonia), there was deep dismay. On 3 August cardinal Granvelle was at San Lorenzo, where he kissed the king's hand and received instructions. Shortly after, Philip fell ill of a throat infection and had to be bled. He managed, nonetheless, to discuss business with his new chief minister. In mid-October the royal family moved on to the Pardo. Granvelle on the same day went to Madrid to take control of the councils of Italy and Flanders. Now aged sixty-two, he was the first non-Spaniard ever to assume direction of the affairs of the monarchy.

*

The virtual settlement of the conflict in the southern Netherlands enabled Philip to pay more attention to the urgent matter of the Portuguese succession.

Philip was as Portuguese as he was Castilian. To his own family links were added those of his sister Juana, mother of the ill-fated Sebastian. When the latter succeeded to the Portuguese throne in 1557, at the age of three, Philip began to take an interest in the career of his unpredictable nephew. Sebastian's evident lack of interest in women and in the need to marry and procure an heir, together with his excessive dedication to war games, were alarming signs. He disappeared for three months into northern Africa in 1574, on a reconnaissance visit. In a famous interview between the two kings, held at the monastery of Guadalupe during Christmas 1576, with the duke of Alba present, Philip tried to reason with him. Sebastian, however, was interested only in concrete offers of help for his plans to invade Africa. At a moment when Philip was working to bring about a truce with the Turks in the Mediterranean, it made little sense to open up a new war in the south. He unbent to the extent of offering some support. 'I decided to offer him fifty galleys and 5,000 Spanish troops', for which he would have to pay.[164] He also insisted that, because of the obvious risks, Sebastian must not participate personally. The Spaniards would be drawn from those returning to Italy from Flanders. On his return to Madrid Philip told ambassador Khevenhüller that Sebastian 'has good intentions but little maturity'. 'I have pressed him by word and by letter,' he said, 'but to no avail.'[165] In 1578 he sent Juan de Silva as ambassador to Portugal to try to restrain Sebastian. Benito Arias Montano was also sent to Lisbon with a similar mission.

In spite of Spanish efforts, the famous expedition to Morocco took place. On 4 August 1578 the army of Portugal, comprising the flower of its nobility with the young twenty-five-year-old king at their head, was wiped out by Berber forces at the battle of Alcazar-el-Kebir. Over 10,000 men were taken prisoner. The news reached Madrid on 12 August. The king had only just left the city, alone, for San Lorenzo. He was in the Escorial when messengers brought him the news on the thirteenth. He was visibly shaken, and immediately withdrew.[166] He spent the next few hours walking around the patio garden, alone,[167] and the friars judged that he was overcome with grief. He certainly grieved. But Sebastian's death also opened up the formidable question of the Portuguese succession. When he went indoors the king wrote at once to Cristóbal de Moura.

*

It was not the kindest of autumns. On 22 September the archduke Wenzel, whom Philip had cared for as a son, died in Madrid at the age of seventeen. Barely a month later, it was the turn of the little Infante Fernando, who died on 18 October. Don Juan had died a fortnight before. The loss of two nephews, one son, and a brother in the space of three months was shattering. The king evaded the mourning by immersing himself in the question of Portugal. The day after receiving the news of Alcazar-el-Kebir he went to Madrid and issued orders to the marquis of Santa Cruz to take the Andalusian galleys to protect the Portuguese forts on the African coast. In effect, the battle for north Africa was now lost. The king, significantly, took no further military measures in that zone. Instead, he concentrated his attention on the peninsula.

He sent Cristóbal de Moura, a Portuguese and one of his most trusted advisers, to Portugal to sound out the situation. Moura, aged forty in 1578, had come to Spain in 1554 in the train of the princess Juana. Like several other Portuguese (among them Ruy Gómez) who sought their fortune at the court of Spain, Moura won the king's favour, thanks largely to the patronage of Juana. He proved exceptionally useful in missions involving his native land, and had helped to arrange the meeting with Sebastian at Guadalupe. Moura was informed that his close friend Juan de Silva, Spanish ambassador to Sebastian who was among those captured at Alcazar-el-Kebir, would be reappointed ambassador as soon as he managed to return from Africa. While Moura was assessing matters, Philip despatched letters of sympathy to the chief authorities. Portugal was defenceless and leaderless, and the most urgent issue was the succession.

The nearest male heir was the late king's great-uncle, the sixty-seven-year-old cardinal Henry. He was proclaimed king at the end of August. Henry was deaf, half-blind, toothless, senile and racked by tuberculosis. He was, reported Moura, half-dead with fright at being nominated king.[168] The best legal right to the throne after him was held by Philip, through his mother. There were Portuguese claimants to the throne, notably the cardinal's nephew Antonio, prior of Crato, and a niece who was married to the duke of Braganza.[169] But Philip was determined to assert his own claims.

For the first and only time in his life, he conducted a campaign to win over opinion. Over problems such as the Netherlands, he had limited himself to defending his policies, for he was the legitimate ruler. Now he was obliged to court the support both of the Portuguese and of Europe. He fervently hoped to secure the throne without the expense and blood of a fight, but he also accepted that even strong claims needed the firm consent of the political elite. Three approaches were made. First, leading jurists from all over Europe were employed to write in support of his cause, so as to convince not only the Portuguese but other European powers. Second, his representatives in Portugal, most notably his ambassador Juan de Silva, his representative the duke of Osuna, and his special envoy Moura, attempted to win over individuals as well as cities. Finally, selective bribes were used. Moura orchestrated a brilliant campaign to win support for his master. He talked to nobles and clergy, collected information on Portuguese defences, and distributed money liberally.

Philip was leaving little to chance. Already by the end of January 1579 he was informing Moura of 'how we are, secretly and discreetly, taking the necessary measures for all eventualities'. 'You may be sure,' he wrote, 'that although I hope that none of this will be necessary, on my side nothing is being overlooked.'[170] Moura agreed on the need for military preparations. 'I have great hopes,' he wrote to the king, 'that though the swords are ready there will be no need to draw them.'[171] Philip supervised plans for a possible military and naval intervention. In the spring and summer of 1579 the galleys of Spain were assembled, and a further number of ships brought from Italy under the command of admiral Doria. The joint force, totalling some sixty galleys, was assembled off the coast of Andalusia, under the command of the marquis of Santa Cruz. The ships from Italy brought with them detachments of Italian and German soldiers, as well as a force of Spanish *tercios*, veterans of the war in the Low Countries. Intensive recruitment of Spanish troops took place in Andalusia and the provinces neighbouring Portugal. In October the cavalry troops were put under the command of the Flanders veteran Sancho Dávila. Santa Cruz was to sail for Lisbon immediately on hearing of the death of cardinal Henry. The duke of Medina Sidonia, seconded by other nobles whose estates bordered Portugal, was to help raise troops for a land invasion. The mobilisation was in theory secret, but Philip made sure that the Portuguese knew of it. 'Even if it doesn't come to a use of force,' he informed Moura in April, 'it would be all the more helpful to press ahead with negotiations while keeping up the threat of arms.'[172] He added that when the Portuguese ambassador came to him to complain of the mobilisation, 'I replied that the preparations and military exercises on the frontier were not being done by my order'.[173] It was a truly professional diplomatic lie.

He then, in March 1579, convened the Castilian Cortes. In May, the whole history of the Portuguese succession was presented to the assembled deputies, who responded with enthusiasm. They were less forthcoming over money. Sporadic sessions of the Cortes were held over several months. The assembly was not dissolved until 1582.

On the eve of the Portuguese campaign, pressure on other fronts eased up. In the Netherlands the new commander Alessandro Farnese was to prove himself one of the most brilliant generals of the time. Aged thirty-three when appointed, the son of Margaret of Parma (and consequently nephew of Philip) had been educated in part at the court of Spain, but remained Italian in outlook. He was able to profit from the growing political split, based on religion, in the Netherlands. Early in 1579 a group of northern provinces, led by Holland and Zealand, formed themselves into a Calvinist-led Union of Utrecht. At the same time some of the southern provinces, led by Catholics, formed a Union of Arras. In May this Union, consisting now of six provinces,[174] signed a treaty accepting the authority of Spain. The accord guaranteed all their privileges, but reaffirmed the exclusive position of the Catholic religion. Parma backed up this success by capturing, in June, the important stronghold of Maastricht. 'Good news has now come from Flanders,' Philip wrote cheerfully to Moura in June, asking him to spread the information in Portugal.[175] The return of the provinces to Spanish obedience would confirm him in Portuguese eyes as a successful, but also liberal and magnanimous, monarch.

There was also good news from the Mediterranean. Peace negotiations were in progress which led, in March the following year, to a renewal of the truce between Spain and the Ottoman empire. The king was free to devote himself exclusively to Portugal.

He instructed Osuna and Moura to tell the Portuguese they should not fear any threat to their liberties. Taxation would not rise. In Castile the *alcabala* tax had recently been increased only 'because it had not risen in over forty years'. In Aragon the liberties were fully protected; in terms of taxes, 'they pay none'. As for the union of the crowns in one person, that did not imply any union of the realms. 'Uniting some realms with others does not follow from having the same ruler, since though Aragon and Castile have a single ruler they are not united, but as separate as they were when they had different rulers.'[176] Never before in the history of Europe had a pretender to a crown been so obliged to present his credentials. Even his more unpopular actions in Flanders could be disavowed. Alba, responsible for the repression there, was in disgrace. His name did not feature among the roll-call of nobles who were asked in July 1579 to raise men for the Portugal campaign.[177]

When cardinal Granvelle arrived at San Lorenzo in August 1579, accompanied from Italy by Juan de Idiáquez, Portugal was one of the first matters to be placed in his hands. All through the year cardinal Henry lingered on the point of death, but refused stubbornly to designate a successor. The succession was nonetheless largely resolved in favour of Philip II, who had won (or bought) the clear support of the majority of clergy and nobles in the Cortes held at Almeirim in January 1580. But the situation was no longer simple. Antonio of Crato had active support among very many Portuguese, who hoped for help from abroad, particularly from France. The longer the delay, the greater the risk of foreign intervention.

Philip spent September to mid-October with his family in San Lorenzo. From 11 to 23 September, unfortunately, he was ill in bed. A few days later he suffered a swelling in his right wrist which put him back in bed for four more days. The following weeks, from mid-October to early December, the royal family spent in El Pardo. They went hunting: Philip killed forty rabbits, Anna thirty. On one of the evenings they held a masked ball in the portrait gallery of El Pardo.[178]

During all these weeks the court was busy with activity resulting from the detention of Pérez and La Eboli. It was a wet December in 1579, with continuous rain. This may have helped Philip decide to spend Christmas, for once, in the Alcázar. He busied himself with his papers, with Flanders, with ordering the transfer of La Eboli from her prison at Pinto to the more spacious fortress at Santorcaz. 'He is as shut up as if he were in a monastery,' an observer said of the king, 'only the chamberlains and gentlemen of the household see him.'[179] He was also waiting for the news, expected at any moment, of the death of cardinal Henry. Meanwhile, he fussed over his pregnant queen. On 14 February 1580 she gave birth to a girl, María.

Cardinal Henry died at last on 31 January. 'Nothing else can be attended to until the matter of Portugal is settled,' the king observed.[180] Although he had made a great effort to bring together the men, supplies and arms needed for an invasion, he now opposed any hasty military move. 'I think that everything humanly possible must be done so that a resort to arms is not necessary,' he warned Moura on 6 February.[181] Philip urged his agents in Portugal that 'everything now should be done, I think, very delicately'.[182] By contrast his advisers, headed by Granvelle, felt that invasion was unavoidable. They also urged him to bring Alba out of retirement and put him at the head of the troops.

Alba was in disgrace for what appeared to many to be a small matter. In 1578 his son Fadrique de Toledo, who had a distinguished record of service in Flanders, secretly married his cousin, the daughter of García de Toledo, marquis of Villafranca, against the express orders of the king. Don Fadrique, twice a widower and a well-known gallant, was already pledged to marry a lady-in-waiting of the queen, Magdalena de Guzmán. The matter had caused problems before.[183] Philip's rigidity over questions of marriage among the aristocracy was not new.[184] In 1577 the duke of Feria had been placed under strict house arrest over a similar issue.[185] When Philip learned that Alba had given his approval to the marriage, he ordered Don Fadrique's arrest.[186] Both father and son were banned from court, and the three grandees assisting at the marriage – prior Don Antonio, Fernando de Toledo, and the marquis of Velada – were placed under house arrest.[187] The issue was not simply a matter of the king's preferences. Relationships among the higher aristocracy were always delicate, and nowhere more than in questions of marriage. The king played an essential role as arbiter between the great families. There were hot tempers at court over Don Fadrique's action and the duke waited nervously for the king's response. In September 1578 he embarrassed the king's secretary in the palace at Madrid by taking him aside and complaining about his treatment, 'demanding justice, saying that he could not go on, and that he had to speak to Your Majesty, and that he would leave here, and mentioned going to live in another country'.[188] In November the president of the council, Pazos, threatened Alba verbally.[189] It was not a good year for the Alba family. In July 1578 the young count of Fuentes, brother of the duchess, was thrown into prison because of a quarrel.[190] In January 1579 the duke, duchess and their retinue left Madrid for the tranquillity of house arrest at Uceda, one of Alba's towns. Foreign dignitaries, including the king of France and the pope, pleaded in his favour, but the king, displaying his well-known stubbornness, refused to relent. For him it was a matter of disobedience that brought its own consequences. He studiously excluded the duke from any of the deliberations over Portugal.

Twelve months later, when it became clear that a commander for the Portuguese campaign must be appointed, Philip was faced with the embarrassing prospect of having to choose Alba. His councillors were unanimous that only Alba had the necessary reputation and prestige. The president of the council on 15 February 1580 informed him that 'the council believes that no other person we know is more fitting and suitable than the duke'. The special committee for Portugal[191] sent its secretary Gabriel Zayas to inform Philip that their unanimous choice was the same. The king refused to give way. He wrote to Moura the next day that 'last night Zayas told me that everybody is of the opinion that I must appoint the duke of Alba'. Moura offered no comfort. He wrote stressing that the 'man from Uceda' was the most likely to terrify the opposition in Portugal.[192]

Browbeaten by his advisers, Philip recalled the old duke, now aged seventy-three and (in his own words) 'frail and finished',[193] to active service. Alba received the king's letter at 10 p.m. on 22 February, and replied on the spot. He was grateful 'to be back in the good graces of Your Majesty, which is what I most desired'.[194] The king brushed aside Alba's request to come and pay his respects, and instructed him to proceed within three days to Llerena, where the army was assembling.

Some felt that one way to avoid invasion was, as suggested by both the pope and the five regents who ran Portugal in the interim since cardinal Henry's death, for Philip to submit his claim to arbitration. The king was willing to talk to the regents. On 1 March 1580 he had the Cortes swear to prince Diego as heir, in a little ceremony in the chapel of the Alcázar. The royal family left Madrid on 5 March and made their way to the monastery of Guadalupe, where they spent Holy Week and Easter. Philip met the regents later that month. He refused arbitration, for this would have been to admit the possibility of a doubt over his rights. In any case, prior Antonio was also unlikely to accept any decision based on arbitration. In these circumstances the preparations for an armed strike went ahead.

In May the court transferred itself to Mérida. Alba arrived there on 12 May. The king, who was despatching letters with secretary Zayas, saw him arriving. He immediately sent Sebastián de Santoyo down to tell the duke to come up. When Alba strode in the king refused to let him kneel down. 'He raised him up, embraced him, and with great contentment asked him how he was, and other things.'[195] During the next three days the two men were locked in discussion, morning and afternoon. On 15 May Alba left for Badajoz. The king and queen left three days later.

On 12 June Philip issued the orders appointing Alba as captain-general of the invading army. The opening sentence of the orders reflected the king's decisive stance. The original draft had read: 'Whereas I am the direct and rightful successor to the realms of Portugal, they belong to and devolve on me.' Philip struck out the limp phrase after the comma, and wrote in: 'I have determined to take possession of them'.[196] Strangely, for a nation weary of war abroad, most Castilians warmed to the idea of a conquest at home. An imperialist dream began to take shape. Among the few dissonant voices was that of Teresa of Avila, who commented that 'if this matter is pursued through war, I fear great harm'. A leading Jesuit lamented that Christians should be fighting Christians: 'This realm [Castile] is ailing and has little wish to see any growth in His Majesty's power.'[197]

On 13 June the king, the queen and the Infantas, flanked by Alba and the archduke Albert, reviewed the forces, numbering some 47,000,[198] on an open plain before the camp near Badajoz. A shelter protected the royal group from the burning sun. Alba, who had been ill in bed the day before, was in good spirits. The file-past, which went on all day, left admiring observers almost speechless. 'It is something to see, even as I am writing this,' reported one.[199] The Portuguese, he felt, were crazy even to think of resisting. 'It was a fine sight,' commented a seasoned soldier, 'a great many men, all in good order.'[200] Half the army consisted of Spanish soldiers and veterans from Flanders (among them Sancho Dávila); the other half were German and Italian mercenaries.[201] The land force was to be given naval support by a fleet under the marquis of Santa Cruz. This sailed from Cadiz on 8 July, with orders to make its way up the Atlantic coast.

On 18 June the frontier fort of Elvas surrendered without a fight. On the twenty-seventh the army, after another march-past before Philip and his generals, crossed the frontier in force. Don Antonio had been proclaimed king by dissident Portuguese, but there was little effective resistance to the Spanish army. Meanwhile an army raised by the Spanish nobles whose lands bordered Portugal, protected the rear of the royal forces. In a letter to the pope in July, the king claimed that he had sent the troops in because of the threat of intervention by foreign powers. They were there 'not to wage war against that realm but to save it from oppression and restore it to peace and tranquillity'.[202] In practice, plunder, outrages and brutality occurred throughout the process of occupation. 'We are beginning to feel pity for all the harm that is being done to these poor people,' an officer wrote.[203] Alba hanged the guilty when he could. Setúbal, besieged by land and sea, capitulated on 18 July. The fleet under Santa Cruz sailed in two days later and gave support to the land forces.[204] In Lisbon there was stiff street-by-street resistance, but the city finally surrendered in the last week of August.

Don Antonio fled. He took refuge in the north and was eventually rescued by an English ship. 'Here, Sir, you can forget about the war,' Alba wrote to the king.[205] Coimbra surrendered on 8 September as the forces moved north. Philip was lost for words. 'I don't know how to express the gratitude that I owe you for all this,' he wrote to the duke.[206] On 12 September he was proclaimed king in the capital.

During the weeks of campaigning, he remained behind in Badajoz. An epidemic of influenza was raging through most of the peninsula in the summer of 1580. In Catalonia 'very many are dying'.[207] The outbreak ravaged Madrid, where 'there are so many dead that no one takes note of them, and the deaths continue'.[208] Cardinal Granvelle fell gravely ill, and many members of the administration died. The court in Extremadura did not escape. Philip, prince Diego and Catalina were all laid low, but recovered, thanks in part to the efficiency of Dr Vallés.

Queen Anna was not so fortunate. She was well into another pregnancy when the epidemic caught her. She suffered several days of fever, and had to be bled. 'The doctors say that her illness shows no signs of being dangerous,' reported a court noble on 14 October, 'but as she is six months pregnant they are being careful with her.'[209] Shortly before dawn on the twenty-sixth, at the age of thirty-one, she died in the epidemic. The king was grief-stricken. His love for her had been very great.[210] Saddened and depressed, he felt that he was about to follow her. He sent instructions to his ministers 'in case I should go' and looked over his testament: 'the queen is not here, and this is what has made me look at this now'.[211] The loss was to mark him permanently: he never married again. For years afterwards, Anna remained present in his thoughts. Her body was taken to San Lorenzo. The king ordered his children to be taken back to the Alcázar.

The death soon afterwards of prince Diego (in 1582) half convinced the king that he should remarry, in order to guarantee the male succession. There was no assurance that Philip, now the only male heir, born in April 1578, would survive. But the king's advancing years, bad health and heavy work schedule meant that he was not keen on the idea.[212] Several candidates were suggested and approached. For one reason or another none of the proposals came to anything. The king, as he preferred, remained a widower.[213]

Events in Portugal had to await the end of a short period of court mourning. The king's intended departure from Castile encouraged a group of Moriscos in Andalusia to plan a rising in Seville. It was discovered and dealt with opportunely by the city,[214] leaving the king without worries in his rear. On 4 December he left Badajoz for the frontier. At Elvas he was officially received by Portuguese representatives. From here he issued summons to the Cortes of Portugal to assemble in April at Tomar, selected because Lisbon was suffering an epidemic.

The Cortes of Tomar, which met in April 1581, were a historic occasion. They confirmed the union of the whole peninsula under one crown. The Cortes swore fealty to the king and recognised prince Diego as his successor. In return, Philip confirmed all the privileges and the independence of Portugal, on terms similar to those which had united the other realms of the peninsula with Castile over a century before. The Portuguese overseas possessions fell in line with events at home and accepted Philip. Only in the Atlantic islands of the Azores, where prior Antonio held out with the help of a French force, was there resistance. In July 1582 a fleet was sent out under the command of Santa Cruz, and inflicted a bloody defeat on the French ships. A further engagement took place in the summer of 1583 off the island of Terceira, confirming Spain's control over the islands.

Alba had been appointed at the insistence of those who saw him as the desired symbol of a truly Castilian enterprise. He had also been invaluable for the quantity of men he helped to raise for the campaign. The king was grateful. When the duke intimated in the spring of 1581 that his job was done and he wished to withdraw, Philip protested: 'when you say that you are not needed there I do not agree, for you are much needed'. He went on to thank him profusely for his services.[215] But tensions between the two continued. When Philip appointed an official to inquire into excesses committed by the soldiers during the occupation, Alba pointedly refused to collaborate with him. The king gave in, but complained that 'the duke's arrogance is on a par with his loyalty'.[216] The duke was seriously ailing and died in 1582 in Tomar. The king visited him during his illness and listened to his last words of advice.[217] His passing, and the break-up of the Eboli grouping with the arrest of Pérez and the princess in 1579, marked the end of an era. By coincidence, in 1582 another famous Spaniard, Teresa of Avila, also passed away.[218]

For nearly thirty years the Alba–Eboli polarisation had dominated politics at the court of Philip II. The king had had to manoeuvre his way carefully between the clashes of interest, and did not emerge unscathed. 'The king's government,' fumed a pro-Eboli grandee, the admiral of Castile,[219] early in 1578, 'is not a government of justice but of tyranny and vengeance. Everything is in the hands of lowly and vindictive people, many of whose fathers were Comuneros.'[220] Family hatreds and rivalry of this type would continue to affect government. But from 1582 the king was a free agent.

7

The World of Philip II

The yellow narcissus they brought you from Aranjuez comes, I think, from the fields rather than from the garden, though its perfume is not so sweet.[1]

The Spanish monarchy arrived late in the company of other princely courts. In the fifteenth century the European Renaissance made Italy the principal magnet for scholars, writers and artists who took the new ideas back to their noble and princely courts in France, Germany, Burgundy and England. A circuit of cultural interchange was created, but Spain lay on its fringes. In the time of Ferdinand and Isabella, a few scholars had brought from Italy ideas that took some root in the small noble courts and in the court of Isabella. At the same time, close links with the Netherlands confirmed the influence of Flemish art and, later, of the ideas of Erasmus. The lack of a fixed royal court, and the emperor's absences, made it impossible for these influences to become securely rooted.

Philip's permanence in the peninsula after 1559 changed the scene. He brought back with him a wealth of ideas and schemes. As sovereign of the Netherlands and much of Italy, he had access to the talents of the principal humanists and artists of his time. Despite his state debts, he set aside sums for his cultural plans. In the 1560s he put together a painstaking and impressive programme. Having seen the great palaces and gardens of Italy, southern Germany, England and the Netherlands, he knew that Spain must compete. A new court must be created, dignified as a royal residence, with a fitting environment of art and music.

More than this, the monarchy should be seen as the active promoter of science and learning. He chose humanists as tutors for his son. His chief secretary, Gonzalo Pérez, was a known humanist. The gains of humanism should be extended by reforming the curriculum in the universities, and by launching a new multilingual version of the Bible. Surveys should be made of all that was known. This was particularly important in respect of the Indies. Appointments were made of official historians and official chroniclers.

Spain was in a unique position to launch such a programme. In addition to contacts with Italy and the Netherlands, the peninsula could draw on its own internal experience of the culture of Jews and Arabs. Philip's commitment to Catholic orthodoxy was beyond question. But beyond that he kept his pulse on all branches of enquiry, including both the exotic and the informal.

He never wrote down an outline of what he might do. At one time or other in the 1560s, however, he made decisions intended to set all the above in motion. Looking at the enormous range of matters involved, one cannot fail to admire his energy and purpose. At the same time, there were serious obstacles of which he was perfectly aware. Though there were prominent exceptions, as a class the Spanish elite, nobles and clergy, had little cultural sophistication.[2] An Imperial ambassador to Madrid in the 1570s commented that when the nobles spoke of certain subjects they did so in the way that a blind man speaks of colours. They travelled out of Spain very seldom, he said, and so had no perspective with which to make judgments.[3] They were unlikely to contribute much to creating a new courtly culture. The printing industry in the peninsula was primitive,[4] and largely in the hands of foreigners. Good books would have to be introduced from abroad. Indeed, the problem was that nearly everything would have to be imported if any progress were to be made in Spain. The king even insisted on importing his own writing paper, since he found Castilian paper too coarse.

To keep his programme in action, Philip had to maintain a policy of relatively open frontiers. Protecting Spain against heresy was feasible, and he attempted it; sealing it off from Europe was, by contrast, never his intention. The censorship decree of 1558 and the restrictions on studying abroad were, by their nature, limited in impact. They applied only to the realms of Castile, and were in any case difficult to enforce. In practice, Castilians continued to enjoy the freedoms available to most Europeans: to publish outside the country, and to travel without hindrance. In the non-Castilian parts of Spain a free movement of books, persons and students continued to operate for much of the reign.[5] Foreign scholars, technicians and artists took advantage of the free access in order to come and seek the patronage of the Spanish king.

*

Until mid-century the usual centre of administration in Castile had been Valladolid. Though never quite a capital city, Valladolid had since the days of Ferdinand and Isabella been the regular centre of royal activity. Both Charles and Philip had been crowned there. The outbreak of heresy in the city may have been among the reasons which impelled Philip at the end of 1559 to leave it and install his government in the more central location of the old capital of Spain, Toledo.

Toledo, however, had problems that became evident in the months the court was there. The city formed a spectacular froth of buildings on the crest of a rock. The Tajo, snaking round its base, gave it a picturesque charm. But the medieval centre with its cramped streets and buildings was too small to accommodate the large numbers of the court and bureaucracy. When the court wanted to breathe, it had to go elsewhere. In the spring of 1560, shortly after arriving in Toledo, the king decided to take his wife to see Aranjuez. There preparations had to be made for receiving 'four thousand persons, not counting the carriages'.[6] Aranjuez, of course, had few buildings apart from the palace, and the luckless courtiers had to be accommodated in makeshift tents. Even with its buildings, by contrast, Toledo did not have space. Neither did it have the infrastructure to supply food, and above all water, to the larger population. Its social life was influenced by the presence everywhere of clergy, whose life-style did not coincide with that of the court. Elizabeth of Valois did not like the city.[7] The bitter winter of 1560–1, during which Toledo's death rate doubled, may have been the last straw.

It was unthinkable to go back to Valladolid, which in any case in 1561 suffered a serious fire that destroyed a good part of the city centre. Arson was suspected, and by official accounts 'over 2,200 houses were burnt'.[8] The city was out of commission for several years while plans for rebuilding (personally examined and approved by the king) were drawn up.[9] Philip was forced to put in train a completely new scheme for a capital elsewhere. His choice of Madrid was in no way influenced by its central location in the peninsula. More important was its position relative to the royal residences, which would allow him to commute without difficulty from his administrative capital to his hunting resorts.[10] This enabled him to plan for the growth of Madrid and also to develop the royal palaces within a short radius of the capital.

Among aristocrats and their ladies who had lived in the sophistication of the Netherlands, the return home in 1559 was a severe disappointment. Spain – and above all Toledo – was a backwater. The king, his courtiers claimed, would love to go back. 'We greatly miss Flanders, and though His Majesty pretends otherwise I suspect he feels the way all of us do,' a noble wrote to Granvelle. His wife, he continued, 'wishes more than anyone to go back to Flanders and never has anything good to say of Spain. And of course she is right. It's hardly necessary to say that the cleanliness there and the filth here are two quite different things.'[11] In short, he said, 'we have passed a terrible summer in the most miserable place in the world, which has nothing in its favour but the fame of "Toledo! Toledo!" ' An intimate of the king, the count (later duke) of Feria, had the same impression of Philip's ideas about returning north. 'I swear to you that His Majesty wishes so much to return that I would not believe it if I did not see it.' Feria had an English wife, which influenced his own preferences. 'Spain is the most backward province on the face of the earth, and devil take me if I do not round up half of all I have and return to Flanders. Besides which, my wife pleads with me every day to go back and has not had a day's good health since she came.'[12] These testimonies make more credible the view that Elizabeth Valois also influenced her husband to look for a more cosmopolitan court environment.

The move from Toledo, decreed early in May 1561, took place formally on the nineteenth of the month. In mid-century Madrid had been a small, unexciting town of some 9,000 people.[13] The court occasionally based itself there, as did Philip between 1551 and 1553. After the move of 1561, the town grew rapidly. There were 16,000 residents by the end of 1561 and 34,000 by 1570. A generation after 1560, the population had increased eightfold.

With increased size came problems of supply, sanitation and crime. A few years later, a witness described it as 'full of royalty, priests, nobles, magistrates, officials . . . criminals, thieves, ruffians and vagrants'.[14] When queen Anna came to Madrid in 1570, one of her retinue thought the city 'the dirtiest and filthiest in Spain'. 'After ten at night it is no pleasure to walk through the city and listen to the emptying of urinals and the discharge of filth.'[15] Although Madrid could be on occasion clean, visitors were more usually impressed by its squalor. The king made efforts to remedy the situation, but eventually confessed himself beaten.[16]

The royal residence in Madrid was the Alcázar. A small palace of Mudéjar style, and occasionally used in the Middle Ages by Castilian rulers, it was enlarged from 1536 onwards by Charles V. From the 1540s prince Philip took an interest in the works and in improving the surrounding streets.[17] When the decision to move to Madrid became firm, the building programme speeded up. Juan Bautista, aided by a number of Italian artisans, contributed. In the reformed and enlarged building the king in the 1560s chose as his apartments those on the west, overlooking the river Manzanares and the small Casa de Campo. As with all his architects, he was meticulous and demanding over details. His sketches and notes to Juan Bautista were merciless: 'This has to be the entrance', 'this has to be the chancel entrance', 'this is the gateway where the horses must be when it rains'.[18] He got the changes he wanted. By the late 1560s, long before San Lorenzo had taken shape, the Alcázar had been transformed into the crown's biggest and most imposing residence. It was also the most visible symbol of the adoption of Italianate style and the abandonment of traditional Spanish architecture.

*

Philip's passion for reconstructing the residences was profound. In the 1540s, when he was regent, the passion only grew. In the 1550s his admiration for the noble residences of northern Europe kept him busy sending messages to his architects in Spain. It was from the Netherlands in 1556 that he first sent orders for the site at Aceca to be rebuilt. From there too, in the same year, he arranged for the acquisition of land just over the river Manzanares below the Alcázar. Here, in 1562, under the direction of Juan Bautista, construction was begun of a small Casa de Campo surrounded by gardens.

Philip's lifelong dedication to building had two inseparable components. In the first place, he was fascinated by the aesthetic and technical aspects of palace construction. He knew from direct experience that Spain had nothing to compete with the architecture of Italy or the Netherlands. As a result, he was determined to recreate in Castile, as symbols of his power, residences which could equal anything anywhere else. The rebuilt Alcázars of Madrid and Toledo were the end products, within an urban context, of this desire.

In the second place, however, he never cared for the city as an environment. His first love was always the open air, fields and forests, riding and hunting. He regularly insisted to his children, as well as to his ministers, that they should take fresh air more often. In the Netherlands he first discovered the delight of endless landscaped gardens, and the possibility of combining countryside with palaces. Full of enthusiasm, he brought the idea of the garden back with him in 1559. He received further advice from those who had direct knowledge of the gardens of Italian princes. As each garden developed, he would pass scribbled lists of plants and ideas to the designers. He sent experts abroad. When one of his designers died he asked for his notebooks to be sent to him; and in particular one 'which says it is of gardens in Italy though I think it refers to France or England, which he did when I sent him to see the gardens there'.[19] In his instructions one phrase recurred: the plants must be like those 'in Flanders'.[20] In the hands of the Dutch and Italian specialists whom he attracted to Spain, and notably under the expert guidance of Juan Bautista, Philip's palace gardens became a superb example of Italian Mannerism.[21] Readily accessible from the capital, they offered a haven of peace to which he could escape from his bureaucratic duties. His love of nature also turned him into one of the first ecologist rulers in European history. A constant traveller through the countryside of central Castile, he noticed and was concerned by the condition of the forests. 'One thing I would like to see done,' he stated to a minister in 1582, 'is about the conservation of the forests . . . I fear that those who come after us will have much to complain of if we leave them depleted, and please God we do not see it in our time.'[22] Above all, the country represented for him the pleasures of hunting, his principal and lifelong relaxation. All his residences were developed with hunting in mind.

Philip's palace programme was sketched out by 1567, and no new projects were added to it. The impact of his new ideas could be seen in the palace of El Pardo, which he himself had done much to rebuild in the previous decade. Now in 1559 he ordered his architect to remove the entire roofing and have it covered in the Flemish style. For technical reasons nothing could be done until 1562, when the king repeated his decision to re-roof it 'in the Flanders style'.[23] Experts ('Flemish carpenters') were brought in from the Netherlands to do it. The rooms of the palace had recently been decorated in the traditional Castilian style. Philip now ordered the entire interior to be redecorated in the Italian manner. Finally, the extensive woods and gardens were put under the direction of a Fleming ('the Dutchman'). The evocative drawing that Jean Lhermite made of El Pardo at the end of Philip's reign shows to perfection the balance between countryside and palace which the king desired. One can also, in the drawing, just make out the form of the splendid building, a typical example of the marriage between Castilian architecture, Flemish influence and Italian art.

The secretary of works, Pedro de Hoyo, was kept busy with the extensive paperwork. Philip followed every detail with loving care. In one of his reports in May 1562 Hoyo listed prices. 'I did not think it was so much,' Philip scribbled in the margin. Hoyo: 'They tell me the orange trees in the Pardo are in splendid condition.' Philip: 'I am glad to hear it.' Hoyo: 'And that the flowers that are sown in double rows have begun to come out.' Philip: 'Tell them to take care when watering.' Hoyo: 'Men need to be hired to weed the slopes.' Philip: 'This seems fine. But they need to be trustworthy men who will not steal the birds' nests or the eggs.' Shortly after – this was in Madrid — Philip sent Hoyo a note: 'Send me by dinner tonight the lists of plants so I can check them against what has come from Flanders.'[24]

After El Pardo, the building to which Philip dedicated most enthusiasm on his return from Flanders was Valsaín, frequently referred to simply as 'the Wood (*el Bosque*)', in the woods near Segovia. Originally a residence of the fifteenth century, it was modified on the prince's orders in the late 1540s. In the 1550s further works were undertaken to turn it into a small palace. After he returned from the north, Philip paid special attention to the gardens and fountains.[25] He drew his own sketches, with comments. 'The paths have to be broad like what you see here . . . and the path in the middle has to be as wide as shown here,' he ordered in 1562.[26] When the

French ambassador Saint-Sulpice presented his credentials to Philip that year, the king chose Valsaín for the audience. He quickly got the formalities out of the way, and chose to dilate to Saint-Sulpice instead on the pleasures of the site. The Flemish engineer Jacques Holbecq was in charge of the water and fountains. The gardener was commissioned to import plants and seeds from Italy and Flanders. In May, excited by the glorious colour of the flowers in bloom, he wrote to Philip that 'they have never looked so beautiful as now. Your Majesty must come at once to dinner here.'[27] The final touches were put to the interior of the palace in the 1570s.

Aranjuez was the site which, after the Escorial, most benefited from the services of Juan Bautista. With Philip's encouragement, the architect and the master of works Juan de Castro laid the basis for a superb residence. One of the king's pet schemes, which he pursued throughout his reign, was to make the river Tajo navigable. At Aranjuez Juan Bautista undertook a prolonged effort of engineering which succeeded in improving transport on part of the river.[28] Water for irrigation and watering was an urgent need on this site. Thanks to Juan Bautista, it became possible to transform the entire area of Aranjuez, with a perimeter of nearly twenty-five miles, into a huge garden.

Jean Lhermite's contemporary sketch of the site offers an impressive perspective. Five thousand trees were imported from Flanders. Fruit trees were introduced from France.[29] Exotic plants came from the Indies and from all over the peninsula. Dutch gardeners were put in charge of the landscaping. Philip lovingly planned and modified every detail of the gardens. He was, to a large extent, their architect.[30] 'What needs to be planted,' runs a memorandum by him on Aranjuez, 'is what is listed here, and I would like most of it done this winter.'[31] Mulberries were to be planted in order to cultivate silkworms, 'not for production but as a pastime for the queen'. It was specially important to 'finish the big lake because if it isn't finished this summer there will be nowhere to put the fish this winter'. Covered with woods, parks and gardens, in which an immense variety of trees, plants, fruits and, above all, flowers flourished, Aranjuez was a source of wonder to visitors and of unremitting pleasure to the monarch. He fled there to escape from his papers and to fish in the lakes.

These major residences were situated on the outer edges of the area surrounding Madrid. Philip also arranged for the construction of smaller houses which served as stops on the way, or simply as hunting-lodges. They included the sites at Fuenfría, La Fresneda, Galapagar, El Monesterio and Torrelodones. More substantial houses, veritable palaces in themselves, were built at Vaciamadrid and Aceca. Together, the palaces and lodges formed an area of royal residences without equal in Europe.

The palace or Alcázar at Toledo was not forgotten. The city had been the medieval capital of Castile, and in the 1540s Charles V and Philip had

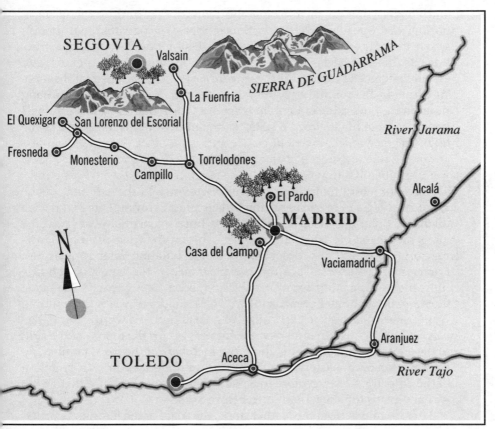

e Residences of Philip II

spent money on restoring the Alcázar. Considerable extra work was done until 1560 in preparing the building for the arrival of the king and his French queen. But the decision to change the capital, and even more the decisive change in Philip's architectural tastes, affected the Alcázar, which was thereafter neglected.

The money and effort devoted to the construction programme was impressive. Thousands of workmen were employed for decades and immense quantities of materials were transported into and across the peninsula. Twelve thousand pines, for example, were purchased from the city of Cuenca for use by the carpenters at San Lorenzo; fleets of carts trundled from the port of Cartagena to the site at Aranjuez with tons of marble imported from Italy; shiploads of nails came from Antwerp.[32]

The king's personal interest in his architectural programme was absolute. His role has frequently been reduced to the level of the trivial and the dilettante. The reality was different. Since the 1540s he had taken a serious and creative interest in restoring the palaces. His direct experience in northern Europe filled his head with new ideas. His personal contribution was not simply as paymaster: he sent rough sketches and specific instructions to his architects. Broad schematisation and minute detail were equally interesting to him, for these were *his* palaces and in great measure *his* ideas. In the middle of a busy session with his papers the building programme would break in on his thoughts. 'Although I have a hundred papers in front of me,' runs a note, 'I thought I would remind you of the following . . .'[33]

*

The major cultural enterprise of Philip's reign was the building of the monastery of San Lorenzo near the village of El Escorial. There were two distinct motives for its foundation. The king intended to celebrate the victory over the French at St Quentin, won on the feast-day of St Lawrence, 10 August. Early descriptions of the building refer to it as San Lorenzo de la Victoria,[34] but the friars persuaded the king that the title 'Royal' would be more appropriate than the warlike 'Victory'. The name therefore became San Lorenzo el Real. The second motive for the building was the need, strongly felt by Philip, to give his father a worthy tomb. The role of the friars was to offer permanent prayers for the repose of the soul of the emperor and, with him, the other members of the royal family. The combination of monastery and tomb was, in some measure, an imitation of the emperor's resting-place in Yuste.[35] There is no evidence that Philip had any plans for such a building before 1558.

After his return from the Netherlands, the friars of the Jeronimite order, his favourite religious order, helped him choose the site of the proposed foundation. They sought a healthy place, away from towns but close to the royal palaces, with good air and water. After three years of searching, the decision (in November 1561) was made in favour of El Escorial. That July, Juan Bautista was named as architect of the project.

The Escorial was in great measure Philip's creation, a projection of his ideas. In the months of consultation in 1561 between Juan Bautista, Pedro de Hoyo and the Jeronimite friars, the king imposed his wishes at every stage. 'If I am not mistaken,' Hoyo observed, 'Your Majesty is quite right to want to do more for San Lorenzo than any other site. Because apart from the service of God one is also dealing with a question of prestige (*reputación*).'[36] The king was determined to create something durable. Because of this in 1562–3 he rejected key features of Juan Bautista's plan, and accepted suggestions by other architects. Construction work began early in 1562 and a foundation stone was formally laid on 20 August 1563. Juan Bautista died in 1567. The work was continued by his disciple Juan de Herrera. Bautista's outline for the building had meanwhile been subjected to the severe (and usually justified) criticisms of the friars, other architects, and the king himself. The master-plan underwent major changes, the most important of which was the decision, in 1564, to construct a further storey in order to house more religious. Through his builders and architects, the king managed to give expression to his concept of the Escorial. The building, though planned in part as a royal residence, was to be pre-eminently religious. It is unlikely that occult ideas played any conscious part in the plans,[37] or that the king had any intention of re-creating the ancient temple of Solomon.[38]

In the peak building years 1562 and 1563 Philip alternated his political and family duties with visits to all the sites where work was going on. His works secretary Pedro de Hoyo had to handle memos, notes and letters from the king. 'I shall go tomorrow to sleep in Aranjuez,' went a typical note in May 1562; 'go there and make Juan Bautista go there tomorrow with the sketches of the monastery'. Philip's attention to detail was unrelenting.

He was no dilettante. Nor did he demand the impossible. He spent long hours discussing plans with his architects, trying to adjust what he wished to what was feasible. There were regular site meetings. 'The weather is so good,' he scribbled to Hoyo on a fine summer's day in 1565, 'that we must not waste it, and so I want to go this afternoon to El Pardo and tomorrow to El Escorial . . . and would like you also to arrive there tomorrow.' His instructions were based on informed discussions with his architects.

His relationship with Juan Bautista was close and friendly, but he was careful not to offend as the architect was of touchy disposition. 'I don't know if he was taken aback by what he was told to do at El Monesterio,' he confessed to Hoyo in 1563, 'I mean with the building.'[39] Seen in perspective, his demands on the architect seem inordinate. The work may well have contributed to Juan Bautista's early death.

The next major influence on the style of the Escorial was Juan de Herrera, who followed Juan Bautista as principal architect. Work picked up rapidly under him. By 1567 enough of it had been completed to allow the monks, the king with some of his court, and part of the stables, to take up residence. There was also a small church, with kitchens and other necessary services.

The next important stage in construction was the building of the basilica, the central feature of the whole edifice, commenced in 1574. The basilica was to be not merely an imposing church, but the resting-place for bodies of the royal family. Its planning and construction was to prove the most problematic aspect of all. Subsequently, other key features of the structure took shape, among them the library, which was completed in 1583.

The king's permanent apartments were not ready until 1585. Before then, the royal family occupied temporary quarters in the south wing. The apartments, when completed, served not only as a residence but also as a court, with public audience halls. This public role never overwhelmed the private character of the palace as a place for retreat and prayer.[40] The private aspect was also foremost in the extensive gardens, no mere background but living space in which the king delighted to walk after the heat of the day.

San Lorenzo was the apple of Philip's eye. If visitors chanced on him in Madrid rather than in San Lorenzo, he packed them off there immediately. Among such visitors were the four young Japanese nobles who came in November 1584 with their Jesuit guides and expressed their admiration for 'a thing more magnificent than any we have seen till now or imagined seeing'.[41]

*

The considerable investment made by the king in art seems to have had a limited impact on Castilian culture. Philip's efforts stand out for their almost solitary splendour. He had enjoyed the close collaboration of Arias Montano and a handful of other intellectuals, but most clergy and nobles seem not to have shared his tastes. A few, such as the duke of Alba or the duke of Villahermosa (who returned to Spain with Philip in 1559 from Brussels), brought with them artworks and tapestries, but the majority remained content with peninsular culture. Antonio Pérez was one of the few advisers who shared in his master's pro-European perspectives. Without the active and intelligent support of an imaginative aristocracy, the king was reduced to producing for himself alone. He tended to become a collector, when he would have preferred to be known as a Maecenas.

Expanding on the material already to be found in the palaces, Philip from the 1560s built up collections in every known branch of the arts. At the Escorial, the centrepiece was the library, housed in a special wing. Its nucleus was the king's own gift, in 1565–75, of 4,000 volumes. He persuaded various prelates and nobles to bequeath their books to the collection, and sent agents throughout western Europe in search of rare editions. In addition to books the collection eventually included precious Latin, Greek and Arab manuscripts. From an early date it also had a special collection of books confiscated by the Inquisition. These could be consulted only by special permission.

The library, as conceived by the king, was meant to have readers and not be a mere deposit. Arias Montano, its first librarian, left his stamp of universal learning on the growing collection. The king explained his project as 'one of the outstanding memorials that I could leave behind for the benefit of all men of letters who might wish to come and study'.[42] But the library also came in for some criticism. Critics applauded the idea but thought it was too far from anywhere, and therefore impossible to consult. They questioned the intellectual capacity of the monks entrusted with the books. As the precious volumes piled up, even the secretary in charge, Gracián, had to admit that 'the whole thing is a worse confusion than the classical Chaos of Hesiod'.[43]

Philip's ambition to do great things in the world of books was continually frustrated by the backward state of both printing and learning in the peninsula. Authors who wished to have their books well printed were as a rule driven to look for publishers abroad. The king himself had to have books printed in Flanders or Italy. There was considerable opposition from within the Spanish Church when Philip decided in the 1560s that the new mass-books sanctioned by the council of Trent could be adequately printed only in Antwerp, by the firm of Plantin. In the same way he decided that the new Royal Bible, whose preparation he entrusted to Arias Montano, could be produced only in Antwerp.

Of other items housed in the Escorial, the most striking was the collection of relics. Philip's search for them was methodical. A typical mission was that entrusted to his annalist Ambrosio de Morales in 1572, to look for relics (and, in passing, rare books) in the north-eastern provinces of Spain. Morales came back with the sensible advice that the king should not, on the whole, take away relics from their sites since 'it would be unjust and cause dissatisfaction and possibly even disturbance'.[44] Philip had long been fascinated by relics, particularly by those he saw in Cologne in 1550. Thereafter he always considered Germany the ideal place to look for them. He brought back from Augsburg relics which the cardinal of that city gave him. At the end of his life, in 1597, he was still financing searches in Germany. The collecting went on until his dying day: in April 1598 four large boxes arrived from Cologne.[45] His final collection amounted to over 7,000 items, among them ten whole bodies, 144 heads, 306 arms and legs, thousands of bones of various parts of holy bodies, as well as hairs of Christ and the Virgin, and fragments of the True Cross and the Crown of Thorns. Relics were usually encased in a rich setting, normally silver, so the collection for this reason did not have the ghoulish aspect a listing of its contents might suggest.

Philip's total faith in relics sustained him in his last days, and relics are given an important mention in his testament. He was much more sceptical about the occult,[46] although his collection of books on magic and the occult was substantial; through the years he continued to add to it. In common with his contemporaries, he treated the unknown with respect. He made use of several astrological advisers (such as the Neapolitan Gesio); was keen to know what comets, eclipses and other unusual phenomena might signify; and consulted horoscopes. When he was in London he had his horoscope drawn up by John Dee, the well-known English magus. But when informed that the Romans had paid attention to the significance of comets, he retorted that 'the Romans were not Christians'.

In 1579 he scolded himself for not ordering the archbishop of Toledo to discipline astrologer-priests. 'I am shocked that they believe in these things, and they certainly do wrong, besides it being a mortal sin'.[47] In matters of magic, as in matters of politics, he collected information without necessarily committing himself. He laid great stress, for example, on searching for the works of the medieval Mallorcan occult philosopher Ramon Llull, for whose doctrines many Spaniards, among them Juan de Herrera, had long shared an admiration. From at least 1577 the king began collecting Llull's works for his library in the Escorial. Translations of the two principal works were made, 'in accordance with Your Majesty's wish [noted the translator] to facilitate the teaching of all sciences'. Llull, for Philip, was an important example of the informal and exotic aspects of knowledge.

He took the same attitude towards all experimental sciences, notably alchemy, and kept an open mind about several attempts which were made in the 1570s, with his approval, to transmute base metals into gold. 'Although I don't believe in these things,' he commented on one experiment, 'I am not so doubting about this one.'[48] The repeated failure of the experiments strengthened his scepticism. When in 1574 Juan de Zúñiga in Rome offered to send him an alchemist, Philip commented that the matter could be 'a hoax like all the other results of this science'.[49] He was more tolerant of other aspects of experimental science, particularly those connected with medicine. His large collection of animal horns, mainly rhinoceros but also including six 'unicorn' horns,[50] may have been connected with their alleged medicinal value. His curiosity for scientific instruments gave rise to the rich collection which he transferred to the library of the Escorial in 1597.

Philip never developed along the lines intended by his tutors, as a humanist and scholar. But he had an insatiable curiosity about everything. He wanted, quite simply, to know. Those who spoke with him were always impressed by his interest in all aspects of art, science and culture. The age in which he lived favoured the spirit of enquiry; not only in traditional branches of learning but also in the sciences and pseudosciences, new frontiers were being explored. Within the king's own generation, the New World had been the greatest stimulus to the imagination. As Spain came into contact with America and with the lands beyond the Mediterranean, the exotic began to form part of everyday reality. From America the bean, the tomato, and later maize, entered peninsular diet; tobacco took its first fatal hold on addicts.[51] As king of a universal empire, Philip was in a unique position to obtain information and specimens. He became, inevitably, a collector *par excellence*.

Collecting was more than a personal hobby. It was also an attempt to give dignity to the monarchy, by furnishing his palaces. He had clear preferences in taste. Sculpture, for example, played only a small part in his interests, even though he managed to obtain the services of excellent sculptors such as Leone and Pompeio Leoni.[52] His partiality was for books and, above all, painting.

He entrusted Arias Montano with (among other things) the collection of Arabic books. The Escorial ended up with one of the finest western collections of works in Arabic. The language was dying in Spain: among a section of the Moriscos it was largely a spoken rather than written tongue, while among the Christians, 'it is no longer understood or used among scholars', according to Montano.[53] For the king his books still had some use. In 1573 he summoned the Morisco scholar and physician Alonso del Castillo to help catalogue the Escorial collection, and let him develop medicines based on the Arab sources.[54] In the subsequent generation, however, the social position of Moriscos in Castile worsened, and Morisco medicine fell into disrepute.

The king's interest in medicine and medicinal plants was well known.[55] From 1557 he encouraged the import and cultivation of ginger and other spices of possible medicinal value. From 1564 a Fleming was 'royal distiller of essences' at the herbarium in Aranjuez. Royal pharmacies were set up in Madrid and San Lorenzo. The most ambitious of all the king's collection schemes was his commission in 1570 to the royal physician Francisco Hernández to go to the New World for information and specimens of the plant life there. Hernández's expedition, which lasted five years, constituted the greatest scientific enterprise of the reign. When he returned, laden with drawings, seeds and live plants, there was no money to publish all his findings and the material was stored in the Escorial.

*

Philip II was Europe's leading patron of artists.[56] His tastes, though nurtured in a Castilian background, were shaped and matured by extensive travelling. Observers of the time, and his own surviving papers, testify that his interest in art was positive, personal and discriminating. At one time he himself had taken up painting.[57] Artists were not, for him, mere artisans. He had a profound but critical respect for them. He wrote to them directly, argued with them personally, and bullied them mercilessly. He cast his eye all over Europe in search of the best.

His first and most enduring enthusiasm was for the work of Titian. In Italy, in Augsburg and from Brussels, he commissioned several paintings. Some of the most famous portraits of Charles V and Philip were done at this time. The most significant canvases of the early period were the series known as 'Poésies', based on themes of classical mythology. The first of them, the intriguing *Danae*, was delivered to Philip in 1554, shortly before his departure for England. The last, the *Diana and Actaeon* and the *Diana and Callisto*, were received after his return to Spain in 1559. The sensuality of Titian's figures, the emphasis on the female nude, the preference for mythological themes, all appealed to a king who at this stage was capti-vated by the world of humanism and chivalry.[58] There was no mystery about his preferences. A taste for sensuality was not exclusive to Philip; it was shared by other European courts as well. Titian continued painting for the king well after this. From about 1560, however, there was a change of mood. All further commissions were for exclusively religious subjects. Since we know that the king had not changed in outlook or character, the reason must be sought in the buildings for which the new paintings were intended. The earlier works were meant for the private leisure of the king, in his country houses at El Pardo and Valsaín. Many of the later works were public pieces. Titian's *Last Supper* (1564), for instance, was meant for the Escorial. Meanwhile, Philip had immeasurably enriched his collection of Titians with the paintings he inherited from his father and from Mary of Hungary. The Italian master remained always one of Philip's favourite artists.

Among the accomplished painters who attracted the king's favour was Antonis Mor. The Brussels-based artist had done a portrait of the prince in 1549. When he returned to the Netherlands six years later Philip adopted him as court painter and invited him to Spain. Mor made three visits. No fewer than fifteen of his works came to hang in El Pardo, and the artist ranked as high as Titian in the king's favour.[59] In the same decade Philip also invited to his court the Italian sculptor Pompeio Leoni and his son Leone. The latter's son Pompeio became in the 1580s official court sculptor of the king. The priority given to Flemish and Italian art in Philip's court can be seen by the roll-call of artists who visited Spain. They included Gianbattista Bergamasco, Anton van Wyngaerde, Luca Cambiaso and Federigo Zuccaro. All the Italian artists were brought in to decorate the Escorial. Among the last of them was Pellegrino Tibaldi, who laboured at the Escorial between 1588 and 1594.

In some matters the king had a decided preference for things Flemish. His collection of paintings by Bosch is an example. He owned at least one work by Bosch in 1564, adding more in subsequent years. Most of the Boschs were hung in the Escorial, though several were to be found in the Pardo, along with works by Mor and Titian.[60] The Flemish artist's primi-tive style, and his obvious moralising, seem to have been the aspects which appealed to the king. The librarian and historian of the Escorial, José de Sigüenza, defended the king's taste for Bosch. The artist, he said, presented 'a satire in paint on the sins of men'.[61] Philip was not unique in his appreciation of this artist. Bosch had a certain popularity in Spain and his works were copied by Spaniards.[62] But for other types of work, such as frescos, the king was more inclined to use Italians.[63]

Peninsular artists were not absent from this gallery. From the 1550s the Valencian painter Alonso Sánchez Coello, who had studied with Mor in Brussels, began to produce portraits of members of the royal family.[64]

Philip set aside special apartments for him and his family in the Alcázar, and loved to slip in unannounced to see the painter at work. Alonso produced a large number of accomplished canvases, and found the time to father eleven children. Royal favour was also extended to Coello's pupil Juan Pantoja de la Cruz. Another favourite of Philip's among the Spanish painters was Juan Fernández de Navarrete, 'the dumb (*el Mudo*)'.

An obvious absentee from the list of artists the king patronised was El Greco. Shortly after his return from Portugal in 1583 Philip had to decide on the future of a large canvas which El Greco delivered to the Escorial in November 1582. Its theme was *The Martyrdom of St Maurice*. According to a friar who was present, the king rejected the painting (on which the artist had been working for two years) because of its exaggerated emphasis on the figures in the foreground.[65] The rejection excluded El Greco thereafter from the ambit of royal patronage.

By the sheer volume of their output, the artists contributed enormously to the grandeur and standing of the king. Philip established a completely new norm for collectors, thanks to the resources at his disposal and the variety of realms over which he reigned. At the time of his death there were about 1,150 major paintings in the Escorial, and 300 in the Alcázar of Madrid.[66]

Philip's close collaboration with Juan de Herrera is perhaps the clearest illustration of the contact between patron and artist. In the 1560s Herrera was doing minor work for the crown. From 1572 he was put in charge of the development of the Escorial, and assigned tasks on other sites. Seven years later, the king appointed him his royal architect. For over thirty years he worked closely as Philip's servant, obediently carrying out instructions but also imposing his stamp on the architecture of Spain. He died in 1597, a few months before his king.

Herrera, under the king's direction, gave a unique character to the royal building programme.[67] In the Alcázar of Toledo, which he modified, he offered a structure of simplicity but also of authority and power. When the king was in Lisbon, he planned and constructed the new royal palace overlooking the harbour. He extended his style to non-royal buildings, such as the merchants' exchange, the Lonja, in Seville. But it was the Escorial which most typified his style and his relationship with Philip.

Thanks to their partnership, architecture in Spain seemed to become an integral aspect of royal policy. Philip was no theorist, and nursed no dreams of grandeur. Simplicity and frugality were among his most basic principles.[68] But he also wished to give Spain the quality that other monarchies already possessed. When he was in Brussels he sent his architect Gaspar de Vega to France to spy out the new buildings of the Louvre and Fontainebleau.[69] It was in public building that the policy aspect of the king's preferences could be most clearly seen. In 1573 he issued to the authorities in America a set of *Ordinances* which they were to follow in

planning new cities. The directive shows his wish for order and simplicity: cities must be practical and beautiful, not mere expressions of
power.[70] He attempted to transform the directive into reality for his own
capital, Madrid, but was frustrated above all by lack of money.

*

The 'court' in Madrid had several functions.[71] At the centre was the king,
served by his household. There were satellite households, of the queen,
the Infantas, and other immediate members of the royal family. Their
combined personnel, adding on the staff in the stables and the guards,
amounted to a small army. The theatre of their activities was the enlarged
and reformed Alcázar. The king as chief actor brought three other spheres
of activity into this scenario: the functioning of government, the manage-
ment of diplomacy and ritual, and the direction of public entertainment.
Fixing the king's residence in Madrid gave for the first time in Spain's
history a permanent location for all these functions. But Philip never
intended to be tied down to this centralisation of the court.

Since the adoption of Burgundian ceremonial in 1548 the size of the
royal household had grown enormously. The main component was the
king's household, divided into five main units: household, kitchen,
chapel, stables and cellar. Each unit was headed by a nobleman in charge
of its administration. The household guard formed an additional unit.
Other immediate members of the royal family had smaller households, all
financed by the king. The most drastic innovation of these years was the
large and expensive retinue which Elizabeth Valois brought and insisted
on maintaining, although many of the servants were sent home a few
weeks later. The Venetian ambassador felt that it was because 'the Frenchmen were very ill-dressed, dirty, careless and disrespectful'.[72] Elizabeth's
demands inflated the queen's household into an entity almost as large as
that of the king.

Burgundian ceremonial at court was exacting in theory, but less so in
practice. It was modified by the king's own impatience with etiquette and
his preference for a simpler life. The king's regular movement between his
palaces also made it impractical to move all the personnel every time. The
court of Philip consequently had little of the rigidity and formality which
scholars have identified with later kings of Spain.[73]

Castilians continued to express a dislike of the new Burgundian ceremonial. Many objected to the expense. The ceremonial also seemed to
distance the king from his subjects. The Cortes of Valladolid in 1558 asked
the king to change it for 'the usages and customs of Castile', made a
similar request in 1580, and in 1593 was still persistently demanding that
the crown abolish these usages which 'are foreign, not ours'.[74] But Philip
was no devotee of formality. Significant moves, in accord with the king's
own preferences, were made towards a simpler public life-style. The

Cortes of Madrid in 1562 petitioned the crown over nobles who dressed extravagantly and banqueted to excess. Their meals were described as 'damaging to the body, a cause of illnesses, and prejudicial to their souls'. One consequence was the important sumptuary law, issued at Monzón in October 1563, controlling the public dress of both men and women.[75]

The king's court in his last dozen years suffered from a lack of social gaiety, due in part to the king's poor health, in part to his absences and travels. But for the first twenty-five years of the reign there was no lack of vitality. There is no evidence for the totally mythical picture, still current, of a royal recluse.[76] Three factors explain the vigorous life of the royal circle. Most nobles took the court seriously; the queens contributed enormously to social life; and the king himself had an active interest in music and entertainment. It is simply untrue to imagine that the court was lugubrious.[77]

No European court could exist without a client nobility. The Spanish nobles continued to have immense military and economic resources, but these were threatened by rising costs and a high death-rate among heirs. The court offered hope, because it presented the chance of employment and influence, as well as contacts which could lead to marriage. For those who liked such things, there was also the life-style, a welcome relief after the monotony of the provinces. As Madrid grew, more and more nobles gravitated there. 'It is terrible,' the king commented, 'that they all want to leave their estates and become residents of the court.'[78] A courtly society came into existence, with its own special rules and, later, its own literature. The court of the king, like the courts of the great nobility, was a theatre not only of ritual but also of entertainment, leisure and diversion.[79] But Philip had no delusions of grandeur. He never insisted on creating, as Louis XIV did later in France, a scenario in which he was the centre of all attention. He allowed his great nobles to do their own thing. The duke of Infantado, for example, presided over his own little court in Guadalajara, and seldom came to Madrid.[80] Philip tolerated this, and instead made courtesy visits to the duke whenever he passed through Guadalajara.

The contribution of the queens to court life was fundamental. Elizabeth of Valois from the beginning tried to reproduce the gaiety (and, in some measure, the decadence) of the Renaissance court she had left behind. She enjoyed parties, masked balls, buffoonery, spectacles, outings to her palaces, and picnics. Ecclesiastical Toledo did not quite offer the environment for all this, and she took a dislike to the city. In jousts, she played the part of liege lady to the three young court princes: Don Carlos, Don Juan of Austria, and the prince of Parma. It gave them a romantic scenario which in turn influenced their chivalric ideals. Elizabeth also contributed to the cultural life of court by her love of music, plays and art: she extended her personal patronage to Sánchez Coello and to the Italian Sofonisba. Anna's role was more subdued and coincided more closely with that of Philip. In the absences of the king's court, the queens had their own social life in Madrid. Anna loved comedies. In February 1571, she 'enjoyed herself in the apartments of the princess [Juana] at a comedy that she ordered to be performed there. At four in the afternoon the Infantas went to join the queen and enjoyed the play as though they were much older.'[81]

The king's sisters also played a crucial role. When the empress María came to reside in Madrid, she contributed powerfully to the prestige of a city which, during Philip's absence in Lisbon, had no king. She set herself up in apartments in the convent of the Descalzas, where she periodically put on musical entertainments.[82] All visiting dignitaries to Madrid were obliged by protocol to make a formal visit to the empress before calling on any other official.

Philip's love of entertainment was profound. The top place in his agenda went to rites of chivalry. In his youth as well as during his years abroad, he had delighted in jousts and tourneys. The *Amadis of Gaul* was one of his favourite books (he later approved it as a set text for his son Philip when the latter began to learn French).[83] Whenever possible, he presided over tournaments at court. Early in February 1566, for example, a small joust on foot was put on in his presence. Those who took part were young nobles, including the archduke Ernst and Don Juan. In the afternoon of Mardi Gras, three weeks later, a more formal tourney was held in the fields just outside Madrid. Eight grandees were the participants. 'They fought first with lances, and then afterwards with swords.' The whole court and many others came to see it and the king and queen watched until nightfall.[84] The king could not always be present at tournaments, which the nobles put on frequently for themselves. His permission, however, was normally required for those held in the capital.

On principal feasts there was always music and dancing and celebration. The king took a close interest in the music of the royal chapels. The Flemish chapel was headed by a number of specially imported composers, of whom the most significant (in residence after 1588) was Philippe Rogier.[85] Ill-health after the 1570s was Philip's only reason for not taking part in festivities. He encouraged, and attended, musical presentations.[86]

By contrast, he had no great fondness for the theatre, though he dutifully sat through performances. On one occasion he admitted to his confessor Chaves that 'I never liked comedies'.[87] It was no doubt his detached attitude to the theatre that freed him from then current prejudices about women on stage. In 1587 he warned his council that if boys were to be employed in the role of women, it did not make sense to ban them using make-up. Why could women not be allowed to act? he asked. Their husbands could chaperone them.[88] His initiative resulted in women being allowed on the stage in Madrid from that year.[89]

It is likely that the king had little time for private reading. Although he had an impressive library, like many book-lovers he had scant opportunity to study the books. Until the 1580s he preferred to spend all his leisure time in the company of his family and the environment of his palaces and gardens. According to the Venetian ambassador in 1563, he was capable of dropping business completely and going off with a small number of people to spend several days 'in extreme tranquillity and rest'.[90] These periods were never spent lazily. If he was not hunting, he was fishing. When the fish-lakes at Aranjuez were eventually stocked, he went there frequently.

A possibly unique aspect of Philip's court, setting it apart from all others, was the frequent *absence* of the king. Other monarchs, such as Elizabeth of England, developed courts which were closely identified with their persons. This did not happen in Spain. Though he respected its formalities, Philip disliked the fripperies and courtesies of protocol. There had been no proper court in the days of Ferdinand and Isabella, and his father had never been around long enough to create one. The adoption of the Burgundian ceremonial, and the choice of a permanent capital, were factors that might have helped powerfully to create a full-blooded court under Philip. In the event, constant movement from residence to residence deprived the royal circle of the continuity which was essential for the development of a Versailles.

Another notable defect in the court of Philip was its cultural level. The Venetian ambassadors sharply criticised it for being ignorant and unlettered.[91] By comparison, Madrid may well have appeared less cosmopolitan than London or Blois or Rome. Many great artists came and went, but there was no continuous cultural atmosphere worthy of the world's most powerful monarch. There were a good number of highly cultured nobles, and culturally distinguished ladies, but if they had salons[92] they held them at the fringes of court life.[93]

The essential feature of the 'court' in Madrid was the royal household. If the king was away, he took most of his household with him. This turned the Alcázar into an empty shell, populated only by its staff, some government officials, and the household of any remaining member of the royal family. Only the presence of other royal persons helped to preserve the vitality of social life. In 1578 an ambassador observed that many nobles who came to Madrid in order to serve the king kept away because of the high costs of staying in a king-less city.[94] This in its turn affected the whole capital. Madrid during Philip's absences tended to turn into a den of bored nobles who, starved of the activity offered by the court's presence, dedicated themselves to gambling, womanising and night revels.[95] By the 1580s the situation had deteriorated to such a point that Philip set up a three-man committee for moral reformation, consisting of cardinal Quiroga of Toledo, the president of Castile (and chief judge of the realm) the count of Barajas, and his own confessor Father Chaves. In November 1586, for example, one of the problems the committee had to deal with was the notorious night-life of the young duke of Feria, who dedicated himself to gaming and low women.[96]

Practical factors, such as the sheer cost of moving around the kingdom, were beginning to distance European rulers from their subjects. Complex ceremonial further helped to isolate the king. Philip was deeply concerned for his people, but had little effective contact with them. He felt that his accessibility on feast-days, which he tried to maintain all his life, was adequate. 'As you know,' he pointed out when urged to pay more attention to popular opinion, 'people talk to me on Sundays and give me petitions.'[97] As often as feasible, he had his lunch 'in public'. But this involved no more than lunching (alone) in one of the large reception rooms of the Alcázar, where members of the court and public might see him.[98] It was a practice he urged his son to follow. He made a rule of being accessible to private petitions while going to or from Sunday mass and deliberately walked slowly, so that people would have a chance to catch up with him.[99] 'On all feast days until now,' a courtier reported in 1583, 'he has gone out, listening to everybody and accepting their petitions.'[100] Though he treated with respect the pieces of paper offered to him on these occasions,[101] they were inevitably handed to officials of the respective councils, and got forgotten in the administrative process. 'When I went to mass today,' he reported in 1575, 'I was given this paper for the council of State, but I did not see who gave it.' It was an anonymous denunciation, but exceptionally he paid attention to it. 'There could be something in what it says, it could be important.'[102]

He did not like crowds. He did not like villagers, who had never seen him, treating him as 'something superhuman', when the truth was that he was a mere human, 'with defects of body and spirit'.[103] During his visit to Andalusia in 1570, he was jostled by thousands of people. He attempted to avoid them. If they were at the front of a building, he went out by the back. On one occasion he refused to go out at all.[104] His opposition to the cult of personality was an extension of his own modesty and austerity. He firmly disallowed any attempts to write his life. He kept his private life totally private. When in 1573 he heard that letters he had written as a child to his old tutor Siliceo were in the possession of people in Toledo, he ordered them to be discreetly ('without fuss') gathered up. 'Even though they are not important,' he reasoned, 'it is not reasonable, out of modesty and respect, that they be passed from hand to hand.'[105]

The ideal ruler for him was Ferdinand the Catholic, who with his queen Isabella had acquired a reputation for being accessible to all. But the fact was that kings, in Spain as elsewhere, were no longer in a position to cultivate the common touch. Their duties inevitably tended to separate them more and more from the public. In any case, personal security had to be assured. Political murder was commonplace in western Europe, and kings were not exempt. An abortive attempt was made on Philip's life in Lisbon in 1581. Thereafter he used greater caution. In 1583 a suspicious Frenchman was followed by officials[106] who feared another assassination plot. He was detained, but 'there is no reason to suspect him'. The murder of Henry III of France some years later, in 1589, horrified opinion in Spain and profoundly worried Philip.

*

The king who had travelled extensively through Europe prior to 1560 may have become in later life unsympathetic to travel. 'Wandering about one's kingdoms for pleasure is neither useful nor becoming,' he is reported (on doubtful authority) to have said. 'The prince should have a fixed base.'[107] In reality, he was never immobile. Like his great forebears the Catholic kings, he remained regularly on the move. His principal area of movement was within the radius marked out by his palaces and Madrid. But he also travelled through much of the peninsula, more than any subsequent member of his dynasty.

His father the emperor became famous for his extensive travels. Philip, by contrast, has always been considered by historians as the exact reverse. A persistent legend presents him after his return to Spain in 1559, as immured in Castile and in the Escorial. The image was one that the Venetian ambassadors, for example, helped to disseminate. The reality was quite otherwise. Philip was glad to return in 1559, but also (as we have seen from the duke of Feria's testimony) deeply missed the Netherlands. He never reconciled himself to being rooted in one spot. His travel record, in fact, was quite as impressive as that of his father. He spent fourteen months in England, and five long years in the Netherlands. Few historians know that his experience of Germany was based on his presence there for one year and three months. His passage through Italy, lasting several weeks, was certainly influential. He had sailed on both the seas of Spain: the Mediterranean and the Atlantic. The best known of his soujourns was the two years and four months that he spent in Portugal. The Portuguese visit has given rise to the impression that Philip neglected his other realms of Spain. It is therefore timely to emphasise that the king, in total, spent more time in the territories of the crown of Aragon – an astonishing three years – than in any part of his monarchy other than the Netherlands.

In the last ten years, when illness kept him bedridden for long periods, he evidently moved little. In the preceding forty years, by contrast, he never stopped. The image of a cloistered king exists only in legend. In the years up to 1571, Philip and his immediate household moved between the several residences in the central area of Castile. There were eleven of them, ranging from fortresses (the Alcázars of Toledo and Madrid) to substantial palaces (Aranjuez, El Pardo) and country houses (Aceca, Valsaín). In 1564, for example, the king's base was the Alcázar in Madrid, but he made regular excursions of two or three days to go hunting at the Pardo, visited the Escorial from time to time to see how the building was coming on, and spent entire weeks in Valsaín and Aranjuez.[108] The summer months of heat tended to be spent, up to 1567, at Valsaín.[109] In this year he made the first changes of routine. He spent March in El Pardo, but Holy Week, Easter and most of August at San Lorenzo.[110] Progress in building work had made space available for the large number of palace officials who had to accompany him.

From 1571 the palace-monastery at San Lorenzo joined the other residences in the permanent ritual of movement.[111] The palaces, hunting-lodges and cottages owned by the crown supplied a network of residences which allowed the royal family to make regular outings to ease the boredom of staying in one place. In May 1572, for instance, Philip informed the queen's chamberlain that his own departure from the Escorial

could be on Monday afternoon for El Pardo, spending Tuesday there, returning on Tuesday to Las Rozas, and on Wednesday morning to El Pardo, then from El Pardo to Galapagar, lunching at Torrelodones. On Thursday [the queen and family] can go to mass, then lunch at La Fresneda, where I will lunch with them, leaving the queen's attendants to go straight to El Escorial where they will dine and sleep that night. This I think will be a good arrangement for the outing.[112]

The somewhat giddy pace was quite usual. Because of the distances involved, and also because he went accompanied either by his family or by his papers, the king normally travelled in his carriage. For short distances, he continued to travel on horseback.[113]

He seldom stayed in San Lorenzo, or any other palace, for more than a short time. For him the Escorial was his perfect office, where he could work peacefully, away from administrators, ministers and petitioners. His librarian testified that 'he completed more business here in one day than in Madrid in four, because of the tranquillity'.[114] The family on these occasions was usually encouraged to stay in some other palace, such as the Alcázar of Madrid. But he did not reserve the Escorial only for work. At Pentecost in 1575, for example, he made a special two-week visit there to celebrate his birthday and to entertain Anna. The evening that the royal party arrived, 20 May, Anna arranged for a group of local shepherds to shear their flocks in the traditional way outside her window. They accompanied their efforts with boisterous and indelicate songs, much to the amusement of the king and queen. The shepherds were plied liberally with wine, which further lowered the tone of the songs but increased the

general hilarity. The day after his birthday, the king and the young archdukes participated in a mounted procession through the cloister. The
following evening, 23 May, Philip acted as guide to his wife, his daughters, the archdukes and a large court following. He took them proudly
through what was going to be his future library: 'he went along chatting
about all the things in the library, showing and explaining them to queen
Anna, so that she saw everything fully and at leisure'.[115] The first delivery
of books had just been made, some 4,000 volumes, from his own
collections.[116]

Despite the separations, at no time in the 1570s was business given
precedence over family matters. He was in constant touch with the queen
and the children. The queen's chamberlain informed him regularly of
every aspect of her household. In the case of Anna, Philip used to write to
her about twice a week during separations, and she did the same. When
their letters crossed, 'it was not necessary to write yesterday [he informed
her chamberlain] since I have seen the queen's reply to mine; and you
may now hand the queen the present letter'.[117] Over and above the letters,
the royal couple would make regular outings (*jornadas*) to see each other,
and in this way would manage to visit the various palaces in turn.

The king could not afford to stop work completely. When the queen
and family came to see him at San Lorenzo on 22 May 1572, he spent most
of his time with them; but in the evening he returned to his papers. It was
a particularly splendid spring that year, and the outings continued regularly through May and June. After a few days in San Lorenzo, with or
without the queen, the king would dash off somewhere else, accompanied by his papers and secretaries. 'I'm off this afternoon,' he wrote from
San Lorenzo in mid-June that year, 'because I have things to do in Madrid;
the queen can leave tomorrow afternoon, but if they are happy here and
she wants to stay longer she may, though I think they will want to go
tomorrow.'[118]

The dutiful balance between work and family was scrupulously
observed by Philip. At no time did he neglect one for the other. Nor did
Anna necessarily come second. Their daytime duties took them in different directions, but when they were together he made sure of seeing her
regularly.[119] Appointments with her were respected. 'Because I have
agreed with the queen to go to the country,' he informed his secretary
during a stifling July, 'I shall not call you at the moment.'[120]

As he travelled between his duties he ruefully commented on things he
was unable to do. Journeying to Madrid in spring 1572, he could not
afford to stop and wander through the countryside. 'I believe that the
woods will be beautiful, and regret the many times that I have passed by
them without having visited one which they say is particularly attractive.
If I ever have the chance I must see it.'[121]

In the hot summers he did not, as is usually believed, lock himself up in

San Lorenzo. The second half of July 1572 he spent in the heat of Madrid, then in early August he moved to the Pardo and from there to San Lorenzo. But in mid-August he was back again in Madrid. The constant movement continued after September, which he spent in San Lorenzo. On 4 October he went off to Madrid. On the fifteenth he went to Aranjuez to spend ten days with his family. On the twenty-fifth he was in the Pardo. Three days later he was back in San Lorenzo. In normal years this pattern of movement was the king's standard routine but by the second half of the reign he preferred to make his Easter retreat at San Lorenzo and tried to spend all the great feast-days there, alternating his stay with visits to other residences. After All Saints', 1 November, he would set off to spend November in El Pardo. At the end of the month he left for Madrid, in order to arrive there by St Andrew's Day, 30 November, when he would celebrate in the company of his knights the founding of the order of the Golden Fleece. The whole Alcázar was usually illuminated and decorated for the brilliant ceremony.[122]

Even when he was tied down in one place, he contrived to go out into the countryside to lunch. After hours and days of paperwork, he yearned to break free, if only for a while, to relax with his family. 'When I finish this,' he wrote after a trying day in San Lorenzo, 'I shall leave here and go to sleep today at La Fresneda and tomorrow at El Pardo, a round route in order to go through some woods. After that I have to leave San Lorenzo on Friday at two, after lunch.'[123] Ambassadors in Madrid interpreted his wish to escape as an urge for solitude. In reality he was simply trying to get away from them.

*

The king's family was not like other families, and his domestic life was accordingly different. Since each principal member of the court had a separate household, their day-to-day existence was normally separate. They very seldom, for example, ate together. The king's meals in Madrid were usually taken alone. Business lunches with his secretaries were common. The timing of supper depended entirely on work. Since childhood he had followed a rule, which he stuck to during his absences abroad in the 1550s, of having supper alone every Friday, Saturday and vigil of a feast.

The princess Juana, always relegated to the background by historians because she abstained from any political role after her short regency in 1554–9, was the effective centre of Philip's family circle. When Philip returned to Spain in 1559, she bought a group of houses in the middle of Madrid and directed the building of a small palace-convent which later received the name of Descalzas Reales. Magnificently decorated and furnished, it became her home and retreat. All her energies were dedicated to helping her brother. Philip in his turn lavished affection on her.[124] She was the inseparable companion of queens Elizabeth and Anna. In 1572 she fell seriously ill, and never recovered. Her early death, in September 1573 at the age of thirty-eight, was a severe blow to the king, who had leaned on her for advice and affection. Philip was at her bedside when she died. Her last request of him was that he advance Cristóbal de Moura in his service. Years later, in a letter to Moura, Philip referred to their common grief during that 'night which you remember very well'.[125] A splendid marble tomb by Pompeio Leoni, similar to others the artist was to make later for the Escorial, marks her resting-place in the church of the Descalzas.

Of Philip's four wives, two profoundly affected his personal and political life: Elizabeth and Anna. They cannot be consigned to the margins of his activity.[126]

Elizabeth was a dark-haired, bright-eyed teenager of immense vivacity and energy, which more than made up for her lack of natural beauty. She brought back to Philip the energy of his youth. He devoted time to her, and even discussed his work with her. It is more doubtful if they had any deep emotional relationship.[127] All the optimistic reports of love emanate from one source only: the French ambassadors, who were anxious to demonstrate to their government that the marriage was a success. Ambassador Saint-Sulpice was under constant pressure from Catherine de' Medici to find out when a birth would be announced. At Monzón in November 1563 he broached the issue by assuring the king of 'the reputation that he has with us of being a good husband'. Philip laughed to hear it. 'He thanked me for my good wishes, and said he would make efforts to keep up the reputation of him that we have in France.'[128]

There were still echoes of past loves. In July 1564 the queen was clearly pregnant. But together with her normal symptoms she began to have serious headaches, nausea and fainting. An incident in August 1564 aggravated these reactions and provoked considerable gossip at court. The king and queen were at a palace window in Madrid with princess Juana, waiting for a big reception to commence. The pregnant queen happened to see Philip's recent mistress, the also pregnant Eufrasia de Guzmán, now the princess of Ascoli,[129] coming into the palace for the reception, dressed to kill. Her expression changed, she started to bleed from the nose, and had to be taken out. 'She later sent a message to the king to say she could not go to the reception, and that she was unwell. So the reception was cancelled, though the palace was already full of guests.'[130] Elizabeth was seriously ill in bed for three weeks. Philip spent all that first night at her bedside. It may have helped to convince her, though in French circles there was a constant suspicion that the king did not love her. By the end of August she had recovered completely. The illness, however, ended the pregnancy.

The king's relations with Elizabeth continued to improve after this crisis. In 1565 Saint-Sulpice observed that Philip showed her 'truly good friendship and perfect goodwill, which makes her as satisfied and happy as she could ever be'. Philip discussed politics with her in the bed-chamber, and talked about his ideas.[131] He never in his life shared intimate secrets with men, nor did he ever have a close understanding with any man in his circle. His links with Ruy Gómez were not based on any personal affection. With Elizabeth it was different. Deprived of his mother when barely in his teens, offered an imperfect love by a foster-mother – Estefania Requesens – he seldom saw, the king found in Elizabeth the opportunity for a degree of affection that no other woman had been able to give him.

The confidence that the king deposited in Elizabeth is clear from the way he put the talks at Bayonne in her hands. Her role there was positive, and delighted the king. Shortly after, she was at Valsaín with Philip. 'Their Majesties go hunting every day,' reported the French ambassador. 'In the evening they walk together through the garden and other cool places of the park, in such a manner that their life is one of happiness and good health.'[132] At the end of 1565 Elizabeth became pregnant again.

The good news made Philip 'more in love every day' (the opinion of the French ambassador)[133] with his wife. From February he tried to spend two hours after dinner each evening with her, and also slept at her side every night.[134] When she was in labour, 'during the night of birth-pains and the birth itself, he never left off grasping one of her hands, comforting her and encouraging her the best that he knew or could'.[135] Isabel Eugenia, born at Valsaín on 15 August, nearly cost Elizabeth her life. She was 'within an inch of death', Fourquevaux reported.[136] Though disappointed that it was not a boy, Philip could not conceal his pleasure and called the French ambassador in to see the baby.

His second child by Elizabeth, Catalina Michaela, was born in October 1567. Though he would again have preferred a son, since he had no male heir other than Don Carlos, the king never ceased to lavish affection on the two girls. This domestic happiness was brusquely shattered by tragedy. A few weeks after the birth of Catalina, Elizabeth became preg-nant again. She also became continuously ill. She died, as we have seen, in October 1568.

Perpetual pregnancy was, unfortunately, the duty of young ladies in high positions. The queen must produce a male heir. Virtually annual pregnancy was the single most important cause of death among ladies of high degree. The social gaiety of court life was tempered by the sober reality of having to move about with a constantly large stomach, and endure regular but dangerous childbirth.

The deaths of Elizabeth and Don Carlos involved the dissolution of their respective households. This usually meant that employees were released, and personal property (clothes, paintings, jewellery) sold. It was the moment to make savings, for both the queen and the prince had been big spenders.

Philip chose in the case of Elizabeth to make a radical change that reveals much about his preferences. He had loved Elizabeth generously. But he had been too generous. For eight years he surrendered to her every whim. In retrospect, he recognised that she was spoilt and capricious, self-willed and with expensive tastes. She had brought an enormous retinue of French ladies, many of whom she succeeded in retaining. She imposed her demands on the king, and influenced his decision to leave Toledo for Madrid. She purchased extravagantly and her expenditure on parties and outings was impressive. She commissioned endless amounts of silver and jewellery from court artists. In 1560 she gave to the wife of the French ambassador 'a necklace of gold with four rubies and four diamonds'.[137] Her household was plunged deeply into debt, to the despair of her chamberlain, Juan Manrique de Lara, a cultured noble who was chosen for the job in part because he spoke French. Nobody, he told the king, wanted to lend money to her because of her debts.[138] She gave sumptuous receptions, and commissioned paintings lavishly. It was said of her that she never wore the same dress twice.[139] An inventory of her jewels made after her death leaves no doubt about the magnificence of her spending.[140] She was no innocent in politics, and used her influence with Philip on several occasions. The king seems not to have showed any impatience, and tolerated her every whim.

A memorandum of Elizabeth's trip to Bayonne in 1565 shows that she spent 80,000 ducats when the king had budgeted only 15,000. In his marginal comments on the report by the aggrieved chamberlain, Philip was left trying to figure out how to cover the costs. The itemised list was appalling. 'For the many expenses in her chamber and in gifts of silks, textiles, cloth of gold, gold and silver', she had spent 20,000 ducats a year in the last few years. 'For outings each year to the woods of Aranjuez and Segovia, with carriages and costs', over 8,000 a year. 'For purchases during three years [1562–5], up to 10,000 ducats in jewels, stones and pearls.' Her gifts of jewels to visiting dignitaries was 'a great quantity', and could not be estimated. For Bayonne she had bought 12,000 ducats' worth of jewels and clothes and in Bayonne had given away gifts of jewellery to the value of 20,000 ducats. During the journey she had spent 12,000 ducats just on banquets.[141]

When in 1570 the new queen's chamberlain, the marquis of Ladrada, was preparing for the arrival of Anna, Philip left him in no doubt that everything must change. The household must revert to the practice of the time of his mother, the empress Isabel. It is one of the moments that his correspondence lets us glimpse his veneration for her. 'It is not acceptable,' he told Ladrada, 'to continue the household practice of the late queen; everything must be done as it was in the time of my mother.' That was over thirty years ago, but 'I believe that the duke of Alba and Ruy Gómez will be able to inform you about it; what used to be done then must be done now'.[142] During the months following his marriage to Anna, he continued to sweep away the customs and changes brought in by Elizabeth. The standard now was to be the peninsular usage of his mother. Asked whether queen Anna should observe the practice of making an offering in church, he replied: 'I cannot recall ever seeing my mother making the offering. I wouldn't do it.' On a point of household procedure, he noted: 'It's what I remember being done in the time of my mother.' On a matter of the queen distributing gifts to all her household at Christmas, he ruled that 'in my mother's time gifts were given, but only to chaplains and cantors; giving more in this past period was, I think, an irregularity, like many other matters'.[143] The last phrase was a cut at the late queen's way of doing things. He remained adamant about the need to run the royal family in the way that his mother had done. The drawback was that he now had only a hazy recall: 'I cannot remember what used to be done in the time of my mother'.[144]

Philip's marriage to Anna brought him a tranquillity that he had never experienced.[145] She was the only one of his wives with whom he could converse in his own tongue, since she was bilingual in Spanish and German. They formed a perfect household. She was delighted to have her brothers Albert and Wenzel around her. Philip treated them in every way as sons. With them and his two daughters for company, he had a complete family circle. 'He loves his wife deeply,' reported a diplomat in 1577, 'and is seldom or never without her.'[146] The queen, happy in an environment she knew, reciprocated the king's affections. Poignant testimony came from Dr Vallés. He related how when the king fell seriously ill in Badajoz, during the Portuguese campaign, Anna expressed her wish to die if necessary in his stead, 'for the great love she bore to His Majesty'.[147] When the king was not with Anna, she was accompanied and entertained by the princess Juana.

When Anna was expecting in 1571, Philip was the soul of concern. In June he observed, from San Lorenzo, that 'the fact is that the queen's rooms [in the Alcázar in Madrid] are hot, at least at night, and so it would be better for her to pass to my chamber for sleeping since it is cooler at night.' 'If the queen wants to leave the palace,' he noted in July, 'remind her to go in a chair so that she doesn't have another fall', apparently a reference to a previous mishap. Near the end of her pregnancy, 'let me know a day ahead if she happens to feel pains, since I don't want to miss the birth'.[148] Through all the days of separation he continued to write twice a week to the queen. She gave birth to Fernando two hours before dawn on 4 December. Philip spent six hours at her bedside.[149] In his years with Anna he continued to suffer bouts of bad health and deep political anxiety, but never lacked personal tranquillity. Twenty years before, in Brussels, the Venetian ambassador had described him as melancholic. In the 1570s he had put melancholy behind him. 'Try,' he urged Mateo Vázquez during one of the secretary's fits of depression, 'to get rid of melancholy, it is very bad for you.'[150]

He was middle-aged before he began to find happiness in marriage, and the same happened with his sentiments as a father. Don Carlos deprived him of the chance to extend his love to his own. He grasped eagerly at the hope of having other sons. He persuaded his sister María, married to the emperor Maximilian II, to allow two of her children to visit him. He was delighted to receive into his household the young archdukes Rudolf and Ernst in 1564. He became fond of them, continued their education, gave them pride of place on his progress through Andalusia in 1570, and was reluctant to let them return home. The stay confirmed both princes in their preference for things Spanish. There is also every reason to speculate that Rudolf's later passion for art and the occult was born during his eight formative years amid the rich and exotic collections of his uncle Philip.[151] It was probably in Spain, for example, that Rudolf first encountered the works of the English astrologer John Dee, whose books Philip bought when in London.[152] The archdukes sailed from Barcelona in July 1571, and were back in Vienna four weeks later.[153] Ernst, later a governor of the Netherlands, died prematurely in 1595. His brother went on to become emperor. Their place in the king's affections was taken by their younger brothers Albert and Wenzel, who came with Anna in 1570.

Wenzel suffered from poor health, and died in 1578. Albert, who was to make the peninsula his home, displayed all the gifts that the king longed for in a son. He shone 'in his studies and in everything',[154] Philip remarked with pride. In May 1577 the king got him a cardinalate, with a view to giving him the see of Toledo. Since Albert was still too young for the position, Philip planned meanwhile to give it to 'some old man who will not live long'.[155] He picked Gaspar de Quiroga, the seventy-eight-year-old Inquisitor-General and bishop of Cuenca. Quiroga, appointed in November 1577, tricked everybody by living nearly twenty years more.

The archdukes were loved as sons[156] but never quite supplanted his own children in the king's affections. As the princesses Isabel and Catalina grew, they came to occupy a profound part of the king's emotional life. He played a direct role in their upbringing. When Isabel was three she was described by a secretary as 'the most comely child in Spain'. Her greatest wish was to imitate her father and 'write like him'. To keep her quiet, 'there's no better way than giving her paper and ink, and with this she is happier than with anything else you could offer'.[157]

His attachment to the girls was such that he allowed them to take part in his office work. In one of the most appealing of all vignettes of his role as king, we see Philip in the summer of 1573 at the Escorial, working at his

papers in the company of Anna and the two girls. He would write and
sign, Anna would scatter sand on the text to dry it, and the girls would
take the papers to another table where Sebastián de Santoyo, the king's
office aide, would arrange them in bundles to be sent out to the secretaries.[158] Anna was heavily pregnant that summer. The plan was to have
the baby in Madrid, for which she set out on 12 August, but the pains
started that evening and she gave birth instead in Galapagar.

Philip was given less opportunity to lavish love on his sons, who by
misfortune died one after another. In the nine and a half years that Anna
was married to Philip, she bore him five children. Fernando, born in 1571,
died in 1578. Carlos, born in 1573 in Galapagar, died two years later.
Diego, born in 1575 just three days after the death of Carlos, became the
apple of Philip's eye and was sworn in as heir before the Portuguese
campaign. He died in 1582. Only the Infante Philip, born to Anna on 14
April 1578, survived the king. The delightful portrait of the two princes
Diego and Philip, done in 1579 by Sánchez Coello, allows us to imagine
the royal residences resounding to the sound of scurrying feet. The scurrying was always brief. Anna's last child, María, born early in 1580, died
in the summer of 1583, shortly after the king's return from Portugal.
Philip was deeply affected. It removed almost his last link with Anna.

*

The king appears to have suffered his first attack of gout in 1563, when he
was thirty-six.[159] Serious attacks began in July 1568, in his foot.[160] The
problem stayed with him for the rest of his life. Possibly because of it, he
was always quick to sympathise with those around him (and they were
many) who had the same misfortune. Once when Mateo Vázquez complained how ill he felt, the king urged him not to worry: 'you know that
this is how things are in the world'.[161] It was the illnesses within his family
that brought out his most profound reactions of concern. In the autumn of
1572 Anna's first child and male heir to the throne, Fernando, was unwell.
The king continued business as usual, but under pressure. Night after
night he literally could not sleep for worry. 'These days that I am away,'
he ordered the queen's chamberlain, 'send me a despatch every night, and
you yourself write every night, so that I know in the morning how the
prince has been that day.' When some days later he received a favourable
report, he sighed: 'I think I shall be able to make up tonight the sleep I lost
the other night'.[162] He felt the same degree of concern for each member of
his family.

The king's own health had never been good. It may not have been
helped by his food intake. In the mid-1550s he had a balanced diet. Meat
and game dominated his table, as was common in all noble households.
But in 1550–1 his meals in the Netherlands and Augsburg also included
salads, cheese, olives, fruit and fish.[163] It is possible that he ate the fish, for

1. Philip's mother, Isabel of Portugal, by Titian.

2. Charles V, Philip's father, by Titian.

3. Silver polychrome bust of Philip by Pompeo Leoni.

4. Elizabeth Valois, Philip's third wife, married 1560–68. Painting by Alonso Sánchez Coello.

5. Philip's fourth and last wife, Anna of Austria, married 1570–80. Painting by Antonis Mor.

6. Infanta Catalina Michaela, the youngest daughter of Philip and later duchess of Savoy. Painting by Sonfonisba Anguisciola

7. Don Carlos, Philip's only child by his first wife María of Portugal. Painting by Alonso Sánchez Coello.

8. Letter from Philip to the duke of Savoy, 7 August 1557, shortly before the battle of Saint Quentin.

9. The battle of Saint Quentin as envisaged by Fabrizio Castello and Niccolò Granello, Italian muralists who painted the Hall of Battles at the Escorial.

10. A contemporary imaginary view of the 1571 Battle of Lepanto by H. Letter.

11. A sixteenth-century design for a tapestry of the Armada.

12. The duke of Alba by William Key.

13. Anonymous portrait of the princess of Eboli.

14. Antoine Perrenot de Granvelle,
later created cardinal Granvelle.
Painting by Antonis Mor.

15. Anonymous portrait of
Antonio Pérez.

NOT LONGE TIME SINCE I SAW A COWE
DID HAVNDERS REPRESENTE
FRON WHOSE BACKE KINGE PHILIP RODE
AS BEING MALECONTNT .

THE QVENE OF ENGLAND GIVING HAY
WHEARE ON THE COW DID FEEDE
A ONE THAT WAS HER GREATEST HELPE
IN HER DISTRESSE AND NEEDE.

THE PRINCE OF ORANGE MILKT
AND MADE HIS PVRSE THE PAYE
THE COW DIDSHYT IN MONSIEURS
WHILE HE DID HOLD HER TAYLE

16. Philip and the Netherlands as portrayed in an anonymous English School painting: the queen of England feeds the allegorical cow which Philip rides and the prince of Orange milks.

17. A contemporary print depicting the execution of counts Egmont and Hornes, which served only to inflame hatred against Spain within the Netherlands.

18. The building of the Escorial, as depicted in an anonymous contemporary drawing entitled *The House of the King of Spain*.

19. Sixteenth-century perspective of the Escorial, based on a drawing by Juan de Herrera.

La Casa Del Bosque De Segobia

20. View of the palace at Valsaín in the 1560s, by Anton van den Wyngaerde.

21. Contemporary print of Philip's palace in Lisbon.

22. (*left*) A Spanish official in Peru dictating to his
scribe. From the *Chronicle* (1615) of Guamán Poma
de Ayala.

23. (*below*) The great Andean mine of Potosí, a major
source of silver from America.

24. (*top*) A view of Cadiz depicting men being paid to
join the Indies fleet

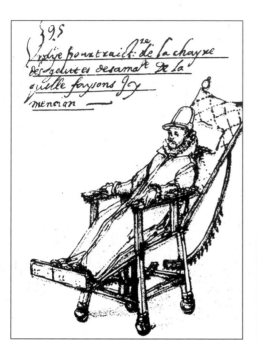

25. Design by Jehan Lhermite of a gout-sufferer's chair for Philip, from *Le Passetemps*, 1595.

26. Portrait of Philip in his last years, by Pantoja de la Cruz, *c.* 1593–5.

it is unlikely that his steward placed before him meals which he did not like. In England in 1555, salads and fruit were regularly on his table. After his return to Spain in 1559 this seems to have changed. In the 1560s and 1570s the Venetian ambassadors stated that the king ate only meat and that 'for many years he has not eaten fish or fruit'.[164] In 1570 a Spaniard (not a courtier and so not necessarily informed) stated that the king 'has not tasted fish in all his life'.[165] The abstention from fish at this date was a fact. But the king certainly consumed fruit.[166] In general, he ate sparingly at meals. He drank a little wine, but never more than two cups. Later in life his health made him restrict all aspects of his diet.

His other faculties were quite normal. Antonio Pérez claimed that the king had insensitivity to smell.[167] This is extremely doubtful, when we consider evidence such as his pleasure in flowers and their perfume. The quotation at the head of this chapter is one example among many. His eyes gave him trouble, a natural consequence of paperwork and middle age. He seems to have used spectacles, though they appear in no portrait of his. His sight, he observed in 1578, 'fails me a great deal at night'.[168]

Precisely because he was forced to rely so much on doctors, he had no faith in any of them. 'Physicians are terrible people', was his opinion. At a pinch, if there was a real need, he might entrust himself and the queen to doctor Francisco Vallés. Otherwise doctors should be avoided. Their resort to bleeding 'may do more harm than good'. Nor did he take to quack remedies. Years later, when his secretary recommended him some herbs, he replied: 'I don't believe that this or anything else is useful or reliable for getting rid of the gout. There are other better things for relieving it.'[169] The best policy was quite simply 'looking after oneself and taking a bit of care with one's health'.[170] Exercise meant walking and lots of fresh air. In 1559 in Brussels he insisted on 'the benefit to my health from exercise and the countryside'.[171] But the exercise must be regular. To keep in shape, he felt, 'it's a good idea to find moments on good days to do a bit of exercise, and neither stop doing it nor do it all at once. Life in the countryside is good for the body and very relaxing.'[172] These good counsels applied above all to his family. When the Infanta Isabel was six he advised that she 'get up early and do exercise', and that both she and her sister go to bed early at night, because 'going to bed early allows you to get up early, and it would be a good idea for both of you to adopt this custom from now on'.[173]

The years, inevitably, took their toll. On the eve of the occupation of Portugal, Philip was all too conscious of his age and infirmities. He had been ruling Spain for well over thirty years. Ill-health was the main threat, but age also pressed. At Christmas 1574 he felt that 'someone who remembers so little and has his head so full as I do', was no longer in possession of a reliable memory. In the spring of 1576 he professed to 'feel so old' that he was ready for 'when Our Lord wishes to call me, which could be very soon'.[174] The hair on his head was beginning to whiten.[175] With age came resignation. 'I don't believe that my life matters so much, at least not to me,' he confided in 1578.

The mid-1570s were, for all that, probably the years in which he experienced the greatest personal tranquillity. A Venetian envoy has left us his observation of the king in 1577:

> He rises very early and attends to affairs or correspondence until midday, when he eats always at the same time and almost always the same type and amount of food. He drinks from an average-size glass, which he drains twice. In general his health is good. However, he sometimes suffers from a stomach illness and a bit of gout. Half an hour after lunch, he despatches all the petitions and other documents that need his signature. Three or four times a week he goes to the country in a carriage, to hunt game and rabbits with a crossbow.

Above all came his devotion to Anna. 'He visits the queen three times a day: in the morning before mass, during the day before he begins work, and at night when he goes to bed. They have two low beds separated by a palm's width, but because of the curtain covering them they appear one bed. The king loves his wife deeply and never fails to visit her.'[176]

He disliked being separated from her. When possible, they spent the entire summer together. During the summers of 1576 and 1577, they spent four or five months at the Escorial. In March 1578 a late snowstorm caught them there. They were forced to spend the whole of Holy Week 'huddled together',[177] cut off from work. When the snows cleared Anna returned briefly to Madrid to give birth to the Infante Philip (on 14 April), but returned a month later and passed the rest of the summer with the king. They made periodic outings to the other residences. In June Philip put on (as we have seen) another of his great chivalric tournaments for her near the abbey at Párraces, with the participation of some 800 knights. It was observed that the king did it all for Anna, 'whom he loves and cherishes', and that 'the king, like a good husband, wished to entertain her with these people'.[178]

8

The Statesman

Kings and princes are instituted primarily to govern, to administer justice to their subjects, and to defend them from their enemies.[1]

Setting up a permanent capital in the 1560s brought a closer attention to the machinery of government. Among the first changes made by the king was a reform in the system of councils. When Philip took over Naples and Milan from his father in 1554 it became obvious that special machinery must be devised for dealing with Italian affairs, normally handled by the council of State. This led to the creation, between 1556 and 1559, of a separate council for Italy.[2] Pursuit of more efficiency was not the only reason. The new council was a linchpin for the whole system of power alliances, based on marriage and influence, which extended throughout the Italian possessions and whose reins were held by Eboli.[3]

Other changes took place when necessary. After Philip's return in 1559 the council of State became limited to a small group of nobles who were also officials of the royal household. After the acquisition of Portugal a council of Portugal was set up in 1582. Subsequently a council of Flanders was created in 1588. Each council, which met in Madrid in the Alcázar, was supposed to include among its members leading figures from the area concerned. In this way all the parts of the monarchy had, in theory, an organ for consulting directly with the king.

In practice, business seldom fell neatly within the ambit of a single council. Regional, and especially non-Castilian, interests were seldom represented adequately. Nor was it possible for each council to handle all the affairs coming before it. From the very beginning of his governorship in the 1540s, Philip found it useful to create special committees (*juntas*) to handle specific business. Some juntas, like that on Works and Forests (1545), became permanent bodies. Others, like the juntas created periodically to discuss the Morisco problem, came and went. In time, Philip came to rely more on these select committees than on the normal apparatus of government.

Beyond the scope of the king's councils, direct royal authority was tenuous. Spain, we have seen, was no centralised state. Its structure was much like that of France and most large European countries. There was no central administration, civil service, army or tax system. For all these things the crown relied on regional officials in the cities, provinces and lands controlled by the Church or nobility. It followed that the king was continually engaged in consultation with the officials and people over whom he ruled. Philip used the process of consultation for two purposes: to obtain information, and to secure consent. On his return from Lisbon to Madrid in 1583, for example, he carried out a survey of public opinion in the sixty-odd Castilian cities with civil governors (*corregidores*). He wanted to know what measures people thought should be taken to deal with inflation.[4] Without such periodic consultation, which had the advantage of covering more townships than were represented in the Cortes, those who ruled in Madrid would have been ill-equipped to make decisions on economic policy.

*

A key part in Philip's style of government was played by his secretaries. These assisted at councils, drew up reports on the discussions, presented summaries of debates and of general correspondence, and countersigned the letters sent out by the king. Their position of direct access to the king made them powerful. But this did not turn the king into a passive servant. An influential study of Antonio Pérez has argued that the secretary from the first managed his master, 'leaving Philip nothing to do but approve'.[5] The reality was otherwise. When Gonzalo Pérez died in 1566 his son Antonio, who was attached to the Eboli grouping, immediately took over temporary care of his section. From May 1566 Antonio was despatching correspondence for the king, even though his formal appointment was not confirmed until July the next year. Philip literally trained the young secretary. He helped him with instructions on how each letter had to be drawn up and where each item should go.[6] Not until around 1572, some six years later, do we find Pérez confident enough to express his opinions on the information he was giving the king. Meanwhile, the king dispensed no special favours to Pérez, and shared his confidences equally with all his private secretaries.

One of these, Antonio Gracián, kept a diary of his work routine for the years 1572 and 1573. From it we get a fascinating picture of the contact between king and officials at that period. Gracián, working mainly from

San Lorenzo, would receive the post when it came from ministers in Madrid, which continued to be the centre of both court and government. The king would make a preliminary distribution of the mail. Specialised letters were dealt with directly by the relevant minister if he were available. The king himself would deal with some correspondence after consultation. The secretary would process most other letters, and often answer them directly. On 9 March 1572, notes Gracián, 'mail arrived with files of papers from the cardinal, Zayas, Antonio Pérez, Escobedo, Juan Vázquez, Eraso, Gassol, altogether fourteen files. His Majesty replied to all, and that night the replies were drawn up.' On 2 May,

His Majesty ordered me to give the Prior Don Antonio the despatches which had come the day before from Genoa, Milan, Rome, Venice, Turin, Sicily, France and Germany; this was done. His Majesty ordered me to reply to a report from the council of Orders: they should keep some papers until he returned to Madrid, send a memorandum to secretary Antonio Pérez, and reply to a letter from Ambrosio de Morales. At night the mail left with despatches for Delgado and Zayas . . . At 10.30 at night mail arrived with a despatch from Zayas, and with great haste I was ordered to give it to His Majesty before he went to bed. It was already 11 o'clock, His Majesty was already in bed, and the letter could not be given.[7]

Of all the aides with whom he worked the king relied most heavily on Santoyo. Sebastián de Santoyo organised all Philip's office papers. He was 'the king's oldest and most intimate servant'.[8] A famous anecdote tells us that very late one night when the king had finished writing a long letter, he handed it to Santoyo to blot with sand. Instead of sprinkling sand over the papers the weary Santoyo by mistake sprinkled ink. Seeing his distress the king merely said, 'You will just have to wait', and proceeded to write the letter all over again.[9] The two made a perfect team. When Santoyo died in February 1588, it 'greatly grieved' the king. Some years later Philip saw an aide searching for a document and mixing up papers he had carefully put in order. 'Tell that man,' he commented half-seriously, 'that if I don't order his head cut off it is because of the services of his uncle Sebastián de Santoyo.'[10]

The first generation of secretaries, such as Gonzalo Pérez and Eraso, faded away in the mid-1560s. Over the next few years Philip exercised no special preferences among the successors. His relationship with Antonio Pérez was not unusually intimate. The crucial moment seems to have come with the advance to favour of Mateo Vázquez after 1573. At once a profound rivalry between Antonio Pérez and Vázquez sprung up. Thanks to Vázquez's complete dedication, Philip was able to hand over to him entirely the crucial task of processing papers when they came in. The king had a clear idea of what changes should be made, and instructed Vázquez accordingly. With the new system, practised until Vázquez's death,[11] the secretary would either report the content of correspondence verbally or by means of a summary written on each paper. Where relevant, he would state the advice offered by himself or by ministers. He would keep back papers that could be dealt with elsewhere. This saved the king a great deal of time. It also brought into existence a fascinating relationship that lasted till Vázquez's death in 1591.

Philip's administration was, like every similar administration of its time, a jungle of bitter personal rivalries and open corruption. The king took care to distribute to each new secretary a firm set of instructions, with particular stress on maintaining secrecy and not taking bribes. The rules were, as always, seldom observed. Individuals such as Pérez made themselves rich. Secretary Gabriel Zayas in 1586 suggested that secretaries should be well paid to avoid possible corruption. The king, he suggested, should follow the example of 'the English, whom we usually consider barbarians'. But the king's memory of English practice failed him. 'I don't very well remember,' was his only comment.[12]

*

From the minute he entered into government as regent in the 1540s, Philip was plagued by papers. As early as the 1550s he was regarded as a 'paper king'. In England he spent every morning with correspondence. In the Netherlands, reported l'Aubespine in 1559, 'the prince is fully immersed in business and doesn't waste an hour, spending all day among his papers'. In 1560 in Toledo he insisted on handling everything, 'acting as master, minister, and secretary, but there is such delay and confusion that everyone here is desperate'.[13] While not relinquishing his hold over his papers, Philip attempted to put more order into the system and adapt it to his needs.

He started work early. In the 1550s and 1560s he was often at his papers before eight in the morning.[14] The image of a slothful king, addicted to long hours in bed, appears regularly in reports by Venetian ambassadors, but is simply untrue.[15] In 1577 another Venetian envoy observed by contrast that 'he rises very early, and attends to affairs and correspondence until midday'.[16] The king gave public audiences 'in the morning before going to mass, and for one hour when he lunched in public. He receives petitions, listens to people, and gives his reply.'[17] He expected the same early timetable from his councillors. The rules he drew up personally for the council of Italy in 1559 required that councillors begin work at 9 a.m. in winter and 8 a.m. in summer.[18]

He regularly called others in to advise him about work on his desk. Unusually for a senior executive, he insisted on keeping the study door open so that ministers and secretaries could go in and out. Once he was sent a confidential paper and advised to lock his door while reading it.

Instead, he waited until the moment of the post-lunch siesta, and looked at it then in bed, 'in order not to draw attention by shutting the door'.[19] The open door was a symbol of his own freedom. One day in Madrid in 1578 the duke of Alba, the prior Don Antonio de Toledo and Alba's son Don Fadrique, came in to see him. They wanted to plead with him about the matter of Fadrique's marriage. Alba made the mistake of closing the door behind him. 'Is this a threat?' the king objected. 'Are you going to attack me?' He went into another room and would not speak to them.[20] They were banned from the palace for a period.

If the king had confidence in a minister he gave him a fairly broad competence over affairs. When his authority over business was still only partial, in the late 1550s, he felt free to entrust Ruy Gómez with unspeci-fied general powers. But as soon as he came to supervise all administra-tion, from about 1560, the king took care to keep spheres of responsibility separate. This prevented quarrels, and also gave him a decisive voice. In this way, many key individuals – not simply Ruy Gómez or Alba – helped in the task of government. In Gracián's notes of 1572–3 the prior of León, Don Antonio de Toledo, Alba's brother-in-law, emerges as the chief voice in foreign policy. On 23 April 1572 'I read to the prior a despatch from Zayas about matters concerning England and Flanders, and he wrote the relevant letters'. On 7 June 1573 'I read to the prior despatches from Flanders about Haarlem, and from Italy from Don Juan, and others. The prior wrote down his opinion and I gave it to His Majesty.' At Easter 1573 the prior handled more correspondence than the king himself.[21]

The king's style of government did not always gain the approval of the public or of politicians. Unlike other European monarchs, he preferred information to be given not verbally but in written form. Council meetings, for instance, were normally held without him: 'He never at-tends the discussions of his councillors,' ambassadors observed in the first decades of his reign.[22] In this he followed his father's advice and his own practice since the 1540s. The rule, never a hard and fast one, was broken when necessary. A written report (*consulta*) of the discussion in council was sent to him after each meeting. This had the advantage of allowing him to consider and reconsider options, and to compare differ-ing views.

Correspondents were only too happy to shower him with advice. Critics – among them his own ministers – held that the resulting mass of paperwork delayed decision-making. Granvelle's brother, the diplo-mat Chantonnay, commented in 1565 that 'as for our master, everything is put off till the morrow, and the main decision taken in everything is never to take a decision'.[23] Slow decision-making in Spain became pro-verbial. Granvelle became one of its fiercest critics. The king himself, it must be said, fought manfully against intolerable delays, but the nature of the system within which he worked made efficiency difficult to achieve.

A different type of criticism concerned what the role of a king should be. Kings, many felt, had a public role to play. They should be accessible to the people. They were not meant to be pen-pushers. Philip's grand almoner Luis Manrique told him frankly in the late 1570s that administration 'through notes and paper' distanced him from his subjects. Other kings, he said, did not spend their time 'reading and writing': business done orally was always quicker.[24]

Philip appreciated the advice but chose to differ. When Vázquez in 1576 suggested that in several matters it might be quicker to conduct business orally with his ministers, he conceded that it might be a good idea. 'But,' he said, 'my experience of nearly thirty-three years dealing with affairs, is that it would be onerous to have to listen to them and afterwards see them to make a reply, and much worse with those who speak a lot.'[25] Reading a ten-minute report was always quicker than enduring a one-hour torrent of words. He carried out faithfully his engagements to speak to ministers, ambassadors and members of the public, but his experience told him that the time spent on such duties was incommensurate with the results achieved. 'I am burdened with so many audiences,' he complained in October 1573, 'that they don't leave me time to settle anything.'[26] It was the same five years later: 'I am burdened with audiences and other things that have prevented me replying until now'.[27] 'Until now, which is very late, the nuncio and others have prevented me seeing this file.'[28] What he needed in order to be able to work was 'time and quiet, and believe me I can't do it with the audiences'.[29] And how was he to remember everything that was said to him? His own method of giving audience was probably no help. He never interrupted speakers, always courteously allowing them to finish before he responded. This possibly turned short audiences into long ones.

Talk, he argued, impeded efficiency in paperwork. 'Here is another pile of letters and petitions which ambassadors and other people have given me today; they all spoke to me at great length, so that I don't have time even to open them.'[30] Talk impeded the work of councils. In 1586 he criticised the council of Castile for 'spending a great deal of time talking, and as a result getting very little done'.[31] Talk, he argued, could not take the place of paper in arriving at administrative decisions. It was one of his quarrels with cardinal Espinosa, who earned a reputation for 'efficiency' because he despatched business verbally rather than in writing.[32]

Meetings with ministers also consumed time, and were difficult to cut down. 'I have had three hours today of a *consulta* from the council of the Indies, and afterwards two hours with Juan de Ovando [president of that council]'.[33] He would frequently invite his secretaries to a working lunch. 'On 3 March,' recorded Gracián in 1573, 'His Majesty went in the morning to El Pardo, and I came to lunch, and after lunch His Majesty dictated to me his replies to two *consultas* from Antonio Pérez.'[34] 'Come to lunch tomorrow,' he ordered Vázquez in July that year, 'and make your report.'[35] On 2 July 1576 Escobedo, who had just returned from Flanders, reported on matters at a lunch with the king and Antonio Pérez.[36] 'Arrange to come to lunch here on Monday, returning in the afternoon', Vázquez was told in June 1588. Philip would also frequently go without dinner and simply have a snack at his desk late in the night.[37] Or he might delay dinner for a moment. Sending off some urgent papers one night, he wrote: 'I didn't think of them until now; it's already nine and dinner has been ordered and I went to take a short walk first. But passing by the study I happened to see them and have now read them.'[38] One night in April 1578 he had just finished a quantity of papers for his secretary at 9.30 p.m. when he was handed yet another report. He continued what he was writing and then scribbled his protest: 'Now they've given me another file from you. I have neither the time nor the head to look at it so I won't open it until tomorrow. It's past ten and I haven't had dinner and my table is full of papers for tomorrow; I can't manage any more for now.' In that half an hour his hand wrote exactly 468 words.[39]

The one constant was his dedication to his work. He tried to despatch in the same day papers he had received that day, setting aside only those which called for further consultation. The aim was sometimes achieved. 'Here goes what came today,' he noted with satisfaction to Vázquez in June 1577, 'and if only it were like that always, it's what we need.'[40] When whole days were lost because of alternative business, the situation simply became desperate. 'Losing a morning for papers, as happened on Sunday and Monday and today, presents me with so many of them that it's impossible to handle, and worse when I have audiences like those this afternoon which I could not avoid, and letters from Italy and Germany, a great many of them.'[41] A Flemish courtier later observed that in the opinion of many the king 'must have during his life written more than four mule-loads of paper'.[42] It was an underestimate.

He seems to have stopped work at the latest just after eleven at night, which is when his body fell asleep. 'Up to now, 11 o'clock, I have been waiting for the file,' he scribbled one night in April 1575, 'but I can't wait any more, I don't have eyes in my head, and tomorrow I have to go to mass to the church.'[43] The letters at the foot of the page become a sleepy scrawl. The capacity, shown in his earlier years, to stay up all night, soon diminished. In 1584 it was reported that he normally slept a healthy eight hours a night.[44]

Since he was always on the move, from one palace to the other, urgent papers came with him in a special bag.[45] He did not let the burden of work disrupt commitments, especially commitments to his family. But the papers would have to come with him. 'I have so many papers today,' he reported in the spring of 1576, 'that I can't see these others now, nor can I today. I think I'll take them with me to read in the coach when I go to the country.'[46] The coach became a travelling office. 'If I can look at it before leaving I'll do so,' he commented of a problem; 'if not it will be in the coach.'[47] 'It's days since I received the letter from cardinal Granvelle but I haven't been able to look at it until today, and I've been reading it on the road.'[48]

Surrounded by papers from every corner of the universal monarchy, the king inevitably found it impossible to keep them all in correct order for easy reference, even with Santoyo to help him. For perhaps the first time, in October 1573 he sent a plaintive note to Mateo Vázquez asking for help. 'My papers are in total confusion,' he wrote, 'and since I want to put them all in order and tear up those no longer needed and arrange the rest', could Vázquez please draw up a list of up to twenty topics for filing correspondence. He wanted the list by lunch next day.[49] All too often, he could not find papers he needed. This happened, for instance, in 1574 when he was thinking of drawing up instructions for his successor, in this case queen Anna. He wanted to base his words on the famous *Instructions* given to him by his father. But now he could not find them: 'I don't know if I have them or where they are, nor do I have time to look for them'.[50] Some papers went adrift permanently. When in 1592 his long-lived confessor Diego Chaves died, the king asked his secretary to look 'if there were any papers there concerning the council of State, which we have looked for on occasion and not found'.[51]

Bound to his desk, he tried to emerge from time to time for fresh air. 'I would like to go out into the country a bit today,' went one note, 'but I don't know if I can with what has come today, which is a great deal.'[52] In April 1575 he passed a little scribble to the secretary: 'I wasn't able to call you because I was finishing off some little things, and now it's rather late, and I'm going to take a much-needed spin round the countryside.'[53] His papers are full of messages informing others that he has had enough and is going to take a break.

*

Decision-making in sixteenth-century government was not what it is today. Modern governments have a 'policy' which they attempt to put into effect. At that time governments had no policy. They simply responded to events as the need arose. Because Philip is often credited with having a firm and aggressive policy, we should glance at his part in the decision-making process.

Top-level affairs of war, peace and rebellion were never in practice the sole preserve of the king. He referred everything, down to the smallest detail, to his councils and advisers. He never made decisions based only on his own opinion or preferences,[54] but always insisted on adequate information and consultation before proceeding to action. Ambassador l'Aubespine stated that in 1559 when he raised a matter with the king, 'he asked me (acting wisely, for fear of being caught in matters of which he has no information or instructions) to refer to his council for them to decide'.[55] In the same way, Philip hesitated to make grave decisions until the force of events pointed in that direction. A subsequent French ambassador, Fourquevaux, commented that 'he decides according to the way things turn out', but that he preferred to judge matters from a distance rather than be pushed into them.[56] 'Very rarely does he depart from the advice of his ministers,' ambassador Tiepolo noted, 'but in the business of Flanders he has shown that he has little confidence in his councillors and has made many important decisions all by himself'.[57] On this last point the Venetian ambassador was absolutely wrong. Important decisions were always referred to many people. The king never acted by himself, and never failed to consult before acting. A classic example is his intervention in the affairs of Aragon in 1591. From the outset, he consulted every relevant official throughout Spain, and did not move a finger without favourable advice. The point at which he did not shirk decision-making was when he had to choose between conflicting opinions. But it never occurred to him to make all decisions by himself.[58]

Low-level decisions were not always easy to arrive at. Much government activity was in response to petitions from subjects. The task of sorting through petitions was a formidable one, carried out initially by officials in the different realms or by secretaries in Madrid. Petitions which passed this first hurdle had to be accompanied by reports and information before they could be allowed into the relevant council. The process could be long. In nearly all cases, firm recommendations were made to the king. His decisions seldom reflected 'policy'. More precisely, they were responses to the opinions of his advisers. The councils were in theory advisory bodies only, in the sense that the king was not obliged to follow their views. In practice, they made very many firm decisions, usually in administrative matters. In 1567 a diplomat complained that the king 'never decides anything by himself but refers everything to his council; it is completely futile to go back to him over something the council has decided'.[59]

Whether decisions were big or small, the king of course accepted ultimate responsibility. Like many executives, he disliked this. He saw no reason, for example, why he should be held responsible for the quality of the bishops he appointed. Some other method of appointing them should be devised, he felt. Inevitably, he would often try to shift the responsibility, and blamed his advisers if things went wrong. This happened with finance, with Flanders, and with the Armada.

It is difficult to exaggerate the enormous range of commitments which the king took on his shoulders. The task, a superhuman one, could not be done without the help of a reliable network of officials and subordinates. At least three main levels of official made up the network of control and information in his monarchy. First, there were the governors or viceroys, located in regional capitals such as Brussels, Saragossa or Naples. They took orders directly from the king, but also linked up with the appropriate council in Madrid, and liaised directly with local organs of government. Second, there were diplomatic personnel, such as Bernardino de Mendoza or Francés de Álava in western Europe, Granvelle or Zúñiga in Rome, the count of Monteagudo in Vienna, who collected information, recruited agents and tried to defend Spain's interests. The diplomatic payroll also included diplomats from other nations, notably Imperial officials such as Dietrichstein and Wolf Rumpf,[60] who cooperated with Philip and thereby extended Spain's influence into the German-speaking lands. Finally, there was a large team of unofficial agents, such as Martín de Acuña in Istanbul, who carried out specific missions when nobody else was available. Fray Lorenzo de Villavicencio falls into this final category. Thanks to all these, Philip was able to carry out an active foreign policy which was not limited to the Atlantic or Mediterranean, but extended even into the Baltic, Poland and Russia.

*

Philip's only working language was Castilian; in this he was unlike his father, who spoke several languages fluently. He was conscious all his life of the deficiency, but never remedied it. It contributed to the tight-lipped impression he gave Italians, Germans and Netherlanders during the tour of 1548. In England in 1554 he 'never departs from his native Spanish'. Once when a lord wrote to him in English, he replied saying that to avoid the need for translation all confidential letters should be in French or Latin.[61] His situation was not unusual. The Castilian elite were extremely poor linguists.[62] When Philip was in the Netherlands in 1550, the Castilian students at Louvain university stuck to speaking Spanish among themselves instead of trying to learn French or Dutch.[63] Secretary Zayas in 1574 could find nobody suitable to appoint as ambassador to the emperor, since not a single Castilian grandee knew German and none could speak Latin. Eventually they had to appoint the Valencian Juan de Borja, who was not a grandee but at least could speak Latin.[64] For sensitive diplomatic contacts where a knowledge of languages might be an advantage Spain tended to use Netherlanders (like Jean Baptiste de Tassis),[65] Franche-Comtois (like Chantonnay), Catalans and others who habitually spoke more than one tongue.

Italian ambassadors spoke to him in Italian and he understood (they said) 'without difficulty'.[66] French ambassadors (and also his wife Elizabeth) spoke to him in French, which he understood for the most part. Germans addressed him in Latin, but the more proficient quickly learned Spanish. In Augsburg in 1550 the princes and electors were ordered by the emperor to address Philip only in French, since some had maliciously addressed him in German. The prince for his part replied only in Latin.[67]

Then and later, he normally conversed with foreigners in Castilian. He himself spoke no Italian or French, though he read both without problems. Years later, commenting on his lack of French, he said: 'it was for lack not of will but of ability. I understand it well enough but never dared to speak it.'[68] His spoken Latin was of very average quality. The Venetian ambassador in 1557 judged charitably that it was 'superior to what is habitual among princes'.[69] We may presume that he understood some Catalan, since he had links with the Requesens household and also sat through debates of the Corts, where the Catalans always spoke in their own language. He picked up the essentials of Portuguese from his mother, and understood it well, but avoided speaking it. He told his children, all the same, that 'you should try to understand Portuguese'.[70]

When it came to studying very long memorials and letters in French and Italian, he seldom coped. He preferred such papers to be translated. In any case, translations were essential if other members of the government were to be able to read the text. When in 1577 just after the death of Hopperus a document in French came from Flanders, neither the king nor any of his ministers could read it, and it had to be set aside until someone could translate it.[71] Now and then he indulged his vanity by correcting French words in letters. On one occasion, he disagreed with a secretary translating the word 'head' by 'tayte': '*head*,' he noted, 'is not *tayte* but *tête*.'[72] Inevitably he used his secretarial staff when documents had to be composed in other tongues. Some of his Latin letters, however, he composed himself. One night he called Gracián in to correct a letter he had just written to the duke of Bavaria.[73] Merely to have composed it was, in Castile, an achievement. Among the Castilian aristocracy of his day few could handle Latin, and almost none Greek.[74] On occasion, Philip put his hand to translation. In 1574 when the Imperial ambassador, Hans Khevenhüller, came to Madrid with a sheaf of confidential documents written in Latin, king and ambassador sat down together and translated the lot into Castilian, 'because of the confidentiality and importance of the subject'.[75]

*

Philip's personal character cannot be separated from his role as king. He was called 'prudent' by his biographers because they saw in him the quality of caution. His slowness in making decisions was, with reason, strongly criticised by those who worked with him. It was part of his nature. 'He who rushes matters in difficult circumstances,' he advised his ambassadors, 'loses credibility (*reputación*)'.[76] His caution and slowness were, clearly, dictated by the circumstances in which he had to rule. Elizabeth of England was also criticised for the same reasons. But Philip was not indifferent to the value of time. His repeated comments show it. He had in his bedroom two ornamental clocks 'that faced him by day and by night and that dictated all the actions of this king'.[77]

Philip was by temperament tranquil, subdued and always in control of himself. For the rest, his character was utterly normal. The point must be made because of the vast quantity of writing, from his day to ours, that has affirmed the contrary.[78] He lacked neither humour nor vivacity. He enjoyed celebrations, feasts, dances and jousts. He delighted in the outdoor life, in riding, hunting and walking. His fondness for women was evident (he was scrupulously faithful to only one of his wives, Anna), but all his pleasures were indulged in discreetly. Some observers referred to his subdued nature as 'melancholic', but the king seems not to have suffered serious melancholy or depression. The outstanding exceptions to this are his reactions to the arrest of Don Carlos, and his response to the Armada defeat.

His reticence has sometimes been seen as indicating a feeling of inferiority. Philip has been presented as essentially shy and withdrawn, afraid of stronger personalities.[79] There is no substance whatever to this. All his life he was a man of silences. He spoke little, and when he did he always expressed himself carefully and courteously. It was precisely his silence that unnerved others. In audience with him, they were given the right to speak first, which made them feel immediately under scrutiny. Worse, the king never interrupted, waiting until the end before he responded, no matter how long the speech.[80] 'He listens patiently,' a diplomat observed in 1567. 'He is amiable to those who speak to him, and accompanies his replies with a friendly smile.'[81] More than one French ambassador was thrown off balance by this politeness. His perfect courtesy was natural and habitual. If addressed by a lady of degree, he immediately removed his hat. On his way to Saragossa in 1585, he was received by the duchess of Infantado and her ladies at the ducal palace in Guadalajara. The speeches of welcome from the duchess, and then from her daughter, were long. 'His Majesty took off his cap and remained uncovered with all the courtesy in the world' while the speeches lasted.[82]

His quietness was also disconcerting. In his audiences, he spoke 'in such a low voice that although we were very close we could not hear him'.[83] Unlike other rulers of the day, such as the pope, Elizabeth of England or Henry IV of France, who gave vent in their audiences to a whole range of emotions, Philip remained always quiet and courteous. Confronted by this silence, even Teresa of Avila was unnerved. 'I began to speak to him when his penetrating gaze, of those that penetrate to the soul, settled on me, so I lowered my eyes and rapidly stated what I wanted.' The king's reserve was natural, not affected. He was aware that it made others uneasy, and usually avoided looking at petitioners,[84] in order not to confuse them. On several occasions the poet Alonso de Ercilla tried to express himself to Philip but was disconcerted by the royal gaze.

The king told him finally, 'Don Alonso, speak to me on paper.'[85] His courtesy was genuine. He tried to be available for consultation. Once when he had to cancel an appointment he hastily told the secretary to inform the petitioner that 'I am not angry, but simply do not have the time I wanted in which to see him'.[86]

His reserve in speech probably arose from his hyperactive mental processes, for his mind had an enormous capacity for storing and using information. He absorbed data from an incredible number of sources, as his ministers and officials never ceased to point out with wonderment. In the course of his letters, he would come across little things, errors of fact or of phrasing, which he could not comment on verbally to those responsible and would therefore annotate. His irritated comments were not a concern for the trivial, as is sometimes assumed.[87] He talked through his pen, and trifles had their normal part in the discourse. Details were never, for him, crucial, and never indulged in to the detriment of the broad view. He seldom lost the overall vision of his strategy. With so much material in his head he was, almost literally, lost for words.

The reticence made an unfavourable impact on some foreigners during Philip's first European visit. But it did not signify timidity. He stood up to his father from the moment he was competent to make his own decisions, and to every other personage he disagreed with. If he distanced himself from his half-brother Don Juan, it was not (as legend would have it) because he feared him, but because he did not sympathise with his highly volatile character. His own self-control in matters of public behaviour was exemplary. His external serenity complemented his natural taciturnity.

There is no evidence to justify the image of a grave and solemn, almost funereal, Philip. Legends about his melancholy extend to his manner of dress.[88] A common view, based it seems on his portraits, holds that his state of mind made him prefer to dress always in black. He can be seen in black in the splendid portrait (c.1575), now in the Prado,[89] by Sofonisba Anguisciola. Throughout his life he had a preference for the colour for solemn occasions. On his grand tour in 1548, when he was barely in his twenties, he frequently dressed in a combination of black and gold. Black helped to set off the Golden Fleece round his neck and the colours of other ornaments on his person. When he went to Barcelona in 1564 he was dressed in black velvet, with a white feather in his cap. When he received the Venetian ambassadors in an audience in Madrid in 1571 he was dressed partly in silver, with a black silk doublet surmounted by the Golden Fleece. But his equally frequent use of other colours, such as red and white for his wedding to Elizabeth, disprove the theory of melancholy. Black, in any case, had a special significance in Spain. It had to be worn for at least a year whenever there was a death in the family. Philip had more than his fair share of mourning. When the rest of Seville was celebrating his visit in 1570, he was still dressed in black for his son and his wife, deceased two years before.[90] But his smile, observers in the city noted, could not have been happier. The truth is that it was difficult for artists to catch the king at a moment when he was not in mourning.

He gave no priority to wearing the colour and on one occasion he positively disapproved. The ambassador of Savoy, who came to the Escorial in 1583 with the proposal of his master's marriage to the Infanta Catalina, happened to be wearing black in mourning for the death of his wife that month. Philip received the proposal happily enough, but later took the ambassador aside and criticised him sharply for wearing a colour quite unbecoming to the good news he was bringing.[91] The miserable ambassador fled to Madrid. It is possible that the king took to wearing black more habitually after the death of Anna. A notable exception to this, however, would be the colourful portrait, for which he presumably sat, of him as king of Portugal.

Although he was uniformly courteous to his colleagues and subordinates he never exuded warmth. His contemporary Henry IV of France had an expansive, affable personality which aroused both love and devotion in his comrades. Philip was different. He refrained from confiding too closely in any of those around him. Well aware that they too had their own volatility and shifted their allegiance, he preferred not to identify with them. He extended his total confidence only to his sisters María and Juana. Of his subordinates, the only one to whom he possibly opened his thoughts was Mateo Vázquez. The king's annotations on correspondence were a manner of thinking aloud, rather than a deliberate baring of feelings. He did not invite an answer. 'There is no need to reply,' he scribbled once to Vázquez. 'I am writing only to relax from weighty matters with you.'[92] 'I am writing only to relax' was a phrase repeated more than once. Complaining to paper was good therapy. He probably expressed the naked truth only to his confessor Diego Chaves. Their correspondence was seized and destroyed shortly after Chaves died.

In the light of all this, there is no reason to believe that Philip was inordinately suspicious.[93] The image of him always suspecting his ministers was first created by a Venetian ambassador. It doesn't stand up to scrutiny. He extended his confidence, as his correspondence shows, without questioning loyalty. But he reserved his right to evaluate positions. The information he accepted in the 1570s from fray Lorenzo de Villavicencio included vicious and poisonous attacks on individuals such as Hopperus, yet it did not make him withdraw his confidence from Hopperus. Well aware that officials might lie to him, he was grateful for alternative reports on their conduct. By the same token, he insisted on all his ministers telling the truth. It was a lie, we have seen, which destroyed cardinal Espinosa. Both ministers and court nobles were pressed to speak freely on all matters. It is one of the significant peculiarities of Philip's rule that flattery was unknown at his court. When a priest began an interview by praising him the king cut in. 'Father,' he said, 'leave that and tell me your business.'[94] At the same time he adamantly refused to accept hearsay or calumny. It was a fundamental principle of social relations that the source of information must be identifiable. Anonymous libels could, in the legal practice of the time, attract the death penalty. The king was quite willing to accept documents from the public, provided they were signed, but he had a firm rule that all unsigned papers should be destroyed on receipt.[95] In retrospect, the way he managed to distance himself from colleagues would do credit to a twentieth-century business executive.

He was an uncompromising partisan of absolute confidentiality in matters of state, a cardinal rule he enjoined on all his secretaries, senior officials and ambassadors.[96] 'Secrecy is essential: without it nothing can be effected,'[97] a norm that today is accepted as essential in politics. In the Spain of his day it was difficult to enforce. Philip was merciless with ministers who leaked confidential information related to their duties. The most notable case was that of Antonio Pérez. In 1579 he was unable to take any action against Pérez because the secretary and his wife hung on to confidential papers which they threatened to use against him. He did not make the same mistake twice. Just before the Portuguese campaign in 1580 the secretary for Church affairs, Gaztelu, died. Philip ordered 'that all notes in His Majesty's hand be put together in a locked case, and kept until His Majesty orders to whom they should go'.[98]

Quite logically he extended the practice of secrecy into the ordinary conduct of diplomacy and state affairs. Ministers were often instructed, in a favourite phrase, to proceed 'with all dissimulation'. The word, literally translated into English, implies 'deceit'. The king's usage carried, rather, the meaning of 'circumspection', not betraying one's purpose. The insistence on state secrecy had no uniquely Spanish moral overtones of secretiveness or deception. The practice of 'dissimulation' in politics was accepted at the time as necessary by a number of commentators, among them the English savant Francis Bacon and the Dutch scholar Hugo Grotius.[99]

Disinclined to speak, Philip always felt more at ease expressing himself on paper. When under stress, or seized by enthusiasm, he could hardly restrain his pen. If an idea gripped him, he could cover reams of paper as his thoughts flowed. The poor legibility of his hand is notorious. It can be blamed in part on his refusal when young to acquire a well-formed script. In part it may also have been a nod to the fashion, then current among many nobles, of writing badly, 'as if [wrote a critic of the fashion] nobility consists in writing badly'.[100] The fact is that there were periods when his script was perfectly neat and legible, which leads to the unexciting conclusion that his poor hand was simply the result of sloppiness or haste.

Although he worked hard, he took as much leisure as possible. He enjoyed company: his personal role in night excursions, entertainments and masquerades continued into the 1560s. He indulged in the revelry of Carnival in Barcelona in 1564. Long after that, well into his years of illness and old age, he was present at masquerades and mass entertainment. But he also appreciated 'rest and solitude, above all in summer; in this part of the year he never grants audiences on affairs of state'.[101] In 1557 in Flanders his favourite reading was history. He also tried his hand at sculpting and painting.[102]

A recurring legend is that of the king's cruelty. No contemporary cites any acceptable evidence for it. As a dispenser of justice he appears to have been rock-hard: there is no record of him ever issuing a pardon after condemnation. But he restrained the severity of his officials on numberless occasions. As a person he was more gentle. He disliked war and violence yet he revelled in the games of war which were an essential rite of male chivalry. And, in common with other members of his class and time, he adored hunting. Though a great devotee of hunting animals, he always managed to distance himself from the suffering of humans. His one direct contact with the horrors of war, the taking of St Quentin, did not make him desire to repeat the experience. Even the sufferings of certain animals gave him no pleasure. Like his great-grandmother Isabella of Castile, he disliked bull-runs[103] and usually avoided them, but took no steps to impose his preferences on Castilians. He prohibited the sport when asked to do so by specific communities (for example the citizens of Ocaña in 1561).[104] On the other hand, when in 1566 the Cortes of Madrid asked him to prohibit bull-runs generally, he refused to do so on the grounds that it was a traditional custom.[105] In 1568 he allowed the publication in Spain of a papal decree of 1567 outlawing them, but otherwise remained neutral on the matter.[106] On great feast-days he would remain all alone in the palace working, 'while everybody else went to the bull-run'.[107] On the feast of San Juan in 1565 one was put on for the court. The three royal princes – Don Carlos, Don Juan of Austria and Alessandro Farnese – went to it; but not the king.[108] At his wedding to Anna in 1570, he disallowed the running of bulls.[109] In September 1576 at the Escorial Don Juan of Austria arranged for bull-runs to be put on to entertain the royal family and the townspeople. But the king would not go. 'He had his own good reasons for not going,' commented a friar.[110] Instead the king went with the prior to see how the building work was progressing. His attitude did not prevent him assisting out of courtesy at bull-runs put on for the court.

*

Philip was not an intellectual. His views followed theories commonly expressed at Spanish universities, and medieval ideas about the reciprocal duties of rulers and ruled. When staying in Salamanca prior to his marriage to the princess Maria, he is said to have listened entranced to the professors as they gave their lectures. He may even have assisted at the lectures of the great master Francisco de Vitoria. But if he absorbed any theory, he made little specific appeal to it. The dominant tradition of political thought in Castile, accepted by the universities, by Charles V, and by Philip himself, asserted that all earthly power came from God, who distributed it to societies and communities. In order to be governed, the community invested this power in a ruler. The ruler derived his authority from the community, but his position made him responsible only to God.[111]

Philip took seriously his direct responsibility to God. Successive Cortes of Castile in the fifteenth century had repeated as an established principle that God 'made kings his vicars on earth'.[112] It became accepted that kingly power drew its origin from God and was based on divine right. Moreover – and Philip demonstrated his belief in this repeatedly – it was undivided power, not to be shared with any person or institution. As the Cortes of Toledo in 1559 stated: the king's authority 'is by nature indivisible, and by both public and royal law must be considered as entire and without division'.[113] But this power brought with it certain duties. Philip's instructions to his viceroys (drawn up by others, but always reflecting his ideas) are a useful guide to his thinking. 'Kings and princes,' he observed in 1559, 'are instituted primarily to govern, to administer justice to their subjects, and to defend them from their enemies.' The statement, a commonplace in the political theory of the time, implicitly rejects absolutist attitudes. It recognises that rulers have one sole duty: to those they rule. Princes have to make laws, but may also change them: 'we are obliged to abrogate or reform those in existence if we know they are harmful to the state'.[114]

Nowhere among Philip's statements is there any unusual emphasis on the rights of kings. Like most rulers, he was attributed 'absolute' power. The concept of *poderío absoluto* in Spain was late medieval in origin, and implied no more than the independence (or indivisibility)[115] of royal power. It was employed habitually by kings of Castile in the fifteenth century, and appeared several times in the will of Isabella the Catholic.[116] It was also applied to Philip when he resumed the government of Spain on his return from Flanders in 1551.[117] In his last testament, over a generation later, he referred to 'my absolute power', but he did not use the phrase during his reign. Charles V had paid little attention to the concept, but encouraged the use of the title 'Majesty', little known in Spain until then.[118] 'Majesty' was also claimed for Philip in the year that he became king, by a Spanish humanist writing in the Netherlands.[119] But he had little need for theory. While university professors in Spain debated political theory, the king avoided any theoretical discussion of his powers, exercised his authority within traditional limits, and was eventually (in 1586) even to discourage the title 'Majesty'.

Occasionally, in moments of crisis, he allowed himself to appeal to the traditional 'absolute' right of life and death which a lord could exercise over his subjects. He made use of this approach only when there was no obvious alternative. His theologians and lawyers advised him in 1590, quite fairly, that he could use it to pursue Antonio Pérez. It would be 'by laws of good government, when punishment cannot be effected through ordinary channels'.[120] Later, during the events of Aragon in 1591, his lawyers again confirmed that he could act without due judicial process. Beyond these cases, which were exceptional, he seems not to have appealed to the right. All the executions known to have taken place during his reign (including that of Montigny) were carried out after due legal process and with the participation of the royal council. Only the mysterious execution of Martín de Acuña (the agent Philip used for negotiations with Turkey), carried out in the fortress at Pinto on 4 February 1585 (the same week as the final arrest of Antonio Pérez), invites speculation.[121]

Many feudal lords, especially in Aragon, claimed to have power of life and death over their vassals. Philip never exercised it over his own vassals, but he acted rigorously in each and every case where his great nobles tried to use it over theirs. His severity in these matters gave him a reputation for firmness which few dared challenge. He never, at any moment of his reign, tolerated rebellion. It was the most profound of all his political convictions. He never pardoned those arrested for it. In his young days, he accepted without reproach the Lutheran companionship of Maurice of Saxony, but never forgave him his subsequent treachery against the emperor. With the unique exception of Martín Cortes in the Mexican conspiracy of 1566,[122] he always approved the execution of rebel leaders. When criticised for his firmness in dealing with the sedition in Avila in 1591, he retorted, 'They know now that words will be translated into actions.' Reminded that Avila had given him many loyal soldiers, he said, 'That is true; but didn't they depose king Henry [IV of Castile] there, and support the tyrant Juan de Padilla?'[123] The memory of the Comuneros never faded from his mind.

Despite his firm belief in royal power, the king made no attempt to mystify it. Previous rulers of Castile and Spain had consciously rejected many of the symbols of power used by monarchies outside the peninsula.[124] They did not consider their office sacred, did not claim (like the rulers of France and England) any power to heal the sick, and enjoyed no special rituals at the time of their birth or crowning[125] or death. The imagery of magical power, common in other monarchies, was notably absent in Spain. Philip followed this tradition perfectly. He encouraged no cult of his person, as Elizabeth of England did in subsequent years and as Louis XIV was to do on a grand scale later. Like his predecessors, he firmly asserted his authority to rule, and the trust he received from God, but he did not inflate these claims into a mystique of royal power. A pragmatic attitude to kingship accorded perfectly with the businesslike approach he preferred. He never encouraged royalist imagery. In 1555, after his marriage to Mary Tudor, he had a medal struck in which he was presented as Apollo, the sun god. The device ran, 'Iam illustrabit omnia'. The emblem never came to acquire special significance, and in subsequent years he did not develop this or any other imagery of his power.[126]

He neither needed nor used special powers to express his displeasure. All who knew him were unanimous in affirming that he never displayed anger. Rarely expressed orally, it was in contrast frequently committed to the annotations on his letters. His desk was a world where he was momentarily isolated and as a consequence could give vent to emotions he would consider wrong to display before others. The Venetian ambassadors are the source for the belief, to be found in most of their reports, that Philip dissimulated grudges until the time was right to strike. 'They say in Spain,' they stated, 'that it is a short distance from the king's smile to his dagger.' The saying was applied to Philip by ambassadors Donato in 1573 and Morosini in 1581.[127] It is likely that some courtiers said it and believed it, but more difficult to find any concrete justification for it.

Philip never accorded special treatment to his own person. The royal portraits show that he never dressed sumptuously, nor did he accept gaudy settings for paintings done of him. The courtesies decree of 1586, in the making for ten years, expressed perfectly his wish to downplay formality. He took no special measures for his own safety,[128] despite the attempt on his life in Lisbon. He had no bodyguards. In 1578 an official expressed anxiety that the king went about 'alone and without any of the measures that are normally taken to put fear into someone with bad intentions'.[129] When in the country, he would wander about alone, without any guard. He also gave audiences alone and unarmed.

While rejecting 'absolutism' of the type claimed by rulers of France, the Spanish monarchy was happy to accept the images of power diffused by the Renaissance. During his visits to the Low Countries, Philip was depicted on triumphal arches as a partner in the glories of his father. In the years after his return to the peninsula, the arches and decorations repeatedly insisted on the themes of justice, religion, triumph and power. Statues from classical mythology mingled with figures from Castilian history, to celebrate the universal status of the crown. No one was more conscious than Philip of this universality. Interestingly, it never led him to try to increase his political power. Philip had long since left behind him the dream, which he no doubt entertained briefly in the early 1550s, of succeeding to the Holy Roman Empire, as the family agreement made at Augsburg in 1551 had stipulated. In 1558, in line with the Augsburg agreement, he approached the emperor Ferdinand about being invested officially as vicar of the empire in Italy. Ferdinand's reply to his nephew, who was then in Flanders, gave clear hints about the uproar that might follow among German princes. However, he said, he was willing to comply with the Augsburg accord, which had supposed that the vicar would reside in Italy. 'On these conditions then, we give our solemn word that the moment His Highness goes to Italy we will send him our patents.'[130] Philip returned to the subject in 1562,[131] but did not insist too strongly. Had he ever seriously lusted after the title, he already (in secret) possessed it. The title of vicar which his father had given him at the abdication in 1556, and which on Granvelle's advice he kept secret, gave him perpetual authority over the territories of the Holy Roman Empire in Italy.[132]

The stories which circulated a few years later among Italian diplomats, to the effect that Philip still yearned for the title of emperor and was thinking of declaring himself emperor of the Indies, were pure gossip.[133] The desire for the supreme title may have existed, but the king seems never to have done anything to realise it. Contemporaries who persisted in fostering the image of a king who lusted after kingdoms and titles either did not know Philip or were deliberately distorting the truth. Philip had no interest in ruling over Germany. 'As to the succession to the Empire,' he reminded his ambassador to Vienna in 1562, 'in the present state of affairs it is not in my interest to claim it, and I wish to help the king [of Bohemia, Maximilian] obtain it.'[134] Because Germany was vital to his general security, however, he pursued an active diplomatic policy there. He was later to get involved in claims to the thrones of Portugal, England and France, but in each case it was because a doubtful succession and pressing reasons of security obliged him to play his hand. A firm anti-expansionist, he felt that each ruler, heretic or not, should rule his country in peace without interfering in the affairs of others. At no time in his life did he express support for the principle that heretics had no right to rule. He was never, in this sense, anti-Protestant. Apart from Elizabeth of England, whose regime he explicitly supported for some twenty years, he had good relations with the Lutheran kings of Scandinavia and several Lutheran princes in Germany.

An astonishing aspect of the Spanish monarchy, especially after union with Portugal in 1580, was the relative absence of triumphalism in literature and the arts. The achievement of peninsular unity fed Castilians with the illusion that they were now masters of Spain. But the resort to ritual celebration was surprisingly muted. Philip had made a great display at his entry into Lisbon in 1581. The occasion, recalling previous entries into Spanish cities and the great triumphal *entrées* of the Renaissance which he had experienced in Italy and Flanders, was quite exceptional, and not repeated during his reign. While the French monarchy in these years was stepping up its ostentations of power, in Spain the trend was the reverse.

Even before the entry into Lisbon, Philip in 1579 looked into the possibility of simplifying the ceremonial of precedence at court. With Granvelle's help, he initiated a review of past and present practice,[135] and in 1584 set up a committee of three on the matter.[136] This bore fruit eventually, in September 1586, with the decree on courtesies or forms of address (*cortesías*) in official letters. The most fundamental change (one which went against the trend in all other western monarchies) was that the king should no longer be addressed as 'Majesty' but only as 'Sir' (*Señor*).

The strong democratic traditions to be found in Spain, and the absence of theories of royal power, might together have produced a down-to-earth, popular monarchy. In practice, foreign observers tended to claim that Philip's monarchy took on the stern appearance of a despotism. A Swiss traveller observed: ' "We are all kings," say the Spaniards, but this has not prevented Philip from being the most absolute monarch in the world.'[137] It was largely an optical illusion. The king's 'unlimited' power was in practice limited by the extensive areas of Spain where the authority of great lords and prelates was, in day-to-day matters such as taxation and justice, greater than his. He could pass few laws without consulting those affected. For money he was heavily dependent on others. Even in matters affecting his own orders, his authority was questioned. In 1577 he ordered the duke of Feria to marry a certain noble lady. The duke refused. 'Your Majesty cannot make the order,' he argued, 'because this is a case affecting honour, and the prince cannot compel a subject to do anything against his own honour.'[138] In 1581 the king sent an apparently simple request to a college in Salamanca, asking for confidential papers on an official who had just been appointed to a government council. The college refused. Confidential papers, it argued, were totally confidential. Not even the king could breach their secrecy. 'To say that Your Majesty is not bound by a precept of natural law, such as that on secrecy, is unacceptable, because the precept binds us all equally.'[139] The examples demonstrate cogently that the king's power was not quite what outsiders imagined it to be.

Like all rulers of Spain, Philip had reason to complain of the famous *fueros* or liberties of the non-Castilian realms. There were always points of conflict where he found his hands tied, whether in dealing with bandits in Valencia or Moriscos in Aragon. Wherever possible, he cut corners, but none of his differences took the shape of serious opposition to the *fueros*. He never harboured any intention of touching them. 'Looked at closely,' he told the French ambassador in Monzón in 1563, the *fueros* 'gave him more liberty than people said. As long as those provinces rendered him fidelity and obedience, he had no wish to innovate there.'[140] In 1589 a Carmelite friar in Catalonia, despairing of the disorder and banditry in that province, suggested to Philip that he should abolish the laws of Catalonia and substitute those of Castile. 'This would perhaps be a good opportunity for Your Majesty to get rid of these laws and put this land in a reasonable state . . . Your Majesty will know best how to do it, and with more thought it will perhaps be easier than it seems.'[141] If Philip ever saw the letter he did not see fit to reply.

The king's power, in brief, was 'absolute' but substantially restricted. A leading legal expert of the time, Castillo de Bobadilla, specified that laws made by the king were not binding if they went against conscience, or faith, or natural law, or accepted laws. The idea of *raison d'état*, he said, existed only in tyrannies and not in Spain.[142] The complex nature of political authority in Spain was ill suited to royal oppression. The king, in any case, had an extraordinary tolerance for those types of dissent which did not threaten to turn into rebellion. When some individuals were arrested for protesting against the increase in taxes in 1575, he ordered their release. 'The prince of whom subjects complain the least,' he is reported as saying, 'is he who gives them most freedom to complain.'[143] Criticism of taxes abounded in the later years of his reign, but with one prominent exception (in 1591 in Avila) he appears to have put up with it.

Despite occasional clashes of interest, Philip did not emphasise royal power at the expense of the liberty of his subjects. In the Castilian countryside, the tranquil advance of local autonomy possibly even worked in the opposite direction: an increase of effective liberty.[144]

*

Philip shared the premiss, derived from Christian tradition, that private sins affect public morality, and that public morality is carefully watched by God. He was singularly careless of his own sexual sins when younger, although, in other respects, he seems on the evidence to have exhibited correct personal behaviour. In religion, he carried out all his duties faithfully, with the required degree of public piety. He heard mass daily. He went to communion four times a year.[145] At no time did he imagine, however, that religious morality could be imposed. When his bishops, full of zeal from their sessions at Trent, attempted in 1565 to put reform of lay morals on their agenda, he warned them firmly to drop the issue. When he was drawn in the 1570s into conflict with the zealous archbishop of Milan, Carlo Borromeo, his confessor Chaves lectured the archbishop that 'a people cannot be forced into perfection'.[146]

Though he felt deeply about religion, not until the later years of the reign did he display signs of religiosity. It is certain that he was not (as his Protestant enemies claimed him to be) a bigot or fanatic in his personal attitudes. His letters to his daughters, written in 1581, virtually exclude religion as a topic. On the other hand, he never ceased to be aware of his personal responsibility as a Catholic ruler. 'The cause of religion,' he informed his envoy in France in 1590, 'has been and is my principal guide in everything I have done and do.'[147] But he normally made such statements when he was about to pursue policies which, in the opinion of others, were *not* primarily serving the cause of religion. This did not prevent him identifying his role as king as the service of God. 'God's service and mine, which is the same' is a phrase that recurs throughout his correspondence. It was a stock phrase, not so different from similar appeals to God made by other rulers. By the 1580s, however, as we shall see, the identification of the two became more obsessive. Another of his declarations – that he would rather lose all his realms than compromise on religion – was also a favourite phrase, repeated frequently in the 1560s. He used it to his wife,[148] to ambassadors, and to his own officials. His harshest comments relating to religion were reserved for political rebels, the Dutch Calvinists and the French Huguenots. The severity was always over rebellion, rather than over religion.

He did not admit the principle of toleration to Protestants within his own states, given the bloodshed caused by religious conflict in other nations of Europe. If his subjects in Flanders wanted to worship as Protestants they could do so, but would have to emigrate. 'To think that a passion so great as this about choice in religion can be resolved by soft means,' he told the emperor Maximilian in 1570, was 'a complete illusion'. Soft measures, if adopted, must always be accompanied by the threat of discipline.[149] But he had good relations with Protestant states, such as Denmark and Sweden. He had German Protestant troop commanders in the army of Flanders.

He also, in contrast to the legendary image of a fanatical king, came to accept the inevitability of toleration in specific circumstances. If England were invaded, he decided in 1576, there must be no religious persecution.[150] His own previous experience there, and the fact that England was not his direct moral responsibility, may have induced this attitude. But it is significant that some years later he was also able to move towards accepting a form of toleration in the Netherlands. Following the Spanish tradition, he likewise accepted – albeit reluctantly – the need to coexist with Muslims (in Spain) and Jews (in Italy and north Africa) as subjects.

His confessors, like those of other Catholic rulers, occupied a special place in government. They were always allotted a place on committees where moral questions were on the agenda. They were also consulted continually by the king on a broad range of issues. On all these occasions, they expressed their views by formal vote or in writing. This gave them a constitutional role which somewhat modifies the popular image of the confessor as an uncontrollable secret influence on the king. Philip, moreover, did not actually have to confess to his 'confessor'. He always had a small group of chaplains to whom he confessed, and when not with them he confessed to any priest he cared to. At San Lorenzo, he confessed to various friars who were not in his team of confessors.[151]

In the absence of documentation, it is difficult to prove that confessors were able to influence the king. During his reign the king had two principal confessors. The first was the Franciscan Bernardo de Fresneda, who served from 1553 till his death in 1577.[152] A fat prelate who thrived on political scheming, Fresneda was a mortal enemy of Carranza and possibly influenced Philip's position in that affair. Philip's second important confessor was the ascetic Dominican Diego de Chaves. There is no evidence to suggest that the king's decisions on any matter were the result of special advice from his confessor alone.

Curiously, Philip showed no special favour to the Jesuits, who were much in evidence both at his court and in Spain generally. He encouraged them in their first phase of expansion in the 1560s. They, in return, gave him invaluable support during the campaign for the Portuguese succession. In the late 1580s, when the order had serious problems with the Inquisition, he seems however to have distanced himself from them, while still keeping up excellent relations with individual Jesuits.

His most profound personal devotion, which he may have picked up from his governess Estefania de Requesens, was to the Virgin of Montserrat. It encouraged his affection for Catalonia, and motivated several visits to the monastery. Above all, it inspired him to rebuild entirely the church at Montserrat. He also had particular respect for the shrines of the Virgin at Guadalupe, and the Pilar in Saragossa. In moments of special crisis, such as the illness of Don Carlos in 1561, or that of Elizabeth in 1564, he contacted the clergy at these sites to ask for their prayers.

Precisely from 1580, after the death of Anna, his tendency to religion became more marked. The monks of San Lorenzo noticed it immediately. He also began to rely more on God for political help, if we may judge by his letters. The setting up in 1583 of a committee to clean up the night-life of Madrid was evidence of his greater concern for public morality. He was, even so, not an extremist about such matters. When in 1583 he received denunciations of moral turpitude in the capital, he demurred. No specific cases, he said, had ever been referred to him. Sweeping statements about immorality were too vague, he said: he received such every Sunday from members of the public.[153] By the time of the Armada, however, God had been enlisted full time in the cause of religion. Philip even permitted himself to question why (after the disaster) God had abandoned His own cause.

He never felt any contradiction between his profound Catholic belief and his high-handed actions in respect of the Church. His continuous hostility to aspects of papal policy was inherited from his father.[154] It also coincided with a common Spanish distrust of the papacy and of Italians in general. From 1555 he had used troops against the pope. He consistently blocked the entry of all papal decrees into his realms and periodically expelled nuncios. 'Secular princes,' he emphasised to his ambassador in

Rome in 1578, 'are not bound to carry out the mandates of the pope in temporal matters.'[155] He cited canon lawyers and his own advisers for this conclusion. An unswerving supporter of the spiritual authority of the papacy, he could not brook its refusal to support him blindly. 'It is intolerable,' he complained to Granvelle, 'that because I am the only one who respects the apostolic see, instead of thanking me as they should they make use of it to try and usurp my authority.' His impatience exploded on paper into little bursts of anger. 'I am fed up and near the end of my patience, and if it should come to that they will very possibly regret it . . . There are many other things that I would like to say on this, but it is midnight and I am very tired.'[156]

Within Spain Philip felt himself completely free to act as he liked in Church matters. With extensive powers over the nomination of dignitaries and the disposal of Church revenue, he was no less head of his Church than the Protestant rulers of northern Europe were of theirs. When in the 1560s and 1580s he gave his support to reforms within the peninsular Church, he did not hesitate to sanction the use of troops against monasteries and convents. The king had total control over appointment of bishops, but always consulted carefully before naming to sees. He once rejected the nominee of his council. 'If we make him bishop,' he asked with a wry irony, 'which of his two sons will inherit the bishopric?'[157]

The king's support for the Inquisition was unswerving. His devotion to it provoked unfounded rumours that he wished to establish it in the Netherlands. Ironically, at the very period that Spain's Inquisition was being attacked by Protestant propaganda in the Netherlands, it was being subjected to criticism within Spain itself. At court, voices questioned the role of the Inquisition in the Carranza case. Philip demonstrated his apparent impartiality by paying for the expenses of the revered canon lawyer, Dr Martín de Azpilcueta, to go to Rome in 1567 and defend the archbishop. Carranza's case dragged on for five more years, largely because of Philip's refusal to let the Inquisition lose face.[158] In 1567 in Valencia, and in 1568 in the cities of Murcia and Mallorca, bitter attacks were mounted against the Inquisition.[159] The most severe problem was Catalonia, where in July 1569 the tribunal, hard pressed by hostile Catalans but stoutly supported by Philip, succeeded in having the constitutional representatives of the province, the *diputats*, arrested for heresy. The storm aroused by the case blew over in a few months.

Criticism of the Holy Office by Italians, Spaniards and others elicited from the king some of his most stubborn defences. He had no doubts in 1569: 'Had there been no Inquisition there would have been many more heretics, and the country would be in a lamentable state, like others where there is no Inquisition as we have in Spain.'[160] It was the only issue on which the king firmly refused to admit any dissenting point of view. His affirmation in October that year to the pope was unwavering: 'I cannot and must not fail to support the Inquisition, as I shall always do all the days of my life'.[161]

'In the days of Philip the Second,' an inquisitor wrote wistfully twenty-five years after the king's death, 'the Inquisition experienced great felicity.'[162] Without doubt, Philip was the tribunal's greatest patron. He obtained from the pope the first regular financing of the Holy Office. He reformed its treasury and personnel. He attended its *autos de fe*. He sanctioned the establishment of new tribunals, in America and in Galicia. He protected it against all critics, most notably during the events in Saragossa in 1591. But he never added to its powers, never used it to advance his political aims, and when possible stepped in to correct abuses.

Neither through the Inquisition nor by any other means did the king ever attempt the impossible task of which he has been most frequently accused: isolating Spain from western civilisation. He actively worked to open Spain's frontiers to the best that Europe could offer in art, technology and science.[163] There were few effective controls on literary publication, and Spaniards actually published more books in Europe during the last decades of his reign than they had ever done before.[164]

*

At the centre of a vast monarchy, the king had the unenviable task of trying to make all its segments work in harmony. Charles V and his advisers never attempted to unify the emperor's dominions and had no concept of a centralised policy. Philip, because of his permanent residence there and the initiative which men and money from the peninsula had begun to take in the European world by the 1550s, began to centralise his policy on Spain. The control was primarily Castilian, given the greater weight of Castile in Spain's affairs. It took two forms. On one hand, Castile ruled over overseas territories that were considered to have been won by conquest, and were treated as colonies, suitable for exploitation and settlement: the Canaries and America fell into this category. On the other hand, Castile's king ruled over sovereign territories in Europe which had come his way by inheritance (the Netherlands, for example) or by agreements (Milan). In the colonies, it was difficult to avoid a domineering and rapacious policy. The problem (common to all empires) was that Spaniards also came to adopt the same rapacious attitudes in the free states associated with their monarchy.

Philip was not a conscious imperialist. He never held or voiced theories about imperial power or status, and never possessed any recognisable principles of empire.[165] His court, except in the triumphalist years of the early 1580s, was not imperialist.[166] One of his own officials in the 1560s, Fernando Vázquez de Menchaca, published a treatise in which he defined political power as the preserve of the people, and dismissed theories about universal power for kings as a fairy-tale.[167] The official attitude remained unchanged throughout the reign.

A dedicated bureaucrat, Philip's intention was above all to make things function efficiently. He had little patience with men or institutions which impeded this aim. Efficiency could be achieved in three main ways: by getting the correct information on which to base decisions, by having reliable officials (where possible, they should be Castilian officials), and by securing adequate sums of money.

The information was vital, since he was well aware of his ignorance of the geography and politics of his realms. From the 1560s he began the task of collecting data on the monarchy. Before leaving the Netherlands in 1559, he commissioned the cartographer Jacob van Deventer to draw detailed surveys of 'all the towns of these provinces'.[168] In 1566 he told the viceroy of Naples that 'since every day there arise matters in which for greater clarity it is necessary to know the distances of the places in that realm, and the rivers and frontiers it has', a detailed map should be sent to him. In 1575 the viceroy was asked for 'a survey of that realm, for business that arises here'.[169] The same procedure seems to have been followed in all his realms. In 1566 Philip ordered the preparation of a completely new geographic survey of Spain, permitting 'not a span of land to pass without inspection'.[170] The survey, unfortunately, was never completed; what was done 'is kept by His Majesty in his study'.[171] Now preserved in the Escorial, it was the most impressive survey of its kind undertaken in any European state of the sixteenth century. In 1570 he commissioned a Portuguese cosmographer, Francisco Domínguez, to carry out a geographical survey of all New Spain. The following year he appointed an official 'cosmographer-historian' for America, Juan López de Velasco.

Lack of information sometimes made it extremely difficult to plan policy. When in 1566 he was asked to make a decision on a voyage of the conqueror Miguel López de Legazpi to the Philippines, he was unsure what to do since he could find no maps of the area. 'I think I have some,' he wrote to his secretary, 'and I tried to find them when I was in Madrid the other day. When I go back there I shall look again.'[172]

His constant interest in maps was not the curiosity of an amateur: he collected few of them. They were, rather, essential instruments of state. Preparations for the Armada against England involved extensive poring over maps. In 1591, when his troops marched into Aragon, he used maps to plan their movement personally. It is a comment on the general backwardness of cartography in Spain that the king's interest did not stimulate the science among Spaniards.

There were not even any reliable maps of the Iberian peninsula. The best map-makers of the time were foreigners, mostly Italians, and they devoted more care to Spain's coastline (for shipping) than to its interior. Philip was therefore highly satisfied with the publication at Antwerp in 1570 of Abraham Ortelius's *Theatrum*, a work dedicated to him. Other Netherlanders also made a crucial contribution to knowledge of the peninsula. Shortly after his return, Philip invited Anton van den Wyngaerde to come to Spain and make a survey of its cities.[173]

From 1575 the councils began preparing the most ambitious of all the survey schemes. In May 1576 Philip issued a detailed list of forty-nine questions which were to be answered by all officials in America. The questionnaire covered every conceivable topic from botany and geography to economy and religion. The answers, the famous 'geographic relations', began to come in from 1577 and trickled through for ten years more.[174]

In Castile a pilot questionnaire was distributed in December 1574 to villages in the area of Coria. On the basis of this, a broad survey was commissioned in October 1575. A list of fifty-seven questions was sent to the villages and towns of Castile, and a subsequent questionnaire was issued three years later. From the document it is clear that the king intended the information to be used also as the basis for a general history of Spain. The 'Survey of Towns', as it was called, foundered on the sluggishness of local officials, who could not be bothered to carry out the task. Only Toledo and surrounding areas took the trouble to send in details.[175]

Behind all these projects, which occupy the 1560s and 1570s, it is possible to see clearly the king's desire to produce a large and encyclopaedic corpus of information on his realms. In detail, some of the individual schemes were the brainchild of officials, but the overall concept came from the king alone. Philip has often been criticised for smallness of mind and correcting grammatical faults in letters, yet in these schemes we have clear proof of his capacity to rise above the detail and envisage wide-ranging and universal schemes. His own incessant curiosity and interest were the driving forces. No other monarch of that time sponsored, as Philip did, a general history, a general geography, a general topographical survey and a general map of his domains. As in all his projects, he wanted research to be based on the methodical use of original data. His purpose was not to impress, but to learn and to achieve. He never became, like some other rulers, a great scholar. But he was without any doubt the most creative sponsor of schemes among the monarchs of Europe.

Philip encouraged the collection of state papers into a central deposit in the old castle of Simancas, near Valladolid. The deposit had been begun by Cobos, but Philip as regent in 1545 took the first steps to store papers officially. In 1578 he approved the construction of a building designed by Juan de Herrera,[176] and bit by bit, administrative papers were sent there for storage. In 1581 he realised that most of the papers on the provincial

Church councils of 1565 had been in the keeping of Gonzalo Pérez and were now in the custody of the disgraced Antonio Pérez. They should immediately be retrieved from Antonio, he ordered, and taken to Simancas.[177] The papers of the crown of Aragon were also carefully conserved. 'They must be kept in the archive in Barcelona,' he ordered in 1552, 'where they are usually taken and preserved.'[178]

Information was also collected for the king through espionage, a policy followed by many governments of the time. In the case of Spain, the espionage network was normally coordinated by the Spanish ambassador in the relevant country. Francés de Álava, when ambassador in France in the 1560s, ran a small team of spies which operated mainly in the south of the country.[179] The ambassador in England ran a similar operation. Lack of finance was the principal barrier to a more efficient espionage system. By 1589 ministers were complaining to Philip that more spies were needed in order to get the information required to run foreign policy.[180]

The ambassadors and other high officials who served the king on an international plane were among the most distinguished in all European history. Curiously, their story has never been told.[181] Philip, evidently, could act only within certain limits when choosing them. The unwritten rules demanded that he appoint from among the grandees of Castile, but he broke the rules often enough, in his preference for Portuguese (Ruy Gómez, Moura) and Catalan (the Requesens family) advisers, and his appointment of Granvelle. Since his was a multinational monarchy, he drew whenever possible on the support of all. It is a comment on his own impartiality that he only asked for loyalty. Beyond that, he allowed his advisers considerable freedom of thought and action. A typical example of this liberal policy was his employment of Jean Baptiste de Tassis in the 1580s and 1590s in several sensitive posts. Tassis was a Netherlander, fluent in six languages, of outstanding diplomatic and military talents. He also supported toleration in the Netherlands, and openly admired Henry of Navarre as 'a great soldier'.[182] None of this disqualified him from the royal service.

Reliable administrative officials, the second of Philip's prerequisites for efficiency, were almost impossible to secure. There was no imperial bureaucracy, and the king had to fend for himself in each country. He attempted to secure nomination of as many senior officials as possible. Appointment to these posts was usually made from among the local elite, a practice which brought stability and bound these elites to the crown. But Philip also insisted that Spaniards must occupy posts. In 1568 he ordered the viceroy of Naples: 'in future, when posts fall vacant, inform us if there are any Spaniards who might be appointed'.[183] Posts involving military security were almost invariably reserved for Spaniards.[184] Non-Spanish elites quickly came to resent this preference. From the 1560s, when cash problems became serious, Philip resorted with frequency to selling offices to local elites. In the American colonies, it was the local elites rather than peninsular Spaniards who came to control the administration.

Trying to get the states of the monarchy to contribute to expenses was the most difficult task of all. No European state of this time, Spain included, had a central treasury or a uniform tax system. Nor were taxes normally raised directly by the parliament or government. Most tax-payers, even in Spain, paid their taxes to a number of different local entities, rather than to the crown. One golden rule, clung to everywhere, was that tax revenue must not be spent out of the country. In these circumstances the king found it extraordinarily difficult to raise revenue for general enterprises, or to persuade each state to contribute to imperial costs. His view was clearly expressed in 1589, when he was asked to reduce his demands for taxes from Sicily. 'Except in pressing cases,' he conceded, 'the burdens of one kingdom are not usually loaded on to another.' However, 'since God has entrusted me with so many, and all are in my charge, and the defence of some preserves the others, it is fair that all should help'. At the same time, he wanted each realm to keep its finances distinct: 'it is better not to mix up the debts and payments of different kingdoms'.[185] Philip was helped by the collaboration of the nobles in each state. He also benefited from the services of the interna-tional financiers, who advanced him cash which he repaid out of taxes.

The desire for efficiency was frustrated, above all, by the immense distances in the monarchy. In order to keep contact with every corner of the world-wide empire, 'Spain waged an unremitting struggle against the obstacle of distance'.[186] Philip's ability to issue commands and control events was determined by the days, weeks and even months that it took for correspondence to reach its destination. Letters to Madrid took just under two weeks from Brussels, over three months from Mexico. Other factors might extend these intervals. In the last week of September 1569 Alba wrote from Brussels to Philip, but the king did not reply until late in November. Alba received the response only in December, a delay of nearly three months which left him fuming.[187] Slowness was not, for all that, the exclusive fault of the king. It was an inevitable defect of the age. Commenting on the delays in letters, Granvelle in 1562 complained that in Brussels they had less contact with Madrid than Americans did.[188] Later, when viceroy of Naples, he quoted a previous viceroy as saying that 'if one had to wait for death he would like it to come from Spain, for then it would never come'.[189]

Control from Spain blurred the important difference between being a colony and being a sovereign territory. 'The other parts of the empire', it has been observed, 'slipped imperceptibly into the role of satellites and Castile into that of the metropolitan power. Hatred of the Spaniard began to smoulder everywhere.'[190] Officials were perfectly aware of the discon-tent. Since the fifteenth century the Spaniards had been the most hated nation in Italy. Italy's political leaders wanted nothing more than to see the back of Spain. 'I don't know what there is in the nation and empire of Spain,' an official in Milan lamented in 1570, 'that none of the peoples in the world subject to it bears it any affection. And this is much more so in Italy than any other part of the world.' An annotation by the same writer goes some way towards showing what Italians had to put up with from Spaniards. 'These Italians,' the writer notes, 'although they are not Indians have to be treated as such.'[191] No less memorable is the observation made by the governor of Milan at this time, Luis de Requesens. 'We cannot,' he stated, 'trust Italy to the Italians.'[192]

Hatred of Spain was not provoked only by Spanish misdeeds. A particularly efficient propaganda campaign was launched at the time by Protestant religious leaders and by Protestant states. From about 1580 the campaign assumed greater virulence as a result of Spanish involvement in the politics of every western European state. Calumnies focused above all on the person of the king of Spain. Legends were born which succeeded in distorting his image down to today.

Curiously, Philip did not believe in the need for propaganda. He believed that the truth – his truth – would triumph over the lies of his enemies. When it was suggested to him in 1593, during his military intervention in France, that he should publish a paper justifying his position to the French people, he refused. 'As for the paper,' he said, 'there's no need to discuss it, because for good people it is our works that count, and for the others we don't need to give them the opportunity for debate.'[193] It was one of the most serious of all his mistakes. By refusing to engage in the propaganda battle, he left the field wide open to the English and Dutch. Their brilliant journalism produced an image of Spain which has since been called 'the Black Legend'.[194] The image succeeded in influencing the way in which even Spaniards viewed their king.

9
War in the West
1580–1586

Strange people, these Portuguese.[1]

Philip was, in 1580, at the height of his power. The first monarch in history to rule over a united peninsula, he could now truly title himself king of 'Spain'. In medieval times, the term 'Spain' (or 'the Spains') had been applied loosely to the sum of states within the whole peninsula, including Catalonia and Portugal. Philip had frequently termed himself 'king of Spain' in documents, but only as a way of abbreviating his titles.[2] From 1580 the loose concept was a political reality. To issue a decree in Lisbon for 'these realms of Spain'[3] was something no ruler of Spain had ever done before. For some, even in Portugal, there was a hope that unity would bring stability and prosperity. When the king entered Lisbon in 1581 one of the triumphal arches erected for him carried the verse: 'Now will be fulfilled the prophecies of the wise, that you will be sole king and sole shepherd on earth.'[4]

The universal monarchy had indeed arrived. A Spanish poet expressed the hope of seeing a world with 'one sole shepherd and monarchy'.[5] These were the years when the veteran soldier Alonso de Ercilla, who had accompanied Philip on both his European journeys and had then served in Peru, composed his epic poem on Spain's imperial triumphs, the *Araucana*. There was reason for the imperial pride. Peace in the Mediterranean was assured. Philip had moved the defence frontier out towards the Atlantic. The one-year truce signed with the Turks was extended in January 1581 into a three-year truce. In the north the richest and most populous provinces of the Netherlands had made their peace. In the New World the Philippines were firmly conquered, viceroy Toledo had put an end to Inca resistance in Peru, expeditions were moving up from Mexico into what is now the southern United States, and in the south Atlantic the city of Buenos Aires was founded. With the absorption of Portugal, Philip's authority now reached also into India, Indonesia and China. The empire, so extensive as to stagger the imagination, was the biggest ever known in history. It was, a Spaniard wrote with pride, 'over twenty times greater than the Roman'.[6] A wave of imperialist pride swept over Spaniards everywhere. Zealous missionaries believed that a universal monarchy would help to conquer the known world for Christ.[7]

Within the range of his war budgets, Philip's most substantial expenditure had been on building up the Mediterranean fleet. In Lisbon, his perspective altered. He now definitively changed his focus from the inland sea out towards the Atlantic.[8] His future strategy, his military efforts, his concern for security, shifted westwards. The choice was not his alone. The growing maritime activity of both the Dutch rebels and the English gave him very little alternative. A programme of shipbuilding was directed from Lisbon and by 1587 Philip was maintaining over one hundred ships in the Atlantic.[9]

He had not been out of Spain for over twenty years. Despite the urgent issues pressing for attention at home, he now took the bold decision to reside away from his capital, his palaces, and his family, in a realm he did not know. His immediate motive was political. In the summer of 1579 he had been advised to give the Portuguese the impression that, once accepted as their king, he would make Lisbon his regular home.[10] It was advice he came to accept. Besides, he was assured, 'the climate of Lisbon is ideal for Your Majesty's health'. Nor was the environment alien: he was half-Portuguese by origin, and could understand the spoken language. He came eventually to spend an impressive two years and four months away from his own nation.

In Lisbon he adapted his living conditions.[11] With some 100,000 inhabitants, the city was the second largest in the peninsula (after Seville) and a fitting capital for a king. The existing waterfront palace of the Paço da Ribera was modified. Its great windows looked directly over the ships in the harbour and gave a panoramic view of the ocean. A new four-storey domed tower, the Torreão,[12] was constructed by Juan de Herrera and Filippo Terzi. It dominated the harbour like a lighthouse,[13] and contained a library as well as a ceremonial throne room and royal lodgings. The Torreão was lavishly furnished, but Philip made no attempt to convert his buildings into expressions of an imperial triumph.[14]

Philip was well aware of popular hostility to Spain among ordinary Portuguese. He was kept informed of 'the stubbornness of the populace in not wanting a foreign king',[15] but made efforts to win them over. He ordered the bodies of two popular saints to be brought back from Spain.[16] He attended an *auto de fe* in Lisbon on 1 April 1582, to show his disapproval of heretics (Portugal had its own Inquisition, dating from 1547). He tried to intervene as little as possible in Portuguese politics, and left nearly all business in the hands of Cristóbal de Moura, who was less likely to offend. Decisions of every sort were put off until 'Don Cristóbal' could be consulted. 'You do well to keep Don Cristóbal informed of these matters (which I can't handle),' he wrote on one memoir; 'inform Don Cristóbal of the details' on another; and 'this can be dealt with in a committee, or by Don Cristóbal' on yet another.[17] The process is expressed neatly in the following order: 'you should draw up a summary that I can give to Don Cristóbal, and on which I can state that he should look into and deal with those matters'.[18]

However, Philip's role in Lisbon was far from passive. For the first time, he came into direct contact with the rich overseas trade of Spain and Portugal. He had the satisfaction of watching from his window as the great galleons came in from the ocean. The Spanish fleets bound for America could now use Lisbon as a departure point. On one occasion, in April 1582, the king actually 'accompanied the fleet out of the harbour' on its first stage to the New World. 'He breakfasted on board his royal galley, and passed the whole day at the mouth of the port.'[19] He took special interest in plans to form a company to organise the trade in pepper from Asia. He was proclaimed king in Goa in 1581. To his other titles, at the end of his reign, he was proud to add that of 'king of Ceylon'.[20] Excited by the new dimensions opening up for Christianity, in 1582 he appointed an Indian from Malabar as one of his chaplains.[21] In practice, it was the possibility of finding new sources of income, through Portugal, that absorbed most of his time. He did not have to tax the Portuguese themselves, since overseas commerce brought in good returns. Half of all Portuguese government revenue came from the lucrative trade to Asia, and a third from trade to Europe and America.[22] The Atlantic trade was booming, thanks to the development of Brazil.

With the acquisition of Portugal, Spain reached the zenith of its status. Contemporaries in Spain, like Philip himself, saw the union of the crowns as a natural aspiration. To give some meaning to the unity of the penin-sula, in 1582 the customs barriers between Castile and Portugal were abolished.[23] The annexation did little to change the practical power or theoretical pretensions of the monarchy. As king of Portugal, Philip could now adopt a broader imperial strategy, but he did not increase his political power, as some Castilian nobles feared he might. Nor did the financial resources of the crown increase significantly.

Possession of Portugal gave new confidence to his policies. After Alcazar-el-Kebir his advisers had stressed that his claim to the crown must succeed, for Portugal was the key to success elsewhere. It would facilitate defence against Islam. Above all it was, as Philip's cosmographer

Gian Battista Gesio put it, the 'brake on Flanders'.[24] Possession of Portugal, Gesio felt, was 'an absolutely sure way of recovering the states of Flanders'. Others advised Philip that from Portugal he could effectively undermine Dutch trade, and deprive the rebels of access to both spices and salt.

*

From Tomar Philip sent his daughters, then at San Lorenzo, comments on the Cortes proceedings, and on how 'they want to dress me in brocade, much against my wishes, for they say it is the custom in these parts'. (He apparently gave in to the demand, for his royal portrait shows him splendid in brocade.) He had bestowed the Golden Fleece on the duke of Braganza and the two had gone to mass together, 'but he went better-dressed than I'. He missed 'the nightingales, though a few can be heard sometimes from one of my windows'. Already, unfortunately, prince Diego was suffering recurrent illness and fever. This worry, together with concern for the health of the three little children he had left behind in San Lorenzo, form the main theme of the letters he began writing in these months to his daughters.

Written in simple language, uncluttered by literary style, formality or learning, the letters are the most charming private correspondence to have survived from the pen of a ruling monarch of those times. In 1581 at least, Philip tried to write every week, usually dictating to a secretary rather than writing in his own hand. If he found that official business got in the way, he gave priority to the letters.[25] He delighted in describing the exotic aspects of his new life. 'We crossed the river to come here to Almada, where I have a very pretty but small house, and from all the windows you can see the river and Lisbon and the ships and galleys. And from an upper room, where I am writing, you can see through the window the whole length of Lisbon ... I very much wish to go to Lisbon, to get on with what I need to do there.'[26]

In Lisbon he passed what, with hindsight, appears to have been the most restful period of his reign. He had serious attacks of gout in the summers of 1581 and 1582 but recovered quickly. His doctors, secretary Gassol reported, attended to him assiduously.[27] Isabel and Catalina wrote to him regularly with news of their activities and health. His replies mention the periodic gout, but also his moments of contentment. Writing that first August: 'Congratulations to you, the eldest, for reaching fifteen years, to reach this age is already to be very old though in spite of all this I think that you are not yet quite a woman. A week ago I wanted to send you my congratulations but when I wrote it slipped my mind. And you, the younger, will soon also be fourteen.'[28] He referred regularly to the things they were enjoying and which he missed. 'You made me very jealous in what you said of El Pardo, which looks better in winter than in summer.' But these were the little pleasantries of a fond father. He was at ease in Lisbon.

The thirty or so letters surviving from this period reveal something more than tenderness and devotion. They also show us aspects of Philip's character. Unlike separated fathers who never refrain from giving sound advice to their children, on their studies or their health or their general development, Philip never once imposed his views or his counsels. He normally gave directives to the chamberlains and tutors, and may have felt that the letters were no place for exhortation. Apart from a recommendation to the girls to learn Portuguese, and an approving comment that 'you do well to exercise whenever you can',[29] he kept the letters free of appeals. Surprisingly, too, in a man frequently accused of being obsessed by religion, the letters are totally free of religiosity. Philip mentioned Church functions as a matter of course, but the tone was wholly secular, with no effusions of pious sentiment. Free both of didacticism and of piety, the letters breathe a freshness and spontaneity unique in the letters of kings.

There was another aspect to them. Philip never referred to his own childhood. He had had no real childhood, and no intimate relationship with his father. Possibly for that reason he did not understand that the missives from his daughters might be treasured by him one day. Shortly before returning from Lisbon he told the girls that he was burning all their old letters, 'in order not to be weighed down with papers'.[30]

*

For a while after Granvelle's arrival in 1579, there was a certain stability of control at the helm of government in Madrid. The antagonisms of the Alba/Eboli days disappeared. On all major matters of policy there was little disagreement among ministers. The king became his own master. In this he was powerfully helped by the cardinal, known among ministers as 'the bearded one' because of his immensely long, white patriarchal beard. Philip put virtually all business into Granvelle's hands and the latter became for several months the real governor of the monarchy.[31]

The situation began to change when Philip left Castile for Portugal. Granvelle was put in complete charge and diplomats and others were instructed to refer directly to him. The new system left many unhappy, and affected the efficiency of consultation and decision-making. Ministers regretted the removal of the king's firm controlling hand. If the king leaves, an observer felt, everything will collapse. 'His Majesty has only to leave Madrid for El Pardo, and the ministers of all the councils drag their feet and don't turn up at appointed hours or meetings.'[32] The pessimism was not misplaced.

Without the king to keep the peace between factions, disputes broke out immediately. 'War and more war is what we have here,' commented the president of the council, Pazos, from Madrid. 'We are all up to our heads in it, though it is true that what you have there is real and what we have here is staged.'[33] The effects on administration were detrimental. 'I admit,' wrote Pazos, 'the importance of His Majesty's presence there, but one must also consider how necessary it is for business here.'[34]

Granvelle was ably seconded in Madrid by Juan de Idiáquez, who had come with him from Italy. Idiáquez, aged thirty-nine when sworn in as secretary to the king in 1579, was a Basque who had spent the last five years as ambassador in Genoa and Venice. He now began a long and distinguished career in the government of Spain. The cardinal, who had spent many years criticising Spain's administration from outside, found that working from within was no easy task. His efficiency clashed with the slower Spanish pace. 'In Spain everything is slow,' he complained. It was common to see him in his office dictating simultaneously in five different languages (which none of the ministers understood) to his team of secretaries. His non-Spanish temperament clashed with that of officials. He had constant battles with the treasury, which he considered both inefficient and corrupt. Above all, it was difficult to influence the decision-making of the king in Lisbon when he himself was in Madrid. Communicating by written word was unsatisfactory. 'No secretary in the world uses more paper than His Majesty.'[35] On policy issues, a gulf began to open up between the chief minister and the king.

In Lisbon, Philip gave priority to Portugal. Granvelle, for his part, felt that the problems of the Netherlands and France were more important. Resolving the threat from France would, he felt, by itself resolve the problems in the Netherlands, Portugal and the Mediterranean. The obvious threat from England could be contained if England were set against France. If necessary, Spain must go to war with France.[36]

*

There is no indication of how long Philip would have stayed on in Lisbon. He missed his family, but the essentials of government functioned well enough and he was personally content. In April 1582 he was visited in Almeirim by his sister the empress María, mother of Anna and the arch-dukes, who had returned to Spain with her thirteen-year-old daughter Margarita in 1581 after the death of her husband the emperor Maximilian. She installed herself in Madrid and then later went to Portugal. Philip was, as he told his daughters, overjoyed to see her. 'You can imagine how pleased she and I were to see each other, after not seeing each other for twenty-six years.'[37] There was a rumour that the king considered making her governor of Portugal in his place, but before leaving Madrid the empress told ambassador Khevenhüller firmly that she had no intention of taking the job. In the event, a governor had to be found. The death of his heir prince Diego on 21 November 1582 altered matters and obliged Philip to return to Spain as soon as possible.[38] He summoned the Portuguese estates to his palace on 30 January 1583, to swear allegiance to the Infante Philip as heir. He then told them that he was going to make a 'brief absence'.

Some months before, the king had issued in Lisbon a decree, dated 29 September, accepting for all his realms the new Gregorian calendar. It created turmoil in the popular mind by abolishing ten days in early October. The king reflected that 'I suppose there will be objections to this, but they will be sorted out'.[39] He no doubt felt the Portuguese would also understand his 'brief absence'. Since his sister María was unwilling to take up the post of governor, he entrusted the governorship to the archduke Albert. Then the court, accompanied by the empress, left Lisbon on 11 February. They passed through Setúbal and Evora, entering Castile via Badajoz. After a stop at the monastery of Guadalupe, they went through Talavera to the Escorial, arriving on 24 March. The king was anxious, after his long absence, to see what progress had been made on the building. The main purpose of his visit, however, was piety. The following day he presided over solemn funeral honours for his late queen. On the twenty-sixth a high mass was sung for her. Afterwards he went round Anna's rooms, awakening memories.[40]

The next day he left for Madrid, by way of Galapagar and El Pardo. He entered his capital on 29 March.

*

It was the beginning of the most solitary phase of his reign.[41] His sister Juana, to whom he had been very close and who was a permanent companion of queen Anna, had died in 1573. After Anna's death, Philip no longer sought love affairs.[42] His closest comfort was his daughters. The family circle now also consisted of the empress, who came straight from Lisbon to take up residence in the convent of the Descalzas Reales. Her 'court' in the convent became a complement to the real court in the Alcázar. All through 1583 the unfortunate Khevenhüller had to commute two or three times a day between the two courts, bearing messages from the empress to her brother.[43] She made at least one major contribution to the cultural life of the city, by bringing with her from Vienna as director of her chapel's music the composer Tomás Luis de Victoria, long absent from his homeland.

After the return from Portugal Philip began to spend more time in San Lorenzo. In 1583, for example, he spent all the great feasts there: Holy Week, Ascension, Pentecost, Corpus, San Juan, and All Saints. Between these visits, he was mostly in Madrid, with stays in Aranjuez or Valsaín. The keynote to his life after Lisbon was loneliness. It was never a matter of solitude, for he spent every possible moment with his children and family. But the quality of his life changed. He became more bound up with the monastery, and the friars commented on the long time he spent in prayer. He also became more obsessive about little details in the church, *his* church. If the doors were not opened at the correct hour, or if relics were placed in the incorrect order on the altar, he got annoyed and scolded the sacristans.[44] Logically, he was able to spend more time on the building programme, but we may suspect also a wish to be in the place where Anna was resting. When their last child, the little María, died in Madrid on 4 August 1583, she was laid to rest solemnly in San Lorenzo two days later. The royal order for her burial referred to her as the child of 'my very dear and much loved wife'. In October, as part of the work entrusted to the newly arrived Genoese painter Luca Cambiaso, Philip commissioned an altar painting of St Anne, as the late queen had apparently once wished for.[45]

That autumn he exercised his sense of humour on the friars. Among the trophies he had brought from Portugal were an Indian elephant and a rhinoceros. In October he arranged for the elephant, driven by a black boy, to saunter round the cloister, up the steps and into the cells of the astonished Jeronimites. A week later it was the turn of the rhinoceros, which was not quite so cooperative. It grunted bad-humouredly and refused to eat the food it was offered.[46]

Autumn 1583 was also the occasion when the marriage of the Infanta Catalina was decided. In mid-September the ambassador of Savoy delivered to Philip in San Lorenzo the formal proposal from his master Carlo Emanuele, duke of Savoy since 1580. Later, while speaking to his daughters, Philip casually handed to Catalina the letter brought by the ambassador. 'Read this letter,' was all he said. Half-knowing its content, Catalina opened the letter enough to see the signature. She immediately blushed a bright crimson, refused to read any more, and handed the letter back.[47] Philip spent the rest of the afternoon in the company of the delighted princesses, and that night there were festivities to celebrate the event. It was probably in this period, as though to complement the celebrations, that Sofonisba began her inimitable portrait of the beautiful young Catalina.[48] Four weeks later the court moved on to El Pardo, where they stayed for two weeks before returning to Madrid.

The king was never a prisoner of the Escorial. The palace was, rather, a convenient base for both business and pleasure. He invariably came accompanied by prince Philip and the princesses, who afforded him company and relaxation. In 1584, once again, he celebrated the great feasts in San Lorenzo. The last week of April and the first of May were spent at Aranjuez, 'going out most days hunting, with the king always taking their Highnesses in his coach, and in the afternoon boating on the river'.[49] On 8 May the royal family took boats upriver to the palace at Aceca, which they reached four days later.

A full-scale deer hunt was put on at Aceca on 12 May. The method of hunting practised by the court was one commonly used at that time in Europe. Beaters, blowing horns and aided by dogs, were sent out to enclose an agreed zone. The required animals in that zone were then driven, terrified, into a target area. The king and members of his family would be waiting in the royal carriage, from which they would pick off the animals they chose.[50] On this occasion fifty carriages participated in the hunt. Twelve deer were eventually killed. The royal party then set off for San Lorenzo, which Philip made his base from 17 May to 2 October. He spent the whole week of his birthday confined to bed by gout, but after Corpus he was well enough to get about. Every afternoon in June, then, he was able to make outings with the children to Fresneda (his preferred site for fishing) and the other residences in the Castilian countryside.[51] It was a special pleasure to teach his daughters how to shoot. In September Isabel went hunting with him and killed a deer. 'Let's see now,' said the king, 'if the younger Infanta can kill a deer as the elder did, so that with this we can take our leave of the hunting here.'[52] Isabel in time, as portraits of her show, became a great devotee of hunting.

Much of October was spent in El Pardo, where on Saturday the twentieth a pastoral comedy was staged in the evening in honour of Catalina's betrothal. It lasted from seven to ten in the evening. 'His Majesty enjoyed it very much and left very pleased.'[53] He returned to Madrid on 4 November.

*

Among the king's first measures on returning to Castile from Portugal was the summoning of the Cortes, which began sessions in the summer of 1583 and continued for a further two years. In November 1584, in a solemn ceremony in the monastery of St Jerónimo, the Cortes deputies swore allegiance to the heir to the throne, the six-year-old Infante Philip. Among the guests present was the duke of Savoy's brother Amedeo, in Madrid to finalise arrangements for the duke's marriage to the Infanta Catalina.

Economic difficulties increased in the peninsula during the 1580s. There were occasional epidemics, particularly in Andalusia. The year 1584 was one of hardship in Madrid: a decree in June referred to 'the great shortage of bread and the drought this year and the want suffered by the poor'. Special measures were taken to bring in grain from the provinces.[54] The state debt, made worse by the expense of the Portuguese campaigns, was at a record level.

The king got back into his work ritual. A daily schedule set out for him in 1583, and presumably reflecting what he really did, suggested that he should awake at 6 a.m. and deal with some public matters, then rise at 8 a.m. and hear mass. From 9.30 a.m. to 11 a.m. he should see ministers.

Lunch, followed by a siesta, was meant to come between 11 a.m. and 1 p.m. The rest of the afternoon was reserved for business and audiences. From 6 p.m. to 9 p.m. he had to despatch papers. From 9 p.m. to 10.30 p.m. he should have dinner, and go to bed at 11 p.m., which allowed him some seven hours of sleep.[55] The timetable seems plausible. A courtier confirms, for example, that the king gave audiences 'from nine to ten in the morning and from five to six in the afternoon'.[56]

There were times when the correspondence simply mounted up. In the hot summer at Badajoz, waiting for the troops to go in, he continued to labour over his papers, which pursued him everywhere. 'Seeing the many papers with which His Majesty has to deal', a minister commented, 'only makes me regret that he wishes to waste his health and shorten his life this way.'[57] 'I can't take any more,' Philip exploded during his stay in Elvas in January 1581. 'Would anyone like to see what I've been through today? Just two men have occupied me for more than two hours and left me with more papers than I can manage in as many hours. I'm completely shattered. God give me strength and patience!'[58] There were days when all the time had to be dedicated to paperwork. 'I've been all day replying to papers,' he wrote from the Escorial in July 1584, 'and can't look now at anything else. It's been a long haul.'[59] It was during this period that he observed: 'I've never seen so many papers mount up as now'.[60]

Family obligations had their due place and might supersede paperwork. February 19, 1584, for example, was a day when the empress María visited him and also a feast-day requiring his presence at mass. All work was shifted to the next day.[61] He took regular rests when he literally saw no papers at all. The most important of these was his annual retreat in Holy Week, which he used to spend in the monastery of St Jerónimo in Madrid, or in some other convent, but which after 1583 he usually took in San Lorenzo.

He was well aware that the task of governing the monarchy was Herculean. Ministers admired his capacity and application. 'His Majesty's head,' his former ambassador in Portugal observed, 'must be the largest in the world, no other human could have one like it.'[62] But without exception they reiterated that he took on too much. Philip agreed in principle, but saw no alternative. Inevitably he had to rely heavily on those around him, and when they failed him (as in the case of Antonio Pérez) he became morose. 'One of the problems I have, and they are many,' he confided six months after the Escobedo murder, 'is having so few to help me, when I need a great many. This discourages me a great deal, because what can I do if I don't have many around to help? And they must be helpers rather than obstructors, as I think some tend to be.'[63] Like most politicians in power, he began to lose confidence in others and feel that he alone was efficient. This became more marked in the 1580s.

*

The victory of the Spanish fleet over the Portuguese and French at Terceira in the summer of 1583 was seen as a basis for security 'for Flanders'.[64] Reflecting on the victory, which was won on the feast of St Anne, 26 July, Philip was convinced that his late wife Anna 'must be playing a big part in these successes. I've always believed that the queen is playing a role in them.' The signs were good: 'it's a good start, but our business is not yet finished'.[65] Santa Cruz wrote to him after the Azores victory to propose an immediate naval attack on England. The king thanked him, and consulted Parma about the feasibility of the idea. England was giving indirect help to the Dutch, and was now also directly aiding Don Antonio of Crato. The time had come to resolve the English question.

The objectives were clear: to settle the Netherlands problem, and (as a prerequisite) to marginalise England. But the solutions proposed were very different. One key that seemed to offer itself was Mary queen of Scots. Her Scottish faction, and her ambassador in France, saw a Spanish military intervention through Scotland as the quickest way to solve the English question. It was a line that they had pursued consistently and never ceased to press on the Spanish representatives in Paris, one of whom as early as 1572 urged his government to invade England, using Alba's troops and ships.[66]

The possibility was never far from Philip's thoughts. In 1576 he had shrugged off Don Juan's proposal for an invasion. But the prince's words triggered a sequence of ideas in his mind. Three weeks later, in November, after Don Juan was deeply embroiled in the affairs of the Netherlands and could hardly spare the time to pursue schemes, Philip sent him a long memorandum.[67] Reading it, one can see that the king was virtually thinking aloud. The pros and cons of invasion are debated, the need for careful planning emphasised. The basis for any invasion must be support *within* the country: 'no kingdom, no matter how weak or small, can be won without the help of the kingdom itself.' An initial force of 4,000 infantry, supported by cavalry, would do the trick. Once the country is secured, there must be no repression of any sort: 'there must be no talk of "rebels" or "heretics"'. In effect, he gave his approval to Don Juan's idea. There was one fundamental prerequisite. 'In no way' must the prince even think about the idea until peace was achieved in the Netherlands. It was the first blueprint for the Armada enterprise. And the details, though based on Don Juan's suggestions, were entirely Philip's.

In August 1580, only a week after Lisbon capitulated, the king wrote to Alba suggesting that the professional troops, rather than being sent to Italy where most of them were based, be employed in pursuance of what the pope had pressed on him 'insistently many times: the conquest of England'.[68] The ease and success of the Portuguese enterprise stimulated him into believing it could be repeated against Elizabeth. There were, obviously, other strategies in respect of England. The Guise party in France, with whom Philip was in close touch, also hoped to be able to rely on Spanish troops. They went further, and plotted to assassinate Elizabeth as a first step to securing the succession for Mary.

Philip, frankly, did not like any of the proposals. He informed his ambassador in France, the Netherlander Jean Baptiste de Tassis, that he was not party to any plots against the thrones of France or England.[69] His first instinct was always to choose peace rather than conflict. In 1582, when Bernardino de Mendoza, his ambassador in England, offered him four possible ways of making Scotland Catholic, he rejected the idea of invasion and chose that of 'preaching'.[70] But conflict could not be avoided for long. In December 1583 in England the government learned of the Throckmorton plot, involving Mary, several great lords, and the Spanish ambassador. Bernardino de Mendoza was summoned before the Privy Council in January and given two weeks to leave the country. Fired by a personal hatred for the queen of England, he continued to dedicate the rest of his active political life to plotting against Elizabeth. He was appointed ambassador in France from September 1584.

By now two different perspectives were to be found in government. The king continued to extend his confidence to Granvelle, but he showed impatience with the cardinal's habit of citing continually what the emperor would have done in such and such a situation.[71] For the cardinal, the enemy was still France. The group of councillors headed by him and Idiáquez felt that war with France was 'the most efficacious and direct solution to the affairs of Flanders'.[72] It was the only way to cut short the military intervention that the duke of Anjou had been carrying out since 1578 on behalf of the rebellious States General.

In order to obtain an alternative outlook on policy the king in 1583 recalled from Italy Juan de Zúñiga, younger brother of Requesens, who till then had served with distinction in Rome and in the viceroyalty of Naples. Zúñiga's outlook, in contrast to that of Granvelle, tended to be more orientated to the Mediterranean. The king agreed with him that the war in the north should end as soon as possible. Philip has often been presented as the knight-errant of militant Catholicism in these years,[73] but his priority was always peace. He never ceased to express his concern for religion, yet in practice his policy decisions were more realistic. No imperialist fever reigned at the king's court.[74] England was for him a political more than a religious problem. The struggle for security and peace in the north looked beyond England to a different prize: the Atlantic, and America.

Fortunately the brilliant strategies of Parma had begun to turn the tide. The Union of Arras, formed in 1579, gave him a strategic base. While he continued his military campaign, the States General and Spain agreed to attempt a negotiated settlement. The Emperor Rudolf II, who from his sojourn in Spain had gained some insight into the Spanish mind, sponsored a peace conference in the city of Cologne.

For a few months in 1579 the eyes of western Europe[75] were on the international gathering in the splendid Rhine city, which Philip knew well. It was probably the first great peace conference of modern times. The Spanish delegation was led by the Sicilian grandee the duke of Terranova. The papacy was represented by the archbishop of Rossano, Castagna, who opened the sessions. The emperor sent the count of Schwarzenberg. Deputations came from the principalities of Trier, Cologne, Juliers and Liège. Parma sent a representative. The States General sent their delegation in three distinct groups: the south (led by the duke of Aerschot), Holland and Zealand, and the spokesmen for Orange. Terranova, who arrived at Cologne early in April, was pessimistic from the start. He wrote: 'I would like to say I have hopes of success, but I do not'.[76] Talks began in May, even while military campaigns continued. But none of the parties was willing to make any significant concession. On the principal issue, religious toleration, Philip refused to budge.

The conference ended in the second week of November, with agreement as far away as ever. Each side in the conflict was now forced to seek its own solution. In Brussels the States General sank their internal differences and after months of negotiation in January 1581 accepted as their new ruler François, formerly duke of Alençon and now duke of Anjou, brother of the French king. Years of French intervention had paid off. The archduke Matthias was induced to resign a few weeks later. The States, assembled in the Hague, then proceeded in July to depose Philip II as ruler of the Netherlands, alleging that he had tyrannically crushed their privileges.

The act of abjuration was a legitimate legal device accepted by western tradition, though little used in the past. In February 1582 Anjou made a triumphal entry into the city of Antwerp,[77] and was crowned duke of Brabant by the prince of Orange. Other triumphal entries followed. In fact, Anjou's success was blighted. His authority coexisted uneasily with that of William of Orange. Several provinces, for reasons of religion or local interest, rejected him. Any semblance of unity in the Netherlands was fast disappearing. 'There is great disorder here,' an English observer wrote, 'for there is no man that will obey.'[78] In Antwerp in January 1583 Anjou used his French troops to try to seize power. The attempt was repulsed by the Netherlanders. His authority evaporating, Anjou left the provinces in June 1583. He was offered more extensive powers a year later, but died in June 1584, of consumption, before he could sign. A month later the rebels were also deprived of the prince of Orange.

The failure at Cologne had persuaded Spain that the issue must be forced. In June 1580 the prince of Orange was declared a traitor by the

Parma government and a price put on his head. The decree received the full support of cardinal Granvelle. It was answered, before the end of the year, by the *Apology of the Prince of Orange*. Drawn up by one of his aides, but reflecting the prince's own sentiments, this brilliant tract vindicated Orange's struggle and denounced the tyranny of the king of Spain. Distributed through the courts of Europe, it set out in black and white the list of Philip's crimes: his murder of Don Carlos and Elizabeth Valois, his personal crimes and lascivious life.

The ban on William of Orange, which declared him to be an 'enemy of the human race', was an explicit invitation to murder. Philip, like other rulers of his time, considered assassination a legitimate weapon of state.[79] His confessor Alfonso de Castro in 1556 published in Paris a treatise which discussed the power of the magistrate to get rid of tyrants. The killing of a 'tyrant' (the word was taken to mean anyone who exercised power illegitimately or abused his power) was a question discussed by many other theologians, both Catholic and Protestant. Most approved of it.[80] In the right circumstances, it might solve a situation and save lives.

Oddly enough, Philip accepted assassination in theory but disliked it in practice. He scrupulously avoided any involvement. As early as 1567 he received an offer to murder William of Orange during a visit the prince was making to Navarre. He rejected the offer indignantly. He would have preferred to hear about it after the deed was done.[81] Being told in advance made him a party to the conspiracy, and this he would on no account permit. For the same reason, he rejected a proposal by the duke of Guise to assassinate Elizabeth of England.[82]

The idea of killing Orange had been around since at least 1573.[83] The prince was under sentence of death by the council of Troubles. This gave legal justification to the idea. Alba's secretary Albornoz had a plan which Philip approved at the time. Later the idea was put to Requesens, was actively pursued by Escobedo in 1577 and subsequently by Bernardino de Mendoza in 1579. At the Cologne conference, Terranova paid a Flemish priest to look into it. After the failure at Cologne, Granvelle suggested the idea to Philip.[84] The first serious attempt on Orange's life was in March 1582. The prince recovered within four months. The mortal blow was finally struck on 10 July 1584, by the Franche-Comtois Balthasar Gérard. The assassin's plan was known to Parma and his family was duly rewarded by Philip.

Parma in these months was pressing home the Spanish advantage. He had the firm support of the southern provinces and a good supply of soldiers, 60,000 men in the summer of 1582. And the king managed to keep the money coming in. Ypres, Bruges and Ghent surrendered in 1584. On each occasion Parma showed moderation to the conquered. Brussels surrendered in March 1585. Finally, in August 1585 he achieved the capitulation of Antwerp. Philip was at Barbastro, in bed, when the news arrived. Overjoyed, he burst into Isabel's room at midnight to wake her. Granvelle was present at court to witness his enormous joy: 'Not for the battle of St Quentin nor for Lepanto nor for the conquest of Portugal nor for Terceira nor for any other past success, has His Majesty shown such contentment as for this of Antwerp.'[85] Parma received a special reward from the king. The Italian fortress of Piacenza, till now garrisoned by Spanish troops, was handed back to the Farnese family. The king's satisfaction with the year's events was completed by the arrival at Seville, early in October, of the silver fleet from America. It brought a rich cargo for the crown. 'And so 1585, which threatened to be most disturbed,' commented the Venetian ambassador, 'by the grace of God will be brought to a happy conclusion.'[86]

The king did not know that three days after the fall of Antwerp, Elizabeth of England committed herself by the secret treaty of Nonsuch to intervene militarily in the Netherlands. The Dutch rebels, deprived of both Anjou and Orange, had hoped that Henry III of France might come to their aid. But the only likely source of help was England, which this time collaborated willingly. In December 1585 the earl of Leicester arrived at Vlissingen to take charge of an English volunteer force of 8,000 men. It was not open war, but in practice England and Spain were now in a state of belligerence.

The situation in France carried if anything even more serious implications for Spain. Anjou's death deprived the king, his childless elder brother Henry III, of an heir. The direct heir to the throne after June 1584 was automatically Henry of Bourbon, the Protestant king of Navarre. The possibility of a heretic ruler caused consternation among the Catholic noble factions in France. It was even more disturbing to Spain. If France became Protestant, the Netherlands would be lost, and all of western Europe beyond the Pyrenees. Philip accordingly instructed Jean Baptiste de Tassis to conclude a treaty of alliance[87] with the Catholic League, the noble front headed by the powerful Guise family.

By the end of 1585, in consequence, Philip had good reason for both confidence and alarm. The impressive conquests of Parma assured control of the greater part of the Netherlands. Through Mary in England, and the Guises in France, he stood a good chance of assuring a Catholic succession in both countries. Bernardino de Mendoza, ambassador in Paris from late 1584, negotiated and schemed to win support for his master: his hatred of Elizabeth kept him busy plotting with the queen of Scots.

The very active diplomacy of Philip and his agents in these months was not to the liking of west European neighbours. Every move by Spain looked like aggression, and it was easy to interpret Spanish policy as a lust for power. In reality Philip was very far from sharing Mendoza's religious crusading zeal or his inflexible hostility to England. The only purpose he had in mind was protecting the Netherlands. He allied with the Guises (whom he never trusted) because in 1584 this seemed the best way in which to destabilise French politics and prevent further French interference in Flanders. The policy worked. Pressed on one side by the Protestants and Navarre, on the other by the Catholic League and the Guises, Henry III was unable to extend his interests to the north. Philip's links with likely rebels in England were inspired by the same motive. From first to last, his ventures into foreign entanglements were a result of his concern to protect the Netherlands.

*

On 19 January 1585, shortly after spending Christmas with his family in San Lorenzo and El Pardo, the king and his court set out for Saragossa for the marriage of Catalina to the duke of Savoy. Granvelle, now in poor health, was openly critical of travelling in mid-winter. He argued that the prince was ill, and the luckless courtiers would have to put up with inadequate lodgings. The king had no worries on this score. His own health was fair, and he would be lodged royally. Some months before, the French envoy judged that Philip had 'a good appearance, full of health, showing by his vivacity his pleasure in his duties'.[88]

An enormous expedition, including the entire royal family and a large group of lords and ladies, set out from Madrid. Only the empress María, in the Descalzas, stayed behind as the king's representative. Granvelle and the councils left separately a week later. Mindful of his position as king of Portugal, the king adopted Portuguese protocol in his procession, which was headed by a group of Portuguese clergy carrying appropriate insignia.[89] Philip accompanied the party on horseback – a gallant display despite his infirmities – as far as the first overnight stop, in Barajas. The next stop was Alcalá, where they stayed nine days. During this time a visit was made to the university of Alcalá. Philip and his daughters slipped unannounced into a lecture being given by one of the professors, Iñigo de Mendoza, brother of the marquis of Mondéjar. They stayed for the entire hour, sitting quietly among the students.[90]

Conditions on the trip turned out to be as Granvelle had foreseen. In Guadalajara the king's party was put up royally for three days by the duke of Infantado. On the first night there was a masque with music, on the last day there was a bull-run with nine bulls. But in Brihuega, where they passed the night after Guadalajara, there was not sufficient lodging for everyone. 'We had a very bad night,' wrote an archer of the king's Flemish guard, Henry Cock, 'because, as the gospel says, there was no room in the inn.'[91] The next day, 6 February, 'it began to rain and sleet and I didn't know where to shelter. The same happened to all those who came with the king.' The following day it snowed, and they had to work at clearing a way for the coaches.

Eventually the royal party entered Saragossa in the afternoon of 24

February. They were given a rapturous welcome by a city packed with people. The courtiers were fortunate enough to coincide with the celebration of Carnival (3 to 6 March), a festivity that had always pleased the king. 'All restraints are thrown off during these three days,' observed Cock of the proceedings, which to his northern temperament seemed licentious. On 10 March the duke of Savoy, Carlo Emanuele, finally arrived from Italy with his escort. The king, accompanied by courtiers and his guards, came out on horseback to meet him, and they rode into the city together at the head of their procession. At 10 p.m., with cardinal Granvelle officiating, Catalina and the duke made their marriage vows.[92] 'The roofs sagged with the weight of the people' who climbed on them in order to be able to see the celebrations that night.

The wedding ceremony was held in the cathedral the day after, 11 March.[93] The king was dressed in black, with the Fleece round his neck. The duke was in a suit of yellow bordered with pearls, with diamonds set in gold as buttons; over it he wore a black cloak. The bride was dressed in red bordered with gold, pearls and precious stones. The elaborate festivities were followed by a ball which ended at ten o'clock at night. The bride retired to her chamber, and the duke was permitted to enter. The following day, everyone was exhausted. 'There was silence throughout the palace the whole day until the evening.'[94]

It rained almost every day but this did not prevent the holding of balls and tourneys. The swollen river Ebro rose, prompting the courtiers to go out on the bridges to see the swirling water. There were celebrations every night, including a tourney in the house of the duke of Medinaceli which lasted until two in the morning. On 31 March the king held a private ceremony at which the duke of Savoy, the Admiral of Castile, the duke of Medinaceli, and four Italian nobles were received into the order of the Golden Fleece. A tourney in the Admiral's house followed the ceremony. In the morning of 2 April the royal party set out for Barcelona. Before leaving, the king signed letters summoning the Cortes of the realms of Aragon to meet in Monzón in May. Leaving Granvelle, who was seriously ill and remained behind in Saragossa, Castilian nobles drifted back to their estates, and the Aragonese capital lapsed once again into tranquillity. 'Wherever you go there is only silence,' an ambassador who remained behind complained.[95]

It was not a fortunate journey to Barcelona. The duke of Savoy was taken ill. The party made a stop at the famous monasteries of Catalonia: after a night at Poblet they went on to Montserrat. But at Montserrat the Infanta Isabel caught a fever, and the Infante Philip was taken violently ill with vomiting. The king was suffering serious pains from his gout. In the circumstances he decided against a ceremonial entry into the city, on the excuse that he was making a purely private visit to see his daughter off. In the first week of May the whole royal group entered Barcelona quietly and informally. They were met by a storm of protest: it was not every day that a city could greet its king. 'The city councillors were angry because they felt they had been cheated, the citizens were angry because His Majesty had not entered in triumph, everybody was angry that the guilds had not greeted him.' The city insisted on declaring a week of feasting, during which 'everything else was dropped and the citizens simply did nothing'.[96] The royal party was in no condition to participate. Besides, the duke again fell ill.

It was five weeks before everybody in the royal party recovered their health. The king could not take part directly in the festivities, but watched from his window. On one of the nights, he and the family 'after dinner stayed a long time at the windows of the palace overlooking Broad Street, watching with great satisfaction the people as they went by and others who were dancing'.[97] He celebrated his fifty-eighth birthday on 21 May. The duke and new duchess of Savoy eventually left on 13 June. The leave-taking at the quayside lasted two hours because Catalina was weeping and unhappy to leave her sister and father. Philip was disconsolate. 'His sadness was very great, and he had never been seen to express his feelings and affection so openly; with a handkerchief to his face, he poured out a flood of tears.'[98] Finally the young couple set sail in the fleet, forty galleys strong, of admiral Gian Andrea Doria.

The departure of Catalina left Philip deeply unhappy. He took up again the correspondence he had begun in Lisbon, and wrote of 'the great loneliness in which you leave me'. The day after she left, the king and his party went to stay in a coastal villa in Llobregat. He went out to gaze at the shimmering Mediterranean. 'I could see all the sea, but you were no longer in the bay.' 'You don't need to ask me to forgive you for leaving,' he responded to the first letter he received from her when she made landfall in Italy. 'I could not take my leave of you or of the duke in the way I wanted, nor could I say some of the things I was thinking, and so I have put down on this paper those thoughts and others I had afterwards.' More relaxed, as always, on paper than in person, he now said what he had meant to say at the quayside. He wrote of 'how much I love you', and said that 'the duke and I have to contend over who loves you most'. 'Here your sister and I cannot stop thinking always of you and missing you very much.'[99]

The Infanta for her part was enchanted by her new existence. Life in Turin was uncluttered by the ceremonial which often made the Spanish court tedious. The ambitious young duke was beginning to convert the city into a worthy European capital.[100] Catalina could go where she liked, invite whom she liked. Her Spanish chamberlain was scandalised by the informality in Savoy. He complained to Madrid of 'the meagre household and few attendants that the Infanta has', and of 'the social contact here, more informal and familiar than over there'.[101] The duke entertained her, and put on parties and plays in her apartments. The new duchess fulfilled her wifely duties and became pregnant immediately.

From Barcelona the king made his way back to Aragon, for the Cortes at Monzón. The general Cortes opened at the end of June 1585, and the sessions dragged on, through the intense heat of the summer. 'My duties don't always give me time for all I would like,' Philip managed to write to Catalina. 'I am very envious of where you go and what you see' was his response to her descriptions of the mountains of Piedmont. 'I would very much more prefer to do the same than to be here.' Meanwhile a severe epidemic broke out in the area of Monzón and several members of the king's court and chapel were among the hundreds who died. The spate of deaths gave rise to the greatest alarm when on 7 October the king was taken ill again with fever and gout. As a precaution, Philip looked over his testament, and made his confession,[102] and prayers were offered for him. Early in November the three realms took the oath to the Infante Philip. By the end of that month, the king was completely well. In deference to his poor health, the final sessions of the Cortes (in December) were held a short distance away at Binefar and were brief. The weather turned cold and it began to snow.

On 13 December the royal party embarked in boats and sailed down the river Ebro. Musicians played to them as they relaxed. They spent Christmas and the New Year in Tortosa by which time the weather had become sunnier. 'Those of us who escaped from Monzón are in good health,' Philip wrote with relief to Catalina.[103] On 2 January 1586 they left Tortosa and headed south towards Valencia. The party entered Valencia city on the nineteenth, to a multitudinous welcome. 'The windows everywhere were full of beautiful girls, whom His Majesty greeted courteously.'[104]

Philip was thoroughly relaxed in the pleasant climate of the Mediterranean. He received news of Catalina's pregnancy and assured her that 'if I could, I would write to you every day out of pleasure'. But 'there is no lack of lots of business'. He also felt the cold ('of course, you young people don't feel it as much as we the old do') but the royal palace in Valencia, with its views and gardens, made up for that.[105] For the first few weeks of his stay there he abstained deliberately from work, and alternated leisure with participation in the festivities (Philip thought they were 'very fine') put on for the royal party.[106] On 2 February the archbishop of Valencia laid on for the royal family a banquet in which enormous quantities of food and wine were made available. The guests sat down to 1,200 bottles of white wine, twenty-one sheep, nineteen turkeys, ninety-six chickens, eighty-three brace of partridge, forty-one capons, 120 pounds of bacon, and an enormous quantity of other items.[107] Vegetables and fish were entirely absent, but fresh fruit was available. The occasion seems not to have had adverse effects on the king.

On 4 February, a Tuesday, he went to visit the port of Valencia, the Grao, and inspected the sea-wall. He delighted in the views of the fields and countryside. On Thursday, the entire royal party went for a picnic beside the lake of La Albufera. The ladies ventured out in boats and were rowed by local fishermen.[108] On Saturday, a bull-run was held; the king watched from a palace window.

That week an observer commented that Philip had never looked better or more relaxed in ten years.[109] He was helped considerably by Isabel, who read him the letters and despatches he had to deal with, adding her suggestions on how they should be answered. Philip even gave her access to the most important papers of state.[110] The repose also allowed him time to think. He became even more convinced that England must be dealt with, and did not attempt to disguise the resentment he felt against Elizabeth.[111] At the end of 1585, when news first reached him of the treaty of Nonsuch, he realised that a confrontation with England could no longer be avoided. But it took several more weeks of thought and consultation before his options became clear.

The king left Valencia, somewhat reluctantly, on 27 February 1586. The trip back from Valencia to Castile was uncomfortable. Philip missed the green of the Mediterranean coast, so green 'that it's unbelievable'. Instead, as they approached Castile they were buffeted, he complained, by 'much cold and a terrible wind always in our faces'. The hills were covered with snow and it was bitterly cold.[112] Whenever they entered a town, the king took care to ride in formally on horseback. The whole royal family wore black, in mourning for Margaret of Parma, who had just died.

Philip's first care on his return was to see how far, after fourteen months of absence, the building programme had advanced.

> We thought Aranjuez was terrible, at least I did. We were there four days and then came to Madrid, where I found that the building work I had left was in good shape, though not finished as I had wished. I stayed there four more days and came one evening to El Pardo, where much less has been done than I had thought. Then I came here [San Lorenzo] where a great deal has been done.[113]

He arrived in San Lorenzo on 26 March and spent Easter there. At the end of May he and the court returned there, to spend the whole summer of 1586.

Foreign envoys often clung to their own stereotype of the king. The Venetian ambassador said in 1584 that his character made him 'love retreats and solitude, and flee from nearly every kind of pleasure'.[114] The reality could not have been more different. The visit to the eastern realms, faithfully described by Henry Cock, shows us a king who, in spite of his very poor health, enjoyed to the full the tourist pleasures of the Mediterranean. He also (despite the ambassador) disliked solitude. He loved to be surrounded by his children, and hated the separations after they came back to Madrid. 'I have been lonely without them,' he told Catalina, 'which has also brought back the loneliness I feel without you.' She, however, sent him in April the good news of the birth of her first child, Filippo Emanuele, named after its grandfather. The messenger brought him the letter in Vaciamadrid when he had not yet woken up. 'It has been for me,' the king wrote back, 'the biggest possible satisfaction and I am overjoyed that you have given me my first grandson.'[115] He knew, he added jokingly, that she had given birth in Holy Week in order to miss the long, boring religious ceremonies. He wrote to Carlo Emanuele to congratulate him. 'Let me now guess,' he wrote, 'which of us two loves him more, since I love him greatly for being the son of you both.'[116]

*

Philip was celebrating the feast of Corpus Christi in June 1585 in the Catalan town of Igualada, when he received disturbing news of an insurrection in Naples.[117] His informant, sent specially by the viceroy of Naples, was his subsequent biographer Luis Cabrera. The Spaniards had been present in mainland Italy long enough to be feared and distrusted. They considered Italians a difficult people to deal with,[118] and many Castilian leaders were uncomfortable about having to be in Italy. Only the defence of the Mediterranean justified their stay. Philip, for his part, took the view that Spain was not an oppressor. Italians, he felt, suffered more under their own nobility than under Spanish tutelage.

The king had always expressed fears of the 'excessive number of people'[119] in Naples, at that time the world's largest urban conglomeration.[120] In May 1585 a serious riot took place in conditions of grain shortage, and a prominent magistrate, Starace, was murdered and ceremonially mutilated. Cabrera, an eyewitness, told the king how the mob 'drank the blood of the corpse and ate his heart'. The subsequent popular disturbances were harshly put down, hundreds were arrested and thirty-one people were executed. There was a clear danger for Spain. Threats were made against 'these pigs of Spaniards', and some of the disaffected even warned the viceroy to 'keep well in mind what has happened in Flanders'.[121]

Portugal, governed by the archduke Albert, also continued to be a cause for concern. There were rumours at court early in 1585 that the king might return to Lisbon; the idea of making it the capital instead of Madrid was not out of the question. Cardinal Granvelle informed the Venetian ambassador 'that it would be of little use for His Majesty to visit Portugal for a few days only, but that he was ready to advise him to reside there permanently, as a place excellently suited for France, England, Flanders,

India and also for commanding the Mediterranean.' He added that 'this would be the true way in which to curb the queen of England'.[122] In the spring of 1586 Granvelle was still pressing Philip to go to Lisbon, but without success.[123]

*

The shadow of England, meanwhile, loomed larger. By the beginning of 1585 Philip and his advisers were convinced that the damaging activity of corsairs in the Channel and along the Spanish coast must be checked. To make matters worse, in March the king received information that Francis Drake was being put at the head of a large naval expedition intended to sail to the West Indies and seize the silver fleet before it left American waters. Philip immediately tried to round up enough large vessels to go out and protect the silver shipment. Lacking Spanish vessels, in May 1585 he sent out an order that appropriate foreign ships in peninsular ports be pressed into service for the crown. The order affected German, English and Dutch ships; French vessels were considered too small. The move was interpreted, especially in England, as a hostile act. There was uproar among English merchants; and the government, to placate them, issued letters of reprisal authorising them to seize Spanish vessels to make up for their losses. Philip's action was one normally permitted to governments in cases of emergency. But in this case it had far-reaching consequences.[124] Ever careful not to offend England, he had not singled out English ships in any way. In London, however, the embargo decisively alienated merchants, who normally favoured peace with Spain. From now on they backed a hard line, at the same time that they tranquilly continued to trade wherever possible with Spanish exporters. At the end of 1587, at the very moment that Philip's great Armada was poised to strike against England, the king was astonished to hear that in the port of Bilbao 'the English come and go as if we were at peace with them'.[125] The embargo of May 1585 also, unfortunately for Philip, served to confirm English government intentions.

It gave Elizabeth an excuse for moving on to the offensive. In September 1585, a month after signing the treaty of Nonsuch, she formally authorised the most destructive of Francis Drake's expeditions. Drake had in the years since the incident at San Juan de Ulúa made himself feared in the Caribbean for his piratical attacks on Spanish settlements. Between 1577 and 1580 he capped his achievements by sailing round the globe. He returned to England richly laden with stolen Spanish gold, and was knighted by the queen. The big fleet of twenty vessels put at his disposal by Elizabeth in 1585 was obviously financed by the state. He was now no mere pirate, but a national hero. On 14 September Drake sailed from Plymouth. He had to put in at the port of Baiona in Galicia for refitting twelve days later. During the two weeks his vessels stayed in

Baiona his conduct was exemplary.[126] Such, however, was his reputation that rumours (all false) quickly arose of outrages allegedly committed by his troops. 'Drake is master of the sea,' the Venetian ambassador commented from Madrid. 'No steps are being taken here, not because they do not care, but because of the great deficiency of everything.'[127] After its tranquil stay in Galicia the English fleet headed out across the Atlantic to America. On the way, in November, Drake for the first time resorted to force, and plundered in the Cape Verde islands.

An effective state of war existed. The marquis of Santa Cruz pointed out that Drake's naval attacks had cost the crown four times its current war costs. It now made sense to check a deteriorating situation by striking at England. 'The policy of defence is not enough,' a secretary summed up the king's view early in 1587; 'we need to direct our fire at their own country.' The whole Spanish system was at issue. A naval expedition was called for: 'the objective of this Armada is both the security of the Indies and the reconquest of the Netherlands.'[128]

But the resources were not readily available. By 1585 Spain had not only run down its Mediterranean fleet, it had also dismantled much of the military apparatus used for the conquest of Portugal and the Azores.[129] Materials could not be found inside the country. For some time now, Spain had depended on other European countries (Italy for sails and oars, Flanders for masts and tar, Brittany for canvas, Genoa for seamen) for up to 90 per cent of the equipment for a typical galley.[130] Cannon had to be regularly imported, and there was no cannon-shot available in Spain. At every level, whether touching personnel or material, major changes would have to be effected to enable the operation to be carried out. From the summer of 1586 a number of administrative reforms were rushed through. The council of War was expanded, a second secretary for war appointed and steps were taken to improve recruitment and cannon production.

It was impossible to complete the ambitious programme in the time available. A paper prepared by Santa Cruz in March 1586 called for a naval strength of over 500 ships, 46 galleys and 94,000 men, more than the entire force at Lepanto and twice that used against Portugal. Lepanto, however, had been a joint venture by several nations. The entire burden now would have to fall on Spain. In the event Philip never committed himself to the March paper. What he did intend was to launch the fleet – the Great Armada – within a year. There were serious deficiencies in all supplies, but the most crucial of all, namely money, was quickly resolved. From 1586 the crown's Italian bankers were happy to lend substantial sums, which gave them continuing access to the silver coming in from America.

Both the preparation and objective of the Armada were meant to be secret. In practice, it was impossible to disguise the scale of activities.

Although the government gave out false rumours, these were not sufficient to mask the fact that something serious was going on.

The royal party arrived back from Valencia in Madrid on 21 March
1586. Philip had been away from his capital for fourteen months. Exactly
a week later, on the twenty-eighth, a shattering report reached the court.
The principal Spanish city in America, Santo Domingo, had been seized
and sacked by Drake early in January. The English, with over thirty ships,
had then gone on to attack Cartagena and the Florida coast. Everybody,
from the king downwards, was stunned. 'Struck with terror', was the
phrase used by an observer.[131] Some of Philip's ministers were heard to
say that this, coming on top of recent reverses, meant a turn of fortune
against Spain. The Indies, on which the government relied for its silver,
promptly jumped to the top of the agenda.[132] Some advised the despatch
of a fleet to America, but Philip knew that this was impossible. The news
only confirmed his commitment to the preparation of the Armada. At this
juncture he received the marquis of Santa Cruz's estimate of the forces
required for a military action. In April the bishops of Castile were
instructed to offer prayers for the success of affairs of state.

*

Shortly before Philip's visit to Barcelona a preacher there had commented
in a sermon on 'the king don Philip, an old and sick man'.[133] The words
obviously reflected a perception that many Spaniards had of their king.
He had been at the helm for forty years. Was he losing control? The truth
is that many of his aides now disappeared. Granvelle was unwell during
1585 and 1586. His health did not recover. 'He has lost all his influence in
important matters,' the Venetian envoy reported.[134] He also became more
and more gloomy about affairs. He wrote to Idiáquez, apocalyptically,
that 'we are heading towards the abyss', and referred to 'the final ruin that
we are blindly pursuing'.[135] He died in September 1586, aged sixty-nine.
Commenting on their long relationship of nearly forty years, the king said
that 'this loss affects me deeply, not only because of the gap it leaves in
political affairs but also because I loved the cardinal'.[136]

Margaret of Parma had also died in 1586. She was followed soon after
by her husband Ottavio. Alessandro Farnese, formerly prince, now
became duke of Parma. The loss which the king felt most keenly was that
of Juan de Zúñiga. Both in Rome and in Naples, Zúñiga had served Philip
so faultlessly that he was called specially to Madrid in 1583 and entrusted
(from January 1585) with the governorship of the Infante Philip. Dissatisfied with most of his ministers, the king had great hopes of him. When he
died suddenly in November 1586 at the age of forty-nine, Philip was
appalled. 'This is wretched news for me,' he commented, 'and puts me in
serious difficulties.'[137] He refused to appoint any other governor, and took
charge of the prince himself.

But his own capacities, as he knew, were dwindling. The year 1586 was, in reality, the great turning point of his life. There were three crucial aspects to the change. His life-style altered, his health deteriorated, and he changed his manner of government.

His life-style became more subdued. Deprived now of Catalina, the king was left to pass the spring of 1586 in the company of Isabel and Philip. The Infanta, now aged nineteen, 'has grown quite beautiful and graceful, to the great delight of the king', it was reported. Late in March, when the heavy snows were over, Philip took the court for a week to Aranjuez to enjoy what an ambassador called 'the softness of the air and the beautiful weather'.[138] In April he expressed a wish to go for a while to Toledo, 'where I haven't been for some time', and possibly to see an *auto de fe*, 'which they sometimes have there around this period, it's something worth seeing for those who haven't seen one'.[139] They went to Toledo to celebrate Ascension, but there was no *auto de fe*.

Despite the king's periodic attacks of gout the family enjoyed the first half of May 1586 at Aranjuez, hunting and strolling through the gardens, and the second at San Lorenzo. The French ambassador Longlée felt that it was a calm before the storm. Spain was clearly on the defensive against a belligerent England, and much rested on Philip's decision-making. But many Spaniards were beginning to doubt whether he could cope.

His health that year took a decisive turn for the worse. At the end of May 1586 he suffered an acute attack of gout, which lasted for over two months and made it impossible for him to conduct business normally. Late in June he was confined to bed for a while and periodically bled.[140] 'Now I can walk around,' he reported in July, 'although a bit lame and still with a stick. I had a bad attack in my hand and have not been able to write.'[141] The gout and the bad news from America and Flanders effected a change for the worse in the king's general demeanour. Longlée observed that 'these two reasons, as well as his age, have changed him somewhat and made him seem older, more pensive, and less resolute and expeditious in all sorts of affairs'.[142]

Castilians noted the disappearance of the king. Thanks to his illness, he became almost a recluse.[143] After the summer stay at San Lorenzo his only major outing was the return visit there in the first week of August, when the completed church was finally blessed and inaugurated. In previous months he had been superintending the move to San Lorenzo of a large number of paintings, largely religious in character. The works of Netherlandish painters, notably Michel de Coxcie, formed an important part of this number.[144] They were the artistic contribution to the centre-piece of the building: the church or basilica. Completion of the basilica after two decades of construction was the climax of the Escorial project. The whole enterprise had been a success, and Philip did not conceal his great joy.[145] In a solemn and glittering ceremony, the sacrament was installed on the high altar. The blaze of candles was such that 'it seemed one was entering into an unparalleled glory'.[146] The highest security measures were taken, because the king ordered all the altars of the church to be covered with gold, silver, jewellery and the most select relics. The ceremonies reached their climax with a high mass on 10 August, feast of St Lawrence. In October the royal family moved off to the Pardo, where they went hunting. In the first days of November, a month after the king had returned to Madrid, the friars carried out the final transfer of all the royal bodies, from their temporary sites to the permanent resting-place directly under the high altar. It was a solemn occasion, but too emotionally painful for Philip. He made it plain that he did not wish to be present.[147]

During the late autumn of 1586 his poor health kept him indoors and he seldom left the Alcázar. He spent Christmas at San Lorenzo, but failed to make his usual public appearance at high mass on Christmas Day. The first three months of 1587 he did not stir from the Alcázar, leaving it only to go and spend Holy Week at San Lorenzo with his family. This behaviour, clearly at variance with his previous active life, contributed powerfully to the subsequent legend of a cloistered king.

He was able to continue with some paperwork, but business was slowed down. A minister complained to the Venetian ambassador of inefficiency 'in the conduct of our most vital affairs'.[148] In spite of his health, Philip continued to deal with everything. Through the summer of 1586 there were crucial talks with a Danish diplomat who came to Madrid on behalf of the States General, but the negotiations foundered on the issue of liberty of conscience in the Netherlands. Writing in July to the Lutheran king of Denmark, Philip appealed to the principle maintained by the Protestants themselves in the states they ruled: 'As to liberty of conscience, it is clear that no prince allows to his subjects any other religion than his own. And so I would rather lose all my kingdoms than consent to this.'[149]

Over these months of illness the conduct of government necessarily changed. In October 1585, when he fell ill at Monzón, the king handed over control of business to a small troika of ministers, which became known as the Junta Grande. Its members were Moura, the count of Chinchón and Juan de Idiáquez. Later their number was made up to four by the short-lived addition of Zúñiga. Working in association with Mateo Vázquez, they dealt with virtually all the correspondence of the councils.[150] But the king continued to keep the reins tightly in his hands. 'It is a miracle to see,' commented an observer, 'how he governs this great machine without any council of State and almost without ministers.'[151] Rule by committee became the norm. For all practical purposes, government by council disappeared during the last twelve years of the reign. The situation contributed in no small measure to the dissatisfaction that many nobles, who dominated the councils, felt with the regime of Philip II. The

French envoy Longlée was there to see it. 'The men of judgment of this nation,' he reported, 'foresee a very great change in this state if the king should disappear. This has already begun to cause some disorder in government.'[152]

10

The Time of Thunder
1587–1593

. . . the great peril that we face if we do not impede what is very close to happening. And if it should happen, I expect that I shall not see it, because I shall have gone to carry out my duty.[1]

The early months of 1587 were bitterly cold in Castile, with 'ice and snow never before seen in this time of the year'.[2] In the Casa de Campo all the ponds froze. Several Flemish courtiers put on for the court a display of ice-skating, a sport unknown in Spain. Philip, well wrapped up inside his coach, went out to see the skaters, and made the acquaintance of one of them, the newly arrived Jean Lhermite.[3] At San Lorenzo some weeks later it snowed during Holy Week. The monks on Palm Sunday could barely carry the palms for the bitter cold. 'We thought here this Easter that we would freeze,' the king wrote; 'it cannot be called an Easter of flowers because they all froze, and the fruit as well, so that food will I think be in short supply this summer.'[4] His poor health was now continuous. In May he was 'in bed, crippled by gout'. Confined to a chair, he could barely walk for the gout in his feet. 'This gout is so persistent,' he wrote in July, 'that it won't let me go. It won't let me walk without help, and for five or six days now has not let me walk at all. It has been worst in this hand, not letting me write or do anything. Nor has my eyesight been very good.'[5] Since the previous summer, he had not had full use of his right hand. 'In order not to tire my hand,' he wrote to Carlo Emanuele in May, 'I am leaving some matters for another letter.'[6]

Deprived of Catalina, he relied more and more on Isabel. It was a common sight during their sojourns at San Lorenzo to see father and daughter walking slowly together, unaccompanied, through the grounds of the monastery.[7] When he felt better, the king also went out for excursions into the countryside. His beard and hair now were white, his face thinner and wan. But he held himself firm and erect. His piercing eyes, as we see them in the portrait done by Hieronymus Wierix in 1586,[8] mirrored his undimmed energy. Lhermite, who got to know the king well and very soon managed to have himself appointed assistant gentleman of the royal bedchamber, confirms this picture. Philip was 'very subject to gout, his hair white and balding, but in good physical condition, his mind lively and his memory even better than ever'.[9]

Though adequately served by his ministers and generals, Philip in 1587 could feel that events were slipping out of his control. The instrument of vengeance, the Armada, was almost ready. But the English everywhere – in the Caribbean, in Portugal, in the Netherlands – were actively counter-attacking. Philip's last constitutional excuse to intervene in England itself disappeared when on 18 February Mary queen of Scots went to the block.

The execution was a direct consequence of the Babington plot. In spring 1586 Bernardino de Mendoza, scheming from his base in Paris, fostered a conspiracy among a group of English Catholics to kill Elizabeth. Philip, for the first time, insisted on being in touch with events. He gave his full approval to the conspiracy, but warned Mendoza that he should not put anything in writing. 'As long as you take care on this point, everything else seems fine.'[10] The plot was discovered in September. Philip regretted the stupidity of the plotters. 'All I can say is that I feel very sorry for them; they themselves are in good measure to blame, for not keeping it secret.'[11] The conspiracy had been a justifiable attempt to avoid further bloodshed, since 'the cause is God's'. But he had deep regrets over the consequences for the queen of Scots. It was the end of nearly twenty years of support for 'that poor lady', as he had termed her in 1569. He wrote to Mendoza: 'You cannot imagine the pity I feel for the queen of Scots. It was irresponsible to keep copies of those dangerous papers.'[12] When he received news of her execution, in mid-April 1587, he wept openly.[13] A solemn requiem was held in the Escorial.

An English response to the plots came rapidly in the shape of Drake's descent on Cadiz. On 29 April 1587, supported by a fleet of twenty-three vessels, Drake made a surprise incursion into Cadiz harbour. Over twenty Spanish vessels were destroyed or captured. The shore defences impeded any landing, and the English sailed away on 1 May, going on to occupy the coastal position of Sagres, at the southern tip of Portugal. The attack made it impossible to prepare the Armada for action that year and won a valuable few months for England.

The delay had serious consequences for Spain. The king was well aware of complaints at every level.[14] In the ports there was dissatisfaction over the impunity with which English ships disrupted trade and attacked vessels. 'The English are masters of the sea and hold it at their discretion,' an ambassador at court commented.[15] In Madrid there was murmuring against the government. The king himself, celebrating his sixtieth birthday that year, was preoccupied by the criticism within the council of War. It was at this period that he tried to allay criticisms of the delays in the Armada with his famous phrase, 'the king and time will do everything'.[16]

*

The decisions concerning the Armada, however, were made by an ailing king. The gout had affected him in hands and feet through the spring and summer of 1587. 'The gout has caught me earlier this year than in others,' he informed Carlo Emanuele.[17] He was unable to sign any documents until July, and only a few in subsequent months. The indisposition did not affect preparations, but it did slow down the process of consultation within the government. Late in July the vessels made ready in Andalusia were sent to Lisbon, in the hope of preparing a general rendezvous there. But by September there was still no final decision. Philip sent off detailed instructions to Santa Cruz in Lisbon and to Parma in the Netherlands. He wrote letters to his commanders in November and December charging them, almost desperately, to put the whole exercise in motion.[18] Yet weather conditions were by now wholly unfavourable. The king was clearly not thinking properly. His commanders, quite rightly, delayed and did nothing.

Santa Cruz wrote from Lisbon in January 1588 that his fleet would shortly leave. The council of State in Madrid urged 'that the enterprise be pursued, since this is the only way to protect trade with America, free these coasts from invasion, and preserve Flanders'.[19] In fact, Santa Cruz was seriously ill. In February 1588 the most successful Spanish admiral of his time died at the age of sixty-three. In his place Philip appointed Alonso Pérez de Guzmán, duke of Medina Sidonia. Though the duke had no experience of naval command, he had a respectable military career, was an efficient administrator and had the status required of the leader of an expedition of this size.[20] His orders were to take the Armada out as quickly as possible. It was costing a fortune while it waited (some 700,000 ducats a month, according to the president of the council of Finance), and its supplies were rapidly rotting. In the spring, therefore, hasty preparations were made to put to sea.

Fortunately, other pieces of the grand design now began to fall into place. In December 1587 the earl of Leicester and his troops abandoned the Netherlands and returned to England, after months of fruitless campaigning. Then in May 1588 the Catholic League of the Guises organised an uprising in Paris and effectively took over control of the government. Neither the Dutch nor the French were now in a position to give active help to Elizabeth.

Contemporaries agreed that the Armada had grave deficiencies. Medina Sidonia had himself said so in a letter to the government which Idiáquez did not dare show the king.[21] In spring 1588, however, the obstacles seemed overcome: 130 vessels, carrying over 18,000 men, sailed out from the Tajo on 30 May. The ships made it out of Lisbon against an unfavourable wind but were forced by gales into Coruña. Pinned in, with men deserting, on 24 June Medina Sidonia wrote to the king advising him to abandon the expedition. But new supplies and men were found, and on 22 July the fleet sailed out of Coruña. A week later, favoured by the winds, the enormous concentration of ships and men lay off the English coast, south of Cornwall. It was an awe-inspiring sight for observers on the cliffs.

Medina Sidonia's instructions were to effect a meeting with Parma off the English coast, and take on board the Flanders army which was to carry out the invasion of England. Many councillors in Madrid had grave doubts about whether the rendezvous was feasible.[22] The English had no intention of even allowing it to take place. Their naval forces, organised in small squadrons under Lord Howard of Effingham, Francis Drake, John Hawkins and Martin Frobisher, began to harass the great ships and force them into the Channel. By 6 August, nevertheless, Medina Sidonia was able to bring most of his vessels intact into the waters off Calais.

His chief problem was that he had been unable to make any contact with Parma. Not until he was off Calais did he receive the first response from the duke. The Flanders army, the duke wrote, would not be available for boarding for at least six more days. There was a yet more pressing problem. Parma did not have adequate boats to ferry his men out to the galleons. These could not come in farther because the waters were too shallow. Parma could not venture out because of the waves and the fleet of Dutch vessels patrolling the coasts.

Howard and the English had no intention of waiting until Medina Sidonia and Parma could unite the Spanish forces. On the night of 7 August they sent in six small fireships packed with explosive and shot. The anchored galleons cut their cables in terror and fled. At dawn the next day the remaining galleons saw before them the bulk of the now reinforced English fleet, drawn up for battle. A long and fierce engagement of some nine hours took place.[23] The Spanish ships were at a consistent disadvantage. Few vessels were lost, but the casualties were high. By the end of the day the fleet had to make a run for it, away from Flanders and up into the uninviting waters of the North Sea. The objective of the whole expedition, to take on board Parma's troops and invade, had failed.

The greater part of the Armada, some 112 vessels, was still intact. But the wind had carried it beyond any possibility of returning to Flanders or to the battle. By mid-August it was heading into the Atlantic. Off Orkney Scottish fishermen reported seeing 'monstrous great ships, about a hundred in number, running westwards before the wind'.[24] Medina Sidonia instructed his captains to sail south-west past the Irish coast and thence for Spain. From this point forward the great disasters commenced. Most of the ships perished in the Atlantic storms or on the coast of Ireland, where the natives plundered the wrecks and showed the survivors little mercy.

*

The king in all these months was in chronically poor health. Through January 1588 he was in and out of bed. Mateo Vázquez sent him flowers, which were put on his bedside table.[25] He cut down on the amount of work. 'I have here papers of several days but have been unable to look at them, I don't know if I shall be able to tonight.'[26] When in February a quack wrote offering him some medicine, Philip retorted that he would take only what his own doctor – Dr Vallés – prescribed.[27] 'I am convalescing very slowly,' he noted in March, 'but I can't manage in the way I used to, and there is more work than ever.'[28] 'I have been extremely weak,' he reported a week later. 'I feel better, but I still have to walk with a stick.'[29] He continued to move about, going out into the park of the Alcázar in Madrid, or visiting El Pardo to accompany Isabel on hunts.

But the pain would not go away. It prevented him thinking clearly about anything else. When asked for a decision on a matter, instead of replying he scribbled a note about his state: 'I was better yesterday, but tonight when I got up I had a pain, which lasted two hours.'[30] Mateo Vázquez tried to urge him on: 'if Your Majesty could manage to call me sometimes, we could get through a great deal, and there is much need of it'.[31]

Early in April 1588 the royal family made their now regular visit to San Lorenzo to keep Holy Week. In May the king was well enough to make outings. They went fishing at Fresneda and hunting in the woods nearby. His relaxation ceased on the day the Armada put to sea. Daily processions and prayers were ordered in the Escorial for the expedition's success. In mid-June, when the Armada was at sea, he continued to excuse himself from paperwork. 'I don't dare now to look at papers as long as this,' he scribbled on one.[32] 'The poor health is having its effect,' one of his secretaries commented to another.[33]

Waiting for news, the king was in a constant state of nerves. 'If God sees fit to grant us success with the Armada, all my hope is that he will provide the remedy, if not it will be a very great reverse in every way; I really do not dare think about it.'[34] On the feast of St Anne, 26 July, the date on which his forces had gained the naval victory of Terceira, his thoughts turned to his late wife again. She had helped then; she could help now. He ordered the prior of the Escorial to hold a solemn procession in honour of St Anne, which the monastery should repeat annually.[35]

In the council of State, ministers were fearful that the Turks would choose this moment to attack from the Mediterranean.[36] There were, inevitably, erroneous reports about the Armada ships. In mid-August a letter from Bernardino de Mendoza, dated the seventh of the month from Rouen and announcing a victory, reached Madrid. 'I hope it's true,' commented Philip.[37] He felt hopeful enough to write immediately to Catalina of 'the news we received yesterday that my armada has defeated that of England'.[38] But he refused to accept the news without confirmation.

More than anybody else, the king was aware that his country was facing fearful odds. From the very beginning he had premonitions of disaster. Early in 1588 he drafted in his own hand the text of an appeal which he hoped to address to the Cortes, meeting in April. It presented Spain's 'darkest hour', and appealed for sacrifice:

> We must be fully armed and on guard and ready for whatever may happen. This obliges us to make heavy and unprecedented expenditure, or else leave everything to terrible disaster. Nothing less is at stake than the security of our seas and of America and of our fleets, and the security of our own homes. We can go forward only if the Cortes does something to help, for you know the state of the treasury.
>
> Confirm to me the confidence that I have in such good subjects. Come forward with the speedy supplies that this moment demands, and discuss the matter with the attention and concern that I very much expect from your loyalty and love for God's service and my own.[39]

The same sense of peril haunts a written instruction to the head of Finance, Rodrigo Vázquez, in June. More money, he insisted, is the only solution: 'without it the sailing of the armada is of little use . . . and we will lose all we have spent, and everything else besides'. Above all, there is

> the great peril that we face if we do not impede what is very close to happening. And if it should happen, there will be no safety even in Madrid, though I expect that I shall not see it, because I shall have gone to carry out my duty.[40]

A week after this stoic declaration, the king was informed that a Carmelite nun in Valladolid had cried out 'Victory! victory!' during a trance. She also promised good news. Two weeks later she sent a written message of hope to the king. Philip scribbled on it: 'Please God it be as this paper says. We shall soon know.'[41]

When the first reliable reports arrived in mid-August, their impact was profound. The messenger, on arriving at the Escorial, was received by Moura and Idiáquez.[42] The former volunteered to break the news to the king. Philip was at his desk and broke off to ask if anything was known. Moura replied that the news of the Armada was bad. The messenger was brought in, and delivered his report to the silent king. Philip then said (according to one version), 'I give thanks to God, whose generous hand has helped me with strength and troops, and will make it possible for me to raise another armada. It does not much matter if the flow of water is cut off, so long as its source is still running.' He turned to his desk, and resumed writing. The same day he ordered 50,000 crowns to be assigned to the relief of the wounded, and ordered the churches to give thanks for the safe return of the survivors.

Moura was astonished at the king's resigned acceptance of the disaster. When an anxious Idiáquez asked him what Philip's reaction had been, he replied, 'The king does not make much of this mischance, nor do I.' Philip's stoic response has since passed into the history books. It was a momentary exercise of self-control, but it was criticised by many courtiers, who disapproved of play-acting at such a grave moment.[43] In reality, the king was deeply shocked. He got the first full report in a letter from Parma, dated 10 August, which arrived in Madrid on 31 August. 'His Majesty has felt the blow more than you would believe,' Idiáquez wrote back to Parma that same day. Three days later he wrote, 'Although he felt the news very much at the beginning, he feels it more every day . . . It hurts him immensely that he failed to render a great service to God, after doing more than you could have asked or imagined.'[44] Philip's private reflection was: 'I hope that God has not permitted as much harm as some fear; everything has been done in his service, and we must not stop praying.'[45] The fault was nobody's. In the draft of the king's next letter to Parma, a secretary referred to 'the honour (*reputación*) of all, which is at stake'. Philip scored out the phrase and wrote in the margin: 'see if you can remove this, since in the affairs of God it is not a question of losing or gaining honour'.[46] The Venetian ambassador that week, observing the king closely, commented that he appeared to feel utterly alone.[47]

The full extent of the disaster took some time to sink in. Not until the third week of September did Medina Sidonia stagger into Santander with eight of his galleons. A further twenty-seven battered ships made it into other northern ports. Possibly sixty of the 130 vessels that had sailed out in May had made it home. But some 15,000 of the men on board had perished. The impact on Castilians was devastating. It was, commented a monk of the Escorial, 'one of the most notable disasters ever to have happened in Spain and one to weep over all one's life . . . For many months there were only tears and laments throughout Spain.'[48] That year the inquisitors in Madrid came into possession of an anonymous paper which may have been written after the bad news was known. The author, a priest, described a dream in which he was 'walking through a city in ruins, without buildings because they were all demolished'. A voice addressed one of the figures in the dream: 'You are no longer the shepherd . . . The good shepherd should be watching over and protecting his flock . . . How deceived we have been!' Was the person addressed meant to be the king?[49]

In retrospect, little can be said to defend the enterprise of England. Neither the king nor anyone else was quite sure what it was meant to achieve. No concrete plans were ever drawn up, either military or political, on what was to be done should the invasion succeed. Those with most experience in war, namely Alba and Parma, always had doubts about it and opposed it. Forecasts of its failure which appeared in prophecies of the time very likely drew on a current of opinion circulating among members of the administration.

Those who always had doubts now spoke out. An officer in the Armada sent a report to Idiáquez, dated 20 August. 'You will now not find anyone who is not saying, "I told you so" . . . We found the enemy with a great advantage in ships, better than ours for battle, better designed, with better artillery, gunners and sailors.'[50] There is good reason to support the traditional view of the Armada as the 'supreme disaster of the reign'.[51] It did not destroy Spain's capacity to launch new armadas or new armies. But it severely undermined the confidence of many Spaniards in the king. It gave rise to a new and oppressive cycle of taxation and state debt. It blocked the way permanently to a resolution of the Flanders problem through the removal of English interference. The imperialist triumphalism of the early 1580s, generated largely by the successful occupation of Portugal, now rapidly evaporated. To add to the government's problems, the wheat harvest in Castile in both 1588 and 1589 failed.

The king was ill and depressed. The gout continued its attacks: in late September, 'I cannot write or even sign'.[52] At court it was obvious to all that his outward equanimity was a cover. 'Though he maintains the contrary, he is really deeply wounded,' the Venetian ambassador observed.[53] Philip's depression lasted for weeks, as he searched for solutions. 'I am under great pressure with all this,' he confided to Vázquez, 'seeing how slow we are to find a solution and how the time moves on and how we need to be aware that our enemies do not sleep and are gaining on us. But all this is not so bad as seeing the slackness with which our people move, especially those in the committee of the Cortes, whose slackness I think affects everybody else.'[54]

Who was to blame? Medina Sidonia, a failure at the early age of thirty-nine, was seriously ill. Allowed to retire to his estates without coming to see the king, he was never blamed by Philip for the disaster. Parma also was absolved by Philip. But Spaniards, especially those who did not like to see their armies under the command of an Italian, were quick to criticise Parma.[55] Months later, a leading Spanish noble, commenting on 'the decay of our former military discipline', observed that 'the truth is that for some time our arms have been in decay ... Since the school is in Flanders and the general is Italian, the arms of Italy will improve and those of Spain will decline.'[56] Others, within the highest levels of government, blamed their own ministers. The veteran soldiers were merciless in their criticism. Alba's natural son Hernando de Toledo, now a councillor of state, complained in December 1589 to the Venetian ambassador that 'things must go ill when all decisions are taken by the inexperienced'.[57] His criticism was directed against Moura and Idiáquez. The first, he said, 'has never been out of Spain, the other never in a campaign'.

Philip was not unaware that in these months there was much discontent at all levels. In his own administration there were senior officials who questioned his personal capacity. In August 1589 Vázquez pleaded with him to listen with attention to reports on the state of the finances, 'and also to look at and think over what can and should be done to satisfy, conciliate and get together the ministers in Madrid and those over here, so that business can function to the satisfaction of everybody'.[58] Philip played down the in-fighting. 'Really,' he replied, 'I don't know why you say this is needed, nor do I know of differences between them nor why there should be any.' To him, the conflicts may have appeared normal. He failed to see that criticisms which ministers made of each other were now in great measure being directed against himself.

In Portugal an ex-ambassador, Juan de Silva, count of Portalegre, lamented in 1589 that the English were landing troops without any opposition. In the early summer a considerable English fleet, commanded by Drake and Sir John Norris, ranged off the coasts of Galicia and Portugal, attacking at will, with destructive blows at Coruña, Vigo and the environs of Lisbon. Though the English achieved nothing substantial, Spaniards were indignant that the enemy could ravage their coasts with impunity. 'I must confess that never in my life have I found myself so close to having to flee from danger,' an angry Silva protested. Complaints poured into Madrid, but the authorities could do little. 'And all of this is happening because our reputation is lame and broken, laid low by the defeat of the recent Armada.'[59] A plan for another Armada was presented to the king in May 1589, but nothing came of it.[60] In effective command of the narrow seas, enemy vessels succeeded in cutting off a good part of the vital naval supplies (masts, pitch) on which Spain depended. The Armada defeat threatened to initiate a rapid decline in Spanish shipping.[61] The economic life of the northern coastline decayed. Only the great ports of Andalusia were unaffected, in part because English and Dutch merchants played an important role in the trade of Seville. When the king a few years later tried to control their activities,[62] he was soon persuaded that Spanish interests would be the most hurt if he did so.

In his letters to a senior administrator in Madrid,[63] Silva reflected the views of others who were serving the king:

I agree with everything you say in your last letter, and so would everyone who is disturbed by affairs and deplores what is happening. I have just one thing to add to confirm this view. A man of leisure, a thinker, told me that after examining in detail the actions of His Majesty since he came to the throne, one had to conclude that we cannot blame any of our reverses on bad luck or attribute any of our successes to diligence.[64]

In a biting criticism, he commented that 'as for the attention that His Majesty pays to details of little consequence, we have agreed for years that it is lamentable that he wastes time in these things . . . His Majesty's head is capable of absorbing a vast quantity of business but does not distinguish between what he should reserve for himself and what he should entrust to others.' The king's failure to distinguish between what was important and what was not, led him (Silva said) to make the wrong decisions. 'As a result time and effort is spent in not taking measures which should be taken; and taking them when there is no time or money or reason; and making savings which cost three times more than is saved; and beginning late and therefore in haste, but because in haste beginning inadequately. Whoever doesn't see this is blind.' Thanks to a failure of methods, the king put his trust only in miracles. 'It seems that everybody agrees with this, for I see that all put their faith in miracles and supernatural solutions.' The general mood of criticism was unmistakable. 'For some time now opinion has been so clear-cut,' Silva felt, 'that nobody could mistake it.'[65]

After the long months of illness and disaster, Philip's health was slow to improve in 1589. In early February, 'he rises at midday and sits in his wheelchair, as he cannot walk yet'.[66] A week later he began walking with the help of a stick, but suffered relapses. He was less concerned for his own health than for that of his son. The prince fell seriously unwell late in February, but the king because of his own infirmities was unable to visit him for nearly a week. Not until April was Philip able to break out of this environment. 'I've finally decided to make an outing to Aranjuez, it's nearly two years since I was last there.'[67]

*

His way blocked by England, facing stalemate in the Netherlands, Philip was now abruptly dragged into the affairs of France by the murder of Henry III, last king of the Valois dynasty. Henry's position as king was being steadily undermined in 1588 by the Catholic League, which was led by Spain's allies the Guises. In an abrupt coup just before Christmas 1588, Henry organised the assassination of the duke and the cardinal of Guise. The Venetian ambassador was present on the day Philip received the news. 'When the king heard of the death of the Guises he stood for a space with his eyes on the ground, musing. Then he said, "This is a matter for the pope." '[68] Even kings could not kill cardinals with impunity. The pope excommunicated Henry III. Leadership of the League passed to Guise's brother the duke of Mayenne, who continued to rely on Spanish support.

In his turn the king of France was murdered by a mad monk on 2 August 1589. The killing sent a shiver of fear down the spine of Spaniards. None of the Spanish theologians of the time, significantly, wrote in favour of killing kings, unlike their French colleagues a few miles away.[69] The royal council, concerned for Philip's security, urged him 'not to see or speak to people who are not known'.[70] Since Henry had been excommunicated, Philip on the advice of his council did not order any commemoration masses at San Lorenzo.

Henry III's death automatically meant that the Protestant Henry of Navarre, next in the line of succession, became king. Philip's lifelong attempt to restrain France, a country which in real terms had always been considered a more direct threat than England, now threatened to blow up in his face. 'Truth to tell,' he had confided earlier in the year, 'I have very little confidence in the way things are going.'[71] Though Spanish policy continued to treat with the utmost gravity the continuing menace from England and from the Turk, it was primarily France that occupied Philip's attention during the remainder of his reign.[72]

The international situation now was too complicated for the king to try and impose a single policy, if he could devise one, on his advisers. Armada year had brought differences of opinion out into the open. The king began to be more testy with his ministers and more distrustful of those who claimed to be helping him. When a matter came up concerning the count of Chinchón, Philip snapped: 'In many of the things the count thinks up he deceives himself, indeed I would say in most things.'[73] He refused to accept criticisms, and began to feel that his ministers were undermining his work. In June 1589, in an angry note to the Junta of three, he insisted that money must be found before it was too late. 'And I believe that we are already too late, if you do not suggest a solution at once and bring it to me, since I am making the request not to our enemies but to my own ministers.'[74]

In a remarkable outburst, which Philip confined to his papers, where alone he felt able to give vent to his frustrations, he hit out at his detractors in the administration and criticised his secretary for paying attention to them. Vázquez had commented (without naming them) that many people with opinions on foreign policy favoured a further fleet against England, and a decisive strike against France in order to secure the Netherlands.[75] Philip, in a private note of November 1589, reacted angrily.

Efforts had been made to collect more ships, he asserted, but it was not so easy:

> We shall see if these things are as easy as those who suggest them imagine. I would also like to know from them if they think these things can be done just by wishing and imagining, for if this were so I would be second to none in doing them immediately and without a further thought. But since they are done not like this but with money, one has to go through the process, in which I see how little they are doing and the slackness of every single one of them, from the first to the last.

The important issue was the money, which they were doing nothing to raise; and were it not for the importance of the matter, 'it would be easier not to strain my head, and simply leave things as they are'.

The councillors had suggested recruiting Italian princes to intervene militarily in France, and sending a special Spanish representative to exert influence in the selection of a Catholic alternative to Henry of Navarre.

> On what you say about France and Flanders, not all those who have spoken to you about the matter have the same loyalty as you, and are certainly sowing these ideas for their own private ends. They couldn't come up with a solution to anything and wouldn't even know how to. Their assumptions are false. Nobody in Italy stirs a leg except for private advantage ... And the idea of sending [a representative] is perhaps to avoid sending money, of which they have some, while I who do not have any would be only too glad to have some of it.

What was needed, he said, was not intervention but a miracle. 'If God doesn't work a miracle we cannot expect anything from France or from anything else, except the very worst. Even a child could tell you the problems and dangers, but very few could produce a solution without money.' For some time the king had routinely identified his cause with that of God. When it seemed, particularly after the Armada, that God was not collaborating, the identification became obsessive. He himself could do nothing. It was now therefore the responsibility of God.

Philip no doubt knew who his critics were. But he did not name names either, and merely concluded, to Vázquez: 'You have done well to inform me of all this. You know very well that the way we do things is not how people think we do them, and that if it were expedient to reveal everything they might perhaps judge differently. But it's more important to get on with the job than pay attention to badly informed people.'

Two days later he stated uncompromisingly that he had no intention of interfering in France. 'Until we see how things turn out, we shall not send anyone there.'[76] He consulted closely with Moura and Idiáquez. Don Cristóbal in particular played an influential role in policy. But the division of opinions in the government left Philip frustrated. If no effective decision were taken, it would not be his fault, he told himself. 'In everything I have fears of the little agreement there is among my ministers, who always end up wrecking everything.'[77] The king would not have drawn much consolation from learning that his ministers blamed him. 'It is no comfort to think,' one of them wrote to Philip's chief military administrator, 'that a people might end in disaster through the fault of its ruler.'[78]

*

The political paralysis intensified the frustration felt among all levels of the population. Nowhere was there more unease than in court circles. It had been commonplace in the Spanish tradition for visionaries to state their views on politics, and to do it publicly.[79] From the king downward, everyone felt free to consult seers and prophets who might have access to special sources of information. Even foreign visionaries (such as the French seer Nostradamus) were listened to with respect in Spain.[80] Prophecies were usually tolerated if they remained prophecies, and did not sound like sedition. Philip was nearly always sceptical of visionaries, and unimpressed by them. When informed of the special visions of a priest in 1584, he commented: 'I know the man well and think that he has good motives, because he has spoken to me in Aranjuez and also here. However I don't know if the science is up to much.'[81] But, like his contemporaries, he was not usually so doubting.

The problems of the late 1580s made visions a live political issue.[82] A famous Portuguese visionary, sister María de la Visitación, known as the 'nun of Lisbon', fell foul of the authorities in Portugal because she meddled in politics. She was arrested and lightly penanced in 1588. In Madrid in 1587–8 considerable attention was paid by some members of the elite, and even members of the Cortes, to the presages of doom uttered by Miguel de Piedrola. An ex-soldier but also a man of considerable culture, he adopted the name 'Prospero' and from the 1570s began spreading his message. Luis de León was among those who consulted him.[83] The king, as we have seen, had him investigated in 1578.[84] Among other things, he forecast (precisely for the year 1588) 'the imminent destruction of Spain'.[85] Philip knew him well and had usually treated him as a well-meaning crank. Piedrola continued his strange ways. His letters in 1580 refer to Madrid as 'Babylon', a city doomed by divine wrath.[86] In 1587 he was involved in a killing which brought matters to a head. Despite strong support for him within the king's council,[87] he was arrested in 1588. The

Inquisition, which dealt with his case, put him on show in an *auto de fe* in Toledo in 1589, and sent him off to confinement in a monastery for seven months.[88]

The credit given to prophecies irritated many. A leading writer in 1588 denounced the fact that 'through them bad news has begun to be spread about and even, astonishingly, believed. The talk is of dreams, for example threats of widespread death and destruction, and that the chosen few have to save themselves in caves.'[89]

In this atmosphere the affair of Lucrecia de León assumed considerable importance. Aged twenty-two when arrested by the Inquisition in Madrid in 1590, Lucrecia was a seer whose prophecies and dreams stimulated a small aristocratic circle at court.[90] Her dreams, coming in the wake of the Armada, took on a verisimilitude not to be found in those of Piedrola. She saw a Spain ravaged and invaded, a Philip too feeble to cope. Some dreams were uncanny prognostications. In December 1587, eight months before the event, she saw the defeat of the Spanish fleet by the English. Subsequent dreams, as narrated to her confidants, presented an image of the kingdom which undoubtedly reflected concerns felt and expressed by very many people. In a dream in the spring of 1590 she was told by one of her dream figures: 'Philip does not know, and if he knows he does not want to believe, that his enemies will soon be in his lands. He wants to spend his summers in the Escorial, but he should beware, it is not the time to retire there without fear.' 'Beware,' warned one of the figures, 'for this is the time of thunder.' Another dream a week later presented Philip as a tyrant who 'has destroyed the poor', and who would be punished by God through the agency of Elizabeth of England. Philip lived in his palace, 'his eyes bound and his ears shut', surrounded by a Spain in ruins: 'the hour has come to endure purgatory in Spain'.[91]

Lucrecia's dreams, which seem to have stopped shortly after her arrest, were limited in their impact to a small group of people and were not therefore accorded too much significance by the government. But the inquisitors took a more serious view. They saw that Lucrecia was repeating calumnies which echoed those spread about by William of Orange's *Apology*. She spoke of 'sins committed by the king in killing his son and queen Elizabeth [Valois]'. The king had 'taken the land from the peasants'. God would punish. 'God wished to remove him and his son, and there would remain no one of his seed, and the Moriscos and heretics would destroy Spain.' People had been repeating these things for several months, if not years. Yet until now the government had taken no action. The king himself seemed to accept the criticisms and calumnies as normal.

Philip's own secretary Vázquez told him in February 1591 that the expensive foreign policy could not be sustained, because 'here the people are perishing, and with them very rapidly both agriculture and cattle-farming, and officials are neglecting many matters touching conscience, justice, government and public welfare'. He foresaw the risk of 'everything collapsing all at once'. 'The people are full of complaints, and many say that things are not right . . . There are criticisms and laments and much fear of great punishments from heaven.'[92]

Philip's reflections on Vázquez's comments were those of a tired but patient old man. 'These are not matters to be ignored by someone like me who, as you know, is concerned about his responsibilities, since they distress and grieve nobody more than me. But, all in all, they are much more difficult to deal with than people think. . .' On the 'complaints', he observed that 'I was told that there was a danger of a sedition involving two of the leading persons here (although most of them are, I think, alone in these things), over the woman about whom I wrote', namely Lucrecia.[93]

*

The atmosphere of criticism did not mean that Philip was losing control. His tenacity was astonishing. Nowhere can his firm hand be seen more clearly than in the way he and his ministers kept the higher aristocracy in rein. Conflicts between nobles were always a source of potential disorder. The prominent jurist Castillo de Bobadilla commented in these years on the king's efficiency. 'He did not pardon their faults with his habitual clemency, nor did he respect their estates and power, and there is no peace officer now who cannot act against them.' All this, he felt, was 'a happy situation never before attained'.[94] No offence went unpunished. The most distinguished nobles of the realm found themselves in prison for offences that might have been overlooked in other times. In 1577 the brother of the Admiral of Aragon was executed for raping a nun.[95] The count of Fuentes went to prison in 1578 for a violent quarrel, the marquis of Las Navas in 1580 for sexually harassing a girl.[96] In 1586 the king condemned no less a person than Luis Hurtado de Mendoza, fourth marquis of Mondéjar, to prison and then to military service overseas, for murdering one of his servants in order to enjoy the favours of the man's wife.[97] The marquis spent most of his life in confinement, dying in Africa during his spell of military service. In 1587 the king ordered the imprisonment of the duke of Osuna and his son the marquis of Peñafiel, for gambling. The same year he ordered the detention of the marquis of Carpio. In 1588 the marquis of Alcalá was placed under close arrest in the tower at Mota de Medina and the trial began of the count of Puñonrostro, accused of murdering a man. 'If matters go on at this rate,' an ambassador commented, 'the court will be emptied of grandees.'[98]

The disciplinary decisions were never made by the king alone.[99] They were always backed up by the whole council or by the Junta of ministers.

As in 1579, when Alba and his son were arrested, there was usually a consensus in the government about what action should be taken. Perhaps the most startling arrests of the entire reign took place in 1590. In July that year the duke of Alba, Antonio Alvarez de Toledo, who succeeded to the title in 1585, committed the same blunder that his uncle Don Fadrique, the previous duke, had committed in 1579: he married in defiance of the king's permission. Philip was not to be trifled with. In August 1590 he ordered the imprisonment of the five grandees who were party to the marriage: the dukes of Alba, Francavilla and Pastrana, and the Admirals of Castile and Aragon.[100] It was a very serious case that could have led to vendettas among the nobility. The governing troika consulted all sections of the council, and agreed with the king that 'it would be just and fitting to order the immediate arrest of the duke of Alba and those who went with him, thereby disciplining one side and calming the other'.[101] The king's firmness could also be seen in 1591, when he sacked his chief magistrate and president of the royal council, the count of Barajas, after being warned by Father Chaves that justice was in a deplorable condition. Barajas died later that year, deeply embittered. For years, Philip refused to appoint a successor.[102] Not surprisingly, the great lords breathed more freely when the old man had gone.

*

The arrests of Lucrecia and of the grandees, both in 1590, were probably not connected. But in the case of the grandees the king may well have considered the connection with Antonio Pérez,[103] who in April 1590 escaped to freedom.

In 1580, Antonio Pérez tells us in his memoirs, 'the king left for Portugal. Antonio Pérez remained in Madrid under house arrest in his own house. No moves were made in his case. This was the state of things until the end of 1585.'[104] But the matter was not put on ice. Rodrigo Vázquez de Arce's officials continued to collect evidence. The king wrote to president Pazos from Lisbon in November 1581 that 'if the matter had been one which could have been pursued through a public trial, this would have been done from the first day'.[105] In the spring of 1582 Rodrigo Vázquez, in Lisbon, began to draw up the list of charges. At this juncture the king decided to separate the two cases of Pérez and La Eboli, and to proceed for the moment only against the princess. Pérez would be left for later.

The princess, confined since her arrest in the castle of Santorcaz, was moved later to the family palace at Pastrana. Her case, not directly involving affairs of state, was dealt with simply by a resolution of the king's council in November 1582. In Pastrana she was closely confined to a suite of rooms. Desperate, periodically ill, she here passed the last ten years of her life. A final illness ended her trials in February 1592.

Pérez, meanwhile, lived in Madrid freely and without impediment. Ministers and diplomats visited him. In the summer of 1584, just over a year after Philip's return from Lisbon, official charges were presented against the ex-secretary. The government was slow to act, for a very compelling reason: Pérez was in possession of an alleged 'thirty cases' of the king's confidential papers. When it appeared that Pérez might flee, he was arrested in January 1585, ten days after the king had left to go to Saragossa. He attempted to escape, with the help of his friend cardinal Quiroga,[106] but was seized and imprisoned. Over the next four years he was confined in various locations, often with a surprising degree of freedom. This benevolence ended in 1589. He and his wife still refused to hand over many of the papers. When accused pointedly of the murder of Escobedo, and asked to explain the alleged involvement of the king, Pérez maintained that he knew nothing. Finally, in February 1590, he was put to the torture. Philip, whose gout prevented him going to spend Holy Week at San Lorenzo, was directly at hand following events. At the end of March the king, tranquil, assisted at a splendid joust in which all the young nobility of the court participated. Pérez's friends, meanwhile, made plans to get him out. With their help, on the night of 19 April Pérez escaped from prison and made directly for his homeland, the kingdom of Aragón.

The laws of Aragon gave Pérez complete protection against the king. He appealed to be tried by the court of the justiciar of Aragon, which was independent of crown control. He was lodged for his own security in the justiciar's prison in Saragossa. From here, he began a campaign to win over Aragon to his cause. Several members of the lesser nobility, fired by enthusiasm for the liberties of their country, rallied to him. The king, meanwhile, took urgent steps to prosecute Pérez in Aragon. In these same weeks he was preoccupied with events in France, and an unstable Aragonese frontier was the last thing he wanted. He also pressed the Inquisition, headed by Quiroga, to claim jurisdiction over Pérez on a trumped-up charge of heresy. The idea of using the Holy Office may have occurred to him after a visit to Toledo in February 1591. He attended an *auto de fe* – described by a Flemish courtier who was there as 'a very sad spectacle, distressing to see'[107] – and then went on to San Lorenzo.

Philip followed a 'wait and see' policy over the situation in Saragossa. But he preferred to put on a tough public face. He explained to the viceroy of Aragon, the marquis of Almenara, that 'if it should leak out that I incline to a soft line (which is what I desire whenever possible) there might follow complications of importance'.[108] On 24 May 1591 the inquisitors of Saragossa tried to get Pérez transferred to their own prison in the Aljafería palace. The attempt provoked serious riots in the city; in the tumult Almenara received wounds from which he later died. The king was asleep in bed at Aceca when Chinchón brought him news of the death. 'What?', he is reported to have said, stroking his beard with his hand, 'so they have killed the marquis?'[109] He had himself dressed, and began to dictate letters.

After the May riots his ministers were unanimous that harsh measures, including the execution of implicated nobles, were essential. Philip, however, disagreed and refused to act. 'In good time we can see what is the best course to take, in this as in everything else. I say this because it does not seem to me that we are yet in a situation to be able to resolve these matters.'[110] To help him consider the issues, he set up a special junta on Aragon of thirteen persons, who were to meet under the presidency of cardinal Quiroga in Madrid. He happened to be seriously unwell at the time, and insisted on resting in bed at San Lorenzo rather than returning to Madrid.[111] In the capital, the junta on Aragon were anxiously deliberating while also criticising the king for his inaction.

Philip's deliberate refusal to act was familiar to a key observer of this time, the count of Luna. 'As was usual when he wanted a matter to be resolved in accordance with his wishes, when he sent it to a committee or for the opinion of others,' Luna noted, 'he took to his bed in order to force a reply. And this without ever declaring his will or ordering firmly "I want to do this".'[112] The tactic always worked. Four weeks later he had not changed his mind, preferring caution to the show of force advised by the junta on Aragon. 'There is no doubt that if this can be settled by benign means it will be better than having to use force.'[113] But this was no display of weakness. The king was already furious with the constitutional leaders of Aragon, the *diputados*, who instead of condemning the events of May had tried to *explain* them to him. 'This was like throwing on the fiery disposition of His Majesty,' it was observed, 'not just oil but burning pitch.'[114] In a long, ominous letter to the junta on Aragon, Philip bared his inner thoughts and also revealed a glimpse of cold steel:

> I don't believe there is anybody in the world so blind or so misinformed as not to understand perfectly well the responsibility thrust on me in Aragon; and much less those here in the junta, unless they are blind or misinformed . . . I understand perfectly well this responsibility I now have, and the greatest responsibility of all is the service of Our Lord.

The next important responsibility was the authority that the Inquisition had lost in Saragossa. It was essential to restore this.

> Besides this, there is the responsibility that I also have to the administration of justice in that kingdom, and the punishment of those who have put both Inquisition and justice in the condition in which they are . . . I am determined to resolve this as necessary, even if it means

involving my own person and whatever else is required. If for the sake of religion we have been through and done what you have seen in Flanders, and then in France, the responsibility is even greater to our own people, on our doorstep. For I see very well that if you abandon them and do not help as you should, they will attempt to abolish the Inquisition . . .

For all these reasons, I cannot but be very firm and determined in what I have said. It also seems desirable that before any resort to force other appropriate means be explored, in order to achieve peacefully what I have been saying. But these means must be through the due and fitting use of authority, not through the pardon that I think some of you have proposed in some matters.

It seems to me that it is time now to begin to explore these means, so do not lose any more time.[115]

In the light of his own experience the king was determined not to repeat his mistake in Flanders, of resorting to strong measures when milder ones would suffice. He was also concerned to act within the law, not outside it.

In the process, substantial differences of approach emerged between himself and his ministers. They could not understand Philip's obsessive concern for the Inquisition. To them it appeared obvious that the whole business would never have got out of hand, had it not been for the Inquisition laying its hands on Pérez. They accordingly informed the king that for the Holy Office to preserve its authority, 'it is very important not to involve this tribunal in matters that are outside its competence'. The view was strongly held by the ministers and other advisers.[116] It provoked an angry and long-suffering outburst from the king. 'Maybe,' he responded, 'you will come to realise one day, that these matters are *not* outside the competence of the Inquisition, but among those that most directly concern it.'[117]

The misunderstandings between king and ministers did not stop there. The junta on Aragon drafted a letter to Saragossa in Philip's name, saying that he was 'determined to go there and hold a Cortes'. The king was indignant. 'In the reply I sent you the other day, about going there, it was not a question of "going to a Cortes" but only of "going"; and that was my reply and it still is. I said nothing about going to hold a Cortes. There is no need right now to raise the matter of a Cortes until we see later on how things turn out.'[118]

Fortunately they all agreed on one thing: the probable need to send in an army. From 1 September secret preparations for this eventuality were put into effect, and the king with great precision drew up in his own hand details of recruitment, movements and strategy. Years of political experience, and direct familiarity with the terrain, enabled him to assume the role of strategist.

It was a grave moment. Never since the union of Castile and Aragon in the 1470s had the crown raised an army to act in Aragon. Not since the 1520s (in Castile) had it had to take armed action against its own nobility. The paramount concern now was France. Philip saw the need to 'act quickly because of the business in France'.[119] If there were commitments in France, he could not be tied down in Aragon. But even though the immediate motive was Saragossa, there were long-standing problems of law and order which Philip and his ministers were no doubt anxious to resolve. Preparations were to be kept secret even from the new viceroy, the bishop of Teruel, who was to be told (correctly) that troops were being prepared to secure the frontier with France.

On 24 September the Inquisition once again tried to remove Pérez to the Aljafería. This time there was an even more serious riot in the streets of Saragossa, and the prisoner was set free. Pérez, accompanied by his friends, fled the city and took the road northwards. He eventually made it to France and then to England. The events of September removed any doubts about the need for action. It was less a riot than a massacre: the casualties were twenty-three dead and many seriously wounded.[120] When informed that the army would be ready by January the king commented: 'It seems a very long time to have to wait until January for a solution.'[121] He was now in a hurry to act.[122] Two armies were assembled on the frontiers of Aragon. A small force waited in the north, on the frontier with Navarre. Further south, some 14,000 infantry and 1,500 cavalry were mustered under the command of Alonso de Vargas, an elderly and ailing veteran of the war in Flanders. Apart from some 800 infantry who had been with the ill-fated Armada, the soldiers were, in Vargas's opinion, the worst dregs he had ever seen. Recruited largely by the Castilian nobility from their estates,[123] they were the only troops the government could raise at short notice. On 15 October the king sent a letter to each of the authorities in Aragon, telling them that he was sending in troops. Philip claimed that they were merely 'passing through on their expedition to France'. There was, he insisted, no threat to liberties: 'my will has been and is that the *fueros* be preserved'. Vargas told a friend that 'the king told him that up till then he believed that the affairs of Aragon would be settled without this severe measure of an army'. Still no action was taken. Days passed while the recruited troops straggled in to the rendezvous on the Castile–Aragon frontier.

The option of persuasion was not forgotten. Philip sent in, by way of the frontier town of Calatayud, the Valencian marquis of Llombay. His task was to reassure the Aragonese. Meanwhile, the king consulted with senior officials throughout the peninsula. The viceroy of Navarre, for example, was asked in October for his view of the situation.[124]

At the end of October the four judges in the court of the justiciar, Juan de Lanuza, declared that sending in the army was a *contrafuero*, a contravention of the laws of the realm. This was an open declaration against the king. On 11 November the royal armies entered Aragon. That same day Lanuza with his allies prepared to confront the invaders. Failing to muster sufficient forces in Saragossa, or the help of any other city in the realm, the dissidents fled the capital. Several nobles who had been forced into a compromising role by the events also left the city and went north to the town of Epila. They included the justiciar, Juan de Lanuza; the count of Aranda, Luis Jiménez de Urrea; and the duke of Villahermosa, Martín de Aragón. Vargas faced no resistance, and entered Saragossa peacefully on 14 November. The city was like a tomb, reports a witness: 'it was horrible, because I saw over 1,500 houses with their doors and windows shut and a terrible fear in the spirits of everybody'.[125]

For a month nothing happened. The nobles and justiciar were persuaded to return to the capital. The constitutional bodies met again, and condemned the refugee dissidents. Vargas, a close friend to many Aragonese, advised moderation. He proposed a general pardon, the confirmation of the *fueros*, and the appointment of Aranda as viceroy. He also advised that 'in order to preserve the authority of the Inquisition its officials should not interfere in matters that do not involve it directly'.[126] This last piece of advice, as we have seen, coincided with that of ministers but went directly against the king's views.

His moderate attitude was brusquely rejected by the junta on Aragon in Madrid. The members were all agreed that exemplary punishment should be carried out. They disagreed only on its manner: some felt that the *fueros* should be respected, others held that the *fueros* were not operative in these circumstances. At the end of November they voted unanimously for the immediate execution without trial of the justiciar and of any other leaders caught.[127] On 19 December Aranda and Villahermosa were arrested and despatched immediately under escort to Castile. The next day the justiciar was arrested.

The subsequent repression was controlled at every stage by the organs of government in Madrid. Every step was advised and recommended by officials of the council of Aragon, led by the count of Chinchón. Chinchón's personal animosity towards many of the leaders of Aragon was well known in that realm. The councillors advised Philip that neither formal trials nor evidence were required in cases like the present, 'when there is open sedition and rebellion'; that the army should execute the guilty on the spot; and that the Inquisition must be used against other guilty persons.[128] The junta in mid-December reaffirmed that 'the guilty may be punished without any judicial order or formal accusation or trial or observation of the *fueros*'.[129] The king followed this advice closely. Some in Madrid, in particular Chinchón, had their own reasons for supporting a harsh line. In that same week the order was sent for the execution without trial of the justiciar. The king issued a blanket commission written in his own hand.[130]

Juan de Lanuza had succeeded to the post on his father's death, just two days before the events of 24 September. He was twenty-two years old, without the experience or the authority to control his own judges or restrain the dissidents as his father had done. His compliance with the declaration of a *contrafuero* had provided the legal basis for opposition. On 20 December, just after his arrest, he had his supper tranquilly. Later he was taken to meet a group of officials including the governor of Aragon, Ramón Cerdán, a Flanders veteran. The king's sentence was read to him. He became distraught, but was told to compose himself since he had only twelve hours to live. When the governor in reading the sentence came to the accusation that he was a traitor, the justiciar could only murmur: 'no, not that; ill-advised, yes'.[131] At ten the next morning, he was beheaded in the market square of the city, under the windows of his residence.[132] The streets were occupied by troops, and the windows shuttered: few managed to witness the execution. At midday, in pouring rain, he was buried with full honours.

It was a rapid, efficient and brutal act of surgery. The junta in February felt that 'punishments are best done rapidly and not in cold blood nor half-heartedly, in this way they cause more terror'.[133] Many Aragonese for their part felt that it was the most terrible moment in the history of their nation. 'There are no words,' the count of Luna lamented, 'to express the calamity and sadness of that day.'[134]

Aranda was confined at Medina del Campo, and moved early in August 1592 to the castle at Coca, where within a few days he died, aged only fifty-three, of a sudden illness. Villahermosa was confined in Burgos, and later transferred to Miranda, where he also died of an illness, on 6 November. There were, inevitably, rumours about these sudden deaths. The king, however, had no motive whatever to remove the two men, and no evidence exists of foul play.[135] Philip never in his reign sanctioned an execution, public or secret, without the explicit written support of his legal advisers. The mysterious deaths of the two nobles continue nevertheless to cast a shadow over the reputation of the king. In 1593, on his return from Tarazona, he instructed the council of Aragon to look into their cases. His confessor, Diego de Yepes, warned him about Chinchón's hostility to such a move.[136] With the help of favourable testimony from Vargas and others, at Easter 1596 the council issued a sentence absolving Villahermosa.[137] Aranda also was later declared innocent.[138]

Philip was concerned to reach a general pacification without delay. A general pardon was published in January 1592. It was accompanied by a list of over 150 persons who were excepted. Some of these, such as the rebel leader Juan de Luna, were already in custody. Luna and his accomplices were tried, tortured and executed on 19 October. The Inquisition was also encouraged to play its part. The king was advised that 'this tribunal is the most efficient way of pursuing and punishing those whom Your Majesty feels should not reasonably remain unpunished'.[139] In the spring of 1592 he was in touch with Inquisitor-General Quiroga over the action to be taken. The result was an enormous *auto de fe* held in Saragossa on 20 October that year, when eighty-eight victims participated in the ceremony. The name of Pérez featured among them, on a charge of homosexuality. Many of the others were accused of taking part in the riots against the Inquisition. It was a blatantly political use of a Church tribunal. A further ceremony, including more rioters, was held just over a year later.

Meanwhile, careful preparations had been made to summon the Aragonese Cortes. 'This business of the Cortes,' Philip had observed, 'is not easy to resolve.'[140] The cities and estates were called to meet in Tarazona: the session was opened on 15 June 1592 by the archbishop of Saragossa. Philip was seriously ill, but resolved, against the advice of Dr Vallés, to attend the later sessions. He also subsequently decided to include Navarre in the itinerary. He would take prince Philip with him, to swear to the laws of that realm. In May he went from San Lorenzo with the prince and Isabel, to spend a week at Valsaín and a further week in Segovia. In June they celebrated Corpus at San Lorenzo, and then set out on their journey towards Navarre and Aragon. In Valladolid, which put on celebrations, fireworks and a bull-run, the king was forced to stop several days because of his gout. On days when he felt better, he went visiting. He paid an official visit to the university, and also went to the English College, which he had founded years before as a haven for exiled English Catholic clergy. During the stay in Valladolid he suffered a serious blow: his long-serving and faithful doctor, Francisco Vallés, died. Another casualty was the Valencian humanist Furió Ceriol,[141] who was accompanying the court.

When the royal party eventually got to Burgos the king's condition was clearly serious. Philip insisted on pressing on towards Navarre, travelling part of the route in a litter. 'In the year 1542 when I went to that city with the emperor my father,' he reminisced to the viceroy of Navarre, 'we went from Logroño, and I think this would be the best and most direct route.'[142] Bad weather made the journey extremely difficult. It was 'overcast, stormy, the roads muddy and very dangerous because of the swollen streams and deep torrents which flowed everywhere with great fury'.[143] The royal group entered Pamplona on 20 November; two days later the Cortes of Navarre, assembled in the cathedral, swore to the prince as heir. There were the usual festivities and celebrations, and a special event was put on for Philip's pleasure: a grand tournament in the medieval manner.

The king reached Tarazona on the last day of November. Making a special effort, despite his condition, he entered the city riding a white horse.[144] He was very ill, but also very angry. He entered the Cortes unsmiling, his face like thunder.[145] As the king had promised, no significant changes were made to the liberties of Aragon. But the decisions agreed upon by the chastened deputies defined more rigidly the parameters of law and order in the realm. A repeat of the Pérez episode was made impossible. In future, delinquents in one realm could be repatriated from another, royal officials could enter other jurisdictions in search of those accused, and the office of justiciar was made revocable by the king. Most decisions of the estates could now be passed by simple majority, though the traditional need for a unanimous vote was still preserved in some essential matters.[146] For the first time, the crown stepped in to license printing.[147] Finally, the four estates of the Cortes held a solemn session on 2 December at which prince Philip swore to observe the *fueros*. Three days later the royal party left Tarazona. They were back in Madrid on the thirtieth. The whole trip had lasted eight months, and took its toll on the king's health. Philip looked haggard, old and ill.[148]

The settlement reached at the Cortes brought peace to Aragon but did not reassure the eastern realms. Castilians began to boast that they had 'conquered an enemy kingdom',[149] a consoling achievement at a time when they were everywhere in retreat. The official Castilian version of events spoke of a 'revolt of Aragon', a clear distortion of what had happened.[150] There was corresponding pressure among the ruling class of Aragon to give voice to their version. None of this helped to create understanding between Castile and its neighbours; if anything, it continued to foment suspicion. Two contemporaries, the count of Luna in Aragon and the noble Francesc Gilabert in Catalonia, pointed out that in the long view the troubles had arisen because of Castile's erroneous policies towards the rest of Spain.[151]

*

The Castilian Cortes happened to be in session in 1588 when news of the Armada disaster came through. This helped powerfully to persuade its members to vote to the crown, by a two to one vote in February 1589, one of the most notorious taxes of the century, the *millones* (so called from its value in the monetary unit of maravedis). Details were formally agreed in April 1590. For the first time, a tax was levied directly on basic food items such as wine, oil, vinegar and meat. Hostility to the *millones* was widespread. Philip was not unaware of the injustice of the new taxes, imposed according to census figures which were (the king admitted) fifty years out of date.[152] In Madrid in the spring of 1591 there was a threat of riot. Witnesses said that up to 2,000 people were involved.[153] The city magistrates managed to control the situation, arrested the ringleaders and hanged some of them.[154] At the end of June in Seville leaflets were being distributed. The king urged his ministers to look into the matter 'before it gets out of control'.[155] In Avila in October 1591 seditious papers were found fixed to the main public buildings. 'Spain, Spain,' they said, 'look to yourself and defend your liberty; and you, Philip, be satisfied with what is your own and do not claim what is another's.'[156] Seven people were arrested for the offence. One, the noble Diego de Bracamonte, was executed four months later. The tax burden made even the king's confessor advise him to desist from pressing the towns too far.[157]

When the troubles in Saragossa broke out, on top of the tensions in Castile, it appeared that the whole peninsula might fall apart. Philip's caution was certainly motivated by awareness of the risks. In November 1591, in a last-minute plea to the government to avoid the use of force in Aragon, the duke of Gandía, the principal grandee of Valencia, commented that

> if this matter of Aragon should reach breaking-point I would not count much on those in Castile, for not only are those who have complaints about the burdens and taxes of these last few years happy to spread it around by word of mouth, they even publish it with posters that they have put up in Seville and Avila; and you know the disturbance they caused in Madrid. I also beg you to consider what assurance there is that the Portuguese stay quiet, and how things are going in Italy. The affairs of Flanders, France and England speak for themselves on the little need the king has to seek another war.[158]

The duke had good reason for caution. In Madrid there were many critics of the king who were actively (reports a historian of the time who preferred not to name names) 'hostile to the current situation, which they considered wretched'.[159] The right to express dissent had always been accepted, but the severity to those in Avila appeared to take away the right. Even in Castile the execution of the justiciar appeared to some to be unwarranted. 'Everybody,' observed a monk of the Escorial, 'criticised such cruelty.'[160]

The last Castilian Cortes of the reign convened in the first week of May 1592. It held periodic sessions over the next few years, and was still in existence when Philip III succeeded to the throne. As in previous Cortes, negotiations were often carried out in committee rather than in plenary sessions. In a committee of the Cortes in May 1593 a deputy for Burgos, Jerónimo de Salamanca, laid the blame for the current situation squarely on the wars. 'That in Flanders began twenty-seven years ago, and has shown little sign of improvement until now.' The wars had 'allowed our enemies to seize all the riches that have come from America, as well as the substance of these realms'.[161] In a clearly concerted move, similar speeches were made by the deputies for Seville and Cuenca, and by the deputy for Madrid, Francisco de Monçón. Two weeks later, on 20 May, the tax proposals of the government were put to the vote of the full Cortes. One-third of the thirty-three deputies present followed Salamanca in refusing approval.

This last Cortes of the reign made striking constitutional claims. The desired taxes were duly voted, but in return the deputies demanded that since the taxes were exceptional, they must be treated less as taxes than as a contractual grant. 'It must be a mutual contract between His Majesty and the realm . . . It is a real contract.'[162] They took their demands to further unprecedented lengths. While the Cortes was in session, the king should make laws only through it. Laws made through the Cortes should be revocable only by the Cortes. New taxes should be voted only by the Cortes.[163] The claims were unparalleled in the Europe of their day.

These crisis years had a direct impact on the standard of living. From Mexico a settler wrote back to her brother begging him to come over from 'that poverty and need which people suffer in Spain'.[164] Philip was not blind to the growing distress among his subjects. Armada year marked the beginning of a run of lean years. In the early months of 1588 the influx of transients into the capital provoked concern. A suggestion was made that the city should have a police force to patrol the streets. 'Having men in the streets,' the king noted, 'is a very good idea.' Then he recalled that he had seen it in practice. 'It is done in England, I saw it there and it works well.'[165] In May 1589 the king commented that 'I am most concerned about the poor harvest this year and what I have seen these days of the country-side . . . The shortage can be seen already . . .'. He ordered an examination of food stocks. At the same time, 'it is days since I wrote to Sicily to find out what they have there'. Sicily was the wheat supplier to which Span-iards always turned in an emergency. In the autumn of 1590 the king was alarmed by the food situation in the capital: 'they say there is great trouble in Madrid about the bread shortage, which is like nothing seen before'.[166] He had heard that his officials were seizing the bread for themselves, 'and that they care little for the poor, who are dying of hunger'. He was indignant and ordered an inquiry.[167]

His concern for the poor was demonstrated in sporadic help for schemes of poor relief put forward at the time.[168] He commissioned a report from one of the doctors of the court, Cristóbal Pérez de Herrera. While preparing his study, the latter in about 1594 struck up a friendship with a writer, Mateo Alemán,[169] who was then living in Madrid and was interested in the same problem. Pérez de Herrera's work, the *Relief of the Poor*, was published in a definitive form in 1598. Alemán the year after published his novel *Guzmán de Alfarache*, one of the most famous of satires on the life of the poor in Golden Age Spain.

In Portugal the discontent with a Castilian regime surfaced continually. In the 1590s there were various clashes with the Castilian soldiers there. In 1591 a Castilian friar living in Portugal reported that the situation was intolerable but that those in authority seemed not to care. 'Don Cristobal is blind and the king even more, God enlighten them. The king is not told what is going on.'[170] In 1593 'offensive papers exhorting the people to rise' were found in towns of the Alemtejo. The leaflets complained of Philip that 'he treats his subjects intolerably; the towns must rise and seek another king'.[171] There were continuous incidents. The Venetian ambassador to Madrid reported in 1596 that 'the Portuguese are natural foes of the Castilians and are almost daily at blows with them'.[172]

The other realms of the monarchy were also having problems. Sicily in 1590–1 suffered severe harvest failures, in common with much of southern Italy.[173] In 1592 there were disorders in the city of Messina.[174] That same year there were attempts to provoke a rising in Naples. The crisis of authority was not limited to Europe. In the New World dissatisfaction with Spanish control provoked the city of Quito to rebel in 1592. 'To conquer these realms of Peru,' the city council protested, 'His Majesty did not have to make any contribution. The land was won by those who came over at their own expense.'[175] The authorities played for time, and eventually the viceroy had to send in armed forces to suppress the rebellion.

*

In the Netherlands the position of Parma had worsened as a result of the Armada failure. The great period of convincing victories was followed by one of stalemate. In August 1589 the first of a new spate of serious mutinies in the Spanish army took place. Criticism of the general became more audible as no further victories materialised. Parma attempted to persuade the Spanish government to make a political settlement based on religious concessions. In the autumn of 1589 he sent to Madrid the president of the Netherlands council of State, Jean Richardot, who brought a general proposal for peace covering all the areas where Spain was in conflict. The crucial aspect was the proposal for partial religious toleration by both sides in the Netherlands.[176]

Philip discussed the paper with Moura and Juan de Idiáquez. The proposal, the ministers summed up, was that 'if those there [in rebel Holland and Zealand] for their part allow the public exercise of our faith, His Majesty will allow and tolerate the public exercise of their erroneous opinions in a few select towns'. It was an indication of how far the situation had changed that both king and ministers were now prepared to mention the forbidden word 'tolerate'. Even more significant, they agreed that it was no longer Spain's objective to reconquer the rebel provinces. The ministers stated that 'to seek to conquer them by force is to talk of a war without end, for which there are neither lives nor money sufficient'.

Accepting the concession might seem, they said, a blow to Spain's honour, its *reputación*. But was *reputación* worth preserving at the cost of the souls that might be saved by acceptance? Philip agreed entirely with all this. 'It would be very good to achieve by this means all that is offered.' But, he said, the council must also be consulted; and in any case he could not make any decision without consulting the pope. While they waited for the pope to look at the question, the war dragged on.

Philip's reluctant conversion to the possibility of toleration for his northern subjects showed that he was, at last, ready to recognise the logic of reality. At the end of 1590 the emperor, Rudolf II, began to organise peace talks along the lines of those held at Cologne in 1579. This time the meeting, which took place in 1591, was in Vienna. The king's spokesman was his ambassador there, Guillén de San Clemente. Philip insisted that the papal nuncio preside in order to give legitimacy to the concession of toleration 'for a limited time' in return for the submission of Holland and Zealand.[177] The concession, a big one for Philip, was not enough to achieve peace.

*

The threatened succession of Henry of Navarre to the French crown dominated Spain's foreign policy in the last decade of the reign. The papacy attempted to tread carefully in French affairs, since there were active Catholics on both sides of the civil wars. Philip suspected Rome of supporting the new heretic king. When informed that two of the French cardinals had recognised Henry as heir, he commented indignantly: 'These are splendid cardinals of the Church. Rome is to blame for creating them.'[178] Spain's policy was straightforward: a Protestant ruler in France posed a direct threat to the Netherlands; everything must accordingly be done to oppose Henry of Navarre. To this end, the Catholic League must be supported. But Philip was not convinced that further bloodshed would end the war, and resolutely opposed intervention. He supported a common front of all groups: 'unite both sides, good and bad,' he wrote to his daughter Catalina in 1590, 'and follow the path that causes least conflict.'[179]

In fact, Catalina's husband the duke of Savoy was an unnecessary complication in the picture. In the autumn of 1588 he invaded the territory of Saluzzo, to which he had claims. Other Italian states, particularly the papacy, became alarmed. Carlo Emanuele also made no secret of his claims to parts of French territory. Philip had to try and soothe the protesting powers, while at the same time sorting out his own policy over France.

The situation within France spoke for itself. Navarre's forces, though small, were ably led. In the spring of 1590 they marched on Paris. The way was blocked by the forces of the League, aided at the last moment by a relief force sent from Flanders by Parma. At Ivry, in March, Henry won perhaps the most famous of his victories over the joint Catholic army. Paris lay wide open. At the end of April the siege of the capital began.

Four months of siege created inhuman conditions in Paris. They also forced Philip to take the step he had tried to avoid. In May he sent special instructions to his representatives in France, declaring that he was ordering Parma in. Early in August 1590 Parma crossed the frontier and forced Navarre to raise the siege at the end of the month. Philip in no way intended any more than a one-off intervention. The real military task was to remain in the hands of Mayenne and the League army.

From the first, the king knew that only a political solution was the answer. Yet there was no clear Catholic choice for the crown of France. The one acceptable candidate, the cardinal of Bourbon, died in May 1590, shortly after Spain decided to intervene. Another possibility was the young duke of Guise. But Philip had his own candidate, whom he offered from the very start in order to set matters straight. He had had lawyers working on the problem for some time. They had assured him (he told his agents in France) that 'the Infanta my eldest daughter has a well-grounded right' to the throne, as granddaughter of Henry II.

Philip's chief agents in France were Jean Baptiste Tassis and Bernardino de Mendoza. Philip's instructions to them show that he considered the throne to be the key.[180] The agents must fully back Mayenne, even though he was not to be trusted. The candidature of the Infanta should be broached tactfully, at all levels. Tassis should visit Guise at his home in Lorraine, offer him military help from Flanders and the Golden Fleece. In return, Guise might refrain from offering himself for the throne. Of course, if all else failed then 'the candidature of the duke of Guise is also acceptable'. Meanwhile, the Catholics must be kept divided so they didn't reach any agreement (that is, in favour of Navarre). They must be told not to trust the promises made to them.

While Philip's agents began to spread the message, France was falling into chaos. Philip felt it necessary to make minor interventions. A small force of Spanish troops was sent into Languedoc in July 1590, to help the French Catholic League. This aid vanished when the events in Aragon forced Philip to concentrate his troops south of the border, to repulse attacks from Antonio Pérez's allies in Béarn. Another force under Juan de Aguila was sent by sea from Coruña in September 1590 to help the League's duke of Mercoeur in Brittany. The military intervention was meant to be a strictly limited exercise, until a political solution could be found.

At first, few French Catholic leaders accepted the reassurances of the king of Navarre. Most rallied to the Catholic League, led by Mayenne. There were other foreign interventions. The duke of Lorraine made incursions into France from the north. On the eastern frontier Carlo Emanuele exploited the confusion to invade Provence in the autumn of 1590. Regions and provinces split up; some even threatened to secede from France. Among the separatists were the civic leaders of the city of Marseille, France's chief Mediterranean city. In Paris extremist members of the League set up a virtual commune.

At the end of 1590 the duke of Savoy came to San Lorenzo to consult with Philip. The visit led to the holding in Madrid, in April 1591, of a high-level conference between Philip, Savoy and representatives of Marseille and the League. Various possible solutions to the conflict were mooted. 'All of this,' the king mused, 'is in a terrible state if God does not produce a remedy, since the cause is his.'[181] He agreed to finance a task force in the Mediterranean. Savoy left Madrid at the end of May 1591, passing rapidly through Saragossa which was in upheaval as a result of the Antonio Pérez troubles. He left Barcelona with the promised Spanish fleet in July, and captured the royalist fortress of Berre. But by the autumn the complex politics of Provence collapsed into turmoil. At the end of March 1592 Carlo Emanuele withdrew his forces. Marseille struggled on alone against the royalists. It sent a delegation of three to Philip in the Christmas of 1595; in response Andrea Doria's fleet and two Spanish companies came to relieve the besieged city.[182]

However, no credible political alternative to Henry of Navarre emerged. Philip consequently found himself being sucked into a conflict that prolonged itself for six more long and expensive years. In August 1591 Parma was once again ordered to enter France, this time to relieve Rouen, besieged by Navarre and English auxiliaries. The seige was raised the following April, but Parma was seriously wounded during the campaign and taken back to the Netherlands in a litter. He never fully recovered. When ordered to lead yet another intervention in France, in November 1592, he left Brussels so unwell 'that he kept falling off his horse'.[183] Long before then, Philip had decided to withdraw him. The king seems to have been unhappy over differences of policy, and over the direction of affairs in Brussels, run 'by persons little known over here'.[184] In the summer of 1592 he sent an army veteran, the count of Fuentes, Pedro Enríquez de Guzmán, to replace him. Fuentes arrived in Brussels at the end of November. Just over a week later, on 3 December, the duke of Parma died in France of his wounds, unaware that he had been relieved of his command.

Philip was very likely aware that Parma's victories were not bringing peace any nearer. He committed himself now to finding a political solution at all costs. In June 1592 Mayenne and the Catholic League convoked a meeting of the Estates General, which opened its sessions in the Louvre in January 1593. In May Jean Baptiste de Tassis addressed the Estates. He used the occasion to argue for a legitimate Catholic succession to the throne, but the Catholics found it impossible to agree on any candidate of their own. Tassis therefore formally proposed on his master's behalf the claims of the Infanta Isabel. The biggest obstacle, in principle, was that in France the so-called Salic Law excluded females from the line of succession. Though Philip had instructed his ambassador, the duke of Feria,[185] to press Isabel's claims, he was willing to accept the candidature of any other reliable Catholic claimant, and had no political ambitions in France.[186] His calculations were upset by Henry of Navarre, who in July publicly abjured his heresy and was received into the Catholic Church.

Navarre's move was distrusted by the Catholics and lost him much Protestant support, but it seriously weakened Spanish efforts to get the Estates to accept Isabel. Most Frenchmen preferred a French candidate, however doubtful his religious position, to a foreign one. 'Weary of travails', Tassis reported, and of war and foreign intervention, they bit by bit declared for Navarre.[187] Mayenne proved to be an unreliable ally. In February 1594 Henry IV was formally crowned king of France in the cathedral at Chartres. Early in the morning of 22 March he and his army were let into Spanish-occupied Paris by French officials, and the enemy troops allowed to march out with military honours. Henry gave them a safe conduct, with two officials to accompany them and help obtain provisions. The duke of Feria described the exit:

> I left at two in the afternoon, with all our men in file, flags flying and beating drums. First to leave were the Italians, followed by myself on horseback with all the rest of our men, and the Walloons behind me. The prince of Béarn [Henry IV] was at a window overlooking the Porte St Denis through which we left. I took off my hat to him when I passed and he did the same.[188]

On this note of gallantry another unsuccessful chapter in Spanish imperialism closed. Henry IV's position was infinitely strengthened when, in 1595, his conversion was accepted by Rome and a papal pardon issued. Some months before this, on 17 January 1595, he formally declared war against Spain, which now faced a struggle on all fronts in western Europe.

Long before then, it was plain to the Spanish government that its military interventions in the west must be ended. One final effort against France was made by the governor of Milan, who assembled an army which crossed the passes through Savoy and launched an attack on French Burgundy.[189] But the forces were unexpectedly defeated by Henry IV in June 1595 at Fontaine-Française, and withdrew to Italy. The other interventions in France had collapsed. In Brittany, where Juan de Aguila faced French royalist troops, English troops under Sir John Norris, and Breton peasant rebels, the Spanish position was completely untenable. 'In Brittany there isn't a single man Your Majesty can rely on, nor any who wouldn't give his own or his children's last drop of blood to see the Spaniards out. Anyone who says otherwise to Your Majesty is deceiving you.'[190] In Marseille too the tide turned. Early in February 1596 a coup took place, the brilliant rebel leader Charles de Casaulx was murdered, and the city surrendered to the French. The small Spanish force was expelled. 'Only now am I king of France!' a delighted Henry IV is said to have exclaimed as he entered the city. Wherever possible, the Spanish government tried to suppress news of the reverses. 'They are wrong to ban the publication of news,' protested an official, 'because the way we Spaniards function is that however bad an event may be what we imagine is always worse.'[191]

Profiting from the absence of part of Parma's army in France, Dutch forces under William of Orange's second son, Maurice of Nassau, began a southward drive which netted significant gains. They were enormously helped by the mutinies which racked the Spanish forces. From the Netherlands the bishop of Antwerp complained to Arias Montano of 'this wretched war', saying that it served only to enrich the rebels with all the gold sent from Spain to pay for it.[192] The provinces under Spanish rule were unhappy with Parma's replacement, the count of Fuentes. Philip appointed the archduke Ernst, the emperor Rudolf's brother, as governor. But Ernst arrived only in 1594, and died shortly after, in February 1595. The financial situation in the Spanish exchequer was desperate. Disengagement became inevitable.

In 1593 the Venetian ambassador Contarini felt that the king had reached an age that was 'very perilous in all old men'.[193] He was likely to live several years yet, thanks to the 'good regime' in his diet and way of life. But the government represented a 'heavy and unbearable weight'. Preoccupations of state, the debt, the heavy taxes, the famine (there was a severe drought and harvest failure in 1593–4) were part of his burden. Above all, there was the problem of the succession. 'These travails trouble the king's spirit and do much harm to his appearance.' The portrait done of him, probably in this year, by Juan Pantoja de la Cruz,[194] reflects perfectly the wastage of the years. Philip stands erect, dressed from top to toe in black, with the Fleece as his only ornament. His face is an ashen white, the same colour as his beard and hair. The lips sag. His eyes now, instead of glaring defiantly as in the portrait by Wierix of seven years before, are old and weary, the lids half-closed.

11

Last Years
1593–1598

I don't believe that my life matters so much, at least not to me.[1]

After his return from Tarazona the king's health was poor and he was patently unable to cope. He made it to San Lorenzo for Holy Week in 1593, and then spent a restful May in Aranjuez. Most of the summer was spent at San Lorenzo. But Philip was seriously ill with the gout. Surgeons had to open two fingers of his right hand to let out the pus.[2] He could barely write, and could no longer manage the tasks of government. The troika which had been functioning since 1585 was therefore given a new lease of life. Its membership was the same: Moura, Idiáquez and Chinchón. Their duties were also the same. But since the king could no longer carry out the roles reserved for himself in 1586, a substitute had to be found.

It was agreed that the prince was still too young for the job, so the decision was made to summon the archduke Albert from Lisbon. Philip had been thinking of this possibility since as long ago as January 1589. 'For some days,' he commented then, 'I have been considering this matter of bringing my nephew over here.'[3] Official duties, Philip wrote now to Moura, 'have put even more pressure on me this year than last year, and because of this I wish to see my nephew over here, and have thought hard about it'. The archduke would have to be carefully instructed, a task he entrusted to Moura. The king signed off with a reflective sigh: 'affairs these days are terrible'.[4]

The cardinal archduke Albert was aged thirty-four in 1593. Philip had always placed great hope in his capacities. Albert came directly to San Lorenzo from Lisbon, arriving in the afternoon of 11 September.[5] In a special gesture, Philip went by coach two miles down the road to meet him. He honoured the archduke by placing him between himself and the prince as they entered San Lorenzo. The prince was unhappy at this arrangement and came round to take his father's right hand. The king frowned sternly at him and made him go to the left hand of the archduke.[6] It was a little incident that summed up for observers the problem of the succession.

Shortly after, the king sent Albert a handwritten note (backdated to 8 September) which thanked him for coming and set out his functions. He was to work in Madrid, accompanying the prince to official meetings, celebrations and church services. Public audiences took up much of the king's time. First audiences of ambassadors would be given by himself (the king) or by the prince; all other audiences were to be given, in the morning, by Albert. Afternoons must be kept free for council meetings. The troika, joined by the prince's tutor the marquis of Velada, was to be presided over by the prince, with Albert sitting to one side. The prince, on this showing, attended only the troika and not council meetings. Even then, according to one source, he stayed for only about half an hour,[7] leaving the others to make decisions without him. A few days later the king gave the troika his instructions. They were to meet every afternoon, and could implement all their decisions except for financial ones, which had to go to the king first.[8]

He was, in effect, preparing to hand over the regime. The prince's appearance alone on horseback in a public procession for the Nativity of the Virgin, in December 1593, was taken by some as a sign that his independent role was recognised. He was allowed to sign some documents but as yet did not have formal authority to act for the king.

In Madrid, the reign was drawing to a close. Seriously ill, on 7 March 1594 Philip had his final testament signed and witnessed.[9] It was a long document in forty-nine numbered paragraphs, conventional in phrasing and content, but careful to assert clearly the royal rights he was leaving in the hands of his son. It also carefully laid down the line of succession. Finally came the firm signature, 'I the king'.

When despatching his paperwork the king refused to be separated from Isabel, now his closest comfort. For years she had helped him, reading papers and aiding him with decisions. In 1590 'he wants her always at his side, and she is sometimes with him three or four hours while he attends to petitions, which she helps him to read'.[10] Well into 1595 Philip continued to annotate the principal papers of the Junta. The hours he worked were dictated by his health. In April 1594 he ordered that 'from now on don't send me anything unless it is before lunch, because afterwards I am already burdened with work for the afternoon'.[11] Though final decisions continued to be his, effective direction was in the hands of Cristóbal de Moura and Juan de Idiáquez. The council of State no longer ran affairs.

'And the other councils don't play any part in day-to-day business, but are sent matters of little moment.'[12] All reports on major matters were drawn up by Moura and Idiáquez alone, without going through the council. Idiáquez determined foreign affairs, Moura domestic politics.

As his illness worsened, the king's unmistakable scrawl tended to disappear from state papers, and in its place appeared the terse directions of Don Cristóbal: 'His Majesty says . . .'.[13] Important legal documents were still retained for the king's signature, and well into 1597 he continued to make written comments on select affairs of state. But his role was almost nominal. When the news came in 1595, for instance, that the pope had recognised Henry IV as king of France, he was too tired and unwell to absorb its significance. In large, shaky letters he scribbled: 'There has been so much today from Madrid, that I cannot look at this nor do I dare read or write much.' Let Idiáquez come tomorrow, he wrote, to explain the situation to him; though 'I think I have understood something of it'.[14] Despite Philip's incapacity, the government of the country did not collapse. Never adequately controlled from the centre, the provinces continued in tranquillity under their local authorities. Administrative and defence functions were confirmed in the hands of local nobility, who continued to play an important part in the politics and government of the country.[15]

His family rallied round the invalid. 'He recovers more quickly than before,' Isabel wrote to her sister Catalina in September 1594, 'and has begun again to drink wine, which he left two years ago. You can imagine what sort of summer we have had with all this, since in the whole summer we have not gone out once.'[16] But Philip's body did not respond to his will. In March 1595 the Venetian envoy Vendramin wrote home: 'The doctors say that his body is so withered and feeble that it is almost impossible that a human being in such a state should live for long.' He suffered continuous fever during the first three weeks of May 1595, but recovered from it; 'and as his sixty-ninth birthday fell on the first day that he was free of fever, he insisted on assisting at a procession, being carried to a window in a chair'.[17] Since 1590, he had walked only with the help of a stick.

As his health continued to deteriorate, Philip agreed it was time to hand over some of his powers to his son. The step could no longer be avoided, for he had decided to make use of Albert elsewhere. His original plan was what he had always intended: to appoint his nephew to the archbishopric of Toledo. Hardy old Quiroga died eventually, aged an incredible ninety-four, in November 1594. Albert's succession had been approved by the papacy, and his investiture robes were fitted out for him. But the unexpected death of the archduke Ernst in February 1595 left the Netherlands without a ruler. Philip immediately decided to replace him with his brother. Albert was nominated as the new governor on 26 April. He did not leave at once, because the king's illness took a sudden turn for the worse in May, but eventually left Madrid for the Netherlands in August. As an earnest of his good intentions, the king sent with him the young prince of Orange, whom the Spaniards had spirited away during the troubles over twenty years before. Albert arrived in Brussels in February 1596.

There was a general unease in the administration in Madrid, normal when a regime is about to change. Because the king was installed in San Lorenzo a group of ministers worked there. But another group, mainly those in finance, had to work in Madrid. The government in this way had two groups of ministers. They worked independently of, and sometimes against, each other. In August 1595 the president of the council of Finance, Poza, protested that 'here we try to turn stones into bread, there they turn bread into stones'.[18] In one report he referred inadvertently to a 'committee of chairmen', an informal committee of the heads of councils in Madrid, which had met periodically in the past to consider financial matters. The king was surprised by this constitutional innovation. 'I know of no committee of chairmen,' he said. He wanted to know 'who goes to it and what matters they deal with'.[19] It was something that could not have occurred in the days when he had his hands on the reins.

In September 1595 Poza sent in a report saying that the committee to discuss taxes with the Cortes was not functioning well. Moura scribbled in the margin: 'the same can be said of many other things'.[20] In a lighter moment, Poza dashed off a joke to the chief minister in the middle of a financial report. Moura, with the cares of a monarchy on his shoulders and a dying king on his hands, responded from San Lorenzo: 'the story is very good, and it's even better that someone who is in charge of the king's treasury at this juncture should have time to tell it. It is clear that you are a more capable person than we thought.'[21] The moments of humour were welcome relief. In October Poza laughed in a council meeting on receiving a note from Moura. On hearing of it Moura commented, 'It's encouraging that letters about serious business should contain something to make you laugh.'[22] The burden of work was heavy. But, said Moura, who had the habit of referring informally to the king as 'the Boss (*el patrón*)', 'here we are used to not complaining about anything'.[23]

Philip discussed with Idiáquez the terms on which the prince could be brought into the government. On 30 July 1595 at the Escorial, he wrote out in his own hand a short instruction for his son. The document commences: 'Since God has given you the desired good health and you are of age to carry out your share of responsibilities, it is time for us to help each other.'[24] The prince was to take over all essential public duties, such as attendance at audiences and councils, and was to rely for advice on Don Cristóbal. Where feasible, he was to report back directly to his father. The king in another document supplied some detail of the prince's duties. On feast-days he was to attend mass at 9 a.m., eat in public, and go riding in the park on some afternoons. On work days, he was to rise at 8 a.m., go out riding or hare-hunting, and then return to hear mass and give audiences. On some afternoons he was to study; and from six to eight was to assist in the relevant councils. He must always be in bed by ten at night.[25]

The Infante Philip was in his eighteenth year when he assumed these responsibilities. The king had made no previous attempt to bring him into the process of government, an attitude which contrasts with the confidence he had placed in the Infanta Isabel when she was even younger. The prince was, on all the evidence, a disappointment to his father. When he was twelve the best that his tutor could say of him was that he was 'intelligent, and concerned not to be idle'. By contrast, the tutor went on, he was 'very childish in many things', and of poor health. His favourite occupation was to imitate his father, 'writing memoranda and drawing up reports'.[26] He appeared to have little intellectual capacity. His study of languages did not extend to French. When the prince was sent a letter from the duke of Guise in 1593 his father opened it and explained apologetically to the secretary: 'I opened it because the prince would not be able to read it'.[27] Philip specially contracted Jean Lhermite to teach the prince French, but little progress was made. The ministers at court had little confidence in the prince, even when it was clear that he must succeed his father. Many despised him. When he was fifteen an ambassador described him as 'not very lively, short in stature, of quiet temperament', totally obedient to his father, whom he followed everywhere. He had not yet learned the use of arms, nor knew anything of matters of state.[28] At eighteen he had changed little, imitating his father 'not only in deeds but also in words'.[29]

In October 1596 Velada, who had been the prince's governor for nearly ten years, sent the king a confidential report. In part, it was also a comment on how the prince had managed three months of government. His Highness, he stated, 'is very quiet and withdrawn'. In order to overcome this shyness, he should have more contact with people and go out in public more often. He should be allotted a more active role in the councils where, it seems, he said nothing. 'What some wish for from His Highness, is that he speak on important matters.' He should be encouraged to lead more of an outdoor life and leave his indoors activities. He should get up very early in the morning to go hunting. This would oblige him to 'go to bed early and give up his music'.[30] Apparently the prince preferred to stay indoors, playing the guitar. There was little in the report to give comfort to the king. He was obliged to rely yet more on the good offices of Velada, whom he promoted in 1596 to the council of State in order to back up the prince.

Though largely cut off from his papers, 'the Boss' attempted to continue directing policy. 'As usual, His Majesty does just what he wants,' said Moura resignedly in February 1596, 'no matter how much we lecture him.'[31] Infirmities were no obstacle to the king's amazing resistance. In 1595, under the direction of the resourceful Jean Lhermite, an adjustable chair was constructed for his use.[32] He would get out of bed directly into the chair, which allowed him both to sit up for desk-work as well as recline completely for sleeping. When necessary he would pass the whole day in the chair, climbing back into bed at night. In February 1596 he and the court celebrated a subdued Carnival ('the weather was good but the food awful,' commented Moura)[33] in Vaciamadrid. In March he even went hunting at Aranjuez, though with what success we do not know. That month the court moved to Aceca, where the king was taken seriously ill, sparking off in Madrid rumours of his death. Courtiers were tied down in Aceca for two months. In April 1596 the gout 'increased to such an intensity of pain that his right arm is powerless'.[34] By this time his body was beginning to suffer from dropsy, which caused swelling of the abdomen and legs, while provoking a continuous thirst.[35] He moved only by means of his wheelchair.

Philip by this time was firmly decided on the policy of disengagement in the north, both in the Netherlands and in France. In Flanders a plan was drawn up to give the provinces their autonomy under the archduke. Albert would marry the Infanta Isabel, and the two would become joint rulers. Meanwhile the war against Henry IV was pursued with vigour in order to have a firm negotiating position. Spanish forces scored some notable successes on the French frontier, capturing Cambrai, Calais (April 1596) and Amiens. The last of these posed a significant threat to the city of Paris. Henry IV accordingly made a special effort and eventually recovered the city after a six-month siege.

In mid-May the king felt a bit better and decided to take the court to Toledo, where they stayed for three months. During this sojourn the conflict with England took a dramatic turn. In London the war party in the council favoured a proposal by the earl of Essex, favourite of the queen and patron of Antonio Pérez, for a surprise attack on Spain. On 30 June 1596, a powerful fleet commanded by Lord Howard of Effingham, hero of the Armada, appeared before Cadiz. A local captain estimated there were forty warships and over a hundred smaller vessels.[36] The fleet carried 10,000 English soldiers under Essex, and 5,000 Dutch under count Louis of Nassau. A witness described it as 'the most splendid armada ever seen'.[37] Nowhere in Spain was there a comparable fighting force available.

Some forty large vessels and eighteen galleys were anchored in Cadiz harbour. At 1 p.m. on 1 July the enemy sailed in, taking or destroying all the Spanish vessels. A government official on the spot estimated that 200 ships were burnt.[38] Two hours later the men put ashore and occupied the city. The defenders fled, leaving the English and Dutch in unimpeded control of the city for two entire weeks. They left on 16 July, after burning a good part of the town so that, Essex explained, no further armadas could sail from it. Though small, Cadiz was the main Spanish port for trade to America and northern Europe. A symbol of Spain's sea power, its occupation without hindrance for over two weeks was a serious blow to Spanish prestige.

The humiliation was, seen in perspective, the lowest point to which Spain's honour and reputation could have sunk. As recently as May there had been general jubilation at court when news arrived of the death of Francis Drake (from yellow fever) in the Caribbean. The king had then declared that 'this good news will help me to get well rapidly'.[39] Now the impunity with which the English demonstrated they could take and hold Cadiz shattered the euphoria. Moreover, it was galling that instead of behaving like barbarians they had acted like gentlemen, leaving the churches unprofaned (though they burned many of them) and the women inviolate. 'The nobles showed us all the courtesy you could wish,' reported a local priest, 'but the common soldiers, mainly the Flemings, kept shouting "Hang the pope!" . . . Not a single woman was forced, not a single person was killed in cold blood, virtually no outrages happened.'[40] A Spanish officer confirmed that the English had been 'very disciplined, without the slightest incident'.[41] The king might make gestures of defiance (he 'seized a candelabrum and with energy declared that he would pawn even that in order to be avenged on the Queen'),[42] but the nobles and courtiers were unimpressed and angry. In Burgos a cathedral dignitary referred to the events of Cadiz as the 'shame of our nation'.[43] From Gibraltar a correspondent wrote to one of the royal secretaries that 'affairs are in a state that demands we speak clearly and utter the truth and declare it to the king and his ministers'.[44] The humiliation provoked from the writer Cervantes a sonnet of biting contempt for the impotence of the Spanish. For several years now, everything had gone wrong. Central government had virtually ceased to function during the king's illness. On all sides there was a feeling of dissatisfaction.

Some political leaders were convinced that policies must be reversed. Instead of retreating everywhere, as the king was doing, it was time to go on the attack. Peace was absolutely necessary, but it must be a peace with honour. The most outspoken proponent of this line was one of Spain's chief naval commanders the Adelantado of Castile, Don Martín de Padilla, count of Sancta Gadea and commander-in-chief of the Atlantic fleet. In a remarkable memoir to the king, drawn up immediately after the sack of Cadiz, he stated:

> I see, Sir, that [other nations] are trying to destroy us, and I say 'trying' because they have managed to take Cadiz . . . If this loss is followed by what we may rightly fear should we not overcome our stupefaction, what respect will men have for Spaniards?

No power exists that can maintain continuous wars, and even for the greatest monarch it is important to conclude wars rapidly. There will be many who would consider this desirable, saying that the policy we now follow will never end the war and that the expenditure there [Flanders] in men and money is enormous; and that if another cure is not found the patient will soon die . . .

Padilla proposed what may be called the 'final push' solution. The king should collect all available men and ships and make a final attack on England. Peace would then be attained on Spain's terms, and the reign 'will with reason be called a Happy and Golden Century'.[45] It was a last desperate alternative, a chance to exorcise the ghost of 1588. The ailing Philip took it.

Padilla was given the responsibility of putting together an Atlantic task force. Such a force was an absolute necessity in order to defend the peninsula against the impressive naval threat mounted by England and was intended also to be used in a retaliatory strike. In September the king sent Padilla a memorandum drawn up by the English Jesuit Robert Persons. The paper outlined the situation in Ireland and suggested an invasion through Cork.[46] As it turned out, the real objective was to be France. Philip hoped to exploit the advantage the Spaniards had gained by the capture of Calais in April that year. In October 1596 a fleet of eighty-one large ships, with other smaller vessels, set out under Padilla's command from Lisbon and Coruña. His instructions were to give out that he was heading for Ireland, but he was in reality to make for Brittany and seize Brest.[47] A couple of days out to sea, the fleet was caught by a storm in the Channel and scattered. The largest galleon disappeared, with all the wages – 36,000 ducats – it was carrying. Other vessels straggled into northern ports. By the first week of November, Padilla informed the king gloomily from his base at Ferrol, only forty-nine of his eighty-one ships had returned.[48]

Neither the king nor the Adelantado gave up hope. By January 1597 Padilla had an adequate force with which to defend the coasts. In July the government asked him to consider two possible targets for a mission. The first was Brest. This would give support to the Spaniards and Mercoeur in Brittany and would also provide an excellent port for use against England. The second possibility was England, more precisely the port of Milford Haven in Wales. When Padilla eventually put out to sea again, it was at the head of a fleet even larger than that of the previous year: some ninety-eight vessels, including twenty-four galleons, and over 17,000 men.[49] His instructions were to seize the port of Falmouth.[50] The ships sailed from Ferrol on 19 September but bad weather made them put into Coruña. They left Coruña eventually on 18 October, but after four days at sea were once again scattered by a storm. Padilla rounded up what ships he could and brought his fleet back to Ferrol. A week later, only thirty-eight ships and three galleons had made it back.[51] 'It was exactly a year ago, to the day, that the last disaster happened,' he reflected gloomily. Nobody was blamed, for the winds were the work of God. A month later Padilla was busy transporting men to Flanders. He had a word of advice, however, for the king. 'If Your Majesty decides to continue the attempt on England, take care to make preparations in good time and in good quantity, and if not then it is better to make peace.'[52]

In the peninsula, among the common people, there was a palpable economic crisis. The heartland of the peninsula was afflicted in the 1590s by a number of small epidemics.[53] Then from 1596 a virulent outbreak of plague began to affect northern Castile. Stragglers from Padilla's fleet who made it to Santander found the city in the grip of an epidemic. In many parts of Andalusia there was no food because of drought. The late 1590s were particularly difficult years: after the harvest failure of 1594, production picked up in 1595 and 1596, but fell again steeply in 1597. In August 1598 the harvest in Castile and Andalusia failed.[54] In Castile the tax burden led to protests and demands for the suspension of the *millones*. Villagers refused to pay. One treasury official suggested reducing the *alcabala*, because of 'the shortages at present'. He could vouch for the poverty: 'I have seen it as someone who has been serving Your Majesty for four years'.[55] A petition of 1596, claiming to speak on behalf of the peasants, referred to the realms of Castile as 'wasted and poor'.[56] This time it was not mere hyperbole. 'For many years now,' a senior official observed, 'the harvests have been so poor that there have been famines and suffering for want of bread.'[57] Peasants thronged into the capital to seek relief from taxes. The council of Finance presented a memorial to the king on 'the pitiful sight of so many farmers and villagers coming here to ask for help with their debts'.[58] Commenting on the taxes, a canon of Jaén caused a stir in November 1597 when he declared that 'if we in Spain were governed by a republic as in Genoa or Venice, perhaps there would be no need for all of this'.[59] Similar opinions had been expressed over two generations before, during the revolt of the Comuneros.

On all sides, or so it seemed to the hard-pressed Spaniards, their nation was in retreat. In November 1597 the Constable of Castile and governor of Milan, Juan Fernández de Velasco, reported to Philip that 'there is a general desire in Italy to expel the Spaniards. Our salvation can only lie in more troops, money and above all speed.'[60] But there seemed to be a sort of paralysis at the nerve centre, San Lorenzo. Philip's secretary of war wrote: 'everything is in such a state that just to see the way things are going takes away one's will to work and serve'.[61] Not the least of Spain's problems was the insurmountable debt, a direct result of the cost of war. Philip had suspended payments to creditors in November 1596, but he was obliged to borrow yet more. The result was a further arrangement to clear the debt in November 1597.

In Portugal, constantly restless under Spanish control, resistance centred on hopes of the return of king Sebastian.[62] The king's body had never been reliably identified on the battlefield of Alcazar-el-Kebir. Some remains were brought to Portugal and in December 1582 were solemnly buried, in the presence of Philip II, in the Jeronimite church of the Belem in Lisbon. Among the Portuguese, popular legend refused to believe in the remains and maintained that the king had merely disappeared. He would return after seven years of penitence. From about 1585, accordingly, pseudo-Sebastians began to appear. The myth of the king's return kept alive the hopes of partisans of Antonio of Crato. Other opponents of Spain, in both England and France, lent their support to the story. The most celebrated of the Sebastians was in 1594. A Portuguese priest, Miguel dos Santos, gained the confidence of Anna, illegitimate daughter of Don Juan of Austria, who was living in a convent at Madrigal, south of Valladolid. She was twenty-six at the time. Santos introduced into her household a young pastrycook, whom he later explained was in reality the disappeared king. The two, declared Santos, were destined to marry and bring about the liberation of Jerusalem. The pastrycook, named Gabriel de Espinosa, was an obvious impostor, but he received the powerful support of Antonio of Crato, Antonio Pérez and Henry IV of France. The government treated the case very seriously. In 1595 both Espinosa and Santos were hanged, and Anna confined in a convent. The Portuguese did not give up their desire to find their lost king. In 1598, once again, a Sebastian appeared, this time in Venice.

*

In these last months, Philip turned once again to an issue that had surfaced time and again during his reign: the role of the Jews. The king had, since the 1560s, looked askance at Spaniards of Jewish origin (*conversos*) and had turned his back on the pleas of exiled Jews to be allowed back to Spain. Despite this, he had tolerated Jews in his realms outside the peninsula, notably in Africa and Italy. Then in December 1590, responding to local pressure, he ordered the expulsion of the tiny Jewish community in Milan, an order he was later to suspend. The expulsion was not carried out till the spring of 1597.[63] This apparent move against the Jews was balanced at home by a curious about-turn on a matter affecting *conversos*.

There had always been doubt in official circles about the justice of the blood-purity statutes that existed in some Castilian institutions. Philip himself had intervened in cases where *conversos* were discriminated against on grounds of their Jewish blood. In 1589, for example, he appointed a *converso* to a post in the cathedral of Sigüenza, and refused to back down when the blood-purity rules were quoted at him.[64] The statutes, he decided, must be looked at. He had in the past shown scepticism about their role. When in 1574 a group of nobles attempted to set up a new order of knighthood in which the principle of selection would be purity of blood, he vetoed the plan.[65] Around 1590 he gave his support – 'he has my approval'[66] – to a well-known preacher, Father Salucio, who was preparing a study critical of the statutes. But the king seems to have done nothing on the whole subject of blood purity until about 1597. He then set up a special committee, with the Inquisitor-General among its members, to find ways of reforming the statutes.[67] It was in 1597 also that he did a clear volte-face on the matter. In 1570 he had firmly refused to nominate a *converso* priest to a Church post in Toledo but in 1597 he appointed the same man to be bishop of Córdoba.[68] The evolution of his views on the issue, greeted with satisfaction by many, accorded with the general demand for change and renovation at the end of the reign.

*

Throughout the early months of 1597 illness kept the king immobile in Madrid. He ventured out only in May, when he went briefly to El Pardo. He then moved on to spend the summer at San Lorenzo. In spite of his infirmities, he went out in his coach hunting. After another severe attack of gout, on 24 August he drew up a final codicil to his testament of 1594.[69] In seventeen clauses, it added details to his previous dispositions. He left his keys to Don Cristóbal, with orders that 'all the papers of my late confessor fray Diego de Chaves, written by him to me or by me to him, be burned'. Chaves, keeper of the king's conscience, had died on 21 June 1592 at the splendid age of ninety. At his death the king had ordered his papers to be collected up,[70] but nothing was decided about them. Now the inevitable decision was made. A priceless source for the king's motives and actions was thereby destroyed. From his own personal papers, said the king, 'documents of importance should be taken to Simancas, and other papers of old matters be burned'. He now also formally authorised his son to sign all state documents in his name. His own signature had sometimes continued to appear on papers, but done with a rubber stamp.

The worst personal blow was yet to come. Throughout the 1590s one of the greatest comforts to the bedridden king had been the regular letters from Catalina, to whom he also continued writing.[71] His principal theme was his grandchildren, whom the duchess went on producing. 'I am delighted with what you tell me about my grandchildren,' runs a typical passage, 'and with the little booklet that the duke sent me with portraits of you and the family, although I would be even happier to see both you and them, since they would not fail to give me great pleasure with their mischief.'[72] The intervention in France had drawn Savoy into the military operations, which gave father and daughter an excuse to talk about matters other than family. In her perfectly formed handwriting, the duchess wrote brief letters at the rate of about three a fortnight. When necessary, cipher was used. Philip in his turn gave her advice on political matters, but inevitably did not have so much time to write. 'I admit that I have not written for days, since I have to reply to your letters of 16 May, 23 June, and 11 and 16 July' (August 1590). 'I owe you a reply to seven letters of 12, 14, 28 and 30 July, and 3, 9 and 12 August; you must believe that they always give me the greatest pleasure' (September 1591).[73] His letters also got shorter and shorter. The chief obstacle was his gout. He could neither sign state papers nor write in his own hand to his daughter. He was sometimes too ill even to dictate. In May 1591 he managed to dictate ten lines of a letter, and then added, in his own shaky hand, 'I have left this because I couldn't manage any more'.[74] 'The gout is to blame,' he excused himself in 1593, 'that I haven't been able to reply sooner.'[75]

From 1592 onwards, Catalina's letters were preoccupied with the Spanish-Savoyard invasion of Provence.[76] While the duke was away at the front, she took over the effective government of the duchy, presiding over tribunals and directing ministers. But family matters were still the principal theme of her correspondence, and at regular intervals she gave news of her latest childbirth.[77] Philip in January 1596 routinely congratulated Carlo Emanuele on 'the latest granddaughter'.[78] Catalina's continuous and virtually annual pregnancies contributed to her poor health and eventually to her death. Her last surviving letters to her father are four missives, all written on the same day, 12 October 1597.[79] She died on 7 December giving birth to a baby girl.

The premature death of this intelligent, lively and beautiful woman at the age of thirty devastated husband and father alike. The duke, grief-stricken by the loss of 'all that I had', fell ill and withdrew for three months from his affairs.[80] When Philip received the news in San Lorenzo he immediately called Isabel and the prince to his bedside. The family remained closeted with their grief for three hours.[81] The king was totally shattered. 'Never before or again,' a courtier observed, 'would they see him express such grief as now, not in the death of his sons nor in that of his wife nor at the loss of the Armada . . . and so this deprived him of many days of life and of health.'[82] A special memorial service, presided over by the prince, was held in the chapel. Isabel and the king watched from the chancel. The king ordered theatres to be closed in mourning. The closure had far-reaching consequences, since it unleashed a flood of impassioned debate about the morality of the theatre. The result was an unprecedented ban, issued in May 1598, on all public theatre and comedies.

The reign was drawing to its close in disaster and defeat. Peace talks between France and Spain were held in secret during 1597 and continued early the next year, openly, at Vervins. The archduke Albert negotiated on behalf of both Spain and the Netherlands. On 2 May 1598 the peace of

Vervins with France was signed. One of Henry IV's ministers described it as 'the most advantageous peace France had secured for five hundred years'.[83] At the court of Spain it was recognised for what it was: a humiliation rather than a peace. Spain gave up all its gains, including Calais. 'Here there are no signs of rejoicing,' the Venetian envoy Soranzo reported, 'nor has the peace been even published, nor will it be. The ministers declare that there is no need to publish, as war was never declared. When I asked the count of Fuentes if the peace would be published he replied, "It will not be published at all, for we are ashamed of it".'[84] It was in fact published, to the ambassador's surprise, in the first week of September.

Four days after the peace of Vervins, on 6 May 1598, Philip signed the act handing over the Netherlands to Albert and Isabel, who were to be married as joint sovereigns. The act did not in fact concede independence. If there was no issue of the marriage (as indeed there was not) the Netherlands were to revert to Spanish control on the death of the sovereigns. A proxy marriage was to be celebrated, but it was put off until after the death of Philip.

*

The king was now in the final stages of his illness. During 1597 the gout broke out in four sores on the middle finger of his right hand, and three on the index finger. There was a similar sore on the small toe of his right foot.[85] In September 'the gout attacked his neck and caused him some difficulty in eating. He had a high fever accompanied by great weakness, loss of appetite and loss of sleep.'[86] At the end of June 1598 he insisted, against the doctors' advice, on being taken from Madrid to San Lorenzo. He was transported in a specially adapted form of the chair designed by Jean Lhermite.[87] When extended, it became a litter. It took the attendants four days, with overnight stops, to carry the king to his destination. Lhermite, who accompanied the group, recorded that the heat was unbearable. 'He arrived almost prostrate in his chair,' a friar of the Escorial reported. 'When asked how he felt he replied, with a show of cheerfulness, "Very well".'[88] He was in better condition than expected. Moura reported some days later that 'His Majesty arrived quite well after the journey, and he was also well here to the extent that we had hopes of improvement. Afterwards he suffered relapses.'[89] The effort of the journey brought on a severe fever, which became particularly serious after mid-July. At the end of June an abscess formed on his right thigh just above his knee, and further small abscesses continued to develop on his body. The ulcerous sores on the fingers of his right hand, and on his foot, continued to get worse. At the same time the swelling of his stomach and thighs contrasted with the rest of his body, which appeared to be reduced to skin and bones.[90]

The agony suffered by the king was so great that the doctors dared not move him. He had to lie on his back in bed. For the fifty-three final days[91] of his illness he could not move from this position. The attendants could not change the bedsheets or the king's clothes. When the doctors opened his sores to control the pus in them, the smell that came out was overpowering. The king had to evacuate in his own bed, soiling his sheets, which could not be changed. The sick-room consequently had a 'foul smell'. He had always been meticulous about cleanliness, reported his confessor, and his filthy bed was not the least of his terrible sufferings. The fever never left him. He suffered in addition an insatiable thirst, caused by the dropsy and the fever. The pain was unceasing.

Philip's fortitude was incredible. He put up, when he could, with the surgeon's knife, but could not stifle his groans of agony when they touched him. He drew his strength in these days entirely from religion. The bedroom was filled, wall to wall, with holy images and crucifixes.[92] On 8 August he instructed his confessor fray Diego de Yepes and the prior of the Escorial to bring him a number of relics and sacred stoles. They presented themselves before the king, one with an arm of St Vincent Ferrer, the other with a knee of St Sebastian. The appropriate prayers were said, the king's affected leg was touched with the relics; and the clergy retired.[93] Philip also made generous use of holy water, which was sprinkled regularly on his body. His last communion was on 8 September. Thereafter his doctors prohibited it, for fear that he would not be able to swallow the host. Since he could not hold a book, he also received the ministrations of readers to help him pass the time. In his last years the bookshelf in his small room was limited to about forty items, largely spiritual.[94] The works of Teresa of Avila, of fray Luis de Granada and of the Fleming Louis Blois featured among them. The texts he chose to be read to him included passages from the Bible, and fray Luis de Granada. Among the helpers was the Infanta Isabel, who came frequently to read to him.

On 12 August Soranzo, the Venetian ambassador, wrote that 'the fever is continuous and with violent paroxysms. His strength is failing. The doctors declare that they have little more hope.' Two weeks later the king called in the prince and the Infanta. He gave the prince two sealed packets with instructions to open them after his death. Soranzo was among those deeply impressed by Philip's courage. 'His Majesty has displayed incredible patience in his acute sufferings caused by the gout and the numerous sores all over him. His courage has never deserted him. He has made himself most familiar not only with the thought of death but with the details of all that should be done after he is gone.'[95]

The king told his clergy to give him extreme unction 'while he is still conscious and can make the responses'. On 1 September the sacrament was administered. The king 'asked for the cross which his father the emperor held when he was dying. He sent for the prince and told him to remain during the ceremony and contemplate this example of worldly misery.'[96] The solemn ceremony, a final leave-taking, was also witnessed by the archbishop of Toledo, fray García de Loaysa, who officiated, and twenty-two other clergy, attendants and councillors of state. After the proceedings, Philip asked everybody to withdraw except his son. He then explained to the prince that he had wanted him to see 'the end to which everything comes'.[97] He also enjoined him to be a protector of religion and justice. On Friday, 11 September, the prince and Infanta went to take their leave of the dying king. Philip expressed to Isabel his regret that he would not live to see her married, but asked her to govern the Netherlands well with the help of Albert.

Meticulous to the last, the king in his last weeks had planned everything down to the details of his own coffin. He arranged to die holding in one hand a candle dedicated to Our Lady of Montserrat, and in the other the small crucifix which his father had held in Yuste. He ordered a coffin to be made like that of his father, and stipulated that he be wrapped well in cloths and placed first in a case of lead, well sealed so that no odour could escape.

The night before he died his councillors and clergy were in attendance. At midnight they attempted to position him for the end, but he murmured 'It's not yet time.' At about three in the morning he said 'Give it to me, it's time.' His attendants supported the Montserrat candle in one of the king's hands, and the crucifix in the other. The archbishop of Toledo read from the Passion according to St John, and the prior of the Escorial, on bended knee, recited the prayers for the dying. Philip's last words were that he died in the Catholic faith and obedience to the Church of Rome. As the clergy prayed, he slowly slipped away. He died as the first rays of the sun came over the horizon, at five in the morning on Sunday, 13 September.[98] In the chapel below, the choristers were singing the first mass of the day.

'The king is dead,' Soranzo wrote home. 'His Majesty expired at the Escorial this morning at daybreak . . . Although change is usually popular, yet nobles and people, rich and poor, universally show great grief.' 'Those of us who were present there,' a witness wrote later, 'greeted his passing with floods of tears. And for many the weeping will not end until life itself ends.'[99]

'He was a prince,' the ambassador commented, 'who fought with gold rather than with steel. Profoundly religious, he loved peace and quiet . . . He held his desires in absolute control and showed an immutable and unalterable temper . . . He hated vanity . . .'[100] The state funeral was held the following day, Monday morning. The coffin, carried on the shoulders of the grandees and nobles of the late king's household, was borne in through the main entrance of the church of San Lorenzo. Mass was celebrated, followed by the funeral rites. The new king then accompanied the coffin to the vault of kings. Here Philip II was laid to rest in the place he had chosen, at the side of his wife Anna.

12

Epilogue

No sooner was the king dead than the criticism and quarrelling began. 'There was a great division among those who served him, and some began to show their true colours.'[1] Philip had governed for over half a century. Much had changed in that period, and many Spaniards now wished to breathe a different air. There was public mourning, much of it undeniably genuine. Sermons delivered in pulpits throughout the country were full of praise.[2] One of the late king's longest-serving ministers, then in Lisbon, could hardly believe the news, even though everybody had been expecting it for months. 'The news arrived here on the nineteenth . . . It left me almost stunned, considering that I had served him abroad and at his side for fifty years.'[3] But the praise was also accompanied by a sense of relief. A fortnight after the king's death Soranzo wrote: 'I myself have heard the Adelantado of Castile declare that they would see what the Spanish were worth, now that they have a free hand and are no longer subject to a single brain that thought it knew all that could be known, and treated everyone else as a blockhead'.[4] The tension in the capital, where ministers waited for the inevitable changes in government, was palpable. Out in the provinces the impact was much less. 'King Philip the Second has died in Madrid,' a village priest in Catalonia noted in his journal. The only comment he saw fit to add was that 'in the country there is good health and no talk of wars'.[5]

The king's long illness, economic problems, rising taxes, the failure of the grain harvest, lent substance to the feeling of popular dissatisfaction. A reign of triumphs, but also of disappointments, was ending in disillusion, the keynote of the following century. Madrid had its own particular problems. The plague epidemic which had affected the northern provinces reached the capital in the autumn of 1598. In 1599 the death rate

317

soared. In this climate of misery, grievances were written down and circulated. In October 1598 a tract on the 'confused government' of the late king went round Madrid in different versions.[6] It claimed to show 'how blind and mistaken the late government was'. The author was arrested and imprisoned. Criticisms were also disseminated by the writer Baltasar Alamos de Barrientos. In a discourse of October 1598 he painted for the new king a dramatic (and exaggerated) picture of a Castile in ruins. 'The cities and big towns are empty of people, the smaller villages completely depopulated, the fields with scarcely anyone to till them . . . There is no spot untouched by this misery, which comes principally from the burden of taxes and from spending all the proceeds on foreign wars.'[7] All the burden of the monarchy had fallen on Castile alone. 'In other monarchies the limbs contribute to maintain the head, and in ours it is the head that labours so that the limbs are fed and sustained.'[8]

Alamos was a lawyer and friend of Antonio Pérez. He was also a proponent of the vogue, then spreading through educated circles in Europe, for the ideas of Tacitus. Tacitean precepts implied for these men an injection of reason into politics.[9] By extension, it implied a rejection of the aspects – war, fanaticism, tyranny – that seemed to have gained the upper hand in the late sixteenth century, not only in Spain but throughout the continent. There were still many diehards, particularly in the Church. But, like Alamos, others felt it was time for a new beginning. In the last years of Philip many writers had been developing more liberal ideas. Best known of them was the Jesuit historian Juan de Mariana, who expressed firmly his opposition to tyranny and racism. The strain, repeated everywhere in Madrid, was now in favour of economy, reform, and peace.

It had been a time of war; now the aspiration was only for peace. Spain had been humbled enough. 'The name Spaniard,' the writer Mateo Alemán noted in his 1599 novel *Guzmán de Alfarache*, 'is now of almost no consequence.' We Spaniards, a commentator of those years complained, 'are detested and hated, and all because of the wars'.[10] Peace with France had been the first step. Then in August 1604 the treaty of London brought about peace with the England of James I. The Netherlands was the last big stumbling-block, but it was not insuperable. A writer claimed that Philip II 'sank over 300,000 millons in the bogs of Flanders, the schemes in France and the disasters in England'. 'If 200,000 Spaniards, not to mention other nations, have been deliberately led like sheep to the slaughter to be killed in the bogs of Flanders', then the late king was 'worse than Nero'.[11] The urge for peace was strong enough to influence Spanish negotiators eventually in April 1609 to accept a twelve-year truce with the Dutch.

It had been a time for defence of the Catholic faith. Now the trend was towards recognising the reality that faith could not be imposed. Members of the Cortes had already argued that the Netherlanders could not be forced into their religion. Spaniards who knew of events in France were impressed that king Henry IV should receive implicit papal support for his toleration of Huguenots. This, many felt, was a possible way forward. 'Your Majesty is not compelled,' the Constable of Castile said to Philip III in the council of State, 'to force England and France to be Catholic if they do not want to.' The problems of English Catholics, he said, 'came from the protection of His late Majesty'.[12] The new attitude was reflected in the truce agreed with the Dutch, which deliberately left the question of religion to one side.

It had been a time of absolute power in the hands of one man. Now the trend was to constitutionalism. All political power, some now argued, comes from God but *through* the people. It is the people who concede power to the king. The king has no absolute power. 'The concept of absolute power,' argued the theorist Pedro Agustín Morla in 1599, only one year after Philip II's death, 'is, more exactly, tyranny, and was invented by the flatterers of kings.'[13] The king's power, others argued, was limited by tradition and by fundamental laws. 'The king,' stated Juan de Mariana in a famous treatise *The King* published in 1599, 'must be subject to the laws drawn up by the state, whose authority is greater than that of the king.' The ideas were not new. They were current in the later years of Philip II, who did not frown on them. But they gained force within the context of a reaction against the previous reign. In the Castilian Cortes, too, there were moves, foreshadowed in the final Cortes of Philip II, towards greater autonomy for the representatives of the realm. The democratic notion of a pact between monarch and kingdom was invoked by the deputy Melchor Dávila in 1599.

Some ministers, like some taxpayers, had long since lost faith in their own government. Spaniards were, as always in times of crisis, merciless in their self-criticism. Astonishingly, ministers who had little but reproach for the late king were second to none in their admiration for Elizabeth of England. In 1587 it was observed that at court 'everyone is amazed to see how cleverly that woman manages in everything'. 'The Spanish say that the king thinks and plans while the queen of England acts.'[14] In Armada year, 1588, the pope himself had not disguised his admiration for Elizabeth. 'She certainly is a great queen,' he said, 'and were she only a Catholic she would be most dear to us. Just look how well she governs. She is only a woman, mistress of half an island, yet she makes herself feared by all.'[15] The year after the Armada a minister of Philip II, Juan de Silva, count of Portalegre, commented that 'only England preserves its spirit and increases its reputation. I think that other princes should exchange advisers with the queen, because she alone assaults with impunity the most powerful crowns of the world.'[16] The late king's ministers joined in the paean of praise. Silva wrote to his friend Cristóbal de Moura: 'these last twenty-two years that the queen of England has spent in the service of the world, will be the most outstanding known of in history'.[17] Moura wrote back, heartily endorsing this opinion of the queen. In his residence Silva displayed prominently two highly prized portraits, of the queen and of Drake. These two persons, he told Moura, 'have done more for our knowledge of the world than fray Luis de Granada'.[18]

Since Philip had never run a tyrannical regime, the opinions were a sad verdict on the extent to which he had failed to project his image. All his great protagonists – Elizabeth of England, William of Orange, Henry of Navarre – became legendary heroes in the memory of their own people. They did so in part because of their opposition to him. Philip alone failed to leave his mark. Roughly from the 1580s, when Spain and Portugal were united under him, he had done everything to relax royal control. Royalist public ritual and monarchic imagery all but disappeared. The title of 'Majesty' was dropped from official correspondence. The tasks of government were shared out. At the centre *ad hoc* committees deliberated on everything; in the provinces the nobles were confirmed in their control of authority.[19] Great care was taken to respect the claims of the regions within Spain, a policy interrupted by the events in Aragon.

The late king had always hated war and yearned for peace, but the criticism from his own people was pitiless. They blamed him for the fruitless wars against the Dutch, the English and the French. Little credit was given him for the attempts to put Spain's naval power in the Atlantic on a firm footing, or for his tireless defence of the peninsula.

The day-to-day conduct of affairs changed almost immediately after the king's death. The late king had virtually ceased to use the government councils, preferring to work instead through the juntas. After 1598 Philip III and his chief minister the duke of Lerma restored the old councils to their traditional role.[20] With the councils the aristocracy returned to power. Several other about-turns were made. Perhaps the most tragic of them was the renewal of the decision to expel the Morisco population of Spain. The new regime, though staffed with many of the old king's ministers, notably Juan de Idiáquez, clearly had a new outlook on politics.

Looking back on those years, it seems pointless to assess the king's role in terms of success or failure. Philip was never at any time in adequate control of events, or of his kingdoms, or even of his own destiny. It follows that he cannot be held responsible for more than a small part of what eventually transpired during his reign. To many spectators, he was the most powerful monarch in the world. In the privacy of his office, he knew very well that this was an illusion. 'I don't think that human strength is capable of everything,' he mused in mid-reign; 'least of all mine, which is very feeble.'[21] For all his power, he had been unable to stop his realms being sucked into a whirl of war, debt and decay. The spectre faced him already in 1556. It was still there, larger than ever, in 1598.

He was 'imprisoned within a destiny in which he himself had little hand'.[22] He could do little more than play the dice available to him.

Condemned to spend his days sorting out the workings of his vast web of a monarchy, he was among the few who had access to a broad perspective on its problems. But he was unable to turn that perspective into a vision that might inspire his people. Cosmopolitan and European in his aspirations, he became tied down to the peninsula by the necessities of politics. Eminently efficient and practical, he struggled always with the immediate and the possible. At a time when his disappointed ministers sought inspiration, he offered them only the burden of sacrifice. His reassurance to himself was that he had played his part to the fullest. His conscience was clear. If ruin lay ahead, 'I expect that I shall not see it, because I shall have gone to carry out my duty'.

List of Abbreviations

AE:CP, MD	Archives des Affaires Etrangères, Paris, Correspondance Politique, Mémoires et Documents
AGS	Archivo General de Simancas, Valladolid
AGS:CC	AGS, section Cámara de Castilla
AGS:CJH	AGS, section Consejo y Juntas de Hacienda
AGS:CR	AGS, section Casas Reales
AGS:E	AGS, section Estado
AGS:E/K	AGS, section Estado, serie K
AGS:G	AGS, section Guerra y Marina
AGS: PR	AGS, section Patronato Real
AGS: SP	AGS, Secretarías Provinciales
AHN Inq	Archivo Histórico Nacional, Madrid, section Inquisición
AP	Arxiu del Palau, Sant Cugat
ARSI Epist.Hisp	Archivum Romanum Societatis Iesu, Rome, Epistolae Hispaniae
BCR	Biblioteca Casanatense, Rome
BL	British Library, London, manuscript room
BL Add.	BL Additional MS
BL Cott.	BL Cotton MS
BL Eg.	BL Egerton MS
BNM	Biblioteca Nacional, Madrid, manuscript room
BNP	Bibliothèque Nationale, Paris, manuscript room
BP	Biblioteca del Palacio Real, Madrid
BZ	Biblioteca Zabálburu, Madrid, manuscript collection
CODOIN	Colección de Documentos Inéditos para la Historia de España
CSP	Calendar of State Papers
CSPV	Calendar of State Papers, Venice
Favre	Collection Favre, Bibliothèque Publique et Universitaire, Geneva
HHSA	Haus-, Hof-, und Staatsarchiv, Vienna

IVDJ	Instituto de Valencia de Don Juan, Madrid
leg.	*legajo* (file)
MZA: RAD	Moravský Zemský Archiv, Brno: Rodinný Archiv Ditrichšteinu

Notes

1. *The Formative Years 1527–1544*

1. Philip to Charles V, Valladolid, 17 Sept. 1544, AGS:E leg.64[1].
2. Cited Joseph Pérez, *La Révolution des 'Comunidades' de Castille (1520–1521)* Bordeaux 1970, p.592.
3. The imperial ambassador, cited March, I, 20.
4. J. M. March, 'El aya del Rey D[a] Leonor Mascareñhas', *Boletín de la Sociedad española de Excursiones*, 46, 1942.
5. Letters of Isabel to Lope Hurtado de Mendoza, 14 June and 7 July 1532, BZ 114 ff.108, 111.
6. March, I, 46–7.
7. The humanist was Dr Busto, 'maestro de los pajes de su Majestad': ibid., 68–9.
8. The Siliceo letters that follow are cited from March, I, 68–78, unless otherwise stated.
9. J. Subirá, *Historia de la música española*, Barcelona 1953, pp.210–11.
10. 1540 letters from Siliceo to Charles V, in AGS:E leg.50 ff.47–8.
11. March, II, 31.
12. Calvet always wrote his name thus. For some inexplicable reason, Spanish writers call him Calvete.
13. Quotations from the Zúñiga letters that follow are from March, I, 226–70, unless otherwise stated.
14. Ibid., 221, 249.
15. González Palencia, I, 108.
16. Antolín, p.341.
17. AGS:CR leg.78.
18. March, II, 334.
19. Estefania de Requesens, ibid., 327.
20. In 1543–4, March, I, 259, 261.
21. March, II, 345.
22. Sandoval, p.76.
23. The statement by Parker, *Philip II*, p.6, that 'the young prince led the funeral cortege from Toledo to Granada', is incorrect. The statement is repeated by several other historians. Philip remained in Toledo, where he had to stand in for Charles at official functions. For his movements, see Vandenesse, II, 150–1.
24. March, II, 100.
25. Sandoval, p.76.
26. The anonymous 'Expédition de Charles-Quint à Alger', in Gachard, *Voyages*, III, 403.
27. AGS:CR leg.35 f.24: 'Casa Real del Principe 1543'.
28. Statement of costs for 1543, AGS:E leg.59.
29. AGS:CR leg.76, 'Libro de la des-

pensa del principe', Valladolid 1544. There is no justification for the claim, found in most books, that Philip did not touch fruit or vegetables.

30. AGS:CJH leg.18 f.233, 'Sumario de la despensa hordinaria de Su Alteza del mes de Junio 1549'.

31. AGS:CR leg.78, 'Sumario de la despensa' for 1551.

32. Several historians (Prescott and Bratli, among others) speak of Philip going to Perpignan and participating in the siege. This incident is mythical. Vandenesse, II, 211 lends no support to it. Nor does the near-contemporary life of Alba: Ossorio, pp.53–6.

33. Zúñiga to Constable of Castile, 15 Sept. 1542, 'Ayer juraron los catalanes al principe': CODOIN, XLIII, 268. The Catalans swore to the prince on 14 Sept., the Valencians on the twenty-third, and the Aragonese, last, on 6 Oct.

34. Vandenesse, II, 244.

35. I use the versions printed in March, II, 7–34.

36. Ibid., 71–2.

37. Zúñiga to Charles, 8 June 1543, AGS:E leg.60 f.201.

38. Zúñiga to Charles, 11 May 1543, ibid. f.56.

39. Ibid. leg.59.

40. Siliceo to Charles, 6 Aug. 1543, ibid. leg.60 f.183.

41. Instructions to council of Finance, 1 May 1543, ibid. leg.60.

42. Council of Indies to Charles, 19 Aug. 1543, ibid. leg.59.

43. Mondéjar to Charles, 25 Aug. 1543, ibid. leg.60 f.191.

44. Note by king, 28 Dec. 1574, BZ 144 f.39.

45. Valdés to Charles, 9 Oct. 1543; Cobos to Charles, 7 Aug. 1543; in AGS:E leg.60 ff.78, 174.

46. Alba and Cobos to Charles, 7 Aug. 1543; and Tavera to same, 17 Sept. 1543: ibid. ff.162, 147.

47. Keniston, pp.257–61. The source is cited as BNM MS. 10,300, which I have not consulted. He dates it to before Sept. 1545.

48. A sample: the correspondence for 1544 in AGS:E leg.66.

49. Cobos to Charles, 7 Aug. 1543, ibid. leg.60 ff.174–82.

50. Philip to Charles, 7 Aug. 1543, ibid. f.24.

51. Philip to Charles, 4 Feb. 1544, ibid. leg.64^2 f.402.

52. Philip to Charles, 17 Sept. 1544, ibid. leg.64^1 f.57.

53. Cobos to Charles, 17 Sept. 1544, ibid. f.66.

54. Keniston, p.171.

55. Conde de Cifuentes, AGS:E leg.64^2 f.253.

56. March, I, 162.

57. Chabod, '¿Milán', prints the texts, which I have also consulted in Simancas. An English version is in CSP, VII, 478–96.

58. Prince to Borja, 4 Nov. 1544, AGS:E leg.291 f.6.

59. Philip to Charles, 13 Dec. 1544, ibid. leg.64^1 f.80.

60. Philip to Charles, 27 Dec. 1544, ibid. f.62.

61. Philip to Charles, 25 Mar. 1545, ibid. leg.69 ff.20–6. Printed in part in March, I, 181–4.

62. Philip to Charles, 14 May 1545, AGS:E leg.69 ff.102–8.

63. Parker, *Philip II*, p.22, unaware of the early activity, dates to much later (1551) the moment when Philip 'began to take a direct share in government'. Other scholars choose even later.

64. March, II, 74–5.

65. Ibid., I, 322–4.

66. Pérez to Juan Vázquez, 5 May 1544, González Palencia, II, 377.

67. AGS:E leg.64^1 f.28; Cobos to Charles, 17 Sept. 1544, ibid. f.66.

68. Ibid. f.175.

2.　The Renaissance Prince
1545–1551

1. Philip to Charles, 25 Mar. 1545, AGS:E leg.69 ff.20–6.

2. St Teresa, *Life*, trans. J. M. Cohen, Harmondsworth 1957, chap.37, p.282.
3. Alvarez, p.134.
4. Ibid.
5. Ambrosio de Morales, *Las antigüedades de las ciudades de España*, Alcalá 1575, p.49.
6. Linda Martz, *Poverty and Welfare in Habsburg Spain*, Cambridge 1983, pp. 21–3. The poor law was issued in 1540, but not printed until 1544.
7. The Soto and Robles books both appeared in 1545, with dedications to the prince. For the controversy between these two see ibid., pp.23–30.
8. BZ 158, f.33.
9. In Catalonia his works were on sale until late in the century: Kamen, *Phoenix*, pp.416–18.
10. For postal mail, see Braudel, I, 355–74. Some useful details also in C. Alcázar, 'La política postal española en el siglo XVI', in the volume *Carlos V*, pp.219–32.
11. AGS:E leg.64^1 f.80. For a full survey of the debate, see Chabod, '¿Milán'.
12. The bestowing of Milan on Philip was repeated by Charles in 1546.
13. He had once before, in 1540, offered Milan to France: see Merriman, III, 268.
14. The count of Cifuentes in Sept. 1545, the count of Osorno in Jan. 1546, and cardinal García de Loaysa of Seville in Apr. 1546.
15. Mondéjar was viceroy of Navarre. He was made president of the council of the Indies and member of the councils of War and State.
16. Keniston, p.275.
17. AGS:E leg.73 ff.224, 230.
18. Keniston, p.291.
19. Philip to Charles, 20 Dec. 1546, AGS:E leg.73 ff.158–9. Note the quite mistaken transcription given of this passage in Keniston, p.292.
20. Philip to Charles, 17 Sept. 1544, AGS:E leg.64^1 f.72 is devoted entirely to Aragonese affairs.

21. Las Casas to prince, 20 Apr. 1544, CODOIN, LXX, 519.
22. 'La peticion q dio Orellana y los pareceres del Consejo', AGS:E leg.61 f.19.
23. Calvete de Estrella, *Rebelión*, I, 98.
24. The beautifully measured instructions reveal Charles at his best as a statesman. They are printed in CODOIN, XXVI, 274–84, but erroneously attributed to Philip.
25. Philip to Gasca, 4 May and 14 May 1547, CODOIN, XLIX, 86, 91. Hernando, the other remaining Pizarro brother, had come to Castile with some gold to influence the emperor. Charles ordered his arrest, and Philip wrote: 'I ordered him taken into custody and that justice be done without prejudice in his case': AGS:E leg.75 f.72.
26. Philip to council of Indies, 17 Oct. 1554, AGS:E leg. 808 f.45.
27. Report by Francisco de Luzón, AGS:CR leg.247 f.30.
28. Incident reported by an attendant of the emperor to Jean Lhermite: Lhermite, I, 101.
29. Checa, p.34.
30. Philip to Charles, 25 Jan. 1547, AGS:E leg. 75 f.302.
31. Philip to Charles, 1 June 1547, ibid. leg.75, 72–9.
32. These disagreements are unduly exaggerated in the study by Rodríguez Salgado.
33. BZ 114 f.55–6.
34. Alvarez, p.23.
35. 'With well-deserved enthusiasm,' says the chronicler: CODOIN, LXX, 161.
36. Ibid., 212, 543. Philip to Las Casas: 'As you will see, I have ordered it to be named True Peace.'
37. The candidate was the famous religious leader Juan de Avila: cited in Kamen, 'Limpieza', in *Crisis and Change*, p.330.
38. Unless otherwise noted, the material that follows is from AGS:CC leg.291 f.1.
39. Philip to Lope Hurtado de Men-

doza, ambassador in Lisbon, 11 Dec. 1547, BZ 114 f.57.

40. Cabrera, I, 47.

41. Braudel, II, 904.

42. The various texts of the *Instructions* of 1548 are considered in Berthold Beinert, 'El testamento político de Carlos V de 1548', in *Carlos V*, pp.401–38. No original of the *Instructions* exists; Beinert opts for the version in Sandoval as the most genuine.

43. A preliminary draft of Alba's instructions is in 'Ce quil semble se devra observer pour lencommencement du service de son Alteze a la mode de Bourgoigne', Favre, 59 ff.341–60.

44. Christina Hofmann, *Das Spanische Hofzeremoniell von 1500–1700*, Frankfurt 1985.

45. *Cortes antiguos*, V, 355.

46. Sandoval, p.337.

47. F. Nicolini, 'Sul viaggio di Filippo d'Absburgo in Italia (1547–48)', *Bunco di Napoli. Bollettino dell'Archivio Storico*, 9–12, pt 1 (Naples 1955–6), p.209.

48. Sandoval, p.340.

49. Prince to emperor, Valladolid, 5 Sept. 1548, AGS:E leg.76 f.52.

50. Alvarez, p.17.

51. Calvete de Estrella, 1552, p.5. There were also a number of other vessels for transporting servants and horses.

52. Letter of 30 Nov. to his father, printed in CSP, England and Spain, IX, 318 (from Simancas); and of 1 Dec. 1548 to Lope Hurtado de Mendoza, in BZ 114 f.63. The letters were written by Gonzalo Pérez.

53. Report by the Mantuan envoy Strozzi, Dec. 1547, cited in Nicolini, 'Sul viaggio', p.214.

54. Alvarez, p.43.

55. Brown, p.30.

56. Alvarez, p.56.

57. Calvete de Estrella, 1552, ff.30–1, 49.

58. Venetian envoy Soranzo, in 1565: Alberi, ser.1, vol.v, p.112.

59. Calvete de Estrella, 1552, f.52.

60. Ibid., f.54.

61. Alvarez, p.65.

62. Ibid., p.70.

63. Calvete de Estrella, 1552, f.56.

64. Alvarez, p.71.

65. Philip to Gonzaga, Heidelberg, 8 Mar. 1549, AGS:E leg.645 f.30.

66. Alvarez, p.77.

67. Cited Gachard, *Retraite et mort*, *Introduction*, 18.

68. Alvarez, p.79.

69. Gachard, *Retraite et mort*, II, lxxii.

70. Cited Forneron, I, 11, from Venetian ambassador.

71. AGS:E leg.645 f.1.

72. Motley, p.71.

73. Philip to Prince Palatine, Brussels, Aug. 1549, AGS:E leg.645 f.36.

74. On Binche, Calvete de Estrella, 1552, ff.182–205.

75. Alvarez, p.112.

76. Calvete de Estrella, 1552, f.281.

77. Letters in autograph from Philip to Maximilian, July–Nov. 1549, HHSA Spanien, Hofkorrespondenz, karton 1, mappe 3, ff.143–4.

78. To king of Denmark, Jan. 1550, AGS:E leg.645 f.14.

79. Alvarez, pp.117–18.

80. Calvete de Estrella, 1552, f.325. Fresneda became confessor to Philip, Constantino was later denounced as a heretic, and Cazalla was burned in an *auto de fe* in Valladolid in 1559.

81. Alvarez, p.119.

82. Ibid.

83. Ibid., p.120.

84. Philip to Maximilian, autograph from Cologne, HHSA Spanien Hofkorrespondenz, karton 1, mappe 3 f.161.

85. Merriman, III, 406.

86. Bishop of Arras to Margaret of Hungary, 13 Oct. 1550, CSP, England and Spain, X, 156.

87. Alvarez, pp.131–2.

88. Philip to Juan Hurtado de Mendoza, Augsburg, 12 Sept. 1550, AGS:E leg.645 f.81.

89. Ibid. f.87.

90. Braudel, II, 915.
91. Antoine's father, Nicolas Perrenot, cardinal Granvelle, had died in August 1550. Antoine replaced him as chief adviser to Charles V.
92. There were three documents: a contract between Maximilian and Philip, an undertaking by Philip, and an undertaking by Maximilian.
93. All details of Philip's movements come from Vandenesse, II, 403ff.
94. Philip to Maurice, Augsburg, 16 May 1551, AGS:E leg.646 f.109: 'in nos studio et amore, quem sub adventum nostrum ad Germaniam, multis magnisque argumentis deprehendimus, gratiam habemus maximam'.
95. Constancio Gutiérrez, *Trento: un concilio para la unión (1550–1552),* 3 vols. Madrid 1981, III, 398.
96. 'Plusieurs festins avec force dames': Vandenesse, IV, 4.
97. Calvete de Estrella, *Rebelión,* II, 455.
98. Another source lists forty-four galleys. The naval commander Bernardino de Mendoza, brother to the scholar-diplomat Diego Hurtado de Mendoza, was no relation to the later ambassador of Philip to England.
99. 'Un banquet et force dames': Vandenesse, IV, 6.
100. AGS:E leg.646 f.226.
101. Soriano, in Alberi, ser.1, vol.III. Cf the comments of Merriman, III, 366, who like others accepts the Venetian view.
102. *Dietari de l'Antich Consell Barceloní,* IV, Barcelona 1895, p.227. The prince resided in the palace of the duke of Cardona.
103. Philip to Maximilian, from Barcelona, HHSA Spanien Hofkorrespondenz, karton 1, mappe 4 f.14.

3. *Soldier and King 1551–1559*

1. To duke of Savoy, Cambrai, 9 Aug. 1557, BL Add.28264 f.26.
2. See the report on her made by Francisco de Borja to Philip in 1554: *Monumenta Historica Societatis Iesu: Borgia,* Madrid 1908, III, 161.
3. Philip to Maximilian, 16 Sept. 1551, HHSA Spanien Hofkorrespondenz, karton 1, mappe 4 f.23.
4. Philip to Maximilian, 25 Sept. 1551, ibid. f.27.
5. Vandenesse, IV, 7.
6. Philip to Maximilian, 29 Sept. 1551, HHSA Spanien Hofkorrespondenz, karton 1, mappe 4 f.29.
7. Philip to Maximilian, 2 Jan. 1552, ibid. f.39.
8. Philip to Maximilian, 5 Apr. 1552, ibid. f.44.
9. Braudel, II, 923.
10. Ruy Gómez to Eraso, 19 May 1552, AGS:E leg.89 f.131. Maurice was killed in a campaign in Germany in 1553.
11. Philip to Andrea Doria, Madrid, 12 June 1552, ibid. leg.92 f.106.
12. Zayas to Pérez, 8 Nov. 1552, in González Palencia, I, 135.
13. Juan Vázquez to Pérez, 26 Nov. 1552, ibid., II, 443.
14. 'Minuta de la carta que se escrivió al Principe de Bruselas', 20 Mar. 1553, AGS:E leg.98 ff.118–23.
15. Philip to Charles, 17 Mar. 1553, ibid. ff.88–93.
16. Philip's first wife Maria was also his cousin, daughter of the marriage of Charles V's youngest sister Catherine to the king of Portugal.
17. 'Memorial que embio Francisco Duarte de lo que le dixo Nicolas Nicolai', Sept. 1553, AGS:E leg.98 f.274.
18. G. Constant, 'Le mariage de Marie Tudor et de Philippe II', *Revue d'Histoire Diplomatique,* 26 (1912), p.36.
19. CSP, Spain, XI, 404, 290.
20. The relationship existed prior to Philip's departure from Spain in 1554, and could only have commenced after his return in 1550: cf. González de Amezúa, I, 393. William of Orange in his *Apology*

stated that there were several children by the marriage: cited in Muro, p.243.

21. Cabrera, III, 367: 'ella tanto se ensalzó por amarle mucho'. On the secret document, Forneron, I, 9. Forneron identifies her as the sister of the marquis of Astorga.

22. According to the Venetian ambassadors Badoero and Soranzo, cited in González de Amezúa, I, 407. Forneron I, 11, identifies one of the ladies as Catalina Laínez, married to a Spanish courtier.

23. González de Amezúa, I, 405.

24. Philip to Egmont, AGS:E leg.808 f.11.

25. Cabrera, I, 43.

26. CSP, England and Spain, XII, 316.

27. John Elder, *The Copie of a Letter sent in to Scotlande*, London 1554.

28. Muñoz, p.99. The Venetian ambassador claimed that she spoke Spanish fluently (CSPV, VI, ii, p.1055), but the testimony of Muñoz is firmer. It is noteworthy that Elizabeth also spoke some Spanish.

29. In Charles's system of government, the 'regent' was a senior official who represented his country's interests in the king's council.

30. Figueroa to Charles, Winchester, 26 July 1554, CODOIN, III, 519. Papal investiture of Naples was conceded in October: cf. Braudel, II, 935 n.184. Vandenesse, IV, 15, dates the Figueroa ceremony to the actual day of arrival, Friday the twentieth, on board Philip's ship. This seems less likely than Figueroa's own account.

31. Details in Constant, 'Le mariage de Marie Tudor', pp.244–60.

32. Instruction of 16 Feb. 1554 to Egmont, AGS:E leg.808 f.19.

33. Muñoz, p.71.

34. AGS:CR leg.33 f.8.

35. Soriano to Senate, 1559, CSPV, VII, 330.

36. Philip to Juana, 2 and 18 Sept. 1554, AGS:E leg.808 ff.38, 40.

37. González Palencia, I, 180.

38. Though Amadis was from Brittany, his deeds were performed in Wales.

39. Muñoz, pp.113, 97.

40. Ibid., pp.106–7.

41. Ibid., pp.118, 108, 77.

42. Ibid., pp.119, 106.

43. CSPV, VI, ii, p.1055.

44. Ruy Gómez to Charles V, London, 27 and 30 July 1554, AGS:E leg.808 f.148.

45. Sandoval, p.428. 'Though the queen,' he adds, 'was a saint, she was ugly and old, and the king handsome and young.'

46. Cf. D. M. Loades, 'Philip II and the Government of England', p.190, in C. Cross et al., eds, *Law and Government under the Tudors*, Cambridge 1988.

47. What follows is summarised from Philip's letter to Charles, Sept. 1554, AGS:PR leg.55, doc. 27 (iii).

48. Loades, 'Philip II', p.189.

49. Bartolomé de las Casas, *De Regia Potestate*, ed. L. Pereña, J. M. Pérez Prendes, et al., Madrid 1969, p.lii.

50. Philip to Charles, 16 Nov. 1554, AGS:E leg.808 f.54.

51. Instructions to Eraso, AGS:PR leg.55, doc. 27 (iv).

52. Milhou, p.4.

53. Ibid., pp.37, 39–41. The enslavement of Caribbean islanders had been prohibited by the New Laws of 1542; but it was permitted by Philip for Puerto Rico in 1547, and then for Hispaniola in 1558.

54. Philip to Charles, Valladolid 2 Sept. 1553: 'El asiento de las licencias de los esclavos se a deshecho porq ha parescido a algunos theologos q era cargo de conciencia', AGS:E leg.98 f.263.

55. Milhou, p.47.

56. In 1560, precisely.

57. Philip's general support for Las Casas is emphasised by Fray Alonso Fernández, *Historia Eclesiastica de nuestros tiempos*, Toledo 1611, pp.29–31.

58. CODOIN, LXX, 227.

59. Cited Lewis Hanke, *Aristotle and the American Indians*, London 1959, p.83.
60. CSP, Spain, XIII, 138–9.
61. Cited in Kamen, 'Toleration and Dissent', in *Crisis and Change*, p.14.
62. Castro did not live to take up his post. He accompanied Philip to Flanders, and died in Brussels in 1558.
63. D. M. Loades, *Politics and the Nation 1450–1660*, London 1979, p.236.
64. CSPV, VI, ii, 1065.
65. Loades, *Politics*, p.193.
66. Philip to Maximilian, 24 Apr. 1555, HHSA Spanien Hofkorrespondenz, karton 1, mappe 4 f.137.
67. CSPV, VI, i, 177.
68. Cabrera, I, 24.
69. Gachard, *Retraite et mort, Introduction*, 80–103.
70. In Strada, I, 12, a version given also in Motley, p.57, Charles is described as standing, leaning for support on the prince of Orange.
71. Sandoval, p.479.
72. Gachard, *Retraite et mort, Introduction*, 98, demonstrates that Philip spoke in French. The dramatic version in Motley, p.58, that he spoke in Spanish, is untrue.
73. Gachard, *Retraite et mort, Introduction*, 142. In a detailed 'Relacion de los documentos hechos sobre el Vicariato', in AGS:E leg.646 f.252, Perrenot insisted that the king must *never* make use of the privilege, and must not even admit that such a document existed.
74. Cf. Van Durme, p.188.
75. Gachard, *Retraite et mort, Introduction*, 133.
76. Gachard, *Carlos V*, p.34.
77. CSPV, VI, ii, 863.
78. Ibid., 1179.
79. Ibid., 1063.
80. 'All sinew, little flesh . . . born to command': Cabrera, I, 166.
81. King to Savoy, 26 July 1557, AGS:E/K 1490 no.40.
82. The account that follows is based largely on Philip's original (and hitherto unknown) military despatches, in BL Add.28264. For a splendid but thoroughly hostile account of Philip at St Quentin see Motley, pp.89–99. In Merriman, IV, 11, Philip is caricatured as writing letters instead of doing battle.
83. BL Add.28264 ff.10–12.
84. Ibid. f.17.
85. Ibid. f.19.
86. My italics: ibid. ff.26–7.
87. Savoy to king, 8 Aug. 1557, AGS:E/K 1490 no.65.
88. Savoy to Eraso, 8 Aug. 1557, ibid. no.67b.
89. Philip to Charles, 11 Aug. 1557, ibid. no.72.
90. *La Guerre de 1557 en Picardie*, St Quentin 1896, p.237.
91. His remark to the Venetian ambassador Suriano: CSPV, VI, ii, 1348.
92. Who died that week, of gout, aged only fifty-one.
93. CSPV, VI, ii, 1345.
94. Suriano to Senate, 24 Oct. 1557, ibid., 1354. Suriano's letters make clear that the retreat after St Quentin was a decision imposed by the council. Nearly all biographers present it, by contrast, as a cowardly decision by Philip.
95. Philip to Ferdinand, 29 Aug. 1557, San Quentin, CODOIN, II, 493–6.
96. Bedford to William Cecil, quoted in *La Guerre de 1557 en Picardie*, p.324. Philip, according to his own letters, ordered the evacuation of women and children from the town in order to save them from the soldiers. Motley, p.97, presents this as an act of cruelty.
97. Philip to Juana, 2 Sept. 1557, AGS:E/K 1490 no.82b.
98. Cabrera, I, 243.
99. King to Savoy, Brussels, 8 Nov. 1557: BL Add.28264 f.37.
100. Philip to Juana, 1 May 1558, AGS:CJH leg.34 f.519.
101. Braudel, II, 942 notes it as 'a turning point in western history'.
102. BL Add. 28264 ff.41–4.
103. Vandenesse, IV, 34.

104. AGS:CR leg.78 no.38, 'los retratos q Su Alteça tiene en su camara'. The portrait of Philip is now in the Prado.
105. Gachard, *Carlos V*, pp.38, 93.
106. Feria to Philip, London 11 Apr. 1559: AE:CP, MD vol.233 f.112.
107. Braudel, II, 948.
108. Weiss, V, 454.
109. Ibid., 491.
110. *Cortes antiguos*, V, 717.
111. Memorials and letters of Valdés to king, AGS:E leg.129 ff.110–12, 128.
112. King to Juana, Antwerp, 5 June 1558, ibid. ff.178–83; to Valdés, 6 Sept. 1558, ibid., f.116.
113. King to Juana, Brussels, 20 Feb. 1559, ibid. leg.138 f.23.
114. Sébastien de l'Aubespine, bishop of Limoges, to king François II, Ghent, 27 July 1559, in Paris, pp.49–54.
115. Weiss, V, 594.
116. Ibid., 606.
117. Ibid., 631.
118. Badoero to Senate, Brussels, 1 Mar. 1556, CSPV, VI, i, 363. Viglius's figure is confirmed by the calculations of Alastair Duke, *Reformation and Revolt in the Low Countries*, London 1990, p.71.
119. Strada, I, 75.
120. Gachard, *Carlos V*, translated from a corresponding volume in French, prints extracts from the reports by Federico Badoero (1554–7) and Michele Suriano (1557–9). Though Gachard accepts everything the ambassadors say, much in their reports is both tendentious and incorrect.
121. In the Museo de Bellas Artes, Bilbao.
122. Suriano to Senate, 1559, CSPV, VII, 331.
123. Cf. Boyden, p.66: 'Philip II was a shy, passive, sedentary man'. Boyden creates this image in order to support his view of Ruy Gómez as the real driving force.
124. Challoner to queen, 3 Aug. 1559, CSP, Foreign 1558–9, 503.
125. At the time of Fox's appointment,

126. Checa, p.87.
127. A good overview by J. K. Steppe, 'Mécénat espagnol et art flamand au XVIe siècle', in *Splendeurs d'Espagne*, I, 247–82.
128. Paris, p.64.
129. A subject currently being studied by Professor Friedrich Edelmayer of Vienna.
130. I prefer not to give credence here to the lively incident, narrated by Motley, p.113, in which the king lost his temper with the prince of Orange at the quayside.
131. Challoner to Cecil, 27 Aug. 1559, CSP, Foreign 1558–9, p.503.

Philip was unaware of a denunciation of the philosopher made to the Inquisition in faraway Seville. Fox never took up his appointment: he was drowned at sea on his way to Spain in 1560.

4. The Cross and the Crescent 1559–1565

1. Serrano, III, ciii–cv.
2. Carrasco, *passim*.
3. For the petitions, Danvila y Collado, II, 281–5.
4. Cited in H. Kamen, 'Spain', in B. Scribner, R. Porter and M. Teich, eds, *The Reformation in National Context*, Cambridge 1993, pp.206, 210.
5. AGS:E leg.137 ff.12, 15.
6. Bratli, p.184.
7. Gachard, *Don Carlos*, p.49.
8. 'Were our father a heretic we would carry the faggots to burn him': CSPV, VI, ii, no.1067. The phrase was clearly a traditional one, not peculiar to either the pope or the king. 'If any *converso* were wicked,' wrote a Castilian royal secretary in 1449, 'I would be the first to bring the wood to burn him': cited in Benzion Netanyahu, *The Origins of the Inquisition*, New York 1995, p.409.

9. Vandenesse, IV, 68.
10. Letter from fray Joan Izquierdo to prince Philip, Barcelona 14 July 1552, AGS:E leg.310.
11. CSPV, VII, 132.
12. Alvaro Huerga, *El proceso de la Inquisición de Sevilla contra el maestro Domingo de Valtanás*, Jaén 1958, p.9. Constantino was the preacher Constantino Ponce de la Fuente (see Chapter Two), whose bones were disinterred by the Inquisition after his death.
13. Philip to Valdés, 23 Aug. 1560, Favre vol.29 f.4. These figures are based in part on William Monter, 'Heresy executions in Reformation Europe, 1520–1565', in O. P. Grell and B. Scribner, *Tolerance and Intolerance in the European Reformation*, Cambridge 1996.
14. Bishop of Pamplona to Granvelle, 23 May 1560, BP MS.II/2291 f.128.
15. Autumn of 1552, AGS:E leg.92 f.81.
16. Favre vol.2 f.32.
17. Cited Kamen, *Phoenix*, p.87.
18. Bataillon, pp.723–4, notes 31 and 32; Kamen, *Phoenix*, pp.416–18.
19. 'Lo que parece convernia proveerse', AGS:E leg.129 f.112.
20. King to Inquisition, 6 Sept. 1558, ibid. f.116.
21. Cited in A. Sicroff, *Les Controverses des statuts de pureté en Espagne du XVe au XVIIe siècle*, Paris 1960, p.138 n.184.
22. The original statement by Siliceo, who was a fanatical anti-Semite, occurs in 'Sobre el Estatuto de limpieza de la Sancta Iglessia de Toledo', BNM MS.13267 f.281.
23. Cf. Braudel, II, 802–26. Also R. Bonfil, *Gli ebrei in Italia nell'epoca del rinascimento*, Florence 1991.
24. Abravanel to king, 27 May 1558, AGS:CJH leg.34 f.432.
25. Bishop of Málaga to king, 10 June 1559, AGS:E leg.137 f.307.
26. J. C. Domínguez Nafría, *La Inquisición de Murcia en el siglo XVI*, Murcia 1991, p.32.
27. AGS:E leg.809 ff.75–7, order of 29 May 1555, Hampton Court.
28. Cited in Kamen, 'Limpieza', in *Crisis and Change*, p.330, n.25.
29. Gil Fernández, p.470.
30. Eboli, a town in Naples, was given to Ruy Gómez by Philip in 1559. Gómez later sold the estate, and bought lands in Pastrana, which earned him the title of duke of Pastrana in 1572.
31. Badoero, in Gachard, *Carlos V*, pp.42–4.
32. Muro, pp.37–40.
33. Boyden, p.27.
34. I deliberately avoid the term 'faction' (used by some historians) for a grouping which, on the evidence available, had no clear cohesion and was certainly not factious. Some recent studies in Spanish on a so-called 'Ebolist party' are wholly unconvincing.
35. Gachard, *Carlos V*, p.41. The study by Boyden gives a very good perspective on the role of Ruy Gómez.
36. This modifies the presentation in Lagomarsino, pp.24–6, where Eraso is shown as joining Gómez in 1556. The correspondence of Gómez with Eraso in AGS:E leg.89 shows that the two had their heads together long before.
37. Gómez to Eraso, Toro, 22 Sept. 1552, AGS:E leg.89 f.120.
38. Gómez to Eraso, Toro, 25 Nov. 1552, ibid. f.123.
39. The file on the Chancery is ibid. f.139.
40. Gómez to Eraso, Madrid, 4 Apr. 1552, ibid. f.129.
41. Maltby, p.151 ff.
42. The bulk of consultations over Flanders in 1563 was with Alba: AGS:E leg.143.
43. Lagomarsino, p.28.
44. See also the sensible comments by Boyden, pp.114–15.
45. Lagomarsino, p.30, states that 'Philip was fundamentally flexible at the start of his reign'.
46. Gonzalo Pérez to Granvelle, 16

Apr. 1560, Toledo, BP MS.II/2291 f.103.
47. Weiss, V, 643, 672.
48. King to council of State, 1565, AGS:E leg.98.
49. Juana to king, 9 June 1559, ibid. leg.137 f.213.
50. Marginal comment on letter from Juana, 14 July 1559, ibid. f.227. The passage has been transcribed erroneously by various recent historians.
51. Ortiz to government, 15 Oct. 1558, AGS:CJH leg.34 f.437. Ortiz earlier that year handed to the treasury a now celebrated *Memorial* on finance.
52. Braudel, II, 966.
53. Ibid., 973–87.
54. Paris, p.555.
55. Tiepolo to Sena, 29 Jan. 1560, CSPV, VII, 147.
56. Tiepolo, in Alberi, ser. I, vol. V, 71.
57. Secretary Courteville, cited in Gachard, *Don Carlos*, p.51.
58. Pérez to Granvelle, Toledo, 3 Oct. 1560, BP MS.II/2291 f.229.
59. Marqués de las Navas to Granvelle, Toledo, 4 Apr. 1560, ibid. f.88.
60. González de Amezúa, I, 210.
61. Report by Soranzo, in Alberi, ser.I, vol.V, 114.
62. Paolo Tiepolo, 1563, ibid., 63.
63. González de Amezúa, II, i, 43, 57.
64. Ibid., I, 430.
65. The architect will be referred to in this book simply as Juan Bautista, since his real surname is uncertain.
66. Rivera, p.62.
67. Ibid., p.294.
68. In the Prado, and in the Kunsthistorisches Museum, Vienna.
69. Gachard, *Don Carlos*, p.72.
70. Ibid., p.76.
71. García Ballester, p.178.
72. 'Juan de Padilla, the tyrant', was his view in 1591 of the famous Comunero leader: Cabrera de Córdoba, IV, 504.
73. Paris, p.551.
74. Cabié, p.78.
75. Ibid., p.171.

76. Cf. Gómez-Centurión, pp.25–9, 146–7.
77. Strada, I, 251.
78. The best account of the activities of Villavicencio is in Lagomarsino, pp.42–57.
79. Ibid., p.39 and later, is the best guide to del Canto.
80. Report by L'Aubespine, 26 Sept. 1560, in Paris, p.560.
81. Of 180 orders issued in Brussels in 1563–5, none was signed by Philip: Schepper, p.187.
82. Danvila y Collado, II, 289.
83. King to count of Luna, 25 Apr. 1563, AGS:E leg.141 f.157.
84. The first stone (as distinct from the foundation stone) had been laid on St George's Day, 23 April.
85. To count of Luna, 25 Apr. 1563, AGS:E leg.141 f.157.
86. Courteville, cited Gachard, *Don Carlos*, p.91.
87. In November 1563. Cited in Carrasco, p.142. Events in Aragon are exaggerated by Rodríguez Salgado, p.288, as a rebellion.
88. Gachard, *Don Carlos*, p.94.
89. Parker, *Dutch Revolt*, p.54, suggests that Alba's temporary absence from court facilitated Granvelle's removal. In fact, the king was in constant touch with Alba, as the correspondence in AGS:E leg.143 shows.
90. Lagomarsino, p.70.
91. Alba to king, 21 Oct. 1563, AGS:E leg.143 f.3.
92. Cf. Lagomarsino, p.89.
93. Report by Soranzo, cited Gachard, *Don Carlos*, p.97.
94. Venetian ambassador Soranzo, cited ibid., p.99.
95. Perot de Vilanova, 'Memòries', cited in Kamen, *Phoenix*, p.44.
96. See also Gachard, *Don Carlos*, pp.105–13.
97. Maximilian became emperor shortly after in 1564, on the death of his father (Philip II's uncle) Ferdinand on 25 July.
98. Mayer-Löwenschwerdt, p.11.

99. *Dietari de l'Antich Consell Barceloní,* V, Barcelona 1896, p.27.

100. Cabié, pp.77, 79.

101. HHSA Spanien, Varia, karton 2, n, f.13, report of 1564.

102. The best account of Egmont's visit, and the problems involved, is in Lagomarsino, pp.95–126.

103. Quoted in ibid., p.104.

104. Philip's draft notes and Pérez's draft and comments are in AGS:E leg.527 f.5.

105. After the comment about 'one o'clock' he wrote another six sides, some 1,400 words more: ibid.

106. Ibid. leg.146 f.145.

107. HHSA Spanien, Varia, karton 2, p, f.4.

108. Parker's picture of the king's 'duping of Egmont' (Parker, *Philip II,* pp.69–72) is over-dramatised. It was not Philip's intention to 'dupe' anybody.

109. I follow the translation given by Lagomarsino, p.114.

110. AGS:E leg.527 f.14, 'Puntos que resultan de las cosas de Flandes'.

111. Pérez to Armenteros, secretary of Margaret of Parma, 30 June 1565, cited Gachard, *Correspondance,* I, 358.

112. Evidence for the committee comes exclusively from the verbal testimony given by one of its members to the Jesuit historian Strada: Strada, I, 315.

113. 'Advis des evesques docteurs sur le fait de la religion', AGS:E leg.527 f.1.

114. Cabié, p.357.

115. Manrique de Lara to king, 18 May 1565, AGS:E leg.145 f.196.

116. The route was through Soria, Pamplona and San Sebastian. Pamplona was threatened by plague in these weeks, but could not be avoided.

117. Alba and Manrique to Philip, 15 and 21 June 1565, AGS:E/K leg.1504 ff.15, 17.

118. Alba and Manrique to Philip, 21 and 29 June 1565, ibid. ff.22, 36.

119. AE:CP,MD vol.235 ff.216–19.

120. Yates, p.59.

121. HHSA Spanien, Varia, p, f.25.

122. Álava to Philip, 8 July 1565, AGS:E leg.1504 f.50.

123. Order to council of State, Apr. 1553, ibid. leg.98 f.156. The importance of this order needs emphasising. Most historians present an inexplicable and untrue image of a king opposed to the decrees of Trent.

124. L'Aubespine to François II, 16 Sept. 1560, in Paris, p.551.

125. Martín de Córdoba, bishop of Tortosa, to marquis of Pescara, Trent, 26 May 1562, CODOIN, IX, 217.

126. King to Luna, 12 May 1563, ibid. XCVIII, 438.

127. King to Luna, Aug. 1563, ibid., 482.

128. Philip to Álava, 2 Aug. 1564, AGS:E/K 1502 f.14 bis.

129. Álava to Philip, 9 Aug. 1564, ibid. f.15.

130. A brief survey in Kamen, *Phoenix,* pp.61–4.

131. For the actual success or otherwise of the reform movement in Spain, see ibid., *passim*; and Sara Nalle, *God in La Mancha,* Baltimore 1992.

132. Changes he proposed for the form of the mass in 1575 occupy four sides of paper: IVDJ, 53, carpeta 7, f.51.

133. Comment on letter of Álava to king, 18 Jan. 1565, AGS:E/K 1503 f.20.

134. Nuns, in 1565: ibid. f.43; books, ibid. ff.22, 37.

135. Quadra to king, London, 11 Oct. 1561, AE:CP,MD vol.234 f.105.

136. Guzmán de Silva to king, London, 26 Apr. 1565, CODOIN, XXVI, 540.

137. Del Canto's detailed memorandum of 1563, in AGS:CJH leg.55 f.174, gives a good sketch of Spanish heretics in Europe.

138. Braudel, II, 1007–12; Thompson, *War and Government,* chaps 1, 6.

139. Cited Braudel, II, 1000.

140. Cf. ibid., 1012.

141. Cf. Fourquevaux to Charles IX, 21

Nov. 1565: 'la conjuration des Morisques dont le bruict a esté et est encores grand en ce pais', Douais, Vol.I, p.12.

142. The background to this is studied in Lagomarsino, pp.136–47.

143. A full report on the verdicts, in HHSA, Spanien, Varia, karton 2, r, f.19.

5. *Towards Total War 1566–1572*

1. King to Francés de Álava, 27 Nov. 1567, in Rodríguez and Rodríguez, doc.70.

2. *Filosofía vulgar*, Barcelona 1958–9 edn, I, 55.

3. Thompson, *War and Government*, chap.4.

4. Castillo de Bobadilla, II, 571, 579.

5. Tiepolo in 1563, Alberi, ser.I, vol.V, 17.

6. Parker, *Army of Flanders*, chap.1.

7. Thompson, *War and Government*, p.17.

8. AGS:E leg.154 f.106.

9. Danvila y Collado, II, 306.

10. Douais, xvi–xxi, 69–80.

11. Philip to Francés de Álava, 7 Apr. 1566, AGS:E/K 1505 f.101.

12. Douais, I, 72.

13. AGS:E leg.148 f.50. The armaments included 10,500 cannonballs and 403 barrels of gunpowder.

14. Weiss, IX, 503, cited Lagomarsino, p.133.

15. AGS:E leg.146, no.77.

16. Lagomarsino, pp.174–82.

17. Gachard, *Correspondance*, I, clxxvi.

18. King to Francés de Álava, Madrid, 22 Dec. 1565: in Rodríguez and Rodríguez, p.31.

19. For some Spanish views, see Kamen, 'Toleration', in *Crisis and Change*.

20. Douais, I, 68.

21. King to Francés de Álava, 27 Nov. 1567, in Rodríguez and Rodríguez, doc.70.

22. Fourquevaux to Charles IX, 5 May 1566, Douais, I, 86.

23. HHSA Spanien, Varia, karton 2, r, f.22.

24. Serrano, II, xxxvi.

25. Lagomarsino, pp.240–1.

26. Cited Gachard, *Don Carlos*, p.256 n.2.

27. Del Canto to king, 4 July 1566, Brussels, AGS:E leg.529 ff.61–2.

28. Serrano, II, xxxix.

29. BNM MS.8246 f.176.

30. Letters in AGS:E leg.530.

31. Parker, *Dutch Revolt*, p.78.

32. Gachard, *Don Carlos*, p.264 n.2.

33. 'Lo que contiene el despacho que se embia a Flandes', AGS:E leg.530.

34. Cabrera, I, 487.

35. Douais, III, 18.

36. He looked 'plus beau, plus frais et plus jeune' than ever: ibid., 23. However, the next day he was unwell again.

37. Cabrera, I, 490.

38. Fourquevaux to Charles IX, 9 Dec. 1566, Douais, I, 150.

39. 'Paresciendole que no se puede venir a matar 200,000 personas': Margaret to king, 18 Aug. 1566, AGS:E leg.530.

40. Parker, *Army of Flanders*, chaps 2–3.

41. Lagomarsino, p.262.

42. Cf. ibid., p.263.

43. King to Requesens, 26, Nov. 1566, in Serrano, I, 399.

44. Parker, *Dutch Revolt*, p.85, refers to the sending of the army as a 'mysterious' decision. One should more probably term it a controversial decision.

45. Douais, I, 173.

46. Fourquevaux to king of France, 13 Feb. 1567, in Douais, I, 179; judgment by the Audiencia of Mexico, AGS:E lib.2018 ff.213–16; reports in HHSA Spanien, Varia, karton 2, s, f.34, 37. Cortés, who accompanied Philip to England and the Netherlands, had recently returned to Mexico from Spain (1562). He was fined but pardoned, and died in 1589.

47. They acted with extreme rigour, and had their commissions

revoked. A new team of judges was
sent out in 1568. See Manuel
Orozco y Berra, *Conjuración del
Marqués del Valle, 1565–1568*,
Mexico 1853.

48. Fourquevaux to Charles IX, 24
Aug. 1567, Douais, I, 255.

49. Philip to Alba, 11 Oct., 1567,
CODOIN, LXXV, 15.

50. Philip to Alba, 16 Oct. 1567, AGS:E
leg.537 ff.3–6.

51. Douais, I, 272.

52. CODOIN, LXXV, 20.

53. HHSA Spanien, Varia, karton 2, s,
f.47.

54. King to Francés de Álava, Madrid,
19 Feb. 1568, in Rodríguez and
Rodríguez, doc.88.

55. Alba to Requesens, and to king, 14
Sept. 1567, in Alba, I, 673, 675.

56. CODOIN, XXXVII, 42–70.

57. King to Alba, 19 Feb. 1568,
CODOIN, XXXVII, 156.

58. King to Requesens, 22 Oct. 1567,
Gachard, *Correspondance*, I, 581–96.

59. Gachard, *Don Carlos*, p.135.

60. Fourquevaux to king, 12 Sept. 1567,
in Douais, I, 266.

61. What follows is summarised from
Gachard, *Don Carlos*, esp. pp.335–
62.

62. Cited ibid., p.393.

63. Ibid., pp.437–9.

64. Cabrera, I, 562.

65. Cited Gachard, *Don Carlos*, p.407.

66. Douais, III, 92.

67. King to Francés de Álava, 19 Mar.
1568, in Rodríguez and Rodríguez,
doc.93.

68. Cabrera, I, 562.

69. Reports by Tisnacq and Hopperus,
in Gachard, *Don Carlos*, p.406;
French ambassador, ibid., p.407 n.1.

70. Fourquevaux to king, 5 Feb. 1568,
in Douais, I, 321 and ff.

71. Gachard, *Don Carlos*, p.393. The
papers of the inquiry, lodged
in Simancas, subsequently
disappeared.

72. Cited Gachard, *Don Carlos*, p.476
n.4.

73. King to Francés de Álava, 3 Oct.

1568, in Rodríguez and Rodríguez,
doc.124.

74. Alba to king, Brussels, 6 Jan. 1568,
Gachard, *Correspondance*, II, 3.

75. The sketch of Orange in Motley,
pp.119–26, is still the most
evocative.

76. Ibid., pp.153–63.

77. AGS:E leg.537 f.26.

78. Strada, II, 686.

79. Alba to Chantonnay, Brussels, 14
Sept. 1567, in Alba, I, 673.

80. Strada, II, 686.

81. King to Alba, Madrid, 18 July 1568,
CODOIN, XXXVII, 310.

82. Pedro Cornejo, *Sumario de las
Guerras Civiles y causas de la Rebellion de Flandes*, Leon 1577, p.125.

83. Ibid., p.114.

84. King to Francés de Álava, 14 Oct.
1568, in Rodríguez and Rodríguez,
doc.126.

85. Philip to Alba, 18 Feb. 1569,
CODOIN, XXXVII, 552.

86. Philip's envoy D. Luis Venegas, 11
Oct. 1568, ibid., CIII, 4.

87. King to Chantonnay, 11 May 1566,
ibid., CI, 137.

88. King to Chantonnay, 20 May 1568,
ibid., 422.

89. Ibid., XXXVII, 358.

90. On Charles, see F. Edelmayer,
'Einheit der Casa de Austria?
Philipp II und Karl von Innerö-
sterreich', in *Katholische Reform und
Gegenreformation in Innerösterreich
1564–1628*, Vienna 1994.

91. Douais, III, x. Guise spent Christmas at Montserrat before coming to
Madrid.

92. King to Francés de Álava, 2 Mar.
1569, in Rodríguez and Rodríguez,
doc.162. Marguerite, who subsequently married Henry of Navarre,
shared with the other children of
Catherine de' Medici traits of
mental instability of which Philip
may have been aware.

93. To Granvelle, Mar. 1569, in L. Pérez
Bueno, 'Del casamiento de Felipe II
con su sobrina Ana de Austria',
Hispania, 7 (1947), pp.372–416.

94. There was also a private version of the reply, more outspoken and meant for the emperor alone: Gachard, *Correspondance*, II, 819.

95. 'Respuesta del Rey Católico', 20 Jan. 1569, CODOIN, CIII, 88–107.

96. 'La réplica que hizo el Archiduque Carlos', 22 Jan. 1569, ibid., 108–19.

97. King to Alba, Madrid, 12 Jan. 1569, AGS:E leg.1570² f.112.

98. Alonso del Canto to king, Brussels, 22 Apr. 1566, ibid. leg.529 f.56.

99. The accusations, and Vandenesse's statements, are in ibid. leg.542 f.122; and leg.543 f.2. He was son of the Vandenesse who chronicled the travels of the emperor.

100. Ibid. leg.152 f.162.

101. Ibid. leg.543 ff.67–9.

102. Full details of his last hours ibid. ff.70, 87–8.

103. Gachard, *Correspondance*, II, 161, 169.

104. 'The terrible secret of Montigny's death was one Philip II took with him to the tomb': Marañón (English edn, p.55). A recent scholar also states: 'He believed that his sovereignty gave him the right to execute private and secret justice ... This belief led him to acts of savagery and arbitrary despotism': Lynch, p.259. Philip never had any such beliefs.

105. García Ballester, pp.109–11.

106. Ladrada to king, Madrid, 29 Sept. 1572, BL Add.28354 f.484. The doctor, La Fuente, is described as having 'not a drop of "pure" blood'.

107. García Ballester, p.54.

108. Cited in E. Salvador, *Felipe II y los moriscos valencianos*, Valladolid 1987, p.23.

109. AGS:E leg.148 f.113.

110. Zúñiga to king, 14 Oct. 1569, in Serrano, III, 165.

111. Cf. Braudel, II, 1068.

112. President of Chancery of Granada to king, 28 July 1570, BZ 158 f.3.

113. King to Alba, Madrid, 16 Dec. 1569, CODOIN, XXXVIII, 257.

114. Danvila y Collado, II, 313.

115. Mal Lara, p.68. The author of this description died prematurely six months after penning it.

116. In Jan. 1570, for example, the army received 414 cases of armament from Milan: AGS:E leg.152 f.76. In 1572 it ordered 250 field-guns: ibid. leg.154 f.106.

117. Don Juan's secretary, Juan de Soto, to Escobedo, Granada 20 Nov. 1570, AGS:E leg.152 f.22.

118. Requesens to Zúñiga, 28 Oct. 1570, IVDJ, 70 f.72. Cf. the reaction of another general to an atrocity in our times. General Curtis LaMay was quoted in the *International Herald Tribune* (The Hague, 9 Mar. 1995) as saying: 'We scorched and boiled and baked to death more people in Tokyo on that night [9 Mar. 1945] than went up in vapour at Hiroshima and Nagasaki combined.'

119. Fourquevaux to king, 8 May 1568, in Douais, I, 354.

120. Don Juan to Ruy Gómez, 5 Nov. 1570, CODOIN, XXXVIII, 156.

121. King to Juan Vázquez, San Lorenzo, 22 Apr. 1579, BL Add.28357 f.302.

122. Cabrera, III, 610.

123. Quiroga to Vázquez, 25 Aug. 1582, BZ 135 f.20.

124. Report of committee, 17 June 1587, BL Eg.1511 ff.106–13.

125. Ibid. ff.183–5.

126. Cabié, pp.122, 171.

127. Requesens to Zúñiga, 28 Jan. 1573, IVDJ, 67 f.1.

128. Philip to Alba, Madrid, 18 Feb. 1569, AGS:E leg.542.

129. CODOIN, XXXVIII, 109.

130. Cited Gómez-Centurión, p.57.

131. CSPV, VIII, 296. In private, Alba confessed in 1573 to a 'personal dislike' of the English: Alba, I, xix.

132. Teulet, V, 57.

133. Alba to king, Brussels, 7 May 1571, 'Your Majesty had no interest in this', ibid., 74.

134. 'Lo que se platicó en Consejo', 7 July 1571, AGS:E leg.823 ff.150–8.

The council did not, contrary to what Parker, *Philip II*, p.118, says, *approve* the plot. Merriman also errs. He states, IV, 293: 'On Saturday, July 7, 1571, there was held in Madrid a famous meeting of the Consejo, in which it was decided that Elizabeth must be assassinated.'
135. BNM MS.2751 f.479.
136. Gachard, *Carlos V*, pp.139–40.
137. Jean Baptiste de Tassis, cited in Stirling-Maxwell, II, 359.
138. Cf. Marañón, I, 216–17.
139. HHSA, Spanien, Varia, karton 2, p, f.19.
140. BZ 186 ff.42–4.
141. See his comments in 1575 in CODOIN, XXXVIII, 284.
142. E.g. the letters in ibid., XXVIII.
143. This is the correct form of her name, and she always signed it this way. The Spanish form 'Ana' was not, to my knowledge, used by her. See her letters in HHSA, Spanien, Hofkorrespondenz, karton 2, mappe 12 ff.1, 5.
144. Lambert Wyts, 'Viaje', in García Mercadal, I, 1173.
145. BL Add.28354 ff.63, 80.
146. 'Her face is small and she is not very tall,' reported a Venetian envoy: Gachard, *Carlos V*, p.119.
147. Philip to count of Monteagudo, 16 Nov. 1570, CODOIN, CX, 113.
148. Gachard, *Carlos V*, p.119.
149. Cabrera, II, 122.
150. See J. L. Phelan, *The Hispanization of the Philippines*, Madison 1959, pp.8–10.
151. A contemporary French estimate: Braudel, II, 1037.
152. Gachard, *Carlos V*, p.118. Philip's alleged impassivity on hearing the news is part of the curious mythology fabricated around him.
153. Cabrera, II, 121.
154. Stirling-Maxwell, I, 450.
155. *Memorias de fray Juan de San Gerónimo*, in CODOIN, VII, 82.
156. Stirling-Maxwell, I, 461.
157. Braudel, II, 1128.

158. More to the point, Alençon was of dwarfish height, slightly hunchbacked, and his face was severely marked by smallpox.
159. Cited J. W. Thompson, *The Wars of Religion in France 1559–1576*, New York 1910, p.443 n.2.
160. Ibid., p.447.
161. BL Add.28355 f.22.
162. Despatches of Zúñiga to king in AGS:E/K 1529 ff.20, 21, 29.
163. Philip to Zúñiga, 18 Sept. 1572, ibid. f.53b.
164. Groen van Prinsterer, p.125.
165. A more recent example: the removal of the leaders of the Indonesian Communist party in 1965 gave great satisfaction to the west. Little consideration was given to the fact that some 500,000 other Indonesians died with them.
166. Philip to Zúñiga, 25 Sept. 1572, AGS:E/K 1529 f.65.
167. Philip to Requesens, 19 Sept. 1572, Favre, vol.30 f.21.
168. Philip to Diego de Zúñiga, 26 Sept. 1572, AGS:E/K 1529 f.66.
169. Gómez-Centurión, pp.72–5.
170. AGS:E/K 1529 ff.95–6.

6. *Dropping the Pilot 1572–1580*

1. Madrid, 10 Dec. 1574: BZ 144 f.34.
2. Notes by king in AGS:E leg.2842.
3. Zúñiga to Granvelle, Rome, 17 Oct. 1574, BZ 62 f.101.
4. Zúñiga to Granvelle, Rome, 11 Dec. 1574, ibid. f.112.
5. Cardinal Cervantes to king, 13 Jan. 1575, AGS:E leg.335 f.285.
6. King to duke of Sessa, Guadalupe, 27 Dec. 1576, Favre, vol.28 f.83.
7. 'Lo que se trato en Consejo a 6 de marzo 1577 sobre lo de los Moriscos', AGS:E leg.335 ff.417–19. Six members, including Alba and Ruy Gómez, were present.
8. King to marquis of Ayamonte, Madrid, 16 Jan. 1578, BL Add.28263 ff.172–3.
9. CODOIN, XXXVIII, 179.

10. I do not share Parker's view (*Dutch Revolt*, p.161) that 'at no stage in 1572 and 1573 does Philip II appear to have considered ending the rebellion other than by force of arms'. It was precisely Philip's drift towards a peaceful solution that alarmed Alba in 1572.

11. Ineptly, it seems: Koenigsberger, p.179.

12. St Gouard to Charles IX, 31 May 1572, in Groen van Prinsterer, p.122.

13. Morillon to Granvelle, 11 Aug. 1572, ibid., p.114.

14. Esteban Prats to king, 30 Nov. 1572, CODOIN, LXXV, 125.

15. Gracián to Zayas, 25 July 1573, AGS:E leg.155 f.52.

16. CODOIN, LXXV, 135.

17. Ibid., XXXVI, 119–30.

18. Ibid., LXXXV, 59, 62.

19. Secretary Prats to king, Nov. 1572, ibid., LXXV, 129.

20. Ibid., 163, 173.

21. Granvelle to Juan de Zúñiga, 8 Oct. 1573: BZ 129 f.148.

22. Requesens to Juan de Zúñiga, 29 July 1573, Favre, vol.30 f.327.

23. Zayas to Montano, 17 July 1573, CODOIN, XLI, 292.

24. Gracián to Zayas, 13 Aug. 1573, AGS:E leg.155 f.63.

25. IVDJ, 76, f.461, 'Presidente Juan de Ovando sobre el desempeño'.

26. CODOIN, LXXV, 190, 199, 236.

27. Cited Marañón, I, 156 n.53.

28. J. M. March, *Don Luis de Requeséns en el gobierno de Milán 1571–1573*, Madrid 1943, p.315.

29. Favre, vol.30 ff.30, 48.

30. A copy, dated 20 Oct. 1573, in ibid. ff.71–4.

31. Cabrera, II, 125–6.

32. BL Add.28354 f.457.

33. Boyden, p.2.

34. A.W. Lovett, *Philip II and Mateo Vázquez de Leca: the government of Spain (1572–1592)*, Geneva 1977, p.29.

35. IVDJ, 51 f.166.

36. Cabrera, II, 449.

37. Requesens to Zúñiga, 18 Jan. 1574, IVDJ, 67 no.5.

38. Requesens to Pedro Manuel, 31 Dec. 1574, Favre, vol.30 f.371.

39. Gómez-Centurión, p.115.

40. Pi Corrales, I, 377–437.

41. Ibid., 462–5.

42. AGS:E leg.156 ff.105, 141.

43. Cited in Gómez-Centurión, p.175 n.207.

44. Hopperus to king, 3 Sept. 1575, AGS:E leg.157 f.229.

45. Cf. Gómez-Centurión, pp.225, 237, and articles there cited.

46. Vázquez to king, 31 May 1574, IVDJ, 51 f.31.

47. Cf. Nathan Wachtel, *Los vencidos. Los indios del Perú frente a la conquista española (1530–1570)*. Madrid 1976, p.277.

48. AHN Inq leg.1650 ff.1250, 1266. Cf. Marcel Bataillon, *Estudios sobre Bartolomé de las Casas*, Barcelona 1976, chap.XII.

49. The president of the Council of the Indies, Juan de Ovando, had the Las Casas manuscripts brought to Madrid for study: L. Hanke, *Aristotle and the American Indians*, London 1959, pp.86–7.

50. The seminal study on missionaries and the frontier is by Herbert Bolton, in *Hispanic American Historical Review*, 22 (1917).

51. Brading, pp.146, 154, 268.

52. 'A detailed examination of the provisions indicates how far the king had departed from early policy': Hanke, *Aristotle*, p.87.

53. An autograph account of an interview with the king on 16 Sept. 1588 is given by Acosta in ARSI Epist. Hisp. 143 ff.293–4. On this occasion Acosta raised the question of the difficulties the Jesuits were having with the Inquisition.

54. BZ 143 f.7. The book was published that year. For an excellent survey of Acosta's thinking, see Anthony Pagden, *The Fall of Natural Man*, Cambridge 1982, chap.7.

55. C. R. Boxer, *The Church Militant and*

Iberian Expansion 1440–1770, Baltimore 1978, pp.16–17.

56. Cited Pagden, *The Fall*, p.160.
57. Cf. Góngora, *Studies in the Colonial History of Spanish America*, Cambridge 1975, p.213; Brading, p.122.
58. Tellechea, I, 75.
59. BL Add.28452 f.248. The document is a copy and the text untrustworthy.
60. Favre, vol.2 f.7.
61. Ibid. ff.26, 28, 29, 31.
62. Quiroga to Juan de Zúñiga, 19 June 1574, ibid., vol.19 f.61.
63. Rodríguez and Rodríguez, p.50, from AGS:E/K 1535 f.109.
64. Letters of Granvelle to Juan de Zúñiga, Philip's ambassador to Rome. The letters date from Oct. 1573 to Aug. 1574, BZ 62 ff.148–63.
65. Gachard, *Correspondance*, V, 69.
66. Vázquez to king, 20 May 1574, Madrid, BZ 144 f.11.
67. Montano to Zayas, Nov. 1573, cited B. Rekers, *Benito Arias Montano*, Leiden 1972, p.31.
68. Marañón identifies Quiroga, on no secure basis, as the leader of the Eboli faction in Madrid.
69. See Bataillon, pp.552, 630. Cf. Lagomarsino, pp.304–15.
70. Postscript of 27 Aug. 1575, in letter to duke of Francavilla dated 26 June 1575: AGS:E leg.563 f.69.
71. Furió died in 1592.
72. See e.g. his 'Memorial touchant le redressement des affaires des Pays Bas': AGS:E leg.531 ff.54–5.
73. Granvelle to Juan de Zúñiga, Naples 22 Mar. 1574, BZ 129 f.150.
74. Granvelle commented that even his memoranda were written in bad French. Hopperus was a Frisian, so French was his second language.
75. Gachard, *Correspondance*, III, 14.
76. Requesens to Zúñiga, 16 Mar. 1574, IVDJ, 67 f.11.
77. Parker, *Army of Flanders*, chap.8.
78. Requesens to D. Pedro Manuel, 31 Dec. 1574, Favre, vol.30 f.378.
79. On letter from Vázquez of 19 Dec. 1574, BZ 144 f.38.

80. 'Lo que Su Magd manda que se platique', AGS:E leg.568 f.51.
81. The four were Quiroga, Luis Manrique, Chinchón, and Andrés Ponce de León.
82. Requesens to king, Antwerp, 9 Jan. 1575, AGS:E leg 562 f.4.
83. 'Los puntos que se comunicaron con Hopperus y lo que el respondió', 29 Jan. 1575: ibid. leg.568 f.30.
84. Note by king in 1576, IVDJ, 53 no.88.
85. The marquises of Aguilar and Los Vélez, 21 Apr. 1576, AGS:E leg.568 f.22.
86. Ibid., f.31.
87. 'Para responder al villete de Hopperus de 12 de abril 1576', ibid. f.10.
88. Note by king, Pardo, 23 Sept. 1576, IVDJ, 53, carpeta 5, f.192.
89. BZ 144 f.114, 'avisando de la muerte de Hopperus', 15 Dec. 1576.
90. 24 Aug. 1576, BL Eg.1506 f.39v.
91. Notes by king, 13 May and 4 July 1574, IVDJ, 53 f.87.
92. King to Vázquez, 18 July 1574, ibid. no.77.
93. Ibid., carpeta 3, f.65.
94. Ibid., f.86.
95. Ibid., f.65.
96. Madrid, Feb. 1576, ibid., carpeta 5, ff.24–5.
97. Fortea Pérez, p.122.
98. IVDJ, 53, carpeta 3, ff.92–5.
99. Note by king, 14 Sept. 1574, BZ 144 f.15.
100. San Jerónimo, *Memorias*, CODOIN, VII, 155.
101. Cf. Thompson, *War and Society*, chap. II, 3.
102. 'This year and last year have been years of bad harvest throughout Castile': Pedro de Solchaga to Juan de Zúñiga, Madrid, 2 Nov. 1578, Favre, vol.16 f.98.
103. D. Pedro Tello, corregidor, to Vázquez, July 1577, IVDJ, 21 ff.181, 506.
104. Philip on a letter from Quiroga, 15 Nov. 1578, BL Eg.1506 f.93v.

105. Cf. Kagan, pp.95–8.
106. 'Espejo que se propone', BL Eg. 330 ff.4–20.
107. Pedro de Ribadeneira to Quiroga, 16 Feb. 1580, *Monumenta Historica Societatis Jesu: Ribadeneira*, Madrid 1923, I, 22.
108. Note of 22 Feb. 1576, Madrid, IVDJ, 53, carpeta 5, f.35.
109. Antonio Pérez to Juan de Zúñiga, 14 Mar. 1577, Favre, vol.19 f.98.
110. Cited in Brown, p.26.
111. Note of 15 May 1577, Aranjuez, IVDJ, 53, carpeta 6, f.51.
112. Quiroga to king, and reply, 24 Aug. 1576, BL Eg. 1506 ff.38–9.
113. Note by Philip to Quiroga, ibid. f.42.
114. Requesens to Pedro Manuel, 31 Dec. 1574, Favre, vol.30 f.371.
115. Requesens to Fresneda, 5 Feb. 1576, quoted Gossart, p.21.
116. But see his subsequent reaction, noted in Chapter Nine, p.252.
117. King to Don Juan, El Pardo, 31 Oct. 1576, AGS:E leg.570 f.123.
118. 'I decided that you should go alone with Ottavio': ibid.
119. Escobedo commented that 'His Majesty feels that it would be helpful to negotiate with Orange and make concessions', to Philip, 27 Feb. 1577, CODOIN, L, 319.
120. Undated note to Quiroga, BL Eg.1506 f.207.
121. BNM MS.2751 f.156.
122. Minutes of council, 2. Feb. 1577, AGS:E leg.570 f.1.
123. King to Vázquez, 6 May 1578, IVDJ, 51 f.178.
124. Cabrera, II, 483.
125. Cervantes, *Don Quixote*, I, xxxii.
126. Report to Adam von Dietrichstein, 5 June 1578, Madrid, in MZA: RAD, cited by Friedrich Edelmayer, 'Honor y dinero. Adam de Dietrichstein al servicio de la Casa de Austria', *Studia Historica. Historia Moderna*, 11 (1993), p.113 n.123.
127. Thompson, *War and Society*, chap. IX, 72.

128. P. de Törne, 'Philippe II et Henri de Guise. Le début de leurs relations (1578)', *Revue Historique*, 167 (1931), p.324.
129. 'Derramado': Cabrera, I, 491.
130. On letter of Pérez to king, 23 Apr. 1576, BL Add.28262 ff.128–30.
131. Ibid., ff.179, 202.
132. IVDJ, 59 no.225.
133. On letter of Pérez to king, 8 Feb. 1577, BL Add.28262 f.225.
134. Only four days before Pérez had suggested to Philip that 'one cannot let Quiroga in on everything': letter of 8 Feb., ibid.
135. On letter of Pérez to king, 12 Feb. 1577, ibid. ff.236–7.
136. The brilliant study by Marañón, full of splendid conjectures, is not a wholly reliable guide to the Pérez affair. The shorter study by Muro is better on some aspects. The brief account I give is a crude simplification of a complex and tortuous story.
137. Philip to viceroy of Naples, 24 Jan. 1584 (copy), BCR MS.2174 f.225. The man was Juan del Castillo. Cf. Cabrera, II, 685.
138. IVDJ, 55 no.102, year 1588.
139. CODOIN, XV, 435; Marañón, I, 351.
140. Those who believe the king to be involved can quite properly suggest that he destroyed incriminating papers. The only document apparently implicating the king is that from the Hague, on which Marañón relies fully. If we discount this unverifiable source (it is a copy), no case whatever can be constructed against the king. The note by the king to Rodrigo Vázquez, 4 Jan. 1590, cited by Muro, p.75, in which the king seems to accept responsibility, can be read in different ways. A proper survey of the Pérez–Escobedo affair needs to be done.
141. Note by king, 1 Apr. 1578, IVDJ, 51 f.161.
142. Both references are cited from the Farnese archive, by F. Pérez

Minguez, *Psicología de Felipe II*, Madrid 1925, p.91.

143. Cf. Marañón, I, 364–6.
144. Ibid., II, 909, doc.88.
145. Philip to Vázquez, Madrid, 15 Nov. 1578, BZ 144 f.224.
146. I refer to the major corruption scandals of the Spanish government in the years 1993–5.
147. On the possibility that she was blind in one eye, see Marañón, I, 177–82; Muro, app.158.
148. Cf. Muro, pp.28–35.
149. On this point Marañón (I, 210–12) is convincing.
150. Cited ibid.
151. King to Vázquez, 28 July 1578, BZ 142 f.7.
152. King to Vázquez, 24 Aug. 1578, ibid. f.8.
153. Muro, app.65; Marañón, I, 281–3.
154. Marañón, I, 400.
155. Cited ibid., 403.
156. Cited ibid., 406.
157. Muro, p.119.
158. San Jerónimo, *Memorias*, CODOIN, VII, 268.
159. Muro, pp.119–24.
160. Ibid., App.53.
161. Ibid., p.129.
162. Letters in AE:CP,MD vol.236 ff.142, 193.
163. 'Very great satisfaction', cited in Muro, App.54.
164. King to D. Juan, San Lorenzo, 1 July 1576, Favre, vol.28 f.17.
165. BNM MS.2751 f.144.
166. San Jerónimo, *Memorias*, CODOIN, VII, 229.
167. Cabrera, II, 484.
168. A. Danvila y Burguero, *Felipe II y la Sucesión de Portugal*, Madrid 1956, p.23.
169. For the various claimants, Merriman, IV, 346–7.
170. Philip to Moura, 26 Jan. 1579: CODOIN, VI, 78.
171. Moura to king, 7 Feb. 1579, ibid., 110.
172. Philip to Osuna and Moura, 14 Apr. 1579, ibid., 350.

173. Philip to Moura, 5 June 1579, ibid., 419.
174. Hainault, Artois, Walloon Flanders, Namur, Luxembourg and Limburg.
175. Philip to Moura, 4 June 1579, CODOIN, VI, 416.
176. Philip to Osuna and Moura, 30 June 1579, ibid., 519–20.
177. Philip's letter of summons was dated 12 July 1579: ibid., 555–6.
178. MZA:RAD, G.140, karton 9, sign. 12a: 'Relacion de algunas menudencias . . . de   1579 . . . para   el Illmo Sr el Baron Adan Dietristan'.
179. Pedro de Solchaga to Juan de Zúñiga, 3 Jan. 1580, Favre, vol.16 f.120.
180. King to Juan de Zúñiga, 13 Feb. 1580, Favre, vol.6 f.44.
181. Danvila y Burguero, *La Sucesión*, p.232.
182. Philip to Osuna and Moura, 25 Feb. 1580, CODOIN, VI, 661.
183. There is a good contemporary discussion in HHSA, Spanien, Varia, karton 2, s, f.36.
184. It is consequently not convincing to attribute the arrest, as Marañón (I, 157) does, to the king's 'vengeful attitude'.
185. Feria (D. Lorenzo de Figueroa, second duke of Feria since his father's death in 1572) was eldest son to the English Lady Jane Dormer. His case was a notable scandal. Having pledged himself to the daughter of the duke of Nájera, he then tried to pledge himself 'all at the same time' to three other aristocratic daughters: Favre, vol.19 f.83. The king ordered him to marry one of the latter, but he refused on the grounds that his honour was involved: BZ 144 f.130. The instructions for his house arrest are in BZ 142 f.1.
186. 'Under arrest by Your Majesty's order in the town of Tordesillas', Pedro de Solchaga to Juan de Zúñiga, 12 Dec. 1578, Favre, vol.16

f.110. It was not Don Fadrique's first imprisonment. In 1567 he had been thrown into gaol for a related offence.

187. BNM MS.2751 f.237.
188. BZ 144 f.242. 'I couldn't get away from him,' Mateo Vázquez reported.
189. Vázquez to king, 30 Nov. 1578, El Pardo, BL Add.28263 f.206.
190. Pedro de Solchaga to Juan de Zúñiga, 12 July 1578, Favre, vol.16 f.45.
191. Its members were the cardinal of Toledo, the marquis de Aguilar, D. Antonio de Padilla and D. Juan de Silva.
192. J. Suárez Inclán, *Guerra de anexión en Portugal*, 2 vols. Madrid 1897, I, 96.
193. Alba to king, 9 Sept. 1580, CODOIN, XXXII, 568.
194. Alba to Zayas, 15 Apr. 1580, ibid., 64.
195. HHSA, Spanien, Varia, karton 3, b, f.59.
196. CODOIN, XXXII, 155.
197. St Teresa and the Jesuit Ribadeneira, quoted in Bouza, 'Portugal', p.96.
198. This is the figure for which the food suppliers catered. The actual size of the army varies in the accounts.
199. CODOIN, VII, 295.
200. Jean Baptiste de Tassis to Juan de Zúñiga, Badajoz, 24 June 1580, Favre, vol.21 f.262.
201. Muster of April 1580, CODOIN, XXXII, 27–9. Alba disliked Italian soldiers. 'Italians, for the love of God,' he wrote, 'Your Majesty must not bring any more, it's money wasted; but as for Germans, bring another 5,000': ibid. p.15.
202. King to marquis of Alcañizes, ambassador in Rome, Badajoz, 10 July 1580: Favre, vol.29 f.103.
203. Juan de Cardona to Juan de Zúñiga, Setubal, 2 Aug. 1580, Favre, vol.21 f.314.
204. This and other details of the Portu-

guese campaign can be found in the excellent journal by a German noble officer, the *Tagebuch des Erich Lassota von Steblau*, printed in García Mercadal, I, 1253–92.

205. Alba to king, 28 Aug. 1580, CODOIN, XXXII, 482.
206. King to Alba, Badajoz, 29 Aug. 1580, BL Add.28357 f.356.
207. Favre, vol.21 f.359.
208. President Pazos to Vázquez, 19 Sept. 1580, IVDJ, 21 f.803.
209. J.B. de Tassis to Juan de Zúñiga, 14 Oct. 1580, Favre, vol.21 f.413.
210. Cabrera, II, 616.
211. King to Juan de Zúñiga, 16 Nov. 1580, BL Add.28357 f.359. The codicil to his will is dated 4 Dec. Cf. CODOIN, VII, 348.
212. Venetian ambassador Zane, Alberi, ser. I, vol.5, p.363.
213. Cabrera, IV, 198: 'he had no wish to repeat the state of marriage'.
214. Asistente of Seville, count of Villar, to Vázquez, 3 Aug. 1580, IVDJ, 21 f.85. The main culprits were executed. See also *Actas de las Cortes*, XII, 183.
215. King to Alba, from Tomar, 10 and 30 Apr. 1581: BL Add.28357 ff.421, 426. See the untrue claim in Merriman, IV, 397 that 'after the fighting had finished the king had no more use for him'.
216. Ossorio, p.518.
217. Cabrera, II, 687.
218. There is a splendid discussion of her death in Eire, pp.369–510.
219. Luis Enríquez de Cabrera y Mendoza, duke of Medina de Rioseco.
220. BNM MS.2751 f.227.

7. The World of Philip II

1. To his daughters, Lisbon, Feb. 1582, Bouza, *Cartas*, p.62.
2. A notable exception was the Mendoza family. For a perspective on

the nobles as a whole, Gil Fernández, pp.299–327.

3. Ambassador Khevenhüller, cited Edelmayer, p.47.

4. Cf. Kamen, *Phoenix*, pp.391–3.

5. For all this, details in my forthcoming *Spanish Inquisition* (1998).

6. Jcsé Antonio de Rojas to Granvelle, 12 May 1560, BP MS.II/2291 f.172.

7. González de Amezúa, I, 215.

8. President of Chancery, Tello de Sandoval, to king, 22 Sept. 1561, AGS:E leg.140 f.156.

9. Cf. B. Bennassar, *Valladolid au siècle d'or*, Paris 1967, pp.147–50.

10. Cf. the useful discussion in A. Alvar Ezquerra, *Felipe II, la Corte y Madrid en 1591*, Madrid 1985.

11. Diego de Córdoba to Granvelle, Toledo, 3 Sept. 1560, BP MS.II/2291 f.224.

12. Feria to Granvelle, 7 Sept. 1560, ibid. ff.205–8.

13. Alvar Ezquerra, p.31.

14. Quoted ibid., p.33.

15. Relation of Lambert Wyts, in Garciá Mercadal, I, 1174.

16. A good overview in Wilkinson, pp.149–52.

17. For what follows, Rivera, pp.198–243.

18. Ibid., pp.215–16.

19. Iñiguez Almech, p.203.

20. BZ 146 f.35.

21. Rivera, p.251.

22. Cited Danvila y Collado II, 389.

23. Rivera, p.276.

24. BL Add. 28350 ff.19–26, 32.

25. Checa, pp.63–4.

26. Cited ibid., p.63.

27. AGS:CR leg.247.

28. For what follows, Rivera, pp.123–83.

29. Lhermite calculated that Aranjuez in the 1590s had 222,695 trees: Lhermite, II, 108.

30. Cf. Wilkinson, pp.140–4.

31. 'Memoria de mano de Su Mgd de lo que es servido que se haga en Aranjuez', 11 June 1563, BL Add.28350 ff.52–5.

32. AGS:CR leg.247.

33. Aranjuez, Apr. 1567, in Iñiguez Almech, p.201.

34. Cf. Kubler, p.34.

35. Ibid., p.42.

36. Hoyo to king, 1562, BZ 146 f.11.

37. Cf. Kubler, pp.170–3, on the interesting views of René Taylor that the building was conceived as an expression of Renaissance magic. Taylor's further arguments in 'Las ciencias ocultas en la Biblioteca del Escorial', *IV Centenario del Monasterio: La Biblioteca*, Madrid 1986, are also weak.

38. Kubler, p.70. For the Solomon thesis, the article by A. Martínez Ripoll, in *IV Centenario del Monasterio: La Biblioteca*, pp.53–73.

39. BL Add.28350 f.100.

40. Cf. Checa, pp.231–2, discussing the secretive aspect of the layout.

41. San Jerónimo, *Memorias*, CODOIN, VII, 396.

42. King to Francés de Álava, 28 May 1567, in Rodríguez and Rodríguez, doc.51.

43. Gil Fernández, pp.710–15. Hesiod describes Chaos in his poem *Theogony*.

44. Ambrosio de Morales, *Viaje por orden del rey Phelipe II a los reynos de Leon y Galicia y Asturias*, Madrid 1765, p.207.

45. Sigüenza, II, 500.

46. What follows is drawn mainly from the excellent essay by Goodman, pp.3–19.

47. 19 Aug. 1579, king on letter from Pero Nuñez to Mateo Vázquez, in Muro, App.62.

48. Francisco Rodríguez Marín, *Felipe II y la alquimia*, Madrid 1927, p.21.

49. To Zúñiga, 29 Aug. 1574, BL Add.28357 vol.1 f.41.

50. The horns and other animal bones are listed in the inventory of his goods sold in 1603: Favre vol.37 ff.123–31.

51. Cf. Braudel, II, 762, for other perspectives.

52. Jonathan Brown, 'Felipe II como

mecenas y coleccionista de arte', in R.L. Kagan, ed., *Ciudades españolas del siglo de oro*, Madrid 1986.

53. García Ballester, p.39.
54. Ibid., p.54.
55. Goodman, pp.233–8.
56. See, in general, Checa, pp.134–61.
57. Badoero, in Gachard, *Carlos V*, p.39.
58. Jane C. Nash, *Veiled Images. Titian's mythological paintings for Philip II*, Philadelphia 1985, is interesting, but posits an unacceptable antithesis between Titian's pagan themes and Philip's allegedly ultra-severe religion.
59. Checa, p.137.
60. Lhermite, I, 98.
61. Sigüenza, II, 635–9.
62. J. K. Steppe, in *Splendeurs d'Espagne*, I, 272.
63. Annie Cloulas, 'Les choix esthétiques de Philippe II: Flandre ou Italie', *Actas XXIII Congreso Internacional de Historia del Arte*, 3 vols. Granada 1977, II, 236–41.
64. I have been unable to consult Stephanie Breuer, *Alonso Sánchez Coello*, Munich 1984. However, her introduction to *Alonso Sánchez Coello y el retrato*, is definitive.
65. On El Greco at this period, see Jonathan Brown, 'El Greco y Toledo', in *El Greco de Toledo*, Madrid 1982.
66. Ibid., p.28.
67. Wilkinson, pp.67ff.
68. Ibid., p.138.
69. Report of May 1556, in Iñiguez Almech, p.165.
70. Wilkinson, pp.148, 165.
71. An overview in Lisón Tolosana, pp.131–70.
72. CSPV, VIII, 223.
73. The sketch of the court given by J. H. Elliott, 'The court of the Spanish Habsburgs: a peculiar institution?', in *Politics and Culture in Early Modern Europe*, ed. P. Mack and M. C. Jacob, Cambridge 1987, is relevant only to the court of *one* Habsburg, Philip IV. On Philip II's court there is no satisfactory study.

74. Danvila y Collado, II, 277, 332, 360.
75. Ibid., 290–1.
76. This view, as stated in 1995, is: 'After the court was established at Madrid, Philip II retreated even farther from public view, firmly establishing the reclusive brand of kingship that would characterize his reign', Boyden, p.83.
77. 'So lugubrious a court': the view of Elliott, in Mack and Jacob, *Politics and Culture*.
78. Comment in 1583: IVDJ, 55 no.85.
79. Cf F. Bouza, 'Cortes festejantes, fiesta y ocio', *Manuscrits*, 13 (1995), pp.185–203.
80. Cabrera, III, 230.
81. Marquis of Ladrada to king, Madrid, 21 Feb. 1571, BL Add.28354 f.158.
82. Cf. Pilar Ramos López, 'Dafne, una fábula en la corte de Felipe II', *Anuario Musical*, 50 (1995), pp.23–45.
83. Lhermite, I, 240.
84. HHSA, Spanien, Varia, karton 2, r, ff.6, 10v.
85. Paul Bécquart, 'La musique', in *Splendeurs d'Espagne*, I, 355.
86. Unfortunately, though much has been published on the music of Philip's chapels, little or nothing has been published on the king's own love of music.
87. IVDJ, 38.
88. San Lorenzo, king to council of Castile, Oct. 1587: ibid. 21, caja 31, f.320.
89. E. Cotarelo y Mori, *Bibliografía de las controversias sobre la licitud del teatro*, Madrid 1904, p.619.
90. Paolo Tiepolo, in Alberi, ser.I, vol.5, p.64.
91. Cf. Prescott, III, 362.
92. No significant literary salons are recorded before the reign of Philip III: see José Sánchez, *Academias literarias del siglo de oro español*, Madrid 1961, p.26.
93. Cf. Danvila y Burguero, pp.97–8, who gives a good list of cultured nobles.

94. Ambassador Badoero, in Alberi, ser.I, vol.5, p.277.
95. Cabrera, III, 205.
96. Barajas to king, 16 Nov. 1586, IDVJ, 21 f.312. Then aged thirty, Feria was the most eligible grandee in Spain.
97. In 1581: BZ 142 f.63.
98. This is explained in the 'Avisos de la Corte', in HHSA, Spanien, Varia, karton 2, p, f.30.
99. Ambassador Soranzo, 1565, Alberi, ser.I, vol.5, p.113.
100. HHSA, Spanien, Varia, karton 3, c, f.21.
101. For two examples, see BL Add.28262 f.290, in 1579; and BZ 141 f.59, in Lisbon in 1581.
102. IVDJ, 53, carpeta 7, f.56.
103. Cited in J. Zarco Cuevas, *Ideales y normas de gobierno de Felipe II*, Escorial 1927, p.48. The source for the statement is spurious; but it reflects other statements by the king.
104. Mal Lara, p.13v.
105. Order to the corregidor of Toledo, 25 Nov. 1573: BL Eg. 2047 f.321v.
106. They were informed by the Catalan cleric Miquel Giginta, who had co-incided with the Frenchman on a journey from Madrid to Barcelona: Giginta to Mateo Vázquez, 11 Jan. 1583, IVDJ, 21 ff.148–57.
107. Cited in Zarco Cuevas, *Ideales*, p.47.
108. HHSA, Spanien, Varia, karton 2, n.
109. Ibid., karton 2, s, f.35.
110. Ibid.
111. Kubler, p.109, states incorrectly that the king slept for the first time in San Lorenzo in 1571. He is also mistaken in stating (p.126) that the king did not stay at San Lorenzo between 1571 and 1575.
112. BL Add.28354 f.392.
113. In 1585, for instance: MZA:RAD, K 9/24, 'Relacion . . . para . . . Dietristan', Feb. 1585.
114. Sigüenza, II, 434.
115. San Jerónimo, *Memorias*, CODOIN, VII, 126–8.
116. Sigüenza, II, 436.
117. King to chamberlain, 10 July 1572: BL Add.28354 f.422. The queen's chamberlain at this date was Antonio de la Cueva, marquis of Ladrada.
118. BL Add.28354 f.414.
119. This was in 1577: see Gachard, *Carlos V*, p.130.
120. King to Vázquez, San Lorenzo, 13 July 1577, IVDJ, 53, carpeta 6, f.39.
121. BL Add.28354 f.370.
122. Khevenhüller (BNM MS.2751 f.734) gives an enthusiastic description of the ceremony at his reception into the order in 1593.
123. King to marquis of Ladrada, 2 Oct. 1572, BL Add.28354 f.490.
124. Cabrera, II, 6.
125. Danvila y Burguero, p.206.
126. Parker, *Philip II*, p.82, says firmly that 'Philip II was simply not interested in women'. The evidence presented in this book demonstrates quite the contrary.
127. The image of a great love was diffused by González de Amezúa's splendid but highly misleading book on Elizabeth.
128. González de Amezúa, II, i, 59.
129. The prince of Ascoli, aged only twenty-three, died in October that year, 1564.
130. HHSA, Spanien, Varia, karton 2, n, f.3.
131. Douais, I, p.68.
132. Cited in González de Amezúa, I, p.388.
133. Douais, I, 45, Fourquevaux's despatch of 17 Jan. 1566.
134. Ibid., 51.
135. Ibid., 106.
136. Ibid., 115.
137. Checa, p.165.
138. IVDJ, 50, report of 1566.
139. Danvila y Burguero, p.102.
140. Checa, pp.167–8; González de Amezúa, III, 414–27.
141. 'Las causas que ay para que la Reyna deva tanta cantidad en fin del año de 1565', AGS:E leg.146 f.35.

142. King to Ladrada, 25 Oct. 1570, BL Add.28354 ff.51–2.
143. King to Ladrada, 23 Dec. 1570, 5 Apr. 1571, and 15 Dec. 1571, ibid. ff.113, 176, 306.
144. King to Ladrada, 9 Mar. 1572, ibid. f.362.
145. His handwriting in 1571, for perhaps the first time since 1559, becomes neater and perfectly legible. Curiously, Anna has been totally ignored by historians.
146. Ambassador Badoero, in Alberi, ser.I, vol.5, p.276.
147. Cabrera, IV, 393.
148. BL Add.28354 ff.230, 240, 294.
149. Gachard, *Carlos V*, p.120.
150. King to Vázquez, 1575, IVDJ, 53, carpeta 7, f.67.
151. Cf. R. J. W. Evans, *Rudolf II and His World*, Oxford 1973, p.50.
152. Barghahn, I, 93.
153. Mayer-Löwenschwerdt, p.40.
154. BL Add.28357 f.359.
155. Philip to sister Maria, 13 Dec. 1576, in Cabrera, IV, 69.
156. Ibid., II, 382.
157. Zayas to Francés de Álava, 16 May 1569, in Rodríguez and Rodríguez, doc.173.
158. Cabrera, II, 198.
159. M. T. Oliveros and E. Subiza Martín, *Felipe II. Estudio médico-histórico*. Madrid 1956, pp.107–18.
160. CODOIN, XXXVII, 310.
161. To Vázquez, 25 Aug. 1578, BZ 144 f.255.
162. BL Add.28354 ff.460, 476, 492.
163. AGS:CR leg.78 no.38; leg.33 f.6.
164. Alberi, ser.I, vol.5, p.60.
165. Mal Lara, p.76.
166. 'Pochissimi fruti', said ambassador Morosini, 1581, in Alberi, ser.I, vol.5, p.322.
167. Marañón, I, 50, quotes Pérez: 'Philip II could not smell and did not distinguish smells'.
168. San Lorenzo, 26 May 1578, BZ 144 f.315.
169. Note of Sept. 1590, El Pardo, BZ 140 f.270.
170. BL Add.28354 ff.480, 490, 506, 542.

171. To Ruy Gómez, in Weiss, V, 491.
172. King on letter from Vázquez, 29 Oct. 1577, IVDJ, 51 f.175.
173. BL Add.28354 ff.394, 408, letters of May and June 1572.
174. King to Zúñiga, 2 Apr. 1576, BL Add.28357 f.111.
175. 'Pelo biondo che incomincia a imbiancare': Badoero, in Alberi, ser.I, vol.5, p.275.
176. Badoero, ibid., p.276.
177. CODOIN, VII, 213.
178. Ibid., 215.

8. The Statesman

1. Instruction by king to viceroy of Naples, Brussels, Jan. 1559, BL Add.28701 f.49v.
2. Manuel Rivero Rodríguez, 'Poder y clientelas en la fundación del Consejo de Italia (1556–1560)', *Cheiron*, 9, nos 17–18, 1992 [1993], pp.37–40. Rivero shows clearly that the new council was derived from that of Castile and not, as many historians had believed, from the council of Aragon.
3. Ibid., pp.41–4.
4. 'Relacion de lo que escriven algunos corregidores cerca de las causas y remedio de la carestia', BZ 149 f.38.
5. Marañón, I, 38. Marañon's discussion of this matter is seriously misleading. His view of a 'capture' of the king by Pérez (I, 51) is mistaken.
6. See the earlier correspondence in BL. Add.28262.
7. BL Add.28355 ff.3, 6.
8. Lippomano to Senate, 13 Feb. 1588, CSPV, VIII, 339.
9. Cabrera, II, 307.
10. Ibid., 452.
11. 'Estilo que guardó el Rey en el despacho de los negozios desde que comenzó a valerse del secretario Matheo Vazquez, hasta que murió': a copy, in BL Eg.329 ff.8–11.

12. Zayas to Vázquez, Madrid, 1 Mar. 1586, BZ 135 f.116.
13. Paris, pp.49, 562.
14. Cf. also Parker, *Philip II*, pp.36, 44.
15. A 1581 report, by Morosini, is largely copied from earlier ones. It states that 'dorme molto . . . la mattina si leva dal letto assai tardi . . . dopo desinare ritorna a dormir': Alberi, ser.I, vol.5, p.322.
16. Badoero, ibid., p.276.
17. Venetian ambassador Tiepolo, 1567, ibid. p.153.
18. BL Add.28701 ff.106–9.
19. Note to Vázquez, 28 May 1590, BL Add.28263 f.522.
20. Cabrera, II, 528; Ossorio, p.466.
21. BL Add.28355 ff.5, 57, 62.
22. Ambassador Tiepolo, in Gachard, *Carlos V*, p.114. Cf. Soranzo in 1565: 'non entra il re nei consigli': Alberi, ser.I, vol.5, p.115.
23. Weiss, IX, 568.
24. 'Espejo que se propone a nuestro gran monarcha para que en el vea el estado infeliz de su monarchia', BL Eg.330 f.8, 10.
25. King to Vázquez, 21 Feb. 1576, BL Add.28263 f.14.
26. 25 Oct. 1573, IVDJ, 51 f.21.
27. Madrid, 6 May 1578, ibid. f.178.
28. 18 Aug. 1575, IVDJ, 21 f.53.
29. Note from Aranjuez, 30 Apr. 1586, BL Eg.28263 f.403.
30. 12 Oct. 1576: ibid. f.58.
31. King to council, 30 July 1586, BL Add.28358 f.386.
32. Cabrera, II, 126.
33. Madrid, 1 Aug. 1575, IVDJ, 51 f.52.
34. BL Add.28355 f.49v.
35. On letter from Vázquez, 26 July 1573, IVDJ, 51 f.19.
36. BL Add.28262 f.207.
37. 22 Jan. 1578, ibid. f.290.
38. BL Add.28263 f.191.
39. 11 Apr. 1578, IVDJ, 51 f.162.
40. San Lorenzo, 25 June 1577, BZ 141 f.11.
41. Note by king, 1 Feb. 1575, IVDJ, 53, carpeta 4.
42. Lhermite, I, 94.
43. 21 Apr. 1575, IVDJ, 51 f.49.
44. Ambassador Zane, in Alberi, ser.I, vol.5, p.363.
45. Cabrera, II, 451.
46. 9 Mar. 1576, San Lorenzo, IVDJ, 53, carpeta 5, f.51.
47. 18 Mar. 1576, El Pardo, ibid., f.63.
48. 26 Sept. 1575, El Pardo, BZ 144 f.72.
49. King to Vázquez, 25 Oct. 1573, IVDJ, 51 f.21.
50. Letter of 28 Dec. 1574, BZ 144 f.39.
51. Note by king, 22 June 1592, Tordesillas, BZ 131 f.41.
52. Jan. 1575, San Lorenzo, BZ 144 f.49.
53. King to Vázquez, 18 Apr. 1575, Aranjuez, IVDJ, 53 carpeta 4 f.59.
54. The best survey of Philip's decision-making is Schepper, pp.173–98.
55. Paris, p.64.
56. Douais, I, 172.
57. Gachard, *Carlos V*, p.115.
58. Cf. H. Koenigsberger, 'The statecraft of Philip II' (an interesting but now superseded essay) in *Politicians and Virtuosi*, London 1986, p.81: 'Philip thought he could make all decisions for himself'. The claim is palpably untrue.
59. Gachard, *Carlos V*, p.114.
60. For Rumpf see F. Edelmayer, 'Freiherr Wolf von Rumpf zum Wielroß und Spanien', in *Die Fürstenberger. 800 Jahre Herrschaft und Kultur in Mitteleuropa*, Korneuburg 1994.
61. CSPV, VI, i, p.31; ibid., ii, p.1061.
62. There were very few exceptions. Virtually none could speak English, Dutch or German. The second duke of Feria, who was half English, was a clear exception. A few with German contacts, like Juan de Borja, chamberlain to the empress Maria, spoke German fluently. Some, like Alba and Don Juan Manrique, spoke a bit of French. Several, thanks to their service in Italy and the similarity of the tongues, spoke Italian well. Contrast the proficiency in Spanish among the English elite: Ungerer, I, 71.

63. Cf. Gil Fernández, p.35.
64. Edelmayer, p.44. Borja's family was Catalan in language; he himself was a gifted linguist, and learned both German and Czech in Vienna.
65. Tassis spoke six languages perfectly: Joseph Rübsam, *Johann Baptista von Taxis, 1530–1610*, Freiburg 1889, p.32.
66. CSPV, VI, ii, p.1061.
67. Ibid., X, p.156.
68. Lhermite, I, 275.
69. Gachard, *Carlos V*, p.39.
70. In 1582: Bouza, *Cartas*, p.75.
71. IVDJ, 53, carpeta 6, f.1. The problem with French was not necessarily the language. Sixteenth-century French script was (as modern researchers can testify) often difficult to decipher.
72. Gachard, *Correspondance*, I, xlix.
73. BL Add.28355 f.58. This was in May 1573.
74. Cf. Gil Fernández, pp.82, 215.
75. BNM MS.2751 f.102. This interesting document is a copy of the memoirs of Khevenhüller, written in the early 1600s.
76. BNM MS.11240.
77. Lhermite, II, 173.
78. The splendid Motley, in his classic *Rise of the Dutch Republic*, pp.75–6, refers to Philip as 'deficient in manly energy, pedant, bigot, cold, mediocre, grossly licentious'.
79. This is the (undocumented) image given in Marañon, I, 44–7, and followed thereafter by most historians.
80. Pérez de Herrera, in Cabrera, IV, 359.
81. Gachard, *Carlos V*, p.112.
82. MZA:RAD, G.140, karton 9, sign. 12a.
83. Gachard, *Carlos V*, p.121.
84. Ibid., p.37.
85. BNM MS.6150 f.115.
86. In March 1581, BZ 142 f.21.
87. Cf. Marañón, I, 48–9.
88. Cf. C. Lisón Tolosana, p.85: 'his expression glacial, always dressed in black ... walking slowly and solemnly'.
89. Previously attributed to Sánchez Coello.
90. Mal Lara, p.47.
91. BNM MS.2751 f.467.
92. On letter of Vázquez, 10 Dec. 1574, BZ 144 f.34.
93. Cf. Koenigsberger 'The statecraft', p.81: Philip's 'suspicion became pathological', a curious claim and totally undocumented.
94. Pérez de Herrera, in Cabrera IV, 359.
95. Pérez de Herrera, ibid., 360.
96. Pérez de Herrera, ibid., 359.
97. Instruction to viceroy of Naples, 1559, BL Add.28701 f.52.
98. Note by Vázquez, 1 Nov. 1580, IVDJ, 37 f.12.
99. Cited in Rosario Villari, *Elogio della dissimulazione*, Bari 1987, p.19.
100. The critic was Juan Costa, in a book of 1578: cited Gil Fernández, p.308. The fashion was still current much later.
101. Gachard, *Carlos V*, p.112.
102. Ibid., p.39.
103. I use the term 'bull-run' deliberately. The 'run' or *corrida*, still commonly practised throughout Spain, was then the standard form of the sport. The modern bullfight was a later evolution.
104. ARSI, Epist. Hisp. 98 f.339.
105. Danvila y Collado, II, 310.
106. Serrano, II, pp.247, 299, 366; IV, p.lix.
107. Archbishop of Rossano, BNM MS.8246 f.97, the reference is to the feast-day of San Juan, 1566.
108. HHSA, Spanien, Varia, karton 2, p, f.18v.
109. Jean Vilar, 'Segovia, 1570', in *Homenaje a José Antonio Maravall*, 3 vols. Madrid 1985, III, 463.
110. San Jerónimo, *Memorias*, CODOIN, VII, 170.
111. This is a crude attempt to summarise a complex question. Cf. Maravall, I, 261–4; and I. A. A. Thompson, *Crown and Cortes. Gov-*

112. The Cortes of Madrigal in 1476: cited Maravall, I, 260.
113. Ibid., 327.
114. Instructions to viceroy of Naples, dated Brussels, Jan. 1559, in BL Add.28701 f.49v. Cf. the views of Koenigsberger on this source: Koenigsberger, pp.172–5.
115. Cf. Jean Barbey, *Être roi. Le roi et son gouvernement en France de Clovis à Louis XVI*, Paris 1992, p.150.
116. Luis Sánchez Agesta, 'El "poderío real absoluto" en el testamento de 1554', in *Carlos V (1500–1558)*, pp.439–60. Cf. also Maravall's views on absolutism: Maravall, I, 279–84.
117. Maravall, I, 253.
118. The word 'majesty' can be found in use in both Castile and Catalonia (see ibid., 255–6), but seldom as an official title.
119. Felipe de la Torre, *Institucion de un rey Christiano*, Antwerp 1556. Torre's book is concerned with education, not power.
120. Cited Marañón, I, 348.
121. Though the execution was secret, the *fact* was made public immediately: 'Relacion . . . para . . . Dietristan', MZA:RAD, K 9/24. The account of his last moments, in BL Eg.357 f.96.
122. Cortés was imprisoned for a while, then banished from court for sixteen years and fined 150,000 ducats: IVDJ, 59 no.48.
123. Cabrera, III, 504.
124. See the important and fundamental study by Teofilo Ruiz on 'Unsacred monarchy. The kings of Castile in the late Middle Ages', reprinted in his *The City and the Realm: Burgos and Castile 1080–1492*, Aldershot 1992, chap.XIII.
125. Spain is notably absent from the essays edited by János Bak, *Coronations. Mediaeval and Early Modern monarchic ritual*, Berkeley 1990.

111. *ernment, Institutions and Representation in Early Modern Castile*, Aldershot 1993, chap.V, 71–3.

126. Here I differ radically from Barghahn, I, 99, 109.
127. Alberi, ser.I, vol.5, p.324. For a sensible comment on the phrase, see Bratli, p.237.
128. Cf. Baltasar Porreño, *Dichos y hechos del rey D. Felipe II*, Madrid 1942 edn, p.286.
129. Cited Muro, App. 12.
130. Braudel, II, 936–7.
131. King to count of Luna, 4 July 1562, CODOIN, XCVIII, 344.
132. See above, Chapter 3, p.64.
133. Braudel, II, 675.
134. King to count of Luna, 28 Jan. 1562, CODOIN, XCVIII, 287.
135. BL Add.28361 ff.10, 11, 24.
136. Barajas, Chinchón and Juan de Idiáquez.
137. Thomas Platter, cited in Thompson, 'Absolutism in Castile', in *Crown and Cortes*, V, 71.
138. BZ 144 f.130.
139. Papers of 7 Sept. 1581: BZ 129 f.61.
140. Cited Gachard, *Don Carlos*, p.93.
141. Kamen, *Phoenix*, p.204.
142. Castillo de Bobadilla, I, 561, 584–6.
143. Cabrera, II, 231.
144. Cf. Helen Nader, *Liberty in Absolute Spain. The Habsburg sale of towns 1516–1700*, Baltimore 1990.
145. Ambassador Soranzo, 1565, Alberi, ser.I, vol.5, p.112.
146. March, *Don Luis de Requeséns*, p.189.
147. To Diego de Ibarra, 18 Nov. 1590, cited in J. Zarco Cuevas, *Ideales y normas de gobierno de Felipe II*, Escorial 1927, p.9.
148. 'L'a dict souvent', Elizabeth Valois stated in 1566: Douais, I, 68.
149. To Maximilian, Guadalupe, 5 Feb. 1570, CODOIN, CIII, 432.
150. See Chapter 9, p.252.
151. E.g. at Pentecost 1575 he confessed to fray Alonso de Sevilla: San Jerónimo, *Memorias*, CODOIN, VII, 127.
152. Fresneda was also appointed bishop of Cuenca in 1562, then of Córdoba in 1571, and finally arch-

bishop of Saragossa in 1577. He died before he could occupy the last of these posts.

153. On letter from Vázquez, 8 Aug. 1583, BZ 142 f.13.

154. The best brief survey of Philip's relations with the papacy is Martin Philippson, 'Felipe II y el pontificado', in Maurenbrecher. It appeared originally in *Historische Zeitschrift*, 1878.

155. Cited Danvila y Collado, II, 271.

156. Cabrera, II, 685.

157. Ibid., 356.

158. Judgment was eventually issued by the papacy in 1572, and Carranza died in Rome in 1576.

159. For Murcia and Mallorca, see Serrano, III, cviii–cxii.

160. Philip to Requesens, Jan. 1569, cited ibid., cii.

161. Philip to Zúñiga, 27 Oct. 1569, in Serrano, IV, xii.

162. Kamen, *Phoenix*, p.258.

163. Cf. Goodman, pp.261–2.

164. Cf Kamen, *Phoenix*, p.404.

165. Koenigsberger, p.58, saw this as a 'grave weakness'. But the relative absence of imperial theory can also be regarded as a reason why the monarchy managed to survive for three centuries, longer than any other empire in history. The British empire, likewise, had no theory until very late in its career.

166. See my comment below in Chapter 9, note 74.

167. Anthony Pagden, *Lords of All the World. Ideologies of empire in Spain, Britain and France c.1500 to c.1800*, New Haven and London, 1995, pp.57–9.

168. G. Parker, 'Maps and ministers: the Spanish Habsburgs', in David Buisseret, ed., *Monarchs, Ministers and Maps*, Chicago 1993. I am grateful to Professor Jeremy Black for this reference.

169. Letters of 1 Feb. 1566 and 11 Mar. 1575, BCR MS.2174 ff.43, 133.

170. Goodman, p.65.

171. Ambrosio de Morales, *Las antigue-* *dades de las ciudades de España*, Alcalá 1575, p.4.

172. Cited by Parker, n.168 above.

173. Splendidly edited by Richard L. Kagan, *Spanish Cities of the Golden Age. The views of Anton van den Wyngaerde*, Berkeley 1989. In the same years Joris Hoefnagel also prepared a series of sketches of Spanish towns for a work he published in 1572.

174. Goodman, pp.68–71, gives a useful brief summary. See also H. Cline, 'The *Relaciones Geográficas* of the Spanish Indies', *Hispanic American Historical Review*, 44 (1964).

175. AGS:E leg.157 ff.102, 104. From this document it is clear that there were no more returns, despite the speculation of Parker (above, n.168) that there were more.

176. Angel de la Plaza, *Archivo General de Simancas. Guía del Investigador*, Valladolid 1962, pp.xxxi–l.

177. 15 Nov. 1581, BZ 142 f.19.

178. Philip to emperor, 9 June 1552, AGS:E leg.92 f.116.

179. Rodríguez and Rodríguez, p.43.

180. Report by Mateo Vázquez on discussions in councils of State and War, Nov. 1589: BZ 143 f.231.

181. The study by De Lamar Jensen, *Diplomacy and Dogmatism*, Cambridge, Mass. 1964, is limited to Mendoza's part in the French civil wars. No other ambassador of Philip has ever been studied. Among ministers, only Granvelle has received full treatment.

182. Report on Tassis contained in 'Copia del papel que el duque de Feria dio sobre las cosas de Flandes', 1596, AGS:E leg.343 f.110.

183. Letter of 15 Dec. 1568, BCR MS. 2174 f.71.

184. As in Naples and Sicily: See Koenigsberger, p.50.

185. AGS:SP leg.984, documents of 11 Nov. 1589.

186. Braudel, I, 374.

187. CODOIN, XXXVII, 228.

188. Gachard, *Correspondance*, I, 199.

189. Granvelle to Morillon, 11 May, 1573, in Charles Piot, *Correspondance du Cardinal de Granvelle*, Vol. IV (Brussels 1884), p.558.
190. Braudel, II, 677.
191. BL Add.28399 ff.7–9.
192. Cited (1565) by González Palencia, I, 259.
193. King to Diego de Ibarra, 25 Feb. 1593, Gachard, *Correspondance*, II, lxxv.
194. Charles Gibson, *The Black Legend. Anti-Spanish attitudes in the Old World and the New*, New York 1971.

9. War in the West 1580–1586

1. San Lorenzo, 27 June 1577: BZ 144 f.158.
2. For example, 'rey de España' in a document of 1574: BL Add.28357 f.85.
3. Order of 18 Sept. 1581, ibid. f.511.
4. Bouza, 'Portugal', p.325.
5. Juan Rufo in his *Austriada* (1584).
6. Pedro Salazar de Mendoza, *Monarquia de España*, written in the 1590s.
7. See e.g. C. R. Boxer, *The Church Militant and Iberian Expansion 1440–1770*, Baltimore 1978.
8. Braudel, II, 1184.
9. Thompson, *War and Government*, p.33.
10. Unsigned memoir, printed in CODOIN, VI, 452.
11. See Barghahn, I, 90–100; Wilkinson, pp.77–9.
12. Destroyed in the 1755 earthquake.
13. I take the phrase from Wilkinson, p.77.
14. Barghahn, by contrast, argues that 'Philip's interest in formulating an imperial vocabulary that would argue the providential rule of the Habsburgs is expressed clearly in the building and decoration of the Torreão': Barghahn, I, 99.
15. Fray Lorenzo de Villavicencio to Philip, Favre, vol.29 f.260.
16. They were returned from Santiago to Braga: ibid. f.132.

17. All in 1582: Favre, vol.33, part 1 ff.10, 137, 155.
18. Favre, vol.33, part 2 f.302, an order of Feb 1582.
19. Venetian ambassador Zane, Madrid, 16 Apr. 1582, CSPV, VIII, 33.
20. Merriman, IV, 381.
21. Claudio Acquaviva to Juan de Zúñiga, 16 Oct. 1582, Favre, vol.23 f.170. The Indian was a priest of the old Malabar rite, studying with the Jesuits in Lisbon.
22. P. T. Rooney, 'Habsburg fiscal policies in Portugal 1580–1640', *Journal of European Economic History*, vol.23, no.3 (winter 1994), p.546.
23. They were restored in 1593, when Philip needed more money.
24. Cited by F. Bouza Alvarez, 'Portugal en la política flamenca de Felipe II', *Hispania*, 181 (1992), p.696.
25. 'I am writing before anything else', June 1581, Bouza, *Cartas*, p.45.
26. 26 June 1581, Bouza, *Cartas*, p.46.
27. Gassol to Zúñiga, 23 July 1582, Favre, vol.23 f.107.
28. Lisbon, 21 Aug. 1581, Bouza, *Cartas*, p.51.
29. Bouza, *Cartas*, p.82.
30. Ibid., p.73.
31. Cf. Van Durme, p.348.
32. The Jesuit Ribadeneira, cited Bouza, 'Portugal', p.101.
33. President Antonio Mauriño de Pazos to Vázquez, Madrid, 9 June 1580, IVDJ, 21 f.782.
34. President to Vázquez, Madrid, 10 Mar. 1582, ibid. f.875.
35. Van Durme, pp.353, 357.
36. Ambassador Zane, in Alberi, ser.I, vol.5, p.358.
37. Bouza, *Cartas*, p.68.
38. 'When he got the news [the prince's death] he decided his departure': Cabrera, II, 686.
39. Lisbon, 25 Oct. 1582, Bouza, *Cartas*, p.78.
40. San Jerónimo, *Memorias*, CODOIN, VII, 364.
41. But not in the sense portrayed in Parker, *Philip II*, p.79, where the

42. Pérez de Herrera, in Cabrera, IV, 353.
43. BNM MS.2751 f.434.
44. San Jerónimo, *Memorias*, CODOIN, VII, 366.
45. On Cambiaso, Checa, p.326; on the painting, San Jerónimo, *Memorias*, CODOIN, VII, 370.
46. San Jerónimo, *Memorias*, CODOIN, VII, 369.
47. HHSA, Spanien, Varia, karton 3, c, ff.12–13.
48. In the Prado; formerly attributed to Sánchez Coello.
49. HHSA, Spanien, Varia, karton 3, c, f.26.
50. Details from Sepúlveda, p.29.
51. San Jerónimo, *Memorias*, CODOIN, VII, 385, 394.
52. San Lorenzo, 24 Sept. 1584: BL Add.28263 f.339.
53. HHSA, Spanien, Varia, karton 3, c, f.37a.
54. Alvar Ezquerra, p.120.
55. Bouza, *Cartas*, p.30, n.25.
56. HHSA, Spanien, Varia, karton 3, c, f.21, Aug. 1583.
57. President to Vázquez, Madrid, 25 July 1580, IVDJ, 21 f.787.
58. 26 Jan. 1581, Elvas, IVDJ, 51 f.187.
59. 17 July 1584, BZ 141 f.90.
60. Memoir by Philip, 3 Feb. 1584, BZ 142 f.67.
61. King to Vázquez, 19 Feb. 1584, BZ 141 f.82.
62. To Esteban de Ibarra, 13 Aug. 1589, BCR MS.2417 f.37.
63. To Vázquez, Madrid, 26 Oct. 1578, IVDJ, 51 f.183.
64. Vázquez to king, 22 Aug. 1583, ibid. f.105.
65. Comments of king on letter of Vázquez to king, 22 Aug. 1583, ibid.
66. Aguilon to Zayas, 6 Nov. 1572, Teulet, V, 109.
67. Philip to Don Juan, Nov. 1576, AGS:E leg.570 f.88.

68. Philip to Alba, Badajoz, 31 Aug. 1580, CODOIN, XXXII, 507.
69. Testimony of Khevenhüller: BNM MS.2751 f.478.
70. King to Mendoza, Setubal, 23 Apr. 1582, Teulet, V, 239.
71. Strada, I, 290.
72. Mousset, p.27, despatch of 29 Feb. 1584. Cf. Van Durme, p.363.
73. E.g. by Braudel, who felt that religious zeal in the 1580s 'turned the Spanish king into the champion of Catholicism': Braudel, II, 677.
74. The claim that 'a unique aura of "messianic imperialism" came to pervade the court' (G. Parker, 'Philip II and his world', in R. L. Kagan and G. Parker, *Spain, Europe and the Atlantic World*, Cambridge 1995, p.259) is made without supporting evidence, and must be seen as baseless.
75. 'Un événement européen', Gossart, p.110.
76. Terranova to Juan de Zúñiga, 10 Apr. 1579, Favre, vol.20 f.75.
77. Cf. Yates, pp.94–6.
78. Parker, *Dutch Revolt*, p.204.
79. This doctrine is still subscribed to by twentieth-century governments.
80. Cf. Roland Mousnier, *The Assassination of Henry IV*, London 1973, pp.86–105.
81. Cabrera, I, 524.
82. Philip said of the Guise proposal, 'It wouldn't be bad if they did it by themselves', but he did not wish to be involved. Marginal note on letter of Tassis to king, Paris, 24 June 1583, Teulet, V, 281. Apart from these cases involving affairs of state, Philip avoided implication in assassination. My discussion of the Escobedo case suggests that the king was not involved in that murder.
83. Cf. Gossart, p.132.
84. Ibid., p.122.
85. Granvelle to Margaret, 20 Sept.; and Venetian envoy to Senate, 21 Sept. 1585 in CSPV, VIII, 121.
86. Ibid., 120.

king and his sisters are shown as solitaries, when in fact they were always socially active, and very close to each other.

87. The treaty of Joinville, signed Dec. 1584, created the Catholic League. A similar league had existed in 1576.
88. Mousset, p.108.
89. MZA:RAD, G 140, karton 9, sign. 12a, 'Relacion . . . hasta los nuebe de febrero de 1585 años para . . . Dietristan'.
90. Ibid.
91. Cock, p.16.
92. This private ceremony was the true marriage; the ceremony next day was merely a blessing. For the distinction between the two, cf. Kamen, *Phoenix*, chap.6.
93. The best accounts of these days in Saragossa are Cock; HHSA; and the 'Relacion de lo que ha pasado . . . para Dietristan mi señor' in MZA: RAD, G. 140, karton 9, sign. 12a.
94. Cock, p.60.
95. Longlée, 13 Apr. 1585, Saragossa, in Mousset, p.130.
96. Cock, p.128.
97. Cited A. Durán i Sanpere, *Barcelona i la seva història*, Barcelona 1972, p.437 n.27.
98. 'Relacion . . . de esta corte para mi señor el baron Adam de Dietrichstan', MZA:RAD, G. 140, karton 9, sign. 12a.
99. June–July 1585, in Bouza, *Cartas*, pp.92–5.
100. Martha Pollak, *Turin 1564–1680: urban design, military culture and the creation of the absolutist capital*, Chicago 1991.
101. Comendador Cristóbal Briceño to Madrid, 1586, Favre, vol.23 ff.435, 438.
102. Longlée, 14 Oct. 1585, in Mousset, p.183.
103. Bouza, *Cartas*, p.103.
104. Cock, p.226.
105. Bouza, *Cartas*, p.106.
106. Longlée to Henry III, 31 Jan. 1586, in Mousset, p.217.
107. Details cited in *Hispania* (Madrid), 2 (1942), pp.286–97. The bottles of wine are listed as 'pounds' (by weight) of wine.
108. Cock, p.253.
109. Longlée to Catherine de' Medici, 8 Feb. 1586, in Mousset, p.226.
110. Longlée to Henry III, 6 Mar. 1586, ibid., p.237.
111. Longlée to Henry III, 8 Feb. 1586, ibid., p.223.
112. Ambassador Zane, 8 Mar. 1586, CSPV, VIII, 145.
113. Bouza, *Cartas*, p.107.
114. Alberi, ser. I, vol.5, p.357.
115. Bouza, *Cartas*, pp.107, 109.
116. King to duke, 25 Apr. 1586, in Altadonna.
117. Cabrera, III, 113.
118. Cf. the opinions of cardinal Tavera in 1535, cited Chabod, '¿Milán', p.343.
119. The phrase is of 1585. From the 1560s the king had shown an interest in limiting the size of the city: BCR MS.2174 ff.4, 11, 29, 143, 258, 315.
120. Exceeded, perhaps, only by Mexico City.
121. Rosario Villari, *La rivolta antispagnola, a Napoli: le origini 1585–1647*, Bari 1973, p.56.
122. Ambassador Zane, 10 Jan. 1585, CSPV, VIII, 129.
123. Ambassador Zane, 8 Mar. 1586, ibid., 145.
124. My account of the 1585 embargo is based on the brilliant piece by Simon Adams, 'The outbreak of the Elizabethan naval war against the Spanish empire: the embargo of May 1585', in M. J. Rodríguez-Salgado and S. Adams, *England, Spain and the Gran Armada 1585–1604*, Edinburgh 1991.
125. Gómez-Centurión, p.197.
126. Adams, 'The outbreak', p.60.
127. CSPV, VIII, 128.
128. Quoted by Gómez-Centurión p.246.
129. Thompson, *War and Society*, chap.IX, 73.
130. Ibid., 71.
131. CSPV, VIII, 150.
132. Longlée to Henry III, 3 and 13 Apr., 4 May 1586, in Mousset, pp.246–52.

133. Kamen, *Phoenix*, p.80.
134. Ambassador Zane, 23 Apr. 1586, CSPV, VIII, 157, 161.
135. Van Durme, pp.364, 366.
136. Ibid., p.372.
137. Cabrera, II, 201.
138. Ambassador Zane, 22 Mar. 1586, CSPV, VIII, 147.
139. Notes on a paper of the Junta, 20 Apr. 1586, IVDJ, 51, f.189.
140. Longlée, 29 June 1586, in Mousset, p.275.
141. Bouza, *Cartas*, p.111.
142. Mousset, p.272.
143. Cabrera, III, 228.
144. Cf. Checa, pp.408, 417.
145. Cabrera, II, 198: 'delighting in what he had awaited so long'.
146. Sigüenza, II, 467.
147. 'In order not to suffer anguish', says a monk, he did not come: Sepúlveda, p.30. 'He did not wish to be present at the translation': CODOIN, VII, 410.
148. Ambassador Lippomano, 20 Aug. 1586, CSPV, VIII, 198.
149. Philip to king of Denmark, 28 July 1586, ibid.
150. 'Estilo que guardó el rey', BL Eg. 329 f.9.
151. Ambassador Lippomano, 12 Jan. 1587, CSPV, VIII, 236.
152. Longlée, 19 June 1586, in Mousset, p.272.

10. The Time of Thunder
1587–1593

1. On letter from Rodrigo Vázquez, 14 June 1588, BZ 146 f.219.
2. San Jerónimo, CODOIN, VII, 419.
3. Lhermite, I, 81–3.
4. Bouza, *Cartas*, p.118.
5. Ibid., p.119.
6. Aranjuez, king to duke, 27 May 1587, in Altadonna.
7. San Jerónimo, CODOIN, VII, 417.
8. Boston Museum of Fine Arts, reproduced in Wilkinson, p.167.
9. Lhermite, I, 94.
10. Teulet, V, 386.
11. Ibid., 413.
12. Ibid., 436.
13. Sepúlveda, p.40.
14. Cabrera, III, 249.
15. Ambassador Lippomano, 21 May 1587, CSPV, VIII, 277.
16. Ambassador Lippomano, 18 Sept. 1586, ibid. 205.
17. Madrid, king to duke, 12 Mar. 1588, in Altadonna.
18. Martin and Parker, pp.110–11.
19. Council resolution of 20 Jan. 1588, AGS:E leg.2855.
20. Thompson, *War and Society*, chap.V, 197–216.
21. Martin and Parker, p.116.
22. Longlée to Henry III, 14 Apr. 1588, Mousset, p.364.
23. Martin and Parker, pp.156–60.
24. Quoted ibid., p.210.
25. Zayas to Vázquez, 'I gave the flowers to His Majesty and they are on his table', BL Add.28363 f.184.
26. Madrid, 4 Jan. 1588, BZ 143 f.4.
27. BL Add.28363 f.188.
28. On a report from Vázquez, 8 Mar. 1588, BZ 143 f.41.
29. Bouza, *Cartas*, p.122.
30. To Vázquez, 16 Mar. 1588, BZ 143 f.46.
31. Vázquez to king, Madrid, 22 Mar. 1588, ibid. f.51.
32. San Lorenzo, 14 June 1588, ibid. f.88.
33. Vázquez to Zayas, 21 June 1588, BL Add.28363 f.234.
34. San Lorenzo, 25 May 1588, BL Add.28263 f.469.
35. San Jerónimo, CODOIN, VII, 429.
36. BL Add.28363 f.235.
37. Mendoza's despatch in CSPV, VIII, 380; Philip's comment in BL Add.28263 f.481.
38. Bouza, *Cartas*, p.125.
39. BZ 142 f.171.
40. King to Rodrigo Vázquez, 14 June 1588, BZ 144 f.219.
41. Favre, vol.31 ff.169, 293.
42. I have followed the version given by Strada, V, 1190, as being the most likely. But neither this nor any

other version of Philip's response is verifiable.

43. Strada, V, 1191.
44. Gachard, *Correspondance*, II, lxxvi.
45. On a letter from Vázquez to king, 4 Sept. 1588, IVDJ, 51 f.190.
46. Gachard, *Correspondance*, II, lxxvii.
47. Lippomano to Senate, 6 Sept. 1588, CSPV, VIII, 386.
48. Sepúlveda, p.59.
49. The manuscript paper was dated March 1588 but may really have been written after August: Miguel Avilés, *Sueños ficticios y lucha ideológica en el siglo de oro*. Madrid 1981, pp.214, 217.
50. Cited Thompson, *War and Society*, chap.VIII, 17.
51. Merriman's view, echoing many other historians: Merriman, IV, 552.
52. BZ 143 f.140.
53. CSPV, VIII, 407.
54. On a letter from Vázquez to king, 13 Nov. 1588, IVDJ, 51 f.145.
55. Longlée to Henry III, 15 Oct. 1588, in Mousset, p.389.
56. D. Juan de Silva to Estevan de Ibarra, 10 July 1589, BCR MS.2417 f.27.
57. CSPV, VIII, 477.
58. Vázquez to king, 5 Aug. 1589, BL Add.28263 f.510.
59. Silva to Esteban de Ibarra, Coimbra, 10 July and 13 June 1589, BCR MS.2417 f.27, 13.
60. Plan by Hernando de Toledo and Cristóbal de Moura, 6 May. 1589, AGS:E leg.2855.
61. Gómez-Centurión, p.255. But the defeat also stimulated some naval activity.
62. In 1595: ibid., pp.282–95, 301.
63. Esteban de Ibarra, a Basque, was at the time quartermaster-general of the Navy and went on to become secretary of the council of Finance.
64. To Ibarra, 22 June 1589, BCR MS.2417 f.19.
65. To Ibarra, 13 Aug 1589, ibid. f.37. These letters are original.
66. Lippomano to Senate, 4 Feb. 1589, CSPV, VIII, 427.

67. Letter of 11 Apr. 1589, BL Add.28263 f.501.
68. Lippomano to Senate, 15 Jan. 1589, CSPV, VIII, 424.
69. The famous writings of the Jesuits Mariana and Suárez, in which they defended tyrannicide, were published only after Philip's death.
70. AGS:E leg.2855.
71. AGS:E/K 1569 f.23.
72. G. Baguenault de Puchesse, 'La politique de Philippe II dans les affaires de France 1559–1598', *Revue des Questions Historiques*, 25 (1879).
73. Note of 18 Feb. 1589, BZ 143 f.199.
74. Note of June 1589, IVDJ, 51 f.150.
75. Memoir by Vázquez, 15 Nov. 1589, BZ 143 f.231; with comments thereon by the king.
76. On letter of Vázquez, 17 Nov. 1589, ibid. f.232.
77. Comment of Oct. 1589, AGS:E/K 1569 f.143.
78. Silva to Esteban de Ibarra, 11 Sept. 1589, BCR MS.2417 f.43.
79. The splendid study by Alain Milhou, *Colón y su mentalidad mesiánica*, Valladolid 1983, touches on several relevant issues. For the period of Philip II, pp.245–8.
80. When Philip sailed from the Netherlands in 1559, the departure was delayed in part because of a forecast of mishap by Nostradamus.
81. Note by king, 4 Aug. 1584, BL Add.28263 f.334.
82. There is a good, brief essay by R. Kagan, 'Politics, prophecy and the Inquisition', in M. E. Perry and A. J. Cruz, *Cultural Encounters*, Berkeley 1991, chap.6.
83. Cabrera, II, 568.
84. Chapter 6 above, p.158.
85. Kagan, p.96.
86. Favre, vol.21 ff.333, 421.
87. In a full council of twelve, six voted against arresting him: Favre, vol.142 f.167.
88. Cf. Sepúlveda, pp.82–3.
89. Juan Horozco Covarrubias, *Tratado*

de la verdadera y falsa prophecia, Madrid 1588, p.42.

90. Kagan, p.127.

91. 'Sueños desde fin de Março de 1588 hasta 18 de abril 1590', AHN Inq leg.3712² exped. 2, pieza 4, ff.25, 27, 33, 38.

92. Vázquez to king, 8 and 24 Feb. 1591, IVDJ, 51/1, 7.

93. Comments on letters of Vázquez to king, 8 and 24 Feb. 1591, IVDJ 51/1, 7.

94. Castillo de Bobadilla, I, p.415.

95. Sebastià García Martínez, *Bandolers, corsaris i moriscos*, Valencia 1980, p.121.

96. Pedro de Solchaga to Juan de Zúñiga, 23 Feb. 1589, Favre, vol.16 f.136.

97. 'Relacion de lo que passa en el negocio del Marques de Mondéjar', 10 July 1586; also plea by marquis, 2 July 1588; both in BZ 135 ff.135, 137. King's order of arrest, 26 Jan. 1586, BL Add.28358 f.350.

98. Ambassador Lippomano, 7 Mar. 1587, CSPV, VIII, 254.

99. The examples that follow are taken from IVDJ, 62 ff.43, 45, 57, 72.

100. Cabrera, III, 446; Sepúlveda, p.115; IVDJ, 62 nos 168, 173, 178. The duke, Don Antonio, married Mencia de Mendoza, daughter of the duke of Infantado, instead of complying with an agreement to marry the daughter of the duke of Alcalá.

101. IVDJ, 38 no.6 ff.13–22. The unauthorised marriage of Alba was referred to Rome, which eventually decided in favour of the duke.

102. Cabrera, III, 474. Barajas claimed he was sacked because of rivalry with the king over a woman.

103. Francavilla and Pastrana were, respectively, father and son of La Eboli. I am not convinced by the suggestion of Kagan, p.130, of a link between Piedrola and Pérez.

104. Antonio Pérez, *Relaciones*, Paris 1598, p.25.

105. Cited Marañón, I, 431.

106. 'It is he who backs them [Pérez and his wife] and has always done': MZA:RAD, G.140, karton 9, sign. 12a, 'Relacion ... para ... Dietristan'. Quiroga owed his nomination as archbishop of Toledo to Pérez's influence with the king.

107. Lhermite, I, 113.

108. King to Almenara, 1590, IVDJ, 62 no.167.

109. Cabrera, III, 554.

110. On a letter of the Junta, 5 June 1591, BZ 186 f.3.

111. Sepúlveda, p.117, says that Philip did not go to San Lorenzo that spring, because of his illness. The count of Luna says that he did.

112. Gurrea y Aragón, p.87.

113. On a letter of the Junta, 5 July 1591, BZ 186 f.9.

114. Gurrea y Aragón, p.86.

115. King to Junta, San Lorenzo, 7 July 1591, BZ 186 f.12.

116. In 1599, significantly, the council of Aragon was instructed 'to see that the Inquisition does not meddle in things that are not its concern, since one can see the harm it caused in Saragossa over Antonio Pérez': cited Kamen, *Phoenix*, p.261.

117. On letter from Junta, 14 July 1591, BZ 186 f.15.

118. On letter of 30 July 1591, ibid. f.20.

119. On letter from Junta, 29 Aug. 1591, ibid. f.21.

120. The names of the dead are given in CODOIN, XII, 418–20.

121. On letter from Junta, 16 Oct. 1591, BZ 186 f.25.

122. 'His Majesty was in such a hurry arranging matters for the entrance of the army, that nothing else was done': Gurrea y Aragón, p.180.

123. 'The whole army was put together from what the nobles, grandees and prelates traditionally offer the king when there is war in Spain': ibid., p.181.

124. AGS:E leg.168 f.11.

125. Gurrea y Aragón, p.227.

126. Cited by Marañón, II, 605.

127. Cf. Danvila y Collado, II, 479.
128. Memoranda of Oct. 1591 by the vice-chancellor of Aragon and two colleagues: BZ 186 ff.66, 72.
129. Opinion of 16 Dec. 1591, ibid. f.85.
130. Cabrera, III, 588.
131. Ibid., 589.
132. This version of his death, given by the count of Luna (Gurrea y Aragón, pp.251–3), who was present in the city and knew all those participating in the execution, must be accepted over the highly dramatic version offered by most historians.
133. Junta, 7 Feb. 1592, BZ 186 f.44.
134. Gurrea y Aragón, p.253.
135. The count of Luna, Villahermosa's brother, reported that 'I made a full and thorough enquiry, and was unable to find any secure basis for the opinion held about this matter': ibid., p.298. Luna also reports that the duke's family learned of his death before they learned of his illness. This must be compared with the fact that in Bayonne an agent of Lord Burghley knew of Villahermosa's illness before he knew of the death: CSP, Foreign, Elizabeth I, vol.III, p.419. Luna was probably guilty of dramatic exaggeration. As in the cases of Montigny and the justiciar, Philip never acted without judicial support. In the case of the two Aragonese nobles, no such support existed, and it is highly unlikely that Philip would have taken any extra-judicial action.
136. Gurrea y Aragón, p.315.
137. The decision was reached at Christmas 1595 but not formally issued until the following Easter: ibid., p.339. The king appealed against the verdict, apparently because he wished to retain control of the county of Ribagorza. In the end he gave up the appeal, in exchange for a formal cession to him of the county.
138. Aranda was subsequently declared innocent on the order of Philip III.
139. Marquis of Llombay to king, 10 Dec. 1591, BZ 186 f.37.
140. Response to junta, 14 Oct. 1591, ibid. f.24.
141. 'My close friend,' wrote Henry Cock, *Jornada de Tarazona hecha por Felipe II en 1592*, ed. A. Morel-Fatio. Madrid 1879, p.27.
142. King to viceroy of Navarre, Burgos, 18 Sept. 1592, AGS:E leg.169 f.25.
143. Lhermite, I, 192.
144. Cock, *Jornada de Tarazona*, p.74.
145. '*Sicut fulgur et acies*,' reports Luna, who was present: Gurrea y Aragón, p.339.
146. This important point has been elucidated by Xavier Gil Pujol, 'Las Cortes de Aragón en la edad moderna', *Revista de las Cortes Generales*, 22 (1991), p.111.
147. Danvila y Collado, II, 353.
148. Cabrera, III, 607.
149. Gurrea y Aragón, p.320.
150. The erroneous phrase is still used in older English textbooks.
151. X. Gil Pujol, introduction to Lupercio Leonardo de Argensola, *Información*, Saragossa 1991 edn, p.xlv.
152. Paper of 1589, BZ 146 f.225.
153. Herrera, III, 402.
154. A dozen were hanged, according to Sepúlveda, p.120.
155. 7 July 1591, BZ 186 f.12.
156. A. Merino Alvarez, *La sociedad abulense durante el siglo XVI*, Madrid 1926, pp.98–102.
157. *Actas de las Cortes*, XVI, 568.
158. Duke of Gandía to Juan de Idiáquez, Nov. 1591, in Gurrea y Aragón, p.178.
159. Herrera, III, 291.
160. Sepúlveda, p.129.
161. *Actas de las Cortes*, XVI, 169–73.
162. Ibid., 305.
163. Danvila y Collado, II, 359–60.
164. J. Lockhart and E. Otte, *Letters and People of the Spanish Indies*, Cambridge 1976, p.136.
165. Papers of Feb. 1588, BL Add.28361 f.160.

166. From San Lorenzo, 8 Oct. 1590, BL Add.28263 f.550.
167. On the crisis, James Casey, 'Spain: a failed transition', in Peter Clark,ed., *The European Crisis of the 1590s*, London 1985, chap.11.
168. Linda Martz, *Poverty and Welfare in Habsburg Spain*, Cambridge 1983, chap.2.
169. See Cristóbal Pérez de Herrera, *Amparo de pobres*. Madrid 1975 (Clásicos castellanos, no.199), pp. xxxiv–xlvi.
170. IVDJ, 55 no.3, letter of fray Pablo de Mendoza.
171. Cited in Bouza, 'Portugal', pp.813–14.
172. CSPV, IX, 226.
173. T. Davies and P. Burke in Clark, *The European Crisis of the 1590s*, chaps 9 and 10.
174. Lorenzo Vander Hammen, *Don Filipe el Prudente*, Madrid 1632, p.111.
175. Cited M. Góngora, *Studies in the Colonial History of Spanish America*, Cambridge 1975, p.76.
176. 'Lo que pareció sobre los quatro papeles que dio a Su Magd el presidente Richardot', Aranjuez, 11 Nov. 1589, AGS:E leg.2855. See the rather different interpretation of Philip's attitude to this document, in Parker, *Dutch Revolt*, pp.222–3.
177. Philip to count of Olivares, El Pardo, 12 Nov. 1590, AGS:E leg.2220/1.
178. On letter from Mendoza, 17 Aug. 1589, AGS:E/K 1569 f.95.
179. Philip to duchess of Savoy, El Pardo, 6 Mar. 1590, BL Add.28419 f.4.
180. 'Lo que vos Juan Bapt de Tassis', issued 1 May. 1590, AGS:E leg.2220/1 f.24. There is a further instruction at f.27.
181. Note of Jan. 1591, Escorial, BZ 141 f.203.
182. Braudel, II, 1215.
183. Gachard, *Correspondance*, II, lxxxv.
184. Ibid., xc, instructions to Esteban de Ibarra, 28 Sept. 1592.
185. Lorenzo Suárez de Figueroa, second duke of Feria, son of Lady Jane Dormer.
186. Cf. the mistaken presentation of Philip as imperialist, repeated by most historians and also by Lynch, p.466: 'Philip was blind to rational argument ... [he committed himself to] a policy of imperialism in France'. The diplomatic documents demonstrate quite the reverse.
187. 'Relacion del estado en que se hallan las cosas de Francia', Paris, 14 Jan. 1594, AGS:E/K 1590 no.10.
188. Feria to king, Laon, 28 Mar. 1594, ibid. no.50.
189. Braudel, II, 1212.
190. AGS:E leg.171, report of 15 Apr. 1594.
191. Silva to Esteban de Ibarra, Madrid, 12 July 1590, BCR 2417 f.74.
192. Arias Montano to king, 25 Nov. 1594, AGS:E leg.171.
193. Alberi, ser. I, vol.5, p.421.
194. Library of the Escorial.

11.   Last Years 1593–1598

1. Madrid, 4 Feb. 1578, BZ 144 f.426.
2. Sepúlveda, p.145.
3. 5 Feb. 1589, Madrid, IVDJ, 37 f.151.
4. Cabrera, IV, 62.
5. Lhermite, I, 233.
6. Cabrera, IV, 63.
7. BL Eg.329 f.10, 'Estilo que guardó el Rey'.
8. Cabrera, IV, 63–8.
9. I have consulted the useful edition by Manuel Fernández Alvarez, *Testamento de Felipe II*, Madrid 1982.
10. Gachard, *Carlos V*, p.157, report of Venetian envoy Contarini.
11. On a report of 4 Apr. 1594, AGS:E leg.2855.
12. Venetian ambassador Contarini, 1593, Alberi, ser. I, vol.5, pp.419–20.
13. See e.g. BL Add.28379, a volume of minutes of Moura from 1594 to 1598.
14. AGS:E leg.2855.

15. Cf. Thompson, *War and Government*, pp.275–7.

16. Bouza, *Cartas*, p.215.

17. CSPV, IX, pp.160, 161.

18. *Consulta* by Poza, 1 Aug. 1595, BL Add.28377 ff.72–3.

19. *Consulta* by Poza, 15 Oct. 1595, ibid. f.158.

20. Report by Poza, 14 Sept. 1595, ibid. f.45.

21. *Consulta* by Poza, 10 Aug. 1595, ibid. ff.81–3.

22. *Consulta* by Poza, 19 Oct. 1595, ibid. f.168.

23. *Consulta* by Poza, 21 Sept. 1595, ibid. f.122.

24. Fernández Alvarez, *Testamento*, p.xxxii.

25. 'Sobre lo con q se a de ocupar el Principe, año de 1595': BL Eg.2052 ff.10v–11.

26. Report by marquis de Velada, tutor of prince, 1590, Favre, vol.37 f.62.

27. AGS:E/K vol.1585 f.80.

28. Ambassador Contarini, 1593, Alberi, ser. I, vol.5, p.425.

29. Ambassador Vendramin, 1595, in Gachard, *Carlos V*, p.161.

30. Cabrera, IV, 200–1.

31. Moura to Poza, 24 Feb. 1596, BL Add.28377 f.233.

32. Lhermite, I, 257ff.

33. BL Add. 28377 f.239.

34. CSPV, IX, 191.

35. Sigüenza, II, 505.

36. An English listing gives 128 vessels, 24 of them Dutch; the duke of Medina Sidonia, who counted them from the opposite shore, estimated 164. See Peter Pierson, *Commander of the Armada. The Seventh Duke of Medina Sidonia*, New Haven and London 1989, pp.193–213.

37. AGS:E leg.177, report of 30 June.

38. Luis Fajardo to Martín de Idiáquez, 17 July 1596, ibid.

39. CSPV, IX, 201. Drake died on 7 Feb. 1596, and was buried at sea.

40. Report by Dr Francisco de Quesada, 'Relacion de lo que sucedió en la perdida de Cadiz, año de 1596', AGS:E leg.177. Cf. Ungerer, I, 310–16, and sources cited there.

41. General Juan Gómez de Medina, 12 July 1596, AGS:E leg.177.

42. CSPV, IX, 223.

43. BCR MS.2417 ff.276–9.

44. Letter of 13 July 1596, AGS:E leg.177.

45. Memorial, ibid.

46. King's letter and Persons' memorandum in AGS:E leg.176.

47. Instructions to Sancta Gadea, 21 Oct. 1596, ibid. These instructions contradict the assumption, common in all English books, that the Armada intended to invade Ireland.

48. Padilla to king, 2 Nov. 1596, AGS Guerra leg.461 f.64.

49. 'Relacion de los galeones que van en la Armada de D. Martin de Padilla', HHSA, Spanien, Varia, karton 3, f, f.276.

50. Instructions, dated 1 Oct. 1597, AGS:E leg.178.

51. 'Relacion de lo sucedido al Armada', AGS Guerra leg.490 f.81.

52. Padilla to king, 28 Oct. 1597, AGS:E leg.180.

53. V. Pérez Moreda, *Las crisis de mortalidad en la España interior*, Madrid 1980, pp.254, 256.

54. 'Great shortage of bread', a chronicler cited ibid., p.269. For a summary view in English, see I.A.A. Thompson and B. Yun, eds, *The Castilian Crisis of the Seventeenth Century*, Cambridge 1994, chap.2.

55. Licenciado Maldonado to Council, Huete, 6 June 1596, AGS:CJH leg.357.

56. *Los comunes labradores y gente pobre destos reynos*, BNM MS. V.E.C–207–35.

57. Castillo de Bobadilla, II, 38.

58. Memorial by marquis of Poza, 10 Feb. 1596, BL Add.28377 f.42.

59. Cited in Fortea Pérez, p.132.

60. Cited Braudel, II, 1219.

61. Letter of Aug. 1597, cited

Thompson, *War and Society*, chap.III, p.284 n.116.

62. Yves-Marie Bercé, *Le Roi caché. Mythes politiques populaires dans l'Europe moderne*, Paris 1990, pp.40–72; Mary E. Brooks, *A King for Portugal: the Madrigal conspiracy*, Madison 1964.

63. Shlomo Simonsohn, *The Jews in the Duchy of Milan*. 2 vols. Jerusalem 1982, I, xxxix–xlix.

64. Letter of appointment, 28 Feb. 1589, BL Add.28263 f.491.

65. Cabrera, II, 239–41.

66. BZ 130 f.94.

67. Kamen, 'A crisis of conscience', in *Crisis and Change*.

68. Serrano, IV, p.lvi.

69. Fernández Alvarez, *Testamento*, pp.69–97.

70. Memoir by king, 22 June 1592, Tordesillas, BZ 131 f.41; Cabrera, III, 600.

71. Original drafts of some of the king's letters, hitherto unknown to historians, can be found in BL Add.28419. Because of the gout in his hand the king normally dictated the drafts, but then if possible corrected them in his own script.

72. Bouza, *Cartas*, p.132.

73. BL Add.28419 ff.8, 17. Cf. Bouza, *Cartas*, pp.138, 146.

74. BL Add.28419 f.23.

75. Bouza, *Cartas*, p.157.

76. BL Add.28419, Catalina to Philip II, Nov.–Dec. 1592, ff.37–8.

77. BL Add.28419, 22 Dec. 1596, f.241.

78. Madrid, king to duke, 12 Jan. 1596, in Altadonna.

79. BL Add.28419 ff.302–8.

80. Duke to Philip II, autograph, 22 Jan. 1598, ibid. f.310.

81. Cabrera, IV, 268.

82. Reported by Sepúlveda, p.182.

83. Pomponne de Bellièvre, quoted in Braudel, II, 1222.

84. CSPV, IX, 332.

85. Sigüenza, II, 505.

86. Ambassador Nani, CSPV, IX, 283.

87. Lhermite, II, 113.

88. Sigüenza, II, 504.

89. Moura to Khevenhüller, July 1598, HHSA, Spanien, Varia, karton 3, e, f.157.

90. Description, taken from doctors' reports, by his confessor fray Diego de Yepes, in Cabrera, IV, 298.

91. Diego de Yepes, ibid., 301. A recent full account of the king's death is in Eire, pp.253–368.

92. Diego de Yepes, in Cabrera, IV, 304.

93. Diego de Yepes, ibid., 305.

94. Antolín, p.400.

95. Soranzo to Senate, 31 Aug. 1598, CSPV, IX, 338.

96. Soranzo to Senate, 5 Sept. 1598, ibid., 341. Soranzo dates the extreme unction to 3 September but Diego de Yepes says clearly that it was on Tuesday, 1 September at 9 p.m.

97. Diego de Yepes, in Cabrera, IV, 317.

98. Diego de Yepes, ibid., 322.

99. Sigüenza, II, 518.

100. Soranzo to Senate, 13 Sept. 1598, CSPV, IX, 342–3.

12. *Epilogue*

1. Lhermite, II, 147.

2. For an analysis, Eire, pp.300–68.

3. Juan de Silva to marquis of Velada, 26 Sept. 1598, BNM MS.6198 f.75.

4. 27 Sept. 1598, CSPV, IX, 346.

5. Kamen, *Phoenix*, p.15.

6. Iñigo Ibáñez de Santa Cruz, 'El ignorante y confuso gobierno', BL Cott. Vespasian C.XIII, ff.375–87. Another version in BL Eg.329 f.16 onwards.

7. 'Discurso al Rey nuestro Señor del estado que tienen sus reynos', dated 'en la carcel y Otubre 7 de 1598': BNM MS.904 ff.284–5. The text has recently been published (Madrid 1990).

8. Ibid., f.285v.

9. The variety of ideas shared by proponents of Tacitus is difficult to summarise.

10. Marcos de Isaba, *Cuerpo enfermo de la milicia española*, Madrid 1594, cited in Ricardo del Arco y Garay, *La idea de imperio en la política y la literatura españolas*, Madrid 1944, p.326.

11. Ibánez de Santa Cruz, 'Confuso gobierno', f.386.

12. Cited by Luciano Pereña in his edition of Francisco Suárez, *De iuramento fidelitatis*, Madrid 1979, p.78

13. Ibid., p.140.

14. Ambassador Lippomano, 6 May 1587, CSPV, VIII, 272, 277.

15. Ibid., 345.

16. Count of Portoalegre to Esteban de Ibarra, 9 Dec. 1589: BCR MS.2417 f.60.

17. March 1601, in CODOIN, XLIII, 570.

18. Silva to Moura, Lisbon, 27 Sept. 1597, BNM MS.6198.

19. Thompson, *War and Government*, chap.V.

20. P. Williams, 'Philip III and the restoration of Spanish government', *English Historical Review*, 88 (1973).

21. In San Jerónimo, Madrid, 15 Oct. 1578, IVDJ 51 no.180.

22. Braudel, II, 1244.

A Note on Sources

The sources for the reign of Philip II add up to thousands of books, articles and documents, dealing with a vast range of subjects. My study could not have been created without drawing on the valuable research done by many other scholars. But it is simply impractical to list the large number of sources, original and secondary, used in writing it. The few references I give are as follows.

The notes, which mainly identify quotations, contain references to manuscript and other sources. The notes also cite, in full, a very limited number of studies. Other studies, which are frequently cited and so given in the notes only in abbreviated form, are listed in the 'Frequent References' appendix, below.

Dates are given as they were in Spain, before and after the calendar change of 1582. Where sources give conflicting dates, I have chosen the most likely. Proper names are given in the form I have considered most suitable.

What follows is (1) a short list of 'Further Reading in English' and (2) a 'Frequent References' appendix, which is in no way a bibliography of Philip II.

Further Reading in English

(Where not detailed, authors mentioned here feature in 'Frequent References'.) Though some popular 'biographies' of Philip II exist, they are derivative and contribute nothing new. The interested reader will profit most from the vivid (and unfavourable) portraits of the king by Motley, and Marañón (abridged English version, 1954). Motley is enjoyable as an extreme statement of the anti-Philip legend. His obvious bias barely detracts from the solid value of his scholarly and passionate account. Marañon's is a brilliant study, but both his premisses and his conclusions are defective and need to be re-examined. A very good brief introduction is Parker (1978), though it repeats a number of common errors about the king. For a student, the most useful political survey is the balanced account by Peter Pierson, *Philip II of Spain* (London 1975), which also has a bibliography valid up to that date. John Rule and John J. TePaske edited an interesting collection of opinions about *The Character of Philip II* (Boston 1963). For background on Philip's Spain the standard textbooks are: Henry Kamen, *Spain 1469–1714. A society of conflict* (London 1991), and Lynch. Those wishing to read history on a grand scale will find a semblance of the king emerging from the pages of Braudel (in English, 1972). The longer political histories, especially Merriman, and the regrettably unfinished work by Prescott, are very informative on the reign but give only secondary importance to the person of the king.

The two English-language historians who in recent decades have done most to illuminate the context within which Philip worked are I. A. A. Thompson and Geoffrey Parker. Thompson's research on politics, the army and the Armada has revolutionised our vision of the reign. Parker's work on Spain and the Dutch has been a model of scholarship. The Armada is also the theme of two different approaches by Martin and Parker, and by Fernández-Armesto (*The Spanish Armada: the experience of war in 1588*, Oxford 1989). The architectural programme is considered in a splendid study by Wilkinson; and a buzz of scandal is discussed in the fascinating study on Lucrecia de León by Kagan, who has done authoritative work on the culture of the reign. The king's death, finally, is one of the themes in the revealing book by Eire.

Frequent References

Actas de las Cortes de Castilla, vols XII–XVI. Madrid 1887–89

Alba, duke of, *Epistolario del III duque de Alba*. 3 vols. Madrid 1952

Alberi, Eugenio, *Relazioni degli ambasciatori veneti al Senato*. Florence 1839–40

Altadonna, Giovanna, 'Cartas de Felipe II a Carlos Manuel II, duque de Saboya', *Cuadernos de Investigación Histórica*, 9, 1986

Alvar Ezquerra, Alfredo, *El nacimiento de una capital europea. Madrid entre 1561 y 1606*. Madrid 1989

Alvarez, Vicente, *Relation du beau voyage que fit aux Pays-Bas en 1548 le prince Philippe d'Espagne*, ed. M.-T. Dovillée. Brussels 1964

Antolín, Guillermo, 'La libreria de Felipe II', *Boletín de la Real Academia de la Historia*, 90, 1927

Barghahn, Barbara von, *Age of Gold, Age of Iron. Renaissance Spain and symbols of monarchy*. 2 vols. New York 1985

Bataillon, Marcel, *Erasmo y España*. Mexico 1966

Bouza Alvarez, Fernando, 'Portugal en la monarquía hispanica (1580–1640)'. Thesis of the Complutensian University 1987

Bouza Alvarez, Fernando, ed., *Cartas de Felipe II a sus hijas*. Madrid 1988

Boyden, James M., *The Courtier and the King. Ruy Gómez de Silva, Philip II and the Court of Spain*. Berkeley 1995

Brading, David, *The First America*. Cambridge 1991

Bratli, Carl, *Felipe II, rey de España*. Madrid 1927 (in Danish 1912)

Braudel, Fernand, *The Mediterranean and the Mediterranean World in the Age of Philip II.* 2 vols. London 1972

Breuer, Stephanie, *Alonso Sánchez Coello y el retrato en la corte de Felipe II.* Madrid 1990

Brown, Jonathan, 'Felipe II, coleccionista de pintura y escultura', *IV Centenario del Monasterio del Escorial. Las Colecciones del rey.* Madrid 1986

Cabié, Edmond, *Ambassade en Espagne de Jean Ebrard, seigneur de Saint-Sulpice, de 1562 à 1565.* Albi 1903

Cabrera de Córdoba, Luis, *Filipe Segundo, rey de España.* 4 vols. Madrid 1876

Calendar of State Papers (London): *Foreign. Edward VI 1547–1553*, 1861. *Foreign. Mary 1553–1558*, 1861. *Foreign. Elizabeth 1558–1559*, 1863. *Foreign. Elizabeth I, vol.II, July 1590–May 1591*, 1969. *Foreign. Elizabeth I, vol.III, June 1591–April 1592*, 1980. *Venice, vol.VII, 1558–1580*, 1890. *Venice, vol.IX, 1592–1603*, 1897. *England and Spain, vol.IX, 1547–1549*, 1912. *England and Spain, vol.X, 1550–1552*, 1914. *England and Spain, vol.XI, 1553*, 1916. *England and Spain, vol.XII, January–July 1554*, 1949. *England and Spain, vol.XIII, July 1554–November 1558*, 1954

Calvete de Estrella, Juan Cristóbal, *El Felicissimo Viaje del muy alto y muy poderoso Principe Don Phelippe.* Antwerp 1552

Calvete de Estrella, Juan Cristóbal, *Rebelión de Pizarro en el Perú y vida de D. Pedro Gasca.* 2 vols. Madrid 1889

Carlos V (1500–1558). Homenaje de la Universidad de Granada. Granada 1958

Carrasco, M.S., *El problema morisco en Aragón al comienzo del reinado de Felipe II.* Valencia 1969

Castillo de Bobadilla, Jerónimo, *Política para Corregidores*, 2 vols. Madrid 1597

Chabod, Federico, '¿Milán o los Países Bajos? Las discusiones en España sobre la "alternativa" de 1544', in *Carlos V*, pp.331–72

Checa, Fernando, *Felipe II, maecenas de las artes.* Madrid 1993

Cock, Henrique, *Relación del viaje hecho por Felipe II en 1585*, ed. A. Morel-Fatio and A. Rodríguez Villa. Madrid 1876

Cortes de los antiguos reinos de León y de Castilla, vol.V. Madrid 1903

Danvila y Burguero, Alfonso, *Don Cristóbal de Moura, primer marqués de Castel Rodrigo.* Madrid 1900

Danvila y Collado, Manuel, *El poder civil en España*, 6 vols. Madrid 1885

Douais, C., ed., *Dépêches de M. de Fourquevaux, ambassadeur du roi Charles IX en Espagne 1565–72*, 3 vols. Paris 1896–1904

Edelmayer, Friedrich, 'Aspectos del trabajo de los embajadores de la casa de Austria en la segunda mitad del siglo XVI', *Pedralbes*, 9, 1989

Eire, Carlos M., *From Madrid to Purgatory. The art and craft of dying in sixteenth-century Spain.* Cambridge 1995

Forneron, H., *Histoire de Philippe II*, 4 vols. Paris 1881

Fortea Pérez, José I., 'The Cortes of Castile and Philip II's fiscal policy', *Parliaments, Estates and Representation*, 11, no.2, 1991, pp.117–38

Gachard, L. P., *Carlos V y Felipe II a través de sus contemporáneos.* Madrid 1944

Gachard, L. P., *Collection des voyages des souverains des Pays-Bas*, 4 vols. Brussels 1876–82

Gachard, L. P., *Correspondance de Philippe II sur les affaires des Pays-Bas*, 6 vols. Brussels 1848–79

Gachard, L. P., *Don Carlos et Philippe II*. Paris 1867

Gachard, L. P., *Retraite et mort de Charles-Quint au monastère de Yuste*, 3 vols. Brussels 1854–6

García Ballester, Luis, *Los Moriscos y la medicina*. Barcelona 1984

García Mercadal, J., *Viajes de extranjeros por España y Portugal*, 2 vols. Madrid 1952

Gil Fernández, Luis, *Panorama social del humanismo español (1500–1800)*. Madrid 1981

Gómez-Centurión, Carlos, *Felipe II, la empresa de Inglaterra y el comercio septentrional (1566–1609)*. Madrid 1988

González de Amezúa, Agustín, *Isabel de Valois, reina de España (1546–1568)*, 3 vols in 5 tomes. Madrid 1949

González Palencia, Angel, *Gonzalo Pérez*, 2 vols. Madrid 1946

Goodman, David C., *Power and Penury. Government, technology and science in Philip II's Spain*. Cambridge 1988

Gossart, Ernest, *La Domination espagnole dans les Pays-Bas à la fin du règne de Philippe II*. Bruxelles 1906

Groen van Prinsterer, G., ed., *Archives de la maison d'Orange-Nassau*. 1er série. Supplément. Leiden 1847

Gurrea y Aragón, Francisco de, conde de Luna, *Comentarios de los sucesos de Aragon en los años 1591 y 1592*. Madrid 1888

Herrera, Antonio de, *Historia general del mundo, del tiempo del Señor Rey don Felipe II el Prudente, desde el año de 1559 hasta el de 1598*, 3 vols. Madrid 1601–12

Iñiguez Almech, Francisco, *Casas reales y jardines de Felipe II*. Madrid 1952

Kagan, Richard, *Lucrecia's Dreams. Politics and prophecy in sixteenth-century Spain*. Berkeley 1990

Kamen, Henry, *Crisis and Change in Early Modern Spain*. Aldershot 1993

Kamen, Henry, *The Phoenix and the Flame. Catalonia and the Counter-Reformation*. New Haven and London 1993

Keniston, Howard, *Francisco de los Cobos*. Madrid 1980

Koenigsberger, H. G., *The Government of Sicily under Philip II of Spain*. London 1951

Kubler, George, *La obra del Escorial*. Madrid 1983

Lagomarsino, Paul David, 'Court factions and the formulation of Spanish policy towards the Netherlands (1559–67)', University of Cambridge PhD thesis, 1973

Lhermite, Jehan, *Le Passetemps*, 2 vols. Antwerp 1890–6

Lisón Tolosana, Carmelo, *La imagen del rey. Monarquía, realeza y poder ritual en la Casa de los Austrias*. Madrid 1991

Lynch, John, *Spain 1516–1598*. London 1991

Mal Lara, Juan de, *Recebimiento que hizo la muy noble y muy leal Ciudad de Sevilla*. Seville 1570

Maltby, William S., *Alba*. Berkeley 1983

Marañón, Gregorio, *Antonio Pérez*, 2 vols. Madrid 1958. A one-volume English abridgment was published in London, 1954

Maravall, J. A., *Estado moderno y mentalidad social*, 2 vols. Madrid 1972

March, J. M., *Niñez y Juventud de Felipe II*, 2 vols. Madrid 1941

Martin, C. and Parker, G., *The Spanish Armada*. London 1988

Maurenbrecher, W., Philippson, M. and Justi, C., *Estudios sobre Felipe II*. Madrid 1887

Mayer-Löwenschwerdt, E., *Der Aufenthalt der Erzherzoge Rudolf und Ernst in Spanien 1564–1571*. Vienna 1927

Merriman, R. B., *The Rise of the Spanish Empire in the Old World and in the New*. New York 1918, repr. 1962. Vol.III: *The Emperor*, Vol.IV: *Philip the Prudent*

Milhou, Alain, 'Las Casas frente a las reivindicaciones de los colonos de ls isla Española (1554–1561)', *Historiografía y Bibliografía Americanistas, XIX–XX*, 1975–6

Motley, John Lothrop, *The Rise of the Dutch Republic*. London 1912 edn

Mousset, Albert, *Dépêches diplomatiques de M de Longlée, resident de France en Espagne (1582–1590)*. Paris 1912

Muñoz, Andrés, *Viaje de Felipe Segundo a Inglaterra*, ed. P. Gayangos. Madrid 1877

Muro, Gaspar, *Vida de la princesa de Éboli*. Madrid 1877

Ossorio, Antonio, *Vida y hazañas de don Fernando Alvarez de Toledo, duque de Alba*. Madrid 1945

Paris, Louis, *Négociations, lettres et pièces relatives au règne de François II*. Paris 1841. (Collection des Documents Inédits sur l'Histoire de France, 1er série)

Parker, Geoffrey, *The Army of Flanders and the Spanish Road 1567–1659*. Cambridge 1972

Parker, Geoffrey, *The Dutch Revolt*. London 1977

Parker, Geoffrey, *Philip II*. Boston 1978

Pérez de Herrera, Dr Christoval, *Elogio a las esclarecidas virtudes de Don Felipe II*. Valladolid 1604

Pi Corrales, Magdalena, 'El declive de la marina filipina (1570–1590)', 2 vols. Thesis of the Complutensian University 1987

Prescott, William H., *History of the Reign of Philip the Second*, 3 vols. London 1855

Rivera, Javier, *Juan Bautista de Toledo y Felipe II*. Valladolid 1984

Rodríguez, Pedro and Rodríguez, Justina, *Don Francés de Alava y Beamonte. Correspondencia inédita de Felipe II con su embajador en Paris (1564–1570)*. San Sebastian 1991

Rodríguez Salgado, M. J., *The Changing Face of Empire. Charles V, Philip II and Habsburg authority, 1551–1559*. Cambridge 1988

Sandoval, fray Prudencio de, *Historia de la vida y hechos del emperador Carlos V*, Vol.III. Biblioteca de Autores Españoles, vol. 82. Madrid 1956

Schepper, Hugo de, 'Ensayo sobre el modelo del proceso de decisión política en los Países Bajos de Felipe II, 1559–1598', *Tussen twee culturen: de Nederlanden en de iberische wereld 1550–1800*. Nijmegen 1991

Sepúlveda, fray Jerónimo de, *Historia*, ed. J. Zarco Cuevas, *Documentos para la Historia del Monasterio de San Lorenzo el Real*, vol.IV. Madrid 1924

Serrano, Luciano, *Correspondencia diplomática entre España y la Santa Sede*, 4 vols. Madrid 1914

Sigüenza, fray José de, *Historia de la Orden de San Jerónimo*, 2 vols. Madrid
    1907–9
Splendeurs d'Espagne et les villes belges 1500–1700, 2 vols. Brussels 1985
Stirling Maxwell, W., *Don John of Austria*, 2 vols. London 1883
Strada, Famiano, *Guerras de Flandes*, 7 vols. Antwerp 1748
Tellechea Idigoras, J. I., *El arzobispo Carranza y su tiempo*, 2 vols. Madrid 1968
Teulet, Alexandre, *Relations politiques de la France et de l'Espagne avec l'Ecosse au
    XVIe siècle*, 5 vols. Paris 1862
Thompson, I. A. A., *War and Government in Habsburg Spain 1560–1620*. London
    1976
Thompson, I. A. A., *War and Society in Habsburg Spain*. Aldershot 1992
Ungerer, Gustav, *A Spaniard in Elizabethan England: the correspondence of
    Antonio Pérez's exile*, 2 vols. London 1974–6
Van Durme, M., *El Cardenal Granvela (1517–1586)*. Barcelona 1957
Vandenesse, Jean de, *Journal des voyages de Philippe II*, in L. P. Gachard, *Collec-
    tion des voyages des souverains des Pays-Bas*, vols II, IV. Brussels 1882
Weiss, Charles, *Papiers d'Etat du Cardinal de Granvelle*, 9 vols. Paris 1841–52.
    (Documents Inédits pour l'Histoire de France)
Wilkinson Zerner, Catherine, *Juan de Herrera*. New Haven and London 1993
Yates, Frances A., *The Valois Tapestries*. London 1975

Index